THE PAPERS OF
BENJAMIN FRANKLIN

SPONSORED BY

The American Philosophical Society

and Yale University

Le Magnétisme dévoilé

THE PAPERS OF

Benjamin Franklin

VOLUME 42   *March 1 through August 15, 1784*

ELLEN R. COHN, *Editor*

ROBERT P. FRANKEL, JR., KATE M. OHNO, AND

PHILIPP ZIESCHE, *Associate Editors*

ALYSIA M. CAIN, ADRINA M. GARBOOSHIAN,

JOHN M. HUFFMAN, AND ELLEN M. PAWELCZAK,

Assistant Editors

KATE G. WOODFORD, *Editorial Assistant*

JONATHAN R. DULL, *Consulting Editor*

New Haven and London   YALE UNIVERSITY PRESS, 2017

This edition was made possible through the vision and generosity of Yale University and the American Philosophical Society, which continue to support the enterprise, and by a substantial donation from Henry R. Luce in the name of Life Magazine. *Additional funds were provided by a grant from the Ford Foundation to the National Archives Trust Fund Board. Subsequent support has come from the Andrew W. Mellon Foundation, The Pew Charitable Trusts, the Norman and Lyn Lear Foundation, the New York Times Foundation, the* Saturday Evening Post *Society, the Friends of Franklin, and the Friends of the Franklin Papers. Major underwriting of the present volume has been provided by the Packard Humanities Institute through Founding Fathers Papers, Inc., and the Florence Gould Foundation, with additional support from the Cinco Hermanos Fund.* The Papers of Benjamin Franklin *is a beneficiary of the generous and long-standing support of the National Historical Publications and Records Commission under the chairmanship of the Archivist of the United States, and the National Endowment for the Humanities, an independent federal agency. To these long-standing sponsors we offer once again our profound gratitude. We gratefully acknowledge the bequest of Raymond N. Kjellberg, which will continue to sustain our enterprise. We offer particular appreciation to Richard Gilder, Charles and Ann Johnson, Mason Willrich, the Yale Class of 1954, and the Benjamin Franklin Tercentenary for generous donations that will ensure the future of the edition. Since the inception of the project we have benefited from the generosity of many individuals whose names have been noted in previous volumes. We acknowledge here the recent contributions from Sheldon Cohen and Joe Rubinfine. For the assistance of all these organizations and individuals, as well as for the indispensable aid of archivists, librarians, scholars, and collectors of Franklin manuscripts, the editors are most grateful.*

Library of Congress catalog card number: 59–12697
International standard book number: 978-0-300-22269-2

♾ The paper in this book meets the guidelines for permanence and durability of the Committee on Production Guidelines for Book Longevity of the Council on Library Resources.

Printed in the U.S.A.

Administrative Board

Contents

Foreign-language surnames and titles of nobility often run to great length. Our practice with an untitled person is to provide all the Christian names at the first appearance, and then drop them; a chevalier or noble is given the title used at the time, and the full name is provided in the index.

*Denotes a document referred to in annotation.

CONTENTS

xviii

List of Illustrations

Anonymous engraving issued after the publication, *circa* August 21,
of the report on animal magnetism by the royal commissioners from the
Académie des sciences and the Faculté de médecine. (The report is summarized below under its submission date of August 11.) The commissioners are shown at the left, entering what appears to be the inner sanc-
tum of Mesmer's clinic. As head of the commission, Franklin is in the
lead, brandishing the "Rapport des Commissaires," whose all-powerful
light banishes chicanery and creates pandemonium: the iron bands
of the magnetic tub burst, a bat-like owl is startled into flight, and ter-
rified patients cower as three demonic magnetizers flee on broomsticks.
One, who sports an ass's head and tail and who may represent Mesmer,
flies ahead of the others holding a bag of money. A second (possibly
Deslon) grabs him and clutches at the bag. A third, depicted with the
hindquarters of an ass, pursues them, holding a whip. Collapsing inside
the broken tub is a half-naked figure wearing ass's ears and a blindfold
that identify her as Ignorance. Barely visible creatures, half-woman and
half-serpent, writhe in the shredded curtains framing the scene. In the
foreground, a shell game and mask reinforce the association with fraud,
deception, and theater. To the left of Franklin, a figure resembling the
late Voltaire, symbol of the Enlightenment, invites viewers to witness
the scene. The engraved title, *Le Magnétisme dévoilé*, has been cropped
in this example, and written in pencil by an unknown hand. Reproduced
by courtesy of the Yale University Library.

A series of ink-and-wash illustrations by Julien-David Le Roy that accompanied his memoir of [April 10–11, 1784]. Figures 1 and 2 show a
gondola attached to a balloon by means of a solid frame, a concept that
Le Roy would explain in the continuation of his memoir, written [after
August 12, 1784]. The frame would help preserve the shape of the globe
should it rupture during flight, facilitating a slower and safer descent.
Figures 4 to 7 depict cone-shaped balloons, which Le Roy argued would
provide greater air resistance in case of accidental descent. Figures 3,
4, and 5 illustrate his proposal to harness flocks of trained birds to steer
balloons. The birds are held in a mesh cage, which is attached to a stick
fastened to the bottom of the gondola. The stick tilts and rotates full
circle, allowing the balloonist to choose the direction of flight. Figures
6 to 9 portray another means of steering: a paddle, protruding below

the gondola, which can be moved in a full circle and opened and closed
like scissors. Le Roy's memoirs are described in annotation of his cover
letter of [April 10–11], below. Reproduced by courtesy of the American
Philosophical Society.

Explanation of the Medal Struck by the Americans in 1782
facing page 140

Engraving by Jean-Baptiste Bradel showing the *Libertas Americana*
medal and the explanation of its iconography that had been written by
Franklin and Morellet for distribution with the medals: XXXIX, 549–55.
Bradel sets the "Explication" inside the skinned hide of a leopard, sym-
bolizing the defeated British empire, that hangs from two roundels, one
bearing a sheaf of thirteen arrows, the other a fleur-de-lis. The image
of the medal is at variance with the actual object, the engraver having added spots to the animal depicted on the reverse, presumably to
conform with Franklin's identification of it as a leopard. Bradel dedi-
cates the engraving "A Son Excellence Monsieur Franklin, Ministre
Plenipotentiaire des Etats-Unis de l'Amerique de l'Academie Royale
des Sciences de Paris, de la Societé Royale de Londres, Président de la
Societé Philosophique de Philadelphie &c." That text flanks an image
of Franklin's coat of arms above a small shield reading "Constitutions
des Etats Unis". A second state of the work corrects the dedication by
specifying that Franklin is the American minister "à la Cour de France":
Waverly Rare Books, Catalogue No. 264 (March 12, 2015), item 239.
There are no mentions of either Bradel or this engraving in Franklin's
papers. Because the piece was advertised for sale in *Affiches, annonces,
et avis divers* on April 15, 1784, we place the illustration at that date. Reproduced by courtesy of the American Philosophical Society.

Cartouche from the *Carte des Etats-Unis de l'Amerique*
facing page 318

From the second state of Jean Lattré's 1784 map of the United States.
The dedication reads "A S. Excellence Mr. BENJAMIN FRANKLIN /
Ministre Plénipotentiaire des Etats-Unis de l'Amérique près la Cour de
France, / anc. Présid. de la conventiõ de Pensilvanie et de la Société
Philosophique de Philadelphie. &c. &c. / Par son très humble et très
obeissant— / Serviteur LATTRÉ." The design is adapted from the cartouche on a map of Holland in Lattré's 1783 issue of the *Atlas Moderne*,
but with three new elements: affixed to the ship's sails are Franklin's
personal seal (left), the Society of the Cincinnati's newly designed Eagle medallion (right), and the Great Seal of the United States (center),
which is also lightly sketched on the flag billowing alongside. The first
known printed announcement of the map's release is below, June 10.
Reproduced by courtesy of the Library of Congress.

The Cliffs
facing page 343

The house outside of Philadelphia belonging to the Fisher family that Richard and Sarah Bache rented, drawing on Franklin's account, in the summer of 1784 as a country retreat for themselves and five of their six children. As Sally wrote to her father on June 20[–21], "I think there is not a more beautiful prospect on the Schuylkill banks." The Cliffs was purchased in 1868 by Fairmount Park, but was destroyed in a 1986 fire: *Philadelphia Inquirer*, February 23, 1986. This photograph was taken in 1931 by the Philadelphia Museum of Art. Reproduced by courtesy of the Library of Congress.

Gustavus III, King of Sweden
facing page 362

One of several engravings after the *circa* 1774–75 portrait in oil by Alexander Roslin: Gunnar W. Lundberg, *Roslin: liv och verk* (3 vols. in 2, Malmö, 1957), II, plate 115; III, 70–1. This one was published in *The Universal Magazine of Knowledge and Pleasure*, LXXXI (1787), opposite page 17. Gustavus was the first monarch to request a treaty with the nascent United States; it was negotiated in secret, as the peace with Great Britain had not yet been concluded. Gustavus ratified the Swedish-American Treaty of Amity and Commerce on May 23, 1783, and ratifications were exchanged on February 6, 1784: XXXIX, 250, 254; XL, 160n; XLI, 516n. In the summer of 1784, the king visited Paris and Versailles under an assumed name. From the fragments of Franklin's journal that survive from this period, spanning June 26–July 27, it appears possible that the two men met on at least one occasion: the dinner for the Swedish court hosted by Ferdinand Grand on July 10. On July 21 Franklin noted that Gustavus sent a card to Passy on the eve of his departure, and was carrying back to Sweden a bust of Franklin that he had purchased. Reproduced by courtesy of the Library of Congress.

Magnetic Tub
facing page 475

This *baquet*, purchased *circa* 1784 by Lyon pharmacist Jean-Baptiste Lanoix, is believed to be the only extant example of the device developed by Franz Anton Mesmer for his magnetic therapy. Bottles filled with "magnetized" water were submerged inside the tub; iron rods, serving as conductors, were extended from the bottles through holes in the tub's lid. At the top of each rod was attached another, movable iron rod that could be applied directly to the area causing complaint. The circuit of "magnetic fluid" was enhanced by means of cords linking patients to the tub or to each other. Mesmer's clinic offered four *baquets* as well as individual treatments for prominent patients: Charles C. Gillispie, *Science and Polity in France at the End of the Old Regime* (Princeton, 1980), pp. 261, 264; Miriam Simon, "Le mesmérisme," in *Benjamin Franklin: un Américain à Paris (1776–1785)*, ed. Simon *et al.* (Paris, 2007), p. 168.

Reproduced by courtesy of the Lyon Musée d'Histoire de la Médecine et de la Pharmacie.

James Cook Gold Medal   *facing page 497*

Medal commemorating the late Captain James Cook, designed by Lewis Pingo, chief engraver of the Royal Mint: Christopher Eimer, *The Pingo Family & Medal Making in 18th-Century Britain* (London, 1998), pp. 25, 65. The obverse features a portrait of Cook, who is characterized in Latin as "the most intrepid explorer of the seas." The figure depicted on the reverse combines characteristics of Britannia and Fortuna. She leans on a rostral column and holds an ancient rudder, which rests on a globe, in her right hand. The surrounding legend translates as "Our men have left nothing untried."

In his letter of August 13, 1784, Joseph Banks notified Franklin that the Royal Society was presenting him with one of the Cook gold medals. The example pictured here belonged to Banks; none of the six others known to be extant have been identified as Franklin's. Reproduced by courtesy of the British Museum.

Contributors to Volume 42

The ownership of each manuscript, or the location of the particular copy used by the editors of each rare contemporary pamphlet or similar printed work, is indicated where the document appears in the text. The sponsors and editors are deeply grateful to the following institutions and individuals for permission to print or otherwise use in the present volume manuscripts and other materials which they own.

INSTITUTIONS

Académie nationale de médecine, Paris
Algemeen Rijksarchief, The Hague
American Philosophical Society
Archives du Ministère des affaires étrangères, Paris
Biblioteca Labronica, Leghorn
Bibliothèque nationale de France
British Library
William L. Clements Library, University of Michigan
College of Physicians of Philadelphia
College of William & Mary Library
Columbia University Library
Gilder Lehrman Collection at the New-York Historical Society
Haus-, Hof- und Staatsarchiv, Vienna

Historical Society of Pennsylvania
Library of Congress
Massachusetts Historical Society
Morgan Library and Museum
National Archives
National Archives, London
National Library of Australia
National Library of Scotland
New York Public Library
Presbyterian Historical Society, Philadelphia, Pennsylvania
Wyndham Robertson Library, Hollins University, Roanoke, Virginia
South Carolina Historical Society
University of Pennsylvania Library
University of South Carolina Library
Yale University Library

INDIVIDUALS

Katherine N. Bradford, Philadelphia, Pennsylvania
Vicomte Foy, Paris
Addinell S. Hewson, Bryn Mawr, Pennsylvania
Myron Kaller & Associates, Inc., Asbury Park, New Jersey
The Scriptorium, Beverly Hills, California
Mrs. J. W. Williams, St. Andrews, Fife, Scotland

Statement of Methodology

Arrangement of Materials

The documents are printed in chronological sequence according to their dates when these are given, or according to the date of publication in cases of contemporary printed materials. Records such as diaries, journals, and account books that cover substantial periods of time appear according to the dates of their earliest entries. When no date appears on the document itself, one is editorially supplied and an explanation provided. When no day within a month is given, the document is placed at the end of all specifically dated documents of that month; those dated only by year are placed at the end of that year. If no date is given, we use internal and external evidence to assign one whenever possible, providing our explanation in annotation. Documents which cannot be assigned a date more definite than the entire length of Franklin's stay in France (1777–85) will be published at the end of this period. Those for which we are unable to provide even a tentative date will be published at the conclusion of the series.

When two or more documents have the same date, they are arranged in the following order:

1. Those by a group of which Franklin was a member (*e.g.*, the American Commissioners in Paris)
2. Those by Franklin individually
3. Those to a group of which Franklin was a member
4. Those to Franklin individually
5. "Third-party" and unaddressed miscellaneous writings by others than Franklin.

In the first two categories letters are arranged alphabetically by the name of the addressee; in the last three, by the name of the signatory. An exception to this practice occurs when a letter to Franklin and his answer were written on the same day: in such cases the first letter precedes the reply. The same rules apply to documents lacking precise dates printed together at the end of any month or year.

Form of Presentation

The document and its accompanying editorial apparatus are presented in the following order:

1. *Title.* Essays and formal papers are headed by their titles, except in the case of pamphlets with very long titles, when a short form is substituted. Where previous editors supplied a title to a piece that had none, and this title has become familiar, we use it; otherwise we devise a suitable one.

Letters written by Franklin individually are entitled "To" the person or body addressed, as: To John Adams; To John Adams and Arthur Lee; To the Royal Society.

Letters to Franklin individually are entitled "From" the person or body who wrote them, as: From John Adams; From John Adams and Arthur Lee; From the Committee of Secret Correspondence.

Letters of which Franklin was a joint author or joint recipient are titled with the names of all concerned, as: Franklin and Silas Deane to Arthur Lee; Arthur Lee to Franklin and Silas Deane. "Third-party" letters or those by or to a body of which Franklin was a member are titled with the names of both writers and addressees, as: Arthur Lee to John Adams; The American Commissioners to John Paul Jones.

Documents not fitting into any of these categories are given brief descriptive headings, as: Extract from Franklin's Journal.

If the name in the title has been supplied from external evidence it appears in brackets, with a question mark when we are uncertain. If a letter is unsigned, or signed with initials or an alias, but is from a correspondent whose handwriting we know, the name appears without brackets.

2. *Source Identification.* This gives the nature of the printed or manuscript version of the document, and, in the case of a manuscript or a rare printed work, the ownership and location of the original.

Printed sources of three different classes are distinguished. First, a contemporary pamphlet, which is given its full title, place and date of publication, and the location of the copy the editors have used. Second, an essay or letter appearing originally in a *contemporary* publication, which is introduced by the words "Printed in," followed by the title, date, and inclusive page numbers, if necessary, of the publication. Third, a document, the manuscript or contemporary printed version of which is now lost, but which was printed at a later date, is identified by the words "Reprinted from," followed by the name of the work from which the editors have reproduced it. The following examples illustrate the distinction:

Printed in *The Pennsylvania Gazette*, October 2, 1729.

Reprinted from William Temple Franklin, ed., *Memoirs of the Life and Writings of Benjamin Franklin* ... (3 vols., 4to, London, 1817–18), II, 244.

The Source Identification of a manuscript consists of a term or symbol (all of which are listed in the Short Title List) indicating the character of the manuscript version, followed by the name of the holder of the manuscript, as: ALS: American Philosophical Society. Because press copies replicate the manuscripts from which they were made, we indicate the character of the original manuscript, as: press copy of L. Since manuscripts belonging to individuals have a tendency to migrate, we indicate the year in which each private owner gave permission to publish, as: Morris Duane, Philadelphia, 1957. When two or more manuscript versions survive, the one listed first in the Source Identification is the one from which we print.

3. An editorial *Headnote* precedes some documents in this edition; it appears between the Source Identification and the actual text. Such a headnote is designed to supply the background of the composition of the document, its relation to events or other writings, and any other information which may be useful to the reader and is not obtainable from the document itself.

4. The *Text* of the document follows the Source Identification, or Headnote, if any. When multiple copies of a document are extant, the editors observe the following order of priority in determining which of the available versions to use in printing a text: ALS or ADS, LS or DS, AL or AD, L or D, copy, and transcript (a copy made at a later date). An AL (draft) normally takes

precedence over a contemporary copy based on the recipient's copy. If we deviate from the order set forth here, we explain our decision in the annotation. In those instances where multiple texts are available, the texts are collated, and significant variations reported in the annotation. In selecting the publication text from among several copies of official French correspondence (*e.g.*, from Vergennes or Sartine) we use the version which is written in the best French, on the presumption that the French ministers used standard eighteenth-century spelling, grammar, and punctuation.

The form of presentation of the texts of letters is as follows:

The place and date of composition are set at the top, regardless of their location in the original manuscript.

The signature, set in capitals and small capitals, is placed at the right of the last line of the text if there is room; if not, then on the line below.

Addresses, endorsements, and notations are so labelled and printed at the end of the letter. An endorsement is, to the best of our belief, by the recipient, and a notation by someone else. When the writer of the notation has misread the date or the signature of the correspondent, we let the error stand without comment. Line breaks in addresses are marked by slashes. Different notations are separated by slashes; when they are by different individuals, we so indicate.

5. *Footnotes* to the Heading, Source Identification, Headnote, and Text appear on the pages to which they pertain. References to documents not printed or to be printed in later volumes are by date and repository, as: Jan. 17, 1785, APS.

Method of Textual Reproduction

1. *Spelling* of all words, including proper names, is retained. If it is abnormal enough to obscure the meaning we follow the word immediately with the current spelling in brackets.

2. *Capitalization and Punctuation* are retained. There is such variety in the size of initial letters, often in the same manuscript, that it is sometimes unclear whether the writer intended an upper or lower case letter. In such cases we make a decision on the basis of the correspondent's customary usage. We supply a capital letter when an immediately preceding period, colon, question

mark, exclamation point, or dash indicates that a new sentence is intended. If a capital letter clearly indicates the beginning of a new thought, but no mark of punctuation precedes it, we insert a period. If neither punctuation nor capital letter indicates a sentence break, we do not supply them unless their absence renders comprehension of the document nearly impossible. In that case we provide them and so indicate in a footnote.

Dashes were used for a variety of purposes in eighteenth-century personal and public letters. A dash within a sentence, used to indicate a break in thought, is represented as an em dash. A dash that follows a period or serves as a closing mark of punctuation for a sentence is represented as an em dash followed by a space. Occasionally correspondents used long dashes that continue to the end of a line and indicate a significant break in thought. We do not reproduce the dash, but treat it as indicating the start of a new paragraph.

When there is an initial quotation mark or parenthesis, but no closing one, we silently complete the pair.

Words underlined once in a manuscript are printed in *italics*. Words underlined twice or written in either capitals or unusually large letters are printed in SMALL CAPITALS.

3. *Contractions and abbreviations* are retained. Abbreviations such as "wd", "honble", "servt", "exclly", are used so frequently in Franklin's correspondence that they are readily comprehensible to the users of these volumes. Abbreviations, particularly of French words, that may be unclear are followed by an expanded version in brackets, as: nre [navire]. Superscript letters are brought down to the line. Where a period or colon is a part of the abbreviation, or indicates that letters were written above the line, we print it at the end of the word, as: 4th. for 4.ᵗʰ. In those few cases where superscript letters brought down to the line result in a confusing abbreviation ("Made" for "Madᵉ"), we follow the abbreviation by an expanded version in brackets, as: Made [Madame].

The ampersand by itself and the "&c." are retained. Letters represented by the "y" are printed, as: "the" and "that". The tailed "p" is spelled out, as: "per", "pre", or "pro". Symbols of weights, measures, and money are converted to modern forms, as: *l.t.* instead of ₶ for *livres tournois*.

4. *Omissions, mutilations, and illegible words* are treated as follows:

If we are certain of text that is missing or obscured because a manuscript is torn, faded, stained, or otherwise damaged, or that is hidden because a letterbook is tightly bound, or that is illegible because of poor handwriting, we supply that text silently.

If we cannot be certain of the text, but have a high degree of confidence in our conjectural reading, we supply such text in brackets. When we are less confident, we supply the text in brackets with the addition of a question mark, as: [treaty?], constitu[tional?].

When we cannot make even a reasonable guess as to the text, we provide an editorial insertion in brackets that describes the nature, and sometimes the extent, of the problem, as: [*torn*], [*illegible*], [*faded*], [*torn: several words missing*], [*one line illegible*].

If a writer has omitted a word absolutely required for clarity, we insert it in italics within brackets, as: sailed [*to*] Boston.

5. *Interlineations* by the author are silently incorporated into the text. If they are significant enough to require comment a footnote is provided.

Textual Conventions

/	denotes line break in addresses; separates multiple endorsements and notations.
⟨roman⟩	denotes a résumé of a letter or document.
[*italic*]	editorial insertion explaining something about the manuscript; or supplying an omitted word to make the meaning clear.
[roman]	editorial insertion clarifying the immediately preceding word or abbreviation; or supplying a conjectural reading for missing, hidden, or illegible text.

Abbreviations and Short Titles

AAE	Archives du Ministère des affaires étrangères.
AD	Autograph document.
Adams Correspondence	Lyman H. Butterfield, Richard A. Ryerson *et al.*, eds., *Adams Family Correspondence* (12 vols. to date, Cambridge, Mass., 1963–).
Adams Papers	Robert J. Taylor, Gregg L. Lint *et al.*, eds., *Papers of John Adams* (18 vols. to date, Cambridge, Mass., 1977–).
ADB	*Allgemeine Deutsche Biographie* (56 vols., Berlin, 1967–71).
Adm.	Admiral.
ADS	Autograph document signed.
AL	Autograph letter.
Almanach des marchands	*Almanach général des marchands, négocians, armateurs, et fabricans de France et de l'Europe et autres parties du monde* . . . (Paris, 1779).
Almanach de Versailles	*Almanach de Versailles* (Versailles, various years). Cited by year.
Almanach royal	*Almanach royal* (91 vols., Paris, 1700–92). Cited by year.
Alphabetical List of Escaped Prisoners	Alphabetical List of the Americans who having escap'd from the Prisons of England, were furnish'd with Money by the Commissrs. of the U.S. at the Court of France, to return to America. A manuscript in the APS, dated 1784, and covering the period January, 1777, to November, 1784.
ALS	Autograph letter signed.

Amiable, *Une Loge Maçonnique*	Louis Amiable, *Une Loge maçonnique d'avant 1789* . . . (1897; reprint, followed by an introduction, commentary, and notes, separately paginated, by Charles Porset, Paris, 1989).
ANB	*American National Biography.*
APS	American Philosophical Society.
Archaeol.	Archaeological.
Assn.	Association.
Autobiog.	Leonard W. Labaree, Ralph L. Ketcham, Helen C. Boatfield, and Helene H. Fineman, eds., *The Autobiography of Benjamin Franklin* (New Haven, 1964).
Bachaumont, *Mémoires secrets*	[Louis Petit de Bachaumont *et al.*], *Mémoires secrets pour servir à l'histoire de la république des lettres en France, depuis MDCCLXII jusqu'à nos jours; ou, Journal d'un observateur* . . . (36 vols. in 12, London, 1784–89). Bachaumont died in 1771. The first six vols. (1762–71) are his; Mathieu-François Pidansat de Mairobert edited them and wrote the next nine (1771–79); the remainder (1779–87) are by Barthélemy-François Mouffle d'Angerville.
BF	Benjamin Franklin.
BF's accounts as commissioner	Those described above, XXIII, 20.
BF's journal of the peace negotiations	Described in XXXVII, 291–346. This refers to the copy in Josiah Flagg's hand with corrections by BF, at the Library of Congress.
BFB	Benjamin Franklin Bache.
BFB's journal	Described above, XXXVII, 682n.

Bigelow, *Works*   John Bigelow, ed., *The Works of Benjamin Franklin* (12 vols., New York and London, 1887–88).

Biographie universelle   *Biographie universelle, ancienne et moderne, ou histoire, par ordre alphabétique, de la vie publique et privée de tous les hommes qui se sont fait remarquer . . .* (85 vols., Paris, 1811–62).

Bodinier, *Dictionnaire*   Gilbert Bodinier, *Dictionnaire des officiers de l'armée royale qui ont combattu aux Etats-Unis pendant la guerre d'Indépendance* (Château de Vincennes, 1982).

Bradford, *Jones Papers*   James C. Bradford, ed., *The Microfilm Edition of the Papers of John Paul Jones, 1747–1792* (10 reels of microfilm, Alexandria, Va., 1986).

Burke's Peerage   Sir Bernard Burke, *Burke's Genealogical and Heraldic History of the Peerage Baronetage and Knightage with War Gazette and Corrigenda* (98th ed., London, 1940). References in exceptional cases to other editions are so indicated.

Butterfield, *John Adams Diary*   Lyman H. Butterfield *et al.*, eds., *Diary and Autobiography of John Adams* (4 vols., Cambridge, Mass., 1961).

Chron.   Chronicle.

Claghorn, *Naval Officers*   Charles E. Claghorn, *Naval Officers of the American Revolution: a Concise Biographical Dictionary* (Metuchen, N.J., and London, 1988).

Cobbett, *Parliamentary History*   William Cobbett and Thomas C. Hansard, eds., *The Parliamentary History of England from the Earliest Period to 1803* (36 vols., London, 1806–20).

Col.	Column.
Coll.	Collections.
Comp.	Compiler.
d.	*deniers.*
d.	pence.
D	Document unsigned.
DAB	*Dictionary of American Biography.*
DBF	*Dictionnaire de biographie française* (20 vols. to date, Paris, 1933–).
Deane Papers	*The Deane Papers, 1774–90* (5 vols.; New-York Historical Society *Collections*, XIX–XXIII, New York, 1887–91).
DF	Deborah Franklin.
Dictionary of Scientific Biography	Charles C. Gillispie, ed., *Dictionary of Scientific Biography* (18 vols., New York, 1970–90).
Dictionnaire de la noblesse	François-Alexandre Aubert de La Chesnaye-Dubois and M. Badier, *Dictionnaire de la noblesse contenant les généalogies, l'histoire & la chronologie des familles nobles de la France . . .* (3rd ed.; 19 vols., Paris, 1863–76).
Dictionnaire historique de la Suisse	*Dictionnaire historique & biographique de la Suisse* (7 vols. and supplement, Neuchâtel, 1921–34).
Diplomatic Correspondence of the United States	*The Diplomatic Correspondence of the United States of America, from the Signing of the Definitive Treaty of Peace, 10th September, 1783, to the Adoption of the Constitution, March 4, 1789* (7 vols., Washington, D.C., 1833–34).
DNB	*Dictionary of National Biography.*
Doniol, *Histoire*	Henri Doniol, *Histoire de la participation de la France à l'établissement des*

Etats-Unis d'Amérique. Correspondance diplomatique et documents (5 vols., Paris, 1886–99).

DS   Document signed.

Dubourg, *Œuvres*   Jacques Barbeu-Dubourg, ed., *Œuvres de M. Franklin* ... (2 vols., Paris, 1773).

Ed.   Edition or editor.

Edler, *Dutch Republic*   Friedrich Edler, *The Dutch Republic and the American Revolution (Johns Hopkins University Studies in Historical and Political Science*, ser. XXIX, no. 2; Baltimore, 1911).

Etat militaire   *Etat militaire de France, pour l'année* ... (36 vols., Paris, 1758–93). Cited by year.

Exper. and Obser.   *Experiments and Observations on Electricity, made at Philadelphia in America, by Mr. Benjamin Franklin* ... (London, 1751). Revised and enlarged editions were published in 1754, 1760, 1769, and 1774 with slightly varying titles. In each case the edition cited will be indicated, *e.g., Exper. and Obser.* (1751).

f.   florins.

Ferguson, *Power of the Purse*   E. James Ferguson, *The Power of the Purse: a History of American Public Finance* ... (Chapel Hill, 1961).

Fitzpatrick, *Writings of Washington*   John C. Fitzpatrick, ed., *The Writings of George Washington* ... (39 vols., Washington, D.C., 1931–44).

Fortescue, *Correspondence of George Third*   Sir John William Fortescue, ed., *The Correspondence of King George the Third from 1760 to December 1783* ... (6 vols., London, 1927–28).

France ecclésiastique	*La France ecclésiastique pour l'année* . . . (15 vols., Paris, 1774–90). Cited by year.
Gaz.	Gazette.
Gaz. de Leyde	*Nouvelles extraordinaires de divers endroits*, commonly known as *Gazette de Leyde*. Each issue is in two parts; we indicate the second as "sup."
Gen.	General.
Geneal.	Genealogical.
Gent. Mag.	*The Gentleman's Magazine, and Historical Chronicle.*
Gillispie, *Montgolfier Brothers*	Charles C. Gillispie, *The Montgolfier Brothers and the Invention of Aviation, 1783–1784* (Princeton, 1983).
Giunta, *Emerging Nation*	Mary A. Giunta *et al.*, eds., *The Emerging Nation: a Documentary History of the Foreign Relations of the United States under the Articles of the Confederation, 1780–1789* (3 vols., Washington, D.C., 1996).
GW	George Washington.
Harlow, *Second British Empire*	Vincent T. Harlow, *The Founding of the Second British Empire, 1763–1793* (2 vols., London and New York, 1952–64).
Hays, *Calendar*	I. Minis Hays, *Calendar of the Papers of Benjamin Franklin in the Library of the American Philosophical Society* (5 vols., Philadelphia, 1908).
Heitman, *Register of Officers*	Francis B. Heitman, *Historical Register of Officers of the Continental Army during the War of the Revolution* . . . (Washington, D.C., 1893).
Hillairet, *Rues de Paris*	Jacques Hillairet, pseud. of Auguste A. Coussillan, *Dictionnaire historique des*

	rues de Paris (2nd ed.; 2 vols., [Paris, 1964]).
Hist.	Historic or Historical.
Idzerda, *Lafayette Papers*	Stanley J. Idzerda *et al.*, eds., *Lafayette in the Age of the American Revolution: Selected Letters and Papers, 1776– 1790* (5 vols. to date, Ithaca and London, 1977–).
JA	John Adams.
Jay Papers	Elizabeth M. Nuxoll *et al.*, eds., *The Selected Papers of John Jay* (4 vols. to date, Charlottesville and London, 2010–).
JCC	Worthington Chauncey Ford *et al.*, eds., *Journals of the Continental Congress, 1744–1789* (34 vols., Washington, D.C., 1904–37).
Jefferson Papers	Julian P. Boyd, Charles T. Cullen, John Catanzariti, Barbara B. Oberg, *et al.*, eds., *The Papers of Thomas Jefferson* (42 vols. to date, Princeton, 1950–).
Jour.	Journal.
JQA	John Quincy Adams.
JW	Jonathan Williams, Jr.
Kaminkow, *Mariners*	Marion and Jack Kaminkow, *Mariners of the American Revolution* (Baltimore, 1967).
L	Letter unsigned.
Larousse	Pierre Larousse, *Grand dictionnaire universel du XIXe siècle . . .* (17 vols., Paris, [n.d.]).
Lasseray, *Les Français*	André Lasseray, *Les Français sous les treize étoiles, 1775–1783* (2 vols., Paris, 1935).
Laurens Papers	Philip M. Hamer, George C. Rogers, Jr., David R. Chesnutt, *et al.*, eds., *The*

	Papers of Henry Laurens (16 vols., Columbia, S.C., 1968–2003).
Le Bihan, *Francs-maçons parisiens*	Alain Le Bihan, *Francs-maçons parisiens du Grand Orient de France* . . . (Commission d'histoire économique et sociale de la révolution française, *Mémoires et documents,* XIX, Paris, 1966).
Lewis, *Walpole Correspondence*	Wilmarth S. Lewis *et al.,* eds., *The Yale Edition of Horace Walpole's Correspondence* (48 vols., New Haven, 1939–83).
Lopez, *Mon Cher Papa*	Claude-Anne Lopez, *Mon Cher Papa: Franklin and the Ladies of Paris* (rev. ed., New Haven and London, 1990).
Lopez and Herbert, *The Private Franklin*	Claude-Anne Lopez and Eugenia W. Herbert, *The Private Franklin: the Man and His Family* (New York, 1975).
LS	Letter or letters signed.
l.t.	*livres tournois.*
Lüthy, *Banque protestante*	Herbert Lüthy, *La Banque protestante en France de la Révocation de l'Edit de Nantes à la Révolution* (2 vols., Paris, 1959–61).
Mag.	Magazine.
Mass. Arch.	Massachusetts Archives, State House, Boston.
Mazas, *Ordre de Saint-Louis*	Alexandre Mazas and Théodore Anne, *Histoire de l'ordre royal et militaire de Saint-Louis depuis son institution en 1693 jusqu'en 1830* (2nd ed.; 3 vols., Paris, 1860–61).
Medlin, *Morellet*	Dorothy Medlin, Jean-Claude David, Paul LeClerc, eds., *Lettres d'André Morellet* (3 vols., Oxford, 1991–96).

xli

Métra, *Correspondance secrète* — [François Métra *et al.*], *Correspondance secrète, politique & littéraire, ou Mémoires pour servir à l'histoire des cours, des sociétés & de la littérature en France, depuis la mort de Louis XV* (18 vols., London, 1787–90).

Meyer, *Armement nantais* — Jean Meyer, *L'Armement nantais dans la deuxième moitié du XVIIIe siècle* (Paris, 1969).

Meyer, *Noblesse bretonne* — Jean Meyer, *La Noblesse bretonne au XVIIIe siècle* (2 vols., Paris, 1966).

Morison, *Jones* — Samuel E. Morison, *John Paul Jones: a Sailor's Biography* (Boston and Toronto, 1959).

Morris, *Jay: Peace* — Richard B. Morris *et al.*, eds., *John Jay, the Winning of the Peace: Unpublished Papers, 1780–1784* (New York, 1980).

Morris, *Jay: Revolutionary* — Richard B. Morris *et al.*, eds., *John Jay, the Making of a Revolutionary: Unpublished Papers, 1743–1780* (New York, 1975).

Morris Papers — E. James Ferguson, John Catanzariti, Mary A. Gallagher, Elizabeth M. Nuxoll, *et al.*, eds., *The Papers of Robert Morris, 1781–1784* (9 vols., Pittsburgh, 1973–99).

MS, MSS — Manuscript, manuscripts.

Namier and Brooke, *House of Commons* — Sir Lewis Namier and John Brooke, *The History of Parliament. The House of Commons 1754–1790* (3 vols., London and New York, 1964).

NNBW — *Nieuw Nederlandsch Biografisch Woordenboek* (10 vols. and index, Amsterdam, 1974).

Nouvelle biographie	*Nouvelle biographie générale depuis les temps les plus reculés jusqu'à nos jours* ... (46 vols., Paris, 1855–66).
ODNB	*Oxford Dictionary of National Biography.*
Pa.	Pennsylvania.
Pa. Arch.	Samuel Hazard *et al.*, eds., *Pennsylvania Archives* (9 series, Philadelphia and Harrisburg, 1852–1935).
Palmer, *Loyalists*	Gregory Palmer, ed., *Biographical Sketches of Loyalists of the American Revolution* (Westport, Conn., 1984).
Parry, *Consolidated Treaty Series*	Clive Parry, comp., *The Consolidated Treaty Series* (243 vols., Dobbs Ferry, N.Y., 1969–86).
Peach and Thomas, *Price Correspondence*	W. Bernard Peach and D. O. Thomas, eds., *The Correspondence of Richard Price* (3 vols., Durham, N.C., and Cardiff, 1983–94).
Phil. Trans.	The Royal Society, *Philosophical Transactions.*
PMHB	*Pennsylvania Magazine of History and Biography.*
Price, *France and the Chesapeake*	Jacob M. Price, *France and the Chesapeake: a History of the French Tobacco Monopoly, 1674–1791, and of Its Relationship to the British and American Tobacco Trade* (2 vols., Ann Arbor, 1973).
Proc.	Proceedings.
Pub.	Publications.
Quérard, *France littéraire*	Joseph Marie Quérard, *La France littéraire ou Dictionnaire bibliographique des savants, historiens, et gens de lettres de la France, ainsi que des littérateurs étrangers qui ont écrit en français, plus*

	particulièrement pendant les XVIIIe et XIXe siècles . . . (10 vols., Paris, 1827–64).
RB	Richard Bache.
Repertorium der diplomatischen Vertreter	Ludwig Bittner *et al.*, eds., *Repertorium der diplomatischen Vertreter aller Länder seit dem Westfälischen Frieden (1648)* (3 vols., Oldenburg, etc., 1936–65).
Rev.	Review or revised.
Rice and Brown, eds., *Rochambeau's Army*	Howard C. Rice, Jr., and Anne S. K. Brown, eds., *The American Campaigns of Rochambeau's Army, 1780, 1781, 1782, 1783* (2 vols., Princeton and Providence, 1972).
Roberts and Roberts, *Thomas Barclay*	Priscilla H. Roberts and Richard S. Roberts, *Thomas Barclay (1728– 1793): Consul in France, Diplomat in Barbary* (Bethlehem, Pa., 2008).
s.	*sous.*
s.	shillings.
Sabine, *Loyalists*	Lorenzo Sabine, *Biographical Sketches of Loyalists of the American Revolution* . . . (2 vols., Boston, 1864).
SB	Sarah Bache.
Schulte Nordholt, *Dutch Republic*	J. W. Schulte Nordholt, *The Dutch Republic and American Independence* (trans. Herbert M. Rowen; Chapel Hill, 1982).
Sellers, *Franklin in Portraiture*	Charles C. Sellers, *Benjamin Franklin in Portraiture* (New Haven and London, 1962).
Sibley's Harvard Graduates	John L. Sibley, *Biographical Sketches of Graduates of Harvard University* (18 vols. to date, Cambridge, Mass.,

xliv

	1873–). Continued from Volume IV by Clifford K. Shipton.
Six, *Dictionnaire biographique*	Georges Six, *Dictionnaire biographique des généraux et amiraux français de la Révolution et de l'Empire (1792–1814)* (2 vols., Paris, 1934).
Smith, *Letters*	Paul H. Smith *et al.*, eds., *Letters of Delegates to Congress* (26 vols., Washington, D.C., 1976–2000).
Smyth, *Writings*	Albert H. Smyth, ed., *The Writings of Benjamin Franklin* . . . (10 vols., New York, 1905–7).
Soc.	Society.
Sparks, *Works*	Jared Sparks, ed., *The Works of Benjamin Franklin* . . . (10 vols., Boston, 1836–40).
Taylor, *J. Q. Adams Diary*	Robert J. Taylor *et al.*, eds., *Diary of John Quincy Adams* (2 vols. to date, Cambridge, Mass., and London, 1981–).
TJ	Thomas Jefferson.
Tourneux, *Correspondance littéraire*	Maurice Tourneux, *Correspondance littéraire, philosophique et critique par Grimm, Diderot, Raynal, Meister, etc. revue sur les textes originaux comprenant outre ce qui a été publié à diverses époques les fragments supprimés en 1813 par la censure les parties inédites conservées à la Bibliothèque Ducale de Gotha et l'Arsenal à Paris* (16 vols., Paris, 1877–82).
Trans.	Translator, translated, or transactions.
Van Doren, *Franklin*	Carl Van Doren, *Benjamin Franklin* (New York, 1938).

Van Doren, *Franklin-Mecom*	Carl Van Doren, ed., *The Letters of Benjamin Franklin & Jane Mecom* (American Philosophical Society *Memoirs*, XXVII, Princeton, 1950).
Villiers, *Commerce colonial*	Patrick Villiers, *Le Commerce colonial atlantique et la guerre d'indépendance des Etats-Unis d'Amérique, 1778–1783* (New York, 1977).
W&MQ	*William and Mary Quarterly*, first or third series as indicated.
Waste Book	BF's accounts described above, XXIII, 19.
WF	William Franklin.
Wharton, *Diplomatic Correspondence*	Francis Wharton, ed., *The Revolutionary Diplomatic Correspondence of the United States* (6 vols., Washington, D.C., 1889).
Wolf and Hayes, *Library of Benjamin Franklin*	Edwin Wolf 2nd and Kevin J. Hayes, eds., *The Library of Benjamin Franklin* (Philadelphia, 2006).
WTF	William Temple Franklin.
WTF, *Memoirs*	William Temple Franklin, ed., *Memoirs of the Life and Writings of Benjamin Franklin, L.L.D., F.R.S., &c...* (3 vols., 4to, London, 1817–18).
WTF's accounts	Those described above, XXIII, 19.

Note by the Editors and the Administrative Board

As we noted in volume 23 (pp. xlvi–xlviii), the period of Franklin's mission to France brings with it roughly two and a half times as many documents as those for the other seventy years of his life. In the present volume once again we summarize a portion of his incoming correspondence in collective descriptions; they appear in the index under the following headings: emigrants, would-be; favor seekers; offerers of goods and schemes.

A revised statement of textual methodology appeared in volume 28 and is repeated here with slight updates, principally to the method of textual reproduction. The original statement of method is found in the Introduction to the first volume, pp. xxiv–xlvii. The various developments in policy are explained in xv, xxiv; xxi, xxxiv; xxiii, xlvi–xlviii.

As noted in volume 39 (p. liv), the digital *Papers of Benjamin Franklin,* conceived and sponsored by the Packard Humanities Institute, is freely accessible at franklinpapers.org. It contains texts of all the documents in our archive up to Franklin's death, including those that are only summarized or mentioned in the letterpress edition. It also contains biographical sketches of all Franklin's correspondents and an introduction by Edmund S. Morgan. Readers are advised that documents marked "unpublished" are preliminary transcriptions whose dates and attributions may change with further research. They will be replaced with final, verified texts as the letterpress edition proceeds.

In 2014, digital versions of the first thirty-nine volumes of *The Papers of Benjamin Franklin* were made available through Founders Online, a database that includes the published volumes of the papers of John Adams, Alexander Hamilton, Thomas Jefferson, James Madison, and George Washington. Created under the auspices of the National Archives and funded by the Congress of the United States, Founders Online is freely accessible at founders.archives.gov.

Researchers are also invited to make use of our preliminary Cumulative Index to the published volumes, available through our project website, franklinpapers.yale.edu.

As with all the volumes in this series, volume 42 is the product not only of the editors whose names appear on the title page but also of the generations of editors who came before us. Our predecessors located and collected thousands of manuscripts, accessioned and transcribed them, identified correspondents, supplied dates for undated documents, and left us the benefit of their research notes and, in some cases, drafts of proposed annotation. We acknowledge here with special appreciation the expertise of former Senior Associate Editor Jonathan R. Dull, who, before retiring in 2008, drafted footnotes for the documents within his areas of expertise, up through the end of Franklin's stay in France. We continue to benefit from his work, and deeply appreciate his service as a consultant who reviews our final manuscripts before publication. We also thank former Assistant Editors Alicia K. Anderson and Michael Sletcher, whose research and textual readings informed many of the documents that appear within these pages. Finally, we express our appreciation to Assistant Editor Alysia Cain, who left the project shortly before this volume went to press, and to Editorial Assistant Kate Woodford, who left after the final corrections were made to the manuscript. We thank them for their contributions and wish them well.

Introduction

The winter of 1783–84 was one of the harshest on record. Extreme cold and heavy snows impeded land travel in North America, making it impossible until mid-January for Congress to assemble the number of delegates required to ratify the definitive treaty of peace. Frozen rivers and harbors paralyzed maritime traffic as well, further delaying the transmission of the ratification across the Atlantic. As this volume opens, Franklin was waiting anxiously for the ratification to arrive, and with it the recall he had so ardently requested of Congress. He was feeling old, he wrote, and wanted to die in his own country. Weather and infirmity, moreover, kept him largely housebound at the Hôtel de Valentinois. Roads and rivers around Paris were just as choked with snow and ice as those surrounding Annapolis. Firewood had become so difficult to transport, in fact, that the French government rationed supplies, giving preference to bakers.[1]

In early March, a letter finally arrived from Congress that explained the delay in ratifying the treaty. By then, the six-month time limit for exchanging ratifications had passed. Hoping that this set of "Accidents unforeseen & unavoidable" would not necessitate a formal convention to extend the deadline, Franklin wrote to inform British negotiator David Hartley that he expected the congressional ratification to arrive within the month.[2] It did so, barely. On March 31, Franklin and John Jay sent Hartley official word that the treaty as ratified by Congress was now in hand and that they were ready to make the exchange. George III ratified the treaty on April 9, and Hartley brought it to Paris, arriving around April 27.

With John Adams in Holland, where he had negotiated a new loan, and Henry Laurens in England, where he was preparing

---

1. BF's request for his recall, a renewal of earlier pleas, was dated Dec. 26, 1783: XLI, 356. For the shortage of wood see XLI, 256–8, where BF's design for a rotating space heater is also illustrated.
2. To Charles Thomson, March 9; to David Hartley, March 11.

for his return to America, Franklin and Jay exchanged the ratifications with Hartley on May 12. Four days later, Jay and his family departed for New York. It was to Franklin alone, therefore, that Hartley communicated the objections of the British foreign secretary to the form of the congressional ratification. The American's response was so thorough and forceful in its clear, simple explanations that it remained the last word.[3] Franklin, on his own, had negotiated the basic framework of the peace, and, at the end, he was the one who dispelled all the petty objections to the ratification's final wording.

Hartley would remain in Paris for four more months, pursuing the chimera of concluding the British-American commercial treaty that he and Franklin had discussed the previous summer. We publish under the date of [after April 27] a list of articles that Hartley drew up for Franklin's review; this is the sole surviving document attesting to the ongoing negotiations. Franklin was skeptical of their success, and for good reason. Hartley had never received authorization to continue these discussions, and he remained in Paris despite the unequivocal instructions he had received to return to London as soon as the ratifications were exchanged.

As winter turned to spring, Franklin set about concluding whatever official business was as yet unresolved. On May 28, he settled the long-disputed account between Congress and his landlord, Le Ray de Chaumont, agreeing to pay rent retroactively for lodgings that had initially been offered gratis. He urged Vergennes to conclude the Franco-American consular convention that they had negotiated the previous year. The two men signed the convention on July 29, at Versailles. This may have been the first time the American minister had traveled to court since the previous September, when the peace was signed.

The man who had found the French such congenial hosts for so many years also began to prepare for what he anticipated would be a bittersweet farewell. Hoping to find relief from the bladder stone that made travel so painful, he sought the advice of William Withering, an English physician whose specialty was "calculous Complaints," sending him on March 1 a

3. Hartley to BF, June 1; BF to Hartley, June 2.

1

case history of his affliction. In early April, with the assistance of a compositor he hired, Franklin finished printing his collection of bagatelles, intended as keepsakes for his French circle of friends.[4] On April 22, reflecting on his remarkable life and judging that his death could not be far off, he composed a poignant verse that gave thanks to his "Landlord" and bid farewell to his friends as he prepared to "retire to Rest."

Retirement in any of its forms, however, was still a long way off. Congress had no intention of releasing Franklin from his diplomatic duties. On May 7, it appointed him, John Adams, and Thomas Jefferson to a new commission charged with negotiating and concluding treaties of amity and commerce with some twenty European and North African powers. Spurning Franklin's request that his grandson Temple be granted another diplomatic assignment, however, Congress appointed David Humphreys, a former aide-de-camp to Washington, as the commission's secretary. This appointment, orchestrated by Franklin's enemies, wounded grandfather and grandson alike.

Franklin received official word of the new commission in early August. Along with it came news of the reduction of the commissioners' salaries. When notifying Adams, who was still at The Hague, of the assignment he knew to be nearly impossible, Franklin resorted to irony. The three commissioners, he wrote, were "not likely to eat the Bread of Idleness; and that we may not surfeit by eating too much, our Masters have diminish'd our Allowance." On August 6, the day Franklin wrote these words to Adams, Thomas Jefferson arrived in Paris. Adams followed soon thereafter, stopping first in London to pick up his family.

Idleness, despite whatever his detractors may have claimed, had never been part of Franklin's constitution. Although his mobility was curtailed during the spring and summer of 1784, his intellect remained as vigorous as ever, and he gave it free range as he considered the follies of human nature and thought deeply about some of the most important scientific problems of his time. In March, struck by the absurdity of an aristocracy that professed to love "économie" while sleeping away half the daylight hours, he wrote his now-famous satire advocating the

4. See BF to Mme Brillon, April 8.

economic advantages of rising with the sun. This essay, published as a letter to the editors of the *Journal de Paris*, also skewered the growing number of charlatans, self-styled discoverers, and self-important experts whose vaunted innovations and opinions were described in the journal's pages. The impetus for this satire may have come from the spectacle of two Parisians trying to claim credit for a new oil lamp whose design they had stolen from a friend. What no one in Paris seems to have known was that the inventor, Ami Argand, had incorporated key elements of his "new" design from an oil lamp he had seen in Switzerland that Franklin himself had invented more than a decade earlier. In May, turning to science, Franklin wrote a piece on climatic conditions in which he correctly posited that the so-called "dry fog" of the previous summer might explain the exceptionally cold winter that followed and may have been itself the result of a recent volcanic eruption in Iceland. In June, he set down on paper what he called "Loose Thoughts on a Universal Fluid," an attempt to produce a unified theory of light and heat. In July, he reflected on luxury in a letter to Benjamin Vaughan.[5]

Even if Franklin was not getting out much in the world, the world continued to come to him. The fragments that survive from his journal, as well as the diary entries of his grandson Benny Bache (for whom French was still the more comfortable language), reveal a vibrant social and intellectual life. Franklin received a visit from the comte de Mirabeau and his co-author Chamfort, with whom he discussed their manuscript on the absurdity of hereditary nobility. He offered them, on the promise of anonymity, the text of an essay he had written the previous January on that same subject. (True to their word, they used passages from his essay without attribution.) On August 4, according to Benny's diary, Franklin hosted a dinner for the British ambassador, the Duke of Dorset, "avec grande Compagnie." Among the guests was John Paul Jones.

Gustavus III, king of Sweden, came to Paris incognito in the summer of 1784. Franklin met with members of his court on

5. The pieces were: "Aux Auteurs du *Journal de Paris*," [before March 31]; "Meteorological Imaginations and Conjectures," [May]; "Loose Thoughts on a Universal Fluid," [June 25]; BF to Vaughan, July 26[–c. Aug. 15].

several occasions and dined with them at least once, at the home of his neighbor Ferdinand Grand. Whether the king was present on that occasion is not recorded. We assume that Gustavus, who had the highest regard for Franklin, would have wanted to meet him in person; in 1782, he had insisted that a Swedish-American treaty be negotiated with no one else. Whether the two men met, however, remains at present in the realm of conjecture. We know only that the king left his calling card at Passy, and bought a bust of Franklin to bring back to Stockholm. If they dined together at Grand's or anywhere else, Franklin was discreet enough not to leave a written record.

Musicians were invited to perform. The celebrated Mlle Paradis gave a concert on Franklin's fortepiano on May 2, to the acclaim of all the assembled guests. (Benny alone, it seems, did not care for her style of playing.) Two weeks later Franklin hosted a performance by the famous Italian violinist and composer Giovanni Battista Viotti, accompanied on fortepiano by one of the abbé Morellet's nieces. Mme Brillon also played that evening.

Benny Bache, a bright and curious fourteen-year-old, added immeasurably to life at the Valentinois. Franklin arranged for him to take a course in natural philosophy taught by M. Charles, the eminent physicist, and enrolled him in thrice-weekly drawing lessons. Benny kept canaries, which occasionally escaped from their cage, and carefully observed their brooding habits, noting when one of them (erroneously referred to in the masculine) laid its first egg. As soon as the Seine was of a tolerable temperature—there were still snow squalls in mid-April—he took to swimming daily, undoubtedly coached by his grandfather. He spent the long summer days outdoors with his friend Bob Alexander, two years his senior, who was living with the Franklins.[6] The boys made a series of kites, adjusting their size based on the tensile strength of the string, which was prone to snapping under the strain of the winds blowing across the Seine. Benny thought nothing of stripping off his clothes and swimming to the opposite bank of the river to retrieve a battered kite when it plummeted. On one particular day, he described an incident in which a deranged man appeared at the gate of the Valentinois,

6. See XLI, 524n.

insisting on an audience with his grandfather. The man's lackey admitted that his master had recently gone mad. Placated somewhat by the offer of pen and paper, the visitor scrawled a letter that was barely coherent. According to Benny, he was not easily evicted from the property.

Franklin received several letters from his daughter, Sally, Benny's mother, written in June from a country house on the banks of the Schuylkill River, whose rental Franklin had subsidized so that the Bache family could escape the heat of a Philadelphia summer. The change in the children was delightful, she wrote; they were all healthier and in great spirits. Their one searing disappointment was that Franklin—contrary to what Sally had been led to expect—had not yet returned to them. Were it not for her domestic obligations, she wrote, she would go to him in France.

Sally's abiding affection, and the devotion Franklin received from the two grandsons who accompanied him to France— Benny and his older cousin William Temple Franklin, the illegitimate grandchild whom Franklin had adopted—compensated to some degree for the deep bitterness that existed between Franklin and his Loyalist son, William, Temple's father and the former royal governor of New Jersey. Estranged from Franklin since the outbreak of the war, William had become a leader of the Loyalists in London. In the summer of 1784, thinking perhaps of his departure from Europe, of Temple's future prospects, and of Temple's desire to see his father, Franklin made a subtle overture to his son. Communicating through a third party who was on his way from Paris to London, Franklin intimated that he would welcome a renewal of relations. If countries could reconcile after a revolution, then surely individuals who had taken opposite sides in the conflict could do so as well. On July 22, William wrote his father a letter that was by turns respectful, conciliatory, and unrepentant. Having personal matters to discuss that could not be committed to paper, he asked permission to visit Passy. Franklin received this letter, filled with as much defiance as affection, as the present volume comes to an end. William would not be allowed to come to Paris. On August 16, Franklin would inform him that Temple would go to London as his proxy.

One important story spans nearly the entire period of the present volume: Franklin's appointment to a French royal commission to investigate a highly suspect medical practice, the use of what was called animal magnetism, a doctrine brought to Paris by the Viennese doctor Franz Anton Mesmer. The commission included some of the most distinguished scientists and physicians of Paris. They were charged with investigating animal magnetism as practiced not by Mesmer, who refused to cooperate, but by Dr. Charles Deslon, his disciple and a member of the Faculté de médecine. Rather than examining the effects of Deslon's medical treatments, however, the commission set itself the goal of determining whether animal magnetism existed at all. Initially, twelve commissioners were appointed, four each from the Académie des sciences (of which Franklin was a member), the Faculté de médecine, and the Société de médecine. When hostilities between the Faculty and the Society made cooperation impossible, two separate commissions were established, with the members of the Academy working with both factions. Franklin hosted meetings of both commissions at the Hôtel de Valentinois, beginning in late April. By May, however, he and his colleagues from the Academy had decided to ally themselves exclusively with the Faculty, leaving the commissioners from the Society to proceed on their own. Franklin was elected the head of the joint Academy-Faculty commission. Over a period of four months, it completed a series of groundbreaking experiments that would prove that physical symptoms could be caused by the "imagination," and that the symptoms experienced by magnetized patients were, in fact, psychological in nature. The commission's report, signed on August 11 and published later that month, caused a sensation at the time and is still considered a milestone in the history of science.

With the arrival of Thomas Jefferson in August, Franklin embarked on his new diplomatic assignment just as his work on the French scientific commission came to an end. The congressional commission would tackle a challenge that would prove more formidable than investigating an invisible, omnipresent force: persuading the nations of Europe to accept the United States as an equal trading partner.

Chronology

March 9: John Adams signs contract for a new loan with the Dutch banking consortium on behalf of the United States, preventing the protest of Robert Morris' bills in Europe.

March 25: George III dissolves Parliament, leading to general elections in April–May that strengthen the coalition of Prime Minister William Pitt.

March 27: William Carmichael arrives in Paris to settle accounts with John Jay.

March 29: Josiah Harmar delivers Congress' ratification of the definitive peace treaty to Franklin.

c. April 2: Baron de Breteuil appoints Franklin to the royal commission to investigate animal magnetism.

April 9: Great Britain ratifies the definitive peace treaty.

April 15: David S. Franks arrives in Paris with a second copy of Congress' ratification of the definitive peace treaty.

April 27: David Hartley visits Franklin at Passy.

May 7–12: Congress commissions Franklin, John Adams, and Thomas Jefferson to negotiate commercial treaties with twenty European and North African nations; appoints John Jay secretary for foreign affairs; elects David Humphreys secretary of the commission.

May 12: Franklin and John Jay exchange ratifications of the definitive peace treaty with David Hartley.

May 14: French government establishes free ports in Lorient, Bayonne, Dunkirk, Marseille, and St. Jean de Luz.

May 16–July 24: The Jay family travels from Paris to New York.

June 7–July 20: Gustavus III visits Versailles and Paris under the alias the comte de Haga.

June 17: The Royal Society awards Cook medal to Franklin.

June 22–August 3: Henry Laurens sails from Falmouth to New York.

June 30–August 4: Lafayette sails from Lorient to New York.

July 5–August 6: Thomas Jefferson travels from Boston to Paris.

July 29: Vergennes and Franklin sign the consular convention between France and the United States.

August 7–13: The Adams family reunites in London, travels to Paris.

August 11: After a four-month investigation, the royal commission to investigate animal magnetism signs their report.

THE PAPERS OF
BENJAMIN FRANKLIN

VOLUME 42

March 1 through August 15, 1784

Editorial Note on Franklin's Accounts

The following accounts, identified in previous volumes, cover the period of this volume: VI and VII (XXIII, 21); XVII (XXVI, 3); XIX and XXII (XXVIII, 3–4); XXV, XXVII (XXXII, 3–4); XXX (XXXVI, 3). We offer here a summary of items that have not found a place elsewhere in our annotation but provide insights into Franklin's private and public life.

Account XVII (Franklin's Private Accounts with Ferdinand Grand, XXVI, 3). On March 16, Jacques Finck, *maître d'hôtel*, received three sums: 5,000 *l.t.*, the first of what were to be quarterly payments under his February 1, 1784, contract; back wages amounting to 900 *l.t.*; and 254 *l.t.* to cover the cost of the December, 1783, illuminations at Passy in celebration of the peace.[1] After the first quarter, Franklin resumed his practice of paying Finck monthly: 2,737 *l.t.* 12 *s.* on May 10 and 2,500 *l.t.* on June 22. Franklin's secretary Jean L'Air de Lamotte received 1,200 *l.t.* on May 10, July 1, and August 15. Durandy, from whom the Franklins leased horses, was paid on March 23, April 26, and June 22. The bills of Broudgoust, the smith, and Bousie, the wine merchant, were honored on June 15 and August 12, respectively.[2]

Account XXV (Account of Postage and Errands, XXXII, 3). These records, kept by L'Air de Lamotte, survive for every month covered in this volume except August. As usual, they include the monthly statements submitted by the postman Berthelot and reflect the

1. For Finck's Feb. 1 contract with BF, and the receipt for these payments that he signed on March 16, see XLI, 521–5. For the illuminations see XLI, 266–7n.

2. Not itemized in these accounts are the biweekly payments of 6 *l.t.* that BF gave BFB as an allowance, beginning (apparently) on Jan. 1, 1784. BFB recorded these payments in a small account book he kept, entitled "Depences de LAnnée 1784 à Passy" (Castle Collection, on deposit at the APS). On the income side of the ledger, in addition to his allowance payments, are BFB's winnings at Saturday card games. On the expenditure side, during the period of this volume, are his losses at cards, money lost while swimming, the cost of an occasional trip across the Seine, and a variety of small purchases such as arrows, kite-making materials, fishing equipment, shuttlecocks, a stick and hoop, flowerpots, and, for his canaries, seed, a birdbath, and baskets for their nests. BFB paid for the washing and mending of his own clothes out of his allowance, and twice gave money to paupers, one of whom was an American sailor.

errands performed by Bonnefoÿ, Franklin's domestic, who received twice his usual amount on April 13 for a trip to Versailles. (His errands are otherwise unspecified.) On May 23 William Temple Franklin was reimbursed for two inkwells purchased for the office at the cost of 54 *l.t.*, and on July 14 Lamotte furnished 12 *l.t.* to a "pauvre Matelot Americain" without taking a receipt. Letters and packets that Franklin received on behalf of others are also recorded: on April 12 Lamotte paid 15 *l.t.* 11 *s.* for a packet addressed to John Adams, and on May 19 he paid 2 *l.t.* 2 *s.* for two letters, one for John Jay and the other for Peter Munro.

Account XXVII (Accounts of the Public Agents in Europe, XXXII, 4). L'Air de Lamotte received six months of salary on May 10, amounting to 840 *l.t.*, and was reimbursed monthly for his postage and miscellaneous expenditures detailed in Account XXV. Francis Coffyn's bill of 1,251 *l.t.* 12 *s.* 8 *d.* was paid on June 19. Cabaret, the stationer, received 220 *l.t.* 4 *s.* on July 11. On August 19, William Temple Franklin received 22,000 *l.t.* by order of Franklin and Adams for his services as secretary of the peace commission from October 1, 1782, to September 3, 1783.

To Félix Vicq d'Azyr

ALS: Académie Nationale de Médecine, Paris

Sir,   Passy, March 1. 1784

I should be very happy to be present at the Reading of your Eloges of Messrs Sanchez & Hunter;[3] but my Indisposition, the Stone, makes it extreamly inconvenient to me to use a Carriage on the Pavement, or to be confined long in a Room, so that I cannot have the Pleasure you propose to me so kindly of meeting the Society whom I highly respect, on Tuesday. With great Esteem I have the honour to be Sir, Your most obedient & most humble Servant   B FRANKLIN

M. Vicq d'azyr

To William Withering

ALS: American Philosophical Society

Sir,   Passy, March 1. 1784

Mr Vaughan communicated to me a very ingenious & judicious Letter (as it appear'd to me) written by you on the Subject of calculous Complaints & the Remedies that had been propos'd for them. You were so good as to say that if I would send you a state of my Case, you might perhaps be able to point out some Plan of Proceeding that would be serviceable.[4] I omitted it then, thinking the Disease had left me; & hoping by the Use of Honey to prevent its Return. I was however mistaken, as you will see in the Case, but have not since had recourse to any Medicine. I now request your Opinion and Advice;[5] and

---

3. At the public meeting of the Société royale de médecine the next day, March 2. Vicq d'Azyr had invited BF to the meeting on Feb. 25; see XLI, 583–4.

4. Benjamin Vaughan had solicited this letter from Withering when BF suffered an acute attack of the stone in 1782. The letter is now missing, but Withering used it as the basis for his 1782 essay entitled "On Calculous Complaints"; see XXXVIII, 39–41.

5. The enclosed case study is immediately below. BF made arrangements to pay Withering for this consultation: on the same day as the present letter he wrote an order for William Hodgson to remit five guineas on his account to "Dr Withering of Birmingham": BF to Hodgson, March 1, 1784 (press

am, with great Esteem, Sir, Your most obedient & most humble
Servant,   B FRANKLIN

Dr Withering.—

Franklin's Case

D and incomplete press copy of D:[6] American Philosophical Society

[c. March 1, 1784][7]

Case

The Patient is now in his 79th. Year. When a Young Man he was
sometimes troubled with gravelly Complaints; but they wore off
without the Use of any Medecine, and he remained more than
Fifty Years free from them.

In the Autumn of 1782, he had a severe Attack accompanied
with what was thought to be a Gouty Pain in the Hyp, and down
the Thigh of the left Side. Some Means were us'd to bring the
suppos'd Gout down into the Foot, by warm Bathing, and a
Poultis of Mustard. A Swelling was produc'd in the Foot, but
not attended with much Pain there; a considerable Pain still continuing above. He daily voided Gravel Stones the Size of small
Pease, took now and then some Decoctions of Herbs & Roots
that were prescribed him by Friends or Physicians, but persisted
constantly in nothing except the Use of Honey at Breakfast instead of or sometimes with Butter on his Bread, he remembring
to have heard in the Conversation of Physicians, Honey mentioned as of great Service in Gravelly Cases.[1]

At length the painful Part of the Disorder left him, and no
more large Gravel offer'd; but observing Sand constantly in his

---

copy of ADS), APS. BF added this sum to the account Hodgson had sent him
on Oct. 30, 1783: XLI, 160n.

6. In the hand of L'Air de Lamotte.

7. The day BF enclosed the present document in his letter to Dr. Withering, immediately above. Being in his "79th. Year," as he wrote, he must
have composed this case since turning 78 in January.

1. For BF's 1782 attack of bladder stones and the various suggestions for
remedies he received from friends and strangers see XXXVIII, 30–4, 39–42.

6

Urine, he continued the Use of the Honey to the Amount of perhaps a Pound per Week; notwithstanding which the Malady return'd in the Autumn of 1783, when he first perceived after going in his Carriage on the Pavements, that he felt Pain & made bloody Water.[2] At times when he was making Water in full Stream, something came and stopt the Passage; this he suspected to be a small Stone, and he suffered Pain by the Stoppage. He found however by Experience that he could by laying down on his Side cause the Obstruction to remove and continue the Operation. He now thinks the Stone is grown bigger & heavier as he is sensible of its falling from Side to Side, as he turns in his Bed.

He has made it a Rule for some Months to walk an hour in his Chamber every Night. This Exercise is of service to him in other Respects; but he has observed that if he has emptied his Bladder just before he begins his Walk, the Stone is apt to hurt him, and he makes bloody Water. He therefore of late avoids beginning his Walk, till he supposes the Bladder to be refurnish'd.

His Inclination to make Water is sometimes very sudden & very violent, tho' the Quantity small.

He feels no Pain, nor is at all sensible of the Existence of the Stone, except when it obstructs his Making Water, or when he is in his Carriage on a Pavement, or on some sudden Motion or Turn of the Body; and he enjoys the Conversation of his Friends or his Books as usual.

Thus if it does not grow worse, it is a *tolerable* Malady, and may be supported for the short time he has a Chance of living. And he would chuse to bear with it rather than have Recourse to dangerous or nauseous Remedies.

If therefore no safe and sure Dissolvent of the Stone is yet known, he wishes to be informed whether there is a Regimen proper to be observ'd for preventing its Increase, as he can without Difficulty conform to any Manner of Living that shall be prescrib'd to him.

In the last Attack no large Gravel has offer'd, and much less Sand appear'd in the Urine, whence he suspects that it attaches

2. In late August, 1783, BF began to refrain from traveling to Paris and Versailles unless it was absolutely necessary. He did travel to Paris to sign the definitive peace treaty: XL, 495n, 505–6n, 566.

itself to the Stone. His Urine has however been unusually turbid till lately, when a Fit of the Gout came on, & swell'd both Feet, since which the Urine has been very clear.—

From Jean-Jacques Bachelier[3]

Printed invitation with MS insertions: American Philosophical Society

M*onsieur*   A Paris, ce *1er Mars* 1784.
Vous êtes invité de la part de Monsieur le Lieutenant général de Police, et du Bureau d'Administration de l'Ecole royale gratuite de Dessin, d'honorer de votre présence la distribution des grands Prix et Maîtrises, qui se fera aux Tuileries, Cour des Princes, Galerie de la Reine, le *8. du present* à *5.* heures précises.[4]
Je suis avec respect, M*onsieur* Votre très-humble et très-obéissant Serviteur,   BACHELIER

From Anne Johnson Clarke[5]

ALS: American Philosophical Society

Honored Sir,   London March the 2d. 1784.
Permit me again to take up the pen (after many years being deprived the pleasure of writing to You) to inquire after your

3. Painter and director of the Ecole royale gratuite de dessin, which he founded in 1766. The school received support from various members of the royal family and a wide range of benefactors throughout France: Ulrich Leben, *Object Design in the Age of Enlightenment: the History of the Royal Free Drawing School in Paris*, trans. Sharon Grevet (Los Angeles, 2004), pp. 47, 53–4. In 1777 BF and Bachelier had discussed a proposal for establishing a school for the arts and crafts as well as manufactures in the United States: XXIII, 619; XXIV, 143n; *DBF.*

4. Lenoir, the lieutenant general of police, was president of the school's administrative board: *Almanach royal* for 1784, p. 525. The ceremony was described in the *Jour. de Paris* of March 11, where Bachelier's address was published and the names of the grand prize winners announced.

5. BF's grandniece. She had lived with BF on Craven Street during 1768 and 1769; in the latter year she was joined there by her brother, Samuel, and their widowed mother, Martha Johnson: XV, 46–7, 271–2; XVI, 211–12.

health, and to give You some account of myself since I last wrote to You. I have long wish'd for a proper opportunity to pay my Duty to You, even at this distance and yesterday Mrs: Woolford call'd to inform me a Relation of Hers was going to Paris for His education, and She wou'd forward a letter for me; which I readily accepted of.[6] Great has been my change in this life. In March 1776 I had the great misfortune to loose one of the most indulgent of Husbands (after lingering some years in a Consumption)[7] and with Him almost every prospect of future happiness. His elder Brother had so involved Himself by extravagence, that He was, at the time of Capt. Clarkes death two Hundred Thousand Pounds worse than nothing, and had given mortgages and judgments to Mr. Daniel Lascelles upon all the Estate (where our interest lay,) prior to my Husband;[8] but as there was a doubt about the legality of Mr. Gedney Clarkes proceedings, I was advised to join in a bill in Chancery, and have been eight years involved in a Lawsuit 'tho no nearer than when I first set out. In 1780 I lost every thing I had in the World in a dreadful Hurricane and thank'd Providence I escaped with Life and

---

The most recent extant letter from her dates from 1771, when she was newly married and living in Barbados: XVIII, 99–100. Her mother wrote BF news of her in 1781: XXXV, 608.

6. Mrs. D. Woolford, a friend of Mrs. Stevenson (XXII, 27) and of Anne's mother (XXXV, 606n), had written a chatty letter to WTF on Feb. 29 (APS) and in a postscript explained that she was enclosing this one from Mrs. Clarke. The bearer must have been Thomas Hyde, whom WTF invited on April 16, 1784, to Sunday dinner; the young man had to decline because on that day he would be arranging for his "schooling": Thomas Hyde to WTF, April 17, 1784 (APS). Thomas was presumably related to Mrs. Woolford's sister Mrs. Hyde. (Her name is established from Woolford's correspondence with WTF, including WTF to Mrs. Woolford, Aug. 23, 1781, APS.)

7. Capt. Peter Clarke: XXIV, 221n.

8. In 1774 Capt. Clarke's older brother Gedney Clarke, Jr. (XVIII, 99–100n), lost the fortune inherited from his father, a Barbadian merchant and planter. After years of business reverses and mounting debts, Clarke suffered a complete financial collapse at the hands of his English bankers, the Lascelles, who foreclosed on their loans and took possession of his plantations: S. D. Smith, "Gedney Clarke of Salem and Barbados: Transatlantic Super-Merchant," *New England Quarterly*, LXXVI (2003), 499–500, 503, 533–4, 538–41, 545–6, and *passim*.

whole bones.[9] My Dear Brother[1] arrived from America shortly after and supplied with Cloths and some money and assisted me in returning to England. Upon my arrival in London, I went to Beaufort Buildings to seek my Mother, but judge Sir, what was my feelings when I beheld the spot laid in ashes,[2] and for some time cou'd get no intelligence of my poor Mother. At last a Girl from a Neighboring Alehouse directed me to Her. We were both so much altered by time and misfortunes, that I scarce knew Her, and She wou'd not believe for some time I was Her Daughter. I immediately took a comfortable Lodging and we have lived together ever since. You will perhaps wonder when I inform You, that notwithstanding the large sums that was sent to Barbados for the reliefe of the Sufferers, my Attornies wrote me by the last Pacquet that my part amounted to no more than £4..4..4 ½ Currency. My income as a Captains Widow is £45 a Year My Mothers £15 so with good management we do tolerably well. You early taught me our real wants were few. We look'd forward with pleasing hopes of my Amiable Brothers return to us, which We daily expected, and promised ourselves many happy Days, but oh! Sir, how short lived was that pleasant prospect. I am sure You sympathetie will melt when I tell You, He was amongst the unfortunate sufferers on board the Vielle de Paris coming from Jamaica. Long were we kept under a painful suspence, but We have now no hopes of ever hearing of Him.[3] My Cousin Franklin knew Him in New York and was much pleas'd

9. See xxxv, 608.

1. Samuel Johnson, who (as she writes later in the letter) had been a lieutenant under Adm. Rodney's command. Part of Rodney's squadron was in New York during the hurricane: xxxiii, 333n, 528n; David Spinney, *Rodney* (London, 1969), pp. 346–7, 353–6.

2. Martha Johnson described this fire to bf in her letter of October 18, 1781. He and other family members had sent her assistance: xxxv, 606–8.

3. Anne Clarke had asked Edward Nairne to communicate this sad news to bf three months before: xli, 252. The *Ville de Paris*, a French ship of the line captured by Adm. Rodney in the Battle of the Saintes, left Jamaica for the British Isles at the end of July, 1782, and foundered off Newfoundland in September: xxxvii, 314n; xxxviii, 212n; W. M. James, *The British Navy in Adversity: a Study of the War of American Independence* (London, 1926), p. 356; Spinney, *Rodney*, pp. 415, 416; *London Chron.*, Sept. 17–19, 1782.

with Him. Mr. Foxcraft saw him at a Coffeehouse, knew and introduced him to Your Son, who has been kind enough to visit Us since His arrival in England.[4] Our loss is irreparable. He was a Dutiful Son, an affectionate Brother, a sincere Friend and an excellent Officer. Lord Rodney had so good an opinion of Him, that He kept Him always his Sons first Lieut. and promised him from time to time to make him a Captain, but never perform'd his promise indeed upon being urged on that head by a Friend of mine, He said his Son must not yet part from so good an Officer. When his Lordship came home my Brother was hurt, quited his Son with the Admirals leave and went into the Vielle de Paris; an unfortunate change for him and Us![5] It had near kill'd my poor Mother, but thank God! She is now more reconciled to our loss, and We are both in tolerable health. Your old Friend Mr. Petrie of Enfield died the 26 of January aged 78 years. Miss Petrie desired me some time before, to acquaint you when I wrote, it was his earnest wish to take You by the hand once more before he died.[6] Mrs. Hewson and her little ones are well. She is in Craven Street for a few days. My Mother presents Her Duty, join'd with mine to You and Compts. to Cousin Williams,[7]

4. Her cousin WF arrived in London in September, 1782: XXXVIII, 182n. The introduction in New York was probably performed by John Foxcroft: XL, 502n.

5. John Rodney (*ODNB*) was only 15 when promoted to captain by his father, Adm. Rodney, in 1780. After the admiral's 1782 recall, the *Anson*, with John at the helm, escorted him most of the way back to England, sailing from Jamaica separately from the ill-fated convoy that included the *Ville de Paris:* Spinney, *Rodney,* pp. 353–4, 380, 407–13; *London Chron.,* Sept. 17–19, 1782.

6. William Petrie, a Scottish-born merchant, operated a business in Tokenhouse Yard, London, with his son Samuel. When it failed in 1776, William retired to Enfield and Samuel began to spend time in Paris, where he maintained a friendly relationship with BF: XXIV, 543n; *London Gaz.,* April 23–27, 1776; Samuel Petrie to William Petrie, June 4, 1777, in Benjamin F. Stevens, ed., *Facsimiles of Manuscripts in European Archives Relating to America, 1773–1783* (25 vols., London, 1889–98), II, no. 169; Worthington C. Ford, ed., *Letters of William Lee, 1766–1783* (3 vols., Brooklyn, N.Y., 1891), II, 683–4; *Morning Chron., and London Advertiser,* Jan. 28, 1784; *Gent. Mag.,* LIV (1784), 75, 150.

7. JW.

and Mr. Temple Franklin. It will give Us great pleasure to hear from You, and them, whenever it is convenient to You. We are in the Lodgings Mrs: Woolford had, when I lived with You. Please to direct at No. 46 Strand, and excuse this long epistle from Honored Sir, Your Dutiful Niece, and Humble Servant,   ANNE CLARKE

Doctr: Franklin

From David Hartley

Two ALS: Library of Congress, William L. Clements Library; transcript: National Archives

My Dear friend   London March 2 1784

Will you be so good as to transmitt the enclosed to Mr Jay. I am sorry that we are going to loose him from this side of the atlantic.[8] If your American ratification shd arrive speedily, I might hope to have the pleasure of seeing him again before his departure. As soon as I hear from you of the arrival of your ratification I will immediately apply for the dispatch of the British Ratification.[9] I wish very much to have the pleasure of conversing with you again. In hopes that that time may come soon, I have nothing farther to say at present. Believe always to be what you have always known me to have been; a friend of general Philanthropy, and particularly Your ever most affecte

D HARTLEY

To Dr Franklin &c &c &c

Endorsed: D Hartley Esqr to B F. March 2. 1784—

8. The enclosed letter, dated March 2, was a response to Jay's farewell letter to Hartley of Feb. 22, announcing his intention to return to America in the spring. Jay was awaiting the settlement of his public accounts before leaving France: *Jay Papers*, III, 561, 565–6, 572–3, 579.

9. Congress had ratified the Definitive Treaty of Peace on Jan. 14 and immediately dispatched the ratification to Paris for an exchange with the British: XLI, 456–7, 464–6.

From James Hutton

ALS: American Philosophical Society

Dear Sir   Pimlico March 2. 1784.

The Bearer of this, George Livius Esqr,[1] is a many years friend of mine, and one whom I very much Love, as He is going to Paris, I am very glad of the opportunity of calling myself to your Remembrance, and of sending you an extract of the last Appendix to the Monthly Review, which is in one of your Branches of usefulness.[2] I beg you to recieve my worthy friend as a Portion of myself. He is well acquainted with our Brethren, and has shewn those in the East Indies many kindnesses. This will certainly give him a Distinction in your Eyes.[3]

I saw Dolly Blunt last Sunday well in Spirits, and saw Mr West the Painter & his Wife, He is painting five pieces for the Kings House or Chapel at Windsor.[4] I saw there young Trumbull, who had just finishd an excellent Portrait of your acquaintance

1. George Livius (1743–1816), the younger brother of Peter Livius (xx, 325–6), was an active supporter of the Moravian Church. He had recently returned to England after a decade in India: Walter A. Reichart, "Washington Irving's Friend and Collaborator: Barham John Livius, Esq.," *PMLA*, LVI (1941), 514–15; J. C. S. Mason, *The Moravian Church and the Missionary Awakening in England, 1760–1800* (Woodbridge, Eng., and Rochester, N.Y., 2001), pp. 81–2.

2. Article VIII of the appendix to the most recent volume, covering the second half of 1783, summarized Faujas de Saint-Fond's *Description des expériences de la machine aérostatique de MM. de Montgolfier . . .* (XLI, 81–2), and chronicled the balloon experiments conducted in December, after Faujas' book was issued. That review was followed by an article criticizing Faujas' speculations on the gas used in Montgolfier's balloons, and offering a different explanation. Though the critique was unsigned, the editor, in denying that national prejudice had informed it, attributed the piece to a "distinguished philosopher who . . . is not a native of this country." As the article named BF as one of the signatories to the affidavit of Montgolfier's first manned balloon experiment (XLI, 210–12), Hutton would have known of BF's involvement. Though Hutton's enclosure is missing, it is likely that he sent an extract of this article: *Monthly Review*, LXIX (1783), 561–8.

3. The sole surviving note from Livius to BF, written on a "Friday morng.", informed BF that he would not be able to visit on Sunday, but would call early the next week "to receive [BF's] commands for London": George Livius to BF, [after March 2, 1784] (APS).

4. Over more than two decades, possibly beginning as early as 1778, West executed or began paintings for two chapels, an audience chamber,

Mr Temple.[5] I think Trumbull will do well. I saw a most exquisitely fine marble Bust of you at Mr West's, I never saw a finer or more ressembling.[6] You say in that Bust—*ye are very welcome to claim all ye please.* I *do not care.* Something like what you said to me in Jan. 1778.[7] Good morrow, Dear Sir I am your most obliged and Obedient Servant[8]   JAMES HUTTON

Addressed: To / Doctor Franklin / Passy / near Paris / with a small parcel.

From Jacques Leveux, with Franklin's Note for a Reply

ALS: American Philosophical Society

Monsieur   Calais le 2 Mars 1784.

J'ay reçu la lettre que vous m'avez fait L'honneur de m'ecrire le 21 du mois passé,[9] & Je saisis avec le plus grand empressement cette occasion de vous etre bon a quelque chose.

J'ay exibé de Suite aux employés des fermes du Roy l'ordre de M. de Calonne. Ils en avoient recu un pareil en consequence les couteaux & fourchette & deux Serrures appartenant a Mr Jay m'ont été remis & ils partiront demain par la Diligence a votre adresse. Mes Debours a ce Sujet Sont de L9. *l.t.* 15. *s.*

---

and other settings at Windsor Castle. At least two paintings and a number of preliminary works were completed by 1784, and any number of others may have been under way by the date of the present letter; see Helmut von Erffa and Allen Staley, *The Paintings of Benjamin West* (New Haven and London, 1986), pp. 89–102, 577–81.

5. John Temple (x, 389–90n). John Trumbull was at this time a student of West's. The master evidently gave his "approbation" of this portrait shortly after Hutton saw it: Irma B. Jaffe, *John Trumbull: Patriot-Artist of the American Revolution* (Boston, 1975), pp. 56–7, 62–3, 311.

6. West himself praised the likeness in a letter to BF: XXXVII, 236.

7. When Hutton had visited BF on an unsuccessful mission to broker peace between America and Britain: XXV, 401–2, 402–3n.

8. At the bottom of the sheet BF wrote "Sir Charles Raymon & Co Bankers London". Sir Charles Raymond was at this time the principal of Raymond, Harley, Lloyd and Cameron: F. G. Hilton Price, *A Handbook of London Bankers . . .* (1876; reprint, New York, 1970), p. 73.

9. Not found.

Depuis le compte que J'ay eu l'honneur de vous adresser le 7 Mars 1779,[1] J'ay continué a Secourir les Prisonniers americains qui Se Sont echapés d'angleterre & qui ont passés icy. Mes avances depuis ce moment montent a L1712.10. tournois. Quand vous le desirerez, Monsieur, Je vous en adresserai le compte des quittances pour que vous ordonniez que je Sois remboursé.

Depuis Sept a huit mois, J'ay refusé a plusieurs prisonniers les Secours d'usage, parceque J'ay craint qu'ils ne fussent anglois & non americains, d'ailleurs comme il y avoit deja quelque tems que la paix etoit faite, Je ne pouvois pas presumer qu'il y eut des prisonniers detenus apres plusieurs mois de paix; Je crois, Monsieur, que vous ne desapprouverez pas ma conduite.

J'ay toujours esperé de recevoir une commission de consul americain; Je ne Scais S'il y en a eû de distribuées dans quelque port de france; J'ose me Rappeller a votre Souvenir, en vous Suppliant de me faire passer ce titre que je desire depuis longtems. Vous pouvez etre assuré, Monsieur, de tout mon devouement au Service des Etats unis de l'amérique, & de mon zele pour les interets de Leurs Sujets. Ce Sera un nouveau Surcroit d'obligation qui, ne poura qu'ajouter au respect avec Lequel J'ay l'honneur d'etre Monsieur Votre tres humble & tres obeissant Serviteur   JES. LEVEUX

M. francklin

Endorsed:[2] Thanks for his Care &c That I should be glad to have his Acct. in order to its Discharge, and approve of his not advancing more Money to pretended Americans.

From Charles-Eléonor Dufriche de Valazé

ALS: American Philosophical Society

⟨Paris, Hôtel d'Orléans, March 3, 1784, in French: I have one more thing to tell you, not wanting to take more of your time in person. I had the honor of giving you two copies of *Loix*

1. That invoice, which BF had requested, and its cover letter have not been found; see XXIX, 4, 172.

2. The full reply, written in French, is below, March 8.

pénales; you accepted one, and promised to send the other to Congress.[3] That book alone will not achieve its aim: it calls for a new penal system, but does not specify the manner of implementing it. I have a manuscript prepared on that subject, which I have given to the king's brother. I beg you to offer a copy on my behalf to Congress. Though my plan is designed for France, it could easily be adapted for other countries, and I seek your advice on making it suitable for America.[4] The balloon experiment conducted yesterday by M. Blanchard leaves no doubt that one might be able to navigate by using different air currents found at different heights of the atmosphere.[5]⟩

3. Dufriche must finally have obtained the interview that he had twice requested, first on Jan. 14 and again on Feb. 10 when sending a copy of *Loix pénales:* XLI, 458. It was presumably during that interview that he jotted down the title of his book and the shop where it could be found (Royez, on the corner of the quai des Augustins) on the verso of an unrelated, undated note from L'Enfant *et al.* That note, without Dufriche's notation, was published in XLI, 480.

4. The author delivered the 31-page "Etablissement et administration Des Maisons de Correction" to Passy on April 8 (Hist. Soc. of Pa.). On April 9, he wrote to BF suggesting ways of editing the text to suit America, and repeated his request that BF send it to Congress along with *Loix pénales*. On May 26, writing from his home in Essay, lower Normandy, Dufriche asked whether BF had thought the treatise worth forwarding. Having heard nothing, on June 8 he wrote again, concerned that BF's silence indicated ill health. The king's brother had inquired about the book's reception in America, and Dufriche asked BF to confirm, at least, that it had been sent. (All three letters are at the APS.) The following week, Dufriche asked BF for a personal favor; see his letter below of June 15.

5. On March 2 Jean-Pierre Blanchard launched a hydrogen balloon from the Champ de Mars to which he had attached a rudder and a primitive motor: double-bladed paddles shaped like wings, operated by a treadle. The launch of this supposedly steerable airship turned unexpectedly dramatic when a would-be passenger attacked the inventor. Blanchard was wounded, instruments were broken, and the propeller mechanism was destroyed. The experiment proceeded, regardless. Blanchard later claimed to have steered the ship by means of an improvised sail; in fact, he had been buffeted by various air currents at different altitudes. BFB, who attended the launch, recorded in his journal that Blanchard had done nothing more than repeat the experiment performed by Charles on Dec. 1, 1783 (for which see XLI, 248–51). In this, he voiced the opinion of many spectators: Gillispie, *Montgolfier Brothers*, pp. 95, 97; BFB's journal, entry of March 2, 1784.

From Marie-Françoise-Dominique Brouttin Mollien
de Sombres   AL: American Philosophical Society

paris ce 4 mars 1784

Jai eu lhonneur Monsieur de vous adresser un memoire pour
M. Morel de dunkerque, mon parens. Il y a deux mois en joi-
gnant mes prieres aux siennes. Depuis jai eu celui de vous écrire
et de vous prier Monsieur de vouloir me mander Sil pouvait
ésperer quelque chose?[6] Afin de lui en rendre compte; privé de
l'honneur de votre reponce jai etté a passy pour avoir Celui de
[vous y voir il y] a eu samedi huit [*torn: several words missing*] Sa
hais de [*torn: two words missing*] [Jai laissé] a votre laquais pour
vous en informé un mot créonné, avec prierres de me donner
votre reponce. Ne l'ayant pas recûe jai prié mde cadet de vaux,
qui va a passy, de se charger de la presente. Vous priant Monsieur d'avoir la bonté de me donner une reponce. En l'attendant
jai l'honneur detre Monsieur Votre tres humble et tres obeissante servante [*torn*]

From the Comte de Vergennes

LS: American Philosophical Society; AL (draft): Archives du Ministère
des affaires étrangères

A Versailles le 4. Mars 1784.

J'ai reçu, Monsieur, la lettre que vous m'avez fait l'honneur de
m'écrire le 26. du mois dernier en faveur du Sr. Williams votre
Neveu.[7] J'ai le plus grand desir de vous prouver le cas que je
fais de votre recommandation; mais pour que je puisse mettre
sous les yeux du Roi la demande que le Sieur Williams fait d'une
troisiéme lettre de surséance, il est absolument nécessaire qu'il
me fournisse la preuve légale des arrangements consignés dans
l'etat qui etoit joint à votre lettre. Aussitôt, Monsieur, que cette

6. She enclosed the memoir with her letter of Jan. 2. Her subsequent
letters were dated Jan. 18 and Feb. 21: XLI, 399–400.

7. XLI, 584–5. JW delivered it to Versailles along with his own appeal
(written the same day) for a third *lettre de surséance;* see XLI, 584–5n.

preuve me sera parvenüe, je ferai le raport de la demande du Sr. Williams au Roi dans son Conseil.

J'ai l'honneur d'être très-sincérement, Monsieur, votre très humble et très obéissant Serviteur./. DE VERGENNES

M. francklin

To [Madame Brouttin Mollien de Sombres]

AL (draft): American Philosophical Society

[after March 4, 1784][8]

That I am sorry I was not at home when she did me the honour of calling on me. That the Appointment of Consuls does not belong to me: but That whenever one is appointed for Dunkirk, I imagine it will be Mr Coffyn, who for seven Years past has constantly served the United States in taking Care of & relieving their poor Prisoners escaping from England & other very troublesome Services without any Reward or Recompence whatever.

Notation: No name.—

To Vergennes

LS:[9] Archives du Ministère des affaires étrangères; AL (draft): American Philosophical Society

Sir,   Passy, March 5. 1784.

I received the Letter which your Excellency did me the honor of writing to me, respecting the Necessity of producing legal Proof of the Arrangements made with the Creditors mention'd in Mr. Williams's State of his Affairs.[1] I am much obliged by the Attention you are so good as to afford this Business on my Recommendation, and I send herewith the Originals of those Ar-

---

8. This draft of a reply was written on the verso of Mme Brouttin's letter of March 4 (above).

9. In the hand of WTF.

1. Vergennes to BF, March 4.

rangements for your Inspection.—[2] With great Respect I am, Sir, Your Excellency's most obedient and most humble Servant.

B. FRANKLIN

These Papers being Mr. Williams's only discharge, he requests they may be return'd to him after Examination.

His Exy. The Ct. de Vergennes.—

Notation: M De Rayneval.

From the Comte de Sarsfield

AL: American Philosophical Society

Friday the 5th at night [March 5, 1784?][3]
Count sarsfield hoped to receive today the Collection of Some of those little pieces which mr franklin had promised to him & which he had forgot yesterday.

He cannot help writing again about them to mr franklin. He is So much the more impatient of receiving them that he is very

2. BF sent the contract that JW signed with his creditors at Nantes, the acknowledgments JW had received for his promissory notes, and receipts for debts already repaid. JW took the packet to Versailles with a cover letter of his own, itemizing the enclosures and pressing his case: JW to Vergennes, March 5, 1784 (AAE).

The following day, March 6, JW wrote to WTF that he had been unable to see Vergennes, and so left the packet. He begged WTF to take up his cause, and hoped that by the following Tuesday, March 9 (the day of the next weekly ambassadors' audience), WTF would bring back good news. JW would remain at St. Germain until then: APS.

On March 13 the Conseil des dépêches, to whom Vergennes had applied, granted new *lettres de surséance* for Williams, Moore & Co. of Lorient and JW's Nantais firm for six months: Vergennes to the *conseil*, March 13, 1784; JW and Williams, Moore & Co., application [n.d.]; both at the AAE.

3. A likely possibility, given what we know of Sarsfield's travels and the few times during BF's stay in France that Friday fell on the fifth of the month. In 1784 Sarsfield arrived in The Hague on April 30, and was back in Paris by the end of July: Frans Hemsterhuis to the princesse de Golitsyn, April 30, 1784 (Universitäts- und Landesbibliothek Münster); Medlin, *Morellet*, I, 526–9. The editors thank Jacob van Sluis, University of Groningen, for his online publication of the Hemsterhuis correspondence.

near his departure for the Hague. He Desires mr franklin never to forget his most Sincere and devoted Attachment.

Addressed: a monsieur / Monsieur Franklin ministre / plenipotentiare des Etats Unis / d'Amerique / A Passy / hotel de Sarsfield

Endorsed: Sarsfield the Count.—

From Paul Strattmann[4]   ALS: American Philosophical Society

Monsieur!   Paris rüe Plâtriere No. 14. ce 5. Mars. 1784.

J'ai l'honneur, de vous envoyer le catalogue de la bibliotheque de M. le Duc de la Valliere,[5] et de vous prier, d'en disposer éntiérement à vôtre plaisir; les feuillets des vacations, que j'ai joint au tome premier, vous indiqueront les numeros des livres, qui viennent d'être vendus; si j'etois assez heureux, de pouvoir me ranger au nombre de vos serviteurs, et vous vouliez bien disposer de mes services en tout ce, qui dependra de moi, vous obligerez infiniment celui, qui est avec un attachement sans égal, et avec un profond respect votre très humble et très obeissant

PAUL STRATTMANN.

From Richard Bache   ALS: Yale University Library

Dear & Hond: Sir   Philadelphia March 7th. 1784

A few days ago your Friend Mr. Alexander forwarded to me from Virginia your favor of the 2d: November accompanied with a packet for Dr. Cooper of Boston, which I shall forward to him by some private hand, to save expence of postage;[6] hav-

---

4. One of the Viennese court librarians, who had come to Paris for the auction of the duc de La Vallière's library: XLI, 215.

5. Guillaume Debure, comp., *Catalogue des livres de la bibliothèque de feu M. le duc de La Vallière* ... (3 vols., Paris, 1783); Quérard, *France littéraire*.

6. William Alexander had left for the United States in November: XLI, 180–1. None of the letters BF sent with him has been located. For the packet, which we believe contained letters supportive of BF in the face of JA's "Calumnies," see XLI, 351n.

ing already found that expence from Virginia pretty heavy, for not withstanding your name was on the packet, as a frank, the post Office paid no regard to it— Not many hours after the packet reached me, Mr. Alexander appeared in person here, I introduced him, as you requested, to Mr. Morris[7] as well as to several other of my friends, and during his short stay here, shewed him every civility in my power; he left Town two days ago on his return to Virginia— Our Navigation is still impeded by Ice, tho' at present there is an appearance of a Thaw taking place; we have had a remarkable severe & tedious Winter, and we are looking impatiently for the approach of Spring. There are now at our Capes & in the Bay, between 20 & 30 Sail of Vessels inward bound, some of whom have been there ten Weeks; so long a stagnation of business, occasions those who live by it, ardently to wish for a renewal of it— Your kind introductions in the Mercantile line, have thrown a pretty large scene of business into Bache & Shee's hands, and we have a good prospect before us of its being profitable, our connections with Trieste in the Empire of Germany, are likely to be very considerable, & our prospects very flattering—[8]

I think I communicated to you some time ago, that we expected an increase of our family, but lest I may have omitted it, I have now to tell you that Sally expects to be up Stairs in a Week or two; at present she is in perfect health & good spirits, as are all the children; I wish you could see what a pleasing group they form, I am sure you would be delighted with them— Will with an excellent capacity, promises to be a good Scholar; Betsy a most admirable woman at her Needle; Louis, is all life, spirits & activity, and little Debby, the greatest pratler & singer you ever heard. They all join me in Love & Duty to yourself, Temple & Ben.

I am ever Dear Sir Your affectionate Son & very Hble Servt.

RICH BACHE

7. The introduction took place on Feb. 27: *Morris Papers*, IX, 149. BF had written to Morris about Alexander on Dec. 25: XLI, 349.

8. BF had recommended the Compagnie de Trieste to Bache & Shee in the spring of 1783 (XXXIX, 600–1). On Jan. 29, 1784, RB sent WTF letters to be forwarded to Trieste (APS).

I send you a large packet of News papers, put up seperately, under the supposition, that they will pay no postage—

Addressed: Dr. Franklin E / Passy—

To Leveux[9]　　　　　LS:[1] American Philosophical Society

Passy ce 8 Mars 1784.

Je suis bien reconnoissant, Monsieur, de la peine que vous avez bien voulu prendre pour retirer de la Douane de votre Ville les Effets appartenans à M. Jay, et Je vous prie d'en recevoir mes Remercimens, ainsi que pour tous les Soins que vous avez eu des Prisoniers Americains échapés d'Angleterre. Je serois bien aise de recevoir votre Compte afin de vous faire le Remboursement de toutes les Avances que vous avez bien voulu faire pour eux Jus qu'a ce Jour, et Je ne puis qu'approuver le Refus que vous avez fait aux Pretendus Americains qui se sont presentés chez vous depuis sept à huit mois, les Raisons qui vous y ont determiné étant très vraisemblables. Quant à la Nommination des Consuls, elle ne depend point de moi, et le Congrès n'a accordé de Commission particuliere pour aucun Port de France. Il est à présumer, que, si cette Nommination à lieu pour votre Ville, les Services que vous avez rendus aux Citoyens des Etats Unis engageront le Congrès à vous donner la Préférence.

J'ai l'honneur d'être, Monsieur, Votre très humble et très obeissant Serviteur./.　　　　　B FRANKLIN

M. Le Veux.

Addressed: A Monsieur / Monsieur Le Veux / Negt. / à Calais.

Endorsed: Passy franklin R le 11 Mars 1784 Rpu le 30

---

9. Written in response to his letter of March 2, above.
1. In the hand of L'Air de Lamotte.

From Antoine La Sablière de La Condamine[2]

ALS: American Philosophical Society

au château de calet à st. roman de beauvoir, par
Monsieur   st. marcellin, en dauphiné Le 8. mars 1784

J'avois envoyé la petite rapsodie cy-jointe[3] à l'auteur du journal général de france pour l'insérer dans une de ses feuilles pèriodiques, ce qu'il n'a pas jugé à propos de faire, je ne sçais pour qu'elle raison,[4] ce refus me détermine à prendre la Liberté de vous l'addresser: ce n'est pas, monsieur, que j'attache la moindre prétention, ni la moindre importance à cette production éphèmere, et encore moins que je la regarde comm'un présent qui soit digne de vous être offert; non, monsieur, je suis bien éloigné de le penser.— Quel est donc, me direz vous votre objet?— Vous m'avez peut-être dèja deviné, monsieur, et vous avez pressenti sans doute que cet envoi, ridicule en apparence, n'étoit qu'un prétexte dont je me servois pour avoir l'occasion de pouvoir vous exprimer directement, et non sous le voile de l'anonyme les sentimens de respect, d'admiration et de vénéra-

2. A physician (1724–1817) who practiced in his hometown of St.-Romans. He became mayor in 1790, and subsequently served in the Legislative Assembly: Louis-Marie-Antoine Miquel-Dalton, *Les Médecins dans l'histoire de la Révolution* (Paris, 1902), p. 22.

3. The three-page enclosure, dated Feb. 10, 1784, and addressed to "mr de xxx," is a critique of balloons written by "un philosophe campagnard," an invalid who finds sudden inspiration while staring into his fireplace. It begins with a 15-line "Epigramme sur les balons aérostatiques": balloons may be magnificent, but God assigned each animal its domain, and man's is the earth; cultivating it will do more for human affairs than "prendre la lune avec les dents" (pursuing the impossible). Next come two pages of "Réflexion": he praises BF and lauds his *bon mot* about balloons and newborn babies (XL, 545–7), but deplores the fortune spent on balloons that could have alleviated poverty and hunger. He calls for abandoning the infant monster before it wreaks unforeseeable ills and spawns a race that will deplete the country's resources. In a postscript, La Condamine adds that these reflections do not diminish the admiration he and all Europe feel for the inventors and the discovery itself.

4. The editor of the *Jour. général de France* was Louis-Abel Bonafous, who had written to BF two weeks earlier: XLI, 277. On April 5 the poem was published on the front page of the *Jour. de Paris* under the title "Vers sur les ballons." It was credited to "Me De La C****."

23

tion dont je suis pènètré, monsieur, pour vôtre personne, vos talens et vos vertus.

J'entends beaucoup parler, monsieur, dans ma retraite (c'est-a dire aux journaux et aux gazettes) et parler diversement de comus, de mesmer &c, le premier paroît avoir l'approbation de la faculté de médecine et opère sans mystère sous ses yeux, ou, ce qui revient au même, sous ceux de ses députés, tandis que le second, quoique médecin, paroit avoir la faculté et tous les médecins de la capitale contre lui.—[5] Je ne suis ni absolument incrédule, ni enthousiaste, . . . mais, je doute et je dis comme montaigne—*que sçais-je?*

Vous m'obligeriez infiniment, monsieur, si vous vouliez m'éclairer, et prendre la peine de me dire vôtre avis sur ces objets importans—si j'étois assûré que ces agens si puissans, quoiqu'invisibles, (du moins quant au magnétisme animal) fussent aussi merveilleux et aussi efficaces que le disent leurs auteurs et leurs prôneurs, et qu'ils pûssent me fournir un moyen de plus de guérir ou de soulager dans leurs meaux les pauvres habitants de la campagne au service desquels je me suis dévoué depuis au moins quinze ans; je vous avouë, monsieur, que je se- rois tenté de faire encore une fois le voyage de paris, (que je n'ai pas revû depuis plus de 36 ans) pour être témoin oculaire de ces merveilles, et tâcher, s'il étoit possible, de me faire initier dans ces sombres mystères, ou du moins, De dérober, nouveau prométhée, une ètincelle de ce feu sacré, mais plus encore, mon- sieur, pour jouir du bonheur de vous voir et de vous présenter en personne l'hommage des sentimens respectueux avec lesquels je suis Monsieur Vôtre très humble et très obéissant serviteur

LA SABLIERE DE LA CONDAMINE

5. BF had visited the clinics of both men. "Comus" (Nicolas-Philippe Ledru) had recently been installed in a clinic sponsored by the government: XLI, 120n. Franz Ánton Mesmer's practice, which BF visited in 1779, re- mained decidedly private. He had developed the theory that an invisible magnetic fluid present throughout nature exercised a strong influence upon the body, particularly the nervous system. All diseases resulted from an obstruction or imbalance of this fluid, which Mesmer claimed to remedy by manipulating the patient's fluids with his hands or an iron wand. Despite being denounced in 1781 by the medical and scientific establishments, Mes- mer continued to attract large numbers of patients: XXXI, 5–6, 8, 186–7; XXXV, 634n.

From Samuel Vaughan

ALS: American Philosophical Society

Dear Sir.   Philadelphia Mar. 8. 1784

An unwillingness to encroach upon your time unless for an object of importance has hitherto witheld me from congratulating you on the late glorious Revolution, in which you have borne a part so conspicuous as to entitle you not only to my gratitude but that of every present & future Inhabitant of these States.

The liberty of the Country Secured, I ardently wish to see you return to your former objects of pursuit & to renew your wonted exertions for the promotion of Knowledge & philosophical pursuits, from which the publick Necessities has called your attention. Persuaded this wish is also yours I am happy in being the Instrument of conveying you a plan the Completion of which is much to be Desired & which will assuredly take place if it meets with your Sanction. I mean the union of the Philadelphian & Loganian Libraries, the latter of which tho' extremely valuable is of very little use to the public contrary to the Intent of the Donor.[6] The present Idea is to house them under Trustees in the Same building but in different appartments, & with the former names in order to perpetuate that of the Benefactor One librarian (if Sufficient) to attend on both, at such distinct times as shall be judged most for public Utility. Dr Logan wishes to promote it, but his Uncle who is averse from business wishes to postpone his assent 'till he hears from you, who are only surviving trustee.[7] It were therefore earnestly to be wished, if we are to be deprived of the pleasure of seeing you

6. The institutions in question were the Library Company of Philadelphia and the Loganian Library, the latter of which, after James Logan's death in 1751, was turned into a public trust with Logan's eldest son, William, as librarian. After William died in 1776, the library remained effectively closed to the public. The Loganian Library would finally be annexed to the Library Company in 1792: I, 191n; XXXIII, 315n; Edwin Wolf 2nd, *The Library of James Logan of Philadelphia, 1674–1751* (Philadelphia, 1974), pp. xvii–li.

7. William Logan's son George was the current librarian: XXXIII, 314–15. George's uncle James Logan, Jr. (III, 390n), and BF were the last surviving trustees of the library: XXXV, 272n.

early in the Spring, that you would send Mr Logan your opinion fully on this Subject, & on some others I shall now hint to you.

Great pains are taking to give importance to the Society above mentioned & the Philosophical—[8] The assembly enter into these views & it is proposed making Mr Writtenhouse State Astronomer,[9] & to aid the P.S: by a grant of 150 $£^1$ encouraged by these favorable appearances, they wish to make an application to the Legislature for a grant of Ground on the S.E. & S.W. corners of the Statehouse yard for the erecting of two buildings one for the library, another for the Society, which are meant to be sufficiently ornamental not to interfere materially with the views of making a publick walk— Committees from the two bodies meet tomorrow to Confer on the proper mode of application—[2] Many advantages will result from this

8. Vaughan had been elected to membership in the APS in January: *Early Proceedings of the American Philosophical Society* (Philadelphia, 1884), pp. 121–2.

9. In February, 1784, Francis Hopkinson petitioned the Pa. Assembly to create the position of salaried state astronomer with Rittenhouse in mind. A bill was brought before the Assembly on March 2 by an enthusiastic committee, but it was ultimately rejected: *Jefferson Papers*, VI, 556; Brooke Hindle, *David Rittenhouse* (Princeton, 1964), pp. 248–9. Though no English text of the bill has been located, a French translation was printed in the *Jour. de Paris* on May 25, 1784, leading us to wonder whether a copy of the bill had been enclosed in the present letter. One of the responsibilities of the state astronomer would have been to correspond with European scholars, and on May 28 BF proposed Rittenhouse as a foreign correspondent to the Académie des sciences: *Procès-verbaux*, CIII (1784), 144. To our knowledge, he was never appointed.

1. The Assembly bestowed the grant on the APS on Feb. 16, and on March 5 the APS appointed a committee to collect it from the state treasurer: *Pa. Arch.*, 1st ser., x, 204; *Early Proceedings of the American Philosophical Society*, p. 123.

2. In early 1784, because of a rent increase and the plan to associate with the Loganian Library, the Library Company sought to move from its quarters in Carpenters' Hall to a more spacious location. The APS, also looking for a permanent home, invited the Library Company to join in petitioning the Assembly for a grant of two opposing lots on the east and west sides of State House Square. The organizations submitted a joint petition on March 12, prepared by a committee of which Vaughan was a member: Charles E. Peterson, "Library Hall: Home of the Library Company of Philadelphia, 1790–1880," APS *Proc.*, XCV (1951), 267–8. Vaughan sent the petition to BF with his letter of May 3, below.

arrangemt. if it meets with Success, some of them will necessarily Strike you— The Society felt the necessity of a resting place so Strongly that they a few meetings ago purchased a large lot of Mr Hopkinson near the Observatory,[3] upon which they propose building if the Assembly should reject the petition, & we flatter ourselves Subscriptions will not be wanting to enable them to do it; should they Succeed which is not improbable, it may either be resold or be converted into a Botanical Garden—

I could wish you would communicate any ideas which may occur tending to the advancemt. of these Interests, as there seems to be a Strong disposition to forward them in the members of the different Societies & the publick at large.

I remain, with the greatest respect & attachment, Dear Sir Your obliged & affe. hble servt.　　　　　SAML VAUGHAN

P.S. The family all join in affectionate greetings

His Excellency B Franklin Esqr.

To Charles Thomson

Transcript: National Archives

Sir,　　　　　　　　　　　　Passy, March 9th. 1784.

I received a few Days since a Letter from Annapolis dated June 5th.[4] in your handwriting, but not signed, acquainting the Commissioners with the Causes of Delay in sending the Ratification of the Definitive Treaty.[5] The Term was expired before that Letter came to hand,[6] but I hope no Difficulty will arise from a Failure in a Point not essential, and which was occasioned

3. In February the APS purchased for £600 a lot on Arch Street, next to David Rittenhouse's observatory, from its treasurer, Francis Hopkinson: *Early Proceedings of the American Philosophical Society,* pp. 122–3; George E. Hastings, *The Life and Works of Francis Hopkinson* (Chicago, 1926), pp. 356–8; Hindle, *David Rittenhouse,* p. 242.

4. Actually, Jan. 5.

5. Though in Thomson's hand, the letter was from Thomas Mifflin, who had not yet signed when the letter was sent: XLI, 407–8.

6. Article 10 of the peace treaty, signed on Sept. 3, 1783, called for ratifications to be exchanged within six months, or by March 3, 1784: XL, 574.

by Accidents. I have just received from Mr. Hartley a Letter on the Subject, of which I enclose a Copy.[7] We have had a terrible Winter too, here, such as the oldest Men do not remember; and, indeed, it has been very severe all over Europe.

I have exchanged Ratifications with the Embassador of Sweden, and enclose a Copy of that I received from him.[8]

Mr: Jay is lately returned from England, Mr: Laurens is still there, but proposes departing for America next Month,[9] as does also Mr. Jay with his Family.[1] Mr: Adams is in Holland, where he has been detained by Business and bad Weather. These Absences have occasioned some Delays in our Business, but not of much Importance.

The War long expected between the Turks and Russians is prevented by a Treaty;[2] and it is thought an Accommodation will likewise take Place between them and the Emperor.

Every thing here continues friendly, and favorable to the United States.

I am pestered continually with Numbers of Letters from People in different Parts of Europe, who would go to settle in America; but who manifest very extravagant Expectations, such as I can by no means encourage; and who appear otherwise to be very improper Persons. To save myself Trouble I have just printed some Copies of the enclosed little Piece, which I purpose to send hereafter in Answer to such Letters.[3]

Be pleased to present my dutiful Respects to Congress, and believe me to be, with sincere Esteem, Dear Sir, &c.

(signed) B. FRANKLIN.

7. Hartley to BF, March 2, above.

8. The ratifications of the March, 1783, treaty with Sweden (XXXIX, 250–85) were exchanged on Feb. 6: XLI, 516n.

9. As Laurens had written at the end of February: XLI, 592.

1. On May 7, when the present letter was received, Congress immediately elected Jay secretary for foreign affairs: *JCC*, XXVI, 355. Jay arrived in New York on July 24: Smith, *Letters*, XXI, 746.

2. A Russo-Turkish agreement had been signed on Jan. 8 (new style): XLI, 352n.

3. No doubt his "Information to Those Who Would Remove to America": XLI, 597–608.

From ———— Thruffé and Other Favor Seekers

ALS: American Philosophical Society

During the period covered by the present volume, Franklin continued to receive a steady stream of letters asking for favors, most of them from people he did not know. We summarize them here, beginning with those individuals seeking help with financial predicaments ranging from temporary indebtedness to outright poverty. A particularly dramatic appeal for money, involving John Jay as well, is the letter from Thruffé, printed below as a sample.[4]

Inspired by Franklin's reputation for benevolence, Madame Baudoüin Barre writes from Nantes on March 11 in the first of what will be a series of five letters. Without telling her husband, she had assumed the large debts of their wayward son. Now she finds herself unable to meet the payments, but is afraid that her husband, a former *avocat général* at the Chambre des comptes de Bretagne, will never forgive her indiscretion. She needs Franklin to send her twelve thousand *livres* in secret.[5]

Monsieur de Laubaréde sends the first of four letters from Paris on April 6. Thirty-eight years ago he lived in London, where he was highly esteemed in society and counted the Duke of Newcastle among his friends. In the intervening years, misfortune struck; now sick and impoverished, he is paralyzed on his left side, nearly blind, and utterly dependent on the charity of kind and virtuous men, among whom Franklin is of the first rank. He begs for some kind of consideration, and prays for Franklin's health. Laubaréde writes again on May 15, enclosing a copy of his earlier letter. Franklin had promised the carrier of that letter that he would respond, but Laubaréde is still waiting. Only a few *louis* would save his life. Chaplains Armand and

---

4. Unless otherwise indicated, all the documents summarized here are in French, are at the APS, and elicited no extant response.

5. Angélique Baudoin ("Baudoüin") was the wife of Toussaint-Pierre Barre (b. 1711) and mother of Bon-Emmanuel (b. 1760): Gaëtan de Ternay, *Dictionnaire des magistrats de la chambre des comptes de Bretagne* (Paris, 1995), under Barre. Convinced that BF has not responded because her letter had not reached him, she renews her plea on April 17: now willing to settle for only 6,000 *l.t.*, she asks BF to keep her secret by replying to Mlle Pouponeau, rue du Moulin, Nantes. She writes three more letters, on July 6, Aug. 11, and Sept. 20, insisting that such an amount would be insignificant to BF, whereas it would mean the world to her.

Marron at the Hôtel des Ambassadeurs de Hollande can confirm his unfortunate situation.[6]

The baronne de Drummond contacts Franklin on May 15. The day before, she had asked a favor of him, related to a lawsuit, that he claimed to be unable to perform. Now she counts on Franklin and his beneficence to help her out of her terrible situation by giving her money to pay her lawyer. After all, she notes, it is more blessed to give than to receive. She will pick up her gift whenever convenient, and asks Franklin to burn her letter. She writes again on May 20 from Paris to express her disappointment at not having received a reply.

Bassi begins his May 26 letter by recalling that it has been three years since he arrived in Paris, recommended by Beccaria, and that Franklin accepted one of his works and aided him during an illness.[7] Now Bassi has fallen so ill that he has to write from his bed and fears he will not be able to finish a long-gestating project, of which he encloses the prospectus.[8] It pains him to ask Franklin to send by the bearer however much money his heart dictates, but knowing that he is writing to the great Franklin soothes his spirit.

On June 27, J. Thiriot, a sixty-five-year-old private tutor, relates that, after an injury the previous winter, a surgeon's incompetence left him permanently disabled. Thiriot is able to move only on two crutches and with great pain. His last hope is to collect thirty *louis* through charity, which would enable him to open a private school

6. Jacques-François Armand and Paul-Henri Marron were pastors of the Protestant chapel in the Dutch embassy, where jw and Mariamne Alexander were married in 1779: xxx, 315; L. A. van Langeraad, *De Nederlandsche Ambassade-Kapel te Parijs* (The Hague, 1893), pp. 187–201, 222–33. Laubaréde reiterates his request twice more. On June 12 he reminds bf of his promise, and on Nov. 6 he encloses yet another copy of his first letter, misdating it 1783.

7. Anton-Benedetto Bassi, an Italian poet, came to France in 1780. His previous communications are summarized in xxxiii, 35; xxxvii, 37n.

8. The prospectus has not been found, but it probably was *Lycée de Paris: Club littéraire qu'on va former dans les bâtimens nouveaux du Palais Royal, sous la protection immédiate de S. A. A. Monseigneur le duc de Chartres, & sous la direction de M. Bassi* (Paris, 1784). As described in the *Mémoires secrets* on April 28, the establishment—similar to one created by Bassi in Lyon in 1777—was to include a library, classrooms, a meeting hall, and gallery space for the display of fine art, models, maps, and scientific instruments. The *lycée* was scheduled to open on Nov. 1: Bachaumont, *Mémoires secrets*, xxv, 257–8; Dena Goodman, *The Republic of Letters: a Cultural History of the French Enlightenment* (Ithaca and London, 1994), pp. 278–9.

in or around Paris. Would Franklin be among his benefactors and perhaps share the story of Thiriot's troubles with others?[9]

Lemoyne, signing himself the former mayor and deputy of Dieppe,[1] writes on August 9 that because Franklin seemed sympathetic to the story of the merchant d'Argainarats,[2] he encloses a memoir on the merchant's behalf and copies of two supporting documents: a letter dated March 27, 1782, that d'Argainarats received from Létombe, French consul in Boston, and a document enclosed in that letter, a three-page extract from the register of the consulate general, certifying the deposit of money and documents. Lemoyne emphasizes the justice of d'Argainarats' claim for compensation from Congress, the distress of his family, and his qualifications for an American consulship.[3]

9. Thiriot asked the comtesse de Beauharnais to forward this letter; she did not do so until Aug. 20, 1784 (APS).

1. Simon-Sylvestre-Clément Lemoyne had also been a naval administrator. He became known for his invention of an improved lighthouse mechanism, approved by the Académie des sciences in August, 1783: Philippe-Jacques-Etienne-Vincent Guilbert, *Mémoires biographiques et littéraires . . . sur les hommes qui se sont fait remarquer dans le département de la Seine-Inférieure . . .* (2 vols., Rouen, 1812), II, 149–50; Henri de Sénarmont *et al.*, eds., *Œuvres complètes d'Augustin Fresnel* (3 vols., Paris, 1866–70), III, xi.

2. BF must have expressed sympathy on the basis of an undated *mémoire* concerning d'Argainarats that remains among his papers. (The hand is neither Lemoyne's nor that of the secretary who prepared the enclosures described in the following note.) The memoir tells about this French merchant of St. Jean de Luz who shipped a cargo of military supplies, including 20 cannon, to America in 1778. The cargo landed in Salem, Mass., and was sold by the merchant Lafitte (XXXIV, 485), who accepted paper money in payment; that emission is deposited in the consul general's office in Boston. As the value of the stores formed his entire fortune, and the paper money is now nearly worthless, d'Argainarats has been plunged into poverty. He, his wife, and their six children are living in a state of extreme deprivation, and the French minister has assured him that the United States will want to help. He begs Congress to render him payment, in recognition that his own situation differs from that of other merchants. APS.

This same memoir, copied by Lemoyne's secretary, was sent to John Jay on Sept. 6, 1785, by Lafayette (National Archives).

3. The enclosed three-page memoir, twice as long as the one described in the previous note, is written in a more formal manner and provides more detail.

There is no evidence that BF acted on this matter. The memoir that Lafayette sent to Jay (mentioned in the previous note) was delivered to

Four supplicants need Franklin's help in getting money owed to them by others. Lefebvre d'Abancourt, a Paris merchant, writes on May 5. On March 18 he had given Ferdinand Grand three United States loan-office bills, which he had received from a merchant at Reims named Brier, and Grand had promised to return them within two weeks. The writer now begs Franklin's help in facilitating their return, either accepted or protested.[4]

A Paris iron founder named Chevalier explains on May 16 that in 1777 Monsieur Feutry, a machinist claiming to act on Franklin's behalf, ordered some bombshells and cannonballs of his own design, promising that Franklin would pay for them.[5] Chevalier filled the order, thinking that it would be disrespectful to Franklin if he did not do so. He has never been paid. He has been to Passy several times, but Franklin was either occupied or not at home. He writes now because he retired a year ago and needs to close his books. Chevalier encloses an invoice dated September 11, 1777, for the account of "Monsieur le Docteur franklin, par order de Mr feutry, machiniste." It lists two shells and two pierced cannonballs, the cost of repairing the models, and the cost of delivery by diligence, for a total of thirty *livres*.

On June 29 the Nantes firm of Wilt, Delmestre & Cie. inquires on behalf of Mr. Sparhawk, in Philadelphia, whether Franklin was ever presented with four bills of exchange of the United States in favor of Sparhawk, dated September 12, 1780. If not, the firm asks him to send a signed certificate so that replacements can be issued by Congress.

Jean-Pierre Carayon and the widows Blaud and Ducastel send a tightly packed eleven-page letter from Nîmes on July 9, the first part of which recapitulates what they had written in an earlier letter.[6] They go on to describe in detail why they believe that Vanschellebeck and Mailhot are defrauding them. They have even heard rumors that their husbands, Blaud and Ducastel, did not die of natural causes.

Congress in January, 1786, and the matter was tabled until Congress could consider a report of the Board of Treasury on the depreciation of paper money owned by French subjects: *Diplomatic Correspondence of the United States*, I, 437–8; *JCC*, xxx, 19, 21n.

4. Lefebvre d'Abancourt appends to his letter a copy of one of the receipts Grand gave him for the bills in question.

5. In the spring of 1777 Feutry, better known as a writer than a "machiniste," designed several military machines, including a cannon, and sent the drawings to BF. Other than the present letter, we have no record of BF's promising to underwrite Feutry's project. See XXIII, 570, 587.

6. Dated Feb. 16, 1783, and summarized in XXXIX, 12–13.

They ask Franklin to help them recover their money and receive justice.

On July 27 the Paris bankers Daume & Cie. hope that Franklin can help them locate Monsieur de Loyauté, formerly a colonel in the Continental Army. They hold his promissory note for 2,750 *l.t.* in favor of Lazare Chavere, who had sent it to his indigent mother in Marseille. Having been hired by the mother, the bankers have searched in vain for either Loyauté or the chevalier de Loyauté, who holds his power of attorney in France.[7]

Three correspondents ask Franklin's assistance in claiming inheritances. On March 23 the baron de Berenger de Beaufaïn, privy counselor of the Duke of Saxony-Coburg-Saalfeld,[8] writes a long and complicated account from Erlangen. He is the sole heir of his uncle Hector Berenger de Beaufaïn, who died in 1766 after having served as a customs official at Charleston and as a member of the Royal Council of South Carolina. The inheritance included two estates on the Savannah River and several debts owed to his uncle. His claims were verified by the British government, but further steps were halted by the war. He requests Franklin's help in appealing to Congress to restore to him both the property of his debtors that was confiscated by Congress and the estates he inherited from his uncle, in case they should have been confiscated as well. He is destitute and the future of his children depends on this; moreover, his uncle was a well-respected figure in South Carolina. Berenger reminds Franklin that he wrote to the American commissioners on May 19, 1783; he encloses the reply he received from Henry Laurens, dated June 3, assuring him of a successful outcome and promising to write again. Since then, however, Berenger has heard nothing: would Franklin assist him, and send him Laurens' address? He also encloses a statement of how much the estate has expended to recover his uncle's property and a copy of the epitaph on his tomb.[9]

On April 3 Simon Kuppler writes in German from Ulm. He is a

7. Anne-Philippe-Dieudonné de Loyauté (XXVI, 35n) was commissioned by Silas Deane in 1776, served as inspector of artillery, fortifications, and stores in Virginia, and rose to the rank of lieutenant colonel in the Va. militia. On the first page of the letter, BF drafted a reply: "That I have no Knowledge of either of those Gentlemen; & that there are in Paris a Number of Officers who have returned from the War in America, some of whom, may probably be able to give the Information desired."

8. Ernst Friedrich Herzog zu Sachsen-Koburg-Saalfeld: *ADB*, VI, 317.

9. Laurens' answer to Berenger's now-missing May 19 letter was written on behalf of the commissioners. He knew Berenger's uncle as well as

resident of Little Oley, Douglass Township, Berks County, who has lived in America for twenty-nine years and has defended the liberty of his adopted home on three different occasions as a militiaman.[1] Kuppler mortgaged a small piece of land and a farm in Chestnut Hill to one Katharina Remssartin, and it is on her behalf that he claims an inheritance in Ulm. The local lawyer he hired did nothing until a magistrate in Frankfurt, eight months later, contacted the mayor of Ulm on Kuppler's behalf. The mayor promised to write to officials in Pennsylvania, but Kuppler decided that it would be more expedient to ask Franklin to certify the enclosed papers. Should his case in Ulm fail, he will not have enough money to return home.[2]

Marie-Thérèse de Lamothe Cadillac seeks to claim property in America, as she explains on May 24 from London. She inherited from her father lands in Acadia that had been granted to her grandfather Antoine de Lamothe Cadillac[3] in the late seventeenth century. Her grandfather served the French crown in Canada and lived on the estate, Douaquec, before the king appointed him governor of Louisiana. Her late father never visited this Acadian estate, but she is determined to take possession of it. Having carried the deed to London, she has learned that, according to the peace treaty, her lands now lie in the province "de Boston." She hopes to avoid a voyage to Quebec, where the original deed was recorded, and needs Franklin's advice on

---

David Rhind, the uncle's executor, and was certain that Berenger would be awarded either the property in question or monetary compensation. He promised to make further inquiries during an upcoming trip to London. The issue was still pending at the end of 1787, when Berenger appealed to TJ: *Jefferson Papers*, XII, 402–3, 433.

1. A Simon Kepler is listed as a taxpayer in Oley Township, Berks County, Pa., in 1757: I. Daniel Rupp, *History of the Counties of Berks and Lebanon . . .* (Lancaster, 1844), p. 238.

2. Filed with Kuppler's letter at the APS are three related documents in French, all in the same hand. The first is a translation of Kuppler's letter to BF, on which BF interlined the correct American placenames. The second is a two-page affidavit detailing the family history of the late Chretien Rimsshard, and making the case that his wife and daughter have a legitimate claim to his and his parents' fortune. The third is an undated copy of a certificate by the Lutheran minister of Germantown, authenticated by the chancellery of Ulm, confirming that Chretien married Marguerite and that they had a daughter, Marie-Catherine (apparently the woman on whose behalf Kuppler had come to Ulm).

3. The founder of Detroit: *ANB*.

how to proceed. She sends an almost identical letter (undated) about one month later.[4]

James Fanning, writing in English from Angers on June 5, is also pursuing a property claim in America, as explained in the memorial he encloses. A native of Ireland, in 1775 he sold his property and moved his family to France to escape the penal laws. There he purchased the estate of La Roche Talbot, and he and his family have become naturalized French citizens. Before leaving Ireland, Fanning and his brother Mathew received from the British crown a total of four thousand acres of land in West Florida, which was surveyed in 1779. The estate, near Natchez, is now part of the United States, and Fanning, having bought his brother's share, wants to send a power of attorney to America to take possession. He asks Franklin to certify that he is a French subject, and is ready to send his letters of naturalization and a certificate of residence if required.[5]

Two petitioners hope that Franklin can help them obtain employment. An undated plea comes from Roché, who lost his father at the age of ten and must support his mother and siblings. He is about to lose his position with the project renovating the Palais-Royal, as the work is coming to a close. Having been an estate manager in Avaray, Roché came to Paris hoping to find employment that would leave him time to study mathematics and improve his skills, but instead fell into debt and now faces utter indigence. He was advised to appeal to Franklin's generous soul to help him find work in either France or America.[6]

Masse, originally from Marseille, writes two rambling letters from

4. Her second letter states that she has been in London for two months; her first says one month. According to a 1786 letter she wrote (as Mme de Gregoire) to TJ, BF acknowledged the justice of her claim and recommended that she draft a memoir to John Hancock and the French consul Létombe, which BF then forwarded to America: *Jefferson Papers*, x, 239.

5. BF endorsed the letter "answer'd the 11th." No trace of that reply has been found. For details on Fanning's life and family, which confirm his own account, see Comte de Beauchesne, "Le Château de la Roche-Talbot et ses seigneurs," *Revue historique et archéologique du Maine*, XXXIV (1893), 77–88; Walter F. Brooks, *History of the Fanning Family* (2 vols., Worcester, Mass., 1905), II, 808–9.

6. March, 1784, is the earliest likely date for this letter, as construction on the remodeled Palais Royal was scheduled to be completed by April 1 of that year. In fact, the renovation of the interior continued until the end of 1785: Anne Forray, "Le Palais Royal de Philippe Egalité," in *Le Palais Royal: Museé Carnavalet 9 Mai–4 Septembre 1988* (Paris, 1988), p. 152.

Paris, where he arrived about ten months earlier. On July 1 he fills eleven pages with his outrage at the hypocrisy and selfishness of the city's inhabitants and of his compatriots in general. He asks Franklin, his last hope, to find him a position as a servant to an Englishman, although he freely admits to having no relevant experience or skills. He encloses a certificate and a letter from Désormeaux, a member of the Académie des inscriptions et belles-lettres.[7] In Masse's second letter, undated and nearly as long as the first, he bemoans Franklin's cruel and, especially for an English philosophe, inexplicable silence in the past week, as well as the general depravity of the times. He wants the certificate and letter back.

Franklin receives letters from three men seeking consulships. On March 10, writing from Sète, C. Barthélemy Martin fils aîné reminds Franklin of his long-standing ambition to serve as the American consul in that port, which they discussed during Martin's visit to Passy. His wife, who signs herself "Martin Degand," adds a note to her husband's appeal. She prays for Franklin every day. The manner in which he received her raises her hopes that she will see her husband in "l'uniforme Americain."[8]

Also on March 10, Pierre Carrèl encloses a duplicate of the *mémoire* he had sent on September 17, 1783, regarding Monsieur Larrouy's application for the vice-consulship in Andaye. Larrouy, a perfectly honest man, is as dedicated as ever, and the Conseil du roi has just declared the nearby city of Bayonne a free port for American shipping.[9]

On March 17, Imberty fils, a lawyer, writes from Menton. The peace secured by the Americans promises to open a flourishing trade with Italy. Nice is the only commercial port in the kingdom of Sardinia and Piedmont, and the United States will want to appoint a con-

---

7. The enclosures have not been found. Désormeaux was one of the members of the academy who thanked BF for his gift of a *Libertas Americana* medal: XL, 118.

8. Martin had been seeking this consulship since February, 1782. His wife accompanied Mme de Le Roy to Passy in March, 1783: XXXVI, 304; XXXIX, 373–4, 455.

9. Carrèl's earlier letter and its enclosure are summarized in XLI, 306–7. At the top of the present letter BF wrote, "Answer to be translated / Sir, I received the Letter you did me the Honour of writing to me the 10th Instant, accompanied with a Memoire, wch I shall communicate to the Consul-General Mr Barclay, who alone has the Power of appointing the Vice Consulship desired. I have the honour to be, Sir, &c."

sul there. If Franklin's government is willing to consider a foreigner, Imberty asks for his patronage and offers to furnish references.

Several correspondents seek help in contacting or locating persons who went to America. Pierrard, an *avocat en parlement* and *curateur en titre pour les absents*, writes from Strasbourg on March 29 searching for some of Franklin's "concitoyens," the five children of the late Henri Pierson and Elisabeth Schweitzer of the village of Schalback (Schwalbach). The five emigrated to Pennsylvania about thirty years ago. Because of a lawsuit pending in Fénétrange, in German Lorraine, which concerns their inheritance, it is necessary to certify whether Jean Philippe, Laurent, Marguerite, Anne-Marie, and Sara Pierson are still alive or have descendants. The last letter their parents received from them dates from 1760, and it appears that they changed their name from Pierson to Birsson. Gérard had assured him that the French vice-consul for Philadelphia would make the necessary inquiries, but Pierrard fears that the vice-consul might have lost the *mémoire* or forgotten about the case. Pierrard writes again on July 28, this time from Fénétrange. He begs Franklin to acknowledge his first letter and provide an estimate of when he might receive the required information.[1]

Jerome Regnier, writing from Tourcelles on May 23, wants Franklin to forward a letter to his son Pierre, who currently resides in New York as a cavalry colonel in the Continental Army.[2] Pierre wrote his father that he was the only Frenchman to have commanded a regiment of American troops before the arrival of Lafayette and that he had fought in ten battles. In twelve years Jerome has received only two letters from his son, one in 1783 and one in 1784, and this is the first he himself is sending. Two of Jerome's other sons hope to travel to America in September.

On May 25 Roulhac of Limoges, who signs himself as "lieutenant Général civil de Police," seeks information about his younger

1. Pierrard contacted TJ with the same request on Aug. 3, 1785. TJ recommended that he consult Otto, the French chargé d'affaires in the United States: *Jefferson Papers*, VIII, 339–40, 363.

2. Pierre Regnier, who added "de Roussi" to his name, joined the militia in Quebec in the fall of 1775, and in 1776 served as lieutenant colonel in the 4th and 2nd New York Regiments. He resigned his commission on March 29, 1780, citing health reasons and "other Circumstances." GW described Regnier as "a brave active and intelligent Officer": Heitman, *Register of Officers*, p. 195; W. W. Abbot *et al.*, eds., *The Papers of George Washington*, Revolutionary War Series (22 vols. to date, Charlottesville and London, 1985–), VII, 178; Fitzpatrick, *Writings of Washington*, XVIII, 176.

brother, who sailed to America in February, 1777, as the representative of the Bordeaux merchant house Reculès de Basmarein & Raimbaux. In early 1778 he moved from Boston to Edenton, North Carolina, where he continued to work as the firm's agent.[3] When the misfortunes of war caused the firm to declare bankruptcy, his brother gave up trade. The family has not heard from him since his letter of May 20, 1781, informing them that he had married the daughter of a prominent local lawyer and had settled near Bath. Another Roulhac brother, who is even younger, sailed for America in November, 1782, to join his sibling. This brother wrote from Baltimore the following January, but since then the family has heard nothing from either one of them and is deeply worried. They fear that the elder brother may have engaged in some ill-advised speculations with the funds of Reculès de Basmarein & Raimbaux. The family implores Franklin to use all the means at his disposal to find out what happened to the two young men.[4]

A former infantry captain named Du Petit-Vendin, writing from Arras on June 19, reminds Franklin that it has been nearly two months since he spoke to him at Passy about his son, Louis de Maresquelle, an artillery colonel and inspector general of the foundry in Boston. Since the young man's return to America, Petit-Vendin has heard nothing except that he arrived at the end of 1781. Fearing

3. In 1778, at the behest of Turgot, BF wrote two letters of recommendation for this brother, Psalmet-Grégoire de Roulhac Dethias. Adopting Turgot's language, BF described him as "the Son of a Magistrate distinguish'd in his Province, being Lieutenant General, and chief in that Quality of the Presidial of Limoges." The father, Joseph-Grégoire de Roulhac Dethias, died in 1781; he was not (as we wrote in a previous volume) a delegate to the Assembly of Notables in 1787. That delegate was the author of the present letter, Guillaume-Grégoire de Roulhac de La Borie, who also served in the Estates-General: XXV, 737; XXVI, 531–2, 559, 597; Helen M. Prescott, *Genealogical Memoir of the Roulhac Family in America* (Atlanta, 1894), pp. 9–13, 15–18, 27–32.

4. Psalmet de Roulhac lived in Beaufort County, N.C., for the rest of his life. His younger brother Jean-Baptiste-Ignace-Grégoire de Roulhac, known as John Gregoire Roulhac in America, succeeded in locating his older brother and also settled in North Carolina, where he became a lawyer: Prescott, *Genealogical Memoir of the Roulhac Family*, pp. 20, 28–32, 59–63. BF was aware that Reculès de Basmarein & Raimbaux went bankrupt in February, 1779 (XXVI, 677n); various French investors in the company asked his help in trying to recover funds thought to be in Psalmet de Roulhac's hands in America.

that he might be dead, the family hopes that Franklin will be able to obtain information.[5]

One of the sons of Madame de Baluze went to war in America and currently resides near Philadelphia, as she explains from Paris on July 31. Their letters to each other have failed to reach their destinations, and she asks Franklin's help in finding a safe conveyance across the Atlantic.

Other requests for information are of a more general nature. James Barrett, writing in English from Bordeaux on May 4, explains nothing about himself other than that he has obtained passage to Philadelphia on an Irish ship. The captain claims that he will have to prove upon arrival that he is able to support himself. Is this true? He hopes that Franklin will be able to send an answer by return mail, since the ship is scheduled to depart in eight days, and the friends in America who could vouch for him live a fair distance from Philadelphia.

Roubaud, a lawyer and professor from Aix-en-Provence, writes on June 18 that he was surprised to read in the Avignon paper published on Sundays and Tuesdays that there are not thirteen United States, but fourteen, since Vermont joined the union, as announced in the *Courier de l'Europe*, sometime around 1780. As history is a sacred *dépôt* and must not be violated, Roubaud turns to Franklin for accurate information.[6]

Some writers ask for personal appointments. On June 9, Monsieur de Lacroix, the most miserable of men, writes from Marly-le-Roi. His misfortunes are endless, he feels betrayed by his native land, and

5. Ansart du Petit-Vendin was interested in mechanics and hydraulics; he was a correspondent of the Académie des sciences and a member of the Académie d'Arras: E. van Drival, *Histoire de l'Académie d'Arras* . . . (Arras, France, 1872), p. 328. He met BF *c.* 1777 when delivering a letter of introduction from Thomas Walker, a friend of his son's in Boston. "Colonel de Marasquelle" (as Walker introduced him) was described by his son as a genius and a patriot. The son was Louis Ansart de Maresquelle, who, far from being dead in 1784, was married to an American woman and living in Massachusetts: XXV, 112; Lasseray, *Les Français*, II, 617.

6. This letter was forwarded to BF from Vergennes' office. Roubaud sent it to Vergennes under cover of a letter of the same date, explaining that he first drafted it on Dec. 9, 1783. Now that he had decided to send it, he did not know whether BF was still in France. Roubaud noted that he had never met BF and first heard of him in connection with his *bon mot* comparing the balloon to a newborn baby (for which see XL, 545–7). A notation in Rayneval's hand indicates that he believed the enclosed letter to be about balloons, which may explain why it was forwarded: AAE.

he begs for help so that he can resume work on "une Entreprise utile au bien du peuple." He can produce authentic certificates for all his claims and would like to explain his situation in person. He signs as "cy devant controleur des fermes du roy de Prusse."[7]

Monsieur de Junquieres, *intendant* of the prince de Conti, writing from Paris, needs Franklin to enlighten him on a matter involving the worthy widow of one of their most amiable Masonic brothers.[8] Junquieres believes that Franklin knew this man, who left estates in Virginia. What he needs to know will take only a few minutes of Franklin's time: could he call between nine and ten o'clock the next morning? His letter is dated July 6.

A woman whose signature we read as Harding-Gaschez writes on July 20 from Cap-Français on Saint-Domingue. She has just discovered that her children's paternal grandmother, who was of English ancestry, was named Franklin. Her son, who is going to France to join the military, will deliver her letter along with evidence of the family connection. Surely Franklin will forgive her son's eagerness to see up close a man who is an honor to humanity.

On July 30 a certain Jacob, in Paris, tells Franklin the amazing tale of how rays of light suddenly began streaming from his eyes following the July, 1783, earthquake in Dijon. Moreover, he found that he was able to produce lightning and bright explosions by blinking his eyes during storms. His powers diminished during the cold season, but now that summer has returned, Jacob is eager to demonstrate them to Franklin.

Two people ask Franklin to forward letters. Lieutenant Colonel Giles,[9] writing in English from New York on August 1, hopes that he will be able to direct the enclosed letter to Giles's friend Colonel Clarkson. V. P. Bridon de la Maillardière of Nantes[1] asks Franklin

7. The Prussian tobacco monopoly, established in 1766 by Frederick II in imitation of the farmers general, was staffed mainly with French personnel: William O. Henderson, *Studies in the Economic Policy of Frederick the Great* (London, 1963), pp. 71–2, 152.

8. Louis-Jacques-Antoine de Junquieres was a member of the Etoile Polaire Masonic lodge: Le Bihan, *Francs-maçons parisiens.*

9. Most likely Aquila Giles: W. T. R. Saffell, *Records of the Revolutionary War . . .* (New York, 1858), p. 420; W. W. Abbot *et al.,* eds., *The Papers of George Washington,* Presidential Series (17 vols. to date, Charlottesville and London, 1987–), III, 417n.

1. Vincent-Pierre Bridon de la Maillardière was a clothing merchant: Stéphane de La Nicollière-Teijeiro *et al.,* eds., *Inventaire sommaire des archives communales antérieures à 1790: ville de Nantes* (4 vols., Nantes, 1888–1948), IV, 61.

on August 7 to forward an enclosed letter to Jonathan Williams, Jr., whose address he does not know.

C. Drogart, writing in English from Paris on June 7, needs Franklin to certify three signatures on the power of attorney he encloses, which he must send to Boston immediately. The signatures are those of Caumartin, lord mayor of Paris, and Pelé and Mercier, two aldermen.[2]

Finally, a confused man named Huguet has heard that Franklin helps people emigrate to "La moscovie" in order to farm. Huguet was born in the country, knows the art of agriculture, and has experienced hardship. In a letter of June 1, he asks Franklin to sponsor his journey and give him land to clear and cultivate. He currently resides in Paris on the rue St. Victor, chez Pelissier, a blanket merchant.

Monseigneur   Troyes Le 9e. Mars 1784
Guidé par les Sentimens de L'humanité, permettés que j'aye L'honneur de vous en peindre icy un Tableau qui en est des plus Susceptible. C'est au Sujet d'une de vos compatriottes Jeune femme d'environ Vingt[-ans?] d'une education aussi belle quelle est jolie et qu'elle inspire d'interest. La Situation critique dans laquelle elle Setrouve y contribue encore pour beaucoup. Madame Rebecca Allere c'est Le nom de Son mary actuellement à Philadelphie ou Newyork pays de L'origine de ce Couple. Le dernier est parti en May der. D'Ostande Sur Le Vaisseau . . . .[3] Laissant Sa femme dans un Couvent d'augustines à armentieres avec un enfent de deux ans qu'elle à avec elle, alors encore trop jeune pour faire un trajet en mer aussi considerables. Mr. allaire dans Lintention de faire des remises à Son epouse aussitôt Son

2. Drogart, a French businessman whose earlier letter to BF was written from Nantes in 1782, had an excellent command of what he called "the American Language": XXXVII, 683–4. The officials were Antoine-Louis-François Lefèvre de Caumartin de Saint-Ange, Pierre-Jacques Pelé, and Nicolas-Jean Mercier: Michel Antoine, *Le Gouvernement et l'administration sous Louis XV: dictionnaire biographique* (2nd ed., Paris, 2004), p. 213; *Almanach royal* for 1784, p. 440.

3. Rebecca Allaire was the wife of N.Y. merchant Peter Allaire (XXIV, 470), who was expelled from France in May, 1780, after serving three months in the Bastille on suspicion of poisoning BF and being a British spy: XXXII, 387–9. His story is told in Claude-Anne Lopez, *My Life with Benjamin Franklin* (New Haven and London, 2000), pp. 61–72.

arrivée, n'avait Laissé d'argent que pour Six mois de pension, probablement il Sera arrivé quelque accident à Lequipage dont on à aucunes nouvelles, ce qui met La personne en question dans Le plus cruel embarras. Les Dames D'armentieres voyant cette dame Sans argent Lui Signifierent plusieurs fois qu'il n'etait pas d'usage de garder des pensionnaires etrangeres Sans pension payée d'avance et finalement on conduisit, avec charité, la pensionnaire. Sortie de ce digne lieu elle vint à Lille ou dabort, elle fût comme etrangere, obligée de payer Le double de ce quelle aurait du, pour Se faire conduire à Amiens, ou elle esperait trouver une anglaise de Sa connaissance qui lui doit 25. Louis, qui devaient la mettre à Son aise pour rentrer au Couvent. A Amiens, ce fut la ou je La rencontrai point d'anglaise et par consequent point d'argent, que faire Sans ce nerf. Par hazard j'eus conversation avec cette Dame qui Venait d'arriver comme moy Le 9e. Jeanvr. dernier, je n'eus pas de peine à m'appercevoir qu'elle etait dans Le chagrin. Mon ame en fut autant emüe que penetrée de la voir avec un enfent de deux ans, Seule dans une voiture de Louage exposée à la rigueur du froid Le plus excessif, Surtout Sans argent. Piqué de curiosité je voulois Savoir ce qui la chagrinait, et elle me raconta avec confiance Son avanture en me disant quelle ne Savait de quel côte donner de la tête, que Son parti etait pris de S'empoisonner et Son enfant, Ne pouvant Sortir de L'hotel faute D'argent. Je fremis de cette resolution et alors je pris celle de la conduire moy même a Paris, dans ma voiture, Sur ce qu'elle me dit encore que Monsieur Gay, connaissait beaucoup Son mari, et qu'elle pourrait implorer Sa protection pour repondre d'elle dans un Couvent. Nous partons Le 11e. pour Paris et arrivons Le même jour; Le Landemain rien de plus empressée que d'aller trouver elle même, Mr. Gay alors absant.[4] Madame fit beaucoup plus de Caresses à L'enfent qu'à la mere qui revint à L'hotel d'hollande rüe du douloy, mon hotel ordinaire, ou Made. allaire est encore aujourdhuy. C'est alors que

---

4. After his return from England in late January, John Jay found Mrs. Allaire in a "distressed Situation," as he wrote to his brother Frederick in April. He lent her 30 guineas as well as money for her voyage home: *Jay Papers*, III, 580.

Son desespoir redoubla; il falloit que je partes Le Landemain
pour regagner mes foyers que j'avais quittés depuis quatre mois;
Le chagrin de cette dame augmentait, à Paris Sans argent, Sans
connaissances, Sans ressources, c'est une Situation bien cruelle.
Enfin Sa resolution d'amiens me revenait Souvent, je parvains
à Savoir d'elle de quelle maniere elle devait executer Son projet. Elle etait munie d'un paquet d'arsenic en poudre dont je
m'emparai, malgré elle à L'ouverture de Ses malles assès bien
fournie en Linge en general, quelques pieces d'argenterie à
Lusage de la table, Tayere [Théiere] &a &a. même quelques
bijoux. Comme il fallait que je quittâ paris, je pris Le parti de
la reccommander à L'hôte de L'hotel d'hollande en lui raccon-
tant à peu prés L'avanture de L'infortunée et je fis prix avec lui à
raison de Trois Livres par jour pour Logement et nouriture de
la mere et de L'enfent, juscesque ce qu'elle eut trouvé quelques
anglais ou ameriquains de Sa Connaissance qui puissent lui
procurer les resources Necessaires pour attendre des nouvelles
et des remises de Son mary ou de Sa famille. Suivant ce quelle
me marque, en consequence des demandes de L'hôte pour être
payé, elle est dans Le plus grand desespoir, puisqu'elle m'avoüe
un Second projet d'aller Se jetter à la riviere avec Son enfent, Si
je ne Lui procure des ressources necessaires à Sa Situation. Je
ne crois pouvoir mieux m'adresser pour un acte genereux, qu'à
un Compatriote bienfaisant après vous même vous êtes ecclerci
de L'aventure par L'avanturiere elle même. D'aprés Les Lettres
quelle porte du Negt. d'ostande qui à fait embarquer Son
mary, les quittances du Couvent d'armantieres, vous ne trouverés que des marques de vraisemblance. Ajoutés à cela Son
intention de Se faire mettre au Couvent Par Monsieur Gay ou
autres en arrivant à Paris, Sa conduitte à L'hotel depuis qu'elle
y reside, Le refus qu'elle à fait d'aller Loger, chés une Dame
Marquise ou Contesse de Sancour, qui avait été penetrée de
Sa Situation, Sur ce qu'en avait racconté un Comte de . . . . . .
Logé au même hotel, de peur de Se Compromettre, par-
cequon lui avait peint Paris comme une antre d'indignités
pour une femme honnete. Elle vous dira en outre qu'elle est
connue des parents de Madame La Duchesse de Manchester à
Londres, je ne Sais même Si elle ne Leur à pas ecrit . . . mais

on est plus affecté du malheur des gens, quand on les y voit reèllement.

Suis avec Le plus profond respect Monseigneur Votre trés humble & trés obeissant Serviteur,   Thruffé Negt.

Notation: Truffé 9 Mars 1784

From the Comtesse d'Houdetot

ls: American Philosophical Society

paris Le 10. mars 1784.

Rien n'est plus Vray, Mon Cher Et Venerable Docteur que la Guerison De Mr De Breget a Laquelle il Est impossible D'attribuer aucunne cause aparente que L'application Du Magnetisme.[5] J'ay Eû ce Matin une Conversation a fond Sur Son traitement avec un De Ses amis qui n'a pas quitté Son Chevet Depuis le Commencement De Sa Maladie, Et qui m'a Confirmé, que Condamné par Les Medecins on a Envoyé Chercher Deslon[6] qui la traité avec un De Ses Diciples, nommé Bien Aimé: ils Sont ar-

5. The cure of the military officer Joseph-Philippe, baron de Bréget (XXVII, 79n), was discussed by physician Louis Desbois de Rochefort in *Cours élémentaire de matière médicale, suivi d'un précis de l'art de formuler* (2 vols., Paris, 1789), I, 41–2. Desbois de Rochefort visited Bréget with Deslon, who had magnetized him, and decided that his recovery from pneumonia could be easily explained by causes other than the application of animal magnetism. Bréget may have been the "Baron de ***" whose case was mentioned in the Aug. 11, 1784, report of the royal commission to investigate animal magnetism (summarized below) as the one most often cited as proof of the existence of "Magnétisme." The commissioners cautioned against the fallacy of ascribing curative powers to any one treatment on the sole basis of the patient's having subsequently recovered: *Rapport des commissaires chargés par le Roi, de l'examen du magnétisme animal* (Paris, 1784), p. 12.

6. Charles-Nicolas Deslon (d'Eslon), regent doctor of the Faculté de médecine and physician-in-ordinary to the comte d'Artois, met Mesmer in September, 1778, and soon became the leading French advocate of animal magnetism. In 1780 he published *Observations sur le magnétisme animal* in an attempt to convince his colleagues on the Faculty of the legitimacy of Mesmer's methods. Instead, the Faculty censured Deslon, suspended him

rivés Le Cinq De La Maladie ont Suprimé tout Remede, oté Les Vessicatoires Etablies Et ont Borné Leur traitement a L'administration Du Magnetisme nourrissant le Malade avec De L'Eau D'orge Et De La Limonade Le premier jour, Ensuitte Bouillon Et Gelée De Viande puis De La nourriture Solide. Les accidents ont Etés Encore assés Graves quoique Diminués jusqu'au Sept qu'ils ont Encore Diminués Et ont Disparû Le huit Et Le neuf; Le Malade Se Sentant Si Bien qu'il S'est Levé Et a fait Sa toilette, il Revient ce Soir a paris quitte De Sa Maladie Et Enchanté comme Vous pouvés penser De Son traitement. Je me Borne a Vous Dire Les faits que Vous avés Demandés. Il m'Est fort Dificile De Croire ce que je ne puis Comprendre, je n'ay aucunne opinion Sur ce prodige Mais je Serais Bien Charmée De Sçavoir La Vôtre. Versailles Retentit de ce Miracle, j'aurais Desiré que quelque Medecin Eut Suivi Le traitement Et En Eut fait un procès Verbal. Je Verrés Bientot Mr. De Breget Et je Vous ferés passer Les Eclaircissemens que Vous Desirés; Le Detail que je Vous Envoye Me Vient D'un homme qui a la tête tres froide Et qui ne croit pas plus au Magnetisme que Moy, Voila Les faits Dont il a Eté temoin. Adieu Mon Cher Et Venerable Docteur, jay Eté trop heureuse De Vous Voir pour ne pas Chercher Encore à jouir de ce Bonheur Et j'iray assurement Vous Demander a Diné, noubliés pas La personne La plus Remplie De tendresse Et De Veneration pour Vous

La Ctesse d'houdetot

---

for a year from all its assemblies, and required him to disavow his book within a year or face expulsion. A decree of Aug. 20, 1782, excluded Deslon from the Faculty's meetings for another two years, when his expulsion would become final, if he remained unrepentant: *DBF;* A. Pinard *et al.,* eds., *Commentaires de la Faculté de médecine de Paris, 1777 à 1786* (2 vols., Paris, 1903), II, 567–73, 943–4.

In late 1783 Mesmer and Deslon turned against each other publicly in letters to the *Jour. de Paris.* On Nov. 25 Mesmer accused Deslon of trying to steal his discovery (which Mesmer regarded as his property) and of breaking their written contract by treating patients without fully understanding Mesmer's method. On Dec. 28 Deslon responded that it was Mesmer who had broken the contract by failing to teach Deslon his method. Deslon claimed that his treatments were based on his own research: *Jour. de Paris,* supplements to issues of Dec. 13, 1783, and Jan. 10, 1784.

To David Hartley

Press copy of ALS:[7] Library of Congress; copy: William L. Clements Library

Dear Sir,   Passy, March 11. 1784

I received duly your Favours of Jany. 28. and March 2.——[8] I find Dr Ross to answer the Character given of him by Mr Dempster, and shall give him the Letters of Recommendation desired.——

I have wondered at the long Delay of the Ratification; but a Letter I have just receiv'd from the Secretary of Congress explains it to me.[9] I enclose a Copy. The Winter it seems has been as severe in America as in Europe, and has hindred the Meeting of a full Congress: but as the seven States who were met were unanimous in the Intention of ratifying, and they are a large Majority of the nine States necessary to be assembled for such a Transaction, there is no doubt of its being done as soon as they could get together, and I expect it will certainly arrive by the Washington Packet, in the Course of this Month. There does not therefore appear to me any Necessity for extending the term by any formal Convention, the Sincere intention of both Parties being to ratify, wch if not done within the time mentioned was only prevented by Accidents unforeseen & unavoidable. With great Esteem & Affection I am ever Dear Sir, Your [*torn*] & [*torn*]   B FRANKLIN

P.S. I forgot to acknowledge the Receipt of another Letter from you dated the 23d of February.[1] I have heard nothing of the Resolutions of Congress you mention, and believe there are none such. Particular States, offended with the Restrictions of your Proclamations, may have made similar ones;[2] but liberal

---

7. The press copy is mutilated, and some words are missing. We supply them, when possible, from the copy.

8. For the former see XLI, 513–14; the latter is above.

9. [Mifflin] to the American Commissioners, Jan. 5: XLI, 407–8.

1. XLI, 579.

2. BF might have learned that states like Maryland and Virginia had taken measures in reaction to British trade policy: *Adams Papers*, XVI, 57, 58–9n; *Courier de l'Europe*, XV (1784), 144 (issue of March 2).

Measures on your part will wipe away all such foolish Projects of commercial War, which are ever hurtful to both sides and produce no Good to either.—

David Hartley Esqr. &c &c &c.

To Henry Laurens

ALS: South Carolina Historical Society; press copy of ALS and transcript: Library of Congress

Dear Sir,   Passy, March 12[−13], 1784

I received your kind Letter by Mr Cholet, with the Pamphlets and Newspapers;[3] and since a Paper of the 5th which came under Cover to Mr Grand.[4] I am much oblig'd to you for these Communications.—

Your Sentiments and mine respecting the continual Drafts on Europe coincide perfectly. I have just received a Letter from Mr. Carmichael, dated the 14th past, in which he says, "Bills from Congress come to hand from time to time, some of which Mr M. has advised me of; the others I am at a Loss what to do with; but having no Instructions to the contrary, I cannot refuse accepting them. I should be glad to know your Sentiments thereon."—[5] All I can say to him in answer is, that it will behove him to consider where he can find Funds for Payment, since there is not the smallest Probability that I shall be able to

3. Laurens introduced Samuel Chollet as the bearer of that letter, written at the end of February: XLI, 588−92.

4. We find no record of a March 5 enclosure from Laurens to BF by way of Ferdinand Grand. On March 9, however, Laurens did send BF, under cover to Grand, "this Evening's Paper containing the Representation of the House of Commons" (University of South Carolina Library). This "Representation" was the March 8 remonstrance to the king, drafted by the opposition in response to his refusal to dismiss Pitt: *Whitehall Evening-Post,* March 6−9, 1784; John Cannon, *The Fox-North Coalition: Crisis of the Constitution, 1782−4* (Cambridge, 1969), pp. 199−202. For additional background on this political crisis see XLI, 528, 590−1.

5. XLI, 568−9.

assist him from hence. Sure it must be some invincible Necessity that induces so prudent a Man as Mr Morris to take such Measures: and the several States must be much to blame to leave him under that Necessity.—

I heartily wish you Success in your Endeavours to recover your 2800£ from the Treasury. I know too well the Dexterity of that Board (Dexterity is acquir'd by much Practice) in fighting-off Payments, not to think you very lucky if you can obtain your Right by only mounting twice more their Seventy Steps.—

The Commission for a Commercial Treaty ordered to be prepared by the Vote of May last, is indeed not yet come to hand;[6] but by their sending us repeatedly Copies of that Vote, & nothing more, it looks as if they thought we might proceed by Virtue of it, to prepare a Plan of a Treaty.— Having written expresly on the Subject,[7] we may expect soon to know their Minds more perfectly.

I thank you much for your Information of the Proceedings of the West India People. It seems to me, that we cannot be much hurt by any selfish Regulations the English may make respecting our Trade with their Islands.— Those who at present wish to kick the Hedge hog, will grow tired of that Sport when they find their own Toes bleed.—

I have just received a Letter from the Secretary of Congress, Mr Thomson, of which I inclose a Copy.[8] The Term for exchanging the Ratifications was expired before it came to hand. Mr Hartley having frequently written to me to know if the Ratification was arriv'd I have communicated to him this Letter,[9] that he might see the Delay was occasioned only by unforeseen Accidents, and that we had reason to expect receiving it by the Return of the Washington Packet. I do not imagine that any Difficulty will be occasioned by this Circumstance, but perhaps it may not be amiss, if you are well enough, to see Mr Hartley

6. BF had reported the same news to Laurens on Dec. 6: XLI, 264. The American commissioners were awaiting instructions from Congress to negotiate a commercial treaty with Great Britain.

7. Most recently to President of Congress Mifflin: XLI, 339.

8. In Thomson's hand, but written by Mifflin: XLI, 407–8.

9. BF's covering letter is above, March 11.

on the Subject; and should any Agreement to extend the Term be necessary, you can enter into it as well as if we were all present.—

I write this in great Pain from the Gout in both Feet;—but my young Friend your Son having inform'd me that he sets out for London to-morrow,[1] I could not slip the Opportunity, as perhaps it is the only safe one that may occur before your Departure for America. I wish mine was as near. I think I have reason to complain that I am so long without an Answer from Congress to my Request of Recall.[2] I wish rather to die in my own Country than here; and tho' the upper Part of the Building appears yet tolerably firm, yet being undermin'd by the Stone and Gout united, its Fall cannot be far distant. You are so good as to offer me your Friendly Services. You cannot do me one more acceptable at present, than that of forwarding my Dismission. In all other Respects as well as that I shall ever look on your Friendship as an Honour to me; being with sincere and great Esteem, dear Sir, Your most obedient humble Servant

B. FRANKLIN

P.S. March 13.—

Having had a tolerable Night, I find myself something better this Morning. In reading over my Letter I perceive an Omission of my Thanks for your kind Assurances of never forsaking my Defence should there be need.[3] I apprehend that the violent Antipathy of a certain Person to me may have produc'd some Calumnies, which what you have seen and heard here may enable you easily to refute. You will thereby exceedingly oblige one, who has liv'd beyond all other Ambition than that of dying with the fair Character he has long endeavour'd to deserve. As to my Infallibility, which you do not undertake to maintain, I am too modest myself to claim it, that is *in general*; tho' when

1. Henry Laurens, Jr., joined his father in Bath on March 20: *Laurens Papers*, XVI, 420.

2. For BF's most recent plea see XLI, 356–7.

3. XLI, 592. Laurens was reiterating what he had already assured BF in September, after BF demanded testimonials from his fellow peace commissioners to counter the malicious rumors about him circulating in America: XL, 606–7, 607–8n, 614–15, 626–8; XLI, 26–7.

we come to *particulars*, I, like other People, give it up with Difficulty. Steele says, that the Difference between the Church of Rome and the Church of England on that Point, is only this, That the one pretends to be *infallible*, & the other to be *never in the wrong*.[4] In this latter Sense, we are most of us Church of England Men, tho' few of us confess it and express it so naturally and frankly as a certain great Lady here, who said, I don't know how it happens, but I meet with nobody, except myself, that is always in the right: *Il n'y a que moi qui a toujours raison*.[5]

My Grandson joins me in affectionate Respects to you & the young Lady, with best Wishes for your Health & Prosperity.

BF.

His Excelly. H. Laurens, Esqr

Endorsed: Doctr. Franklin 12th. & 13th. March 1784 Recd 20th— Answd. 28th. requesting me to solicit his recal & return to America—

To Benjamin Rush
ALS: Yale University Library

Dear Friend, Passy, March 12. 1784

This will be delivered to you by Dr. Ross, who is strongly recommended to me by Persons of Distinction in England,[6] and who, after travelling over a great Part of the World, wishes to fix himself for the rest of his Life in America. You will find

4. The words, "You are Infallible, and We always in the Right," appeared in the dedication to Pope Clement XI published at the outset of Richard Steele's *Account of the State of the Roman Catholic Religion* (1715). Though signed by Steele, the dedication was written by Bishop Benjamin Hoadly: *ODNB*, under Hoadly. BF repeated this phrase and the story of the "great Lady" (which follows) in his Sept. 17, 1787, speech to the Constitutional Convention: Max Farrand, ed., *The Records of the Federal Convention of 1787* (4 vols., New Haven and London, 1966), II, 642.

5. Mme de Staal attributed the variant "je ne vois que moi qui aie toujours raison" to the duchesse de la Ferté: *Memoires de Madame de Staal, ecrits par elle-meme, ou anecdotes de la Regence, premiere partie* (Amsterdam and Leipzig, 1756), p. 127.

6. For Andrew Ross see XLI, 513n; his recommendations from David Hartley and William Strahan are in XLI, 513–14, 527.

him a very ingenious sensible Man, and be pleas'd with his Conversation: and you will therefore excuse my requesting for him those Civilities which you have a Pleasure in showing to Strangers of Merit, and such Counsels as from his Unacquaintedness with our Country may be useful to him.[7] With great Esteem I am ever, my dear Friend, Yours most affectionately

B FRANKLIN

Dr Rush

From ———— Milet l'aîné, with Franklin's Draft of a Reply, and Other Applicants for Emigration

ALS: American Philosophical Society

Beginning in March, 1784, Franklin was able to send would-be emigrants copies of his "Information to Those Who Would Remove to America," which he had printed in English and French versions.[8] The draft reply to Milet l'aîné, which he wrote at the top of Milet's letter and presumably gave to L'Air de Lamotte to translate, is our earliest evidence of his having sent one of those pamphlets. Milet's letter is published in full as an example of the applications Franklin received from would-be emigrants during the period of this volume. The others, to which no replies have been located, are summarized below.[9]

Leonhard Magnus Broell of Nuremberg writes in German from Paris on April 6. In 1780, while living in Amsterdam, he decided to go to America and applied to Captain Gillon of the frigate *South Carolina;* Gillon hired him as a valet. After serving for fourteen months, he fell ill and had to leave the ship at Corunna.[1] As Gillon was very

---

7. Rush and Ross were amicable colleagues until the 1790s, when they differed over Rush's treatments of yellow fever. In 1797 Rush believed that Ross had written an article attacking him; this misunderstanding escalated into Ross challenging Rush to a duel, which Rush refused: L. H. Butterfield, ed., *Letters of Benjamin Rush* (2 vols., Princeton, 1951), II, 675, 676n; George W. Corner, ed., *The Autobiography of Benjamin Rush . . .* (Princeton, 1948), pp. 101n, 369–70.

8. See XLI, 597–608.

9. All these documents are at the APS and, unless otherwise specified, in French.

1. Alexander Gillon, commodore of the S.C. navy, was in Amsterdam in the summer of 1780, hiring crew and preparing the *South Carolina* for her voyage. The ship sailed in early October, and stopped at Corunna at the

fond of him, the captain encouraged him to proceed to America once he recovered, and gave him the names of four merchants in Philadelphia who might hire him: Phul, Thiriot, Radel, and Dessessement. Broell now asks Franklin to help him find an affordable passage to Philadelphia. His current employer, Locré,[2] will provide a recommendation.

On April 14, a widower from lower Normandy with two children writes from Fécamp (where he has business) because he knows that Franklin welcomes "tout honnête homme." For years he has longed to live under freedom. Now that the United States has triumphed over England, he wishes to emigrate, placing himself under Congress' and Franklin's protection to obtain lands in Pennsylvania, Virginia, or New York. He is sure that his neighbors the La Luzernes—the comte de La Luzerne and the bishop of Langres[3]—will provide him with letters of recommendation to their brother, the French minister to the United States. The most precious recommendation of all, of course, would be from Franklin himself, and he begs Franklin to supply one. The writer signs himself "De mauviel Du Boüillon."[4]

Thirty-five-year-old Dalzan Delapierre writes on April 25 from Florac in Languedoc.[5] He has long wanted to transplant himself to

---

end of September, 1781, for a stay of three weeks: James A. Lewis, *Neptune's Militia: the Frigate* South Carolina *during the American Revolution* (Kent, Ohio, and London, 1999), pp. 25, 45.

2. Jean-Baptiste Locré de Roissy was the founder of a Paris factory that specialized in imitations of German porcelain: Xavier, comte de Chavagnac and Gaston Grollier, *Histoire des manufactures françaises de porcelaine . . .* (Paris, 1906), pp. 489–91.

3. For the comte see XXXII, 54n. The bishop of Langres was César-Guillaume de La Luzerne (1738–1821): *Nouvelle Biographie.*

4. Probably Marie-Pierre-Thomas Mauviel du Bouillon (b. *c.* 1735), an officer of the corps of engineers. Suspected of royalist sympathies, he was executed in May, 1794: Robert Sinsoilliez, *Etienne-François-Louis-Honoré Le Tourneur: le Normand qui a gouverné la France* (Condé-sur-Noireau, France, 2002), pp. 91–4.

5. François-David Delapierre, *dit* Dalzan (b. 1747), a Protestant notary and lawyer, never emigrated. During the French Revolution he served as public prosecutor in the tribunal of Lozère for the district of Florac: Jacques Poujol and Patrick Cabanel, "'Tout protestant doit être vrai républicain . . .': pasteurs et fidèles du synode des Hautes-Cévennes pendant la Révolution (1789–1799)," *Bulletin de la Société de l'histoire du protestantisme français,* CXXXV (1989), 659–62, 680–1; Lise Dupouy, *Les Protestants de Florac de la Révocation de l'Édit de Nantes à l'Édit de Tolérance, (1685–1787)* (Paris, [1968]), pp. 7, 70, 88.

the country now called the United States of America. That desire has only increased with time, as he wishes to live under civil and religious freedom and observe the effects of independence on the American people. He deplores discrimination against non-Catholics, which he himself has suffered. The execution of Calas at Toulouse, which he witnessed, was a frightening example of iniquity and barbarism. He begs Franklin to inform him of what he can expect in America, and what resources he would need in order to live comfortably. He proposes to devote himself to agriculture, although he is a lawyer. The comte de Nozières[6] will deliver his letter and can vouch for his character. Dalzan is hoping to settle along the Pee Dee River in Carolina and wants Franklin's opinion of this locale.

On April 30 Piere Louis Stouppe, the scion of a military family, writes in German from Ach in Upper Austria to request information about America with a view toward emigrating there. He asks that Franklin's reply be sent to Franz Ferdinand von Prielmayr.[7] On the letter itself, Ferdinand Grand translated into French the salutation and wrote a brief précis of the substance of the inquiry, suggesting that Franklin send Stouppe a copy of "Information to Those Who Would Remove to America." Although the writer does not know any trade, Grand noted, he nevertheless was offering his services.

A. J. Renaux, an engineer who tells Franklin that he is acquainted with Le Ray de Chaumont, writes on May 19 from the Hôtel de Poitou in Paris.[8] He will soon be free to embark for the United States, and asks how he might be useful to the new republic. He is forty years old, in good health, and has traveled to several European countries. His two defects are his lack of English and his uncertain finances. If

6. Vital-Auguste de Grégoire, comte de Nozières, had been governor of Martinique from 1772 to 1776: XXII, 444n; David P. Henige, *Colonial Governors from the Fifteenth Century to the Present* (Madison, Milwaukee, and London, 1970), pp. 43–4.

7. Prielmayr, in the service of the Elector of Bavaria, had been the head of the financial administration of the regency of Burghausen since 1777: Fritz Demmel, *Die Burghauser Stadtmaurermeister: Franz Anton und Joseph Glonner: ein Beitrag zur Architektur der Stadt zwischen 1777 und 1842* (Burghausen, Germany, 1995), p. 12.

8. Alexandre-Joseph Renaux was a noted engineer, mechanic, and mineralogist. He wrote a work on mines for the Estates General in 1789, and later published *Précis des voyages et travaux d'Alexandre-Joseph Renaux . . .* (Angoulême, France, 1792): Arthur Birembaut, "L'Enseignement de la minéralogie et des techniques minières," in *Enseignement et diffusion des sciences en France au XVIIIe siècle*, ed. René Taton *et al.* (Paris, 1964), pp. 405–6.

he could choose an occupation, he would clear lands, locate and excavate mines, and write a natural history of the lands he would survey. In winter he could teach courses in French on mechanics, hydraulics, mineralogy, and assaying, perhaps in Boston. For twenty-one years others have benefited from his work in the mines, but he has not gained personally, nor is he certain that the French government will reward him for it.

On May 23 Matthew Young[9] writes in English from Trinity College in Dublin. He is sending Franklin, through a London bookseller, a copy of his new treatise on "Sir Isaac Newton's theory of the pulses of the air."[1] He now seeks Franklin's advice on a scheme he formed with several other students in 1773 but abandoned at the outbreak of the late war: emigrating to America and founding a college. His ardor for this dream remains strong, but in the meantime he has started a family and has earned a position at the college with a good salary and the promise of advancement. He believes that the benefits of living in America, under its freedoms and among its virtuous people, will more than compensate for the inevitable loss of income. Would Franklin be willing to advise him? Young begs Franklin not to reveal his plan to anyone in Ireland, and to send his answer care of the Forster brothers at Bordeaux.

In a letter written on a Sunday, July 4,[2] the marquise de Lafayette asks Franklin to see a gentleman from Auvergne who wants to emigrate to America. This man is a relative, though she and her husband do not know him well; his lands adjoin those of her husband's. Would Franklin please advise him on what opportunities might exist?

Also on July 4, Georges Le Cerf,[3] in Paris, asks whether Franklin

---

9. The natural philosopher who spent his entire academic life at Trinity College, from his matriculation in 1766 to his election as professor in 1786: *ODNB*.

1. *An Enquiry into the Principal Phænomena of Sounds and Musical Strings* (London, 1784).

2. No year is specified, but it must have been 1784. The only other Sunday, July 4, during BF's stay in France was in 1779, when the ongoing war would have precluded such a casual inquiry about emigration.

3. A Genevan watchmaker and inventor of watchmaking tools. In 1775, Le Cerf had tried unsuccessfully to establish a factory in Geneva to manufacture blank movements. In 1778, he sent two of his instruments to the Royal Society, with an article describing them; it was read to the society on July 9, 1779: Luc van Aken, "Louis Faizan, horloger et révolutionnaire. 1725–1781," *Genava: Revue d'histoire de l'art et d'archéologie*, XLIX (2001),

had yet heard anything about the possibility of Le Cerf's establishing a watchmaking manufactory in America. Whether or not his proposal was approved, he is still eager to emigrate with his small family. If an American ship will be leaving for Philadelphia from Le Havre or Rouen around September, he would make arrangements to depart. His address is "Mr Le Cerf. horloger au grand Monarque," rue des Bourdonnais.

On July 21 Frohard de Lamette, writing from Dunkirk and signing himself as an officer in the Couronne regiment,[4] appeals to "Monsieur le Docteur" to assist some of his relatives in emigrating to America. Several generations of Lamettes had served in the military; they had achieved glory but not wealth. His ancestors, who emigrated from England more than two hundred years since, once owned grand estates in Picardy, but all that remains is a small farm. The recently widowed mother, living on the farm, is barely able to provide the necessities of life for her eight children, the eldest of whom is around twenty. Lamette hopes to settle them in Pennsylvania. They would be ideal immigrants: virtuous, wise, hardworking, and sober. Vices common to city folk are unknown to them. If all emigrants to the United States possessed these traits, America would see the rebirth of a golden age. Lamette beseeches Franklin to serve as their father and protector, and help them find a farm, perhaps near Franklin's own relations. He would receive their unbounded gratitude.

On August 4, Madame Des Mignons Dusaray addresses Franklin in phonetic French, sending for the fifth time a letter to "votre othel â chailliot."[5] (Whether the previous four letters found their way to

---

154–8; Le Cerf, "Account of the Advantages of a newly-invented Machine . . . ," *Phil. Trans.*, LXVIII (1779), 950–98; *Monthly Review,* LXII (1780), 44–8, 176.

4. François-Joseph de Frohard de Lamette (Lameth) (1751–1844) was currently a lieutenant in that regiment. He was eventually promoted to captain and made a chevalier of St.-Louis and of Notre-Dame du Mont-Carmel and St.-Lazare: Paul Denis du Péage, "Notes d'Etat Civil de la région du nord," *Recueil de la Société d'études de la province de Cambrai,* XI (1924), 279; *Etat militaire* for 1784, p. 212.

5. Françoise Guillien des Mignons was the wife of Joseph Dusaray, who had applied to BF for assistance in emigrating to America in 1778: XXVII, 16. She remained in Burgundy and remarried in 1812: Archives départementales de Saône-et-Loire, *Canton de Mont-Saint-Vincent* (2 vols. to date, Mâcon, France, 1982–), I, 99–100.

Passy, rather than Chaillot, is not known.) She requests free passage to Philadelphia as well as land for herself and ten other people, including her seven children. She is the descendant of a long line of military officers who left her with nothing but debts. Her relative L'Averdy had given her husband employment; since then, their income has fallen from four thousand to fifteen hundred *livres*. If it were not for her extreme distress she would not trouble respectable people with her requests, as it is difficult for someone so well-born to be reduced to supplication. She hopes that Franklin has more regard for her than do the farmers general and will grant her lands. She would rather leave than starve to death.

Monsieur   Neuville ce 12[–19] mars 1784
   Je prens la liberté de vous écrire pour un jeun homme, qui désireroit passer en amérique, mais non pas sans recomandation, c'est pourquoi il m'a chargé de vous écrire a ce sujet, bien informé que vous vous employez volontiers; pour un homme dans lequel vous reconnoissiez quelque qualité; en Effet, le jeun homme en a quelques unes; il sait écrire correctement, ayant fait de bonnes Etudes, il aime baucoup cultiver; ce qui l'engage a partir le plus c'est qu'il à apris que lon donnoit un certain terrain a ceux qui passoient; mais il désireroit auparavant etre un peu au fait des meurs des habitants, connoitre Surtout la qualité et l'Exposition du sol pour voir Ce qu'il pouroit produire avec plus d'avantage: D'ailleurs, Monsieur, si vous daignez agreer ma lettre; et m'honorer d'une réponse, le jeune homme ira lui meme a paris ou il aura l'honneur de vous voir, en attendant l'honneur de la vôtre. Jai l'honneur D'Etre avec la plus haute Estime Monsieur Votre tres humble et tres obeissant Serviteur

MILET L'AINÉ

Mon adresse est à Neuville sur seine par bar sur seine

[*In Franklin's hand:*]
Sir,   Passy, Mar. 19. 1784
   I have no Orders or Authority to encourage any Persons to go to America, by promising Lands or other Favours from the Government there. The enclos'd printed paper will give such an Account of that Country as may perhaps convince your Friend that he had better stay where he is. I have the honour to be &c

From Nicola Victor Mühlberger[6]

ALS: American Philosophical Society

Monsieur   Lisbonne le 13e. mars 1784.

Sans avoir l'honneur d'Estre personellement Connue de Vous je prend la Liberté de Vous adresser la présente.

Je Suis Mühlberger de Dresde Negotient que vôtre Complaisançe a bien voulu a la requete de nôtre Embassadeur Monsieur le Baron de Schönfeld a Paris accorder la recomandation de Mr. Robert Morris Intendent des finances en avril dernr.[7] de quoi je ne scaurois assé vous Exprimer ma reconnoissençe de m'avoir procuré la Conoissençe d'une ausi respectable maison; il est Seulement triste pour moi que le premier essai n'ai point répondu a l'attente par l'abondançe des marchandises Sur la plaçe, Cependent nullement découragé dans le moment je prie le partie éstent sur Les Lieux de prendre Connoissençe de l'interieur du paÿ affin d'estre a même de Voir se qui seroit le plus analogue & Lucratif avec le nôtre, je poussé mon Voÿage jusques a Niagara a mon retour je Comuniquai mes idées a Monsieur Morris qui me fit l'honneur de les approuver de sorte qu'après avoir prie touttes les mesures pour une heureuse reussite dans des affaires de Cette Conséquençe, je chargé mon Batiment a la Nouvelle York pour Les Isles azores, la Surveille de mon départ je trouvé au fond d'une armoire dans la maison ou jetois Logé le Paquet, Cÿ joint, je demendai aussitot a mon hote d'ou il venoit à une tel Plaçe lequel me dit avoir fait acquisition de Cette maison après l'evacuation des anglois[8] & qu'il n'en avoit aucune Connoissençe, d'après quoi je le gardéz affin de vous le faire parvenir au plutot.

---

6. A Dresden merchant who also acted as a commissioner for the court of Saxony. In the spring of 1783 the Saxon Commerce Commission reported that he had bought Saxon textiles at the Leipzig fair for sale in America and intended to embark at Hamburg: William E. Lingelbach, "Saxon-American Relations, 1778–1828," *American Hist. Rev.*, XVII (1911–12), 518n, 530n.

7. Not found, but see XXXIX, 311–12, for Schönfeld's March 9, 1783, letter to BF introducing another representative of the Saxon court.

8. *I.e.*, after Nov. 25, 1783: Harold E. Selesky, ed., *Encyclopedia of the American Revolution* (2nd ed.; 3 vols., Detroit, New York, and San Francisco, 2006), II, 834.

Le malheur m'ayant empeché de pouvoir terminer mon voÿage aux azores, car a lentré du Port de Lisle St. Michel une Tempete affreuse survint qui nous mit dans un Triste etat emporta touttes les Voiles & nous jeta sur Cette Cote ou avec le plus grand bonheur nous avons avec bien des Peines été a même de gagner dans nôtre détresse le Port de Lisbonne. J'espere d'ans le Courrent de lété êstre a même de vous rendre mes tres humbles devoirs personellement, Si dans cette intervalle vous deignéz m'honorer de quelques uns de Vos Ordres quelconque je vous prie vouloir me les adresser chéz Mr. Mark Gregori a Dunkerque.

Vous prient de me croire avec Le respect le plus parfait de Votre Excellençe Votre tres humble & tres Obeissant Serviteur

NICOLA VICTOR MÜHLBERGER

From Anne Ogle[9] ALS: American Philosophical Society

Sr. March 13. 1784

Mr. Sam: Ridout, my Grandson, purposing to pass a few weeks at Paris previous to his leaving Europe—wishes to have the honor of paying his respects to your Excellency. I therefore take the liberty of using this method for introducing him—

I am Sr. your most Obedien Servant ANNE OGLE

Addressed: A Monsieur / Monsieur Franklin / Ministre Plenipotentiaire / des Etats Unis de L'Amerique

Endorsed: W T. F. to visit him, and invite him to dine, &c

Notation: Anne Ogle March 13, 1784—

To John Adams ALS: Massachusetts Historical Society

Sir, Passy, March 15. 1784.

We have lately received a Letter from the Secretary of Congress,[1] of which I enclose a Copy, accounting for the Delay of

9. Anne Ogle (XXXI, 238n) was living in Boulogne-sur-Mer. In 1782 BF helped secure permission for her grandson Samuel Ridout to join her there; see XXXVII, 200, 408, 413, 420–1.

1. [Mifflin] to the American commissioners, Jan. 5: XLI, 407–8.

the Ratification; & we have sent a Copy of it to Mr. Laurens,[2] who being on the Spot can easily negociate an Agreement to extend the Term if necessary; but I imagine it can hardly occasion any Difficulty, since the Ratification will certainly be made, seven States being unanimously for it, and the Delay was only occasion'd by Accidents unforeseen & unavoidable.

I send herewith a Packet & two Letters left with me for you, which I hope will come safe to hand. I have the honour to be Sir Your Excelly's most obedient & most humble Servant

B FRANKLIN

His Excellency John Adams Esqr

From the Abbé André Morellet

AL: American Philosophical Society

On January 26, Franklin wrote a critique of hereditary nobility in general and of the Society of the Cincinnati in particular, couched as a private letter to his daughter, Sarah Bache.[3] After keeping that essay secret for "some Months," he asked Morellet to make a translation, which the abbé returned with the present letter. In response to the concern that Morellet expresses here, Franklin agreed that the piece would not appear during his lifetime.[4] Nonetheless, the two men continued to work on the French translation. None of the manuscripts they exchanged has survived. The last extant letter in the series, sent by Morellet on an unspecified "samedi" and published below under the date [after March 16], enclosed a revised translation marked with suggestions for further passages that might be cut if Franklin saw fit.

In September 1784, Franklin gave Mirabeau letters of introduction when the Frenchman fled Paris for London and sought a British publisher for his own work against the Society of the Cincinnati and hereditary nobility.[5] When published later that year, the book, which Mirabeau and his co-author Chamfort had discussed with Franklin

2. BF enclosed it in his letter of March 12[–13], above.
3. XLI, 503–11.
4. See BF to Morellet, March 16, immediately below.
5. BF to Richard Price, Sept. 7, 1784 (APS); to Benjamin Vaughan, Sept. 7, 1784 (Library of Congress).

in July, incorporated passages (without attribution) from Franklin's satire.[6] The doctor may have promised Morellet on March 16 that he would not publish his "letter" and allow his name to be associated with such harshly anti-aristocratic views, but he was evidently keen, nonetheless, to see his arguments circulate.

It was Mirabeau who announced Franklin's death to the French National Assembly on June 11, 1790. Six weeks later, a French version of Franklin's satire was published in Paris. Shorter and milder in tone than the English original, the translation appeared in the journal of a recently formed association of which Mirabeau was a member, the Société de 1789.[7] The text published in the *Journal de la Société de 1789* appears to have been adapted from the now-missing translation that Morellet and Franklin had prepared. A compelling indication of this is the way the piece ends: the version published in the *Journal de la Société de 1789* concludes with the modified final sentence that Morellet proposes in the present letter.[8] One notable change, however, must have been made by the journal editors: the salutation was dropped and the first sentence was revised so that instead of addressing his daughter, Franklin is addressing an unnamed male "ami,"

6. See the entry of July 13 in BF's journal, [June 26–July 27], below. The work in question was in French. The passages taken from BF's essay are literal translations of his English. They differ substantially from the translation published in 1790, discussed later in the headnote.

7. "Lettre de Franklyn, du 26 Janvier 1784," *Jour. de la Société de 1789*, July 24, 1790, pp. 9–16. For Mirabeau's announcement of BF's death to the French National Assembly see *Jefferson Papers*, XIX, 79–80. The Société de 1789 was a political club of moderate supporters of the constitutional monarchy. Among its members were many of BF's friends and colleagues, including Lafayette, Condorcet, Bailly, Cabanis, Lavoisier, Du Pont de Nemours, and La Rochefoucauld. Morellet was not a member: Mark Olsen, "A Failure of Enlightened Politics in the French Revolution: the Société de 1789," *French History*, VI (1992), 303–34; Durand Echeverria, "Franklin's Lost Letter on the Cincinnati," *Bulletin de l'Institut Français de Washington*, nouvelle série, III (1953), 119–22.

8. The text of this sentence, showing the addition suggested by Morellet, is quoted below, in annotation of the letter itself. A further indication that the 1790 translation derives from the Morellet/BF translation is that it includes the sentence that BF inserted after the one surviving press copy of his English original was taken (XLI, 503n, 509). Finally, the 1790 translation does not include BF's table for calculating the number of a future knight of the Cincinnati's ancestors, but, rather, summarizes the conclusion. This may well have been suggested by Morellet, who was urging BF to shorten the piece.

and instead of thanking Sarah for newspapers, Franklin thanks this friend for news of the unspecified "pays que vous habitez." Despite these alterations, the reference to "votre bonne mère" remained. Franklin's satire was introduced in the journal's pages by a letter of submission from Philippe-Antoine Grouvelle, one of the editors. How he obtained the manuscript is as yet unknown.[9] Grouvelle wrote that Franklin's piece was "tres-peu connue," and that current events had given it new relevance: "elle est neuve aujourd'hui pour ceux même qui l'ont lue en son tems." He evoked "l'ombre de Franklyn" to bestow legitimacy on the new revolutionary order, in particular on the recent and highly controversial abolition of noble privileges. Franklin's reasons for attacking the cult of nobility at its inception in America, Grouvelle argued, were the same that led the French revolutionaries to fight it in its decline.[1]

In 1792 this French translation was reprinted, with a rephrased opening, in *La Feuille villageoise*, a revolutionary newspaper co-founded by Grouvelle, published in Paris, and distributed in the provinces for the political education of rural villagers. Again, Franklin's words served to justify the suppression of noble titles and arms. But the editors considered it necessary to explain in a footnote that the concluding sentence, which in fact had been revised at the behest of the cautious Morellet, should be understood as "une raillerie douce, une ironie fine," aimed by Franklin at the swarm of young courtiers who, assuming the airs of protectors and liberators and exhibiting the insolent manners of the French nobility, pestered him with requests for the medal of the Cincinnati.[2]

Paris mardi [March]. 16. [1784]³

Je vous renvoye mon respectable ami votre original et la traduction.[4] Je crois y avoir conservé le ton de raison et de plaisanterie

9. Grouvelle was active in the Lodge of the Nine Sisters during the period when BF attended meetings, though we have no direct evidence of their friendship. See XXXIV, 470n; Olsen, "A Failure of Enlightened Politics," p. 312.

1. "Lettre de Franklyn, du 26 Janvier 1784," *Jour. de la Société de 1789,* July 24, 1790, pp. 1–2, 7.

2. *La Feuille villageoise,* Jan. 26, 1792, pp. 421–7; Melvin Edelstein, "*La Feuille villageoise,* the Revolutionary Press, and the Question of Rural Political Participation," *French Historical Studies,* VII (1971), 175–203.

3. The date is based on BF's reply, the following document.

4. The two enclosures are missing. Because Morellet, in the present letter, calls attention to a change he made to the last sentence, BF must not have

sourde que vous y aves mis. Examines pourtant si j'ai bien saisi
vôtre sens par tout. J'ai ajouté de mon chef la derniere ligne
comme un correctif necessaire sans lequel vôtre phrase enoncoit
un peu de mepris pour *les officiers qui ont servi en amerique* mepris qui n'est pas sans doute dans vôtre intention.[5] Au reste si
vous me permettes de vous le dire ce papier qui est excellent
en lui même peut donner de l'humeur à quelques personnes
que vous ne voules pas desobliger et par cette raison il ne faut,
sauf vôtre avis, que le donner à des gens qui ont assés de philosophie pour connoitre et sentir toute l'absurdité et tout le ridicule du funeste préjugé que vous combattes si bien. Je me flatte
d'etre de ce nombre mais je suis aussi flatté d'etre au nombre de
ceux à qui vous aves montré quelque estime et quelque amitié et
que vous aves jugé dignes de vous entendre. Je vous embrasse
avec toute la tendresse et tout le respect que je vous ai voués
pour la vie.

To Morellet   AL (draft):[6] American Philosophical Society

Passy March 16. 1784
Your Sentiments and mine, my dear Friend, are exactly the same
respecting the Imprudence of showing that Paper; it has therefore, tho' written some Months past, never been communicated
to any one but your self, and will probably not appear till after
my Decease, if it does then. You see how much I confide in your
Friendship and Discretion.

---

given him the final two paragraphs of the English original, which discuss
the Cincinnati's insignia and Latin mottoes.

5. The sentence that Morellet modified begins in the original, "For
my own Part, I shall think it a Convenience" (XLI, 509). The concluding
sentence of the letter as published in the *Jour. de la Société de 1789,* cited
above, reads: "Cette distinction visible sauve au mérite modeste l'embarras
d'attirer l'attention et de m'apprendre toujours avec un peu de gaucherie
que je parle à un homme employé ci-devant comme officier au service de
l'Amérique, et qui a contribué à la liberté et au bonheur de mon pays."

6. Written on the verso of Morellet's letter, immediately above.

The Translation appears to me in general good, and in some places better than the Original; in a few only it seems not fully to render the true Sense. When I next have the Pleasure of seeing you; we will read it together, and you will easily correct those Faults if they are such.
Yours most affectionately

From Anne-Louise Boivin d'Hardancourt Brillon de Jouy

AL: American Philosophical Society

ce 16 mars [1784]

Monsieur gosséc[7] qui vous reméttra cétte léttre, mon cher papa et auqu'el je prends beaucoup d'intérest a déja eu l'honneur de vous voir, ou monsieur votre fils l'année derniére il vient de négotier des papiers que vous avés trouvés bons, et compte repasser incéssament en amérique ou il a été déja employé, il voudroit avant son départ avoir l'honneur de vous voir, de causér avec vous, et de vous demander qu'elques recomandations, je lui ai fait esperer que vous auriés la bonté de le recevoir et de faire pour lui ce qu'il seroit possible;[8] adieu mon bon papa mon bon ami, voila le soleil et les feuilles qui viennent et moi qui vais bientost vous retrouver et vous embrasser de tout mon coeur. Mille amitiés de tous les miens.

7. François-Philippe Moufle Gossec, originally from Maubeuge in northern France, served as the royal land surveyor in Pointe-à-Pitre, Guadeloupe, in the 1770s. He left the office in 1780 and became a prominent investor in housing construction and real estate on the island: Anne Pérotin-Dumon, *La Ville aux Iles, la ville dans l'île: Basse-Terre et Pointe-à-Pitre, Guadeloupe, 1650–1820* (Paris, 2000), pp. 350, 459–60, 475–7, 490–1, 766.
8. Gossec wrote to BF on March 24, 1784, from Paris. He intended to return to Guadeloupe to realize his assets and in September leave for the United States with all or some of his wealth. He planned to travel through all the states before deciding where to settle. The letters of recommendation that BF agreed to give him would allow him to meet prominent individuals and help him in making his decision. APS.

From Morellet

From Morellet   AL: American Philosophical Society

Samedi. [after March 16, 1784][9]

Voilà Monsieur la copie de la traduction que vous aves lüe avec les retranchemens que nous sommes convenus d'y faire.[1] Je crois même que vous féres encore bien d'en retrancher encore les deux endroits que j'ai renfermés entre des lignes. Vous saves avec quelle facilité on saisit icy toutes les occasions de nuire. Pour moi je voudrois avoir tous les jours des occasions de vous servir et de vous temoigner mon tendre et respectueux devouement.

From William Hodgson[2]   ALS: American Philosophical Society

Dear sir—   London 17 March 1784

I recd yours of the 11th Instant[3] as also a preceeding Letter inclosing Dr Wrens Diploma, which I forwarded to him immediately,[4] as I have also that to Dr Withering & shall discharge the Draft in his favor when presented—[5]

Church Bells are sold by weight ½ [1s. 2d.] per lb. or £6..10.8 per Cwt. [hundred weight] when wanted, the weight of the Tenor Bell must be given & then the weight of the Peal may be easily computed from 5 to 12— The Stocks & Wheels are separate Charges & on an Average are about £7— per Bell— The Exportation of Bells is prohibited (for what reason God knows) but leave may be obtained to export them upon Application to the Treasury for a *Fee* of about £6— On an Average the

9. The date is based on BF's March 16 exchange of letters with Morellet, above.
1. Not found.
2. This is the last extant letter from William Hodgson, who died on Oct. 20, 1784: Sheldon S. Cohen, *British Supporters of the American Revolution, 1775–1783: the Role of the 'Middling-level' Activists* (Woodbridge, Eng., 2004), pp. 22–3, 45–7.
3. Not found.
4. BF's letter of Dec. 10, 1783, enclosed an honorary doctorate for the Rev. Thomas Wren from the College of New Jersey: XLI, 271. Wren expressed his thanks in a letter to Elias Boudinot of Feb. 12: Cohen, *British Supporters*, pp. 78–9.
5. See BF to Withering, March 1.

weight of a Peal of Bells, more or less in No. is about 4 Times the weight of the Tenor, & there is no difference in the price per Cwt if the Peal be 6 or 12. Light or heavy Bells— A Peal of 6 Bells supposing the Tenor to weigh 12— Ct will weigh about 48 Ct & the Expence according to the above will be £366.12—[6]

I am very sorry I have not yet had it in my Power to furnish you with the Information respecting the Ships sent into Bergen[7] & I much fear I never shall be able to procure it, my Correspondent at Liverpool cannot learn any thing about the amount of Insurance—

I thank you for your Complimts on my Success against the Secretarys of State— It was your Information (that the passes were delivered gratis,) that determined me to try the Cause,[8] the money must now all be refunded 'twill make a great saving to the Merchants, I believe more than I stated it at, for I believe more than 200 passes were exchanged, with great & Sincere Respect I am Dr sir Yr most Obedt Hble Servant

WILLIAM HODGSON

If you were to be wafted into this Country you wou'd think we were all run mad, stark staring mad for prerogative & our Loyalty & adoration *for the best & most glorious of Kings,* exceeds a Frenchman's Vive le Roi— The Ton is, Honor the King— despise Parliament—especially the Commons—& what is scarcely credible the Dissenters allmost all join the Cry. I met your old Friend Dr. Price, yesterday, he has got as high a Prerogative Fever upon him as the veriest page of the back Stairs— In my poor Judgment they are stabbing the Constitution to the Heart—[9]

Addressed: To / His Excellency Benj. Franklin Esqr / Passy near / Paris

Notation: Wm. Hodgson, 17 Mars. 1784—

6. BF's inquiry into church bells was prompted by his learning that the town of Franklin, Mass., wished for him to donate one: XLI, 476.

7. Requested by BF in a now-missing letter of Dec. 26, 1783; see XLI, 495–6.

8. For this suit, see XXXIX, xxix, 209, 306.

9. For the most recent conflict between the king and the House of Commons, see BF to Henry Laurens, March 12[–13], and the annotation there.

To Mary Hewson   ALS:[1] American Philosophical Society

Passy, March 19. 1784

You will forget me quite, my dear old Friend, if I do not write to you now and then.

I still exist, and still enjoy some Pleasure in that Existence, tho' now in my 79th Year. Yet I feel the Infirmities of Age coming on so fast, and the Building to need so many Repairs, that in a little time the Owner will find it cheaper to pull it down and build a new one.

I wish however to see you first, but I begin to doubt the Possibility.

My Children join in Love to you and yours with Your affectionate Friend

Mrs Hewson

Endorsed: Passy Mar 19 — 84 45

To La Condamine

AL (draft):[2] American Philosophical Society; LS:[3] Bakken Museum

Sir,   Passy, March 19 1784.

I receiv'd the very obliging Letter you did me honour of writing to me the 8th Inst. with the Epigram &c. for which please to accept my Thanks.

You desire my Sentiments concerning the Cures perform'd by Comus, & Mesmer. I think that in general, Maladies caus'd by Obstructions may be treated by Electricity with Advantage. As to the Animal Magnetism, so much talk'd of, I am totally unacquainted with it, and must doubt its Existence till I can see or feel some Effect of it. None of the Cures said to be perform'd by it, have fallen under my Observation, and there being so

1. Or so we assume. The signature has been cleanly cut away.
2. BF drafted this reply on the letter it was answering: La Condamine to BF, March 8 (above). Because it is complete, and conveys BF's thoughts in his own words, we publish the draft rather than the French translation that BF signed and sent.
3. In French and in the hand of L'Air de Lamotte.

many Disorders which cure themselves, and such a Disposition in Mankind to deceive themselves and one another on these Occasions; and living long having given me frequent Opportunities of seeing certain Remedies cry'd up as curing every thing, and yet soon after totally laid aside as useless, I cannot but fear that the Expectations of great Advantage from this new Method of treating Diseases, will prove a Delusion. That Delusion may how ever in some cases be of use while it lasts. There are in every great rich City, a Number of Persons who are never in health, because they are fond of Medicines and always taking them, whereby, they derange the natural Functions, and hurt their Constitutions. If those People can be persuaded to forbear their Drugs in Expectation of being cured by only the Physician's Finger or an Iron Rod pointing at them, they may possibly find good Effects tho' they mistake the Cause. I have the honour to be, Sir, &c

To ———— Mazue   AL (draft):[4] American Philosophical Society

Sir,   Passy, March 19. 1784—
   I received your Favour of the 27th. past, proposing the Cultivation of the Vine in America. Our People[5] conceive that it is yet too early to put such a Project in Execution. Labour is too dear there, and the Culture of Wheat more profitable & certain; in Exchange for which either directly or indirectly, we can procure the Wines of Europe.[6] I cannot therefore give you any Hopes of Success in such an Enterprize; for tho' proper Land & Climate might be found, the Wines could not be produc'd so cheap as they are imported.— I have the honour to be Sir,

Proposal to make Wine in America & Answer

4. Written on a blank leaf of the letter to which it was a response: Mazue to BF, Feb. 27, 1784 (summarized in XLI, 448). At the top of the draft, WTF wrote "Letter (in French)", probably a note to L'Air de Lamotte to prepare a translation for BF's signature.
5. BF interlined the phrase "Our People". He originally wrote "I".
6. BF had first written "France".

From Charles-Guillaume-Frédéric Dumas

ALS: American Philosophical Society

Monsieur, Lahaie 19e. Mars 1784

Dans la supposition que vous avez plaisir de lire de temps à autre une relation fidele des affaires ici, je continue de faire passer sous vos yeux mes Lettres au departement, au lieu de les envoyer directement d'ici à l'orient;[7] & aussi parce que cela me procure l'occasion de me rafraichir dans l'honneur de votre souvenir, & de vous faire agréer les assurances du respectueux attachement avec lequel je suis toujours De Votre Excellence Le très-humble & très-obéissant serviteur C. W. F. DUMAS

A Son Exce. Mr. Franklin

Addressed: à Son Excellence / Monsieur Franklin, Esqr. / Ministre Plenipo: des Etats-Unis / d'Amerique, &c. / Passy./. / près Paris. / France

Thomas Mifflin to Franklin and John Adams

Press copy of copy:[8] American Philosophical Society; copy: National Archives

Gentlemen Annapolis March 20. 1784.

I have the Honor to transmit to you an Act of Congress of the 16th. Inst: together with Copies of the several Papers to which that Act refers.[9]

---

7. Dumas must have enclosed his letter of Feb. 24[–March 12] to the Department of Foreign Affairs. An English translation is in *Diplomatic Correspondence of the United States*, VII, 33–7.

8. In L'Air de Lamotte's hand.

9. The enclosed resolutions of March 16 (Hist. Soc. of Pa.; see *JCC*, XXVI, 144–5) stated that they were passed following the receipt of BF's letters and enclosures of Nov. 1 and Dec. 25, as well as letters from Thomas Barclay dated Oct. 20 and Nov. 14. The first resolution, however, responded to BF's recommendation of William Hodgson as American consul in London, contained in his Dec. 26 letter to Mifflin (XLI, 358–9). Congress resolved that only U.S. citizens would be appointed to civil positions such as ministers, consuls, etc., and directed that copies of this resolve be sent to BF, JA, and Jay. It further directed that the American commissioners inform Hodgson

I am with the Greatest Respect, Gentlemen, Your obedient &
humble Servant   (signed) THOMAS MIFFLIN

The Honrble Benjn. Franklin & J. Adams.

From Jane Franklin Case[1]   LS: American Philosophical Society

Newburgh ulster County State of Newyork
Honourd Sir   march the 22d—1784
Altho I am but a Child of Eight years of age And you Dear
Sir to me Intirely unknown I make Bold to Send you these few
Lines to Inform you that my Parents Informs me that I Receivd
one part of my Christian Name in honour to you and to manifest
their Regard for you as a friend to america my Native Country
and In order to Shew the Great Regard I have for your Person
and Character I Beg of you to accept of the Enclosed Piece as a
token thereof it was wrote by So near a Connection to me that I
would wish to Conceal his name[2] So wishing you all health and

---

of its gratitude for his services to American prisoners. The other resolutions were as follows: (1) to send to the supreme executive of Massachusetts
the paragraph from BF's Dec. 25 letter to Mifflin concerning the capture
of the *Providentia*, and the letter from Danish minister von Blome that
BF's letter enclosed (XLI, 342–3); (2) to send all Congress' correspondence
with Robert Montgomery to the American ministers in Europe so that they
could inquire "on what grounds Mr. Montgomery has undertaken to write
in the name of the United States to the Emperor of Morocco" and could
take all appropriate actions; (3) to send the American ministers a copy of
Barclay's Oct. 20, 1783, letter to Robert R. Livingston on the advantages of
Lorient as a free port (Giunta, *Emerging Nation*, II, 235–7), and to instruct
them to obtain at least two free ports on the French coast, one on the Atlantic and one on the Mediterranean. BF had BFB make copies of the March 16
congressional act and of Barclay's Oct. 20 letter; press copies of them are
at the APS.

1. The eight-year-old daughter (b. 1777) of Stephen and Glorianna
Meritt Case. Stephen, after writing this letter for his daughter, wrote his
own letter to BF, immediately below. Genealogical information on the Case
family was kindly provided by Barbara Wich and the Orange County Ge-
neal. Soc.

2. Her demonstration of personal regard for BF came in the form of a
55-page pamphlet published anonymously by, and privately printed for, her

Happiness Both here and Hereafter I Remain your most Loving friend and Humble Servant   JANE FRANKLIN CASE

PS I Should be Happy to hear by a Line from your honour that you had Receivd this Letter Safely if Sir you Should Condecend to write to me please to Direct to the Care of Coll Thomas Palmer at the above Named place   J F C

To Doctor Benjamin Franklin—&c

Addressed: To Doctr / Benjamin Franklin / att / The Court of versallies / Near Paris

From Stephen Case[3]   ALS: American Philosophical Society

[March 22, 1784][4]

I Do hereby Certify to you that the name Signd is in the proper hand writeing of my Daughter who has Long been Desirious of writeing to your Honour. She is a fine Beautifull Child of fine witt and Exceeding apt to Learn more So than any one of my Children to the amount of 11 which I have had born to me.

From Sir your unknown friend   STEPHEN CASE

To Doctor Benjamin Franklin Esq

Addressed: To Doctor / Benjamin Franklin Esq / Near or at Paris / in old France— / Pr. Packet

---

father: *Defensive Arms Vindicated; and the Lawfulness of the American War Made Manifest. To which Is Added, A short Receipt for a Continental Disease, &c. Dedicated to his Excellency General Washington. By A Moderate Whig* ([New-Marlborough, N.Y.], 1783). Stephen Case inscribed the title page "For The Honourable Benjamin Franklin Esq". BF's copy is at the APS.

3. Stephen Case (1738–1794) was appointed to the Newburgh Committee of Safety and Observation in 1775 and served as an officer in the Ulster County militia during the Revolution: Ruth P. Heidgerd, *Ulster County in the Revolution* . . . ([New Paltz, N.Y.], 1977), p. 34; Edward M. Ruttenber and Lewis H. Clark, comps., *History of Orange County, New York* . . . (1881; reprint, 2 vols., Interlaken, N.Y., 1980), I, 256.

4. This letter accompanied the one immediately above. The date was written in pencil at the top of the letter but in a different hand.

From John Paul Jones   ALS: American Philosophical Society

Sir,   Paris March 23d. 1784
    The Marquis de la Fayette was so obliging as to translate and
enforce my two last Letters, which I had the honor to communicate to you of the 6th. and 13th. Current, to the Marechal de
Castries, on the subject of the Prize-money due to the Officers
and Men who served in the Squadron I commanded in Europe.[5]
But, from a Letter written the 29th. of May 1780 from M. De
Sartine to Mr. le Rey de Chaumont, of which I had the honor
to shew you an Extract,[6] the Marquis informs me, that it is the
opinion of the Marechal de Castries that you have agreed to the
Settlement of the Prize-money *in the manner that was proposed
by Mr. le Rey de Chaumont*; whereby the whole expence of the
Squadron in the Texel is charged to the Captors.[7] The Marechal
finds it difficult to alter what he thinks has been settled by his
Predecessor; but if you would be so good as to enable me to
convince him that you never consented to the Settlement proposed by Mr. le Rey de Chaumont, the Marquis de la Fayette
is of opinion that you would thereby remove the greatest difficulty that now opposes a final Settlement of the Business. I am,
Sir, with the greatest Respect, Your Excellency's most obedient
and most humble Servant   J PAUL JONES

    5. In the March 6 letter, Jones criticized Le Ray de Chaumont, the
former liaison between the French government and Jones's *Bonhomme
Richard* squadron of 1779, for claiming to have had authority over that
squadron: Bradford, *Jones Papers*, reel 7, no. 1505. Chaumont had acted on
behalf of the French monarchy as the squadron's paymaster: XXIX, 240n.
The March 13 letter has not been located (the copies that Jones sent to BF
are missing), but on Feb. 18 Jones had also written to Castries, criticizing Chaumont: Bradford, *Jones Papers*, reel 7, no. 1503. For Jones's current mission to obtain prize money from the French government, see XLI,
261, 298.
    6. BF comments on that now-missing extract in his reply of March 25,
below. Sartine, at that time, was minister of the French navy. Most of the
letter concerned the sale of the *Pallas* and the *Vengeance*, two ships from
Jones's squadron (New York Public Library).
    7. After the Battle off Flamborough Head the Jones squadron had sailed
to the Dutch naval base of the Texel, arriving in early October and sailing
just before the end of 1779: XXX, 442; XXXI, lxv.

His Excellency B. Franklin Esqr. American Minister Plenipotentiary at the Court of France

Notation: Paul Jones March 23. 1784—

To John Paul Jones   ALS: British Library

Sir,   Passy, Mar. 23. 1784
    I received the Letter you did me the honour of writing to me
this Morning respecting the Settlement of Charges incurred in
Holland, &c. Be so good as to send me a Copy of the Letter
written by Mr. de Sartine, which you mention. On Sight of that
I shall immediately give you an explicit Answer.
    With great Esteem, I am, Sir, Your most obedient & most
huml Servt   B. FRANKLIN

Honble Paul Jones Esqr

Addressed:[8] A Monsieur / Monsieur Le Capitaine / Paul Jones,
Hotel de / Londres / rue de Richelieu.

From Joseph Banks   ALS: University of Pennsylvania Library

Dear Sir   Soho Square March 23 1784
    After the Storm which has agitated the Royal Society since
Christmas with no Small degree of Violence We have drop'd
into a flat Calm. It seems as if the debates have exhausted the
annual supply of genius or at least skimmd off the Cream of
it as nothing very interesting appears either in Presence or
Prospect.[9]

    8. In L'Air de Lamotte's hand.
    9. The resignation on Nov. 27 of Charles Hutton (x, 303n), the Royal
Society's assistant secretary of foreign correspondence, became the occasion for a challenge to Banks's leadership of the institution. Between December and February, Banks's critics charged that he had interfered in the
election of officers and fellows and that he did not possess sufficient creden-
tials as a scientist to head the society. Banks's supporters, rallied by Charles

The best papers we have had is Dr. Blagdens general thoughts on Meteors in which he has made an Observation gatherd from the Examination of as many accounts as he Could procure from all periods which is, that Meteors appear always to have followd a direction somewhat near the Magnetical meridian which analogy between Magnetism & Electricity seems likely to produce discoveries.[1]

Mr. Herschel has given us Some good Observations on the Planet Mars[2] in the Couse [Course] of which he has descanted much on large luminous Areas seen in the Polar regions of that planet which in the Course of some years Observation he has Observd to increase or diminish as their respective poles were oppos'd to or inclind from the Sun whence he concludes them to be Masses of Snow & Ice accumulating about the poles of that planet in a manner similar to what happens on ours the first Observation I think that we have had tending to *Prove* a similarity of Creative arrangement in the Similar parts of our System.

The business of Aerostates seems to Come now towards rest in France no advances appear to have been made by the Clumsey means hitherto propos'd of guiding them indeed any one who Sees a bird strugling against the wind notwithstanding his shape is apparently contrivd to Present the Smallest possible Surface to it will hesitate much in beleiving it possible for men

---

Blagden, submitted a resolution of confidence that was carried overwhelmingly at the meeting of Jan. 8, 1784. Resolutions by the opposition to reinstate Hutton and to limit the role of the president in the admission of fellows were defeated on Feb. 12 and 26, respectively. Paul Henry Maty, principal secretary of the society and a leader of the opposition, resigned as secretary during the next regular meeting on March 25. The election of Blagden as his successor on May 5 further consolidated Banks's position: Harold B. Carter, *Sir Joseph Banks, 1743–1820* (London, 1988), pp. 194–201.

1. In his "An Account of some late fiery Meteors . . . ," read before the Royal Society on Feb. 19, Charles Blagden hypothesized that meteors were not combustible vapors or solid bodies, as previously thought, but that they instead consisted of electricity. Based on his claim that all large meteors move along the magnetic meridian, Blagden postulated a resemblance between electricity and magnetism: *Phil. Trans.*, LXXIV (1784), 201–32.

2. William Herschel's "On the remarkable Appearances at the Polar Regions of the Planet Mars . . ." was read before the Royal Society on March 11: *Phil. Trans.*, LXXIV (1784), 233–73.

to Give *usefull* direction to a machine which always must present an enormous one increasing in Proportion as it Carries up additional Strengh to move it.

Smeathmans Idea is ingenious but I fear impraticable the weight of his Plane must if it is made of Materials sufficiently strong to support its own extention be more than the Proportion of Ballon fit to Ride upon it Can Support to say nothing of the danger of Oversetting nor is it new for it was suggested in Conversation to me Some Months before I receivd it from Smeathman.[3]

Mr. Argand has procurd a Patent for his Lamp which the officers of Police at Paris Seem to have borrowd from him without any valuable consideration[4] it appears to me A real improvement

3. Henry Smeathman had been in Paris since August, 1783, hoping to find sponsors for the establishment of a free-labor colony in Sierra Leone: XL, 426–7. Unable to raise funds for that project, he designed a steerable flying machine that he hoped would earn him sufficient capital to finance the colony himself. He wrote a memoir on Feb. 2, 1784, describing his invention, which the Duke of Dorset reviewed and certified. Having thereby established his rights to the invention, Smeathman showed the memoir to BF on Feb. 6, and later claimed that BF approved of his sending it to Banks as the first step in his quest for sponsorship. According to Smeathman, "As soon as Dr. Franklin had read my Memoir, he launched half a sheet of paper obliquely in the air, observing, that that was an evident proof of the propriety of my doctrines."

Smeathman described his machine as "a mixed form of a fish, a bird, and a bat, flat-bottomed, and presenting a large membrane on each side, and two wings of very simple construction, and a very broad tail or rudder." In the drawings he sent to Banks on Feb. 11 (Royal Society Archives), an elongated balloon sits atop a frame resembling a hull with wings on each side and a back rudder; this is what Banks calls a "Plane." A passenger car hangs suspended below the hull by four ropes. Smeathman posited that once the machine was in the air, it would be able to glide on the wind like a bird or a boat on water, and be steered by the rudder: Smeathman to John Lettsom, Feb. 7, April 17, and July 16, 1784, in Thomas J. Pettigrew, ed., *Memoirs of the Life and Writings of the Late John Coakley Lettsom* ... (3 vols., London, 1817), II, 270, 275–80. In his Feb. 11 letter to Banks, Smeathman asserted that none of the three men to whom he had shown his plan—the Duke of Dorset, BF, and Dr. Broussonet—had doubted that the vessel could easily be steered: Neil Chambers, ed. *Scientific Correspondence of Sir Joseph Banks, 1765–1820* (6 vols., London, 2007), II, 258–61.

4. For Ami Argand's oil lamp, see XLI, 144n, and the headnote to "Aux Auteurs du Journal de Paris," [before March 31], below.

I only Lament that we are to pay the piper to whom in all likely-hood all Europe will dance.

Our old Friend Smeaton is just About to publish his Account of the Building of Edistone Lighthouse.[5] I was with him this morn & lookd over the plates most of which have been engravd these 20 years but he left off business with the last year & now means to amuse himself with this publication.

Yours Faithfully   Jos: BANKS

From Amelia Barry   ALS: American Philosophical Society

My Dear Sir,   Pisa 24th March 1784

Mr. Partridge, one of the principal Merchants at Leghorn,[6] and who is universally esteemed for his knowledge and virtue, will have the honor to present you this letter. As he takes Paris in his way to England, I wish to introduce to you a Gentleman of his merit, and who has long been a warm and sincere friend to me and my little family. As his stay upon the Continent will not be sufficiently long for you to have a proper knowledge of his character, permit me to entreat your best offices to him on my account;—and every attention he receives from you, will be considered as immediately confered upon, My Dear Paternal Friend, Your grateful, obliged & affecate. Humble Servant,

A. BARRY.

His Excelly. B. Franklin Esqr.

Endorsed: Mar. 24. 84

Notation: A Barry 24 Mars 1784

5. *A Narrative of the Building and a Description of the Construction of the Edystone Lighthouse with Stone* . . . by John Smeaton (XIX, 158n) was not published until 1791.

6. James Partridge, an Englishman, had established himself in Leghorn nearly 20 years earlier: John Ingamells, *A Dictionary of British and Irish Travellers in Italy, 1701–1800* (New Haven and London, 1997), p. 744.

To John Paul Jones

ALS: British Library; copies: Archives Nationales, Library of Congress, National Archives

Sir,   Passy, March 25. 1784

I return herewith the Papers you communicated to me yesterday.[7] I perceive by the Extract from M. de Sartine's Letter, that it was his Intention all the Charges which had accru'd upon the Serapis & Countess of Scarborough should be deducted from the Prize-money payable to the Captors, particularly the Expence of Victualling the Seamen & Prisoners; and that the Liquidation of those Charges should be referr'd to me.[8] This Liquidation however never was referr'd to me; and if it had, I should have been cautious of acting in it, having receiv'd no Power from the Captors, either French or Americans, authorizing me to decide upon any thing respecting their Interests.— And I certainly should not have agreed to charge the American Captors with any Part of the Expence of maintaining the 600 Prisoners in Holland till they could be exchanged, when none of them were exchanged for Americans in England, as was your Intention, & as we both had been made to expect.[9] With great Esteem, I have the honour to be, Sir, Your most obedient humble Servant   B. FRANKLIN

Honble Paul Jones Esqr.

Addressed:[1] A Monsieur / Monsieur Jones Chevalier de / l'Ordre Royal du Merite No. 3 / rue du Reposoir / à Paris

7. See the exchange between Jones and BF on March 23.

8. According to an Aug. 13, 1779, agreement of the captains of the squadron (cited in XXX, 223n), the distribution of prize money was to be regulated by the French naval minister and BF.

9. Jones placed prisoners taken during the squadron's cruise under French control at the instance of the French government. They were exchanged for Frenchmen: XXXI, 120n. On March 26, Jones sent a copy of the present letter to Castries: Bradford, *Jones Papers*, reel 7, no. 1510.

1. In L'Air de Lamotte's hand.

To Edward Nathaniel Bancroft

ALS: Yale University Library

My dear young Friend,   Passy, March 26. 1784

I have received two Letters from you,[2] and am pleas'd to see that you improve in your Writing and Language, and to read your dutiful Expressions of Respect and Love for your Parents, which is very commendable. My Grandson Benja. Franklin Bache, who is lately return'd from Geneva,[3] answer'd for me your first Letter, and hopes you receiv'd it, tho' you mention nothing of it in your second.— You are happy in being under the Care of so good a Master as Mr Rose,[4] whom I much esteem, and desire you would present my Respects to him. Pursue your Studies diligently: they may qualify you to act in some honourable Station hereafter, and distinguish you from the ignorant Vulgar. Strive to be one of the best Boys among your Acquaintance; 'tis the Road that leads to the Character of a Good Man. Be dutiful & affectionate to your good Mother, particularly now in the Absence of your Father; which will draw down upon you the Blessing of God, and procure you the Regard of all your Father's Friends, and of every one that knows your Family. I am, my dear young Friend, Yours very affectionately

B. FRANKLIN

This Family join in respectful Compliments to Mrs Bancroft

Master E. N. Bancroft.—

Addressed: To / Master Edwd. Nathl Bancroft / No 6. Dukestreet / St. James's / London

From David Hartley

ALS: Library of Congress

Dear Sir   London March 26 1784

I have received yours of the 11th instant. I am to inform you in answer that it is not thought necessary on the part of Great

2. XLI, 201, 433–5.
3. BFB had returned to Passy the previous July: XL, 267n.
4. William Rose: XI, 98n, 100n.

Britain to enter into any formal convention for the prolongation of the term in wch the ratifications were to be exchanged as the delay in America appears to have arisen merely in consequence of the inclemency of the season. There will be no delay on our part in exchanging the ratifications of the definitive treaty with the united States as soon as that on their part shall arrive.—[5] I shall be very happy when you send me notice of that arrival, for the pleasing opportunity that it will afford me of seeing you again. I beg my best Compts to Mr Adams if at Paris and to Mr Jay & all friends. I am with the greatest affection & Esteem ever Yours   D HARTLEY

To Dr Franklin &c &c &c—

Endorsed: D Hartley Esqr to B F. March 26. 1784

John Adams to Franklin and John Jay

Copy: Massachusetts Historical Society

Gentlemen   The Hague March 27. 1784

I have the Honour to inclose a Letter from Mr Edward Browne of Ostend and another from Mr De Berdt.—[6] Mr Browne was introduced to me in London by Mr De Berdt, and appears to be an accomplished Person well acquainted with the Language Laws and Commerce of the Place where he is.— If your Excellencys judge proper, I should be obliged to you if you would transmit to Congress, Mr Brownes Letter and Mr De Berdts, for the Consideration of that Body.

With great

Their Excellencies Mr Franklin & Mr Jay.

5. Hartley had presented the issue to Carmarthen in a letter of March 22, which enclosed the letter from Mifflin to BF that BF had sent on March 11 (National Archives, London). For more background see Laurens to BF, March 28.

6. The first was a now-missing Jan. 27 letter from Browne to JA requesting appointment as American consul at Ostend, and the second was a Feb. 6 cover letter for the first, from the London merchant Dennis De Berdt, Jr. (XXVII, 515n). JA responded to both men on March 27: *Adams Papers,* XVI, 17–18.

From John Adams

Copy: Massachusetts Historical Society

Sir   The Hague March 27. 1784

I have received the Letter you did me the Honour to write me the 15th with the Letters Packet and Copy inclosed. I think with you that the Delay of the Ratification cannot occasion any Difficulty, but it was very proper to Send a Copy of the Secretarys Letter to Mr Laurens, who may negotiate an Agreement to extend the Term or at least may explain the Cause of delay.

I have comfortable Assurances of Saving our Financiers Credit for this time,[7] but if he repeats these bold Measures I shall not be able I fear to rescue him again.

Dr Franklin.

From ———— de Gourdon[8]

AL: American Philosophical Society

ce Samedy 27. mars 1784.

M. de Gourdon a l'honneur de Présenter Ses Respectueux homages a Monsieur franklin, et de Luÿ Renvoÿer Les 10 Volumes qu'il a Bien voulu Luÿ Prester: il Se Seroit fait un devoir de les luÿ Reporter Luÿ même Si Sa Santé Luÿ Eut Permis de sortir ces jours cÿ.

Il Supplie Monsieur franklin, Si il a quelque Suplément à Cette histoire qui l'amene jusqu'a La conclusion, de Vouloir bien Le luÿ prester: il Le luÿ Rendra avec La même Exactitude, et Saisira Le premier moment d'aller Renouveller Sa Reconnoisance a Monsieur franklin.

Mad de Gourdon a l'honneur de Luÿ Presenter Ses très humbles civilitées.

---

7. The financier in question was Robert Morris. On March 9 JA had signed a contract to raise a 2,000,000 f. loan for the United States with the same Dutch consortium that had handled his 1782 loan (XXXVIII, 433n). By March 27 enough of the loan had been subscribed to pay all of the outstanding drafts: *Adams Papers*, XVI, 79, 80–5, 93, 103.

8. This French army captain, now living at Passy, had been introduced to BF by Kéralio in November, 1783. In February, BF invited Gourdon and his wife to dinner: XLI, 244.

From the Marquis and Marquise de Lafayette and Jean-Baptiste de Gouvion
L: American Philosophical Society

Paris Ce 27. mars [1784?][9]

Mr et Mde. La Marquise De lafayette et Mr. De Gouvion profiteront avec grand plaisir de l'Invitation de Monsieur Franklin et auront l'honneur de Diner chez lui Dimanche.

From John Witherspoon[1]
ALS: American Philosophical Society

Sir   London March 27. 1784

I had some Expectations of seeing you before this Time at Paris. Please to know that the Trustees of the College of New Jersey contrary to my Judgement and Inclination were induced by some Things they had heard to suppose that this would not be an improper Time to Solicit Benefactors for the College which is known to have suffered so much by being seated in the Center of the Theatre of the late War. They therefore gave a Commission to Genl Reed & myself to make Application for the Purpose both in England and France.

There is little or no Prospect of Success here[2] and though I should be well pleased to visit Paris for my own Satisfaction I was somewhat unwilling to add to the Charge unless there is some Reason to hope it may be useful. I have Letters of Introduction

9. The earliest possible year, though the note could also have been written in 1785. Lafayette's former aide Gouvion (XXIII, 160–1n) was in America on March 27 from 1777 through 1781 (XXXVI, 527) and again in 1783. The year 1782 is impossible, as Lafayette was not in Paris on that date: Idzerda, *Lafayette Papers*, V, 25, 116n; *Morris Papers*, VIII, 646n.

1. Witherspoon, president of the College of New Jersey, had been in London since the end of January. For more details of his commission to raise funds, see XLI, 270–1n.

2. Witherspoon's solicitations produced less than £6: Ruth L. Woodward and Wesley F. Craven, *Princetonians, 1784–1790: a Biographical Dictionary* (Princeton, 1991), p. xxvii. For an account of his trip see Varnum L. Collins, *President Witherspoon: a Biography* (2 vols., Princeton, 1925), II, 138–43. Joseph Reed, Witherspoon's co-commissioner, reported, in letters to JA in February and May, that the British public was little disposed toward reconciliation with Americans: *Adams Papers*, XVI, 49–51, 191–3.

to the Comte de Vergennes &c from the Minister of France and other Letters from Mr Marbois & Genl Washington. These Letters however I suppose are general and not relating to the Purpose abovementioned.[3] What I would particularly request of you is to give your Opinion candidly whether in Case of my going to Paris it would be at all proper to make Application to any Persons for the College either as to Subscriptions or Books or Apparatus. I will be governed in this Matter by your Opinion & Mr Jays and either not go to Paris at all or when there be entirely silent as to this Business and only gratify my Curiosity & pay my Compliments where they are due.

I retain a very grateful Sense of the Attention you paid to my Son while in Paris.[4]

I have the Honour to be Your Excellencys most obedt humble Servant   JNO WITHERSPOON

P.S. Please to direct for me to the Care of Mr Dennis Deberdt Mercht in London

His Excellency Benjamin Franklin Esqr

Notation: Witterspoon March 27 1784.—

From ———— Beaumont[5]   ALS: American Philosophical Society

Son Excéllance,   Ce Dimanche 28. Mars 1784./.

Jai L'honneur de vous prévenir qu'après avoir presenté le Sr. Schaffer à Monsieur le Marquis de La fayette, ce Seigneur la recû avéc Bonté; et lui a offert de le remener avéc lui en Amérique; cette circonstance est unique dans Son Espéce et trop intéréssante pour le Sr. Schaffer pour qu'il n'en profite avéc joie. J'ose me flatter que votre Excéllance ne dira rien au Marquis qui puisse diminuer Son Zêle dans Cette occurrence.

3. In a letter to Jay of May 7, Witherspoon implied that the letters to French officials, which were sealed, might indeed have mentioned his mission; see the annotation of Henry Hunter to BF, May 27, below.

4. John Witherspoon, Jr., had been taken prisoner in 1781 and BF helped secure his release; see, in particular, XXXV, 48, 169–70; XXXVI, 62, 67, 68.

5. The lawyer representing John Shaffer. For background on the hapless young American see the annotation of his April 8 letter, below.

Mr. le Mis. connoit parfaitement le Beau frere du Sr. Schaffer. Ils ont vecû ensemble en Virginie et sont amis.[6] Le Sr. Schaffer a eû L'honneur de Se trouver Sous les mêmes Drapeaux que Mr. le Mis. ils ont Souvent Mangé Ensemble chéz Son Excéllance Le Général Wasginston.

Je viens d'apprendre à L'instant que Mr. le Marquis doit Se rendre aujourdhuy chéz Votre Excéllance pour y diner probablement il S'agira dans la Conversation du Sr. Schaffer dans Ce Cas je vous Suplie d'en parler de manière à ce que Mr. De la fayette conserve Sa Bienveillance au Sr. Schaffer à qui il a fait tout L'acueil possible, et promis toute protection. Il est déja prevenû [de?] la Bonté que Votre Excéllance á eû de Laisser toucher les 60. dollars déposés au greffe.

Enfin Son Excéllance, Si vous ne dites rien de désavantageux au marquis Sur le Compte du Sr. Schaffer, j'aurai La Consolation d'avoir conduit toute cette affaire à Son terme le plus heureux. Je ne vous en aurai pas moins d'obligation que Si Lobjet M'etoit personel.

Je vous prie de croire au Respect avec lequel Je Suis de Votre Excèllance Le tres humble Et très obeissant Serviteur.[7]

avocat DE BEAUMONT

Notation: De Beaumont 28 Mars 1784.—

From Henry Laurens

LS: Library of Congress; copy: University of South Carolina Library

Dear Sir,   Bath, March 28. 1784

The 20th. Instant I had the honor of receiving your favor of the 12th. with Postscript of the 13th. by the hand of my Son, who will be the Bearer of this. I should have replied immediately, and

6. Shaffer's sister's brother-in-law, Brig. Gen. John Peter Gabriel Muhlenberg (XXXV, 12n), fought under Lafayette's command in Virginia and at Yorktown: XL, 620n; Paul A. W. Wallace, *The Muhlenbergs of Pennsylvania* (Philadelphia, 1950), p. 224.

7. Beaumont also wrote to WTF, asking him, too, to say nothing negative about Shaffer in front of Lafayette: Beaumont to WTF, March 28, 1784, APS.

at all hazards to my health have made a Journey to Whitehall, on the subject of Mr. Secretary Thomson's Letter, which considering Times & Tempers, I felt as demanding immediate Attention. But luckily for me, our friend Mr. Hartley was at Bath and just going to London. I requested him to propose to Lord Carmarthen, a convention for extending the stipulated Term, for exchanging the Ratifications of our Definitive Treaty of the 3d. September, and to say I would, without delay, repair to London for executing on our part if necessary—that if the Formality might be dispensed with, without prejudice to the contracting Parties, the assent of the Minister should be signified to me in writing. This morning brought me a Letter from Mr Hartley, a Copy of which will be inclosed.[8] I flatter myself, the Contents will afford the same satisfaction, to yourself and the other Gentlemen on your side the Channel, as I feel upon the occasion.

Mr. Carmichael's intelligence of new Draughts, "some advised of," is further alarming. Your answer is sage and good. I am weary of conjectures upon this Business. Is there a Worm at the Root of the hasty grown Gourd? I find however some consolation, in foreseeing that there must be a Stop to the Evil, and hoping the Day cannot be distant. That several of the States are to blame for deficiencies I have no doubt, but according to my Ideas, no Necessity could sanctify continued Draughts under a moral certainty of Dishonor. Abundantly more prudent would it have been, to submit to every Inconvenience at home. Creditors there would have worked out their own Salvation, and People's Eyes would have been opened. The Work must still be performed with accumulated Weight.

I have heard nothing since I left London the 16th. relative to the intended Regulations of Commerce with America, except the Extension of the Intercourse Bill,[9] and from Mr Bourdieu who writes in general terms.

8. Hartley to Laurens, March 26, containing the same information that Hartley had written to BF that same day. The letter is published in Wharton, *Diplomatic Correspondence*, VI, 789–90.

9. In the absence of an Anglo-American commercial treaty, Parliament passed a bill (which received the royal assent on March 24) to extend the king's authority over regulating trade with America to June 20: *Laurens*

"I could have wished to have carried him better accounts of the Conduct of Administration, touching the American Intercourse Bill, but there are strong remains of the old Leaven among us, and the same Disposition for monopolizing the Trade and Navigation of the World to ourselves."

But as this Gentleman intends to make you a Visit in a few days, You'll have an Opportunity of learning particulars from himself.[1]

I sent you some time ago a Pamphlet entitled Considerations &c.[2] The Author having entreated my Opinion, I have pointed out several parts which will probably be ill taken by our People. They may ask, is this the Work of a Friend? Harry will shew you my Remarks, such as they are. I was too sick to be minute and could only dictate in brief.

As for the Treasury Affair,[3] being well acquainted with their tricks and not ignorant of their present Necessities, I think nothing more about it, except that when I am able to walk up the Steps, I will once firmly request a categorical Answer, persuaded at the same time, that the Chance, even of recovering the authenticated Account lodged in their Office, is against me. This and much greater Losses in my Estate are to my feelings trifles, compared with the destruction of all my papers, a savage Work which my Attornies inform me was perpetrated by the British troops when they were in possession of South Carolina. The Papers had been lodged under the protection of an old Gentleman Seventy miles from the Sea.[4]

My late Journey to London in January was made in full de-

Papers, XVI, 422; Public Advertiser, March 24 and 25, 1784. For the original authorization of 1783 and a subsequent extension of it see XLI, 579n.

1. See Laurens to BF, March 29.

2. The pamphlet was [Richard Champion], Considerations on the Present Situation of Great Britain and the United States of North America . . . (London, 1784). On the half-title page, Laurens wrote that the text had been read to him while he was sick in bed, and that he had drawn X's in the margins where he intended to make comments "at the Author's reque[st]". (This annotated copy is at the Hist. Soc. of Pa.) For the origins of the pamphlet and Champion's visit with BF in 1783 see XL, 515n.

3. For Laurens' claim against the British Treasury see XLI, 532–3.

4. Laurens lost 21 boxes of his papers: Laurens Papers, XVI, 770.

termination to provide proper Embarkation hoping to have been this day on my Voyage, but sickness rendered me wholly incapable of taking the necessary Steps. At this moment I feel a double Regret from losing the advantage of a long continued Easterly Wind, and from feeling the same Wind piercing thro' all my joints. An Accident however has lately happened which would arrest my attempts for some days, even if I had strength enough to stir about. My Son's late journey to France was intended for conducting his widowed Aunt and his Sister to this Kingdom, but the former being very infirm was incapable of proceeding in the late severe Season. He is now going to make a second Attempt.[5] The concerns of two distressed Families render it necessary for me to wait the Event, hoping no Offence will be taken on the other side of the Water, when no Expence or Loss will be incurred by the delay.

Thus circumstanced I do not expect to begin my Voyage till the middle of May. When please God I arrive at the proper place, I shall pay full attention to the desires respecting yourself.

The good old Lady's sole claim to Infallibility conveys to the World in general a Satire, as severe as Sir Richard's Lampoon upon the Church established by Law, but I had something else in contemplation, when in the fullness of my heart, the intimation, which you have treated with so much pleasantry, gushed forth. I could honestly make an Explanation to a third Person, and to the satisfaction of every unprejudiced impartial Person. To such I appeal. An attempt here, I am sure would be disgusting.

I have desired my Son to present you with the latest News Papers and Pamphlets and not to forget the Letters of Marius.[6]

With repeated good wishes for your health and happiness, And with sincere Attachment I have the honor to be, Dear sir Your faithful & Obedt servant   HENRY LAURENS.

His Excellency Benjamin Franklin Esqr. Passy.

5. Henry Laurens, Jr., had left his aunt Mary and sister Mary Eleanor at Nîmes. He now was returning to escort them to England: *Laurens Papers*, XVI, 420n, 437–8, 445.

6. Thomas Day, *The Letters of Marius: or, Reflections upon the Peace, the East-India Bill, and the Present Crisis* (2nd ed., London, 1784). The copy that BF received from Laurens is at the Hist. Soc. of Pa.

From Graf von Brühl   ALS: American Philosophical Society

Sir   Dover St. March 29th. 1784.
I presume to trouble you with an Application for a Letter
of Recommendation in favour of Mr Biederman Dr of Law in
the University of Leipzig who in the Course of last year set
out for America in the Capacity of Agent & Manager of the
Concerns & Interest of many of our principal Manufacturers
& Merchants.[7] If you should be inclined to comply with my Request, I beg you will trust me with the Care of transmitting
your recommendatory Letter to that Gentleman. I need not
point out to you the advantages that will arise to both Countries
from the Countenance with which you will be pleased to honour Dr Biederman's Undertaking. It is with singular pleasure I
embrace this opportunity to assure you of the high Esteem &
great respect with which I have the honour to subscribe myself,
Sir Your most obedient & most humble Servant   CT DE BRÜHL

Notation: Cte. De Bruhl March 29. 1784—

From Antoine-Alexis-François Cadet de Vaux

AL: American Philosophical Society

Ce 29 Mars 1784
M. Cadet de Vaux présente l'assurance de Son très humble re-
spect à Monsieur franklin.
Sa commission pour la farine de Mays est faite, du moment ou
Elle Sera arrivée, il en Sera prevenu.[8]

7. Ehrenhold Friedrich Biedermann met with BF in March, 1783, having
been introduced by the Saxon minister, Schönfeld: XXXIX, 311–12. On
March 22, 1783, BF wrote recommendations for him to Jonathan Williams,
Sr., and RB. (These letters were located only recently; copies are in the
Goethe- und Schiller-Archiv and reproduced in the work cited below.) Biedermann traveled to America in June, 1783: Christian Deuling, "Friedrich
Justin Bertuch und der Handel mit Nordamerika," in *Friedrich Justin Bertuch (1747–1822): Verleger, Schriftsteller und Unternehmer im klassischen
Weimar,* ed. Gerhard R. Kaiser and Siegfried Seifert (Tübingen, 2000),
pp. 199–200, 221, 225.
8. For a previous shipment of corn flour that Cadet had arranged, and
the bread that BF made from it, see XLI, 457, 535–7.

La cheminée poele réussit à merveille. M.M. le grand et molinos auront l'honneur d'aller en rendre compte à Monsieur franklin, un jour avec moi.[9]

M. Cadet prie Monsieur franklin d'accepter un Exemplaire des deux mèmoires cy joints[1] et d'en faire passer un a m. l'abbe de la Roche et a M. le Veillard.

Notation: Cadet de Vaux 29 Mars 1784—

From Henry Laurens

ALS: Library of Congress; copy: University of South Carolina Library

Sir.   Bath 29th. March 1784.

Mr. Bourdieu of London intending shortly a visit to France is desirous of paying his Respects at Passy. Permit me Sir, the liberty of introducing him in person to your acquaintance. To say Mr. Bourdieu merits the regard & acknowledgements of the Citizens of our United States would be only repeating what I have heretofore signified in private conversation, but over & above such considerations I feel a satisfaction in foreseeing that while I gratify the request of one friend the other will be no loser by devoting an hour to a Gentleman of eminent character in the commercial World & of much intelligence in Political affairs.[2]

9. The stove, based on a design proposed by BF, was fabricated in February. Cadet had hoped, in vain, that BF would be able to get to Paris to inspect it. Legrand and Molinos were prominent architects whom Cadet had introduced to BF the previous October: XLI, 120, 534–5.

1. Cadet may have enclosed his two recent pamphlets, *Mémoire historique et physique sur le cimetière des innocents* . . . [Paris, 1783], and *Mémoire sur le méphistisme des puits* . . . [Paris, 1783]. BF's copies are at the APS.

2. The merchant James Bourdieu was a business associate and friend of Laurens' who had sympathized with the American cause. He had aided Laurens when the latter was confined in the Tower of London: XXXVII, 710; XLI, 590n; *Laurens Papers*, XV, 390, 406–35. His purpose in going to France was to negotiate an agreement between the East India Company and the newly constituted French East India Company, for which his firm, Bourdieu, Chollet & Bourdieu, hoped to secure the London agency. It also sought to become the London purchasing agent of the farmers general for American tobacco: Lüthy, *Banque protestante*, II, 382–3, 415–17, 674–82; Price, *France and the Chesapeake*, II, 687–90, 739–41.

I have the honor to be With the highest Esteem & Respect Sir Your obedient & most humble servant   HENRY LAURENS

His Excellency Benjamin Franklin Esquire Passy.

Endorsed: Mr Laurens to BF. Feby. March, April & May 1784—

To John Jay   ALS: Columbia University Library

Dear Sir,   Passy, March 30. 1784
    Yesterday late in the Evening arrived here an Express from Congress with the Definitive Treaty ratified, which I enclose with the Resolutions, Proclamation, and the President's Letter.[3] The Congress anxious that the Ratification should arrive within the Term stipulated, dispatch'd it seems three Expresses, by different Vessels, with authenticated Copies. This came by the French Pacquet Boat; Major Franks sail'd before, with another, in a Ship for London.[4] As the Term is long since expired, and I have already sent to Mr Hartley the Excuse for the Delay;[5] and as Majr Franks may probably be arrived in London, and have delivered his Copy to Mr Laurence;[6] and the Post going on Thursday; I hardly think it necessary to send an Express on the Occasion to London; but shall be glad of your Advice, and to consult with you on the Steps to be taken for the Exchange, in Case Mr Laurens has not already made it, which I wish he may, as it will save Trouble.

    3. Of Jan. 14 (XLI, 456–7), informing BF that the courier would be Josiah Harmar. Harmar's departure on the French packet was delayed until mid-February (XLI, 465n); he arrived in Lorient on March 25. According to his diary, he delivered his dispatches to BF on Monday, March 29, at five o'clock in the afternoon, and retired that evening to a hotel in Paris. He was invited back to dine with BF on Wednesday, March 31: Josiah Harmar's diary, Clements Library, entries of March 25–31, 1784.
    4. In addition to the copies carried by Harmar and David Salisbury Franks, a third was sent to Robert Morris to be forwarded (XLI, 465).
    5. Above, March 11.
    6. Franks arrived in London on April 7 and left for Paris the following day: *Public Advertiser*, April 9, 1784.

All the News I learnt from Col. Harmar who brought the Dispatch, is, that the Winter has been uncommonly severe in America; that the Pacquet Boat was long detain'd in New-York by the Ice; and that one which sail'd from hence in October, was lost on Long Island going in,[7] some of the People and Passengers saved tho' much frozen, others froze to death. With great Esteem, I am, Your most obedient humble Servant

B FRANKLIN

The Post has the Mail with all the common Letters and the Dispatches for the Court. Our Express is a Day before him.— I have receiv'd no private Letters from any of my Friends.

His Excelly. John Jay Esqr

Endorsed: Doctr Franklin 30 march 1784

Certification for Jacques Le Maire de Gimel[8]

ADS: University of Pennsylvania Library

Passy, March 30. 1784—

I do hereby certify whom it may concern, that Col. Lemaire came from Virginia to France in the Year 1778, with Letters of Recommendation to me from Patrick Henry Esquire then

7. The *Courier du Port Louis* was shipwrecked on Jan. 19: *Pa. Gaz.,* Feb. 4, 1784.

8. A French military man whom BF had evidently recommended to GW at the beginning of the war and assisted when Le Maire came back to France on a mission for the state of Virginia: XXVI, 34–6; XXVIII, 611–12. Le Maire sailed to America again in early 1779 and stayed until 1782. On his attempted return to France, he was captured at sea and lost all his property. It is not known when he finally reached Paris. On March 30, 1784, he wrote a three-page petition to the French government recounting his military service and his captures, and asking for a post in St.-Domingue. He then asked BF to append a note of verification. BF's note, published here, was written on the final page of Le Maire's petition. This petition, however, was not submitted. Three months later, Le Maire asked BF to copy his certification onto a revised petition: Le Maire to BF, [June 28], below.

Governor of that State, by whom he was employed to procure Arms and military Stores here for the Use of their Army; which Commission, as far as I have ever heard, he executed with Fidelity & Ability, to the Satisfaction of the Government there.

B FRANKLIN

From Leveux

ALS: American Philosophical Society

Monsieur   Calais le 30 Mars 1784.
J'ay reçu la Lettre que vous m'avez fait l'honneur de m'ecrire le 8 de ce mois. En consequence de vos ordres Je Joins a la presente le compte de mes Debours pour les prisonniers americains échapés d'angleterre depuis 1779 Jusqu'a ce Jour.[9]

Il Se monte a	1712.10. *l.t.*
mes Debours pour les Effets de Mr Jay	9.15.
	1722. 5

J'attendray vos ordres pour le remboursement de cette Somme. Quand le Congrès accordera des Commissions de Consul des Etats unis de l'amerique dans quelque port de france, Je vous Suplie, Monsieur, de faire en Sorte que Je ne Sois pas oublié.
Je Suis avec respect Monsieur Votre tres humble & tres obeissant Serviteur   JES. LEVEUX

Monsieur le Docteur francklin

Notation: Le Veux, Calais le 30 Mars 1784.—

---

9. The bill, signed and dated March 30, 1784, listed disbursements made to 23 escaped American prisoners between March 26, 1779 and July 11, 1783. The men received between 24 and 96 *l.t.* apiece, for a total of 1,704 *l.t.* To this was added a ½ percent banker's commission of 8 *l.t.* 10 *s.*

Aux Auteurs du *Journal de Paris*

(I) French translation: press copy of D:[1] American Philosophical Society; printed in *Journal de Paris*, April 26, 1784;[2] (II) Reprinted from *The Repository*, I (1788), 5–10; partial copy: Historical Society of Pennsylvania; fragment: American Philosophical Society[3]

In February, 1784, a Parisian apothecary named Quinquet and his friend Lange, a distiller, began to demonstrate in Paris a new kind of oil lamp that they claimed to have invented. That claim was exaggerated. What they had done was to reproduce the closely guarded design of their friend Ami Argand, who had taken them into his confidence the previous September.[4] Argand was no longer in Paris; he

1. In the hand of BFB. The translator is not known.
2. The *Journal* deleted three passages, noted below. In September, 1795, the full French text appeared in *La Décade philosophique* under the title "Lettre de Franklin aux auteurs d'un journal." Stating that the piece had never before been published, the editors claimed to have received one of BF's own MSS from a friend of his: *La Décade philosophique*, VI (An III), 549–55. The Republican editors of the *Jour. de Paris* in 1795 did not recognize the essay either. Citing *La Décade* as their source, they published on Nov. 30, 1795, a condensed version—abridged this time out of space considerations—and erroneously stated that it had been written at Passy in 1786. That text is reprinted in A. M. Roederer, ed., *Œuvres du comte P. L. Roederer* . . . (8 vols., Paris, 1853–59), V, 183–4.
3. No complete MS of BF's English text has been located, but parts of what may be a single copy, made by BFB, do survive. The fragment at the APS is a half page of text from near the end of the essay; on its verso, BF wrote "Lamps" and "Economy". The portion at the Hist. Soc. of Pa. consists of four complete, continuous pages and four half-pages. (In all cases, it is the bottom half of the sheets that survive.) These contain a small number of edits and interlineations made by BF at an unknown time; they do not appear in the text published by Benjamin Vaughan in the inaugural issue of his journal, *The Repository*. Vaughan wrote that his version was "the original piece, with some additions and corrections made in it by the author." We reproduce that version here, believing it to be the closest to what BF originally intended for publication. A slightly variant text (which also does not incorporate the edits made by BF to the now-mutilated copy in BFB's hand) is in WTF, *Memoirs*, III, 350–4, under the title "An Economical Project."
4. Argand had recruited Quinquet (whom he had known for many years) and Lange to help construct a replacement balloon, on very short notice, for Montgolfier to demonstrate at Versailles on Sept. 19. During the bustle of sewing and piecing the balloon, Quinquet and Lange overheard Argand discussing his lamp with the physicist Meusnier, and persuaded him to explain it to them as well: XL, 609–10; XLI, 81, 563n; John J. Wolfe,

had left for London in November, 1783,[5] to obtain a British patent and recruit English workmen to manufacture the metal bases and flint-glass chimneys.

Cadet de Vaux, editor of the *Journal de Paris*, was an early champion of Quinquet and Lange. After having told Franklin about their lamp, on February 13 he sent word that Quinquet and Lange wished to demonstrate their "discovery" in hopes of obtaining the doctor's endorsement.[6] There is no evidence that Franklin saw the lamp before Cadet published his article about it five days later. By the time he wrote the satire published below, however, he had examined it carefully.

The February 18 article in the *Journal de Paris* appeared under the heading "Economie." It informed readers about a newly invented lamp that emitted a brilliant light, did not produce smoke, and consumed very little oil. A foreign scientist, "Monsieur A.," had conceived the design but had refused to divulge its mechanism. Quinquet and Lange, recognizing its "avantages économiques," had penetrated the mystery. They not only replicated the lamp but even improved it by adding a glass chimney. The same quantity of oil and cotton that in ordinary lamps emitted a dull, weak light would produce, in this one, a light that shone as brightly as ten candles and was infinitely more beautiful. All classes of citizens would soon be adopting this economical invention. Quinquet and Lange had no interest in keeping the mechanism secret; on the contrary, they had explained it to scientists (unnamed) and "MM. Montgolfier, Faujas de St. Fond, &c." The Lieutenant General of Police was interested in using the technology to light the streets of Paris, and Quinquet and Lange, along with the official in charge of street lamps, were planning a trial. The pair deserved even more honor than would ordinarily be

---

Brandy, Balloons, & Lamps: Ami Argand, 1750–1803 (Carbondale and Edwardsville, Ill., 1999), pp. 2–5; Argand [and Abeille], *Découverte des lampes a courant d'air et a cylindre* (Geneva [Paris], 1785), p. 12, reprinted in Michael Schrøder, *The Argand Burner, its Origin and Development in France and England 1780–1800* (Copenhagen, 1969), p. 205.

5. When trying to date the letter from Le Roy published in XLI, 143–4, we deduced that Argand had to have left Paris on either Oct. 27 or Nov. 3. Having now located Argand's own account of his discovery, we can eliminate the first of those dates. Argand wrote that he left Paris in early November. That would place his departure on Nov. 3, and date Le Roy's letter as Sunday, Nov. 2: Argand [and Abeille], *Découverte des lampes a courant d'air et a cylindre*, p. 18.

6. XLI, 563–4.

due to a discovery because the lamp was of a "utilité generale." In a final flourish of hyperbole, the article concluded that the lamp was the "perfection de la combustion des huiles." Interested parties could see a prototype in the shop of M. Daguerre, who would manufacture them in whatever size was required.

Three days later, on February 21, Quinquet and Lange presented their lamp to the Académie des sciences, representing it as their own invention. (They may not have known that Argand had already demonstrated his lamp to several members of the academy, as well as many government officials.) If Cadet had believed them to be offering their innovation to the public without regard for personal gain, he was mistaken: seeking an *approbation* from the academy was the first step toward their ultimate goal of obtaining a royal *privilège*. It was also the opening volley in what would become a prolonged fight over rights to what became known in France as a *quinquet* and what in the English-speaking world is still known as an Argand lamp.[7]

While the self-styled inventors were chasing official recognition, the new lamp was transforming the nightlife of Paris. With its brilliant, smokeless light, and its promise of fuel economy, it was universally acclaimed and was soon illuminating homes and public spaces.[8] Yet Franklin, who had himself invented a circular wick oil lamp in London, and who continued to improve it (showing his new design to Sebastian Clais, a visiting engineer, in 1781),[9] was more

7. Quinquet and Lange parted company later in 1784 and began publically fighting with one another, as well as with Argand, in the pages of the *Jour. de Paris* and elsewhere. Argand was slow to respond to their betrayal, being preoccupied with obtaining and then defending his patent against such relentless challenges that it was eventually nullified. The complicated story is told in the several works cited above, although each version differs. As for the academy, the committee appointed to evaluate the lamp did not deliver its report until September, 1785; by that time they concerned themselves only with Lange, and restricted their *approbation* to the redesigned chimney that Lange submitted in December, 1784. They declared that the basic wick mechanism had been known for a long time, and the first person to adapt it to a lamp had been Ami Argand: *Procès-verbaux*, CIII (1784), 37; CIV (1785), 203.

8. See, for example, the description of how the installation of 40 *quinquets* solved the lighting problem of the Comédie Française in April: Bachaumont, *Mémoires secrets*, XXV, 260–1. See also Wolfe, *Brandy, Balloons, & Lamps*, p. 49.

9. BF had given Clais a prototype in 1772, which Clais showed to Argand in 1782; see XLI, 144n. It is not known whether Argand showed his closely guarded design to BF. When he arrived in London, however, his associates

aware than most of his contemporaries of the caveats that would apply to such a device. Did the lamp really consume very little oil?

Franklin probably drafted his letter to the *Journal de Paris* in mid-March. An internal clue—the author's observation that for three days in a row the sun rose at approximately six o'clock in the morning—places the conceit around March 18–20. (According to the meteorological data published at the top of the front page of the *Journal,* the sun rose at precisely six o'clock on March 18.) A French translation was ready by March 31, when Franklin sent a copy to Mme Brillon.

"Aux Auteurs du *Journal de Paris*" lampooned human nature in general, as well as specific aspects of the society from which Franklin was preparing to take his leave: charlatans and amateurs who advertised fantastic claims; credulous audiences who flocked to demonstrations; aristocrats who advocated conserving resources while profligately wasting them; a court that justified its imposition of onerous regulations by claiming to be concerned for the welfare of its citizens. When Cadet de Vaux sent the author a set of typeset pages on April 23, three of the sharpest barbs had been excised. Otherwise, the text was unchanged. (The three censored sections are noted, below.) Cadet ran the article on the front page of the April 26 issue. As with the February 18 article about the lamp of Quinquet and Lange, this letter to the editor was published under the heading "Economie."

The English text of Franklin's anonymous letter was first published in January, 1788, by Benjamin Vaughan, and has been a favorite among editors and anthologizers of Franklin's writings ever since. Though written for a Parisian audience, the author considered the practical implications of his "discovery"—the sun gives light as soon as it rises—as equally relevant to the capital of Britain. He would address it in the third part of his autobiography, written in August, 1788: "The Inhabitants of London chusing voluntarily to live much by Candle Light, and sleep by Sunshine; and yet often complain a little absurdly, of the Duty on Candles and the high Price of Tallow."[1]

---

recognized the similarity between the lamp he showed them and the prototypes they remembered Matthew Boulton having made for BF in the early 1770s. They immediately sent to Boulton for an example and found the two lamps essentially identical. Argand was advised to travel to Birmingham and talk to Boulton before pursuing a patent. That meeting resulted in Boulton joining Argand and Parker in a partnership; Argand's patent was granted on March 15, 1784: Wolfe, *Brandy, Balloons, & Lamps,* pp. 12–25.

1. *Autobiog.,* pp. 25, 207.

Franklin's letter is best known for its satire and the suggestion of rising with the sun, which in our time has led readers to conclude, falsely, that he invented Daylight Saving Time. Focusing only on the humor, however, misses the important scientific question that Franklin poses at the outset. He writes of having attended a gathering at which the lamp of Quinquet and Lange was examined. It produced a brighter light than ordinary lamps, but was not the amount of oil it consumed in proportion to the light it afforded, in which case it represented no savings at all? Though no one present could answer that question, Franklin wrote, everyone agreed on its importance.[2]

The question of the lamp's economy was as yet unanswerable. Three years after Franklin's death, Count Rumford invented a shadow photometer capable of measuring the relative luminosities of various light sources. One of his first experiments set out to answer the question that Franklin and others had posed. According to his data, the Argand lamp consumed more than one and a half times as much oil, but considering the amount of light it gave, it represented a saving of approximately 13 percent. Whether that savings was offset by the costs of manufacture, Rumford could not say.[3]

[before March 31, 1784]

I.

Aux Auteurs du Journal de Paris.

Messieurs,

Vous nous faites souvent part de Découvertes nouvelles;[4] permettez moi de vous en communiquer une, dont Je suis moimême l'Auteur, et que je crois pouvoir être d'une grande Utilité.

2. The chemist Macquer, a member of the Académie des sciences who was asked by the ministry to examine Argand's lamp in August, 1783, had concluded that it did consume more oil than ordinary lamps, but produced light in proportion to the amount of oil burned. This was not necessarily a disadvantage, as the intensity of light could be adjusted up or down: Schrøder, *The Argand Burner*, pp. 62–3, 161.

3. Benjamin Thompson, Count Rumford, "An Account of a Method of measuring the comparative Intensities of the Light emitted by luminous Bodies," *Phil. Trans.*, LXXXIV (1794), 98–9. Rumford made a miscalculation that we have here corrected; he figured the saving at somewhat more than 15 percent.

4. The *Journal* was indeed a source of astonishing information, and did little to distinguish between discoveries made by rigorous scientists and those promoted by amateurs or even tricksters. A dowser from the countryside demonstrated his ability to find water while blindfolded; he had

Je passois il y a quelques Jours la Soireé en grande Compagnie, dans une Maison ou l'on essayoit les Nouvelles Lampes de Mrs Quinquet et Lange; on y admiroit la Vivacité de la Lumiere qu'elles repandent, mais on s'occupoit beaucoup de savoir si elles ne consumoient pas encore plus dHuile que les Lampes communes, en proportion de l'Eclat de leur Lumiere: au quel cas on craignoit qu'il n'y eut aucune *épargne* a s'en servir. Personne de la Compagnie ne fut en état de nous tranquilliser sur ce point, qui, paroissoit a tout le monde très important a éclarcir, pour diminuer, disoit'on, s'il étoit possible, les Frais des Lumieres dans les Appartements, dans un tems où tous les autres Articles de la Depense des Maisons augmentent si considerablement tous les Jours.

Je remarquai avec beaucoup de Satisfaction ce goût général pour l'Economie; car j'aime infiniment l'Economie. Je rentrai chéz moi, et me couchai vers les trois heures après minuit, l'Esprit plein du Sujet qu'on avoit traité. Vers les Six heures du Matin Je fus réveillé par un bruit audessus de ma tête, et Je fus fort étonné de voir ma Chambre très éclairée. Encore moitié endormie, J'imaginai d'abord qu'on y avoit allumé une douzaine de Lampes de M Quinquet: Mais, en me frottant les yeux, Je reconnus distinctement que la Lumiere entroit par mes Fenêtres. Je me levai pour savoir dou elle venoit; et Je vis que le Soleil s'élevoit a ce moment même des Bords de l'Horison, d'où il versoit abondament ses Rayons dans ma Chambre, mon Domestique ayant oublié de fermer mes Volets. Je regardai mes Montres, qui

---

been brought to Paris by a respected physician. (See La Condamine to BF, April 12, below.) A chess-playing automaton toured Europe, winning many of its games: XL, 80. A watchmaker announced the invention of shoes that enabled him to walk on water; among his many subscribers were Lafayette, Castries, and Bariatinskii: *Jour. de Paris*, Dec. 8, 15, 18, 26, 1783, and see Robert Darnton, *Mesmerism and the End of the Enlightenment in France* (Cambridge, Mass., 1968), pp. 23–4. Montgolfier's balloons rose into the sky, levitated by a secret gas. (It turned out to be heated air.) Various fantastic mechanical flying machines were announced that, in the end, never left the ground; see, *e.g.*, XXXVII, 246–7n. Perhaps the most astonishing and controversial discovery, which occupied many columns of print over many months, was Mesmer's method of manipulating an undetectable fluid to cure disease. BF would soon delve deeply into this problem as a member of a commission investigating animal magnetism.

son fort bonnes, et Je vis qu'il n'étoit que six heures; mais trouvant extraordinaire que le Soleil fut levé de si bon matin, J'allai consulter lAlmanach, ou l'heure du Lever du Soleil étoit en effet fixeé à six heures precises pour ce jour là. Je poussai un peu plus loin ma recherche, et Je lus que cet Astre continueroit de se Lever tous les Jours plus matin jusqu'a la fin du Mois de Juin, mais qu'en aucun tems de lAnneé il ne retardoit son lever jusqu'a huit Heures. Vous avez, surement, Messieurs, beaucoup de Lectures des deux Sexes, qui, comme moi, n'ont Jamais vus le Soleil avant onze Heures ou midi, et qui lisent bien rarement la partie astronomique du Calendrier de la Cour, Je ne doute pas que ces Personnes ne soyent aussi étonnées d'entendre dire que le Soleil se leve de si bonne heure, que je l'ai été moi-même de le voir. Elles ne le seront pas moins de m'entendre assurer qu'il donne sa Lumiere au même Moment ou il se leve; mais J'ai la preuve de ce fait. Il ne m'est pas possible d'en douter. Je suis témoin oculaire de ce que j'avance; et en répétant l'Observation les trois Jours suivans, J'ai obtenu Constamment le même Resultat. Je dois cependant vous dire que lors que J'ai fait part de ma Decouverte dans la Société, J'ai bien démêlé, dans la Contenance et l'air de beaucoup de Personnes un peu d'Incredulité, quoi qu'elles aïent eu assès de Politesse pour ne pas me le témoigner en termes exprès.[5] J'ai trouvé aussi sur mon chemin un Philosophe, qui m'a assuré que j'étois dans l'Erreur sur l'Article de ma Relation, ou Je disais que la Lumiere ENTROIT dans ma Chambre; que je concluois malàpropos ce pretendu fait de ce que mes Volets étoient demeurés ouverts; et que cet Evénement accidentel n'avoit pas servi a INTRODUIRE la lumiere, mais seulement à faire SORTIR l'Obscurité; Distinction qu'il appuyoit de plusieurs Arguments [ingénier?] en m'expliquant comment J'avais pu me laisser trompe par l'Apparence. J'avoue qu'il m'embarassa, mais sans me convaincre; et mes Observations postérieur, dont J'ai fait mention c'y dessus, m'ont Confirmé dans ma premiere Opinion.

Quoiqu'il en soit, cet Evénement m'a suggéré plusieurs Reflections sérieuses, et que Je crois importantes. J'ai considéré que sans lAccident qui m'a éveillé ce Jour la [*illegible*] matin, j'aurais dormi environ six heures de plus, pendant les quelles

---

5. The remainder of this paragraph did not appear in the *Jour. de Paris.*

le Soleil donnoit sa Lumiere; et par consequent J'aurois vécu six heures de plus a la Lueur des bougies. Cette derniere maniere de s'éclairer etant beaucoup plus Couteuse que la premiere, mon Gout pour l'Economie m'a conduit a me servir du peu d'Arithmetique que Je saïs, pour faire quelques Calculs sur cette Matiere; et Je vous les envoye, Messieurs, en vous faisant observer, que la grand mérite d'une Invention est son Utilité; et qu'une Decouverte dont on ne peut faire aucun Usage, n'est bonne a rien.

Je prens pour Base de mon Calcul la Supposition qu'il y a 100 mille familles à Paris qui Consomment chacune, pendant la Durée de la Nuit, et les unes dans les autres, une Demie Livre de Bougie ou de Chandelle par heure. Je crois cette Estimation modéré, car quoique quelques unes consomment moins, il y en a un grand nombre qui consomment beaucoup davantage. Maintenant Je compte environ sept Heures par Jour pendant les quelles nous sommes encore couchés, le Soleil etant sur l'Horison; Car il se leve pendant six Mois entre six et huit heures avant midi, et nous nous éclairons environ sept Heures dans les Vingt quatre, avec des Bougies et des Chandelles. Ces deux faits me fournissent les Calculs suivans.

Les Six Mois du 20 Mars au 20 Septembre me donnent 183 Nuits. Je multiplie ce nombre par sept, pour avoir le nombre des Heures pendant lesquél nous brulons de la Bougie ou de la Chandelle, et J'ai 1281. Ce nombre multiplié par 100 Mille, qui est celui des Familles, donne 128,100,000. heures de Consommation. A Supposer, comme je l'ai dit, une demi Livre de Bougie ou de Chandelle consommée par chaque heure dans chaque Famille, on aura 64,050,000 Livre pesant de Cire ou de Suif, consommées à Paris; et si l'on estime la Cire et le Suif, l'un dans l'autre, au prix moyen de 30 Sols la Livre, on aura une Dépense annuelle de 96,075,000 livres Tournois, en Cire et Suif: Somme enorme! Que la seule Vi[lle] de Paris épargneroit en se servant, pendant les six mois d'été seulement, de la Lumiere du Soleil, au lieu de celle des Chandelles et des Bougies: Et voila, Messieurs, la Decouverte que J'annonce, et la Reforme que Je propose.

Je sais qu'on me dira que l'Attachement aux anciennes Habitudes est un Obstacle invincible a ce qu'on adopte mon Plan; qu'il sera plus que difficile de déterminer beaucoup de Gens a se lever avant 11 heures ou midi; et que par consequant ma Découverte restera parfaitement inutile. Mais Je répondrai, qu'il ne faut desesperer de rien. Je crois que toutes les Personnes raisonables, qui auront lu cette Lettre, et qui par son moyen auront appris qu'il fait jour aussitôt que le Soleil se leve, se determineront a se lever avec lui; et quant aux autres, pour les faire entrer dans la même route, Je propose au Gouvernement de faires les Reglemens suivans.

1° Mettre une Taxe d'un Louis sur chaque fenêtre qui aura des Volets empechant la Lumiere d'entrer dans les Appartements aussitot que le Soleil est sur lHorison.

2° Etablir pour la Consommation de la Cire et de la Chandelle dans Paris, la même Salutaire lois de Police qu'on a faite pour diminuer la Consommation du Bois pendant lHiver que vient de finir;[6] placer des Gardes a toutes les Boutiques des Ciriers et des Chandeliers, et ne pas permettre a chaque Famille d'user plus dune livre de Chandelle par Semaine.

3° Placer des Gardes qui arrêteront tous les Carosses dans les Rues après la Nuit ferme é, excepté ceux des Médecines, des Chirugiens et des Sages femmes.[7]

4° Faire Sonner toutes les Cloches des Eglises au Lever du Soleil; et si cela n'est pas suffisant, faire tirer un coup de Canon dans chaque Rue pour ouvrir les yeux des Paresseus sur leur veritable Interet.

Toute la Difficulté sera dans les deux ou trois premiers Jours, apres lesquels le nouveau Genre de Vie sera tout aussi naturel et tout aussi commode que l'irrégularité dans laquelle nous vivons; car; il n'y a que le premier pas qui coute. Forcez un Homme de se lever a quatre heures du Matin, il est plus que probable qu'il se Couchera très volontiers a huit heures du Soir; et qu'après

---

6. In February, 1784, when snow and ice impeded the delivery of firewood into Paris, municipal authorities imposed a strict rationing system to ensure that bakeries had sufficient fuel, an established practice in times of scarcity: *Ordonnance de police, concernant la distribution des bois à brûler aux boulangers & au public. Du 7 Février 1784* ([Paris], 1784); Steven L. Kaplan, *The Bakers of Paris and the Bread Question, 1770–1775* (Durham, N.C., and London, 1996), p. 76.

7. This third proposed regulation was not included in the *Jour. de Paris*.

avoir dormi huit heures, il se levera sans peine a quatre Heures le landemain matin.

LEpargne de cette Somme de 96,075,000. livres Tournois qui se depensent en Bougies et Chandelles n'est pas le seul Avantage de mon Economique Projet. Vous pouvez remarquer que mon Calcul n'embrasse qu'une moitié de l'Anneé, et que par les memes raisons on peut épargner beaucoup, même dans les Six mois de lHiver, quoique les jours soient plus courts. J'ajoute que l'immense quantité de Cire et des Suif qui restera apres la Suppression de la Consommation de l'Eté, rendra la Cire et le suif à méllieur marché l'Hiver suivant, et pour l'avenir, tant que la Reforme que je propose se soutiendra.

Quoique ma Découverte puisse procurer de si grands Avantages, je ne demande, pour lavoir communiqueé au public avec tant de Franchise, ni Place, ni Pension, ni Privilege exclusif, ni aucun autre genre de Recompense. Je ne veux que l'honneur qui doit m'en revenir si l'on me rend Justice. Je prévois bien que quelques Esprit étroit et Jaloux me le disputeront; qu'ils diront que les Anciens ont eu cette Ideé avant moi; et peut être trouveront-ils quelques Passages dans de vieux livres pour appuyer leur Prétention. Je ne leur nierai point que les Anciens ont connu en effet les Heures du lever du Soleil; peut être ont-ils eu comme nous des Almanachs ou ces heures etoient marquées; mais il ne s'ensuit pas de là qu'il aient sû ce que je pretens avoir enseigné le premier, qu'il nous éclaire aussitôt qu'il se leve. C'est là ce que je revendique comme ma Decouverte. En tous Cas si les Anciens ont connu cette Verité, elle a été bien oubliée depuis et pendant longtems, car elle est certainement ignorée des modernes, ou au moins des Habitants de Paris; ce que Je prouve par un Argument bien simple. On sait que les Parisiens sont un Peuple aussi éclairé, aussi judicieux, aussi Sage qu'il en existe dans le Monde: Tous, ainsi que moi, ont un grand Goût pour lEconomie, et font proffession de cette Vertu; tous ont de très bonnes Raisons de l'aimer,[8] chargé comme ils le sont des impots très pesants qu'exigent les Besoins de lEtat. Or, cela posé, je dis, qu'il est impossible qu'un Peuple Sage, dans de semblables Circonstances, eut fait si longtems usage de

8. The rest of the sentence was omitted in the *Jour. de Paris.*

la Lumiere fuligineuse, malsaine, et dispendieuse, de la Bougie et de la Chandelle, s'il eut connu, comme je viens de l'apprendre et de l'Enseigner, qu'on pouvoit s'éclairer pour rien, de la belle et pure Lumière du Soleil.

Jai l'honneur d'être &a. UN ABONNÉ.

II.
To the AUTHORS of the JOURNAL.

MESSIEURS,

YOU often entertain us with accounts of new discoveries. Permit me to communicate to the public through your paper, one that has been lately made by myself, and which I conceive may be of great utility.

I was the other evening in a grand company, where the new lamp of Messrs. Quinquet and Lange was introduced, and much admired for its splendor; but a general enquiry was made, whether the oil it consumed was not in proportion to the light it afforded, in which case there would be no saving in the use of it. No one present could satisfy us in this point, which all agreed ought to be known, it being a very desireable thing to lessen, if possible, the expence of lighting our apartments, when every other article of family expence was so much augmented.

I was much pleased to see this general concern for œconomy; for I love œconomy exceedingly.

I went home, and to bed, three or four hours after midnight, with my head full of the subject. An accidental sudden noise waked me about six in the morning, when I was surprized to find my room filled with light; and I imagined at first that a number of those lamps had been brought into it; but rubbing my eyes I perceived the light came in at the windows. I got up and looked out to see what might be the occasion of it, when I saw the sun just rising above the horizon, from whence he poured his rays plentifully into my chamber, my domestic having negligently omitted the preceding night to close the shutters.

I looked at my watch, which goes very well, and found that it was but six o'clock; and still thinking it something extraordinary that the sun should rise so early, I looked into the almanack, where I found it to be the hour given for his rising on that day. I looked forward too, and found he was to rise still earlier every day till towards the end of June; and that at no time in the year he retarded his rising so long as till eight o'clock. Your readers, who with me have never seen any signs of sun-shine before noon, and seldom regard the astronomical part of the almanack, will be as much astonished as I was, when they hear of his rising so early; and especially when I assure them *that he gives light as soon as he rises*; I am convinced of this. I am certain of my fact. One cannot be more certain of any fact. I saw it with my own eyes. And having repeated this observation the three following mornings, I found always precisely the same result.

Yet so it happens, that when I speak of this discovery to others, I can easily perceive by their countenances, though they forbear expressing it in words, that they do not quite believe me. One indeed, who is a learned natural philosopher, has assured me that I must certainly be mistaken as to the circumstance of the light *coming* into my room; for it being well known, as he says, that there could be no light *abroad* at that hour, it follows that none could enter from *without*; and that of consequence my windows being accidentally left open, instead of *letting in the light*, had only served *to let out the darkness*; and he used many ingenious arguments to shew me how I might by that means have been deceived. I own that he puzzled me a little, but he did not satisfy me; and the subsequent observations I made, as above-mentioned, confirmed me in my first opinion.

This event has given rise in my mind to several serious and important reflections. I considered that if I had not been awakened so early that morning, I should have slept six hours longer by the light of the sun, and in exchange have lived six hours the following night by candle light; and the latter being a much more expensive light than the former, my love of œconomy induced me to muster up what little arithmetic I was master of, and to make some calculations, which I shall give you, after observing that utility is, in my opinion, the test of value in matters of invention, and that a discovery which can be applied to no use, or is not good for something, is good for nothing.

I took for the basis of my calculation the supposition that there are 100,000 families in Paris, and that these families consume in the night half a pound of bougies, or candles, per hour. I think this a moderate allowance, taking one family with another; for though I believe some consume less, I know that many consume a great deal more. Then estimating seven hours per day, as the medium quantity between the time of the sun's rising and ours, he rising during the six following months from six to eight hours before noon; and there being seven hours of course per night in which we burn candles, the account will stand thus:

In the six months between the 20th of March and the 20th of September, there are

Nights,	183
Hours of each night in which we burn candles,	7
Multiplication gives us for the total number of hours,	1,281
These 1281 hours, multiplied by 100,000, the number of families, give	128,100,000
One hundred twenty-eight millions and one hundred thousand hours, spent at Paris by candle-light, which at half a pound of wax and tallow per hour, gives the weight of	64,050,000
Sixty-four millions and fifty thousand of pounds, which, estimating the whole at the medium price of thirty sols the pound, makes the sum of ninety-six millions and seventy-five thousand livres tournois,	96,075,000

An immense sum! that the city of Paris might save every year, only by the œconomy of using sun-shine instead of candles.

If it should be said that people are apt to be obstinately attached to old customs, and that it will be difficult to induce them to rise before noon, consequently my discovery can be of but little use; I answer, *nil desperandum*. I believe all who have common sense, as soon as they have learnt from this paper that it is day-light when the sun rises, will contrive to rise with him; and to compel the rest, I would propose the following regulations:

First. Let a tax be laid of a louis per window, on every window that is provided with shutters to keep out the light of the sun.

Second. Let the same salutary operation of police be made use of to prevent our burning candles that inclined us last winter to be more œconomical in burning wood; that is, let guards be placed in the shops of all the wax and tallow chandlers, and no family permitted to be supplied with more than one pound of candles per week.

Third. Let guards also be posted to stop all the coaches, &c. that would pass the streets after sun-set, except those of physicians, surgeons, and midwives.

Fourth. Every morning, as soon as the sun rises, let all the bells in every church be set ringing; and if that is not sufficient, let cannon be fired in every street, to wake the sluggards effectually, and make them open their eyes to see their true interest.

All the difficulty will be in the first two or three days; after which the reformation will be as natural and easy, as the present irregularity: for *ce n'est que le premier pas qui coute*. Oblige a man to rise at four in the morning, and it is more than probable he shall go willingly to bed at eight in the evening; and having had eight hours sleep, he will rise more willingly at four the morning following.

But this sum of ninety-six millions and seventy-five thousand livres, is not the whole of what may be saved by my œconomical project. You may observe, that I have calculated upon only one-half of the year, and much may be saved in the other, though the days are shorter. Besides the immense stock of wax and tallow left unconsumed during the summer, will probably make candles much cheaper for the ensuing winter, and continue cheaper as long as the proposed reformation shall be supported.

For the great benefit of this discovery, thus freely communicated and bestowed by me on the public, I demand neither place, pension, exclusive privilege, or any other reward whatever. I expect only to have the honour of it. And yet I know there are little envious minds who will, as usual, deny me this, and say that my invention was known to the antients, and perhaps they may bring passages out of old books in proof of it. I will not dispute with these people that the antients might know the sun would rise at certain hours; they possibly had, as we have, almanacks that predicted it; but it does not follow from thence that they knew *he gave light as soon as he rose*. This is what I claim as my discovery. If the antients knew it, it must have been long since forgotten, for it certainly was unknown to the moderns, at least to the Parisians, which to prove, I need use but one plain simple argument. They are as well-instructed, judicious, and prudent a people as exist any where in the world, all professing like myself to be lovers of œconomy; and from the many heavy taxes required from them by the necessities of the state, have surely an abundant reason to be œconomical. I say it is impossible that so sensible a people, under such circumstances, should have lived so long by the smoaky unwholesome and enormously-expensive light of candles, if they had really known that they might have had as much pure light of the sun for nothing. I am, &c.

AN ABONNÉ.

Franklin and John Jay to David Hartley

ALS:[9] American Philosophical Society; copy: William L. Clements Library

Sir,   Passy, March 31. 1784

We have now the Pleasure of acquainting you, that the Ratification of the Definitive Treaty is arrived here by an Express from Congress. You have already been informed that the Severity of the Winter in America, which hindred Travelling, had occasion'd a Delay in the assembling of the States. As soon as a sufficient Number were got together, the Treaty was taken into Consideration, and the Ratification pass'd unanimously. Inclos'd you have Copies of the Proclamation issued on the Occasion, and of the recommendatory Resolution. The Messenger was detained at New-York near a Month, by the Ice which prevented the Packet-Boat's sailing, otherwise he would probably have been here in February. We are now ready to exchange the Ratifications with you, whenever it shall be convenient to you. With great & sincere Esteem, we have the Honour to be, Sir, Your Excellency's most obedient & most humble Servants

B FRANKLIN
JOHN JAY

His Excellency David Hartley Esqr &c &c &c—

Endorsed: Amern Ministers to D H Mar 31 1784

9. In BF's hand.

To John Adams   ALS: Massachusetts Historical Society

Sir,   Passy, March 31. 1784
    I have the honour of acquainting Your Excellency, that an
Express from Congress is at last arrived, with their Ratification
of the Definitive Treaty. Inclosed I send Copies of the President's Letter, the Recommendatory Resolution, and the Proclamation, together with three Letters for yourself.[1] We have written to Mr Hartley, that we are now ready to make the Exchange.
With great Respect, I am, Sir, Your Excellency's most obedient
& most humble Servant[2]   B. FRANKLIN

To Madame Brillon   ALS (draft): American Philosophical Society

                                      Passy, March 31. 84
Voici, ma trés cher Amie, une de mes Plaisanteries serieuses, ou
sourdes,[3] que je vous envoie, esperant qu'elle pourra peutétre
vous amuser un peu. Au quel cas, vous me recompenserez en
me donnant, je n'ose dire un Baiser, car les votres sont trop pre-
cieux, & vous en étes trop chiche; mais vous me jouerez un Noel
et l'excellent Marche des Insurgents—[4]   B F.—

    1. The editors of the *Adams Papers* speculate that BF enclosed four
letters—one from Elbridge Gerry, one from Arthur Lee, and two from
Samuel Osgood: *Adams Papers*, XVI, 105–6n.
    2. JA answered on April 10, acknowledging receipt of the papers and
the three letters, and expressing the hope that the exchange of ratifications
would take place soon. Mass. Hist. Soc.
    3. BF's letter to the editors of the *Jour. de Paris* (published under the date
[before March 31]), as acknowledged by Mme Brillon in her response of
March [*i.e.*, April] 4, below. BF borrowed the phrase "plaisanterie sourde"
from Morellet, who had used it in his letter of [March] 16, above, to characterize BF's letter on the Society of the Cincinnati.
    4. A composition by Mme Brillon: XXXVIII, 218n.

To Henry Laurens

ALS: American Philosophical Society; ALS (draft): Library of Congress

Dear Sir, Passy, March 31. 1784

The Ratification of the Definitive Treaty is arrived, and we have written to Mr Hartley that we are ready to exchange with him whenever it is convenient to him. Enclos'd you have Copies of the Recommendatory Resolution, Proclamation, & President's Letter.[5] We imagine Mr Hartley has an Inclination to come hither on the Occasion. Perhaps we are mistaken, and that he would as willingly make the Exchange there. In that Case, as a Duplicate is sent via London, by Major Franks, who probably is arriv'd by this time, and may have delivered it to you, it will be very agreable to us, if you, who are equally impowered, should finish the Business. With great and sincere Esteem, I am, dear Sir, Your most obedient & most humble Servant

B. FRANKLIN

His Excelly. Henry Laurens Esqr

Endorsed: Doctr Franklin 31st. March 1784 Recd & Answd. 7th. April

To Charles Thomson

ALS: Library of Congress

Dear Sir, Passy, March 31. 1784

I write this Line by the English Packet, just to inform you that Col. Harmar arriv'd here last Monday Evening with the Ratification, &c. and that Mr Jay & myself, (Messrs Adams & Laurens being absent) have written to Mr Hartley at London, that we are ready to exchange with him. I have not heard that the Delay is likely to occasion any Difficulty. I had before communicated to him your Letter of the 5th of January, which gave the Reasons of it.[6] With great Esteem, I am, Dear Friend, Yours most sincerely B FRANKLIN

5. BF also enclosed a copy of his March 31 letter to Charles Thomson; see Laurens to BF, April 7.

6. See BF to Hartley, March 11. The Jan. 5 letter was actually from Mifflin.

Cha. Thomson, Esqr

Addressed: To / Charles Thomson, Esqr / Secretary of Congress / at / Annapolis

Notation: Doctr. Franklin

From ———— de Joly   ALS: American Philosophical Society

A Toulouse haut Languedoc
Son excellence   31. Mars 1784.
Voudra telle me permetre de luy demender si tous les capitaines de vaisseau du Roy peuvent esperer d'etre admis dans le nombre des *cicinnati?*[7]
Une vaine curiosité n'excite pas en moy cette question: un interet personnel m'engage de La faire a son excellence.
Mr. joly de Cabenoux (mon gendre) est l'un des capitaines de vaisseau du roy, il comendoit a la derniere campagne Le vaisseau L'indien de 64. et dans les precedentes campagnes, a *Boston*, a *la grenade*, a *Savanae* en amerique, il a toujours combatu et servi sur le meme vaisseau a cotté de M. Le comte D'estaing.[8]
Si son excellence veut bien me faire l'honneur de m'expliquer

7. Many officers and their relatives wrote to BF about membership in the Society of the Cincinnati in the mistaken belief that Congress had established the society and authorized him to make appointments. For background on the establishment of the society's French branch see XLI, 314–16, 480. Naval officers were not admitted until after the charter was amended in May, 1784, at the request of the French admiralty: XLI, 480n. Thereafter, French captains of ships who ranked as colonels were eligible, along with (as honorary members) specially recommended officers of lower rank who had distinguished themselves in service on the American coast: Asa B. Gardiner, *The Order of the Cincinnati in France . . .* (n.p., 1905), pp. 20–22, 38.
8. After serving under d'Estaing in 1778–79 as a *lieutenant de vaisseau* aboard the *Languedoc*, Joseph-Louis Joly de Cabanoux (1744–1827) rose to the rank of captain of *l'Indien* in 1782. He was admitted to the society on Aug. 16, 1784: Gardiner, *Order of the Cincinnati in France*, p. 216; Christian de La Jonquière, *Les Marins français sous Louis XVI: Guerre d'indépendance américaine* (Issy-les-Moulineaux, France, 1996), p. 48; Ludovic de Contenson, *La Société des Cincinnati de France et la guerre d'Amerique, 1778–1783* (Paris, 1934), p. 148.

ce que les papiers publics ou gazetes ont deja fait entendre a cet egard, elle m'obligera d'autant plus, que j'attends dabord apres les fettes de paques prochaines ma fille et mon gendre en visite. Je serois bien flaté, si a cette epoque, je le voyois decoré d'une distinction aussi flateuse, surtout des qu'il peut esperer par son etat de revoir quelque jour vos contrees, a La liberté desquels il a côoperé au peril de sa vie. Je suis avec Respect de son excellence Le trés humble et tres obeissant Serviteur.　　　　　De joly

ecuyer rue *Montoulieu*.

From Jean-Baptiste Le Roy

ALS: American Philosophical Society

ce Lundy [March, 1784?][9]

Pardon Mon Illustre Docteur Si je ne vous ai pas envoyé plutôt La note Sur L'auteur de cette espece de Fourneau où on met le feu par dessus et où la flamme descend et remonte ensuite par un Tuyau de façon qu'on ne voit pas Sans étonnement la fumèe Se precipiter en bas et passer ensuite dans le tuyau qui Sert à L'emporter. J'ai été Si occupé depuis Jeudy que bien malgré moi je n'ai pu remplir ma Promesse.[1]

Lauteur de cette espece de Poële est feu M Dalesme reçu à lAcadémie en 1699 et mort en 1727 il a certainement presenté cette espece de Poele à lAcadémie avant 1686[2] cependant Je n'en

---

9. Dated on the basis of the English newspaper item mentioned in the final paragraph, which appeared in late February.

1. BF may have asked for this information in preparation for writing the description of his smoke-consuming stove that he had promised friends and fellow scientists for over ten years. The most recent request for it had come from Cadet de Vaux and Lenoir in December, 1783. BF wrote the piece during his return voyage to Philadelphia in August, 1785, by which time he had forgotten the name of the "ingenious French philosopher" who had given him the idea: XX, 25–6, 159; XXXV, 8–9; XXXVIII, 177; XXXIX, 93; XL, 9; XLI, 256–8; Smyth, *Writings*, IX, 443–62.

2. In fact, the engineer André Dalesme presented a memoir on his oven design to the Académie royale des sciences on Jan. 28, 1699: *DBF*.

ai point trouvé de description dans ce qu'on appelle nos anciens mémoires et il n'y en est pas même fait mention autrement que par ce que M De la Hire en dit page 692 du Tome 10me de ces anciens mémoires.[3] Mais vous en trouverez la description dans la Collection Académique Tom 1r pag 309 Sous le titre à ce que je crois de Machine pour Consumer la fumée.[4] Au reste vous Savez mon Illustre Docteur que les fours de nos fayenciers Sont échauffés de cette manière on met les buches et le feu dans une espece de berceau fait avec des barres de fer et la fumee et la flamme Se précipitent en dessous et vont passer dans le four &c.

Je Suis désolé Mon Illustre Docteur de ne pouvoir avoir Lhonneur de diner avec vous Jeudy avec Me Le Roy mais nous avons un Engagement qui nous prive de ce plaisir là. Nous Esperons bien que vous voudrez bien nous donner Notre revanche.

Permettez vous que Je vous demande Si M. Barclay votre Consul général dans le Royaume a recu enfin des ordres pour nommer des Consuls particuliers dans Nos villes de commerce et dans les differrentes parties de L'Europe. Parceque Je vous demanderois votre recommandation aupres de lui pour un M. De la Porte qui mest fort recommande et qui a une tres bonne maison de commerce à L'ile de Ténériffe il Souhaiteroit beaucoup davoir Lhonneur d'y etre Le Consul de Messieurs Les Américains.[5]

Vous m'aviez promis Mon Illustre Docteur une certaine Gazette angloise où il est question de ce barbier Juif qu'on a payé

3. "Reflexions de M. de La Hire, sur la Machine qui consume la fumée, inventée par M. Dalesme," *Memoires de l'Académie royale des sciences depuis 1666. jusqu'à 1699* (11 vols., Paris, 1729–1734), X, 692–4.

4. "Machine qui consume la fumée, inventée par M. Dalesme," published in *Collection Académique* (13 vols., Dijon, 1755–1779), I, 309–10, was reprinted from the *Jour. des sçavans* of April 1, 1686.

5. Among BF's papers at the APS is an undated petition from Jacques de Laporte, who along with his two brothers had appealed to BF for help in 1779: XXIX, 76. The 30-year-old, originally from Bigorre, argues that his devotion to the American cause qualifies him for the job of American consul for the Canary Islands. Captured at sea in 1778 while trying to emigrate to America, he spent nine months in a British prison and thereafter started a business in Tenerife. He encloses recommendations (now missing) from friends there. He aided several Americans during the war, including Commodore Gillon and Capt. Joyner of the frigate *South Carolina*. BF endorsed his request "Consul."

pour monter dans un ballon.[6] Adieu Mon Illustre Docteur Vous Savez combien Je vous suis passionnément attache pour la vie

LE ROY

John Jay: Account of Conversations with Franklin[7]

AD: Columbia University Library

[March–April, 1784]

March 1784

Doctr Franklin, who has lived long & much with Quakers, tells me that he thinks the far greater part of them approve of defensive tho not of offensive War— In the Course of the War wh. ended in 1748, It was thought necessary to erect a Battery at Pha. & a Lottery was made to defray part of the Expence— At that Time the Doctr. was of a fire Company of thirty Members, twenty two of whom were Quakers— They had sixty pounds of public or Company Stock—and the Dr. proposed to lay it out in Lottery Tickets. It was their Custom in all Money Matters to give Notice or make the Motion a Week before its Determination— When the Dr. moved his Proposition Anthy Morris a Quaker Member opposed it strenuously observing that the Friends cd. not apply Money to Purposes of War & that if the Dr. persisted in this Motion, it wd. be the Means of breaking up the Company— The Dr. observed that the Minority must be bound by the Majority, & as the greater part of the Co. were Quakers it wd. be in their power to decide as they pleased.— When the Day for the Determination came, Any Morris was the only Quaker who appd— The Doctr. observing that Circumstance pressed for the Vote, Morris sd. he expected that other Members wd. soon come it, & begd that the Vote might be

6. The British press reported that on Feb. 16 a Jewish barber in Ross, Gloucestershire, was carried by a balloon to a height of 116 yards and descended safely, amazing a thousand spectators. The account we have located does not mention the aeronaut's being paid: *Whitehall Evening-Post,* Feb. 24–26, 1784; *Morning Post and Daily Advertiser,* Feb. 26, 1784.

7. These are the final three of five casual conversations that Jay recorded in a small quire. The first two are dated July 19 and September, 1783, when the Jay family lived at the Hôtel de Valentinois: XL, 342–6; XLI, 59–60.

deferred for an Hour— While that Matter was in agitation, the Waiter called him out, telling him that two Men below Stairs wanted to speake to him— He found they were two Quakers, Members of the Company— They told him they came from six or seven others who were in a House next Door but one— They came to inquire whether he was strong enough to carry his Mo. [Motion] If not that on being sent for they wd. attend & vote with him—but they whd. to avoid it if possible lest they shd. give offence to certain of the Friends who were more scrupulous on that Head— The Docr. returnd & agreed to Anthony Morris's Request for another Hour— The Hour elapsed and not a single Quaker appd— The Question was then put and carried.—[8]

While Govr. Thomas was Govr. of Pensylvania shortly after the taking of Louisbourgh by an armarmt. from Boston, advices came to Pha. that the Garrison was in great want of Gun powder— Govr. Thomas communicated it to the Assembly & wanted them to afford Supplies— The Quaker Majority in the assembly wd. not consent to supply any Gun powder—but they granted three thousand pounds to be laid out in Flour Wheat or other *Grain* for the use of the Garrison— Govr. Thomas said that by *other Grain* was meant Gun powder— He laid the money out accordingly & nothing was sd. about it.—[9]

8. This meeting of the Union Fire Company took place on Jan. 4, 1747/8, during King George's War. However, both in his conversation with Jay and in the third part of his autobiography, written in 1788, BF apparently misremembered most of the details. The Quaker assemblyman Anthony Morris (1682–1763) was never a member of the company. In the autobiography BF identified the sole Quaker member voting against the first Philadelphia lottery (for which see III, 220–4, 229–31) as James Morris. Morris was indeed a leading pacifist in the Pa. Assembly and resigned from the company over the lottery the following month. Yet according to the company's minutes, Morris did not attend the Jan. 4 meeting: *Autobiog.*, pp. 186–7; J. A. Leo Lemay, *The Life of Benjamin Franklin* (3 vols., Philadelphia, 2006–09), III, 36–8.

9. On July 24, 1745, the Pa. Assembly allocated £4,000 for "Bread, Beef, Pork, Flour, Wheat or other Grain, or any of them, . . . to be shipped from hence for the King's Service, as the Governor shall think most fit." BF, the Assembly's clerk at the time of the vote, included this transaction in the autobiography: *Pa. Arch.*, 8th ser., IV, 3042; *Autobiog.*, p. 189; Lemay, *Life of Benjamin Franklin*, III, 36.

March 1784
Doctr. Franklin told me that the Quaker Morris Family of Pha. are descended from anthy Morris a Quaker who came here from England about the Beginning of this Century— It was said among the old People, that he was a natural Son of a Spanish Embassador in England— The Doctr says he always thought he looked a little like a Spaniard— He was an industrious money gathering Man, as well as a *rigid* Quaker—[1] He once found a friend of his reading a large Book— What says he *art thee reading that Book? Why a Man might earn forty Shillings in the Time necessary to read it thro'*—

[April, 1784][2]
Dr. Franklin says he knew the Father & Grandfather of W. Bingham the continental Agent at Martinico— The Grandfather was a Sadler—the Father a mercht.—

From Matthew Ridley[3]   Copy: Massachusetts Historical Society

Paris le 1r. avril 1784
Mr Ridley fait à Monsr. Franklin Ses très humbles remerciements de l'envoy des 29. Vol. qui completent *les 39. de L'ency-*

1. Morris (1654–1721) was born in London and immigrated to Burlington, West Jersey, arriving in February, 1682/3. About three years later he moved to Philadelphia. A successful brewer, substantial property owner, and leading Quaker, Morris also served in various public offices, including as mayor of Philadelphia in 1703–04. He was the father of the Anthony Morris mentioned above: Robert C. Moon, *The Morris Family of Philadelphia* ... (5 vols., Philadelphia, 1898–1909), I, 32, 39, 45–8, 52, 77, 86–9, 156–7.
2. Directly below this entry, Jay wrote a final one (the rest of the page is blank) dated April 17, 1784, which also concerns William Bingham. Because Jay drew a line before these last two related items, he may have entered them around the same time.
3. This letter, in French, survives only in Ridley's letterbook. It must have been written on the merchant's behalf by his clerk Nicolas Darcel, who kept the letterbook and handled Ridley's correspondence when he was away: XXXVII, 278n. Ridley had gone to England in mid-March: Darcel to Neave & Son, April 3, 1784, Mass. Hist. Soc.

clopedie dont le porteur lui comptera la valeur en 228 *l.t.* 12.—[4]
Au cas que Monsieur Franklin ait été muni du titre de la Sous-
cription il obligera Mr. Ridley de vouloir bien le lui faire remettre à loccasion.[5]

Mr Franklin Passy

John Adams to Franklin and John Jay

Copy:[6] Massachusetts Historical Society

Gentlemen   The Hague April 2. 1784
I duely received the Letter, you did me the Honour to write
me, on the Subject of a Treaty with Prussia and have communicated it to the Baron de Thuelemeier.[7] The King agrees to take
the Treaty with Sweeden for a Model[8] and if your Excellencies

4. BF evidently sold Ridley the pirated Swiss edition of Diderot's *Encyclopédie* that BF had ordered in 1778 but neglected to claim or pay for until—
it seems—the beginning of 1784. Ridley, through his clerk, is here sending
the purchase price of 225 *l.t.* plus 3 *l.t.* 12 *s.*—presumably the cost of cart-
age. The volumes had been sitting in a residence at Fontainbleau for well
over a year before the first ten were delivered to BF at Passy sometime before August, 1783. The remaining 26 volumes of text and three volumes of
plates were then transferred to Pierre-Sylvain Maréchal in Paris, to whom
BF was to remit payment: XXVII, 594–5; XXXVIII, 297–8; XL, 552–4. It is
possible that Ridley had taken the first ten volumes from BF's residence,
and that BF arranged for the remaining volumes to be shipped directly to
him from Maréchal.

5. During the months covered by this volume, Darcel also sent BF on
Ridley's behalf three letters requesting BF's examination of bills of exchange. The letters are dated March 4, May 12, and June 2: Ridley letterbook, Mass. Hist. Soc.

6. In JA's hand. Unless otherwise noted, copies of his letters at the Mass.
Hist. Soc. are in JA's autograph letterbooks.

7. The Feb. 28 letter from BF and John Jay to JA approved of his holding
preliminary discussions with Thulemeier about a Prussian-American commercial treaty. JA showed it to Thulemeier on March 8, and the baron was
"well satisfied" with it: XLI, 593–4; *Adams Papers*, XVI, 78.

8. Thulemeier informed JA on March 14 that Frederick II had agreed to
use the Swedish-American treaty (XXXIX, 250–85) as the basis for negotiations and requested a copy of it: *Adams Papers*, XVI, 90–1.

have any Alterations to propose I should be obliged to you for the Communication of them. The Baron waits the further Instructions of the King, before he proposes any Additions or Substractions.[9] I should be obliged to your Excellencys for a Copy of the Treaty with Sweeden as I am so unlucky, as not to have one here.

Inclosed is a Copy of a Petition to Congress transmitted me, from Boston by which it appears that the Britons in New York have condemned many Vessells taken after the Commencement of the Armistice.—[1] This Judgment Seems to me to amount to this that a Parrallel of Latitude is not a Circle which surrounds the Globe. If your opinion, Gentlemen is clear upon this head, as I doubt not it is, I think it would be a publick Service to write it to Congress, as this will at least determine the Sufferers to pursue their Rights by Appeal to England. There can be no dispute about it in England I think.

With great Regard

Their Excellencys Benjamin Franklin & John Jay Esqrs

From Mary Hewson

ALS: American Philosophical Society

Dear Sir   Black Friars Apr. 2. 1784

I received your kind letter of the 19. of March this morning, and thank you most heartily for it, tho; I confess it lowers our spirits, as it seems to take away the hope of seeing you here. The

9. JA asked Thulemeier, in the meantime, to compile a list of merchandise that might be exchanged between Prussia and the United States. Thulemeier sent it on March 25. The commodities proposed were largely those discussed by BF and Prussian minister Goltz in July, 1783: XL, 363; *Adams Papers*, XVI, 97–100, 101n.

1. JA had received a copy of this Aug. 18, 1783, petition from Boston merchant John Hurd, one of the 70 signatories: *Adams Papers*, 107n. (The petition itself is at the National Archives.) In response to it, article 7 of Congress' Oct. 29, 1783, instructions to the American Peace Commissioners (XLI, 157) asked them to clarify the timetable of the Jan. 20, 1783, armistice, which had confused Americans ever since it was announced; see XLI, 157n.

papers tell us you are soon to return to America,[2] and I begin to fear you intend to do so without giving a look at poor Old England.

I am much in your debt every way. This morning's letter is the third I have had from you since I wrote you a single line. I had determined to write by this days post to thank you for the two former letters, and the books with which they were accompanied.[3] You desire me to tell you whether I have received the complete set of *l'ami des enfans* for the year 1783. We have all but the month of Sepr. Your last packet contained the three last months, and you sent us the first eight in the two former.[4] We are much obliged to you for thinking so constantly of us. My son was highly delighted with your present of the *Synonimes François* as coming from you, and his French master no less so with the Grammars.[5] I receive instruction from them all. I can assure you my knowledge of the language is greatly increased. My daughter[6] learns of her brother's master, and for her sake I am attentive to her lessons.

Mr Viny fetched me last tuesday to spend a few days here. The family is all well. We keep up the gothic custom of drinking your health every day, and our best wishes always attend you. Mr Viny is uneasy at not hearing from you since he sent your wheels, which were put on board a vessel for Ostend last December.[7] He fears you either have not received them or are not pleased with them.

Return my cordial Love to your dear children, and believe me Dear Sir your gratefully affectionate MARY HEWSON

Addressed: A Monsieur / Monsieur Franklin / á Passy / prés de / Paris

Notation: Mary Hewson Apl. 2 1784.—

2. This rumor appeared in the March 20–23 issues of the *London Chron.* and the *Whitehall Evening-Post* and was widely reprinted thereafter.

3. See XLI, 353–4, 392.

4. For BF's shipments of the 1783 installments of *L'Ami des enfans* see XXXIX, 504; XL, 588; and XLI, 392.

5. BF enclosed them with his letter of Dec. 26, 1783: XLI, 354.

6. Elizabeth: XXXIV, 524n.

7. John Viny had earlier informed BF that the wheels were shipped at the end of November on a vessel bound for Rouen: XLI, 239.

From Amelia Barry

ALS: American Philosophical Society

My Dear Sir,   Pisa 3d April 1784.

After I had given Mr. Partridge a letter for you,[8] it occurred to me that we are famous at this Place for making Hare-down Gloves. I take the liberty of entreating your acceptance of 2 pair. If you approve of them have the goodness to signify it to me by a line, and I shall think myself equally honored and obliged by being permitted to supply you with them so long as you and I remain on the Continent.

The Gloves will be presented you by Mr. Mallack, a Gentleman who has spent the early part of his life in the East Indies, and has resided at Pisa some time with his family. He goes to England with Mr. Partridge you will find him very well informed in subjects relative to the E. Indies, which at present engage general attention—and when I add that he is a most worthy man, I am sure he will need no recommendation to my dear Docr. Franklin.

It is an age since I have received the least accounts of my dear Mrs. Bache,—the Papers occasionally give me your news.— I should be mortified at having it in this manner only, were it not for the conviction that the private ought to give place to the Public. Yet tho' you do not write to me, I am persuaded that no engagements can entirely banish from your remembrance Most Dear Sir, Your affecate. Obliged & devoted   A. BARRY.

His Excelly. B. Franklin Esqr.

Endorsed: April 3. 84

Notation: A Barry: 3 April 1784

From Jean-Antoine de Rubigny de Berteval[9]

ALS: American Philosophical Society

Monsieur   Paris ce 3e. Avril 1784

Je suis on ne peust plus reconnoisant de la bonté que vous avez Eut de repondre à La Lettre que Javois Eut L'honneur de

---

8. Dated March 24 (above).

9. A prominent Paris tanner who published numerous pamphlets against taxation of the leather industry and on other political subjects from the

vous Ecrire[1] Je suis pleinement satisfait de votre reponse. Le
1e. moment ou mes áffaire me permetront de quiter Je nauray
rien de plus pressé que daller Vous presenter mon Respect. Jay
L'honneur d'Estre avec Une grande consideration Monsieur
Votre trés humbles Et trés obeissant Serviteur
    DE RUBIGNY DE BERTEVAL
    Rüe Censier fausbourg st Maceau [St Marceau]
Endorsed: Rubigny de Bertheval 3. avl. 1784.—

From Madame Brillon   AL: American Philosophical Society

     ce 4 mars [*i.e.*, April 4, 1784][2] a paris
Je vous dois mil remercimens mon bon papa de votre joli billét et
de votre lettre aux auteurs du journal de paris,[3] mais je vous en
devrés deux mil, si vous y joignés l'avis a Ceux qui veulent passer en amérique,[4] j'éspérois aller vous le demander aujourd'hui
et m'etablir pour six ou sept mois a passy mais mon pauvre mari
a la goutte aux deux jambes, et la guérison de cétte mauditte
goutte peut seule nous rendre notre libérté; priés pour lui mon
bon papa tout hérétique que vous estes, j'ai plus de foi en vos
priéres qu'en toutes celles de nos dérviches; adieu mon ami aimés moi bien et comptés que de toutes célles qui vous ont aimés
et vous aiment aucunes ne vous aime autant que moi;
  Mil hommages de toute ma famille et complimens a mr votre
fils; je lui en veut bien a mr votre fils ainsi qu'au grand voisin[5] et
ils doivent bien sçavoir pourquoi.

---

late 1780s through the French Revolution and the Consulate: *Catalogue
général des livres imprimés de la Bibliothèque nationale: auteurs* (231 vols.,
Paris, 1897–1981); Giorgio Riello, "Nature, Production and Regulation in
Eighteenth-century Britain and France: the Case of the Leather Industry,"
Hist. Research, LXXXI (2008), 76, 82, 92–4.
 1. Neither letter has been found.
 2. In response to BF's letter of March 31, above.
 3. BF's letter to the editors of the *Jour. de Paris* (published under the date
[before March 31]) that was enclosed with his letter of March 31.
 4. "Information to Those Who Would Remove to America": XLI,
597–608.
 5. Le Veillard.

Addressed: A Monsieur / Monsieur Benjamin Franklin / ambassadeur des états unis de / L'amérique / a Passy

From Charlotte de Cheminot[6]

AL: American Philosophical Society

paris ce 4 d'avril 1784

Madame de cheminot presente ces civiliteé a monsieur francklin et prend la liberteé de luy mender que demain Lundy 5 d'avril elle profitera de la permission quil a bien voulu luy donner daller dejeuner chez luy elle ŷ menera messieurs le roy[7] gudin[8] quointin[9] qui sont penetree de cette marque de bonte de monsieur francklin.

Addressed: A Monsieur / Monsieur francklin / ministre plenipotentiaire / des etats unis de lamerique / en son hotel / a passy—

Notation: Cheminot 4 avl. 1784

To John Witherspoon

ALS: Presbyterian Historical Society; copies: Columbia University Library, New Jersey Historical Society, New York Society Library

Revd Sir, Passy, April 5. 1784.

I have received the Letter you did me the honour of writing to me the 27th past. It would be a pleasure to me to see you here, but I cannot give you any Expectations of Success in the Project

6. A former dancer who entertained prominent men of letters, including Diderot and Beaumarchais, at an *hôtel* on the rue Neuve-des-Mathurins: XXX, 166n; XXXV, 431.

7. Either Jean-Baptiste Le Roy or his brother Julien-David (XXIX, 634n), who, after BF's return to America, included news of Mme Cheminot in almost all his letters: Julien-David Le Roy to BF, June 20, 1786; March 23 and April 27, 1787 (all at the APS).

8. Poet and playwright Paul-Philippe Gudin de la Brenellerie (1738–1812). Gudin was a longtime friend of Beaumarchais and edited his complete works: *DBF*.

9. Most likely the chevalier de Cointin: XXXV, 431n.

of obtaining Benefactions for your College.[1] Last Year Messrs. Wheelock came hither with the same Views for their College at Dartmouth in New-England; and they brought a Recommendation signed by a great Number of the principal People of our States.[2] They apply'd to me for Advice & Assistance, and I consulted some knowing prudent Persons, well acquainted with this Country, & Friends of ours. After well considering the Matter, they gave their Opinion that it was by no means adviseable to attempt a Collection here for such a purpose; for tho' possibly we might get something, it would not be equal to the Expence and Trouble attending the Solicitation; and the very Request would be disgraceful to us, and hurt the Credit of Responsability we wish to maintain in Europe, by representing the United States as too poor to provide for the Education of their own Children.— For my own part, I am persuaded we are fully able to furnish our Colleges amply with every Means of public Instruction, and I cannot but wonder that our Legislatures have generally paid so little Attention to a Business of so great Importance.— One Circumstance in Messrs. Wheelock's Application here made me somewhat ashamed for our Country. Being ask'd by a Gentleman, what Sums had been subscribed or Donations made by the many eminent Persons who had sign'd the Recommendation, they were not able to say that more than one had given any thing.— Meeting with no Encouragement from any other Quarter here, they went to Holland & England. What Success they had in those Countrys, I have not heard.[3] With great Esteem & Respect, I have the honour to be Revd Sir, Your most obedient & most humble Servant   B. FRANKLIN

Revd Dr Witherspoon

1. John Jay, to whom Witherspoon had also written on March 27, responded similarly on April 6: *Jay Papers*, III, 573–5.
2. See XXXIX, 176–7n.
3. In fact, John Wheelock had reported on his successes in Holland in a June 12, 1783, letter to BF. When that was delivered is not known; a month later Wheelock had not received an answer: XL, 154–5, 322–3.

From Jonathan Trumbull
LS: American Philosophical Society

Honord. sir,   Lebanon Connecticut 5th. April 1784—
I take the liberty to introduce Messrs. Gerrey, and Bucking-
ham, the Bearers to your kind notice to advise means for thier
recovering some money due on some French Bills of Exchange,
which they lost by accident and were accepted for payment
premiture to thier presentation: probably you may put 'em in
a way for to assert thier Rights if the evidence they have procured is sufficient— The young men, are of good Families, and
young men of good reputation—and your assistance in thier
matter, wou'd be gratefully acknowledged by them, and at the
same time wou'd gratify the request, Honord. Sir, of your obedient, humble Servant,   JONTH; TRUMBULL

Benjamin Franklin Esqr.

Addressed: The / Honorable Benjamin Franklin Esqr.— /
Minister, / from the United states of / America, at the Court
of / France.—

Notation: J. Trumbull 5. Apl. 1784.—

From Joseph (Jean) Dupas de Iden de Valnais

AL: American Philosophical Society

Monday the 5th. april 1784./.
Mr. de Valnais presents his Respects to Dtr. Franklin. He has
the honor to inform his Excellency that Mrs. de Valnais is happily delivered this morning of a Son: Both are very well—[4]

Addressed: Monsieur / Monsieur le Docteur Franklin / Ministre
plenipotentiaire des / Etats Unis de L'Amerique du N. / auprés
de la Cour de France / A Passy—

4. The former French consul at Boston and his wife, Eunice Quincy,
were social acquaintances of BF's. They named their son Henry Quincy
Joseph Dupas de Valnais, after his grandfathers: XL, 261; XLI, 42, 318;
Edward E. Salisbury, *Family-Memorials: a Series of Genealogical and Biographical Monographs . . .* (New Haven, 1885), p. 321.

From Richard Price

ALS: American Philosophical Society

My Dear Friend   Newington-Green Ap. 6th. 1784

I have been long intending to write to you, and I feel ashamed that I have not done it Sooner. Your letter wch: was brot: me by Mr Bingham gave me great pleasure.[5] It inclosed a case for an air Balloon and a print wch:, in conformity to your desire, I deliver'd to the President of the Royal Society. Soon after Mr Bingham's arrival, Mr Daggs brot: me your paper on a Mathematical prize Question proposed by the Royal Academy of B———. I convey'd this to Dr Priestley, and we have been entertained with the pleasantry of it and the ridicule it contains.[6]

The discovery of air Balloons Seems to make the present time a new Epoch; and the last year will, I Suppose, be always distinguish'd as the year in which mankind begun to fly in France. Nothing has yet been done herein this way of any consequence— In the Royal Society a great part of the winter has been employ'd in a manner very unworthy of Philosophers. An opposition has been formed to the President. Motions for censuring him have been repeatedly made at our weekly meetings, and Supported by Dr Horseley, the Astronomer Royal, Mr Maseres, Mr Maty &c. &c. and these motions have produced long and warm debates. Lately there has been a suspension of these debates, but there is now Some danger that they may be revived again, for Mr Maty has just resigned his place of Secretary in resentmt:.[7]

In your letter you have intimated that you then entertained Some thots: of visiting London in the Spring. This is much wished for by your friends here; and, particularly, by the Club at the London-Coffee-House wch: you have so often made happy by your company. Dr Priestley intends coming to London from

5. It was dated Sept. 16, 1783: XLI, 6–8.

6. BF's letter to Price stated that he was also enclosing a "little jocular Paper," which he asked Price to pass on to Priestley. The piece was "To the Royal Academy of Brussels" (XXXII, 396–400), but it was not enclosed. BF sent it to London with a letter from Henry Dagge to his brother, who evidently delivered it to Price; see XLI, 7, 44–5.

7. For the discord within the Royal Society see our annotation of Joseph Banks to BF, March 23, above.

Birmingham in about a fortnight, but could he reckon upon the pleasure of meeting you in London at any time he would contrive to come up at that time. He has, I find, been chosen a member of the Royal Academy of Sciences at Paris.[8] This is indeed a Singular honour, and it must give him particular pleasure. I can Scarcely tell you with what emotions of concern I have heard that you have for Some time been Suffering under Symptoms of the Stone. What a Sad calamity it is to be visited in the last Stage of life by so dreadful a distemper? Dreadful I know it to be from experience. I have, however, been so happy as to discharge the Stone; and my only present trouble is the Sad State of health into which my wife is fallen. About a month ago She was Struck a third time with Paralytic Symptoms. She is extremely debilitated, and I live in a constant State of painful apprehension about her.[9] She hopes you will accept her best respects.

Political affairs in this country are at present in great confusion. The King, after dismissing from his Service the leaders of the late odious coalition, and appointing other ministers in their room to the great joy of the kingdom, has at last found it necessary, in order to maintain the new ministers in power and to carry on the public business, to dissolve the Parliamt:. We are, therefore, now in the midst of the heat and commotion of a general Election; and Such is the influence of governmt: on Elections and also the present temper of the people, that probably the new ministers will have a great majority in their favour in the new Parliamt:—[1] The more wise and virtuous part of the nation are Struggling hard to gain a Parliamentary reform; and

8. Priestley was elected *associé étranger* of the Académie royale des sciences on Feb. 26: *Index biographique des membres et correspondants de l'Académie des sciences de 1666 à 1939* (Paris, 1939), p. 375.

9. Sarah Blundell Price (1728–1786) suffered the first of her palsy attacks in 1762: D. O. Thomas, *The Honest Mind: the Thought and Work of Richard Price* (Oxford, 1977), pp. 15, 127; *ODNB*, under Richard Price.

1. William Pitt became prime minister in December, 1783, bringing to an end the Fox-North coalition government. George III dissolved Parliament on March 25, and the general election took place over five weeks in April and early May. When Price wrote this letter, the first electoral results had already appeared in the newspapers. In the end, Pitt's supporters made substantial gains: XLI, 349; *London Chron.*, March 25–27, 1784; John Cannon, *The Fox-North Coalition . . .* (Cambridge, 1969), pp. 210–16.

think, with great reason, that while the Representation continues Such a mockery as it is, no change of ministers can do us much good. But an equal representation is a blessing wch: probably we Shall never obtain till a convulsion comes which will dissolve all governmt: and give an opportunity for erecting a new frame.

In America there is, I hope, an opening for a better State of human affairs. Indeed I look upon the Revolution there as one of the most important events in the History of the world. Wishing, for the Sake of mankind that the united States may improve properly the advantages of their Situation, I have been lately employing myself in writing *Sentimts of caution and advice* which I mean to convey to them as a last offering of my goodwill.[2] I know I am by no means qualified for Such a work; nor can I expect that any advice I can give will carry much weight with it, or be much worth their acceptance. I cannot however Satisfy my own mind without offering it, Such as it i[s].

I always think of your friendship with particular Satisfaction, and consider it as one of the honours and blessings of my life. You have attained an eminence of credit and usefulness in the world to which few can aspire. That it may be continued as long as the course of nature will allow, and that you may enjoy every comfort that can make you most happy is, Dear Sr, the Sincere wish of yours most affectionately   RICHD: PRICE

Should Mr Jay or Mr Adams be at Paris, be so good as to deliver my respectful remembrances to them when you See them. You probably well remember Mr Paradise, a friend of Sr Willm: Jones's and a very worthy man, who has considerable property in Virginia and to whom you have been kind.[3] He has lately been in great trouble. The folly, ill temper and extravagance of his wife produced for Some weeks a Separation between him

2. Price finished this pamphlet by July 12, when he sent an advance copy to BF. See Price's letter of that date.

3. Price and Priestley had effectively introduced Paradise and Jones to BF in 1779, when asking the pair to deliver some of their publications to BF in Passy. BF subsequently wrote letters on Paradise's behalf to help him save his wife's estate in Virginia from forfeiture: XXIX, 524–5, 570–1; XXXV, 26; XXXVII, 629–32; XXXVIII, 311–12.

and her and made him one of the most unhappy men I ever Saw. But they are now come together again.[4]

Addressed: Benjamin Franklin Esq: / At Passy / Near Paris

From Henry Laurens

LS: Library of Congress; copy: University of South Carolina Library

Dear Sir.   Bath 7th April 1784.

I had the honor of addressing you under the 31st Ulto,[5] by the hands of my Son, who I hope will pay his Respects at Passy the present Day. This Morning I am favored with yours of the same Date, enclosing the several Copies of Papers from Congress, which you have enumerated, & also an open Letter to Charles Thompson Esqr,[6] not mentioned. From the Contents of which, I presume you intended it should go by the April Packet from Falmouth. I shall therefore seal & send it forward by to-morrow Nights, which will be the first Post. It will arrive at Falmouth exactly in time, according to the Rule of making up the Mail in London.

I have written to Mr Hartley upon the Business of the Ratification, & lodged in his hands a Letter for Major Franks—[7] Should Mr Hartley prefer making the necessary Exchange on this side the Water, I shall be ready to attend him upon the first Intimation of his Pleasure. I have requested Mr Bourdieu, who will probably be the Bearer of this,[8] to take with him some of

4. Paradise and his wife maintained a lavish lifestyle based on the mistaken belief that income from their estate would pay their bills: Archibald B. Shepperson, *John Paradise and Lucy Ludwell of London and Williamsburg* (Richmond, 1942), pp. 181–5.

5. Not found. Henry Laurens, Jr., did deliver to BF Laurens' letter of March 28.

6. BF to Thomson, March 31, above.

7. Laurens' April 7 letter to Hartley asked him to inform Franks where the exchange of ratifications would take place. His letter to Franks, also dated April 7, alerted him to the possibility that the exchange of ratifications might occur in London: *Laurens Papers*, XVI, 426n. Franks arrived in London that same day; see our annotation of BF to Jay, March 30.

8. He carried the letter only as far as Dover; see the notation on the address sheet.

the latest Newspapers for your Perusal, you will at least see how the Elections go forward, except which there is very little in them worth Notice.

I continue in very infirm health, but in sound & perfect Mind & Memory of the Esteem & Regard with which I have the honor to be. Dear Sir. Your obedt hble Servt. HENRY LAURENS His Excellency. Benj. Franklin Esquire Passy.

Addressed: His Excellency. / Benjamin Franklin Esqr. / Minister Plenipotentiary from / the United States of America at / the Court of France / Passy. / [*Notation by Bourdieu?:*] Forwarded from Dover, 10th. April 1784 by J.B.

Endorsed: Recd April 14.

To Madame Brillon

Press copy of AL: American Philosophical Society

à Passy, ce 8 Avril 84—

Je vous ai envoyé, ma trés chere fille, par Mr. le Roy, *l'Avis à ceux qui veulent passer en Amerique,* que vous m'avez demandé, & j'ai joint *les Remarques sur la Politesse des Sauvages.*[9] Avec ce Billet, je vous envoye plusieurs autres petites choses, dont on a imprimé quelques Exemplaires dans la Maison, seulement pour nos Amis. Je vous demande bien pardon d'avoir mis parmis les miennes, une de vôtre façon,[1] qui est certainement trop joli pour être placée en telle compagnie.— Si par hazard vous n'avez pas perdu *la belle & la mauvaise jambe,* & *la Morale des Echecs,*[2] vous avez, avec celles-ci, une Collection complette de toutes mes Ba-

9. "Avis à ceux qui voudraient s'en aller en Amérique" ("Information to Those Who Would Remove to America") and "Remarques sur la politesse des sauvages de l'Amérique septentrionale" ("Remarks concerning the Savages of North America"); see XLI, 412–23, 597–608, and for the French imprints in particular, pp. 413–14, 598–9.
    1. "Le Sage et La Goutte," written by Mme Brillon: XXXIII, 529–31.
    2. Sent by BF under cover of the undated letter published in XLI, 380. For the first piece see XXXIV, 41–6. No Passy imprint of "The Morals of Chess" (XXIX, 750–7) has been found in either French or English.

gatelles qui ont été imprimées à Passy.—³ Je suis bien faché que Madme la Goutte afflige notre cher Ami. Vous sçavez qu'elle m'a donné de bons Conseils autrefois, mais malheureusement ayant trop de foiblesses pour en profiter, je ne puis mieux faire, il me semble, que de les envoyer à notre Ami, à qui ils pourront peut-étre étre utiles. Cette Dame m'a donné trés souvent beaucoup de Chagrin, mais jamais autant qu'à present qu'elle vous empeche de revenir à Passy.— Je prierai pour vous, & pour notre pauvre Malade, puisque vous le desirez. Mais si vous étes aimés de Dieu autant que je vous aime, mes Prieres seront inutiles & superflus. Et tout Heretique que je suis, je ne doute pas qu'il aime des Catholiques tels que vous.—

From John Shaffer⁴   ALS: American Philosophical Society

Sir   Paris ce 8 avril 84./.

As the Marquis de la fayette is Kind Enough to Suply me with Every Nessary to Return to my Native Country, and as I intend

---

3. It is not known which of the bagatelles not already mentioned were enclosed with the present letter; the two surviving collections (Yale University Library and Bibliothèque nationale) are not identical, the former containing 15 items whereas the latter contains only 12. Both begin with "Dialogue entre La Goutte et M. F.," as the title page is affixed to that piece (see XXXIV, 11–20). Assuming that BF would have sent Mme Brillon only French pieces, as she did not read English, the others would have been: "Lettre à Madame B." ("The Ephemera"), XXVII, 430–5; letter to Mme Brillon, Nov. 10, 1779 ("The Whistle"), XXXI, 69–77; one or both versions of "M. F———n A Madame H———s." ("The Elysian Fields"), XXXI, 322–7; "Parabole Contre la Persécution, à l'imitation du langage de l'Ecriture," XXXI, 570–3; "Les Mouches à Madame He———s.," XXXIV, 226–7; and "M. F. à Madame la Fr———é.," XXXVI, 348–9. The only other French bagatelle, the one-page "Conte" (XXVIII, 308–9), was printed in the same pamphlet as "To the Royal Academy of ＊＊＊＊＊", which BF shared with certain friends though considered too vulgar to publish: XXXII, 396–400. A facsimile of the Yale collection of bagatelles, containing all of the above, is in *The Bagatelles from Passy by Benjamin Franklin* (New York, 1967).

4. BF could not have been unhappy to see the last of John Shaffer (now spelling his surname with a "c"; see XL, 618n), who brought warm letters of recommendation when he arrived in France in 1781, but who had exhausted BF's patience and goodwill by the time of his most recent arrest in August,

to Leave paris in a day or two I beg you will Kind Enough to send me a Pasport for *LOrent*. As to the small Sum of Money you was Kind Enough to lend me you may be assured that as Soon As I arrive in America I will Reimburce you with Intrest,[5] or if you think Proper I will Give you a bill payable at Sight upon My father at *Philada.*, if you will Honour me with your Comands to that Country I will Charge my Self with Pleasure.

I am with Respect sir your Humble servant

J. SCHAFFER
Rue St Jacque de la
Boucherie Ches Antoin
Peruquier *a Paris*

PS. I beg you will without los of time Send me the Past Port En question[6] and if you thinck Proper I will Send you the bill I Propopose to you—

Notation: Schaffer 8 avril 1784

1783, on charges of fraud. For his introduction to BF and an overview of his misdeeds, including the felonies he committed after returning to Philadelphia, see XXXIV, 364. For his arrest, imprisonment, trial, appeal, and unexpected acquittal at the end of January, 1784, see XL, 618–20; XLI, *passim*.

5. An oft-repeated assurance, which had little chance of coming true. Around the same time as the present letter, BF and WTF both received pleas from a cook named Denis Germain Gien, who had supplied Shaffer with food in prison and had housed him after his release, even lending him clothes. It was the lawyer Beaumont who had persuaded him to accept Shaffer's credit, but Shaffer vanished without paying a single bill. After much sleuthing, Gien found that Shaffer was living at a wigmaker's on the rue St. Jacques de la Boucherie (the address Shaffer gives BF here) under the name "Lewingston." Fearing that he will never be paid once Shaffer leaves for America, Gien asks BF's help in recovering the 353 *l.t.* he is owed by this "fripon." APS.

6. BF did so. On "Saturday Morning," which must have been April 10, Shaffer wrote a final note informing BF that he would leave Paris the next day and would not have time to pay his respects in person. He was also "much mortified" at not being able to thank WTF in person, and wished him "health and happiness." APS.

David Hartley to the American Peace Commissioners

Two copies:[7] National Archives; ALS (draft): Williams L. Clements Library

Gentlemen, [April 9, 1784]

I have received the honour of your Letter dated March 31. 1784 with the enclosures, wch. I have communicated to his Majesty's Ministers. I have the Pleasure to inform you that the Ratification on our Part, is now making out, and that I have received orders to prepare for the Exchange at Paris with all convenient Speed.[8]

Before my Departure I shall propose such general Sentiments for the Consideration of his Majesty's Ministers, as have occurred to me in our former Negotiations; my utmost Wish at all times being to give every possible Assistance in my power to effect a cordial & conciliatory Intercourse & Connexion between our Countries.

I have the honour to be Gentlemen, Your Excellencies most obedt. humble Servt. (signed) D. HARTLEY.

Copy of a Letter from D. Hartley Esqr. to the Ministers Plenipotentiary of the United States of America &c. dated London April 9. 1784.—

From Anthony Todd: Two Letters

(I) Copy:[9] American Philosophical Society; (II) ALS: American Philosophical Society

I.

Sir, General Post Office April 9th. 1784.

I have received a long Letter by this Days post from the Baron d'Ogny Postmaster General of France relative to the Treaty

---

7. Both in the hand of L'Air de Lamotte.
8. The king ratified the definitive treaty on April 9. For the text see Wharton, *Diplomatic Correspondence*, VI, 757–8n. (A copy in L'Air de Lamotte's hand, and a press copy of it, are among BF's papers at the APS.) Hartley did not leave London until April 18, when he received two letters from Laurens that he promised to deliver to BF: Laurens to BF, April 18; BF to Laurens, April 29; both below.
9. In BFB's hand. BF probably gave the original to the baron d'Ogny

between the two Kingdoms[1] which will require mature Consideration and I am not at present enabled to answer it, but great Difficulties already occur with regard to the Letters from North America by the French Pacquet Boats a great Number of which came hither to day by the French Mail charged with an high rate of Postage, and you well know we are restrain'd by our Laws from taking more than 10 d. for a single Letter from France.[2] In this Situation it will be necessary that all Letters from the United States for Great Britain or Ireland by the French Pacquets should be put under Cover to some Correspondent in France agreably to the sketch of an Advertisement which I submitted to your Consideration in my Letter of the 17th. of October Last, and which would have been better if it had also named Letters from, as well as to America to be put under Cover to some Correspondent in France, & I shall be exceedingly obliged to you if you will recommend it in the strongest Manner to the United States to publish an advertisement at New York and elsewhere to that Effect as the likeliest means to obviate all Difficulties.[3]

(XLI, 87n), to whom Todd asked him to show it; see Letter (II).

1. That letter has not been located. British and French postal authorities were in the midst of negotiations to replace a 1713 postal treaty slated to expire in June, though already nullified by France during the war: Eugène Vaillé, *Histoire générale des postes françaises* (6 vols., Paris, 1947–55), VI, 461; Brian Austen, "Dover Post Office Packet Services, 1633–1837," *Transport History*, V (1972), 33–4. BF had been acting as an intermediary in the negotiations between the two nations, and was trying to coordinate their packet-boat services to the United States: XL, 240–1, 501–2, 558–9; XLI, 85–7.

2. Rates chargeable by the British Post Office were restricted under the Post Office Acts of 1711 and 1765; foreign rates in excess were not recoverable. Postage on a single letter between Paris and London had remained 10d. from 1713 until 1779, when France, now sending letters for London via Flanders, added a charge of 4d. per letter. Britain expected that this surcharge would be removed after the war, but France retained it: XLI, 117; Herbert Joyce, *The History of the Post Office from its Establishment down to 1836* (London, 1893), pp. 138–9, 187, 296–7; Vaillé, *Histoire générale des postes françaises*, VI, 464.

3. The advertisement that Todd sent on Oct. 17 was a revision of the advertisement slated for British papers he had sent on Sept. 19; it included a final paragraph concerning French packets that conforms to what he stipulates here. He issued the advertisement on Nov. 18, after incorporating BF's suggestions. The corresponding advertisement for the American market, which BF had sent to the American postmaster general, Ebenezer Hazard,

I was in hopes it had been sufficiently understood that all Letters for Great Britain or Ireland should be conveyed from New York by our Packet Boats unless directed *Viâ France* and Vice Versa; but I am sorry to find that out of 233 Letters and Packets there are no less than 196 by the French Mail today not directed Via France.

This is such an evident mark of Partiality that I must entreat it of you to cause such directions to be given to the Postmaster of New York[4] as may prevent the like in future, but the best and only way would and must be on due Reflection to send all Letters without Exception for France and the whole Continent of Europe by the French Packets and all Letters for Great Britain and Ireland by our Boats. I am, Sir, Your most Obedient and most humble Servant   (sign'd) ANTH. TODD Secy.

Copy

His Excellency Dr. Franklin

II.

Dear Sir   General Post Office London 9 Apl. 1784.

Though I write You a Public Letter herewith it is really as a private one in the Truth of my Heart, and all I wish for You to dissemble on my Account is, if not very much against Your Conscience, that You would be pleased as of Your own Accord to show it in common Conversation as soon as ever it may be convenient, to the Baron d'Ogny, who will I hope feel the Force and Truth of it, but I cannot write to him on that single Subject having a very long Letter to day on the Proposal of a new Treaty in the Place of that in the Year 1713. which for France and us too had better not have been broken, but this is the Age of Novelty in every Quarter of the Globe.

---

in December, remained unpublished. Unbeknownst to Todd and BF, however, the substance of the British advertisement had already been reprinted in American newspapers: XLI, 21–4, 116–17, 153, 200, 352–3; *Pa. Packet*, March 4, 1784; *Independent Ledger*, March 8, 1784; *U.S. Chron.*, March 11, 1784.

4. William Bedlow: XXII, 398n; Philip L. White, *The Beekmans of New York in Politics and Commerce, 1647–1877* (New York, 1956), p. xix.

To quit Politicks You will I am sure be glad to hear that my daughter who has been married to Lord Maitland Elder Son of Lord Lauderdale whose whole Family Male and Female are Virtuous and good, in these Times rather rare, except amongst You Americans, has produced him an Heir[5] and they are both in good Health as at present is the Case with My Dear Sir Your most humble obedient Servant ANTH TODD

His Exy Dr Franklin.

John Adams to Franklin and John Jay

AL (draft): Massachusetts Historical Society

Gentlemen   The Hague April 10. 1784

Inclosed is Copy of a Letter from the Baron de Thulemeier and Copy of a Project of a Treaty transmitted to me by order of the King of Prussia:[6] I should be glad if your Excellencies would examine it, and write me your objections, and proposals of alterations, which I shall immediately communicate to his Majesty through his Minister. I presume too that your Excellencies will transmit it to Congress that when they send a Commission to conclude, they may Send their Instructions concerning any Changes to be made in the Project.[7] Your Excellencies

5. James Maitland, the future ninth Earl of Lauderdale, who was born Feb. 12 to Todd's daughter, Eleanor, and James, Viscount Maitland, the future eighth earl: *ODNB*.

6. Thulemeier's letter, dated April 9, enclosed the original draft treaty he had received from Frederick II, and asked JA to copy and return it to him as soon as possible: *Adams Papers*, XVI, 130–1. JA himself made a copy, which he retained; it is published in *Adams Papers*, XVI, 132–56, document (I). The copy enclosed in the present letter was made by JQA and docketed by him, in French, as having been copied from the original at The Hague on April 13. BF and Jay returned the copy with their comments under cover of their April 29 letter, below. As it was forwarded to Congress, that version is at the National Archives; JQA's notation is quoted in *Adams Papers*, XVI, 162n.

7. After finishing the present letter, (judging by the order of the drafts in JA's letterbook), JA himself wrote to President of Congress Mifflin

I flatter myself will think with me, that We Should execute the Treaty in our own, as well as in the French or German.

I am Gentn, your

Their Excellencies Benjamin Franklin Esq and John Jay Esq. Ministers Plenipotentiary.

From Uriah Forrest[8]   ALS: American Philosophical Society

Sir   London 10. April 1784.

The enclosed[9] came to my hands this day and as it appears to have met with rough treatment on it's Passage I have done myself the Honor to put it under Cover.

Shou'd there be any thing at this place which your Excellency can Charge me with that will be usefull to yourself or Our Country It will afford me real pleasure Being with all possible Respect Yr. Excellency's Most Obedt. & Very hble St.

URIAH FORREST

Addressed: His Excellency B. Franklin Esquire / Ministre Plena. of the United States / Passy / near / Paris.—

Notation: Uriah Toncet 10 April 1784—

---

enclosing a copy of the Prussian draft treaty, asking for instructions regarding any desired changes, and reiterating, for the third time since March 9, his suggestion that Congress send the commissioners powers to conclude the treaty: *Adams Papers*, XVI, 79, 102–3, 161–2.

8. A former lieutenant colonel in the Md. militia who was now a principal in the Baltimore-based mercantile firm of Forrest & Stoddert. Forrest moved to London in June, 1783, to establish a branch in that city. He returned to America in 1786 and settled in Georgetown, Md.; he was a member of the U.S. House of Representatives (1793–94), and the Md. Senate (1796–1801): Edward C. Papenfuse, *In Pursuit of Profit: the Annapolis Merchants in the Era of the American Revolution, 1763–1805* (Baltimore and London, 1975), pp. 183–5; Edward C. Papenfuse et al., *A Biographical Dictionary of the Maryland Legislature, 1635–1789* (2 vols., Baltimore and London, 1979), I, 324–5.

9. Not found.

From Julien-David Le Roy

L:[1] American Philosophical Society

This is the first known letter to Franklin from Julien-David Le Roy, one of the three brothers of Franklin's close friend and neighbor Jean-Baptiste. Franklin had met the brothers during his first visit to Paris in 1767.[2] Julien-David, though best known as an architect, was also an expert on ancient ship design and navigation. He had begun studying lateen (triangular) sails in the 1760s, and presented his first paper on the subject in 1770.[3] In 1782, he conducted a series of experiments designed to prove the advantages of using ancient sail designs on modern vessels. On September 24 of that year, with Franklin as a witness, he sailed a small boat rigged with lateens down the Seine from Paris and performed dexterous maneuvers in front of the Hôtel de Valentinois. Julien-David described those trials in a work published at the end of 1783, *Les Navires des anciens*, in which he paid homage to Franklin as "le pere de tant de découvertes."[4]

Franklin began a written response to what he called Le Roy's "learned Writings on the Navigation of the Antients" in February, 1784, proposing to offer his own thoughts on sail design. Before having completed those thoughts, however, he put the letter down, and only

1. The letter and the enclosed memoir are in a secretarial hand. Le Roy made minor changes to the text of the memoir, and at the bottom of its final page added the date "11 avril 1784." At the end of the summer Le Roy submitted to BF a second memoir (described below); it is in the hand of the same secretary who wrote the first memoir, with the exception of the final five pages, which were written by Le Roy. We are indebted to Abigail E. Shelton of the APS for identifying Le Roy's handwriting and to Prof. Christopher Drew Armstrong for confirming it.

2. XV, 82–3; XXIX, 634n.

3. Christopher Drew Armstrong, *Julien-David Leroy and the Making of Architectural History* (London and New York, 2012), pp. 242–5, 254n; Le Roy, "Premier mémoire sur la marine des anciens," *Histoire de l'Académie royale des inscriptions et belles-lettres* for 1770–72, XXXVIII (1777), 542–97. BF's copy of the latter is at the APS.

4. Julien-David Le Roy, *Les Navires des anciens, considérés par rapport à leurs voiles, et à l'usage qu'on en pourroit faire dans notre marine* (Paris, 1783), pp. 87–91. The experiment was witnessed by at least one other member of BF's circle, [Philip?] Keay (XXV, 725n), whom the author considered knowledgeable about naval matters: Julien-David Le Roy, *Nouvelles recherches sur le vaisseau long des anciens . . .* (Paris, 1786), p. 29; Julien-David Le Roy to BF, June 20, 1786 (APS). We have no record of when Le Roy gave BF a copy of *Navires des anciens*, but suspect it was in mid-December, around the same time that he sent a copy to the Royal Society of London: *Phil. Trans.*, LXXIV (1784), 503. BF's copy is now at the APS.

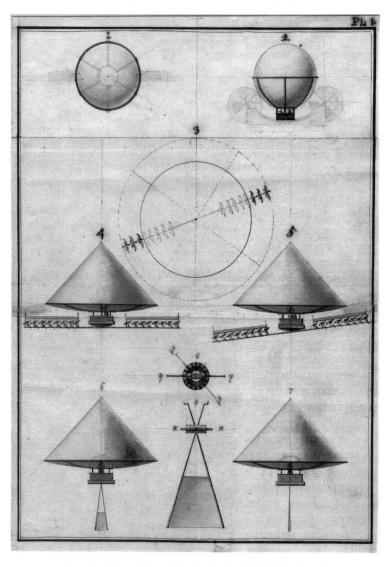

Julien-David Le Roy's Designs for Improving Hot-Air Balloons

resumed it during his voyage to Philadelphia in August, 1785. As the weeks wore on and more ideas occurred to him, Franklin expanded his letter to Le Roy into the paper now commonly known as "Maritime Observations," which he submitted to the American Philosophical Society upon his arrival.[5]

Les Navires des anciens contained an appendix in which Le Roy wrote a series of speculations on how balloons could be useful in a maritime context: to save shipwrecked sailors, to improve naval maps, to explore ocean currents, and even to function as sails.[6] In the spring of 1784 he wrote a memoir that expanded on those ideas, attempting in part to lend his expertise to the problem of how to steer balloons. He sent that memoir to Franklin under cover of the present letter.

Monsieur, [April 10–11, 1784][7]

Vos profondes connoissances dans la Physique et dans les Arts, le génie également Simple et Sublime qui vous en a fait tirer des résultats si utiles et si nouveaux, et l'intérêt que vous prenez à mes recherches sur la Marine; m'enhardissent à vous Soumettre quelques idées que j'ai eues sur les moyens de diriger l'Aérostat.[8]

5. BF's draft of "Maritime Observations" is at the Library of Congress. His initial dateline read "Passy, Feb. [*blank*] 1784". After finishing the MS he added lines above and below that dateline in a different ink: "Began at" / "but finished at Sea. Aug. 1785". Because the bulk of the paper was written in August, 1785, we will publish it under that date.

6. "Observations Sur la Machine Aërostatique, relatives à la Marine & à la Géographie," in *Navires des anciens*, pp. 225–39.

7. Although Le Roy added the date of April 11 at the bottom of his first memoir, as noted above, the second memoir is entitled a continuation of the letter written on April 10, 1784.

8. The enclosure, "Différentes idées Sur la maniere de diriger l'Aérostat," is 17 pages and divided into four sections. In the first section, Le Roy addresses the urgent problem of how to protect balloonists in case of crash landings on land and in water. He suggests giving balloons the shape of a cone to increase air resistance during an unplanned descent. He also recommends making the gondola detachable, so that it can serve as a boat when landing on water. In the following sections, he offers on three methods of steering balloons: with a harnessed flock of trained birds, a fan-like paddle, and a set of windmill blades. These proposals are illustrated in two professionally drawn plates, the first of which is shown on the facing page. (For more information, see the List of Illustrations.)

Ces moyens different essentiellement les uns des autres. Je n'aurai l'honneur, Monsieur, de vous en proposer qu'un petit nombre, parceque, d'après vos principes, j'ai rejetté tous ceux qui se présentant à mon esprit, ne m'ont pas paru marqués au caractere de Simplicité qu'on observe dans les inventions les plus utiles aux hommes./.[9]

Addressed: A Monsieur Frankclin, / Ambassadeur et Ministre plénipotentiaire / des Etats Unis de L'Amérique.

9. Sometime after Aug. 12, Le Roy submitted to BF what he called a continuation of his earlier memoir, entitled "Sur divers moyen de diriger Les Aérostats" (27 pp. including one plate of professionally drawn illustrations and a crude pencil sketch of an unidentified apparatus). It was written in two stages. The first part, in the hand of Le Roy's secretary, concerns the near-disastrous balloon experiment by the Robert brothers and Meusnier at Saint-Cloud on July 15 (for which see the July 15 entry in BF's journal, [June 26–July 27]). Le Roy criticizes the oblong shape of the balloon and its all but useless paddles and rudder. Still concerned about balloonists' safety during falls, he dismisses parachutes designed by Blanchard as ineffective and instead proposes encasing the lower half of the globe in a frame resembling an inverted umbrella. As an alternative to a rudder at the tail of the gondola, Le Roy would install a windmill propeller. Rather than an oblong shape, he proposes a cylinder with cones tapering to a point at either end, or else two cones attached at their circular bases. In a final section, handwritten by Le Roy, he recounts a discussion he had on Aug. 12 with a physicist (identified in the margin as "Mr. Testu") and imagines an improved method of managing atmospheric pressure during flight.

At some point Le Roy had his secretary make a fair copy of a revised version of the memoirs, cover letters, and plates. Beneath the title of the first memoir, which begins with a variant of the cover letter published here, Le Roy added the date "du 10 Avril 1784". Beneath the title of the second memoir, he added "du 5 Septembre". We do not know for whom the packet was intended; the MS is now at the National Library of Scotland. Le Roy deleted from the first memoir the section about harnessing trained birds, and they are likewise omitted from the illustrations. In a postscript, he admitted that the method was too complicated. Le Roy also added a footnote to the section on windmill blades stating that subsequent to writing the original memoir, he learned from BF about previous uses of windmill blades to move bodies on water. To the second memoir, Le Roy added three final paragraphs that relate to the illustrations.

From Valnais   ALS: American Philosophical Society

Sir   Paris. april the 11th. 1784./.
I have but this day Received the Billet your Excellency has
honored me with.[1] It is directed to the hotel *d'angleterre* & I
Lodge at the hotel *de Londres*. Its not Coming Sooner is the
Cause I have not answered before.
    I am penetrated with the warmest Sentiments of the most Re-
spectful gratitude for your Kind attention for Mrs. de Valnais.
She charges me to thank you heartily for the tender Concern,
you have been pleased to Shew her at all times & particularly
on this occasion: She ever will Remember it with an encreasing
Satisfaction Since it Comes from a Gentleman Born in her own
Town & who is So Justly esteemed & Revered through all the
Civilised world.
    Mrs. de Valnais & her little infant are Both tolerably well.
    I am with Respect. Sir Your most obedient & most humble
Servant   DE VALNAIS

Notation: Valnais M. de, Paris 11. Avril 1784.

From La Condamine   ALS: American Philosophical Society

                                       à calet. le 12. avril 1784.
Que je vous sçais gré, monsieur, d'avoir bien voulu prendre la
peine de me répondre, malgré les grandes et importantes occupations dont je vous suppose environné![2] Vos travaux littéraires
et politiques m'avoient inspiré pour vous, monsieur, de profonds
sentimens de respect et d'estime; vous venez d'y ajoûter ceux de
l'amour et de la reconnoissance; je vous admirois, je vous re-
spectois comme un grand-homme, je vous vénère, je vous chéris
maintenant comme un père!— Pardonnez, monsieur, je vous
supplie, cet épanchement naïf d'un cœur trop plein.
    Ce que vous me dites, monsieur, au sujet de comus, de mes-
mer, des remèdes & des malades m'a paru très raisonnable et

    1. A now-missing reply to the April 5 birth announcement of Valnais'
son, above.
    2. BF's answer is above, March 19.

très vrai; cela pourroit me fournir matiere à bien des réflexions, je les supprime pour ne pas abuser de vôtre complaisance ni de vos momens précieux.

J'avois oublié dans ma précédente lettre de vous parler aussi, dès prodiges prétendus du chevalier graham à londres, de sa musique divine, de son lit célestial, &c &c—[3] c'est bien une autre histoire, cela! Si tout ce qu'on en débite étoit vrai, les comus et les mesmer ne seroient que de bien petits garçons auprès de lui; mais je ne vois dans tout ce merveilleux prétendu que du charlatanisme raffiné pour éblouir les sots et faire des dupes. Vous ne mavez rien répondu, monsieur, au sujet du voyage de paris?— Je suis cependant décidé à le faire, dès que l'état de mes finances et de ma santé pourront me le permettre, ne fut-ce que pour jouir du bonheur de vous voir, et de vous présenter mes hommages en personne. Alors je pourrai dire comme le st. homme simeon: *nunc dimitte*, &c.[4]

Voici encore, monsieur, une rapsodie fruit de l'oisiveté d'un pauvre convalescent, que je prends la liberté de vous addresser.[5] Je vous prie, monsieur, si vous jugez à propos de la faire insérer dans le journal encyclopédique dans lequel a été consignée l'an-

3. The "celestial bed" of Dr. James Graham (the "Prince of Quacks": XXXIII, 123–4), promised to cure impotence and infertility and could be rented for £50 per night. Located in Graham's Temple of Health, it was elaborately decorated, charged with electricity and strong magnets, perfumed with exotic spices, and enhanced by music from mechanical instruments. A skeptical report on the bedchamber and the Temple itself, written by a physicist, circulated in French periodicals during the fall of 1783 and early 1784; for an early example see Métra, *Correspondance secrète*, XV (Oct. 8, 1783), 152–6. See also Lydia Syson, *Doctor of Love: James Graham and His Celestial Bed* (London, 2008), pp. 5, 138–40, 182–5.

Graham claimed to have met BF during a trip to France in 1779, when he was discussing electro-medical treatments with physicians and dignitaries: James Graham, *Travels and Voyages in Scotland, England and Ireland, France . . .* (London, 1783), p. 139. Though that claim cannot be substantiated, two of Graham's pamphlets, published in 1778 and 1779, found their way into BF's library: Wolf and Hayes, *Library of Benjamin Franklin*, p. 349.

4. The opening of the Canticle of Simeon (Luke 2:29): "Nunc dimittis servum tuum, Domine" (Lord, now lettest thou thy servant depart). Simeon, who had been told he would not die before seeing the Messiah, uttered these words as he cradled the infant Jesus in his arms.

5. This may have been a duplicate of the "rapsodie" he sent on March 8, above. Only one version is extant.

nonce qui y a donné lieu, je vous prie, dis-je, d'avoir la bonté de
l'envoyer aux auteurs, ou au bureau du dit journal.

Je suis avec un profond respect, Monsieur Votre très humble
et obéissant serviteur   LA CONDAMINE

P.S. J'avois demandé des renseignemens sur l'origine de bletton[6]
&c. à un homme à portée de s'instruire sur les lieux; j'en reçois la
réponse dans le moment, et je la joins ici, pour que vous puissiez,
monsieur, voir et juger par vous-même. Vous y verrez que le berceau de bletton, comme celui de tous les hommes extraordinai-
res, a été entouré d'une espèce de merveilleux:—[7] qu'en faut-il
croire?— C'est à vous, monsieur, qu'il appartient de prononcer. Au reste, je ne sâche pas qu'il soit question de ces sortes de
gens-là dans les autres pays, les françois auroient-ils ce privilège
exclusif, et parmi ceux-cy, les dauphinois seroient-ils plus spé-
cialement privilégiés que ceux des autres provinces du royaume?
Cette question (supposé qu'il y ait lieu à la faire) pourroit-
être ajoûtée à la fin de mon mémoire.

6. Barthélemy Bleton (*DBF*), a peasant from the Dauphiné region who
claimed to be able to sense underground water and minerals, ignited a
public controversy over the scientific merits of dowsing. The support he
received from the public and the court during a series of experiments in
Paris, Passy, and Auteuil in the spring of 1782 challenged the authority
of scientific experts, most of whom remained skeptical. In a final series
of experiments overseen by members of the Académie des sciences and
the Faculté de médecine, his powers proved unreliable. The *procès-verbaux*
of those controlled experiments were published in *Jour. de physique*, XX
(1782), 58–72. They were countered by articles in the *Jour. de Paris*, most
of which were written by Bleton's chief supporter, Pierre Thouvenel, who
claimed that BF witnessed one of the experiments in company with Diderot
(issues of May 21 and June 26, sup.). The articles were reprinted in Thouvenel, *Second Mémoire physique et médicinal* . . . (London, 1784). See also
Michael R. Lynn, *Popular Science and Public Opinion in Eighteenth-Century
France* (Manchester and New York, 2006), pp. 108–18.

7. La Condamine's correspondent, writing from Bleton's native village
of Bouvante, provided a long account of the dowser's personal history.
Born on Sept. 7, 1737, to an impoverished mother, he showed a gift—as
evidenced by pallor and convulsions—almost from birth. It was not until
he was seven or eight years old that the cause of the convulsions was discovered to be the child's proximity to water. His talent, tested by various
academicians, had gained him international fame and a substantial fortune:
Terrot to La Condamine, April 7, 1784, APS.

Pardon, monsieur, j'abuse de votre patience, et je finis en vous réiterant les assûrances de tous les sentimens dont je suis pénétré pour vôtre sçavoir, votre mérite et vos vertus.

From Dumas

AL (draft): Algemeen Rijksarchief

M.   Lahaie 15e. Avr. 1784
Je continue d'adresser à V.E. [Votre Excellence] la Lre. ci-jointe pour le Congrès,[8] vous priant, M, après l'avoir lue de vouloir bien la fermer & lui donner cours par premier Navire qui fera voile pour le Continent.

J'ai tiré le 5 de ce mois sur V.E. le semestre de mon salaire échu le 30 Juin prochain, savoir come à l'ordinaire £2700 tournois à une usance à l'ordre de Mrs. Wm. & Jn. Willink d'Amstm., à laquelle Traite il plaira à V.E. de faire en son temps l'honneur accoutumé.[9]

Il y a longtemps que j'ignore, Monsieur, l'état de votre Santé Daignez en instruire celui qui est avec le respectueux attachement que vous connoissez.

Passy à S. E. [Son Excellence] Mr. Franklin M. P. [Ministre Plénipotentiaire]

From Benjamin Webb

ALS: American Philosophical Society

Dear Sir   Geneva April 15th. 1784
I took the Liberty of writing to you by the favour of your Grandson sometime since[1]—and It is only from very urgent

8. Most likely his April 15 letter to the president of Congress. Dumas had learned that the office of secretary for foreign affairs was vacant and hoped that his previous dispatches to that department had been read by Congress. He also appealed for financial support. With that letter, Dumas probably sent his latest dispatch on events in the Netherlands, dated April 10. (Both are at the National Archives.) For English translations see *Diplomatic Correspondence of the United States*, VII, 37–40, 40–1.

9. On May 13 Ferdinand Grand paid Dumas' bill of 2,700 *l.t.*, half of his annual salary: Account XXVII (XXXII, 4).

1. Webb sent the letter, dated July 7, 1783, by way of BFB: XL, 287–8.

Explanation of the Medal Struck by the Americans in 1782

Reasons that I am induc'd again to trouble you, which I hope you will be so good to pardon. I have not ever mentioned to you myself, any other part of my unfortunate History, but that of being intirely deprived of the Society of my amiable little Woman by Ill health.[2] This had been the Case three years before I left England. But this is not all. The total deprivation of the Means to support Her—her dear Babes and myself, is also a part of my sad Story.[3] The Limits of a Letter will not admit of the particulars—as well as that I should be sorry to pain you with the Recital of certain Circumstances that led to, and finished this sad Catastrophe. Your former Acquaintance with the parties, about whom Truth & Justice to my own Character would oblige me to speak plainly, must give you pain to hear.

Let It suffice therefore at present to say, that with a fine Fortune in my pocket—& with the highest Ideas that the sweetest Enjoyments of Life were only to be found In Its most private Walks—thus provided for—and Seemingly guarded against the Whirlpools of Speculation & Schemeing, I was so weak to suffer myself to be prevailed on, to embark on those dangerous Waters, & was swallow'd up—without having first of all made a Settlement for Subsistance on my dear Wife, and her Issue.— Thus I became totally ruined—however, having always bore an unimpeachable good Character, & what is more material, wishing, from principle I trust, to deserve It, I had no doubts of being able in some way or other to provide for myself and Family. I gave up my All, as the Law justly requires, at the third Meeting,[4] and was on the point of being made a free man—When Those who owed me Respect and Honour to my Live's-end, dared to insinuate that I had Somewhere secreted property, to a large Amount.

2. On his wife's poor health, see Webb's letter cited above and XXXVI, 322.

3. Webb and his business partner, William Curteis, who was also his father-in-law, went bankrupt in 1778: XXVI, 432; XXXVI, 322n; *London Gaz.*, April 21–25, 1778.

4. Webb was obliged to surrender himself by the third meeting of the commission that had determined his bankruptcy, and he also had to account for his holdings and give up what property he could. The third meeting was scheduled for June 6, 1778: *London Gaz.*, April 21–25, 1778; Julian Hoppit, *Risk and Failure in English Business, 1700–1800* (Cambridge, 1987), p. 36; William Blackstone, *Blackstone's Commentaries on the Laws of England*, ed. Wayne Morrison (4 vols., London and Sydney, 2001), II, 388–9.

This occasioned a most unnecessary Adjournment at the Moment I had as good a right to be liberated as ever unfortunate Bankrupt had.— And in Its Consequences involved everything I did or said in the thickest Mists of Suspicion & prejudice. My honour thus deeply wounded, Nay—my Character—the only Wherewithall I had left to provide for my helpless Family hereby fatally stab'd—instead of staying to vindicate and recover It as I ought to have done—driven almost to Desperation—I acquainted no one in the World with my Intention, but in the moment of Despondency took the fatal Step that landed me on a foreign Shore—with my son Charles however as some Solace, and Guard perhaps to a miserable Being.[5] The Circumstance of quitting my Country made so against my Cause, that my Enemies of course triumph'd, & some of my best Friends were stagger'd.— But Time will convince them all, that reasoning on probabilities is not the surest Basis. I have long since had the Satisfaction to know, that the three Assignees who have been setling our Affairs, have given up every Idea that I had secreted property. One of them the late Mr. Polhill[6] did invite me to return, and the present Judge Kenyon early gave It as his Opinion that I might with perfect safety to my person,—[7] but I am too well acquainted with Parties, & still too sore from the Wounds of past Ill usage to dare to trust them, 'till by a petition to the Chancellor signed by all the Creditors, shall put me out of the reach of Malevolence— That, now is impeded by only One, who is perhaps turned of Ninety.—[8] His inexorabil-

5. He fled to Switzerland: XXXVI, 321–2.
6. Nathaniel Polhill, M.P., a tobacco merchant and banker who died in 1782: Namier and Brooke, *House of Commons*, III, 306; *London Gaz.*, Dec. 18–22, 1792.
7. Lloyd Kenyon, an illustrious barrister who was named attorney general in 1782. Webb's reference to his judicial status could have applied either to his 1780 appointment as chief justice of Chester or, if the news had reached Geneva, his recent ascent to the office of master of the rolls. Ultimately, Kenyon became lord chief justice: *ODNB*.
8. An individual could obtain a release from bankruptcy when the lord chancellor allowed a certificate signed by four-fifths (in number and value) of a bankrupt's creditors: Blackstone, *Commentaries*, II, 389; E. Welbourne, "Bankruptcy before the Era of Victorian Reform," *Cambridge Hist. Jour.*, IV (1932), 54.

ity to my certain Knowledge has been Kept alive by Artifice and Falshood. The Support of myself and Child have ever since my Absence, depended on the Bounty of a few particular Friends in England—and some of their Contributions on the Success of Trade & Commerce, which was never at a more uncertain or lower Ebb than now in England. I cannot with propriety say more.

In short I am under the Necessity to apply by a more general Memorial to those Who Knew me in my days of prosperity— and It has occurr'd to me, that if It could be presented to you, Sir, you would be so good candidly to think of, and help me. I was obliged however to Send the Memorial to England with all Expedition, but I herewith send a Copy of It to you, as also of the Certification of It by my two valuable Friends Mr. Pigott & Mr. Clason.[9] I beg your pardon most sincerely for this long Interuption. I have slid into a Prolixity I did not intend. I have the Honour to subscribe myself with the highest Respect Sr. Yr. much obliged and obedt. hble Servt   B: WEBB

Charles & myself desire to join in Love to your Grandson.

The greatest fall of Snow here yesterday that has happen'd in the memory of Man at this Season. In nine hours, It was thirteen Inches & a half deep.—[1]

Mr. & Mrs. Pigott desire me to present their Compliments.

My present Direction I will take the Liberty of Subjoining. At Mr. Roux near the Great Coffeehouse. Geneva.

Addressed: To / The Honble: Benjn Franklin / Esqr. / at / Paris.

Notation: Webb M. Benjn.

9. Patrick Clason, a Scotsman who was a friend of Adam Smith's and resided for a time in Geneva: John Rae, *Life of Adam Smith* (London and New York, 1895), pp. 191, 263, 432.
    1. This sentence appears at the bottom of the fourth side of a folded sheet of paper. Webb filled the first two sides of a second sheet with a copy of his memorial, which duplicated the information contained in his letter. He then added the postscripts (published immediately below) on the third side of this sheet and, on the fourth side, wrote the address. The memorial included the certifications by Pigott (dated April 7) and Clason (dated April 8).

From Wilhem & Jan Willink, Nicolaas & Jacob van Staphorst, and De la Lande & Fynje ʟs: Library of Congress

Sir   Amsterdam 15 Apr: 1784
We take the liberty to inform your Excellency that in consequence of the Success of the new Loan, his Excellency John Adams Esqr authorised us to open for acct of Congress,[2] we have become in the Situation to pay due honor to every disposal, we have hitherto advice, his Excellency Robt. Morris Esqr. Super Intendant of Finance has been pleased to make on us.[3]
We have the honour to remain with respectfull regard. Sir Your most Humb Servts.   Wilhem & Jan Willink
                                             Nic: & Jacob van Staphorst.
                                             de la Lande & fÿnje.

To his Excellency Benjn. Francklin Esqr in Paris.

Franklin and John Jay to Thomas Mifflin

ALS[4] and copy: National Archives; press copy of ALS: Library of Congress

Sir,   Passy, April 16. 1784.
We duly received the Letters your Excellency did us the honour of writing to us the 14th of January by Colonel Harmar & Lieut. Col. David Franks, with the Ratification of the Definitive Treaty, the Proclamation, & the Recommendatory Resolves of Congress.[5] On the Arrival of Col. Harmar, we immediately wrote to Mr Hartley, acquainting him that we were now ready to exchange with him; sending him at the same time Copies of the Proclamation and Resolutions. We have this Day

2. See the annotation of JA to BF, March 27, above.
3. The consortium opened the loan on Feb. 18, before the contract was signed: *Adams Papers*, xvi, 38n. Their letter to Morris, informing him that they would honor all his bills, was dated Feb. 19: *Morris Papers*, ix, 126, 312–14.
4. In BF's hand.
5. xli, 456–7, 464–6. For Harmar's arrival see BF to Jay, March 30. Franks arrived in Paris on April 15: Josiah Harmar's diary, entry of April 15, 1784 (Clements Library).

receiv'd from him the enclos'd Answer,[6] and we expect he will soon be here, and put with us the finishing Hand to this important Business.

With great Respect, we have the honour to be, Sir, Your Excellency's most obedient & most humble Servants—

B. FRANKLIN
JOHN JAY

His Excellency Thomas Mifflin, Esqr President of Congress

To John Adams

ALS: Massachusetts Historical Society; press copy of ALS:[7] Columbia University Library

Sir,   Passy, April 16. 1784—

We duly receiv'd (Mr Jay & me) the Letters you did us the honour of writing to us the 27th of March & the 2d Instant. We shall transmit, as you desire, the Recommendation of Mr Browne to Congress;[8] and enclos'd we send a Copy of the Treaty with Sweden.

We expect Mr Hartley here very soon, to exchange the Ratifications of the Definitive Treaty; when we shall endeavour to obtain an Explanatory Article relating to the Limits & Term of Captures. The Form used in the last Treaty is precisely the same that has been used in all the Treaties of Peace since that of Nimeguen;[9] and I therefore imagined that Cases must have arisen at the End of every War, in which it was necessary to decide on the Meaning of that Form of Words wherein the

6. BF and Jay to Hartley, March 31, and Hartley's reply of April 9, both above.

7. Made for Jay, who endorsed it.

8. They must have done so, as De Berdt's recommendation of Edward Browne is now among Charles Thomson's papers at the Library of Congress: *Adams Papers*, XVI, 17.

9. The 1678 treaty of Nimeguen (Nijmegen) between France and the Netherlands was only slightly less ambiguous regarding when the armistice was to take effect in different parts of the world. It suggested, but did not explicitly state, that this would happen by latitudinal zones: Parry, *Consolidated Treaty Series*, XIV, 369.

Canary Islands are mention'd; and I desir'd Mr Barclay when he went to London to procure from the Records of the Admiralty Court some of those Cases as decided there; but he tells me none are to be found.[1] May there not be some in Holland? I should suppose they must have been adjudg'd by the Parallel of Latitude of those Islands; and I should be glad to have such a Decision to produce to Mr Hartley.

With great Respect, I have the honour to be Sir, Your Excellency's most obedient & most humble Servant   B FRANKLIN

His Excellency John Adams, Esqr

Endorsed: Dr Franklin 16. Ap. ansd. 20. 1784

To Charles Thomson   ALS: Library of Congress

Dear Friend,   Passy, April 16. 1784—

I received your kind Letters by Colonel Harmar, & Lieut. Col. Franks; with the Dispatches in good Order; Triplicates of which are since come to hand.[2] You will see by our Letter to the President,[3] that we daily expect Mr Hartley from London with the British Ratification to exchange with us. There was no Difficulty occasion'd by the Lapse of the Term. I send you herewith four Packets of Newspapers, by which you will be inform'd of the Confusions that have reign'd all Winter in England, and the Probability of their being finish'd by the Choice of a new Parliament, in which the present Ministry will have a great Majority.— The N. [News] Papers are directed for the Presidt.[4]

You are good in excusing the Trouble I have given you with so many little Affairs & Enquiries, and for enabling me to give

1. Barclay had returned to Auteuil on April 11. He had reported on his search in a letter of Feb. 17: XLI, 574–5.
2. Thomson's letter of Jan. 14 was delivered by Josiah Harmar and his letter of Jan. 15 by David S. Franks, each of whom also carried a copy of the congressional ratification of the peace treaty: XLI, 463–4, 472–4. The triplicate of the ratification had not yet arrived when BF wrote to Jay on March 30.
3. BF and Jay to Mifflin, April 16.
4. This sentence was added in the margin, its placement indicated by an asterisk.

some Answer to the Persons who make them. I am pester'd continually with such Matters.

I am happy to learn from you, that a Disposition begins to prevail in the States to comply with the Requisitions of Congress, and to grant Funds for the regular Payment of the Interest, and Discharge of the Principal of the Debts contracted by the War.[5] Punctuality and exact Justice will contribute more to our Reputation, & of course to our Strength, than People generally imagine. Without those Virtues we shall find it difficult, in case of another War, to obtain either Friends or Money; and a Reliance on that may encourage and hasten another Attack upon us.— Gratitude to our former Benefactors is another Point we should seize every Opportunity of demonstrating. I place with you much Confidence in the good Sense of our Countrymen, and thence I hope that the Endeavours of some Persons on both sides the Water to sow Jealousies and Suspicions, and create Misunderstandings between France and us, will be ineffectual.

A Commission from Congress for a commercial Treaty with Britain has long been expected.[6] If the Intention of sending such a Commission is not changed, I wish it may arrive before Mr Laurens leaves us, who has a more perfect Knowledge of the Subject than any of us, and might be greatly useful.—

A Minister from Denmark has been waiting in Paris all Winter for the Result of Congress on the propos'd Treaty, a Plan of which was long since sent; as also one for a Treaty with Portugal.—[7] I hope by the Return of the Washington Pacquet, we may receive some Directions respecting them.

I am, with sincere & great Esteem, my dear Friend, Yours most affectionately   B FRANKLIN

Cha. Thomson, Esq;

Endorsed: Letter Doct B Franklin April 16. 1784 Recd. July 30. 1784

5. BF quotes almost verbatim Thomson's letter of Jan. 15: XLI, 473.

6. Congress resolved to prepare such a commission on May 1, 1783, and Elias Boudinot informed the commissioners on June 16 that it was in the works. However, Congress abandoned the project soon after: XL, 178–80.

7. BF sent the draft treaties with Denmark and Portugal to Congress in late July, 1783, and since then had repeatedly requested instructions: XL, 123–4, 360–1, 367–8, 621–2; XLI, 166, 342.

From Francis Coffyn

ALS: American Philosophical Society

Hond. Sir.   Dunkerque 16. April 1784.

I had the honnor to address your Excellency on the 6th. inst,[8] whereunto I beg leave to refer. This cheafly Serves to enclose a Copy of a letter I Just now received from my friend M. Bodin at Lille, to whom I wrote to enquire about the price of Bells.[9] If that which was offer'd me here at 30 s. per pound all charges included, as mentioned in my Said letter, would Sute, it would be preferable to those at Lille, where they demand 34 s. per lb. exclusif of the duty & the expences of transporting it here; The Three Bells my friend mentions that are to be Sold in the course of Eight days are I apprehend too large,[1] if not I beg your Excellency will favour me with his orders per return of the post, & rely on my attention to execute the Same. Interim I have the honnor to remain very respectfully. Your Excellencys Most obedient & most humble Servant   F. COFFYN

His Excy. Dr. B. Franklin at Passi

Notation: Coffyn, Dunkerque 16 Avril 1784.—

From William Withering[2]

Printed in William Withering, *The Miscellaneous Tracts of the Late William Withering; to Which is Prefixed a Memoir of His Life, Character, and Writings* (2 vols., London, 1822), II, 485–6.

[before April 17, 1784]

Believing the passing of the stone to be impossible, the extraction of it unadvisable, and that no known medicine can dissolve

8. Not found.

9. The enclosure is a copy (in Coffyn's hand) of an April 15, 1784, letter from P. J. H. Bodin. APS. Coffyn had consulted him as a result, apparently, of an inquiry posed by BF in the wake of his hearing about the town of Franklin's wish for him to donate a bell: XLI, 476–7; William Hodgson to BF, March 17 (above).

1. Bodin's letter indicated the availability of four bells from a church slated for demolition.

2. On April 17 (below) BF informed Benjamin Vaughan that he had finally received Dr. Withering's letter—presumably the response to BF's appeal

148

it, I shall turn my attention to such methods as will be most likely to prevent its increase. These consist in

Encouraging perspiration, in order to pass off as much as possible of the excrementitious animal matter through the pores of the skin, and to leave less to be discharged with the urine.

Strengthening the solvent powers of the bile, by which the excrementitious part of the urine is rendered soluble in its watery part.

Diluting freely, as well with a view of supporting an abundant insensible perspiration, as of supplying a sufficient proportion of watery menstruum to the kidneys and bladder.

To fulfil these intentions, I advise the patient

To wear a flannel shirt next his skin.

To use a warm bath once a fortnight or three weeks, and whilst in the bath to have the skin chafed with a piece of coarse cloth.

To avoid those exposures which check the insensible perspiration.

Eat a plentiful dinner of animal food, using salt freely, and every vegetable except those usually eaten without boiling. All the onion tribe are particularly recommended: ripe fruits are not included in the exception. Supper, a basin of gruel, well impregnated with onions. Fruit will be best eaten an hour or two before dinner. Strawberries, two or three pints a day through the season, if the bowels will bear them in such quantity.

To dilute freely, with

Spring water, hard or soft. Chalybeate waters, as those of Spa or Pyrmont. Wine in moderation; but good small beer is one of the best liquors.

Infuse an ounce of liquorice-root, sliced in a pint of boiling water, all night: to drink one half fasting every morning, the other half at bed-time.

I hardly know a medicine I wish you to take.

---

of March 1, enclosing a case history of his stone. Withering's letter has not been found, but we believe the undated text published here to be the substance of it. The text appeared in a posthumous collection of Withering's writings, prefaced by the heading: "Directions for the Treatment of the Case of B. F——, LL.D. an aged Patient, suffering from a large Stone in the Bladder. Addressed to Dr. Vaughan, at Paris." Vaughan had written to Withering from Paris in 1782 about BF's case, but in 1784 he was in London.

If again troubled with kidney concretions, you will probably find that fifty drops of balsam of capivi, taken twice a day, will prevent their further formation. Equal weights of essential oil of juniper and sweet spirit of nitre, mixed with an equal bulk of mucilage of gum arabic, I have sometimes thought useful in detaching the looser lamina of stones. I direct two spoonfuls of the mixture to be taken daily in half a pint of small ale: to some patients it proves too heating.

To David Hartley

Copy: William L. Clements Library

Dear Sir   Passy April 17 1784

The Commissioners have received the Letter you did them the honour of writing to them the 9th Instant, and are glad to learn that they may expect the Pleasure of seeing you soon again at Paris. It is a particular Satisfaction to me, as it will give me an opportunity of communicating an Idea to you in Conversation which may tend to promote your excellent views of "effecting a cordial & conciliatory Intercourse between our Countries," but which I cannot so well explain at present by writing.

The Bearer, Col. Harmar, is an American of good Character, who visits England in Curiosity to see the Country and People he has been fighting against.[3] I wish to give him a good Opinion of them by the Sample he may be acquainted with, and therefore beg leave to recommend him to your Acquaintance & Civilities.[4] With great & inalterable Esteem & Affection I am ever my dear Friend Yours most sincerely   B FRANKLIN

David Hartley Esqr

3. Harmar left for England on April 19 and arrived in London on April 25. He was back in Paris on May 17: Josiah Harmar's diary (Clements Library).

4. On April 26 Harmar delivered "several" letters of introduction from BF (Josiah Harmar's diary, Clements Library), of which this one alone has been located. He carried now-missing letters from BF to Edward Bridgen (who responded on May 11) and Anthony Todd (who responded on May 18). He may also have carried BF's April 17 letter to Henry Laurens, who replied on May 6. Harmar carried back to Paris at least two letters for BF: Edward Nairne's of May 5 and Laurens' of May 10.

To Henry Laurens ALS: New York Public Library

Dear Sir, Passy, April 17. 1784.

I have received your Favours of March 28. and April 7.— I am glad that Mr Hartley's being luckily at Bath, sav'd you the Fatigue of a Journey to London. His Letter to you, of which you sent us a Copy, was very satisfactory.[5] By one he has written to us, of the 9th Instant, we find that he expects to be here in a few Days.—

I have not yet had the Pleasure of seeing Mr. Bourdieu, and apprehend he is either gone back to London, or has taken some other Route, as I find on the Back of your last, "Forwarded from Dover, 10th April by J.B." Your Son went well from hence the Day after his Arrival here.—

I thank you much for your Remarks on the *Considerations*, &c. They appear to me very judicious & just, and show so extensive a Knowledge of the Subject, that I regret exceedingly your Purpose of leaving Europe before the Commercial Treaty is settled; and if the Commission for that Treaty arrives soon, as I expect it will in the Washington, I hope you will conclude to stay and see that important Business finished. The Congress, tho' they have given you leave to return, appear by all their Letters to consider you still in their Service, and Mr Grand holds himself ready to pay the Continuance of your Salary as you shall demand it. We are none of us otherwise paid at present, for they have omitted sending us any Bills since June last.[6] You have not mention'd to me the Name of the Author of the Considerations. Is it a Secret?—

I sympathise with you in the Loss of your Papers in America, I too having lost a great Part of mine there:[7] But I cannot with the same Justice as you do blame the Enemy. It was my own Imprudence, in trusting them to the Care of a pretended Convert to our Cause, who after my Departure for France went over to the Enemy.

5. Laurens sent that copy on March 28.
6. Those bills of exchange were sent by Lewis Morris: XL, 115.
7. The British pillaged a chest of papers that BF had stored at Joseph Galloway's country house: XXVII, 90, 605; XXXII, 610.

151

Mr Jay is preparing for his Departure,[8] and Mr Adams is still in Holland, and likely to continue there some time, being engag'd in forming the Plan of a Treaty with another Power.— My Grandson joins in best Wishes for your and the young Lady's[9] Health and Happiness, with Dear Sir, Your most obedient & most humble Servant   B. FRANKLIN

His Excy. H. Laurens Esqr

Endorsed: Doctr. Franklin 17th. April 1784 Recd 26th Answd. 6 May.

To Benjamin Vaughan

Transcript:[1] American Philosophical Society

My dear Friend,   Passy, April 17. 1784

Since I wrote to you respecting Dr. Withering, I have received a very satisfactory Letter from him.[2] So this Affair need not give you father [farther] Trouble.— I am sorry to hear you are hurt by a Fall from your Horse. I hope the Effects will not be lasting; and that by this time you are recover'd.

It will give me great Pleasure to hear that our Friend has an Opportunity of doing all the Good he wishes; as he [is] capable of doing a great deal.

I do not understand well a Paragraph of your last (dated

---

8. With Carmichael on the way to Paris to resolve the accounts of the Spanish mission, Jay had written to Benjamin Vaughan on March 21 that he was "preparing to go to New York by the first good vessel that may sail for that port": Henry P. Johnston, ed., *The Correspondence and Public Papers of John Jay* . . . (4 vols., New York and London, 1890–93), III, 117. He would not, however, be able to leave Paris until mid-May; see the annotation of Carmichael to BF, April 20; BF to John and Sarah Jay, May 13.

9. Laurens' daughter, Martha: *Laurens Papers*, XVI, 438, 464.

1. In a hand we do not recognize, and filed in the Benjamin Vaughan Collection.

2. BF's letter to Vaughan is missing. Withering's letter (or the main portion of it) is above, [before April 17].

April 2)[3] relating to the Subscription of the 39 Articles.[4] Please to explain in your next.—

It would be well not to think of a new Edition of that Collection, 'till I can from America render it more compleat. Have you ever enquir'd of Govr Franklin, what supply he can furnish? He had a great many Things.—[5]

To John Walter   Copy and transcript: Library of Congress

Sir,   Passy April 17. 1784

I have received a Book for which I understand I am obliged to you, the Introduction to Logography.—[6] I have read it with Attention, and as far as I understand it am much pleas'd with it. I do not perfectly comprehend the Arrangement of his Cases; but the Reduction of the Number of Pieces, by the Roots of Words and their different Terminations is extreamly ingenious; and I like much the Idea of cementing the Letters, instead of casting Words or Syllables, which I formerly attempted and succeeded in, having invented a Mould and Method by which I could in a

3. Missing.

4. The Thirty-Nine Articles were a set of dogmas first issued by the Church of England in 1563. It was mandatory for Anglican clergy and the members of Oxford and Cambridge to subscribe to all of the articles and for Dissenting ministers and teachers to subscribe to most of them. In 1772 BF had supported an unsuccessful petition by Dissenters to be exempted from subscription: XIX, 163–8; F. L. Cross and E. A. Livingstone, eds., *The Oxford Dictionary of the Christian Church* (rev. 3rd ed., Oxford and New York, 2005).

5. Vaughan was the editor of BF's *Political, Miscellaneous, and Philosophical Pieces* . . . (London, 1779). Soon after its publication, BF informed Vaughan that he could supply "Materials for 2. or 3. Volumes more" once he returned to America: XXXI, 210–18, 458. Thereafter, Vaughan periodically reminded BF to think about materials for an expanded edition; see XXXVI, 416.

6. Walter had written to BF about this pamphlet the previous December, but had not enclosed a copy: XLI, 371–2. He sent this one to Passy with Thomas Barclay: Walter to BF, May [*blank*], below. Written by Henry Johnson, the pamphlet was titled *An Introduction to Logography: or, the art of Arranging and Composing for Printing with Words Intire, their Radices and Terminations, instead of Single Letters* (London, 1783).

few Minutes form a Matrice and adjust it, of any Word in any Fount at pleasure, and proceed to cast from it. I send inclosed a Specimen of some of my Terminations,[7] and would willingly instruct Mr. Johnson in the Method if he desired it, but he has a better.— He mentions some Improvements of Printing that have been proposed, but takes no Notice of one published here at Paris in 1776; so I suppose he has neither seen nor heard of it. It is in a Quarto Pamphlet, intitled, *Nouveau Systéme typographique, ou Moyen de diminuer de moitié, dans toutes les Imprimeries de l'Europe le travail et les frais de Composition, de Correction et de Distribution; découvert en 1774 par Madame de ****. Frustra fit per plura quod potest fieri per pauciora. *A Paris de L'Imprimerie Royale*. M.DCC.LXXVI.— It is dedicated to the King, who was at the Expence of the Experiments. Two Commissaries were named to examine and render an Account of them; they were M. Desmarets of the Academy of Sciences, and M. Barbou an eminent Printer.[8] Their Report concludes thus—"Nous nous contenterons de dire ici que M. de St. Paul a rempli les Engagemens qu'il avoit contractés avec le Gouvernement; que ses Experiences projetées ont été conduites avec beaucoup de Méthode et d'Intelligence de sa part; & que par des calculs longs et pénibles, qui sont le fruit d'un grand nombre de combinaisons raisonnées, il en a deduit plusieurs résultats qui meritent d'être proposés aux Artistes, & qui nous paroissent propres à éclairer la pratique de L'Imprimerie actuelle, et à en abréger certainement les procédées. . . . Son projet ne peut que gagner aux contradictions qu'il essuiera sans doute, de la part des gens de l'Art. A Paris le 8 Janvier 1776."— The Pamphlet consists of 66 Pages containing a Number of Tables, of Words and Parts of Words, Explanations of those Tables, Calculations, answers to Objections, &c. I will endeavour to get one to send you if you

---

7. These "Terminations" were listed in the running inventory of types cast at Passy: XXXIV, 323–4. For an overview of BF's foundry see Ellen R. Cohn, "The Printer at Passy," in *Benjamin Franklin: In Search of a Better World*, ed. Page Talbott (New Haven and London, 2005), pp. 241–9.

8. Nicolas Desmarest (XXXVI, 384n) and Joseph-Gérard Barbou (*DBF*), a printer, bookseller, and publisher. For the latter see also Frédéric Barbier, *et al.*, eds., *Dictionnaire des imprimeurs, libraires et gens du livre à Paris, 1701–1789* (1 vol. to date, Geneva, 2007–).

desire it. Mine is bound up with others in a Volume.[9] It was after seeing this Piece that I cast the Syllables I send you a sample of. I have not heard that any of the Printers here make at present the least Use of the Invention of Madame de ***. You will observe that it pretended only to lessen the Work by one half; Mr. Johnson's Method lessens it three fourths. I should be glad to know with what the Letters are cemented. I think cementing better than casting them together, because if one Letter happens to be battered, it may be taken away and another cemented in its Place.— I received no Letter with the Pamphlet. I am Sir, Your most obedient humble Servant   (sign'd) B. FRANKLIN

Mr. Walter

From Edward Nathaniel Bancroft

ALS: American Philosophical Society

Honoured Sir   Chiswick April 17th 1784
    I have received your two very kind letters of which the first was not dated & the last dated Passy March 26th. 1784[1] & I am very happy to find that you are well & I hope your Grandson Benjamin Franklin Bache is also. I received Mr Bache's letter & answered it & which I hope, by this time, he has received.— My dear Mama, whom I have seen not long ago, has been very indifferently; but is now getting better: She has recd. a few days ago two letters from my dear Papa: the first dated the 15th of Januy. & the last dated the 25th of Januy. which informs us that he was just agoing to sail for *South Carolina* & where he expected to be in 4 or 5 days & of his expectations of being in England about the end of June next & I flatter myself to see him in June.—

---

9. BF's copy, still bound with other pamphlets, is at the APS. It was, as stated on the half-title page, an account of commissioned experiments conducted in 1775 by Francisco (François-Paul) Barletti de Saint-Paul to evaluate the new method of composing type by syllables that had been proposed by Mme de ***. The passage that BF quotes here is the extract from the commissioners' report that appears in the pamphlet, pp. vii–viii.
    1. The former has not been found; the latter is above.

My dear sisters & brothers[2] are in charming health except the last little one whose name was *Sophia* & who lately died of the Small-pox. All my sisters & brothers have been inoculated & now look as well as ever & they all join in giving their restpect-ful love to you & your beloved family.— I remain, Honoured Sir, Your affectionate Sert.   EDWD. NATH. BANCROFT

P.S. Mr. Rose & his family give their best respects to you & pray if you please give mine to your Grandson.—

Addressed: A Monsieur / Monsieur Le Docr. Franklin / Ministre plénipotentaire des / Etats. unis d'Amérique. / A Passy.

Notation: Bancroft M. Edd. Nath. Chiswich, April 17. 1784

From Louis de Boislandry and Other Offerers of Goods and Schemes
ALS: American Philosophical Society

Between March and mid-August, 1784, Franklin received far fewer unsolicited letters concerning commerce with America than he did during and immediately following the peace negotiations. The one from Louis de Boislandry, printed as a sample, is from an already established firm. As before, a number of authors sent or threatened to send copies of their work, and Franklin received accounts of several inventions.[3]

The German firm Conrad Walter & Cie. contacts Franklin on March 15 from Hildesheim. Thanks to Franklin's wisdom, all the nations of Europe now enjoy the freedom to trade with America. Formed a couple of years ago under its present name, the firm trades in wools, threads, and linens produced in lower Saxony.[4] It exports large quantities of wools to France and Brabant, while its threads and linens are sent to Holland, Spain, and England. It is from these latter countries that their merchandise would be shipped to the United States. The firm is interested in a direct exchange with American merchants and asks Franklin to recommend it to some dependable houses.

Masson cadet and Geofroy, papermakers, write on April 5 from

2. For Bancroft's siblings see XLI, 434n.
3. Unless otherwise noted, all the documents summarized in this headnote are in French, are at the APS, and produced no known response.
4. Henri Walter had offered the same wares to BF in late 1777: XXV, 72–3.

Carpentras in the papal enclave of Comtat Venaissin in southern France. They wish to establish a paper mill in New England that will manufacture sheets of a superior quality. Would Franklin intercede with Congress to help them secure the necessary funds and arrangements, as well as travel expenses for themselves and their families?

James Hill, an engraver and jeweler, sends a series of letters from London in florid, if not stilted, English.[5] He introduces his proposed scheme on June 4. As the "late Quixotian Contest" has depressed his employment, he has begun to craft and sell hair lockets and "fancies." Hoping to increase this side of his business, he is making an ornament that he wishes to send, through Franklin, to the comte d'Artois: "a Handkerchief Locket For His Princess." The locket will feature an allegorical representation of the three nations involved in the war, set in pearl and enamel. Hill hopes to be named as hairworker to the comte d'Artois, since anything in the count's taste is extremely fashionable in England. If he does not hear otherwise, Hill will send the gift to Franklin's address in four weeks; the count cannot refuse it if presented by "so Distinguish'd a Character." In a postscript, Hill adds that another of his artworks, a "monumental Trophy" to the memory of fallen Americans, has been exhibited by Mr. Scott on Tower Hill.

On Tuesday, July 20, Hill writes that the locket is now ready. He will send it the following Tuesday, either by an American traveling to Paris or else by mail. After dropping off the locket at the post office he writes again, informing Franklin that he sent the box unsealed and hopes that Franklin will admire the work—which he describes in detail—before delivering it. The seed pearl design is intended to emulate the Order of the St. Esprit. The allegory features a female figure representing America about to take up arms; Minerva, as France, holds a shield and protects her against a woman wearing plaid (Britain), whose standard is being struck by lightning, suggesting divine intervention.[6] Hill neglected to date this letter, which was probably written on Tuesday, July 27.

5. Hill gives his address as No. 9 Ball Alley Lombard Street. He was still listed at that address, as an engraver, in the 1790s: Ian Maxted, *The London Book Trades, 1775–1800: a Preliminary Checklist of Members* (Folkestone, 1977), p. 110.

6. A French translation of the description of the locket, in L'Air de Lamotte's hand, is filed with this letter at the APS. It is likely that the locket and a copy of this translation were delivered to the count by WTF, who functioned during this period as BF's representative at court. WTF called on Hill during his trip to London the following fall, and seems to have inquired about ordering a trinket. On the eve of WTF's departure, Hill,

On April 24, Desfours of Lyon, a captain of cavalry, writes what is his third letter, though he does not acknowledge that fact. Certain that Franklin will want to examine a scheme that will be of essential use to the United States, he encloses it. (His previous letters had only offered to send the scheme, pending Franklin's response.)[7] Desfours has always regretted not bearing arms for America; during the war, he was attached to a service that required him to stay in France. The enclosed work is his own small contribution to the cause, and he hopes it meets with Franklin's approval.[8]

Niel Brioudes, a lawyer in Toulouse, writes on April 28. He asks Franklin to accept as an homage a discourse on the grandeur and importance of the American Revolution, his submission to a competition held by the academy of Toulouse. If it had won a prize, he would have offered it to Franklin with more confidence, but he remains convinced that it contains some truths.[9]

Reports of negotiations of an Anglo-American commercial treaty prompt Johann Schmoldt[1] to write, in German, on July 16 from Osten in the Duchy of Bremen. He urges that the treaty should include a provision exempting the residents of the German states under the dominion of George III[2] from the 10 percent duty on the belongings of emigrants to the United States. The reciprocal right could be given to Americans who wish to settle in the king's dominions in Germany. Many people in Bremen wish to go to America, including

---

believing him to have already left, wrote WTF a letter insisting that his prices were fair, and concluded by asking WTF to convey his thanks to BF "for His Condescension to My Requests": James Hill to WTF, Nov. 25, 1784 (APS).

7. See XLI, 451–2. In those letters, he signed himself Desfours l'aîné.

8. Desfours' letter is at the Hist. Soc. of Pa. The enclosure has not been located.

9. His 41-page MS is entitled "La Grandeur et l'importance de la Révolution qui vient de s'opérer dans l'Amérique septentrionale," the theme of the prize in rhetoric for 1784 offered by the Académie des jeux floraux. The prize for that year carried an extra premium. On May 18, 1783, Vergennes announced that in order to encourage studies of the American Revolution, a sum would be added to the usual award, raising its value to 1,200 *l.t.*: Axel Duboul, *Les Deux Siècles de l'Académie des jeux floraux* (2 vols., Toulouse, 1901), I, 107, 548–9; II, 175–7.

1. In the return address he provides, Schmoldt adds to his name "Johans Sohn," *i.e.*, son of Johan. A French summary of this letter, in a hand we do not recognize, is also among BF's papers at the APS.

2. The Duchy of Bremen was ruled by the House of Hanover and therefore by the British crown.

himself, but the duty deters them. If Franklin should reply, Schmoldt begs him not to use his personal seal or otherwise give any indication that the letter came from him. Otherwise, it could cause Schmoldt trouble.

William Doyle, a clergyman of the Church of Ireland, on leave by permission of his bishop, writes in English on July 10 from Flushing, Cornwall. Though unknown to Franklin, he is no stranger to Generals Washington and Gates, Samuel Adams, and Thomas Mifflin, to whom he has sent letters similar to the present one. Doyle identifies himself as a monarchist and the author of a refutation of Paine's *Common Sense*,[3] and offers an elaborate plan for redrawing the political maps of North America and Europe. As for North America, he would jettison the "absurd" Articles of Confederation and transform the United States and Canada into one state, divided into provinces of equal size that would be governed by the same laws and be represented in Congress based on their population. Europe should likewise consolidate adjacent territories under the same government, which would reduce the potential for conflicts.[4] Doyle intends to put his scheme before the English king and the stadholder. He will take no credit for it, as his only ambition is world peace.

Bouébe, writing from Paris on August 9, does not doubt that Vergennes, who had previously asked him for several memoirs about his invention, has communicated these memoirs to Franklin. They are of interest to the navy and even to places on earth where the water is unhealthy. Bouébe hopes that Franklin will approve of what he now encloses, and will grant him an interview either that same day or at some other time.[5]

3. Doyle advertised for subscribers to this work, titled *Good Sense*, in New York in the summer of 1780, but it does not appear to have been published: Michael J. O'Brien, "Some Pre-Revolutionary Ferrymen of Staten Island," *Jour. of the American Irish Hist. Soc.*, XV (1917), 393.

4. Doyle developed some of the same ideas in a dedicatory letter to the Prince of Wales (whom he mentions in his letter to BF as another of his illustrious contacts): *Some Account of the British Dominions Beyond the Atlantic...* (London, [1770?]), pp. i–vii. BF endorsed the address sheet of the present letter, "Wm Doyle".

5. Bouébe's letter, without its enclosure, is at the Hist. Soc. of Pa. In 1787, he sent the same proposal (also missing) to TJ. TJ answered Bouébe that although his "procès" and "machines &c." appeared to be useful, Congress did not support such projects, and it would not be worth his while to apply to the individual states for exclusive manufacturing rights: *Jefferson Papers*, XII, 119, 164, 196–7, 217.

Among BF's papers at the APS is a one-page printed memoir advertising

Finally, we take note of a one-page undated printed prospectus for a combination movement designed by Lafontaine: "Prospectus du mouvement de combinaison." The mechanism can be adapted to all kinds of locks, from the simplest to the most complicated, and can be fitted to locks already made. After the Académie des sciences examined and approved the invention, the government granted Lafontaine a monetary award and an exclusive right to manufacture his device for fifteen years. On the verso of the sheet, a note in an unknown hand (perhaps that of the inventor himself) announces that the sieur Lafontaine has just opened a subscription: he will sell three hundred locks at thirty-six *livres* apiece, of which half must be paid in advance, to be completed by January 1, 1785.[6]

Monsieur   Paris le 18. avril 1784

Je me présentai l'anné derniére chez vous appuyé d'une lettre de Monsieur Vieillard de Passy,[7] rélativement à diverses opérations de commerce qu'une compagnie se proposait de faire avec l'amérique Septentrionale. Elle a commencé depuis ce tems quelques opérations dont plusieurs ont été assez heureuses, d'autres n'ont point eu de succés. Elle attribue ce defaut de réussite, prémiérément a la concurrence générale eprouvée au

---

an invention by an unnamed "auteur" who may possibly have been Bouébe: it announces a machine that produces fresh water on shipboard, and can also serve as a fire pump. The machine received the approbation of the Conseil de Marine on Jan. 18, 1783. Interested parties may apply to the author chez M. Rouen Notaire, rue neuve des Petits-Champs, Paris.

6. The inventor was Claude Lafontaine: *Catalogue général des collections du Conservatoire royal des arts et métiers* (Paris, 1818), p. 61. Le Roy and Brisson were the academicians assigned to evaluate the invention, and their report was submitted on March 27, 1784: Académie des sciences, *Procès-verbaux*, CIII (1784), 75–7. The subscription was announced in the *Jour. de Paris* on July 25, 1784.

7. Le Veillard's letter of introduction of Jan. 12, 1783, identified Boislandry as a relative by marriage and a merchant from L'Aigle (Normandy); it is summarized in XXXVIII, 479. The Boislandry family ran an extensive textile business based in L'Aigle, with branches in Orléans and Paris and customers in Spain, Italy, and England: E.-B. Dubern, "Boislandry, député aux Etats-Généraux de 1789," *Annales historiques de la Révolution française*, XV (1938), 345–8.

moment de la paix, secondément a la médiocrité des entréprises qui n'etant pas assez considérables, ne permettaient pas d'entre-ténir dans le pays un agent immédiat. Comme elle est determinée à augmenter & à etendre autant qu'il séra possible les rélations d'un commerce qui doit a la fin devenir réciproquément utile, il à été résolu qu'un des principaux intéressés se fixérait dans celui des ports de l'amerique qui sérait le plus convénable à leurs spéculations; mais avant tout on desirérait avoir sur ces objets les eclaircissémens que votre Excellence voudra bien procurer. Je la prie donc d'avoir la bonté de m'indiquer pour l'un des jours de cette sémaine un moment d'audiance à l'heure qui lui conviendra, & s'il se peut vendredi prochain, comptant partir ce jour la pour l'angléterre.

J'ai l'honneur d'etre avec les sentimens du plus profond [respect] Monsieur Votre trés humble & trés obeissant Serviteur.

Ls. DE BOISLANDRY
Negt. Rue du chevalier du Guet

From Henry Laurens: Two Letters

(I) and (II) ALS: Library of Congress; copy: University of South Carolina Library

I.

No. 32. Norfolk Street London 18th. April 1784

Dear Sir.

I beg leave to refer to my Letter of the 7th. Inst. by the hands of Mr. Bourdieu.

Mr. Hartley call'd upon me the 13th. at Bath & return'd a verbal answer. "The King had ordered him immediately to Paris for exchanging the Ratifications." & he accordingly goes & will do me the honor of delivering this.

Nothing further done by Administration respecting American Intercourse & Commerce, but 'tis said they are doing. A judicios intelligent friend who has been much consulted call'd upon me last Night, & assured me "nothing liberal or to good effect would be done, or he very much fear'd so, that he was tired & would be done with them. Mr. Pitt is well disposed having been well advised but the weight of the Council is against him." I feel no regret on this account, difficulties will have an excellent effect on our side, I think my Countrymen appear to most advantage when they have a Rub to encounter & they seem to be at this moment taking measures which should have been adopted upon the first appearance of the Proclama: of 2d July '83. The West India Merchants & Planters, every sensible Man in Trade with whom I converse, every unemployed Manufacturer & many who dread loss of future orders are uneasy. & all will come right when we determine to act right.[8] I am come to London tho' in poor health to provide for embarkation & hope to get away about the 15th. or 20th. May. I have the honor to be With the highest Esteem & Respect Dear sir Your Obedient humble servant   HENRY LAURENS

This will be accompanied by two of the latest News Papers.

I see last Night's Gazette contains a Proclamation or enlargement of the term for American intercourse to the 20th June.[9] But this I count Nothing probably Parliament are to be consulted. If I can get one of the Gazettes in time it shall go with this but no doubt Mr. Hartley will have a Copy.

His Excellency. B. Franklin Esquire &c &c

8. In March, Pitt created a new Committee of Council on Trade and Plantations to review American trade policy. West Indian planters and merchants lobbied against the system established by the Order in Council of July 2, 1783 (XL, 289n), which restricted trade between the islands and the United States to British-built, British-owned, and British-manned ships. Despite these efforts and Pitt's own preference for a more liberal policy, he endorsed the committee's report, which was issued at the end of May and recommended the continuation of the restrictions: John Ehrman, *The Younger Pitt* (3 vols., New York and Stanford, Calif., 1969–96), I, 307–8, 332–6. Laurens' "judicios intelligent friend" might have been Benjamin Vaughan.

9. In its issue of April 13–17 the *London Gaz.* printed the April 16 Order in Council extending existing trade regulations to June 20.

II.

P.S. to a Letter of this date 18th. April 1784
already deliver'd to Mr. Hartley's care.

Dear Sir

In writing in haste this Morning fearing to lose the opportunity an Instance of egregious weakness & folly which I learn'd from my friend last evening escap'd my memory, but as Mr. Hartley stays an hour longer I will communicate it, although I hear you say this is nothing extraordinary in these people.

Some of them & from circumstances attending, there must be a Majority, meaning no Man Eastward of Charing Cross, still entertain an opinion that America, say, the United States must & will infallibly return to Great Britain & upon her own terms— What new Maggot has bitten them? See say they & assert it very possitively, there's already a defection of four States, only Nine could be convened for Ratifying the definitive Treaty.[1] I don't think this is merely the effect of ignorance, or not in all of them, therefore to me it proves a determin'd resolution in such, not to return to America, but to urge a Commercial in hopes in time of provoking an hostile War & of improving upon late errors. Happy for us if this be the design, their horns are shortned, & their hands restrain'd by manyfold ties, we nevertheless may read the Heart & should be upon our Guard.

Mr. Hartley had not the Gazette, I have put one into his hands with your Name to it, the Proclamation is almost verbatim a Copy of the former.[2] This really, considering they are inform'd of the resentment on our side, looks hardy.

God bless you Sir.   HENRY LAURENS

His Excellency Doctor Franklin

1. For the difficulties in assembling the requisite number of states for the ratification of the peace treaty see XLI, 407, 456n; BF to Laurens, April 29, below.

2. *I.e.*, the order of Dec. 26: XLI, 579n.

From Jean-Baptiste Le Roy

ALS: American Philosophical Society

Lundy après midy [April 19, 1784?][3]
Mon Illustre docteur Je comptois bien avoir Lhonneur de vous aller voir ce Soir et de me dèdommager du tems que jai passe Sans aller vous attaquer ou me deffendre aux echcs Mais malheureusement un petit accès de fièvre m'empêche de Sortir. Une autre raison qui me faisoit desirer d'avoir Lhonneur de vous voir ce Soir c'etoit pour vous rappeller que Les Commissaires viennent diner demain mardy chez moi. J'espere et je me flatte que vous ne les abandonnerez pas dans cette Occasion nous aurons grand Soin de vous et ce n'est qu'a un pas de votre Jardin je crois que je n'ai pas besoin d'ajouter combien Monsieur Franklin votre petit Fils nous fera de plaisir. Jespere qu'il Se regarde toujours comme prié chez moi.[4]

Recevez Mon Illustre docteur les Sincères assurrances de tous les Sentimens de tendresse que je vous ai vouès pour la vie

LE ROY

Addressed: A Monsieur / Monsieur Le Docteur Franklin

Notation: Le Roy—

3. This undated letter urges BF to attend a dinner for "Les Commissionaires" at Le Roy's home in Passy. Because of the references to commissioners, to BF's fragile health and immobility, and to Le Roy's entertaining at his Passy residence, the invitation most likely dates from the spring or summer of 1784. BF and Le Roy served on two commissions that year: the Académie des sciences commission to examine the installation of lightning rods on powder magazines, and the royal commission to investigate animal magnetism. We tentatively date this invitation on the earliest of the possible Mondays associated with the former investigation. April 19 was the Monday before the lightning-rod commission submitted its report, published below under the date of April 24.
4. On another occasion, WTF issued an invitation to Le Roy and "the commissioners" to dine at BF's house. Le Roy answered this now-missing note, writing to WTF in English on an unspecified "Thursday morning": he would inform the others and was sure that they would all be pleased to accept this invitation to dine with BF and WTF the following day. APS.

From Charles Thomson   ALS: American Philosophical Society

Dear Sir,   Annapolis 19 April 1784

In my last I informed you that I had taken measures to gain information respecting Mr Marggrander and the other persons enquired after.[5] The enclosed is a copy of letter I have received from our old neighbour Reuben Haines in answer to my enquiries touching Marggrander.[6] With respect to the others I have yet heard nothing—

Give me leave my dear Sir to recommend to your friendly notice and protection Mr Isaac Norris a son of our old friend Norris.[7] He is young & inexperienced but of a good disposition and with proper care may become a useful member of Society. The last letter I had from him informs me that he was at Leige in Flanders, but that he intended to visit Paris. Should he still be at Leige I would take it as a favour if you would send him a letter to introduce him to proper company and to make his travels useful to himself and to his country. He left home too young and too little informed respecting the affairs of his own country he will therefore stand in need of more advice abroad, and I know none more capable of advising him or whose advice will have more weight with him than yours, as he has a strong desire of being under your patronage.

I am with the greatest Esteem & respect Dear Sir Your affectionate old friend & obedt humble Servant   CHAS THOMSON

Doctr B. Franklin,

Notation: Chas Thomson Esqr to B F. Ap. 19. 84.

5. Thomson's last letters, sent by different couriers but covering the same material, were written on Jan. 14 and Jan. 15: XLI, 463–4, 472–4.

6. The copy, in a secretarial hand and written on the same sheet as Thomson's letter, is of Haines's reply of March 24, 1784. Haines writes that Marggrander had worked for him for several years as a brewer and cooper but left Philadelphia in 1777. From what Haines could determine, Marggrander then moved to Lancaster County and served in the militia.

7. Thomson had recommended Norris the previous September: XLI, 45–6. He also wrote on Norris' behalf to Jay and Jefferson: Smith, *Letters,* XXI, 693–4, 695, 746n.

To Jonathan Williams, Sr.

ALS: Biblioteca Labronica

Dear Kinsman, Passy, April 20. 1784

The Bearer, Mr Biederman, is recommended to me by Persons of Distinction, as a Gentleman of Worth & very respectable Character, charged with the Concerns and Interest of many principal Manufacturers and Merchants in Saxony, between which Country and ours I should be glad to see a commercial Intercourse opened and established, as it might be advantageous to both.[8] I recommend him therefore very earnestly to your Civilities, and to all the Information & Advice that as a Stranger may be useful to him, wherein you will very much oblige Your affectionate Uncle B FRANKLIN

Jonathan Williams Esqr

John Adams to Franklin and John Jay

ALS: Columbia University Library; copy: Massachusetts Historical Society

Gentlemen The Hague April 20. 1784

I have just now received the Letter which Dr Franklin did me the Honour to write me on the 16th. with the Copy of the Treaty with Sweeden. I have before inclosed the King of Prussias Project of a Treaty, prepared as I am assured by his Minister with his own Hand in his private Cabinet.[9]

---

8. This is the second time that BF recommended Biedermann to Williams; see the annotation of the March 29 letter from Graf von Brühl. Biedermann was back in Hamburg by August, 1785. Although his business ventures in Philadelphia were unsuccessful, his sanguine assessment of the prospects of trade with America contradicted the gloomy reports of Saxony's official commercial agent, Philipp Thieriot (XL, 350–1, 555). Biedermann later claimed that Saxon government officials had led him to believe that he would be chosen for the mission assigned to Thieriot. Instead, Biedermann had to go into debt to finance his journey and went bankrupt: Christian Deuling, "Friedrich Justin Bertuch und der Handel mit Nordamerika," in *Friedrich Justin Bertuch (1747–1822): Verleger, Schriftsteller und Unternehmer im klassischen Weimar,* ed. Gerhard R. Kaiser and Siegfried Seifert (Tübingen, 2000), pp. 199–205.

9. Graf von der Schulenburg-Kehnert (*ADB*), known to BF as the baron de Schulenburg, was the Prussian minister for war and maritime trade. He

I believe it has been reserved to the present Age when the subtilties of Aristotle and the schools are transferred from Theology to Politicks, to discover Room for a Doubt in the Construction of the Armistice. And therefore We shall Search in vain in any Admiralty, for a Precedent. The Words are "Le terme Sera d'un mois depuis la manche et les mers du Nord, jusqu'aux Isles Canaries inclusivement, Soit dans l'Ocean, Soit dans la Mediterranée."[1]

This Limit is to extend to the Southermost Point of the Southernmost Canary Island, from the Channell. This is the Extent from North to South.— What is to be the Extent from East to West? is it to have none. is it to be confined to a mathematical Line, running from the Middle of the Channel to the remotest Part of the remotest Canary? or is it to be a Space as Wide as the Channel, running from it to that Canary? or is it to be as wide as that Island. if none of these Constructions have common sense in them, what can We suppose to have been the Meaning of the Contracting Parties? They have ascertained the Space very exactly from North to South, and as they have left the Extent from East to West without limits, it is very clear they intended it should be unlimited and reach all round the Globe, at least where there is any Ocean or Mediterranean.

I have the Honour to be, Gentlemen your most obedient and most humble servant   JOHN ADAMS

Their Excellencies Benjamin Franklin Esq John Jay Esqr.

Addressed in another hand: à / Leurs Excellences / Messieurs B. Franklin et J. Jay / Ministres Plenipotentiaires des Etats Unis / de l'Amerique / à / Passy / près / Paris— / France

---

corresponded with the American commissioners in early 1777 about establishing commercial relations, after receiving from them a copy of the Declaration of Independence: XXIII, 327–8, 495–6, 591–2. In a letter of March 7, 1784, Frederick instructed him to carefully review the Swedish-American treaty and to prepare a draft suited to Prussia: Geheimes Staatsarchiv Preußischer Kulturbesitz.

1. A quotation from Article 22 of the preliminary British-French peace treaty that also applied to the armistice between Britain and the United States: XXXIX, 7n, 190–2; Parry, *Consolidated Treaty Series*, XLVIII, 238–9.

Endorsed by John Jay: Mr. Adams' Letter of 20 Ap. 1784 to Mrs. Franklin & Jay

From William Carmichael[2] ALS: American Philosophical Society

Dear Sir   Paris 20th April 1784

Inclosed I have the honor to send you a Letter from the house of Drouilhet advising me of their having drawn upon your Excellency for £s [*l.t.*] 13447.5. *s.* at 60 days date making the Sum of 54000 Rials de Vn. [Veillon] or 2700 Dollars for the payment of a bill drawn by Mr Morris on me which bill became due since my Departure from Madrid.—[3] I intended to have had the pleasure of waiting on you this morning but am prevented by a bilious vomiting which confines me to the house & I am afraid will the whole day.

I have the honor to be with Much respect your Excellencys Most Obedt & Most Humble Sert[4]   WM. CARMICHAEL

His Excy. Benjn. Franklin—

2. Carmichael had been summoned to Paris by Jay to settle the accounts of the Spanish mission with Thomas Barclay: XLI, 158n, 569n. He arrived on March 27, but the audit was held up first by Barclay's delayed return from England and then by Carmichael's procrastination as well as Jay's charges that Carmichael had mismanaged Jay's personal account. Barclay finally settled the personal and public accounts in mid-May, allowing the Jay family to return to America: *Jay Papers,* III, 552–4.

3. The enclosed April 5 letter from Drouilhet & Cie., the bankers to the Spanish mission (XXXIX, 463n), requested BF to pay the money to Jean Frans. Lopez (APS). Grand paid the bill on June 14: Account XXVII (XXXII, 4).

4. Among BF's papers is an unsigned note in Carmichael's hand, addressed to "His Excy. B. Franklin" and dated "Tuesday 12 OClock": "Not being in the least acquainted with the manner of making out Memorials I can not pretend to say whither or no the enclosed will answer the purpose. Shall take the liberty to call tomorrow or next day that in case it be not right I may new model it as you think proper." The note was undoubtedly written during Carmichael's 1784 stay in Paris. While it could have been written on Tuesday, March 30, we think a date of [April?] more likely.

From David Barclay   ALS: American Philosophical Society

Respected Friend   London 21st: 4th/mo: 1784.

My Nephews Daniel Bell & David Barclay[5] being likely to spend a few days at Paris, I take the freedom to introduce them to Thee, as well for the favour of Thy Countenance, as to bring me Information of Thy Welfare—[6] The long Winter and uncommonly late Spring have been disadvantageous to many Constitutions, in wch I have had a Share, & hope, Thine has not suffered by it.

I am Respectfully Thy Affectionate Friend.

DAVID BARCLAY.

Addressed: Honble Benjamin Franklin / &c &c / Passy.

Notation: Barclay David, London 1784.—

5. Daniel Bell (1753–1834) was a son of Barclay's sister Catherine and her husband, Daniel Bell. The other nephew, David (b. 1763), was a son of John Barclay (IX, 190–1n): Charles W. Barclay, Hubert F. Barclay, and Alice Wilson-Fox, comps., *A History of the Barclay Family* . . . (3 vols., London, 1924–34), III, 243, 248, 251; [Edward M. Chadwick], *The Chadwicks of Guelph and Toronto and their Cousins* (Toronto, 1914), p. 67.

6. Daniel Bell had also been charged by his uncle John Barclay to deliver to BF a letter that Barclay's firm had received from one Thomas Blackburn of the Isle of Thanet, Kent. Blackburn wished to be appointed U.S. agent or consul along the Kentish coast, where American ships were running aground on the shoals and being attacked. Blackburn asked the Barclays to recommend him to President of Congress Mifflin. John Barclay, through Bell, evidently asked BF to place the matter before Congress. According to Bell's later account, he also delivered to BF a batch of "Papers." Filed with Blackburn's letter at the APS is an undated, incomplete memorandum in Blackburn's hand explaining how he could help American captains, and asking that the consulship be procured from "Mr Hancok": Daniel Bell to BF, July 29, 1785; Thomas Blackburn to John and Robert Barclay & Co., April 6, 1784; undated, incomplete memorandum; all at the APS.

From Jacob Duché, Jr.[7]   ALS: American Philosophical Society

Sir   Asylum, Lambeth, April 21, 1784

I take the Liberty of addressing your Excellency on a Subject, in which I am sure you will find your Philosophy as well as
Humanity not a little interested.

The eldest Daughter of Mr George Meade, a respectable
Merchant & Citizen of Philadelphia,—a young Lady of about
15 Years of Age,[8] has now been above Six Months in England,
under the Care of some of the most eminent Physicians, for
the Recovery of her Health. Her Complaint is of the Epileptic
Kind; and her Fits return at Intervals of a Week or Fortnight, &
sometimes of a longer Continuance. They began, when she was
7 or 8 Years old. At first they had only the Appearance of Gid-
diness, and a short Absence of Mind, and were supposed to be
occasioned by over Exercise in a Swing with other Children—
They have been increasing ever since; till they are now generally attended with some Degree of Convulsion—

Every Method of Cure, that could be thought of, was tried
by the Physicians at Philada without Success. Sir Richard Jebb,
old Dr Pitcairn, and your Friend Dr Watson[9] have been consulted since her Arrival here. Various Courses of Medicine have
been ineffectually tried. A Perpetual Blister as it is called, on her
Back, has proved useless: And she is now under the Experiment
of a large Issue, which, we are apprehensive, will have as little
Efficacy as the former Attempts.

Under these Circumstances her Friends have received Letters
from Philada by the New-York Packet, dated March the 1st last,
from her Father, in which he earnestly desires, that she may be
sent immediately over to France, in order to be put under the

7. This former Philadelphia cleric, who had opposed the Revolution and
left for England in 1777, renewed his acquaintance with BF after the preliminary articles were signed: XXXIX, 72–5, 491.

8. The eldest daughter of George Meade (*DAB*) was most likely Catherine Mary Meade: John H. Campbell, *History of the Friendly Sons of St. Patrick* . . . (Philadelphia, 1892), p. 121.

9. Sir Richard Jebb and William Pitcairn were both distinguished
practitioners in London affiliated with the Royal College of Physicians:
ODNB. William Watson had long been a student of electricity, and was
instrumental in introducing BF's work on the subject in England: III, 457–8.

Direction of a Monsr *Le Drue*, known in England by the Name of *Comus*,[1] who, it seems, has published a Pamphlet, containing an Account of some extraordinary Cures of the Epilepsy, by the Electric Shock. The Physicians & Surgeons here, I believe, are not acquainted with his mode of applying the Stroke: And they apprehend it to be a dangerous Experiment. Mr Meade, however, is extremely earnest to have the Experiment tried.

A Lady of Mr Meade's Acquaintance is to be applied to, to accompany his Daughter, and return with her, after proper Time allowed for the Experiments to take Effect.

But as Mr Meade has written to me on the Subject, and wishes me to assist his Correspondent with my Advice in this Matter, I thought I could not serve him more effectually, than by endeavouring to obtain from your Excellency the best Information relative to this new Parisian Experiment, which could not have escaped your minute Enquiry & Examination; and, which I could wish might not be hazarded, in the present Case, without your Approbation.

I should be much honoured by an early Intimation of your Thoughts on this Subject; and would choose to postpone the young Lady's Excursion to France, which must be attended with great Expence to her Father, 'till I can be indulged with your Opinion and Advice. Your Tenderness & Delicacy will naturally suggest the Propriety of concealing the young Lady's Name.

Mrs Duché and my young Folks desire to be affectionately remembered; and we shall all be happy to hear of your Health, and that of Mr & Mrs Bache and their Children—

I have the Pleasure of informing you, that I expect my dear aged Father in one of the first Ships from Philada— As there was no Probability of his Son's ever returning to his Native Land,[2] he has disposed of Part of his Property, and arranged the Rest, so as to embark in May next—

1. For this popular Parisian physician who specialized in electrical therapies see XLI, 120.

2. Duché did return to Philadelphia in 1792: Whitfield J. Bell, Jr., comp., *Patriot-Improvers: Biographical Sketches of Members of the American Philosophical Society* (3 vols., Philadelphia, 1997–2010), II, 17.

I have the Honour to be, Sir, With sincerest Respect Your Excellency's most obedient Friend & Servant   J. DUCHÉ

Notation: Duché, April 21. 1784.

From Gaetano Filangieri

Translation of ALS in Italian:[3] Historical Society of Pennsylvania

Sir,   La Cava, April 21, 1784

On the 20th of November of last year, 1783, I sent you the fourth volume of my work on *La scienza della legislazione,*[4] and a few days later I shipped, via Marseille, a trunk containing more copies of the same volume, in the same quantity as the other volumes you had previously received through Mr. Pio.[5] Before that, I had sent you a copy of the third volume as well as another trunk, addressed to Mr. Pio, with the corresponding number of copies of that volume.[6] However, I did not receive, either from you or from Mr. Pio, a confirmation that these books of mine had actually reached their destination. This silence from both of you makes me fear they are lost, and since in this case I would like to repair the loss, please send a response on this matter. My work proceeds quickly in my solitude, where all possible causes of delay are removed by the isolation that separates me from the rest of mankind. I hope to receive news of your precious health, and I remind you of the most sincere admiration and respect from Your most humble and devoted servant,

GAETANO FILANGIERI

3. Prepared by Roberto Lopez. The Italian original is published in Antonio Pace, *Benjamin Franklin and Italy* (Philadelphia, 1958), pp. 401–2, and in Eugenio Lo Sardo, ed., *Il mondo nuovo e le virtù civili: l'espistolario di Gaetano Filangieri (1772–1788)* (Naples, 1999), pp. 260–1.

4. Filangieri's cover letter is dated Oct. 27. Luigi Pio, in Paris, forwarded the volume to BF on Dec. 12: XLI, 148, 286. Perhaps Nov. 20 was the day Filangieri sent the book to Pio.

5. In March, 1783, Pio informed BF that 12 copies of the first two volumes of Filangieri's work had arrived for him: XXXIX, 360–1.

6. BF's personal copy of the third volume was forwarded by Pio on Aug. 10, 1783: XL, 460. No record of either of the trunks has been found.

From Samuel Cooper Johonnot

ALS: American Philosophical Society

Hon'd Sir— Boston 21st April 1784

I arriv'd here the 12th Jany., after a Voyage, & Journey, exceedingly laborious, & disagreeable.— Fourteen Days sooner, I could have had the Satisfaction, of seeing my Grandpappa.— Why did I arrive later?— I acknowledge the Fault. It will not bear Reflection:— May the Lesson prove as useful, as 'tis severe. I really deserv'd a harder Stroke, than Your friendly Reproach, which I rec'd at Nantes.[7] From the 16th Septr., to the 22'd of Decr., I was floating between Nantes, & Baltimore. I am now in Boston, having had my Degree of Batchelor of Arts, last Year.[8] I expect to study, 12 or 18 Months, as a Graduate, at Harvard College: then, to enter Judge Sullivan's Office, as a Candidate for the Bar.[9] My hon'd Grandpappa has left Me one Third of his estate, the income of which, will, it is expected, with Œconomy, compleat my Education; & at 21, set Me out handsomely in the

---

7. XL, 488. Johonnot's grandfather, Samuel Cooper, died on Dec. 29: XLI, 372.

8. In June, 1783, Samuel Cooper (a member of the Harvard Corporation) arranged for Harvard to award Johonnot a bachelors degree in absentia at the upcoming commencement to credit him for his studies in Geneva: Cooper to Johonnot, June 23, 1783 (Yale University Library); Charles W. Akers, *The Divine Politician: Samuel Cooper and the American Revolution in Boston* (Boston, 1982), pp. 168, 183, 215, 356, 426n.

9. James Sullivan (XXXVIII, 77n) was a close friend of Cooper's. On Dec. 17, 1783, upon hearing that young Johonnot would be sailing into Philadelphia, he addressed a letter to him there, urging him to come to Boston as soon as possible on account of his grandfather's failing health. Johonnot endorsed it as not having been received in time: Yale University Library. A few weeks after Cooper's death, Sullivan received permission from the Suffolk County bar to take Johonnot "into his office as a student": George Dexter, ed., *Suffolk County Bar Book: 1770–1805* (Cambridge, Mass., 1882), p. 19. Johonnot practiced law in Portland, Maine, from 1789 to 1791, and subsequently moved to Demerara (part of present-day Guyana), where he became U.S. consul. He died there in 1806: James D. Hopkins, *An Address to the Members of the Cumberland Bar* . . . (Portland, 1833), p. 59; *Jefferson Papers*, XXV, 308, 309n; W. W. Abbot, *et al.*, eds., *The Papers of George Washington*, Presidential Series (18 vols. to date, Charlottesville and London, 1987–), XII, 233n.

world. Meanwhile, Sir, let me beg the continuation of your useful Correspondence; & though I may have been heedless, I still presume, to ask your good Advice. My future Behaviour will prove whether I deserve it.—

As I know Ben would not receive an Apology, for not writing to Him, I will not make One. A Letter, shortly, will be the best Method of appeasing Him. You have so many abler Correspondents, that it would be equally presumptuous & useless, to write any thing concerning the state of Affairs; But, though many write with more Elegance, none can with more Gratitude, Esteem, & Affection,—than Your humble Servant,

SAM'L COOPER JOHONNOT.

P.S. Grandmama acknowledges the Receipt of your Letter, dated 26 of December;[1] & desires her best Regards. Please to remember me affectionately, to your two Grandsons.

Addressed: A Son Excellence / Monsr. le Doctr. Franklin / Ministre Plenipotentiàire des Etats / Unis de l'Amerique, près sa Majesté / tres Chretienne. / à Passy près Paris.

To Benjamin Webb
Transcript: Library of Congress

Dear Sir   Passy, April 22d. 1784

I received your's of the 15th. Instant, and the Memorial it inclosed. The account they give of your situation grieves me. I send you herewith a Bill for Ten Louis d'ors. I do not pretend to *give* such a Sum. I only *lend* it to you. When you shall return to your Country with a good Character, you cannot fail of getting into some Business that will in time enable you to pay all your Debts: In that Case, when you meet with another honest Man in similar Distress, you must pay me by lending this Sum to him; enjoyning him to discharge the Debt by a like operation when he shall be able and shall meet with such another opportunity.— I hope it may thus go thro' many hands before it meets with a

1. Samuel Cooper's widow was Judith Bulfinch Cooper. BF had dined with her on at least one occasion, in 1775: XXII, 387n; Akers, *The Divine Politician*, pp. 18, 208. The letter she here acknowledges was written to her husband: XLI, 350–2.

Knave that will stop its Progress. This is a Trick of mine for doing a deal of good with a little money.[2] I am not rich enough to afford *much* in good works and so am obliged to be cunning and make the most of a *little*.— With best wishes for the success of your Memorial and your future prosperity, I am, Dear Sir, Your most obdt. Servt.   B. F.

Please to present my affectionate Respects to Mr. & Madam Pigot.—

Mr. Benjn. Webb.

If Life's Compared to a Feast

AD: New York Public Library; transcript: Library of Congress

William Temple Franklin found this poem among his grandfather's papers and claimed that it was entitled "B. F.'s Adieu!"[3] The sole extant autograph, written on a small sheet of paper, has no title. Beautifully penned, as though intended for presentation, it fills the sheet, with the dateline placed in the bottom left corner. Whether the top of the sheet originally bore a title and was subsequently trimmed is not known.

This verse takes as its point of departure a poem by Isaac Watts that Franklin had reprinted in the *Pennsylvania Gazette* some fifty years earlier along with the essay in which it appeared.[4] The essay tells of an indolent, self-indulgent man who has an epiphany at the age of thirty. Devoting himself thereafter to leading a useful existence, he performs good works and dies content in the knowledge that his life was of value. At the end of the essay, Watts quotes in Latin and loosely translates three "Scraps of Horace."[5] The one that Franklin references is the following:

2. BF had made a similar loan to William Nixon in 1781: XXXV, 445.

3. WTF, *Memoirs*, I, 417.

4. The essay, titled "The Waste of Life," appeared in Watts's *Reliquiæ Juveniles: Miscellaneous Thoughts in Prose and Verse* . . . (London, 1734), pp. 57–63. As noted in II, 150, BF reprinted it in the *Pa. Gaz.*, Nov. 18, 1736.

5. BF quoted, evidently from memory and somewhat inaccurately, a couplet from another of these "Scraps of Horace" in "Information to Those Who Would Remove to America": XLI, 602.

> Life's but a Feast; and when we die,
> *Horace* would say, if he were by,
> Friend, thou hast eat and drunk enough,
> 'Tis Time now to be marching off:
> Then like a well-fed Guest depart,
> With cheerful Looks, and Ease at Heart;
> Bid all your Friends Good Night, and say,
> *You've done the Business of the Day.*

Temple published Franklin's poem beneath what he characterized as "the original (with various corrections)" of the epitaph Franklin wrote in 1728.[6] Although the autograph of that version of the epitaph has not survived, both it and the autograph verse published here were owned by the bookseller and collector William Upcott in the early nineteenth century. Around 1836, Upcott permitted a one-page facsimile to be made of the two pieces, which was subsequently published.[7] On the facsimile, they appear as Temple placed them: the epitaph on top, followed by a rule; the poem at the bottom, with the dateline in the lower left corner of the sheet. At the top of the sheet, above the epitaph, appears the title "Epitaph written 1728," in a hand that imitates Franklin's. Whoever wrote this title took it from Temple's edition, where it was an obvious editorial insertion, set in italics within square brackets.

The Upcott facsimile has been the cause of much confusion. Lyman Butterfield, in his comprehensive study of the handwritten and printed epitaphs, regarded it as proof that Franklin had written both pieces on the same sheet of paper on April 22, 1784.[8] We disagree. A close comparison of the handwriting of the autograph verse (which Butterfield did not see) with that of the facsimile of the epitaph reveals enough differences to convince us that the two pieces were written with different pens at different times. Moreover, But-

6. For the three known epitaphs see I, 109–11.
7. The facsimile appeared in the second part, published in 1836, of a series of facsimiles and engravings issued between 1835 and 1840 by Charles J. Smith and his successor (who released the final two installments after Smith's death in 1838). A compilation was first published under Smith's name in 1840: Charles J. Smith, *Historical and Literary Curiosities* . . . (London, 1840), plate 18; *The Mirror of Literature, Amusement, and Instruction*, XXVII (1836), 163.
8. L. H. Butterfield, "B. Franklin's Epitaph," *New Colophon: a Book-Collector's Miscellany*, III (1950), 12–14. Butterfield criticized WTF for creating the impression in *Memoirs* that the items were found on different sheets, calling it a "deliberate obfuscation."

terfield and many scholars who relied on his judgment, including our predecessors, did not recognize that the facsimile's title was forged.[9] Nonetheless, it is possible that Franklin wrote this version of the epitaph in late 1783 or early 1784, as he anticipated his departure from France and reviewed his early life in preparation for resuming his autobiography.

April 22. 1784.—

If Life's compared to a Feast,
Near Fourscore Years I've been a Guest,
I've been regaled with the best,
And feel quite satisfyd.
'Tis time that I retire to Rest;
Landlord, I thank ye!— Friends, Good Night.

From Robert Pigott   ALS: American Philosophical Society

Hotel d'Angleterre [Fri?]day 4 O Clock.

Dear Sir   [between April 22 and May 18, 1784?][1]

I had proposed myself the honor of dining to day at Passy, but Business of the day has prevented me of having that Pleasure As I propose going to England early on Sunday morning, I shall be proud to receive your commands and of executing any of your orders As I am with the greatest Respect & Regard dear Sir Your most faithful & obed Sert.   R. PIGOTT

Addressed: A Son Excellence / Dr. Franklyn / Passy.

9. See I, 110, where the editors puzzled over what they believed to be BF's own statement that the epitaph was written in 1728.

1. The best we can do with this letter, given that the day of the week is nearly illegible ("Friday" is highly conjectural), is to assign to it a plausible range of dates. When writing to Benjamin Webb on April 22 (above), BF believed Pigott to be in Geneva. By Tuesday, May 18, when Webb wrote to BF (below), Pigott had written Webb three letters from Paris, the last of which indicated that he intended to leave for London the next day. As Pigott here tells BF that he intends to leave for England on "Sunday," his third letter to Webb was probably written on a Saturday. May 8 is the most likely Saturday, given how long it took for a letter to reach Geneva from Paris.

To Jan Ingenhousz

ALS: Myron Kaller & Associates, Inc., Asbury Park, New Jersey (1989)

Dear Friend,   Passy, April 23. 1784.

I did intend to have written you a long Letter by the good Bishop,[2] but cannot now accomplish it.— You will however have it very soon.— Fearing that the Seeds for your Friend might not arrive in time, to be planted this Spring, and having received a Box for some of my Acquaintance here, I sent a Part to you, to be dispos'd of as you please, supposing you might oblige him with them. I hope they got safe to hand.—[3] I am, ever, my dear Friend, Yours most affectionately   B Franklin

Dr Ingenhauss.

From Cadet de Vaux   ALS: American Philosophical Society

Monsieur   ce 23 Avril 1784

J'ai l'honneur de vous Envoyer l'Epreuve de la lettre que vous avés eu la complaisance de me remettre.[4] Je vous prie de la faire *repasser au Bureau du journal de Paris* (rue Grenelle St honoré) DIMANCHE AVANT 9 HEURES, afin qu'elle paraisse dans la feuille du lundi, le dimanche nous laissant un peu plus d'espace dans le Journal du lundi, par la Suppression de plusieurs articles.

La farine de Mays est arrivée.

2. Johann von Gott Nekrep, the eminent Orientalist, had come to Paris with a letter of introduction to BF from Ingenhousz dated Feb. 10: XLI, 542–3.

3. The previous September, Ingenhousz had sent BF an order for American seeds from the Graf von Chotek: XL, 562. For the reasons he explains here, BF divided what he had recently received from America (XLI, 177, 299–300) and gave a box containing some of each kind of seed to Bishop Nekrep, who had promised to forward them to Ingenhousz: BF to Ingenhousz, April 29[–May 2], 1785, in Smyth, *Writings*, IX, 314.

4. BF completed his letter to the editors of the *Jour. de Paris* (of which Cadet de Vaux was the founder and editor: XXVII, 520n) by the end of March. It was published in the April 26 issue; see "Aux Auteurs du Journal de Paris," [before March 31], above.

Je Suis avec un profond respect Monsieur, Votre très humble et très obeisst Serviteur CADET DE VAUX

Notation: Cadet de Vaux, 23 avril 1784—

Franklin *et al.:* Report to the Académie Royale des Sciences

D: Académie des sciences, *Procès-verbaux*, CIII (1784), 90–5.

Samedi 24 Avril 1784

M.M. Franklin, Le Roy, Coulomb, Delaplace et l'abbé Rochon, ont fait le rapport suivant.

M. le Marêchal de ségur ayant envoyé à l'Acade. deux projets, pour armer de paratonnerres, les magasins à poudre de la ville de Marseille et mandé dans la Lettre qui les accompagnoit, que le Roi desiroit que la compagnie les fit examiner et en donnât son avis; l'Académie nous a nommés pour lui en rendre compte.[5] Nous allons le faire avec tout le soin que demande un sujet de cette importance, non seulement par la nature de son objet; mais encore par les heureux effets qui en résultéront. Car rien n'est plus propre à multiplier de toutes parts les paratonnerres, que l'exemple que donnera sa Majesté, est en faisant armer les magasins à poudre de son Royaume.

Mais avant de parler des projets que nous avons été chargés d'examiner; il ne sera pas inutile de rappeller en peu de mots la Théorie qui doit servir de guide dans l'etablissement des Paratonnèrres ou des conducteurs.

Pour armer un édifice quelconque de maniére a le mettre à l'abry de la foudre, au moyen d'un ou de plusieurs conducteurs; il y a differentes circonstances auxquelles on doit avoir une attention particuliére.

1°. Il est nécéssaire de connoître ou de déterminer qu'elle est son étendue, afin de décider s'il faudra en mettre un ou plusieurs;

5. Ségur's letter was read, and the commissioners were appointed, at the meeting of Jan. 10, 1784. The brief minutes of that meeting state that Ségur had sent six proposals: Académie des sciences, *Procès-verbaux*, CIII (1784), 2.

car c'est un point sur lequel il est important de statuer avant de rien entreprendre. Malheureusement les expériences électriques, ne nous ont encore rien appris qui puisse nous mener à connoître l'étendue de la sphére d'action de la pointe d'un conducteur; mais depuis qu'on en a armé des Edifices, plusieurs observations nous ont appris que des parties de ces Edifices qui se sont trouvées à une distance de plus de quarante cinq pieds de la pointe du conducteur, ont été foudroyées, d'où il suit tout naturellement qu'il faut les placer de maniére que leur sphére d'action n'ait à défendre que des parties situées à une moindre distance.

2°. L'orsqu'il y a plusieurs pointes ou flèches sur un édifice, il faut les faire bien communiquer ensemble et faire communiquer de même toutes les parties du comble de l'Edifice qui sont recouvertes en plomb ou qui ont quelqu'autre métal, comme des pointes en fer appartenant à des Girouettes, ou à quelques ornements, afin que le tout ne fasse qu'un système de corps métallique qui avec les barres de transmission soit propre à faire passer la matiére fulminante du haut en bas de l'edifice, de quelque part qu'elle vienne.

3°. Il n'est pas moins important que ces barres soient intimement unies entre elles, afin que cette matiére ne trouve aucune résistance dans son passage de haut en bas. Car la solution de continuité dans ces barres, produit toûjours une résistance plus ou moins grande, sélon l'etendue de leur séparation; parce qu'il faut alors que la matiére fulminante ou électrique saute de l'une à l'autre de ces barres.

4°. Enfin, il faut quelles communiquent bien exactement avec la Terre humide, ou mieux encore avec l'eau, pour qu'il y ait un passage facile et toûjours ouvert le long de ces barres de transmission avec la masse de la terre ou le grand reservoir commun de la matiére électrique.

Quant à la hauteur des pointes, elle doit être au moins de 12 ou 15 pieds et plus même, si l'edifice est fort grand; ce qu'il y a de certain, c'est que plus elles seront élevées, plus leur sphére d'activité s'étendra à une grande distance. On leur donnera deux pouces en quarré par en bas et même plus en proportion de ce que leur hauteur excédera celle de 15 pieds. Et quant à la grosseur des barres de transmission, il paroît qu'en leur donnant huit à 10 lignes en quarré, ou un pouce tout au plus, cette grosseur sera plus que suffisante pour qu'elles transmettent la matiére fulminante du plus violent coup de Tonnèrre. Ce qu'il y a de certain, c'est que l'observation ne nous a encore fourni aucun exemple de barres de fer de cette grosseur qui ayent été en aucune façon fondue ou altérée par le passage de la foudre.

Après ces notions préliminaires sur la maniére d'établir les conducteurs et sur les dimensions qu'on doit donner aux parties dont ils sont composés; il faut en venir à l'examen des deux projets pour armer les magasins à poudre de Marseille, envoyés par M. le Maréchal de ségur et signés par M.M. Ravel, de Puy Contal et Pierron l'un officier dans le corps royal d'artillerie et l'autre dans le corps royal du Génie.[6]

Ces deux projets ont été formés pour le même magasin qui a 31 toises de long sur 8 de large ou à peuprès. Dans le prémier on établit trois pointes ou flèches, sur le faîtage du magasin et dans sa longueur. A celles ci on en ajoûte quatre autres placées réspectivement à chaque angle du bâtiment. Dans le second projet on place de même trois pointes sur le faîtage, mais au lieu d'en mettre aux quatre angles du bâtiment; on les établit en quinquonce des deux côtés du toît avec des barres de fer de transmission horisontales qui régnent tout le long et qui font communiquer ces pointes les unes avec les autres.

Quant à la maniére dont elles sont arrêtées ou scellées sur le faîtage dont les barres de transmission sont assemblées les unes avec les autres; enfin dont elles vont se rendre dans l'eau, elle est la même pour les deux projets. En jettant un coup d'œil sur les déssins, l'académie concévra sans peine tout ce que nous venons d'exposer sur la nature de l'un et de l'autre.

Pour prononcer sur celui des deux qui doit être préféré, nous remarquerons que le second avec les barres de transmission couchées horisontalement le long du toît, entraîneroit une trop grande dépense et qui ne paroît pas nécéssaire; mais pour les pointes qu'on y employe, il faut les conserver, seulement, au lieu de les placer en quinconce comme on le propose dans ce projet;

6. Jean-François de Ravel de Puycontal and Elie-Marie Pierron: Six, *Dictionnaire biographique*, II, 312–13, 348.

on les établira de maniére que chacune d'elles réponde exactement à la moitié de l'intervalle qui se trouve entre la pointe du
milieu du faîtage et celle de l'extremité. Et au lieu de faire communiquer ces pointes ensemble par des barres de transmission
couchées le long du toît, on les fera communiquer avec celles
du faîtage par des barres qui viendront les joindre perpendicu-
lairement en rampant le long du toît. Par là on auroit également la
communication intime de toutes les pointes sans la dépense que
entraîneroit des barres couchées horisontalement tout autour du
toît. Ce point réglé il faut passer à l'examen de la maniére dont
on propose de réunir ou d'assembler les differentes parties des
paratonnèrres de ces deux Projets.

Il paroît que M.M. Pierron et de Ravel, auteurs de ces projets,
pénétrés de la nécéssité d'établir une communication bien intime
entre ces parties, ont crû qu'on ne devoit jamais épargner rien
pour y parvenir, mais nous ne pouvons nous empêcher de penser
que ces Messieurs ont poussé trop loin le scrupule à cet égard, et
que la maniére dont ils proposent d'unir ensemble toutes les parties de leur système conducteur, comporteroit trop de travail et
une dépense superflue. En effet, les vis aux extremités des barres
de transmission, les écrous dans les espèces de pitons chargés
de les recevoir, ne manqueroient pas de demander des frais assés considérables pour être bien faits et remplir leur objet. Nous
croyons qu'on pourroit y procéder plus simplement: voici en
conséquence comment nous pensons qu'on pourroit armer ces
magasins, en parlant d'après ce qui nous est exposé et en réunis-
sant dans l'etablissemt de leurs paratonnèrres la solidité et tout ce
que peut en assurer l'effet à l'economie, conformément à ce que
paroît désirer M. le mal. de ségur, selon les termes de sa Lettre.

On conservera les jambes de force des flèches dans les magasins à poudre qu'on se propose d'armer à Marseille et dans
d'autres Ports où ils se trouvent exposés à de grands vents de
Mer, mais dans d'autres magasins situés dans l'intérieur du
Royaume, on pense qu'on pourroit s'en passer, l'expérience
ayant montré que des pointes avec les dimensions qui sont indi-
quées dans les déssins, sont suffisantes pour résister aux efforts
des vents qu'on y éprouve; mais on donnera plus de hauteur aux
fleches en la portant jusqu'à 15 pieds. Au bas de chaque flèche, et
immédiattement au dessus de l'endroit où elle sera scellée, dans

la pierre de taille on pratiquera ou on réservera de chaque côté une oreille circulaire ayant deux pouces de diamètre ou a peu près et deux lignes d'épaisseur. On y fera au centre un trou de 5 ignes de diamètre au bout de la prémiére barre de transmission qui sera attachée à cette flèche, on pratiquera une oreille toute semblable. On en fera autant à l'autre bout; de maniére que toutes les barres de transmission auront ainsi une oreille à chacune de leurs extremités. Pour faire la réunion de toutes ces parties les unes avec les autres, on appliquera l'oreille d'une de ces barres contre celle d'une autre en mettant entre deux une lame de plomb. Et au moyen d'un écrou entrant sur une vis à tête et dont la tige passera à travers l'œil de ces oreilles, on les serrera fortement l'une contre l'autre. De cette maniére ces barres seront bien assemblées les unes avec les autres; on pourra les séparer facilement et cet ajustement sera très facile a executer. Pour soutenir ces barres de transmission le long du toît, on pourra établir et sceller dans la pierre de taille de distance en distance, des pitons fendus par en haut, pour les récévoir. Quant à la position et à la distribution des pointes ou des fleches, on les établira comme nous l'avons proposé, trois sur le faîte et deux de chaque côté du toît répondant réspectivement au milieu de l'intervalle entre la flèche du milieu du bâtiment et celle de l'extremité. Ces pointes du toît communiqueront avec les barres de transmission régnant le long du faîtage, comme nous l'avons dit plus haut et s'eleveront de maniére a déborder ce faîtage au moins de six pieds. Par cette disposition des differentes pointes de ce bâtiment, il se trouvera que toutes les parties de son comble seront bien défendues par ces pointes n'y en ayant aucunes qui ne soient fort en dedans de la sphère d'activité dont nous avons parlé. On ne peut qu'applaudir d'ailleurs à la maniére dont on a fait communiquer les barres de transmission à l'eau en les ménant jusqu'à la Mer. Cependant si à l'autre extremité du bâtiment il se trouvoit de la terre à la superficie et que le sol ne fut pas entierement de Rocher, on pourroit y faire déscendre des barres de transmission de la pointe placée à cette extremité: cela pourroit servir a diminuer l'espace que la matiére fulminante auroit à parcourir de l'autre côté. La manière dont les pointes en cuivre sont adaptées à la flèche est bien, on les ajuste ici à vis, l'une et l'autre méthode sont bonnes, mais par la derniére, on peut démonter facilement cette pointe et c'est un avantage, car cela est quelquefois nécéssaire; on en a vû de fondus par le passage de la matiére fulminante dans un coup de Tonnerre.

Telles sont les observations que nous avons crû devoir faire sur les deux projets, pour armer de paratonnères les magasins en poudre de la Ville de Marseille, que M. le Mal. de ségur a envoyés à l'Académie, ainsi que les changements que nous avons crû devoir proposer à la maniére de faire communiquer ensemble, toutes les differentes parties de l'appareil mais avant de terminer ce rapport nous devons à M.M. Ravel de Puy comtal et Pierron, la justice de dire qu'on reconnoit par la maniére dont leurs projets sont conçûs, qu'ils entendent très bien la matiére et qu'ils sont très en état de faire armer de paratonnères, les magasins à poudre que M. le Mal. de ségur, les chargera de défendre contre les ravages de la foudre.[7]

From Pierre-Isaac Poissonnier[8]

AL: American Philosophical Society

On March 12, 1784, the French government ordered the Faculté de médecine to conduct an investigation of animal magnetism. It had

7. The academy sent this report to Ségur on April 28, and he passed it on to Ravel and Pierron, who returned their observations and a set of revised proposals. The commissioners responded on July 3 (by which time Le Roy had left the commission): of the four changes, three were of little significance and they opposed the fourth—raising the transmission bars—as it increased the chances of electric sparks escaping from the conductor. Académie des sciences, *Procès-verbaux*, CIII (1784), 126–7, 172–4.

An earlier instance of a governmental entity seeking BF's advice on lightning rods, of which we were previously unaware, occurred in August, 1781, during a visit from the Swiss engineer Johann Sebastian Clais: XXXV, lxii. Clais questioned BF on behalf of the council of Winterthur and relayed BF's detailed instructions on how lightning rods should be installed. The council successfully attached them in 1782 to Winterthur's church steeple, powder magazine, and chancery: Gertraud and Rudolf Gamper-Schlund, *Johann Sebastian Clais (1742–1809): Ein vielseitiger Unternehmer der industriellen Frühzeit* (Meilen, Switzerland, 1990), pp. 64–5.

8. BF had met this distinguished physician and chemist more than a decade earlier, in London. A longtime member of the Académie des sciences, Poissonnier writes here as a member of the Société royale de médecine

been six years since the man who claimed to have discovered it, Franz Anton Mesmer, had established an independent medical practice in Paris, and three years since the last of several attempts to examine his methods had failed.[9] This time, rather than attempt to investigate the uncooperative Mesmer, the government instructed the Faculty to examine his doctrine as practiced by his chief disciple, Charles Deslon, the personal physician to the king's brother and one of the Faculty's elite regent doctors.

The letter to the Faculty came from the baron de Breteuil, minister of the king's household, who stated that the king's order was a response to Deslon's own request. The physician had evidently used his connections at court to obtain one last chance to vindicate his magnetic treatments. The Faculty had long since denounced animal magnetism as quackery and, despite Deslon's status, had suspended him, threatening him with expulsion if he did not renounce Mesmer's doctrine by August. Meanwhile, Mesmer, with whom Deslon had recently quarreled, had turned on him in public, accusing him of being a traitor, not yet initiated into the deepest mysteries of magnetism, and unqualified to operate the independent practice he had just opened.[1] By March, 1784, whatever devotion Deslon may have felt toward his mentor's code of secrecy had evaporated. The baron de Breteuil's letter of March 12 instructed the dean of the Faculty himself, Jean-Charles-Henri Sallin, to form a three-man commission with Jean d'Arcet and Joseph-Ignace Guillotin to investigate how Deslon harnessed this insensible force in the cause of curing disease. Their report was to be submitted to the king.[2]

Between March 12 and the time Poissonnier wrote Franklin the present letter, much had changed in the royal commission. First it was expanded from three members to twelve, with commissioners added from the Académie des sciences (Franklin among them) and

---

(XXIV, 176–7), of which he had served as vice-director in 1779 and 1780, and director in 1781: XIX, 328n; XXVII, 559n; *Almanach royal* for 1779, p. 581; 1780, p. 501; 1781, pp. 513–14. The current director was his brother, Antoine Poissonnier-Desperrières (*Almanach royal* for 1784, p. 528), whose name has been erroneously associated with the Society's report on mesmerism.

9. See XXXV, 634.

1. This last accusation came as a surprise to Deslon. For his dispute with Mesmer see the annotation of the comtesse d'Houdetot to BF, March 10.

2. A. Pinard *et al.*, eds., *Commentaires de la Faculté de médecine de Paris, 1777 à 1786* (2 vols., Paris, 1903), II, 1243, 1246–7. For d'Arcet, a chemist who directed the Sèvres porcelain works, and Guillotin, a doctor regent who later invented a machine that bore his name, see the *DBF*.

the Société royale de médecine. That configuration proving unworkable, the commission was then split in two, with separate Faculty and Society commissions sharing Franklin and his fellow members of the Academy. Later, when the work was under way, the membership would shift once again: the Society would lose the members of the Academy and continue its experiments independently. Those experiments being of little consequence, the Society's work would be eclipsed by the conclusions of the Faculty/Academy commission.

The story of how the king came to appoint two separate commissions with the same task, both of which included Franklin and met at his residence at Passy, is not generally known. Nor has it been understood when and why the members of the Academy allied themselves exclusively with the commissioners of the Faculty of Medicine. The commissioners' private records are gone. Negotiations among the various organizations and the government have left only partial traces, and of the surviving documents, some are undated drafts. The official reports submitted by the two commissions never mention that their members were at any time commingled. Moreover, previous historians appear to have been unaware of certain documents among Franklin's papers, published for the first time in this volume, which contradict aspects of the standard narratives. We therefore attempt to relate this confusing history to the degree we can reconstruct it, so that our readers may understand why Poissonnier was convening the meeting that is the subject of the present letter.

Breteuil's March 12 letter to the Faculty lay unanswered for three weeks. The fact that it had been sent, however, was soon known to the Society of Medicine, which strongly objected to being left out of the investigation. Poissonnier, Vicq d'Azyr, and Chief of Police Lenoir, who was an associate of the Society, lobbied Breteuil to broaden the commission. The Society's argument was indisputable: advising the government on quackery and secret remedies was its explicit mandate, not that of the Faculty. Lenoir must also have discussed with Breteuil the broader issue of public safety. Mesmer's influence had been steadily increasing, and he had become a substantial threat to the health and well-being of a credulous citizenry. His popularity was not only growing in Paris; he had recently begun to invade the purses of people throughout France and the islands by means of the Society of Harmony, which was eliciting huge fees from wealthy "students" who had been promised a copy of his doctrine, which was not yet, and never would be, printed. If the government were to receive a negative report from the Faculty, which had already declared its hostility to Mesmer and Deslon, it would have as little effect on public opinion as all previous censures. If there were to be a government-sanctioned investigation, it should be definitive, and the royal commission had to be perceived as being above any suspicion of bias. In the opinion of Lenoir, Poissonnier, and Vicq d'Azyr, the best chance of securing public confidence would be to expand the commission to include four members of the Faculty, four members of the Society, and four of the most distinguished members of the Academy of Sciences: Franklin, Bailly, Le Roy, and Lavoisier.

By the end of March, Breteuil and Lenoir appear to have come to an agreement and authorized Poissonnier to investigate the feasibility of this plan.[3] On April 1, Poissonnier reported to Lenoir that Bailly, Lavoisier, and Le Roy, whom he had seen at a meeting of the Academy, had all agreed to serve as commissioners. He expected the same response from Franklin, whom he would visit either the next day or the day after. Whether the Faculty would be willing to work with the Society, if the goal were presented as the public good, was as yet unknown.[4] Maloet, a member of both institutions, doubted it, but the duc de Praslin was optimistic. Poissonnier proposed that if the Faculty should refuse to join forces with the Society, each institution could work independently with the four commissioners of the Academy. Maloet had advised that in the letters of appointment to these academicians Breteuil should state that it was the physicians who had requested their counsel. Poissonnier hoped that his views conformed to those of Lenoir and Breteuil.[5]

They evidently did because on April 2, Breteuil sent a letter of appointment to Lavoisier, stating that the king had chosen him to examine Mesmer's methods as practiced by Deslon. He was notably vague on who Lavoisier's colleagues would be. Mentioning neither the Faculty nor the Society by name, he wrote that the commission would include "plusieurs autres personnes distinguées

3. We can find no trace of their discussions, but the wording of Poissonnier's April 1 letter to Lenoir, cited below, suggests that Breteuil and Lenoir were working in concert. If the initial idea to broaden the commission did not come from Lenoir, then it came from the Society of Medicine, which was determined to participate in any royal investigation of mesmerism.

4. The long-standing rivalry between the Faculty and the Society is discussed in XXXI, 229–30n. Poissonnier hoped that the cause of virtue and the public good would induce them to set aside their differences.

5. Poissonnier to Lenoir, April 1, 1784, Bibliothèque de l'Académie nationale de médecine.

par leurs lumières et leur experience." Following Maloet's advice, Breteuil added that it was "les médecins eux-mêmes" who desired the collaboration.[6] We assume that Bailly, Le Roy, and Franklin received similar letters of appointment around the same time. We know, at least, that Franklin's came from Breteuil. When Temple Franklin published an edition of his grandfather's papers, he wrote that when the king appointed a commission to investigate animal magnetism, "Dr. Franklin, at the particular request of his majesty, signified to him by a letter from the minister, consented to be one of the number."[7]

On April 3, the day after Breteuil sent Lavoisier a letter of appointment, the Faculty commissioners—now four in number, Borie having been added—collectively replied to the letter of appointment that Breteuil had sent them on March 12. Their response, as polite as the occasion required, effectively rejected both government plans: the one of March 12 (the only one they explicitly acknowledged) and the expanded one that was being implemented without their consent (to which they gave a subtle nod in their final sentence). They were honored to accept the king's commission to examine animal magnetism, they wrote, but begged to point out that the assignment was not a straightforward one. Mesmer claimed that magnetic fluid permeated the entire universe, extending as far as the celestial bodies. There was nothing in nature, either animate or inanimate, that did not possess its energy and was not subject to its force. It therefore could be said to encompass two kinds of properties: one physical, in the general sense; the other medicinal, in that it was said to produce changes in animal constitution. As practical doctors, they were incapable of investigating the former. They requested that a preliminary study be conducted by some of those illustrious physicists whose work was so celebrated. Those scientists could determine whether this universal agent, said to be newly discovered, existed, and could identify its general properties. If it were proven to exist, then they, the doctors, would investigate its medicinal effects. This would yield a judgment "d'autant plus capable de répondre aux vues du Gouvernement et de

---

6. Antoine-Laurent Lavoisier, *Correspondance*, ed. René Fric *et al.* (7 vols., Paris, 1955–2012), IV, 15. Through April, news accounts portrayed the investigation as one project undertaken jointly by four commissioners from each of the three organizations: Bachaumont, *Mémoires secrets*, XXV, 252 (under the date of April 24); Tourneux, *Correspondance littéraire*, XIII, 515 (April issue).

7. WTF, *Memoirs*, I, 368.

fixer l'opinion publique." They mentioned nothing about the Society of Medicine.[8]

In a letter dated only "Dimanche," which we believe to have been written on April 4, Lassone, the president of the Society, sent an urgent message to Breteuil. He insisted on the Society's being consulted in cases such as this, warned of the dangers of factionalism and misplaced animosity (no doubt alluding to the Faculty's hostility toward the Society), and emphasized the advantages of a collaboration among the three bodies (*i.e.*, the Faculty, the Society, and the Academy). Lassone also proposed the names of four commissioners from the Society.[9]

Breteuil was away from Versailles for almost two weeks. After his return, he settled on the compromise plan suggested by Poissonnier. On April 18 he wrote nearly identical letters to the commissioners of the Faculty and the commissioners of the Society, informing each group (without mentioning the other) that "sur le désir que vous m'en avés témoigné par votre lettre du . . . ," the king had appointed four members of the Academy of Sciences—Franklin, Bailly, Le Roy, and Lavoisier (in that order)—to assist them with the examination of animal magnetism.[1]

The present letter from Poissonnier is the earliest piece of correspondence in Franklin's archive that mentions any aspect of his appointment as a royal commissioner. Its chief significance lies in its indication, hitherto unrecorded, that he was, for a brief period, a member of a joint commission with the Society of Medicine. The initial meeting was held at Passy to accommodate Franklin's limited mobility. What was discussed that day is not known, and the

8. Sallin, d'Arcet, Guillotin, and Borie to Breteuil, April 3, 1784: Pinard *et al.*, eds., *Commentaires de la Faculté de médecine de Paris*, II, 1248–9.

9. After having written this letter, Lassone (XXIV, 177n) informed Poissonnier that he had strongly recommended that all three bodies cooperate, and had insisted, in any case, that the Society had to be consulted in all such situations: Lassone to Poissonnier; Poissonnier to Vicq d'Azyr; both undated (Bibliothèque de l'Académie nationale de médecine).

1. The only difference between the letters is a single phrase. When writing to the Faculty, Breteuil said that he was responding to the desire they had expressed in their letter of April 3. He did not specify any particular letter when writing to the Society: Breteuil to Sallin, d'Arcet, Guillotin, and Borie, April 18, 1784, in Pinard *et al.*, eds., *Commentaires de la Faculté de médecine de Paris*, II, 1249; Breteuil to Mauduit, Andry, Jussieu, and Caille, April 18, 1784, Bibliothèque de l'Académie nationale de médecine.

academicians' role would prove to be extremely limited. Only two members of the Academy—Le Roy and Lavoisier—are known to have attended sessions at which the Society's physicians examined patients. On May 22, the day after they signed their third *procès-verbal*, Lavoisier penned a declaration on behalf of both of them: since they were not doctors, their signatures could signify nothing other than that they had been present.[2] That may have been the day they decided, in concert with their fellow academicians Franklin and Bailly, that their collaboration with the Society of Medicine was pointless. On that spring afternoon, all the members of the other commission, comprising academicians and members of the Faculty, gathered in Franklin's garden and conducted the seventh of a series of systematic, rigorous experiments. With Deslon secretly pointing his rod at a tree he had just magnetized, so as to amplify the effect, his blindfolded, twelve-year-old patient, handpicked by Deslon because of the boy's extraordinary sensitivity to animal magnetism, was led to a group of non-magnetized trees some thirty feet away, and, after hugging them, convulsed so violently that he fainted. That experiment, according to the commissioners' report, was the one that definitively proved that animal magnetism did not exist.[3]

Ce Lundy 26. avril 1784

Mr. Poissonnier a Eté Chargé par mrs. Leroy, Bailly et Lavoisier de demander a Monsieur Francklin sil peut luy Convenir de les recevoir a diner vendredy prochain et s'il trouveroit bon qu'il invita aussy de Sa part les 4. Commissaires de la société Royale[4] pour s'Entretenir Ensemble aprés midy ou plustot a une heure avant midy du Plan qu'ils auront a Suivre pour l'Examen du Procédé de Mr Deslon.

Mr Poissonnier Saisit cette occasion de renouveller a Monsieur Francklin les assurances de son respect et de Son inviolable attachement/

Notation: Poissonier, Paris 26. avril 1784.——

2. *Œuvres de Lavoisier* (6 vols., Paris, 1862–93), III, 500.

3. See Report on Animal Magnetism, [Aug. 11, 1784].

4. The four commissioners from the Society were physician Pierre-Jean-Claude Mauduyt de la Varenne, Charles-Louis-François Andry, Antoine-Laurent de Jussieu, and Claude-Antoine Caille. Poissonnier signed the final report.

David Hartley's "Project of a Treaty"

AD: Library of Congress

On September 4, 1783, the day after signing the definitive treaty of peace with the United States, the British negotiator David Hartley put in writing the assurance he had given the American peace commissioners during the signing ceremony: that "in a very short time" the parties would renew the suspended negotiations for a commercial convention. Hartley delivered this message on behalf of the then foreign secretary, Charles James Fox, unaware that Fox had no intention of agreeing to any of the additional eleven articles that Hartley and the Americans had negotiated in the spring and summer of 1783. The Americans had interwoven those articles—along with the preliminary articles of November 30, 1782—into their "Project for the definitive Treaty of Peace and Friendship" of August 6.[5]

When Hartley carried the signed peace treaty to England in mid-September, he expected that he would soon return to Paris. He received no such instructions, however. On October 4, having heard nothing from Fox, Hartley sent Franklin his own proposal for a temporary convention.[6] In late October and early November, he sent Fox four extremely long letters setting forth his thoughts about the substance and importance of an agreement between the two nations. The first, dated October 27, argued that a further delay in negotiating a commercial convention would be contrary to British interests; with it, he enclosed a copy of Franklin's letter to him of September 6.[7] On October 29 he sent Fox a copy of the proposed temporary convention he had conveyed to Franklin, accompanied by twenty-three pages of explanation. On November 1 he resent the eleven articles that were awaiting "the adjourned consideration of his Majesty's ministers." Following each article was Hartley's personal commentary: he noted when the article had first been sent for the secretary's consideration, pointed out when an article seemed uncontroversial, and for cases that bore further scrutiny offered his opinion as to how the ministry should respond.[8] Finally, on November 6, he sent a sixteen-page analysis of

5. XL, 435–9, 566–7, 578–9.
6. XLI, 72n.
7. Copies of Hartley's four letters to Fox are at the Clements Library. For BF's Sept. 6 letter see XL, 582–3.
8. Hartley labeled each article with a letter of the alphabet, keying them to the way he had labeled the articles in the American peace commissioners' Aug. 6 project for the definitive treaty, which Hartley had forwarded to Fox the day he received it: XL, 435–9.

why Great Britain should care about maintaining the peace with the United States, and how important it was to establish principles upon which such an alliance could hold. He advocated two principles for the foundation of this alliance: (1) that Great Britain and the United States make common cause of defending their respective dominions in North America, and (2) that the British navy should defend and protect the United States, in return for which the United States would support and strengthen the Royal Navy by supplying raw materials and seamen. Hartley would later inform Carmarthen, Fox's successor as foreign secretary, that these four letters recorded the substance of the "many" personal conferences he had had "with Mr. Fox & others of his majesty's then ministers" on Anglo-American negotiations.[9] Whatever the nature of those conferences, the change in the English ministry in December, 1783,[1] put an end to them.

On April 9, 1784, the day George III signed the ratification of the peace treaty, Hartley was instructed to return to Paris to exchange ratifications with the American commissioners. Although he wrote to the commissioners that before leaving England he would seek authorization to resume commercial negotiations,[2] it appears that his request for such authorization went unanswered. Ever optimistic, Hartley arrived in Paris believing that instructions to treat would surely arrive.

The undated document published below, in Hartley's hand and found among Franklin's papers, is our sole evidence of the discussions that must have taken place at Passy shortly after Hartley's arrival.[3] Informal in appearance (the writing is hasty, the columns irregular in width, and some text is interlined), this one-page list records the articles that Hartley wished to see in a British-American treaty of commerce. The first ten refer to articles that he had already negotiated with the American commissioners; they correspond to articles 4, 8, 9, 10, 11, 12, 13, 14, 15, and 17 of the Americans' "Project for the definitive Treaty of Peace and Friendship" of August 6, 1783.

9. Hartley to Carmarthen, May 13, 1784, National Archives, London.
1. Hartley announced this change to BF on Dec. 25, 1783: XLI, 349–50.
2. See Hartley's letter to the commissioners of April 9.
3. Among BF's papers at the Library of Congress is a copy in Hartley's hand of a letter Hartley wrote to Fox on Nov. 19, 1783, the day after Fox had moved for leave to bring in the ministry's India bill to the House of Commons (for the bill see XLI, 233n; John Cannon, *The Fox-North Coalition: Crisis of the Constitution, 1782–4* [Cambridge, 1969], pp. 114–16). The letter includes a plan that Hartley developed in 1766, after a conversation with Lord Chatham, on dissolving the monopoly of the East India Company. We assume that Hartley gave this copy to BF in 1784.

The fourteenth (penultimate) item refers to the "co-partnership in commerce" that Hartley had proposed in the draft temporary convention he had sent to Franklin the previous October. The remaining four items refer to proposals that Hartley had made to Fox in his letter of November 6, 1783. These, presumably, were new to the American minister. The comments in the right-hand column are Hartley's own opinions and queries as expressed (in many cases) in his letters to Fox.

Franklin's reactions to the new articles were not recorded. Hartley may have brought this sheet to his first meeting with Franklin, which took place on the morning of April 27,[4] or else sketched it out during one of their conversations. As it did not represent an official overture, no formal response was required. Two days later, a skeptical Franklin informed Henry Laurens of Hartley's hopes of receiving authorization to treat, and solicited Laurens' views on a commercial treaty in case an official overture should be made.[5] It never was. On May 13, when informing Carmarthen that the exchange of ratifications had taken place, Hartley added that the Americans were "ready and desirous" of negotiating a commercial treaty and wished to sign in the interim a one-year commercial convention.[6] On May 25 Carmarthen responded curtly that Hartley's mission to Paris was completed and that there was "no reason for your continuing there any longer." Further negotiations with the United States would "require a considerable degree of deliberation."[7] Despite these unambiguous instructions, Hartley remained in Paris, having convinced himself, if no one else, that as soon as Parliament had finished formulating a new trade policy he would at last receive his instructions.

[after April 27, 1784]

Debts & Interest suspended.	Appears reasonable but [Quere] whether it can be done by right
Free navigation of River St Laurence	agreed
Account of prisoners to be drawn out &c	not agreed
The Kings good offices with the Emperor of Morrocco &c	agreed

4. Jay to JA, April 27, 1784, in *Adams Papers*, XVI, 178–9.
5. BF to Laurens, April 29, below.
6. Hartley to Carmarthen, May 13, 1784, National Archives, London.
7. Carmarthen to Hartley, May 25, 1784, in Giunta, *Emerging Nation*, II, 379.

Husbandmen & fishermen not to be
    attacked in war. Privateering to cease   agreed
warlike stores supplied to an enemy not
    to be esteemed Contraband   not agreed
mutual denization & naturalization   agreed
Proposal to cut logwood &c   Q
All places upon the boundary line to be
    mutually free &c   agreed
British troops to be kept on the water line   agreed
GB to supply to the Amern states —
    ships of the line & — frigates in case
    of attack   agreed
Amern States to give to GB a certain
    number per annum of timbers for masts
    yards bowsprits &c. And pitch tar &
    turpentine to supply troops & provisions
    if Canada [&c] be attacked   agreed
Amern States not to carry any naval stores
    or military to any nation at war with GB
    during such war [or] take part in any way
    against GB but to furnish — Seamen if
    demanded   agreed
British subjects to carry freely in to
    Amern ports as Amerns. & amerns in to
    British ports in ships half owned by
    british & navigated by equal British &
    Amern Crews   agreed
This treaty to last for 20 years   agreed.

Project of a Treaty

From Richard Bache

ALS: American Philosophical Society

Dear & Hond. Sir   Philadelphia April 28. 1784

    I take this opportunity Via Amsterdam with pleasure to ac-
quaint you, of Sally's safe delivery of a fine boy, whom we in-

tend calling Richard;[8] and that she is well down Stairs again, and the Child perfectly hearty— We have no Letters from you since Barney's arrival,[9] we are however flattering ourselves with the pleasure of seeing you this approaching Summer; Whenever you come you will find the circle of your old Friends decreased; Dr. Bond & Mr. Rhoads are both gone to the Land of Spirits;[1] Mr. Roberts[2] is still alive, but very infirm— The Family is well; I am looking out for a Summer retreat for them, in a healthy spot; but the great demand there is for these kind of places, owing to the number of Strangers lately arrived among us, renders it difficult to procure an eligible place on reasonable terms—[3]

Sally & the Children join me in Duty & Affection to yourself, Temple & Benny— I am ever Dear sir Your affectionate son   RICH. BACHE

Dr. Franklin

To John Jay   AL: Columbia University Library

Passy, April 29. 1784—
Mr Franklin presents his respectful Compliments to Mr Jay, and sends a rough Draft of a Letter to Mr Adams,[4] which he prays Mr Jay to correct to his Mind, and then permit the Bearer[5] to copy it fair in his House, that it may receive his Signature, as Mr F. must send it away early to-morrow morning.

He requests to know how the Family does, fearing there may

8. Richard, Jr., was born on March 11: I, lxv.
9. Capt. Barney arrived in Annapolis on March 5: XLI, 313n.
1. Thomas Bond (II, 240n) died on March 26 and Samuel Rhoads (II, 406n) on April 7: *ANB*, under Bond; Henry D. Biddle, "Colonial Mayors of Philadelphia. Samuel Rhoads, 1774," *PMHB*, XIX (1895), 71.
2. Probably BF's old friend Hugh Roberts (V, 11n).
3. In a now-missing letter of Dec. 27, 1783, BF had directed RB to rent "a house in the Country for the family": Penrose R. Hoopes, "Cash Dr to Benjamin Franklin," *PMHB*, LXXX (1956), 64. This was probably in response to SB's Nov. 5 letter expressing a desire for a summer "retreat" to vitiate the toll the heat took on her children: XLI, 178–9.
4. The following document.
5. Presumably BFB, as the LS of the letter to JA is in his hand.

be some Indisposition, as Company was not receiv'd yesterday Evening

Addressed: His Excellency / John Jay Esqr / &c &c— / Chaillot

Endorsed: Dr. Franklin 29 Ap 1784

Franklin and John Jay to John Adams

LS:[6] Massachusetts Historical Society

Sir,   Passy April 29th. 1784

We received the Letter you did us the honour of writing to us the 10th. Inst, with the project of a Treaty that had been transmitted to you by the Baron de Thulemeier,[7] which we have examined, & return herewith, having made a few small Additions or Changes of Words to be proposed, such as *Citoyens* for *Sujets* and the like, and intimated some Explanations as wanted in particular Paragraphs.[8] The sooner a Copy, with such of these Changes as shall be agreed to by your Excellency and the Prussian Minister, is forwarded to Congress for their Approbation,

6. Drafted by BF and written by BFB; see the preceding document.

7. The draft Prussian-American treaty (*Adams Papers*, XVI, 134–56, document I), modeled on the Swedish-American Treaty of Amity and Commerce (XXXIX, 250–85), differed from it in the following ways. It inserted a new Article 3, specifying merchandise to be traded on a most favored nation status, and a new Article 4, affirming the right of each nation to prohibit any trade for reasons of state. It eliminated Swedish-American Articles 22 and 23 and Separate Articles 1 through 4; Separate Article 5 was moved to the body of the Prussian draft as Article 5. Some of the language of the Swedish-American articles was condensed, and Prussia adapted and combined what had been reciprocal Articles 3 and 4 into a new Article 6. Like the Swedish-American treaty, the Prussian draft was in French.

8. All comments on the MS are in Jay's hand. He pointed out that "Septentrionale" did not belong in the title of the United States of America; the French translation should stop after "Etats unis de l'Amérique." American citizens should be referred to as "Citoyens" throughout the treaty, rather than "Sujets." He corrected certain mistranscribed words. He requested clarification of the restrictions on liberty of conscience in Article 7 and suggested that Article 21, on the right to carry prizes into ports, might conflict with the article on the same issue in the Franco-American treaty (published in XXV, 612–13, as Article 19; it was later renumbered 17).

the better. With regard to the Language of Treaties, we are of Opinion that if the Ministers of the Nation we treat with insist on having the Treaty in their own Language we should then insist on having it also in ours, both to be sign'd at the same time; this was done in our Treaties with France;[9] but if both Parties agree to use a Language that is particular to neither but common to both, as the Latin, or the French, as was done in our Treaty with Sweden, we then think it not necessary to have it also signed in English.

With great Respect, we are, Sir, Your most Obedient and most humble Servants[1]
B FRANKLIN
JOHN JAY

His Excellency John Adams Esqr.

Endorsed: Dr Franklin Mr Jay 1784

Notation: April 29th.

9. XXV, 583–626.

1. JA received this communication on May 4, and met with Thulemeier the next evening to discuss the Americans' proposed alterations. Thulemeier summarized the points they discussed in an undated memorandum (*Adams Papers,* XVI, 158–61) that, after showing it to JA, he sent to Berlin on May 18: Thulemeier to Frederick II, May 18, 1784, Geheimes Staatsarchiv Preußischer Kulturbesitz. On June 6 JA received from Thulemeier the Prussian response: the suggestions were accepted, and as for Article 21, Prussia proposed changing it so that each country was prohibited from bringing prizes into the ports of the other. JA sent to Mifflin Thulemeier's memorandum and the Prussian response on June 7, adding that unless Congress wished further changes, all that was needed was a commission to conclude the treaty, preferably at The Hague: *Adams Papers,* XVI, 161n, 227–8.

Frederick II would have preferred to eliminate Article 21 entirely, because, as he wrote to Schulenburg on May 22, "il pourroit nous compromettre, et que d'ailleurs nous ne faisons point de pirateries." Since there was neither a Prussian navy nor Prussian privateers, the article would effectively apply only to American ships seeking shelter in Prussian harbors. Prussia would assume a burden (antagonizing the European nation from which the Americans took the prize) without receiving a corresponding benefit. On May 27, Schulenburg submitted to the king a point-by-point response to the American requests, including the reformulation of Article 21, which Frederick accepted in his reply of May 29. All three letters are at Geheimes Staatsarchiv Preußischer Kulturbesitz.

To Mary Hewson   ALS: American Philosophical Society

Dear Friend,   Passy, April 29. 1784
    I receiv'd yours of the 2d Inst. dated at Blackfriars. I had but
just receiv'd the Wheels you mention. The Ice had prevented
their coming up the River. I shall write to Mr Viney as soon as
I can. In the mean time please to acquaint him that they came
to hand well and that I like them.—[2] I enclose a Specimen of a
new Work by the Author of L'Ami des Enfans, which I shall
continue to send if you like it.[3] I have now only time to add what
is indeed needless to add, that I am as ever Yours most affectionately   B FRANKLIN
Mrs Hewson

To Henry Laurens
    ALS: Yale University Library; press copy of ALS: Library of Congress

Dear Sir,   Passy, April 29. 1784.
    I received your Favour by Mr Bourdieu, and yesterday another
of the 18th. per Mr Hartley,[4] who also gave me the Gazette with
the Proclamation. I am with you very little uneasy about that,

    2. Rather than summarize BF's message, Hewson sent Viny the letter
itself, writing a letter of her own on the inside leaf. She insisted that Viny
return it to her in person. Moreover, now that summer had come, she hoped
that his wife would begin to return her visits to Blackfriars as well. Her letter to Viny is dated May 10.
    3. Berquin had just announced the first of three volumes that would be
distributed *gratis* to subscribers of *L'Ami des enfans* who would subscribe to
the sequel, *L'Ami de l'adolescence*, scheduled for launch in July. The bonus
publication, published in the same format as the *Ami* series, was *Introduction
familière à la connoissance de la Nature; Traduction libre de l'anglois, de Mis-
triss Trimmer*, Berquin's translation and adaptation of Sarah Kirby Trimmer, *Easy Introduction to the Knowledge of Nature* (London, 1780): *Affiches,
annonces, et avis divers, ou Journal général de France*, April 29, 1784; Angus
Martin, "Notes sur *L'Ami des enfants* de Berquin et la littérature enfantine
en France aux alentours de 1780," *Dix-huitième siècle*, VI (1974), 304–6.
    4. Laurens had recommended Bourdieu in a letter of March 29, above.
On April 18 he actually wrote two letters (above), entrusting both to Hartley. Hartley arrived in Paris around April 27, on which day he visited BF:
Jay Papers, III, 579.

or any other Measures the Ministry may think proper to take with respect to the Commerce with us. We shall do very well.— They have long lost Sight of their true Interest, and are now wandring blindfold in Search of it, without being able to find it;—but they may *feel* what they cannot at present *see*, and all as you say will come right at last.

Mr. Hartley seems to have some Expectation of receiving Instructions to negociate a Commercial Treaty. He thinks he could hardly be sent here merely to exchange the Ratifications. I have not much Dependance on this. Yet as we are authoriz'd to receive Overtures from any European Power, and to plan Treaties to be sent to Congress for Approbation, and I am not yet dismiss'd, I shall much regret your Absence if such a Treaty should be brought upon the Tapis: for Mr Jay will probably be gone, and I shall be left alone, or with Mr A.[5] and I can have no favourable Opinion of what may be the Offspring of a Coalition between my Ignorance and his Positiveness.— It would help much if we could have from you a Sketch of the Outlines, and leading Features of the Treaty, in case your propos'd Embarkation for America should take Place before Mr Hartley makes his Overtures.—

There being but nine States present at the Ratification was owing only to the extreme Inclemency of the Season which obstructed Travelling. There was in Congress one Member from each of three more States; and all were unanimous, tho' the Votes of those three could not be reckon'd.[6] It is therefore without Foundation that those Gentlemen flatter themselves from that Circumstance with a Defection of Four States from the Union, and thence a Probability of a Return of the whole to the Dominion of Britain.— What Folly!—

My Grandson joins in respectful Compliments and best Wishes, with, Dear Sir, Your most obedient humble Servant

B FRANKLIN

His Excelly. H. Laurens Esqr

Endorsed: Doctor Franklin 29th. April 1784. Recd. 6th. May. Answd. same date.

5. JA.
6. See XLI, 456–7.

To Benjamin Vaughan

Reprinted from William Temple Franklin, ed., *Memoirs of the Life and Writings of Benjamin Franklin* . . . (3 vols., 4to, London, 1817–18), III, 466.

My dear Friend,   Passy, April 29, 1784.

I received your kind letters of the 16th and 20th instant.[7] I thank you for your philosophical news. We have none here. I see your philosophers are in the way of finding out at last what fire is. I have long been of opinion that it exists every where in the state of a subtile fluid.[8] That too much of that fluid in our flesh gives us the sensation we call heat; too little, cold. Its vibrations, light. That all solid or fluid substances which are inflammable have been composed of it; their dissolution in returning to their original fluid state, we call fire. This subtile fluid is attracted by plants and animals in their growth, and consolidated. Is attracted by other substances, thermometers, &c. &c., variously; has a particular affinity with water, and will quit many other bodies to attach itself to water, and go off with it in evaporation. Adieu. Yours most sincerely,   B. F.

7. Not found. One of them probably enclosed the "observations on cold by Professor Wilson" that Percival and BF subsequently discussed; see their letters of May 11 and July 17. The astronomer Patrick Wilson (XIX, 228), curious about the temperature differential between snow and the air above it, had tested the cooling properties of various materials (snow, sand, charcoal, metal, etc.) when subjected to the extreme cold of the nights in December and January. His rambling paper, dated Feb. 14, 1784, was titled "Experiments and Observations upon a Remarkable Cold which accompanies the Separation of Hoar-Frost from a Clear Air." It had not as yet found a publisher. The chemist Joseph Black (XXVII, 464), whose theories of heat underpinned Wilson's work, forwarded the paper to the Royal Society of Edinburgh, where it was read on July 5. The society published it in its inaugural volume of transactions, which would not appear for another four years: Royal Society of Edinburgh *Trans.*, 1 (1788), 146–77.

8. For BF's earlier ideas about fire and heat see VII, 184–90; X, 49–50; see also XXXVIII, 127. He developed these ideas further in "Loose Thoughts on a Universal Fluid," June 25, below.

From the Vicomte de Rochambeau

AL: American Philosophical Society

Paris ce 29 avril 1784—

Le Vcte. De Rochambeau a deja eu l'honneur d'envoyer L'année passée a Monsieur Le Docteur franklin Le premier volume du traité sur Les bois.[9] L'auteur vient de lui addresser Le premier cahier du Second volume[1] en le priant d'en faire passer un exemplaire a Passy. Il est enchanté que cette occasion lui fournisse celle de Le rappeller a son souvenir et de l'assurer De L'attachement inviolable quil lui a voué.—

Extracts of Henry Mackenzie's Journal[2]

AD: National Library of Scotland

[April 29–May 2, 1784]

Thursday 29th.

Went to see *Dr Franklin.*— His House elegant & excellently situated at *Passy* on an Eminence commandg a View of the River

9. Dominique-Antoine Tellès d'Acosta, *Instruction sur les bois de marine et autres*. The author was the vicomte's uncle: XL, 493.

1. *Supplément à "l'Instruction sur les bois de marine et autres"* (Paris, 1784): Jean-Claude Waquet, *Les Grands Maîtres des eaux et forêts de France de 1689 à la Révolution suivi d'un dictionnaire des grands maîtres* (Geneva and Paris, 1978), pp. 279, [413].

2. Mackenzie (1745–1831) was a successful Scottish novelist, playwright, editor, and attorney (*ODNB*) who went to Paris in the spring of 1784. He arrived on April 21, stayed until at least May 11 (the extant diary is incomplete), and saw as much as possible. What remains of his MS is published in Horst W. Drescher, ed., *Literature and Literati: the Literary Correspondence and Notebooks of Henry Mackenzie* (2 vols., Frankfurt, Bern, and New York: 1989–99), II, 229–46. We publish here the entries documenting visits to BF.

In the spring of 1783, Mackenzie helped found the Royal Society of Edinburgh, which on Nov. 17 of that year elected BF one of their first foreign members. (WF was also elected.) See Neil Campbell and R. Martin S. Smellie, *The Royal Society of Edinburgh (1783–1983)* . . . (Edinburgh, 1983), pp. 4, 5, 7, 17, 19n; *Trans. of the Royal Society of Edinburgh*, I (1788), 93. No correspondence has been located between the society and BF, but Mackenzie mentioned BF's election in a letter to Carmichael: Drescher, *Literature and Literati*, I, 124–5.

& the Country beyond it.— In good health & a green old Age, except that he has the Stone wh [which] however does not trouble him except when he is driven in a Carriage. Wears now his own thin grey Locks wh look very venerable.— Walks every Day for about 2 Hours.— Would wish to visit England but for fear of the Motion of a Carriage.— Our Conversn chiefly about the *Balloons*, wh He thinks may be turnd to usefull Purposes & that Means may be found of directing them. He saw a Man work a Boat over the River opposite to his House by a machine like the Wings of a Windmill, wh he turnd round wt his Hand— Something like that may guide the Balloon.[3] Surprised as I was, at the Adventurers not complg [complaining] of Dizziness; but some of them did feel it while near the Earth; but afterwds when they lost the Idea of relative Distance they ceased to feel it. One of the things wh appear'd most tremendous to them was the perfect & awfull Silence wh reign'd around them, the Wind having no Subject on wh to make a Noise. He thinks that both Mongolfiers & Charles's Method of filling it will be usefull.[4] The first for War, because they can be always in the Baggage of an Army & can be instantly fill'd; the Second for Journeys, because it is

3. On Jan. 11, a sieur Vallet, who had been experimenting with methods of steering balloons, propelled a boat across the Seine by means of a colossal man-powered fan made from a set of four windmill vanes attached to an axle. He and his crew repeated this experiment on each of the next two days, logging data about their crossing time and the wind direction and velocity. BF saw one of the crossings from a fair distance (Vallet was in Javel, below Paris), and described it in "Maritime Observations" (1785). He said that the wind was calm and the boat reached the opposite shore in three minutes. That would have been on Jan. 13, when Vallet was sailing with the east wind at his back; the return trip took five times as long. BF observed that the "machine" was subsequently adapted for moving balloons, and conjectured that an "instrument similar" could be used under water to move a boat: *Jour. de Paris*, Jan. 9, Feb. 4, 1784; Smyth, *Writings*, IX, 387.

BF may have been alluding to the design of M. Deumier, a flying sailboat suspended from a balloon, featuring a rudder and paddle-wheel. An engraving of it, headed "Essai sur l'art de diriger a volonté la chaloupe d.," was distributed along with the description published in the March 25 supplement of the *Jour. de Paris* and is among BF's papers at the University of Pa. Library.

4. For those methods see XLI, 6n, 218.

less exposed to Accidents, & needs less constant Attention for a long continued Purpose— Query by me of the Danger from the electric Fire in Summer; he answd that he was told the Gaz, tho highly inflammable when mix'd wt a certain propn [proportion] of common Air was quite the reverse when unmixed.

Sunday 2nd May.

Dined with Dr Franklin— Compy [Company] Mr Hartley, Mr Jay, &c. High Eulogium of Ld Chatham— Junius written by Ld Campden.—[5] An Invention of a Grate by Dr F. for clear burning of Coal.—[6] Flame acts as a preservative agt [against] the Burning of any Substance, therefore any thing burns slower when surrounded with Flame.— Young Franklin formerly Temple a Companion of my poor Brother Jamie at Kensington.[7]

To Jacques-Donatien Le Ray de Chaumont

AL (draft): American Philosophical Society[8]

In May, 1784, after a truce of two years' duration, Franklin and his friend and landlord, Le Ray de Chaumont, finally agreed on what

5. BF owned a compilation of the letters of "Junius" (XXXVI, 335), the pseudonym of the author of more than 60 letters on politics first published in the *Public Advertiser* between November, 1768, and January, 1772. His identity has never been proven, but the editor of a modern edition of Junius' letters believes him to be Sir Philip Francis. "Lord Campden," by whom Mackenzie undoubtedly meant Charles Pratt, first Earl Camden (1714–1794), served as lord chancellor, first under Chatham and then in the ministry led by the Duke of Grafton. He was dismissed in January, 1770, after publically criticizing his colleagues. As many of Junius' letters were critical of the Grafton ministry, the identification of Camden was plausible: *ODNB*, under Camden; John Cannon, ed., *The Letters of Junius* (Oxford, 1978), pp. xiii–xix, 348–96, 539–72, 588.

6. For BF's coal-burning fire grate, see XLI, 256–7, and the illustration facing p. 257.

7. Henry's stepbrother James Mackenzie, who died young, had been a pupil at James Elphinston's school in London at the same time as WTF: XXII, 108–9n; Drescher, *Literature and Literati*, I, 69, II, 249; *ODNB*, under Elphinston.

8. Filed with the papers in Account XIX (XXVIII, 3).

was owed to whom. Franklin had tried unsuccessfully to settle their accounts in the spring and summer of 1782, on order of Congress. After Chaumont refused to abide by the ruling of their mutually chosen arbitrator, Ferdinand Grand, and after Franklin (as he explains here) thought better of prolonging the dispute by submitting the accounts to a second arbitrator, the diplomat let matters stand as they were: at an impasse.[9]

Chaumont, meanwhile, continued to press a claim against Congress through his agent in America, Jean Holker, for seventy thousand *livres'* worth of woolens and medicines he had shipped to the Continental Army in 1780 and 1781. He had credited himself with that amount in the account he submitted to Franklin, to the American's surprise. Franklin told Ferdinand Grand during the audit that he knew nothing about that transaction, having never received any orders regarding it.[1]

What spurred the recommencement of negotiations in May, 1784, was the arrival of two letters from Philadelphia: one addressed to Thomas Barclay, the congressional auditor of European accounts, and the other to Chaumont.[2] Both contained information about the merchant's claim and Congress' intention of honoring it. Comptroller of the Treasury James Milligan, after meeting with Jean Holker, had written to Robert Morris on February 4 to explain the history of Chaumont's invoices and inform the superintendent that Chaumont's account with Congress could not be settled until the Treasury had in hand an authenticated copy of the merchant's settled account in Europe. Morris forwarded a copy of this letter to Barclay on February 7, instructing him to send Chaumont's settled account "immediately." Holker sent Chaumont a copy of the comptroller's letter on February 9. Under cover of a long letter detailing his efforts to obtain payment, he also enclosed copies of his recent correspondence with Robert Morris and his statement of what Chaumont was owed by the United States. He stressed that Chaumont's European accounts had to be settled before Congress would act. Chaumont gave all these en-

---

9. See XXXVII, 215–25, 279–81, 473–5, 588–9, 604–6.

1. BF also informed Robert Morris that Chaumont was withholding 70,000 *l.t.* from the debt he owed in Europe. See XXXVI, 673–4; XXXVII, 221, 224–5.

2. It is not known when these letters arrived, but Barclay—who had been out of the country—returned to France in mid-April: BF to JA, April 16, above.

closures to Franklin, who kept them, endorsing the set, "Papers from Mr Holker relating to the Debt due to M. Chaumont in America."[3]

Having received proof that Chaumont's outlay of woolens and medicines was deemed legitimate by Congress, and cognizant that his landlord had been unable to emerge from the bankruptcy into which he had fallen in 1781,[4] Franklin recommenced negotiations in the spring of 1784 with an attitude both shrewd and benevolent. The letter published here is the first evidence of the two men's conversations. Their final agreement was signed on May 28, below.

Dear Sir,   Passy, May 2. 1784

I am sorry to learn from you that Mr Grand declines acting as an Arbitrator in our Affair, because if it must be settled by others than our selves, it is best it should be done by our common Friends.— I have always been ready to submit the Matters in Dispute between us to his Decision with that of M. Dangirard,[5] but knowing that you must be found much in Debt, that it would embarras you to make Payment, and conceiving it was the difficult Situation alone of your Affairs that induc'd you to make certain Objections to my Accounts, and Demands in yours which did not appear to me just, I forbore in Friendship to press the Examination of those Points and a Determination upon them, believing that as soon as your Affairs should be arranged, it would not be difficult for us to adjust our Accounts ourselves, without the help of any Arbitrator. And now I would

3. The enclosures were: Milligan to Robert Morris, Feb. 4, 1784; Holker to Morris, Feb. 6, 1784; Morris to Holker, Feb. 7, 1784; Morris to Barclay, Feb. 7, 1784; and Holker's statement of Chaumont's account with Congress [undated]. All these documents are at the APS; BF's endorsement appears on the verso of the undated statement. The four letters are published in *Morris Papers*, IX, 87–8, 91, 92. Holker's cover letter to Chaumont, dated Feb. 9, 1784, is at the Saint Bonaventure University Library.

4. The French government first issued Chaumont an *arrêt de surséance* to protect him against creditors in January, 1781: XXXIV, 144n. These orders had been renewed annually since then: Thomas J. Schaeper, *France and America in the Revolutionary Era: the Life of Jacques-Donatien Leray de Chaumont, 1725–1803* (Providence, R.I., and Oxford, 1995), p. 307.

5. The Paris banker chosen by Chaumont in July, 1782, to co-arbitrate with Ferdinand Grand the disputed account: XXXVII, 218, 588–9.

propose to you that we should try that Experiment. If we agree and make a Settlement, so that the State of our Accounts may appear clear to my Constituents, I shall make no Difficulty of advancing the Sum you require, tho' it should augment your Debt here, as you can easily make an equal Diminution of your Demand in America. With great Regard, I have the honour to be Dear Sir, &c[6]

Letter from Mr Franklin to M. de Chaumont May 2. 1784— N° 8

From Samuel Vaughan   ALS: American Philosophical Society

Dear Sir,   Philadelphia 3d. May 1783 [*i.e.*, 1784]
Shortly after my last, the foregoing petition was presented to the Assembly;[7] it was referred to the Committee of ways & means, who made a favorable Report, the day before their adjournment; therefore not time to have procured leave to bring in a Bill, which have good reason to believe, would then have

6. On May 10, 1784, BF filled an entire sheet with a reckoning of the items that he and Chaumont had proposed and reproposed at various times. His conclusion was that Chaumont owed him 66,881 *l.t.* 17 *s.* 8 *d.:* Account XIX (XXVIII, 3).

7. See Vaughan's letter of March 8, above, describing the initiative to obtain building sites within State House Square for the APS and the Library Company of Philadelphia. The petition Vaughan copied above the present letter was dated March 12 and prepared by a committee of three representatives from each institution, including Vaughan. Although it specified that the APS would be located along the west side of the square (6th Street) and the Library Company along the east side (5th Street), there appears to have been some disagreement about this decision. On Dec. 9 the APS discussed the draft of an amended joint petition for the two lots that left the assignment of the properties to the Assembly. The Library Company refused to endorse it, however, and, as Vaughan reported to the APS on Dec. 17, he had therefore presented a petition in the name of the APS alone. The Assembly granted a lot along the east side of State House Square to the APS on March 28, 1785: *Early Proceedings of the American Philosophical Society* (Philadelphia, 1884), pp. 128, 130; James T. Mitchell and Henry Flanders, comps., *The Statutes at Large of Pennsylvania from 1682 to 1801* (16 vols., Harrisburg, 1896–1911), XI, 527–8.

been readily granted. But some persons are now making interest against the prayer, saying it would be injurious to the proposed plan of making shady walks, by avenues of Trees. Pity it is that another year has passed without planting them, to bring them the sooner to maturity.

I conceive the Buildings would not only be very ornamental, but contribute to the encrease of cool agreeable shade; should You be of the same opinion, the writing Your sentiments thereon, may have great effect & arrive before the motion is made; as the House has adjourned until the 16th. of August.

I well know this Business is less important than such in which You are generally engaged, nor should I have troubled You with this application, but under a persuasion it will have a tendancy to the advancement of knowledge & Sience, as well as contribute to the health & pleasure of the Citizens at large. The family all join in most affectionate regard, with, Dear Sir, Your assured & mo: obedt. hble Servt   SAML VAUGHAN

Addressed: To His Excellency / Benjn. Franklin / Passy / near Paris

From John Gardner[8]   ALS: American Philosophical Society

Sir,   [*c.* May 4, 1784][9]

I should hardly have presumed to have given this interruption to your important occupations had not an event taken place in which I find my interest and honour too deeply concerned to admit of Silence.

I arrived here 5 Days since in the Ship Amity belonging to Messrs. Cabot of Salem in the Commonwealth of Massachusetts,

---

8. Probably John Gardner (1760–1792), the son and grandson of seafarers of the same name in Salem and Wenham, Mass.: Frank A. Gardner, *Thomas Gardner, Planter* . . . (Salem, Mass., 1907), pp. 168, 198–202.

9. In the postscript to the present letter Gardner indicates that Pierre Texier, a Bordeaux merchant, would write to the farmers general that same day. Texier's letter was dated May 4; see [Saimier?] to BF, May 16.

bringing a Cargo of Rice from Charleston South Carolina.[1] Being unacquainted with the Laws of this Kingdom I was upon my arrival apprised by my Broker (M. Menard) of the necessity of making an exact report of the quantity of Tobacco on board of the Ship, I according sent an express & most positive order to my Mates to collect every Ounce of that Commodity on board the Ship & to make a return to me of the weight of it: this order was faithfully executed & the quantity returned 173 lb weighed with the Steelyards belonging to the Ship, from this amount I deducted 17 lb being as I was informed the difference between the weight of this Country & Ours. Unfortunately I did not mention this circumstance to Monsr. Menard who therefore deducts 16 lb more for the same purpose, so that our report was erronious by this accident 16 lb. The Envoys of the Bureau report that they find 23 lb more of Tobacco than have been reported; of this Quantity about 2¼ lb was by threats drawn from the Pockets & Pouches (I might almost add Jaws) of my Crew consisting of 15 Sailors which did not exceed one Day's consumption for the remaining excess of 4¾ lb I can give no account; it probably arose from a fault in the Steelyards which are seldom very exact, I have the most solemn assurances of my Officers in whom I have every reason to confide that they weighed every Leaf of Tobacco on board of the Ship neither they nor myself had any interest therein.

I have stated these facts to the Directors of the Tobacco revenue but am told that 23 lb of unreported Tobacco have been found on board my Vessel & that I must pay a fine of 50 Livres pr. pound therefor & that if I expect redress I must look elsewhere for it.

This being my situation I must pray your Excellency to use your influence with the Farmers General that this severe & unmeritted fine may be remitted.

Was there the slightest foundation for a suspicion of an unwarrantable intention on my part I should not have had the

1. Gardner had to have been writing from Bordeaux, where Texier, in his May 4 letter, noted the captain's arrival a few days earlier. Gardner's ship had been cleared at Charleston on March 10, bound for that port: *S.C. Gaz., and Gen. Advertiser,* March 9–11, 1784.

assurance to apply to your Excellency in the manner I now do. But however contrary it may appear to the principles of our Order there is no person who views an illicit trade in a light more unfavourable than myself.

Permit me now to subscribe myself with the most profound respect your Excellency's ever obedient & humble. Servt.

JOHN GARDNER
Cr. of Ship Amity

N.B. As I shall sail from hence for America in about 3 Weeks I must pray your Excellency to consider my case as soon as convenient. I am addressed here to Monsr. Pierre Texie who will write this Day to the Farmers General.

His Excellency Benjamin Franklin Esqr. Minister Plenipotentiary of the United States of America at the Court of France.

From Edward Nairne

ALS: American Philosophical Society

Dear Sir   Lond: May 5: 1784

By the favor of Colonel Harman,[2] have sent you three lens's from 40 to 49 inches focus, one of which I hope will prove the right length. Have looked over my books but cannot find any account of those you formerly used. If either of these should not be long enough, their shall be others sent you, by any conveyance you shall mention. Mrs Nairne & my two daughters desire to be remembred to you, I am Dear Sir Your most obliged Hble servt   EDWD: NAIRNE

Dr Franklin

Addressed: Dr Franklin / Passey / near Paris

2. *I.e.*, Harmar.

From Jean-Sylvain Bailly:[3] Two Letters

(I) and (II) AL: American Philosophical Society

I.

ce jeudi 6 may. [1784]

Mr Bailly de L'academie des sciences presente ses respects a Monsieur Franklin. Il est chargé par mrs les commissaires de la faculté de medecine et de L'academie des sciences pour le magnetisme animal, de lui demander s'il veut les recevoir apres demain samedi pour avoir l'honneur de le voir et de conferer avec lui.

Addressed: a Monsieur / Monsieur Franklin ministre / plenipotentiaire des etats unis de / l'amerique septentrionale en son hotel / a passy

Notation: M. Bailly.—

II.

ce jeudi 6 mai [1784]

Mr Bailly a l'honneur d'observer a Monsieur Franklin qu'il serait fort difficile dans ce moment de se concerter avec tous les commissaires sur la proposition qu'il veut bien leur faire de diner chez lui samedi; et d'autant plus que ce jour etant un jour d'academie plusieurs et particulierement Mr Lavoisier, sousdirecteur, sont obligés de s'y trouver.[4] Mr Bailly pense donc qu'il

---

3. The formal tone of letter (I), and the fact that Bailly introduces himself by institution, suggests that he may have been arranging the initial meeting of the Faculty/Academy commission, for which group see the headnote to Poissonnier to BF, April 26, above. Bailly had been on familiar terms with BF since at least 1779, the year of his only previous extant letter. He was also a sometime neighbor, as he divided his time between Paris and a country house in Chaillot, near Passy: XXX, 387; Edwin B. Smith, "Jean-Sylvain Bailly: Astronomer, Mystic, Revolutionary, 1736–1793," APS *Trans.*, new ser., XLIV (1954), 452.
Bailly was inducted into the Académie française on Feb. 26, 1784. Knowing that BF's health did not permit him to travel, Morellet invited WTF to accompany him to the ceremony, on the condition that he be prompt: Medlin, *Morellet*, I, 505–6.
4. Bailly, Le Roy, and Lavoisier all attended the meeting of the Académie des sciences on Saturday, May 8: Académie des sciences, *Procès-verbaux*, CIII (1784), 117.

vaut mieux pour le moment laisser les choses comme elles sont; la visite des commissaires samedi après midi est un hommage qu'ils sont bien aise de rendre a Mr franklin, et il pourra leur faire lui meme pour un autre jour, sa proposition de diner chez lui, proposition qui ne peut que leur etre infiniment agréable.

Addressed: a Monsieur / Monsieur Franklin ministre / plenipotentiaire des etats unis de / l'amerique en son hotel / a passy

Notation: Bailly 6 May 1784.—

From Henry Laurens

ALS: Library of Congress; copy: University of South Carolina Library

Dear Sir.   London 6th. May 1784.

I have been about a fortnight indebted for your obliging Letter of the 17th Ult: delaying from day to day a reply, hoping from expected supplies of Money from my own funds I should have avoided calling upon Mr Grand, but the prospect is vanished. My Attornies had sent me a Bill for £500. which is protested, they had Shiped about three times that value of Rice & Indigo, the Ship struck on the Bar sprung a leak & put back & probably will be condemn'd, the Ministers of this Country will give no answer to my demand for the £2860. Nor will the Judge of the Admiralty condemn or acquit a quantity of Indigo value upwards of £2000—which has been lock'd up in his Court from the Month of July 1780.[5] Besides these I had lent about £1100. to friends who seemed to be more in distress than my self & who cannot at present repay, these disappointments leave me poor & I hold my resolution against borrowing, it is therefore a fortunate circumstance to know that I may be supplied by Mr. Grand on account of the United States. I have requested him to remit me immediately the value of One thousand or twelve hundred Guineas & I intreat you Sir, if it shall be necessary to second the

5. Laurens learned of the government's ruling on May 31; his claim was denied. In the admiralty suit, he finally recovered some of his money in 1787: XLI, 532n; *Laurens Papers*, XVI, 109n, 456.

motion, my affairs will not admit of delay.[6] I hope to embark on or about the 25th. Inst:— The Author of "Considerations" &ca is our friend Mr. Champion, he has thanked me for my remarks & is publishing a second Edition with amendments.— Mr. Edwards (Bryan Edwards Esquire) is likewise about a second Edition of his Tract with a copious Postscript,[7] he has assured me, my remarks & several additional hints in conversation are useful to him, if I have not skill for shaping at the Anvil, I am content with the humbler part of blowing the Bellows. But alas! There remains such a degree of sourness towards us & so great a jealousy of our acquiring the Carrying Trade, as will render all these attempts fruitless. If the intelligence which we have lately received is founded, it will more effectually alarm this Administration, than the sentiments & warnings of fifty Pamphleteers. 'Tis reported the Loyalists in Nova Scotia had quarrel'd with their Governor, complained of a monopoly of the best Lands by the King's Officers, were weary of Military Government, demanded a Representation, many of them had at all hazards returned to the United States &ca.[8]

I thank you Sir, for the friendly terms in which you have invited my stay to see the important business of a Treaty of Commerce finished, but first I perceive not the least disposition on this side to adopt one wise step, except per force of necessity. Secondly I entertain no opinions of my own abilities, the neces-

6. Laurens' letter to Ferdinand Grand, requesting this amount as part of his back salary from the United States, was dated May 7. Grand answered on May 13 that he would need to consult BF. After receiving BF's approval, Grand sent Laurens seven bills between May 15 and May 17 totaling £1,178 5s. 11d., all of which were accepted by June 2: *Laurens Papers*, XVI, 452–3.

7. The second edition of Richard Champion's *Considerations* was advertised for sale on May 22. The second edition of Edwards' *Thoughts . . . Respecting the Trade of the West India Islands with the United States of North America* (XLI, 591), corrected, enlarged, and including a postscript addressed to Lord Sheffield, was announced for sale eleven days earlier: *Public Advertiser*, May 11, 22, 1784.

8. The Loyalists who had fled to Nova Scotia bore such hostility toward crown officials that one deputy surveyor described them as "inclining to be mutinous": Neil MacKinnon, *This Unfriendly Soil: the Loyalist Experience in Nova Scotia, 1783–1791* (Kingston, Ont., and Montreal, 1986), pp. 17, 72–4, 82; *Dictionary of Canadian Biography* (15 vols. to date, Toronto, 1966–), IV, 603–5.

sary work is pretty clearly marked out & I shall leave superior judgement for the Execution; that you were more agreeably Coupled, or single, since Mr. Jay is going, is the friendly wish of my heart.

When I had so far advanc'd My Son arrived & honor'd me with your Letter of 24th. April.[9] We every day repeat the thread bare adage, "I am surpriz'd at nothing." & yet are every day expressing our surprize at some event. I confess it is surprizing to me, our friend D.H. should affect to "seem to have some expectation of receiving Instructions to Negotiate a Commercial Treaty" than which I firmly believe, nothing is more remote from the view of his Court; or is he the least inform'd of every Man of Intelligence in this Country? True indeed, it has been industriously circulated & is credited by the bulk of people, that a Treaty of Commerce is the present employment of our friend & we are charg'd with throwing stumbling blocks in the way, averse to reasonable propositions. "He thinks he could hardly be sent merely to exchange the Ratifications." I can only sigh & lament the frailty of human Nature. How was he sent? It would have been very easy to have saved him the expence & trouble of the journey. But it did not appear expedient, why should we deprive a friend of a little consolatory Éclat? Certainly not for saving Money in the Treasury of an uncordial people. But let this pass.

You know my sentiments Sir, respecting the Politics of this Country; to morrow some Buggaboo may cause a total change in their present Plans. I speak therefore from appearances & from no light Authority, there is no ground for expecting overtures from Mr. Hartley. Take this for granted, nothing further will be attempted before the meeting of Parliament. Quarreling will probably be their first employment & take up no small space of time; firm resolutions on our side to retaliate restrictions on this, may bring on deliberations for a Commercial Treaty. But until such Resolutions shall be formed the unfriendly party will flatter themselves with an assurance of success & of our submission to their regulations. These reflections carry my view of Treaty to a great distance. I shall nevertheless, at your desire, hazard committing my self by communicating such outlines as

9. *I.e.*, April 29.

shall occur to my mind before I leave England. My Son informs me you wish for a Copy of the Remarks, you will receive them by Colonel Harmer, possibly with anecdotes which I think will even "surprize" a Man of your experience, in the mean time be assured the Monarch of this Kingdom, "entertains no ill Will to Doctor Franklin, would be glad to receive at his Court a Character which, tho' formerly misrepresented to him, he now admires & speaks of with respect." This is a truism, as the modern word coiners have it, it came to me from one who deliver'd it, in private conversation, at no second hand, whose veracity & candor I am sure you would depend on.

As soon as I shall have properly lodg'd my Widowed Sister, I shall embark in the first good Vessel, for any Port in the United States not southward of Chesepeake, hoping as I said above to get away about the 25th Inst ready in the mean time to receive your Commands. Being always With sincere Esteem & Regard Dear Sir Your affectionate & Obedient humble servant

HENRY LAURENS

His Excellency Benjamin Franklin Esquire Passy.

From Jérôme-Joseph Geoffroy de Limon[1]

AL: American Philosophical Society

Paris rue du fauxbourg St. honoré
près la rue St. charle, le 6 may 1784.

M. de Limon a l'honneur de faire mille complimens a Monsieur le Docteur franklin et de lui envoyer un boete et un paquet qu'il

1. After being dismissed from a clerical position in the household of Monsieur, the king's brother, Limon went to London in October, 1782, and, claiming intimacy with the court, offered his services to Lord Shelburne as a mediator between Britain and France should the Anglo-American peace negotiations fail. Fitzherbert warned Shelburne against Limon, writing that although he was believed to have performed secret missions for Vergennes, he had a reputation for possessing neither scruples nor morals: Fortescue, *Correspondence of George Third*, VI, 148–9; Fitzherbert to Lord Shelburne, Dec. 4, 1782 (Clements Library); Vicomte de Lastic Saint-Jal, "Notice sur Geoffroy de Limon," *Bulletins de la Société des antiquaires de l'Ouest*, 2nd ser., I (1877–79), 389–400.

a trouvé pour lui dans une caisse qu'il vient de recevoir de M. B.
Vaughan.[2] Si M de Limon ne partoit pas demain matin pour aller passer huit jours a la campagne il auroit eu l'honneur d'aller
lui porter lui-même ces effets et de profiter de cette occasion de
rendre ses hommages à un grand homme qui fait autant d'honneur a son Siécle qu'a son pays

Notation: Limon 6 Mars 1784—

From George Washington

ALS: University of Pennsylvania Library; copy:[3] Library of Congress

Dear Sir,   Philadelphia May 6th. 1784.
    Mr. Tracy the bearer of this, is a Gentleman of Fortune from
Massachusettsbay—on a visit to Europe.[4]

2. Limon met Vaughan in Paris in November, 1782, and impressed the
Englishman with his self-confidence and his alleged connections with Vergennes: Vaughan to Shelburne, Nov. 27, 1782 and Jan. 11, 1783 (APS). The
boxes that Vaughan sent to Paris in June, 1783 (XL, 176), contained items
for Limon, as well as for BF and others: Benjamin Vaughan to WTF, June 6,
1783, APS. Enclosed in the letter just cited was a paper by Benjamin Rush
that Vaughan hoped would be translated into French and sent to Limon, at
the address given in the present letter.
    3. Dated May 5.
    4. Nathaniel Tracy, a prominent Newburyport merchant and shipowner
who had helped provision the American army (XXIX, 332), had by 1779 lost
most of his fleet and was now on the verge of financial collapse: *ANB.* He
was sailing to Europe to settle his accounts. JW, one of his major creditors,
was depending on remittances from Tracy to satisfy his own creditors in
France before the expiration of his *lettres de surséance* on Sept. 13.
    Tracy sailed from Boston on July 5 aboard his new brig *Ceres.* He re-
mained in England through the end of August, arriving in Paris at the beginning of September. It is not known when he delivered this letter, but on
Sept. 5 he and JW were among the guests at a dinner party hosted by the
Adamses (*Adams Correspondence,* V, 444). After another trip to London he
was back in Paris *c.* Oct. 5, still unable to remit to JW any of what he owed:
W. W. Abbot *et al.,* eds., *The Papers of George Washington,* Confederation
Series (6 vols., Charlottesville and London, 1992–97), I, 374n; *Jefferson
Papers,* VII, 363–4n, 395; and for background on Tracy's financial prob-
lems, see Benjamin W. Labaree, *Patriots and Partisans: the Merchants of
Newburyport, 1764–1815* (Cambridge, Mass., 1962), pp. 60–2.

His political character, and character for benevolence & hospitality are too well established in this Country to need any other recommendation, notwithstanding I have taken the liberty of giving him this letter of introduction to you.— With very great esteem and regard—I am—Dr Sir Yr. Most Obedt. Servt GO: WASHINGTON

The Honble. Doctr. Franklin

Addressed: The Honble / Doctr. Franklin / Paris / Favored by Mr. Tracy

Continental Congress to the American Commissioners: Instructions

Copies:[5] Massachusetts Historical Society, National Archives; press copy of copy: American Philosophical Society

The instructions that follow established a new diplomatic commission to negotiate and sign a total of twenty treaties of amity and commerce with European and North African powers. Their creation was a long and contentious process. On October 29, 1783, Congress authorized the peace commissioners to offer a treaty to Joseph II and enter into negotiations with other European states.[6] However, a congressional committee that included Thomas Jefferson pointed out in December that these instructions had failed to empower the commissioners to sign treaties and to negotiate with non-European powers. The committee's report outlined the principles that should guide

5. We publish the one that JA retained; it is largely, if not entirely, in BFB's hand. We silently correct several minor copying mistakes, and note below two instances of BFB's having omitted words, which are supplied from other official versions. The press copy at the APS was made from BFB's copy and was kept by BF, who overwrote in pencil some of the faintest lines at the bottom of the first page. The copy at the National Archives was made by David Humphreys for the commissioners' letterbook. It omits several May 11 instructions that were either for BF alone or did not pertain to the treaty negotiations.

6. XLI, 154–8, 168. BF had written to Congress in July, 1783, that several European powers had signaled their interest in forming commercial treaties with the United States and pointed out the need for a new commission: XL, 360–1, 363, 368.

these negotiations.[7] Congress debated this report over the next five months, as it struggled to maintain a quorum. Among the disputed articles was number three, which stipulated that the United States should be considered in all foreign treaties as one nation.[8] Congress also argued over the demand from southern delegates to appoint two additional ministers from their states in order to ensure the adequate representation of that region.[9] On May 7 the news of Jay and Laurens' impending returns to America, contained in Franklin's March 9 letter to Charles Thomson, created the opportunity for a compromise. Congress elected the New Yorker Jay as secretary for foreign affairs and a Virginian, Jefferson, as minister plenipotentiary to join John Adams and Franklin. It also approved a set of instructions. These were followed by further resolutions approved on May 11.[1] Five days later Charles Thomson sent these instructions to Jefferson to carry to France. After Congress added one final resolution on June 3, Thomson sent the complete instructions, published here, to the commissioners on June 18.[2]

[May 7–June 3, 1784]
United States in Congress Assembled May 7th. 1784

Whereas Instructions bearing date the 29th. day of October 1783 were sent to the Ministers Plenipotentiary of the United States of America at the Court of Versailles empowered to Negotiate A Peace or to any one or more of them for concerting Draughts or Propositions for Treaties of Amity and Commerce with the Commercial Powers of Europe

Resolved That it will be advantageous to these United States to conclude such Treaties with Russia, the Court of Vienna, Prussia, Denmark, Saxony, Hamburg, Great Britain, Spain, Portugal, Genoa, Tuscany, Rome, Naples, Venice, Sardinia and the Ottoman Porte.

---

7. *JCC*, xxv, 812–13n, 821–8; *Jefferson Papers*, vi, 393–402.

8. For the debates in Congress see *Jefferson Papers*, vi, 400–1n; *JCC*, xxvi, 169–70, 176–7, 180–5. Later that year, TJ recalled the difficulties of passing Article 3 but observed that the "majority however is for strengthening the band of Union, they are the growing party, and if we can do any thing to help them, it will be well": *Jefferson Papers*, vii, 478–9.

9. Smith, *Letters*, xxi, 460–1, 583, 612; *JCC*, xxvi, 341–5.

1. *JCC*, xxvi, 355–62.

2. *Jefferson Papers*, vii, 261–71; Thomson to the American commissioners, June 18, below.

Resolved that in the formation of these Treaties the following points be carefully stipulated.

First That each Party shall have a right to carry their own Produce, Manufactures and Merchandize in their own bottoms to the Ports of the other, and thence to take the Produce and Merchandize of the other, paying in both Cases such duties only as are paid by the most favoured Nation, freely where it is freely granted to such Nation, or paying the Compensation, where such Nation does the same—

Second. That with the Nations holding Territorial Possessions in America a direct and similar Intercourse be admitted between the United States and such Possessions; or if this cannot be obtained, then a direct and similar intercourse between the United States and certain free Ports within such Possessions; that if this neither can be obtained, permission be stipulated to bring from such Possessions in their own bottoms the Produce and Merchandize thereof to these States directly and for these States to carry in their own bottoms their Produce and Merchandize to such Possessions directly.[3]

Third. That these United States be considered in all such treaties, and in every Case arising under them, as one Nation upon the Principles of the Federal Constitution.—

Fourth.[4] That it be proposed, though not indispensibly required, that if War should hereafter arise between the two Contracting Parties, the Merchants of either Country then residing in the other shall be allowed to remain nine Months to collect their Debts and settle their Affairs, and may depart freely, car-

3. TJ considered the negotiation of commercial treaties with those European nations that possessed colonies in the West Indies (*i.e.*, Britain, Spain, Portugal, France, Holland, Denmark, and Sweden) to be the most important task of the commissioners: *Jefferson Papers*, VII, 638.

4. BF drafted this article in December, 1782, for inclusion in the definitive peace treaty, but the British ministry rejected it: XXXVIII, 444–5; XL, 257–8, 438. On Sept. 10, 1783, the peace commissioners sent it to President of Congress Boudinot as one of the additional proposals they had made to Hartley, beyond those already accepted in the preliminary treaty: XL, 602. Two members of the congressional committee appointed on Dec. 13, 1783, to examine those documents, TJ and Elbridge Gerry, also served on the committee whose Dec. 20 report formed the basis of the present instructions: *JCC*, XXV, 812–13n.

rying off all their effects without molestation or hindrance; And all Fishermen, all Cultivators of the Earth and all Artizans or Manufacturers unarmed and inhabiting unfortified towns, Villages or Places, who labour for the common subsistence and benefit of Mankind, and peaceably following their respective employments, shall be allowed to continue the same, And shall not be molested by the Armed force of the Enemy, in whose power by the Events of War they may happen to fall; but if any thing is necessary to be taken from them for the use of such Armed force, the same shall be paid for at a reasonable Price; and all Merchants and Traders exchanging the Products of different Places, and thereby rendering the necessaries conveniences and comforts of human life more easy to obtain and more General, shall be allowed to pass free and unmolested, and neither of the contracting powers shall grant or issue any Commission to any private Armed Vessels empowering them to take or destroy such trading Ships or interrupt such Commerce.

Fifth.[5] And in case either of the Contracting Parties shall happen to be engaged in War with any other Nation, it be farther agreed in order to prevent all the difficulties and misunderstandings that usually arise respecting the Merchandize heretofore called Contraband, such as Arms Ammunition and Military Stores of all kinds, that no such Articles carrying by the ships or Subjects of one of the Parties to the Enemies of the other shall on any account be deemed contraband, so as to induce confiscation and a loss of Property to individuals. Nevertheless it shall be lawful to stop such Ships & to detain them for such length of time as the Captors may think necessary to prevent the inconvenience or damage that might ensue from their proceeding on their Voyage, paying however a reasonable Compensation for the loss such arrest shall occasion to the Proprietors; and it shall be further allowed to use in the service of the Captors the whole or any part of the Military Stores so detained, paying the owners the full Value of the same, to be ascertained by the current Price at the place of its destination: But if the other contracting party will not consent to discontinue the confiscation of

5. As with the previous article, the peace commissioners unsuccessfully proposed this article (without the concluding sentence) to Hartley for inclusion in the definitive peace treaty: XL, 258–9, 438.

contraband goods, then that it be Stipulated that if the Master of the Vessell stopped will deliver out the goods charged to be contraband, he shall be admitted to do it, and the Vessell shall not in that case be carried into any port but shall be allowed to proceed on her voyage.

Sixth. That in the same case where either of the contracting parties shall happen to be engaged in War with any other Power, all goods not Contraband belonging to the Subjects of that other Power and shipped in the bottoms of the Party hereto, who is not engaged in the War, shall be entirely free; and that to ascertain what shall constitute the blockade of any place or port, it shall be understood to be in such Predicament, when the assailing power shall have taken such a station as to expose to imminent danger any Ship or Ships that would attempt to sail in or out of the said Port; and that no Vessell of the Party, who is not engaged in the said War shall be stopped without a material and well grounded cause; and in such cases justice shall be done and an Indemnification given without loss of time to the Persons aggrieved and thus stopped without sufficient cause.—

Seventh. That no rights be stipulated for aliens to hold real property within these States, this being utterly inadmissible by their several laws and Policy; but where on the death of any person holding real estate within the territories of one of the contracting parties, such real estate would by their laws descend on a subject or citizen of the other, were he not disqualified by alienage, there he shall be allowed a reasonable time to dispose of the same and with draw the proceeds without molestation.

Eighth. That such treaties be made for a term not exceeding ten years from the exchange of Ratifications.

Ninth. That these Instructions be considered as supplementary to those of October 29. 1783 and not as revoking, except where they contradict them. That where in Treaty with a particular Nation they can procure particular Advantages, to the Specification of which we have been unable to descend, our object in those Instructions having been to form out-Lines only and general Principles of treaty[6] with many Nations, it is our Expectation they will procure them, though not pointed out in

6. BFB's copy did not include the words "of treaty."

these Instructions; and where they may be able to form Treaties on Principles, which in their Judgment will be more beneficial to the United States than those herein directed to be made their Basis, they are permitted to adopt such Principles. That as to the Duration of the Treaties, though we have proposed to restrain them to the Term of 10 Years, yet they are at liberty to extend the same as far as fifteen years with any Nation, which may pertinaciously insist thereon; and that it will be agreeable to us to have supplementary Treaties with France, the United Netherlands and Sweden, which may bring the Treaties we have entered into with them as nearly as may be to the Principles of those now directed; but that this be not pressed, if the proposal should be found disagreable.

Resolved, That Treaties of Amity or of Amity[7] and Commerce be entered into with Morocco and the Regencies of Algiers, Tunis and Tripoly to continue for the same Term of 10 Years or for a Term as much longer as can be procured.

That our Ministers to be commissioned for treating with foreign Nations make known to the Emperor of Morocco the great Satisfaction which Congress feel from the amicable Disposition he has shewn towards these States and his Readiness to enter into Alliance with them;[8] that the Occupations of the War and Distance of our Situation have prevented our meeting his Friendship so early as we wished: But that Powers are now delegated to them for entering into Treaty with him, in the Execution of which they are ready to proceed. And that as to the Expences of his Minister they do therein what is for the Honour and Interest of the United States.

Resolved that a Commission be issued to Mr John Adams Mr Benjamin Franklin and Mr Thomas Jefferson giving Powers to them or to the greater Part of them to make and receive Propositions for such Treaties of Amity and Commerce and to negotiate and sign the same, transmitting them to Congress for their final Ratification and that such Commission be in force for a Term not exceeding two years.

7. BFB's copy did not include the words "or of Amity."
8. As the peace commissioners had reported to Congress on Sept. 10: XL, 605.

May 11. 1784.[9]

Resolved That our Ministers to be commissioned for treating with foreign Nations be referred to the Instructions of the thirtieth Day of May 1783 relative to British debts[1] the Objects of which they are hereby directed to urge with Perseverance.

That they require with Firmness and Decision full Satisfaction for all Slaves and other Property belonging to Citizens of these States taken and carried away in Violation of the Preliminary and definitive Articles of Peace; and to Enable them to do this on precise grounds Congress will furnish them with necessary Facts and Documents.[2]

Resolved, That Doctor Franklin be desired to notify to the Apostolical Nuntio at Versailles that Congress will always be pleased to testify their Respect to his Sovereign and State; but that the Subject of his Application to Doct. Franklin being purely spiritual, it is without the Jurisdiction and Powers of Congress who have no authority to permit or refuse it, these powers being reserved to the several States individually.—[3]

9. On this day Congress concluded its debate of the December report and voted to make several changes. First, it eliminated a paragraph instructing the commissioners to apologize to European powers for the fact that, because of its debts, the United States would not be able to maintain resident ministers at their courts. Second, it substituted the first resolution below for a longer paragraph instructing the commissioners to urge European powers to show "reasonable forbearance in the levy of debts due within these states to British subjects." Congress postponed a decision about where American consuls and consuls general would be stationed. In addition to the following resolutions, Congress also approved a draft commission for the three ministers (see under [May 12], below): *JCC*, xxv, 825; xxvii, 367–74; *Jefferson Papers*, vi, 397, 401–2n.

1. Congress instructed the peace commissioners on that day to negotiate an amendment to the preliminary treaty that would grant American debtors at least three years after the signing of the definitive treaty to repay their prewar debts to British creditors and that would deny all demands for interest accrued during the war. The following day Robert Livingston sent a copy of these instructions to the commissioners: xl, 87.

2. On May 26, 1783, Congress directed the peace commissioners to remonstrate with the British about this issue: xl, 75–6.

3. Papal Nuncio Pamphili inquired of BF in July, 1783, whether Congress would permit the appointment of a bishop or vicar apostolic in the United States. Although BF warned Pamphili that Congress would not

That Doct. Franklin be instructed to express to the Court of France the constant Desire of Congress to meet their Wishes; That these States are about to form a general system of Commerce by Treaties with other Nations; that at this Time they cannot foresee what claims might be given to those Nations by the explanatory Propositions from the Count de Vergennes on the 2d. & 3d. Articles of our Treaty of Amity & Commerce with His Most Christian Majesty; but that he may be assured it will be our constant Care to place no People on more advantageous ground than the Subjects of his Majesty.[4]

Resolved,[5] That the Papers containing the claim of the five Fosters, brothers for the Prize of their Vessel "the three friends" made by Captn. Landais of the Alliance frigate which Papers were communicated by the Count de Vergennes to Doctor Franklin to the end he might apply to Congress for an indemnification of the said Fosters, be remitted to the said Ministers with a Copy of the fourth Clause of the Instructions to them of October 29th. 1783 and the following extract from Dr. Franklin's Letter of July 22. 1783 to the Secretary for foreign Affairs viz "Mr. Barclay has in his hands the Affair of the Alliance and Bonhomme Richard. I will afford him all the Assistance in my Power. But it is a very perplexed Business. That expedition tho' for particular reasons under American Commissions and Colours, was carried on at the King's Expence and under his Orders. Mr. de Chaumont was the Agent appointed by the Minister of the Marine to make the outfit. He was also chosen by all the Captains of the Squadron as appears by an Instrument under their hands, to be their Agent, receive sell and divide Prizes &ca.

---

become involved in church affairs, he forwarded the nuncio's memoir to Congress: XL, 410–12, 516–18, 623.

4. On May 20, 1783, Vergennes proposed three additional articles to the Franco-American treaty, which affirmed that the United States and France would grant each other most-favored-nation status. The peace commissioners did not forward the proposal to Congress until after the definitive treaty with Britain had been concluded: XL, 45–6, 606.

5. Here Congress confused Forster frères' attachment of prize money made by the *Alliance* (for the firm's claim and the papers mentioned here see XL, 207–8, 414–15, 624) with the issue of settling the accounts of John Paul Jones's 1779 squadron, which had been addressed in the Oct. 29 instructions from Congress (XLI, 156) and BF's July 22 letter (XL, 364–5).

The Crown bought two of them at Public sale, and the Money I understand is lodged in the hands of a Responsible Person at L'Orient. Mr. de Chaumont says he has given in his Accounts to the Marine and that he has no more to do with the Affair except to receive a balance due to him. That Account however is, I believe, unsettled, and the absence of some of the Captains is said to make another difficulty which retards the completion of the business. I never paid nor received any thing relating to that Expedition, nor had any other concern in it than barely ordering the Alliance to join the Squadron at Mr. de Sartine's request." From which extract there is Reason to believe the United States of America had no concern in the Expedition; but that it was carry'd on wholly under the Authority and for the Advantage of his Most Christian Majesty. That if this fact should not be so apparent as to give full Satisfaction to his Majesty's Ministers, they then take such Measures as in their Discretion shall be thought most conducive to an amicable and equitable adjustment thereof on the best evidence they shall be able to procure.—

Resolved, That the Claim of the Sieur Bayard against these United States for the sum of 255236 Dollars continental Money is not founded in Justice from the Circumstances of the Case as stated by himself,[6] which are "That a Vessel & Cargo in which he was interested sailing in May 1779 from Charles Town for France was taken by an English Armed Vessel, and retaken by an American Frigate called the Boston that she was carried to Boston and there sold as French Property by Mr. de Valnais Consul for France at that Port that he unfaithfully and irregularly, as is suggested, endeavoured to have the whole adjudged to the Recaptors, but that the Sentence was that they were only intitled to one eighth and the Sr. Bayard's Correspondents obliged Mr. de Valnais to deposit with the Consul of France in Philadelphia 255236 dollars continental Money in part of the proceeds with a reserve to the Sr. Bayard against Mr. de Valnais of every right of redress for his irregular Conduct." That no injurious intermeddling by the United States or any of them or by any of their Citizens is here complained of— That the Money was constantly in the hands of the Sr. Bayard's Correspondents

6. In a memoir, which BF forwarded on Sept. 13, 1783: XL, 435, 623–4.

or of the Consul of his Nation— That he may indeed have suffered by its depreciation as many others have suffered both foreigners and Citizens, but the latter in a much higher Degree than the former— That this Depreciation was not effected by any arbitrary change by Congress in the Value or denomination of the Money which yet has been frequently practised by European States, who never have thought themselves bound to make good the Losses thereby incurred either by their own Citizens or by foreigners, but ensued against the will & the unremitting endeavours of Congress— That in this Case too it might have been lessened, if not prevented by investing the Money immediately in Gold or Silver or in other Commodities. Congress are therefore of opinion that these States are not bound to make Good the Loss by Depreciation—

That as to the Residue of the Claims of the Sieur Bayard, if founded in truth and right they lie only against the State of Georgia, to the Governor of which[7] Congress will transmit Copies of the Papers, expressing at the same time our Confidence that that State will cause to be done in it, what Justice and the respect due between friendly nations require, and that the Sieur Bayard be referred to them.

Resolved, That the friendly Services rendered by the Sr. John Baptist Pequet, Agent for the French Nation at Lisbon, to great Numbers of American Sailors carried Prisoners into that Port during the late War, and his sufferings on that Account merit the sincere Acknowledgements of Congress, and that it be referred to the said Ministers to deliver him these in honourable Terms, & to make him such Gratification as may indemnify his losses & properly reward his Zeal.[8]

Resolved, That the papers relating to the detention of the schooner Nancy, captn. Gladden, belonging to Citizens of these United States residing in North Carolina, be transmitted to our ministers for negotiating Treaties with foreign Powers; and that they be instructed to make enquiry into the cause of the seizure and detention of the said schooner and her Cargo, and if it shall

7. John Houstoun: *ANB*.
8. On Sept. 13, 1783, BF sent Boudinot a memoir from Jean-Baptiste Pecquet that Vergennes had forwarded to him: XL, 243–6, 423, 623–4.

appear that she has been unjustly detained to demand the release of the Vessel and the restoration of her Cargo with adequate damages for her detention—[9]

June 3. 1784.[1]

Resolved, that the Ministers Plenipotentiary of the United States for negotiating Commercial Treaties with foreign Powers be, and they are hereby instructed, in any negotiations they may enter upon with the Court of Spain, not to relinquish or cede in any event whatsoever the right of the Citizens of these United States to the free Navigation of the River Mississippi from its source to the Ocean—[2]   (signd) CHAS. THOMSON. secy.

Notation by John Adams: Instructions. May 7. 1784.

From Thomas Barclay   LS: American Philosophical Society

Sir   Paris 7th May 1784
The Gentleman who will have the Honor to deliver this Letter to you is Mr. Morel du faux of Dunkirk,[3] who has been several Years settled in that place with great reputation, and who when I was at Amsterdam, was recommended to me so warmly by a

9. For the detention of the *Nancy,* Capt. John Gladin, in Castlehaven, Ireland, see XL, 381–2n. According to a report in the *Independent Ledger and the American Advertiser* of Dec. 15, 1783, the crew of the *Nancy* had cut the ship's cables on Aug. 11 and escaped from the harbor, leaving behind their captain. We have no evidence that the commissioners ever acted on this part of their instructions.

1. This final part of the instructions was based on a committee report by Edward Hand, Samuel Hardy, and James Monroe on a May 31 motion by Francis Dana and Elbridge Gerry. On the same day Congress issued commissions to JA, BF, and TJ to negotiate supplementary treaties of commerce with France, the Netherlands, and Sweden (see Charles Thomson's letter to the commissioners of June 18): *JCC,* XXVII, 489–90, 529–30.

2. Although Article 8 of the definitive peace treaty stipulated this right (XL, 574), the issue remained unsettled as Spain controlled both banks of the lower part of the Mississippi River.

3. Who sent a letter of his own, asking for an appointment, on May 12, below.

number of persons for whom I have the greatest respect, that I promis'd to Interest myself in procuring for him the Office of Agent or vice Consul for the United States.—⁴ I mentiond this application already to your Excellency, and informed Mr. Morel of what pass'd. He waits upon you to State some services he has done to America, and will think himself under great obligations to you if he succeeds— As it is highly proper for me to have your approbation of the appointments that are to take place, I have referd Mr. Morel to you, on this occasion and remain with the greatest respect, Sir Your Excellency Most Obedient Most Hume. Servt.⁵   THOS BARCLAY

His Excellency Benjamin Franklin Esqr.

From the Abbé ——— Thomas⁶

Copy⁷ and press copy of copy: American Philosophical Society

à Paris ce 7 may 1784.
Au mois d'Octobre 1781 j'ai fait passer a Mr Williams Negt etabli a Nantes un Ballot de Marchandises marqué T.H. No 1.

4. The position of American consul in Dunkirk was also pursued by Francis Coffyn. In a letter to Coffyn, Barclay claimed that when he agreed to support Morel Dufaux, he was unaware of Coffyn's interest in the post: XLI, 95–6.

5. When BF left France in 1785, the consulship in Dunkirk was still vacant. In an undated "List of American Agents in France" that Barclay made for TJ, he praised Coffyn as dependable, "well informed, and attentive to the Interests of America." The U.S. Senate confirmed GW's appointement of Coffyn as consul for Dunkirk on Dec. 11, 1794: *Jefferson Papers*, VIII, 441; XIV, 60, 62n; *Journal of the Executive Proceedings of the Senate of the United States* . . . (3 vols., Washington, D.C., 1828[–29]), I, 164–5.

6. Since 1780, Thomas had been the preceptor to the son of Louis, comte de Durfort: Honoré Bonhomme, ed., *Correspondance inédite de Collé* . . . (Paris, 1864), pp. 201, 211. According to his later account (Thomas to BF, Sept. 20, 1787, APS), he sent this appeal to a friend of M. Brillon's, asking that M. Brillon communicate it to BF. Brillon gave it to WTF instead. When Thomas complained to M. Brillon the following month that only BF was capable of effecting a resolution to his complaint (see the note below), BF felt obliged to intervene. The matter was not settled until 1789.

7. In the hand of BFB.

contenant toiles de Coton futaines et Bazins, Bas et Bonnets de Coton, enfin grose Draperie en Laine, en le priant d'expedier le dit Ballot pour l'Amerique Septentrionale pour mon Compte et a mes Risques et fortunes, moyennant les Droits de Commission dont nous etions convenus, le laissant au reste maitre du Choix des Corespondants auxquelles il l'adresseroit. Mr Williams l'a envoyé a Mrs. *Bache* et *Shée* Negts a Philadelphie.[8] J'avois expréssement demandé à Mr Williams qu'il m'obtint le plus promptement possible un compte de Ventes et des Observations d'après lesquelles je pusse diriger et étendre cette Speculation, ce premier Ballot ne devant être regardé que comme un Echantillon. Cependant me voici au mois de May 1784 sans avoir pû l'obtenir. Au mois de juin dernier, Mr Williams m'à fait passer une Remise à *Compte*,[9] et dans la lettre qui l'a renfermoit il m'anoncoit que ces Mrs. lui disoient que par leur prochaine ils lui remettroient le Compte de Vente et la Remise pour Solde. A en juger par la datte de l'acceptation de la Traite, il y a plus de 15 mois que Mrs Bache et Shée promettoient compte et remise par leur *prochaine*, et ni l'un ni l'autre ne sont arrivés. Mr Williams a qui j'en ai temoigné mon étonnement, m'a repondu par Ecrit dabord, et tout recemment encore de vive voix qu'il n'en etoit pas moins Surpris que moi même et qu'il me conseilloit de leur écrire directement. Je l'ai deja fait 2 fois, j'enverai un Triplicata par le premier paquebot; mais j'aurai bien plus de Confiance dans une Récommandation de son Excéllence Mr le Docteur Franklin si j'étois asses heureux pour l'Obtenir. Je ne doute pas qu'elle me procurat plus promptement et plus surement ce que je demande avec justice, a ce qu'il me semble, savoir un Compte de Vente, une Remise pour Solde et a court terme. Independamment de l'Ancienté de ma créance, je puis encore représenter les Risques énormes que j'ai courus, ayant fait partir sans assurance, sur l'Avis de Mr Williams, et dans un tems ou nous etions si maltraités que nos Chambres ne vouloient plus assurer a quelque Prix que ce fut. Au reste je rends la plus Haute

8. jw shipped the bale in early April, 1782: jw to Thomas, April 14; to Bache & Shee, May 1, 1782 (both at the Yale University Library).

9. jw received the remittance from Bache & Shee on May 22. They had sent it in January: jw to Bache & Shee, May 22, 1783 (Yale University Library).

Justice a Mrs Bache et Shée; tous les rapports sont a l'avantage de cette maison vraiment Respectable; je suppose seulement que l'Objet pour lequel je réclame, n'étant qu'un Essay, ne leur a pas paru asses important pour meriter toute leur Attention, et qu'ils m'ont oublié./.[1] (Signe) THOMAS

To William Strahan   ALS: Morgan Library and Museum

Dear Friend,   Passy, May 8. 1784
The Bearer Mr Maurice Meyer has lived with me Five Months, is a good Compositor, understands Latin, French & German, and has the Character of an honest Man.[2] If you can employ him, or help him to Employ in London, you will oblige Your affectionate Friend, & most obedient Servant

B FRANKLIN

Wm Strahan Esqr.—

Addressed: To / Wm Strahan, Esqr / Printer to his Majesty / London

1. As noted above, M. Brillon gave this letter to WTF. JW immediately wrote to RB (JW to RB, May 7, 1784, Yale University Library), and sometime within the next month he informed Thomas that he had done so. That letter from JW, now missing, incited Thomas to write a long letter of complaint on June 9 to "les personnes respectables" who he believed had given his memoir to BF. He had not asked BF to contact JW; he wanted BF to write to Bache & Shee. Thomas responded to the explanations JW had offered, and threatened him with prosecution. M. Brillon must have given this letter to BF, as a copy remains among BF's papers at the APS. Also at the APS is a draft "Exposé des Faits" by JW with an explanation begun by JW and continued by WTF. Filed with those sheets is a half-sheet in WTF's hand that appears to be the first part of an intended answer to Thomas: BF had written to Bache & Shee as soon as M. Brillon requested it, but there had not yet been time to receive an answer. BF would send another by the first packet boat (APS). In a now-missing letter of June 17, BF asked RB to send an accounting of Thomas' venture and any balance due: RB to BF, Aug. 28, 1784 (Musée de la Coopération franco-américaine du Château de Blérancourt).
2. Moritz Chretien Meyer, from Saxony, had introduced himself to BF the previous October. On the day BF wrote this recommendation, he paid Meyer 395 *l.t.* in wages: XLI, 162.

From Henry Laurens

ALS: Library of Congress; copy: University of South Carolina Library

Dear Sir,   London 10th. May 1784.

The 6th. Inst: I had the honor of addressing you by Post & availing myself of the encouragement you had given to hope for a supply of Money from Monsr. Grand on account of the United States, I requested that Gentleman by the same conveyance to remit to me the full value of One Thousand or twelve hundred Guineas which I repeat in order to guard against accidents as my affairs will not admit of delay.

I am presently to commence a journey to Bath with my Sister in Law, where I shall stay no longer than shall be necessary to see her settled, perhaps not more than eight & forty hours, then return here & take the first good opportunity for proceeding to America.

Inclosed with this are the Remarks which My Son inform'd me you wish'd to have,[3] I think they are highly honour'd by your attention, the bearer Colo. Harmar does not leave London till Wednesday or Thursday next I have intreated him to take some of the latest News Papers for you.

With great Esteem & Respect I have the honor to be Dear sir Your obedient humble servant   HENRY LAURENS

His Excellency Benjamin Franklin Esquire Passy.

From Edward Bridgen   ALS: American Philosophical Society

London May 11 1784

I was favoured with your Excellency's Letter by Colll: Harmar under the date of April 17th:. In compliance with your request I have delivered to Coll: H's care 3 Roles & 1 parcell the particulars of their contents you will find in the inclosed paper and how they are addressed.[4]

3. Not found.

4. BF's April 17 letter has not been located, nor has the "inclosed paper." Nearly a year earlier, Bridgen had informed BF of the prints and journals that were due to him from the Society of Antiquaries: XL, 145. From the present letter, it appears that BF had been expecting the shipment for some time.

You say truly Sir that I promised to send them by the Count de Moustier, who leaving England sooner that I expected,[5] with the neglect of the Society's porter, prevented it, and having no good opportunity presenting, after that, by which I could send them with safety, and convenience occasioned the delay until I was informed by our Good & Mutual Friend Dr: Price some Months ago that you intended Visiting your Friends here in April,[6] was the reason of a further delay, and I hope my Dr: Sir that you will have the Goodness to admit the above reasons as my Excuse.

As the 12 last prints were not delivered until the 23d of Last Month, you were not intitled to them until your arrears to Xt:mas were paid up, I have taken the Liberty to pay the 2 Guineas for you due at that time, which may be repaid at any time, but if you wish that I should purchase the 2 first Vol: for 30s I will do it and it may be repaid me with the 2 Guineas whenever you please.

It was by the advice of Mr Laurons that I took the liberty to address the outside covers to the Count de Vergennes, and to be lodged at the Custom House at Callais for his orders, as Prints are either prohibited, or pay a heavy Duty in France, so that you must advise the Count thereof, and he will Issue out his orders in consequence for you to receive them safe, which I shall be glad to hear of.

I should have presumed to have purchased for you a work which is just Published by Mr Astle intitled the Origin & progress of Writing[7] 1£:11s:6, but Mr Astle tells me that it is sold by *Barrois le jeune sur le Quay des Augistines*[8] & I thought best not to Load the Coll: with any addittional weight. I think that your

5. The comte de Moustier, interim minister to the British court, returned to France in May, 1783: XXXIX, 546n; *London Chron.*, May 22, 1783.

6. BF had not been quite so specific: XLI, 7.

7. *The Origin and Progress of Writing* . . . (London, 1784), was the most significant work of Thomas Astle (*ODNB*), a fellow of the Society of Antiquaries and of the Royal Society. It traced the history and evolution of hieroglyphics, letterforms and numerals, treated ciphers and secret writing, and included a chapter on the history of printing.

8. Paris publisher and bookseller Pierre-Théophile Barrois, *dit* Barrois le jeune: Frédéric Barbier *et al.*, eds., *Dictionnaire des imprimeurs, libraires et gens du livre à Paris, 1701–1789* (1 vol. to date, Geneva, 2007–), I, 152–4.

Excellency will be much pleased with it besides I beleive that you once did write something yourself on that Subject.

And now my Dr Sir will I repeat my thanks, my most respectful regards & best Wishes to the Good Doctr: Franklin, The Friend of Mankind in behalf of my self & my fellow-men in general, and in particular for your interesting yourself in my Affairs in No Carolina, which I have now reason to hope will have the desired effect.[9] My poor Patty[1] says all that is respectful & Grateful but is in too weak a State to suffer me to pay you my regards in person however I beg your Excellency will be assured of my most sincerely & Affectionately yours whilst

EDWD: BRIDGEN

If Mr Jay is with you pray be so good as to pay him my respects?

I have delivered a packett from Laurens for you to Col: Harmar.[2]

His Excellency Benjn: Franklin

Addressed: His Excellency / Benjn: Franklin Esqr / at Passey / near Paris

Notation: E. Bridgen. 11 May 1784

From the Baron de Feriet   AL: American Philosophical Society

Versailles ce mardi 11 mai 1784

Mr. De Feriet a L'honneur de faire part a Monsieur francklin qu'il est convenu avec Les directeurs de la manufacture de st. cloud, qu'on ferait demain tous Les Verres D'harmonica;[3] en

9. BF's intervention notwithstanding, Bridgen was still waiting for a ruling by the N.C. legislature on restoring his property. See XXXVIII, 243; XLI, 464n.

1. Martha Richardson Bridgen: XXVI, 126n; XXXI, 130.

2. Most likely Laurens to BF, May 10, above, and its enclosures.

3. The previous January, Feriet had been conferring with the duchesse de Villeroi about armonicas: XLI, 493. He had evidently settled on the kind he wanted, and had ordered bowls from the *cristallerie* in Sèvres at the parc de Saint-Cloud. Established *c.* 1782 by Lambert and Boyer, the factory employed a number of English artisans and was one of the first in France to

conséquence, demain dès six heures du matin, il sera rendu a La manufacture avec tous les modéles, et il veillera soigneusement a ce que les verres soyent faits avec toute L'éxactitude possible. Si la santé et les affaires de monsieur francklin lui permettaient d'y venir faire un tour dans le courant de la journée, ses observations pouraient contribuer a la perfection de L'ouvrage, et il pourait juger par lui même si les Moyens proposés par les directeurs pour accorder les verres en les usant, sont praticables ou non.

Mr. de feriet prie Monsieur francklin d'agréer L'homage de son tendre et respectueux attachement que toute sa famille partage.

Notation: Feriet M. De, Versailles 11 Mai 1784.—

From Stephen Hopkins[4]   LS: American Philosophical Society

Sir,   Providence May 11th. 1784.

Mr. Solomon Drown, a native of this place, is a young gentleman of great modesty, and of a very fair character; has spent many years in his Studies here, and in his attendance on the various Medical Lectures at Philadelphia; and is now about to take a Voyage to France, in order to perfect his knowledge in the healing Art, and in the French Language.[5]

---

manufacture English-style crystal: James Barrelet, *La Verrerie en France de l'époque gallo-romaine à nos jours* (Paris, 1953), pp. 109, 171, 177.

4. Chancellor of the College of Rhode Island: XLI, 431.

5. Solomon Drowne (1753–1834), a 1773 graduate of the College of Rhode Island (later Brown University), studied medicine at the College of Philadelphia and served as a surgeon during the Revolution. In 1783 he was elected a fellow of the College of Rhode Island. Drowne sailed for England in November, 1784, and would visit BF the following June. After his return to the United States in the summer of 1785, he practiced medicine and taught, and was instrumental in founding the medical school at Brown University: Solomon Drowne, *Journal of a Cruise in the Fall of 1780 in the Private-Sloop of War, Hope . . .* (New York, 1872), pp. 18–26; Frederick C. Waite, "The Third Medical College in New England, that of Brown University (1811–1828)," *New England Jour. of Medicine,* CCVII (1932), 31; Solomon Drowne's diary, Brown University Library.

Any favours shown, or patronage afforded him while in France, will be very gratefully acknowledged by him, who is with sincere esteem, Your affectionate old Friend,

STEP HOPKINS

His Excellency Benja. Franklin Esqr.

Addressed: His Excellency Benja. Franklin Esqr. / Paris.

Notation: Hopkins May 11. 1784

From Thomas Percival   ALS: American Philosophical Society

Dear Sir.   Manchester May 11th. 1784.

I cannot omit the favourable opportunity, which the Tour of my young Friend Mr. White[6] affords me, of paying my respects to you; and of requesting your acceptance of a Vol. of Moral and Literary Dissertations, which I have just published.[7] Your approbation of my little Work, I should deem a distinguished honour: But whatever opinion you may form of it, I hope and trust it will not be unacceptable to you, as a memorial of my cordial esteem & veneration.

How happy would it render your Friends, to see you once more in England! But with respect to yourself, it is doubtful whether you might not feel more pain than pleasure, from such a visit. Time has produced many changes, which you would lament: and amongst these, the loss of Sir John Pringle has almost ruined the Royal Society. But you are no stranger, I presume, to the disgraceful contentions of that learned body, & to the

6. Thomas White was the son of Percival's friend and colleague Charles White, F.R.S., a prominent Manchester surgeon (*ODNB*). He studied medicine in London and Edinburgh, was elected to the Royal Medical Society of Edinburgh in 1782, and assisted with his father's lectures in 1783. He completed medical training at Leiden after his present "Tour": Edward M. Brockbank, *Sketches of the Lives and Work of the Honorary Medical Staff of the Manchester Infirmary* . . . (Manchester, Eng., 1904), pp. 41, 125–6; *Laws and List of the Members of the Medical Society of Edinburgh* . . . (Edinburgh, 1792), p. 81.

7. *Moral and Literary Dissertations, on the Following Subjects* . . . (Warrington, Eng., and London, 1784).

234

conduct of the President, both to his excellent predecessor and to many of the Fellows.[8]

We have established a very useful Literary & Philosophical Society here, and shall soon publish a Vol. of Memoirs.[9] I shall inclose the account of another Institution, in the success of which, I am much interested. Mr. White, who is an intelligent young man, will inform you of the progress we have made in it, and of the encouragement with which it has been honoured.[1]

I have not heard very lately either from Dr. Price or Dr. Priestley. But I believe they are both well. From Mr. Vaughan I had a letter a few days ago. He has sent me some curious observations on Cold, made by Professor Patrick Wilson, at Glasgow.[2] I would transmit a copy of the paper, but you will probably have it communicated to you, long before this packet arrives.

With the most cordial respect and esteem, I am, Dear Sir, Your faithful, & very affect. hble. Servt.   Tho. Percival

Addressed: To / Doctor Benjn. Franklin / Paris.— / with a Book—by favr. of Mr. White

Notation: Thomas Percival 11 May 1784

8. John Pringle died in January, 1782, several years after resigning as president of the Royal Society: XXVII, 505n; XXXVI, 407n. For the controversy surrounding the leadership of his successor, Joseph Banks, see Banks to BF, March 23, and Richard Price to BF, April 6.

9. The society was founded in Percival's home in 1781, and as of 1782 he served as its president. Charles White was also a founding member: *ODNB*, under Percival and White. Volumes 1 and 2 of *Memoirs of the Literary and Philosophical Society of Manchester* were both published in 1785.

1. The other "Institution" was the College of Arts and Sciences, which Percival, White, and other members of the Literary and Philosophical Society founded in June, 1783, as an educational institution for tradesmen. Percival was its president. The account he enclosed was its first report, which described a course of evening lectures in natural philosophy, belles lettres, mathematics, history, law, commerce, and ethics: *College of Arts and Sciences, instituted at Manchester, June VI, MDCCLXXXIII* (Manchester, 1783). (BF's copy, bound with other pamphlets, is at the Hist. Soc. of Pa.) Despite its promising beginning, the college lasted barely five years: A. E. Musson and Eric Robinson, *Science and Technology in the Industrial Revolution* (Manchester, Eng., 1969), pp. 92–3.

2. For Wilson and a description of the essay referenced here see our annotation of BF to Benjamin Vaughan, April 29.

To Samuel Mather

ALS: Massachusetts Historical Society; transcript: Library of Congress

Revd. Sir,   Passy, May 12. 1784.

I received your kind Letter with your excellent Advice to the People of the United States,[3] which I read with great Pleasure, and hope it will be duly regarded.— Such Writings tho' they may be lightly pass'd over by many Readers, yet if they make a deep Impression on one active Mind in an hundred, the Effects may be considerable. Permit me to mention one little Instance, which tho' it relates to my self, will not be quite uninteresting to you. When I was a Boy, I met with a Book intitled *Essays to do Good,* which I think was written by your Father. It had been so little regarded by a former Possessor, that several Leaves of it were torn out: But the Remainder gave me such a Turn of Thinking as to have an Influence on my Conduct thro' Life;[4] for I have always set a greater Value on the Character of a *Doer of Good,* than on any other kind of Reputation; and if I have been, as you seem to think, a useful Citizen, the Publick owes the Advantage of it to that Book.— You mention your being in your 78th Year. I am in my 79th. We are grown old together. It is now more than 60 Years since I left Boston, but I remember well both your Father and Grandfather[5] having heard them both in the Pulpit, and seen them in their Houses. The last Time I saw your Father was in the Beginning of 1724, when I visited him after my first Trip to Pennsylvania. He receiv'd me in his Library, and on my taking Leave show'd me a shorter way out of the House thro' a narrow Passage which was cross'd by a Beam overhead. We were still talking as I withdrew, he accompanying me behind, and I turning partly towards him, when he said hastily Stoop, Stoop! I did not understand him till I felt my Head hit against the Beam. He was a Man that never miss'd any Occasion of giving Instruction, and upon this he said to me, *You are young and have the World before you;* STOOP *as you go through it,*

3. Mather's letter of Nov. 13, 1783, enclosed a copy of his *Dying Legacy of an Aged Minister:* XLI, 199–200.

4. BF here repeats, in nearly the same words, what he had written about Cotton Mather's *Essays to Do Good* in his autobiography: *Autobiog.,* p. 58.

5. Increase Mather.

and you will miss many hard Thumps. This Advice, thus beat into my head has frequently been of use to me, and I often think of it when I see Pride mortified, & Misfortunes brought upon People by their carrying their Heads too high.—[6] I long much to see again my native Place, and once hoped to lay my Bones there. I left it in 1723; I visited it in 1733, 1743, 1753, & 1763. In 1773 I was in England; in 1775 I had a Sight of it, but could not enter, it being in Possession of the Enemy. I did hope to have been there in 1783, but could not obtain my Dismission from this Employment here. And now I fear I shall never have that Happiness. My best Wishes however attend my dear Country. *Esto perpetua:*[7] It is now blest with an excellent Constitution. May it last forever.—

This powerful Monarchy continues its Friendship for the United States. It is a Friendship of the utmost Importance to our Security, & should be carefully cultivated. Britain has not yet well digested the Loss of its Dominion over us, and has still at times some flattering Hopes of recovering it. Accidents may encrease those Hopes, and encourage dangerous Attempts. A Breach between us and France would infallibly bring the English again upon our Backs. And yet we have some wild Heads among our Country-men, who are endeavouring to weaken that Connection!— Let us preserve our Reputation by performing our Engagements, our Credit by fulfilling our Contracts, and our Friends by Gratitude & Kindness; for we know not how soon we may again have occasion for all of them.

With great and sincere Esteem, I have the honour to be, Reverend Sir, Your most obedient & most humble Servant

B FRANKLIN

Revd Dr Mather

Notation: Dr Franklin to Dr Mather 1784.

---

6. BF had told this story to Samuel Mather ten years earlier; see XX, 287.
7. Translated by BF in the next sentence: May it last forever.

To Thomas Mifflin

Press copy of LS[8] and AL (draft):[9] Library of Congress; copy: Yale University Library; transcript: National Archives

Sir,   Passy, May 12th.[–13][1] 1784

In my last[2] I acquainted your Excellency that Mr. Hartley was soon expected here to exchange Ratifications of the definitive Treaty. He is now arrived, and proposes to make the Exchange this Afternoon: I shall then be enabled to send a Copy.—

Enclosed is the new British Proclamation respecting our Trade with their Colonies.[3] It is said to be a temporary Provision 'till Parliament can assemble and make some proper regulating Law, or till a Commercial Treaty shall be framed and agreed to. Mr Hartley expects Instructions for planning with us such a Treaty. The Ministry are supposed to have been too busy with the new Elections when he left London, to think of those Matters.

This Court has not compleated its intended new System for the Trade of their Colonies, so that I cannot yet give a certain Acct of the Advantages that will in fine be allow'd us. At present it is said we are to have two Free-Ports, Tobago & the Mole;[4] and that we may carry Lumber and all sorts of Provisions to the rest, except Flour, which is reserved in Favour of Bourdeaux;

8. In WTF's hand.

9. At the top of this draft, BF later wrote, "Sent by Mr. Jay who sail'd from Dover the 31st." He must have based this erroneous date on the June 2 letter he received from Thomas Thompson (below). Jay forwarded the present letter to Mifflin on July 25, the day after he arrived in New York: *Jay Papers*, III, 589.

1. BF added the following postscript to the now-missing LS: "May 13. I now enclose a Copy of the Ratification of the Definitive Treaty, on the part of His Britannic Majesty." (The postscript is present in both the copy and transcript listed above.) On Aug. 2 Congress, meeting in Annapolis as the Committee of the States, voted to transmit the British ratification to the governors and have it both entered into the journal and printed in the *Md. Gaz.: JCC*, XXVII, 615–24.

2. BF and Jay to Mifflin, April 16, above.

3. Presumably the copy of the April 16 Order in Council that Laurens had sent BF via Hartley; see Laurens to BF, April 18, and BF to Laurens, April 29.

4. Môle-St.-Nicolas on the northern coast of St.-Domingue.

and that we shall be permitted to export Coffee, Rum, Melasses and some Sugar for our own Consumption.[5]

We have had under Consideration a Commercial Treaty proposed to us by the King of Prussia, and have sent it back with our Remarks to Mr Adams,[6] who will I suppose transmit it immediately to Congress. Those plann'd with Denmark and Portugal wait its Determination.[7]

Be pleased to present my dutiful Respects to the Congress, and believe me to be, with sincere and great Esteem Sir, Your Excellency's most obedient & most humble Servant.

B. FRANKLIN

His Exy. T. Mifflin Esq.—

Commission to Negotiate a Treaty of Amity and Commerce with Prussia[8]

DS: Massachusetts Historical Society

[May 12, 1784]

The United States in Congress Assembled—

To all to whom these presents shall come or be made known Send Greeting—

5. BF had given a similar report to Henry Laurens on Feb. 12: XLI, 557.

6. BF and Jay to JA, April 29, above.

7. Negotiations for treaties with both nations had begun in 1783: XXXIX, 252, 467–8; XL, 63.

8. Congress approved the general language of this commission on May 11, to be adapted for the 20 such documents authorizing BF, JA, and TJ to negotiate treaties with the 16 European and four North African powers specified in the instructions published above under May 7[–June 3]. The text, using Russia as the model, was drafted by Charles Thomson and modified by Elbridge Gerry: *Jefferson Papers*, VII, 261–5. David Humphreys, whom Congress elected as the commissioners' secretary on May 12 (see GW to BF, June 2), copied the text and made a list of the titles of all the other recipients (National Archives). On May 16, Thomson sent all 20 commissions to TJ, who brought them to France. (They are now at the Mass. Hist. Soc.) Each is signed by Thomas Mifflin and attested by Thomson, and bears the seal of the United States. BF labeled all but one of them with the name of the state. The one exception is the Holy Roman Empire, whose commission he labeled "Emperor". We print as a sample the commission to treat with Prussia because that power was the only one to conclude a treaty with the United

Whereas an intercourse between the Subjects of His Prussian Majesty and the Citizens of the United States of America founded on the principles of equality, reciprocity and friendship may be of mutual advantage to both Nations. Now therefore Know Ye that we reposing special trust and confidence in the integrity, prudence and ability of our trusty and beloved the honorable John Adams late one of our ministers plenipotentiary for negotiating a peace and heretofore a Delegate in Congress from the State of Massachusetts and Chief Justice of the said State—the honorable Doctor Benjamin Franklin our minister plenipotentiary at the Court of Versailles and late another of our ministers plenipotentiary for negotiating a peace and the honorable Thomas Jefferson a delegate in Congress from the State of Virginia and late Governor of the said State have nominated, constituted and appointed and by these presents do nominate, constitute and appoint them the said John Adams, Benjamin Franklin and Thomas Jefferson our ministers plenipotentiary giving to them or the majority of them full power and authority for us and in our name to confer, treat and negotiate with the Ambassador, Minister or Commissioner of his said Prussian Majesty vested with full and sufficient powers of and concerning a Treaty of Amity and Commerce to make and receive propositions for such Treaty and to conclude and sign the same, transmitting it to the United States in Congress Assembled for their final ratification. This Commission to continue in force for a term not exceeding two years from the date hereof—

In Testimony whereof we have caused the Seal of the United States to be hereunto affixed Witness His Excellency Thomas Mifflin president this twelfth day of May in the year of our Lord one thousand seven hundred and eighty four and of the Sovereignty & Independence of the United States of America the Eighth. Thomas Mifflin
Chas Thomson secy.

States before BF left France. Textual variations among the 20 commissions are minor; we have silently corrected one copying error in this text.

From Benjamin Morel Dufaux

ALS: American Philosophical Society

Paris 12th May, [1784]

Honourable Sir.   hotel des Prouvairs rue des Prouvairs

If real Services rendered to the Subjects of the united States in the most Critical times when no Soul durst to Employ himself for, fearing blame, can Entitle to Claim of the protection of your Excellency, I flatter I have an undoubtfull right to it. Those Important Services I have already mentioned in a memoir I had presented to your Excellency[9] but having thought it more usefull for me to State them myself, I supposed my Coming to Paris was the real way to pay you my respects. Shall Esteem myself happy your Excellency wou'd permit me to be introduced by M Grand who at all times has honoured my family with his much Esteemed friendship.

I am with Respect, of your Excellency the most humble & most obedient Servant   MOREL DUFAUX
of Dunkirk

His Excellency Benjamin franklin Esqr Passy

Notation: Morel Dufaux 12 May

To John and Sarah Jay

Passy May 13. 1784

My dear Friends, I find I shall not be able to see you again as I intended. My best Wishes however go with you, that you may have a prosperous Voyage and a happy sight of your Friends and Families.[2]

---

9. Petitioning to be appointed American consul in Dunkirk: XLI, 97.

1. Made for the preparation of WTF's edition of BF's writings. It is published in WTF, *Memoirs*, I, 359–60.

2. The Jays left Paris on May 16, sailed from Dover on June 1 on the ship *Edward*, and arrived at New York on July 24: *Jay Papers*, III, 589.

Mr. Jay was so kind as to offer his Friendly Services to me in America. He will oblige me much by endeavouring to forward my discharge from this Employment.[3] Repose is now my only Ambition. If too he should think with me, that my Grandson is qualified to serve the States as Secretary to a future Minister at this Court or as Chargé des Affaires, and will be kind enough to recommend such an appointment, it will exceedingly oblige me. I have twice mentioned this in my letter to Congress,[4] but have not been favored with any Answer; which is hard, because the suspense prevents my endeavouring to promote him in some other way. I would not however be importunate; and therefore if Mr. Jay should use his Interest without Effect, I will trouble them no more on the subject. My Grandson's acquaintance with the Language, with the Court and Customs here, and the particular Regard M. de Vergennes has for him, are Circumstances in his favor.

God bless and protect you both. Embrace my little Friend[5] for me, and believe me ever yours &ca   B FRANKLIN

To Henry Laurens: Extract   Extract:[6] Library of Congress

Passy May 13. 1784.
—I am sorry for the numerous Disappointments you have lately met with. The World it's true is full of Disappointments, but

3. BF's desire to be released from his duties came close to being fulfilled. On March 27, William Ellery made a motion in Congress to allow BF to retire, citing his "repeated applications." The motion was referred to a congressional committee, which did not make its report until May 12, by which time Congress had appointed BF to a new commission to negotiate commercial treaties in Europe; see Congress' instructions to the American commissioners, May 7[–June 3], above. The committee's report, therefore, recommended that a decision about BF's recall be deferred until after the treaties had been negotiated: *JCC*, XXVI, 171; XXVII, 377.

4. In 1781 and in late 1783: XXXIV, 447–8; XLI, 357–8. BF had also raised the topic with Secretary Livingston: XL, 366.

5. The Jays' daughter Maria (b. Feb. 20, 1782), who was part of BF's household for several months in 1783: XL, 180n; *Jay Papers*, I, facing p. lxxvi; II, 670.

6. In WTF's hand and published in WTF, *Memoirs*, I, 360. The present letter responds to points made in Laurens' May 6 letter, above, which BF probably acknowledged in the missing portion of his letter.

they are not equally divided, and you have had more than your share.

The Ratifications of the definitive Treaty are now exchang'd; but Mr. Hartley waits for Instructions respecting a Treaty of Commerce, which from what you observe, may probably never arrive. I shall however be glad to receive what you are so good as to promise me, your Thoughts on the Subject of such a Treaty.

You have been so kind as to offer me your friendly services in America. You will oblige me greatly in forwarding my Dismission from this Employment, for I long much to be at home: And if you should think my Grandson qualified to serve the States as Secretary to my Successor, or Chargé des Affaires 'till a Successor arrives, I shall thank You for recommending him. His Knowledge of this Court, and Acquaintance with the Language; and the Esteem the Minister[7] has for him, are Circumstances in his favor: his long Experience in the Business here is another, he having served an Apprenticeship to it for more than seven Years. His Intelligence, Discretion & Address, you can judge better of than myself, who may be partial. His Fidelity & Exactitude in performing his Duty, I can answer for.

My best Wishes attend you, your very valuable Son, and amiable Daughter. God bless you all, and give you a good Voyage, and a happy Meeting with your Friends, with long Life, Health & Prosperity, is the sincere Prayer of Your affectionate, humble servant   B. FRANKLIN

To Charles Thomson

Two LS: Library of Congress, Historical Society of Pennsylvania[8]

Dear Sir,   Passy, May 13th. 1784.

Yesterday Evening Mr. Hartley met with Mr. Jay and myself, when the Ratifications of the Definitive Treaty were exchanged. I send a Copy of the English Ratification to the President.[9]

7. Presumably Vergennes.
8. Marked "Copy" by WTF.
9. Enclosed in BF to Mifflin, May 12[-13], above.

Thus the great and hazardous Enterprize we have been engaged in, is, God be praised, happily compleated: An Event I hardly expected I should live to see. A few Years of Peace, well improved, will restore and encrease our Strength: But our future Safety will depend on our Union and our Virtue. Britain will be long watching for Advantages, to recover what she has lost. If we do not convince the World that we are a Nation to be depended on for Fidelity in Treaties; if we appear negligent in paying our Debts, and ungrateful to those who have served and befriended us; our Reputation, and all the Strength it is capable of procuring, will be lost, and fresh Attacks upon us will be encouraged and promoted by better Prospects of Success. Let us therefore beware of being lulled into a dangerous Security; and of being both enervated and impoverish'd by Luxury; of being weakened by internal Contentions and Divisions; of being shamefully extravagant in contracting private Debts, while we are backward in discharging honourably those of the Publick; of Neglect in militia Exercises and Discipline, and in providing Stores of Arms and Munition of War, to be ready on Occasion: For all these are Circumstances that give Confidence to Enemies and Diffidence to Friends; and the Expences required to prevent a War, are much lighter than those that will, if not prevented, be absolutely necessary to maintain it.

I am long kept in Suspense without being able to learn the Purpose of Congress respecting my request of Recall, and that of some Employment for my Secretary W. Temple Franklin. If I am kept here another Winter and as much weakened by it as by the last I may as well resolve to spend the remainder of my Days here; for I shall hardly be able to bear the Fatigues of the Voyage in returning. During my long Absence from America my Friends are continually diminishing by Death, and my Inducements to return in Proportion. But I can make no Preparations either for going conveniently, or staying comfortably here, nor take any Steps towards making some other Provision for my Grandson, till I know what I am to expect. Be so good my dear Friend, to send me a little private Information. With great Esteem, I am ever, Yours most affectionately   B. FRANKLIN

Charles Thomson Esqr. secy. of Congress.

Endorsed: Letter May 13. 1784 Doctr B. Franklin Recd. July 26.
1784[1]

From David Hartley[2]   ALS: American Philosophical Society

My Dear friend   Paris May 13 1784 7 o'clock morning
    I shd be much obliged to you if you cd send me *two* or *three*
words this evening after you have seen the Minister[3] viz only
thus much *He can* or *He can not,* because as the time advances
to the meeting of Parlt., It wd be necessary for me to send the

1. On July 28 Thomson forwarded extracts of this letter to Samuel
Hardy, chairman of the Committee of the States: Smith, *Letters,* XXI,
745–6.
2. On March 31 Hartley had stood for election to Parliament for his former seat of Kingston-upon-Hull. The constituency elected two members,
but Hartley came in third. After one of the victors, William Wilberforce,
chose to vacate his seat, Hartley published a pamphlet appealing for it.
Written in the form of a letter dated Paris, May 18, 1784, it is the "Address"
he refers to in the present letter, ultimately published as *Address to the Right
Worshipful the Mayor and Corporation, to the Worshipful the Wardens and
Corporation of the Trinity House, and to the Worthy Burgesses of the Town of
Kingston upon Hull.* Hartley implies here that BF had agreed to ask Vergennes whether the pamphlet could be printed in Paris. We have no record
of BF's intercession, nor any reason to think that the address was printed in
France. The copy owned by BF (APS), whose title page does not specify
the publisher or place of publication, is thought to have been printed in
England. A second version, issued by J. Debrett in London, was announced
in the *Public Advertiser* on June 12, 1784. Hartley's attempt to regain the
seat was ultimately unsuccessful: Namier and Brooke, *House of Commons,*
I, 434–5; II, 592–3; III, 636–7.
3. According to his own account, Hartley believed that he had insulted
Vergennes when, while announcing his mission to exchange treaty ratifications, he referred to the Americans as "those who were your allies." Vergennes responded, "And who still are," to which Hartley countered, "That
is all over." Vergennes answered that "Those who have once been the allies of France are her allies always": George H. Guttridge, *David Hartley,
M.P.: an Advocate of Conciliation, 1774–1783* (Berkeley, Calif., and London, 1926), pp. 318–19.

first part to England by our Courier early tomorrow morning if the printer cannot do the business here. I shall be employed the whole of this day & tomorrow morning, in writing my letters, & in transcribing the first part of the Address. I wd rather receive *two* words from you than *three* But if *three* I must lose no time in England. Yours ever   D H—

Addressed: To Dr Franklin &c &c &c / Passy

From Poissonnier   L: American Philosophical Society

[before May 14, 1784][4]

M Poissonnier a l'honneur de présenter son Respect à Monsieur Franklin et de lui Rappeller qu'il a promis de Vouloir bien signer le rapport des Commissaires de la Société Royale de Medécine, Sur les Bains de Mr Albert.[5] En Conséquence il a l'honneur de lui envoier ce Rapport que M Albert aura celui de lui présenter lui même, avec la Copie de ce même Rapport, afin que Monsieur franklin puisse en faire plus aisement la lecture, S'il juge à propos d'en prendre Connaissance.

Notation: Poissonier.—

4. The date when the report on Nicolas Albert's baths was read to the Societé royale de médecine. For Albert and his baths see XLI, 98–9.

5. The commissioners were BF, Poissonnier, Vicq d'Azyr, Claude-Antoine Caille, and Jacques Dehorne. Dehorne was physician to the duc d'Orléans and the comtesse d'Artois and editor of the *Jour. de médecine militaire:* Jean Sgard, ed., *Dictionnaire des Journalistes: 1600–1789* (2 vols., Oxford, 1999), I, 278–9. After describing the baths and their therapeutic potential, the commissioners lauded Albert for reserving rooms for the poor and recommended the establishment for government protection. (The signed report, which is heavily edited, is at the library of the Académie nationale de médecine.) The society endorsed the commission's findings at its May 14 meeting and further recommended that the price of admission be reduced so that all social classes could enjoy the benefits of the facility: *Rapport sur l'établissement de bains du sieur Albert, au nom d'une commission composée de MM. Poissonnier, Franklin, de Horne, Vicq d'Azyr et Caille, rapporteur* (Paris, 1784).

From Franz Anton Mesmer[6]

Mr. [May 14, 1784]

Vous êtes à la tête des Commissaires que le Gouvernement a envoyés chez M. D'Eslon pour obtenir la révélation de ma découverte, et en constater l'efficacité.

Quand Mr. d'Elon S'est approché auprès de moi et quand J'ai jugé à propos de lui laisser entrevoir quelques parties du Système de mes connoissances, J'ai exigé de lui Sa parole d'honneur, qu'il ne rendroit jamais public, sans en avoir auparavant obtenu mon aveu, le petit nombre d'idées nouvelles que je pourrois lui confier.

M. d'Eslon a depuis Souscrit un acte par lequel il reconnoît que le Magnétisme animal est ma propriété et qu'en disposer Sans mon consentement, c'est se rendre coupable d'un délit aussi odieux que punissable.[8]

6. The present letter was apparently written for Mesmer by Nicolas Bergasse (*DBF*), an *avocat au Parlement* and a devoted patient. Bergasse served as Mesmer's secretary and claimed to have written this and many other letters and pamphlets for the doctor, whose French was not fluent. In 1785, angered by what he perceived as Mesmer's betrayal of him, he published a highly critical pamphlet that purported to set the record straight: *Observations de M. Bergasse, sur un Écrit du Docteur Mesmer* . . . (London [*i.e.*, Paris?], 1785). See, in particular, pp. 4, 11, 22, 24–5.

7. One of three enclosures (numbered 3, 4, and 5) that Mesmer sent on Dec. 3 to Joly de Fleury, the *procureur-général* of the Parlement of Paris, under cover of a letter jointly signed by 14 of his students. The enclosures were the present letter; Mesmer's May 18 letter to the baron de Breteuil, enclosing a copy of the present letter; and BF's response to Mesmer of May 23 (below). Mesmer's appeal of Dec. 3 requested the Parlement's protection against "une persécution méthodique de la part des savants et des sages": Robert Darnton, *Mesmerism and the End of the Enlightenment in France* (Cambridge, Mass., 1968), p. 86n.

Mesmer had actually made the present letter public long before sending a copy to Joly de Fleury. On Aug. 20, having learned that the commission to investigate animal magnetism was about to issue its report, he sent it to the *Jour. de Paris* under cover of a letter rejecting the legitimacy of the commission. The journal declined to print his submission, for unspecified reasons ("considérations particulières"), but instead issued the two letters as a pamphlet: *Lettres de M. Mesmer, à Messieurs les auteurs du Journal de Paris, et à M. Franklin* ([Paris, 1784]).

8. This last phrase is taken from the May 12, 1783, contract between Mesmer and Deslon, in which Deslon recognized Mesmer as the author

247

Cependant au mépris de ses Sermens et de l'acte qu'il a Sous-crit, M. d'Eslon a non Seulement osé disposer de ma propriété pour lui même; mais il a trouvé des hommes qui n'ont pas craint de partager avec lui mes dépouilles. Trente Six Médecins, à ce qu'on m'assure, Sont venus chercher auprès de lui un Systême de connoissances sur lequel il doit se taire, et qu'il ne peut leur révéler Sans manquer aux loix de l'honneur.[9]

Mr. d'Eslon a plus fait, il a osé demander au Gouvernement des Commissaires pour faire constater chez lui, une découverte qui n'est pas à lui, une découverte qu'il a dérobée à celui qui en est l'inventeur, et dont, quoiqu'on en dise, il ne peut faire qu'un usage condamnable.

Le Gouvernement a crû Surement, que M. d'Eslon est l'au-teur de la découverte du Magnétisme animal, et qu'il possède le Systême de connoissances qui y est relatif dans toute son étendue.

Les Commissaires que le Gouvernement a choisis pour aller se faire instruire chez M. d'Eslon dans la Science du magnétisme animal, ont Surement crû la même chose.

Car je ne dois pas présumer, et je ne présume pas que si le Gouvernement et les commissaires qu'il a choisis, avoient pensé que le Magnétisme animal est dans les mains de M. deslon, une chose dérobée, et une chose qu'il ne possède que d'une manière absolument imparfaite; ils eussent pû se résoudre à l'Ecouter, il n'est pas dans les principes du Gouvernement de légitimer un attentat contre la propriété, et il n'est aucun des Commissaires Sur lesquels il a jetté les yeux qui veuille se rendre complice d'une perfidie. De plus le Gouvernement et les Commissaires auroient surement compris qu'en faisant au public le rapport de ce qui leur auroit été Enseigné, ou de ce qu'ils auroient vû chez M. Deslon, ils se mettroient dans le cas de faire ou un faux rapport, ou un rapport incomplet, et ils se seroient abstenus

---

of the discovery of animal magnetism, and considered the attempt to re-veal it to others without Mesmer's consent to be "un délit aussi odieux que punissable": *Jour. de Paris*, Dec. 13, 1783, sup.

9. Deslon himself claimed to have instructed 160 physicians, including 21 members of the Faculté de médecine: Deslon, *Observations sur les deux rapports de MM. les commissaires* . . . (Philadelphia [*i.e.*, Paris], 1784), p. 26.

d'une démarche qui nécessairement doit les exposer à quelque Blâme.

Il faut donc, Monsieur, que je vous apprenne, et que par vous, J'apprenne à tous les Commissaires, que le Gouvernement a nommés, ce que c'est que M. d'Eslon, de quel abus de confiance il s'est rendu coupable envers moi, Et combien sont foibles et imparfaites les connoissances qu'il m'a dérobées; Il faut que je vous l'apprenne, car il est de mon intérêt qu'on ne me juge pas d'après ce que M. d'Eslon pourroit dire; parcequ'encore je dois démasquer cet homme menteur, et qu'étant devenu l'objet public de ses calomnies, après avoir été trahi par lui de la manière la plus odieuse, Je ne veux pas qu'il dispose de la destinée d'une doctrine qui est à moi, dont moi Seul, J'ose le dire, Je connois l'importance et l'étendue,[1] et dont le développement fait avec imprudence, peut être aussi dangereux qu'il Sera bienfaisant si l'on veut enfin m'entendre.

En Conséquence, Monsieur, Je vous prie de lire avec la plus grande attention le mémoire que je joins à cette Lettre; vous y apprendrez une partie des délits que J'impute à M. d'Eslon, et vous ne tarderez pas à connoître combien peuvent devenir embarassantes pour le Gouvernement et pour vous, les relations que dans le dessein Seulement de me nuire, il a trouvé l'art d'établir entre le Gouvernement et vous d'une part, et entre lui et ses correspondans de l'autre.[2]

1. Mesmer previously claimed in letters to the *Jour. de Paris* that he had fully revealed his doctrine of animal magnetism to M. Amic, *médecin du roi* in the naval department, and to the Bailli des Barres, commander of the Order of Malta, who were now authorized to call themselves "possesseurs" of his discovery: *Jour. de Paris*, Oct. 31 and Dec. 13 (supplement), 1783.

2. In the copy of the present letter sent by Mesmer to the *Jour. de Paris*, he here inserted a footnote explaining that the memoir (now missing) was more than 150 pages in length and had not yet been published. "Mais tous les faits qu'il contient, & toutes les pièces sur lesquelles il est appuyé, seront connues quand il en sera tems. Si j'ai fait une grande découverte, je veux prouver que je n'étois pas indigne de la faire": *Lettres de M. Mesmer*, p. 12.

Bergasse asserted that he had written this memoir on Mesmer's behalf based on information provided by the latter; it was titled "Mémoire contre le Docteur d'Eslon." In his 1785 pamphlet Bergasse published an extract which focused on Deslon's breach of contract, and noted that he had since learned that most of the information Mesmer had provided him was false: *Observations de M. Bergasse*, pp. 25, 63–6, 92–3.

Ce mémoire devoit être imprimé dans le courant du mois de Janvier dernier, et devenir la première pièce d'un procès que je me proposois d'intenter à M. d'Eslon, ne pouvant parvenir à lui faire rendre un compte public de sa conduite, et à me justifier des imputations calomnieuses dont il a osé m'accabler. Le procès n'a pas été entrepris parcequ'on m'en a détourné parcequ'on m'a persuadé que le moment viendroit, où la vérité reprendroit son empire, et où tout naturellement M. D'eslon seroit placé dans la classe de ces hommes qui se trouvent toujours à coté de ceux qui ont fait de grandes choses, pour leur dérober, S'il Se peut, la gloire qui leur appartient, et mettre à profit leurs Succès.[3]

Le Mémoire, que je vous envoye a été déposé chez un notaire de Paris, il est également déposé chez un homme public à Londres, et Je viens d'en envoyer une copie à Vienne. J'espère que cette dernière sera remise incessamment aux mains de l'Empereur.[4]

Ma découverte interesse toutes les nations, et c'est pour toutes les nations que je veux faire et mon histoire et mon apologie. On peut donc ici, comme on l'a fait Ju'squa présent Etouffer ma voix, on ne fera que rendre ailleurs ma reclamation et plus imposante et plus terrible.

Je suis, comme vous, Monsieur, au nombre de ces hommes qu'on ne peut opprimer sans danger, au nombre de ces hommes qui, parcequ'ils ont fait de grandes choses, disposent de la honte, comme les hommes puissans disposent de l'autorité quoiqu'on ôse tenter, Mr, Comme vous, J'ai le monde pour Juge; et si l'on peut oublier le bien que j'ai fait, et empêcher le bien que je veux faire, J'aurai la postérité pour vengeur.

Je Suis &c.

Copie de la Lettre adressée à M. franklin par M. Mesmer le 14. may 1784.

3. Rumors circulated in June that a claim from Mesmer against Deslon for 150,000 *l.t.* was about to be argued in court by their lawyers. If Mesmer did file his lawsuit, it never went to trial: Bachaumont, *Mémoires secrets,* XXVI, 39–40, 276.

4. This paragraph was not included in the version Mesmer sent to the *Jour. de Paris.*

From Joseph-Mathias Gérard de Rayneval

ALS: American Philosophical Society

A Versailles le 15. mai 1784

Cette lettre, Monsieur, vous sera remise par m. de chateaufort, qui se rendra incessament en amérique en qualité de notre Consul général à Charlestown, c'est le même par qui vous aviéz bien voulu m'envoyer une letre pour M. le Dr. Price.[5] M. de Chateaufort a desiré d'être connu de vous, et je l'ai assûré que vous lui feriez accueil. J'y serai personnellement on ne peut pas plus sensible, etant depuis bien longtems attaché à M. de chateaufort. J'ai l'honneur d'etre avec un très Sincère attachement, Monsieur, votre trés humble et tres-obeissant Serviteur

DE RAYNEVAL

Notation: De Rayneval 15 May 1784

From John Marsden Pintard[6]

LS:[7] American Philosophical Society

Sir— Madeira 16th. May 1784

I beg leave to hand yr. Excy. the enclosed Introductory letter from my Uncle Elias Boudinot Esqr. & have the Pleasure

5. See XLI, 362. Chateaufort was appointed consul on April 25. His departure was delayed, and he did not reach the United States until the end of March, 1785. He returned to France the following year on account of ill health: Abraham P. Nasatir and Gary E. Monell, comps., *French Consuls in the United States: a Calendar of their Correspondence in the Archives Nationales* (Washington, D.C., 1967), p. 559.

6. An American merchant living in Madeira who solicited from his uncle Elias Boudinot a letter of recommendation (Aug. 23, 1783), which he is now sending to BF. For that letter, and a full identification of Pintard, see XL, 504–5.

7. Pintard must have sent duplicates of this letter and its enclosure to BF: both of the enclosures survive, though the present text, marked "Copy," is the sole surviving example of the cover letter. The copyist made several errors of punctuation that we have been able to silently correct based on a similar letter of the same date that Pintard sent to JA (Mass. Hist. Soc.). JA's letter is nearly the same as this one, except that it lacks one passage: the section relating to the *United States*, followed by Pintard's request that BF recommend Searle & Co. to French merchants.

to inform you that I have Scince recd a Letter from the President of Congress enclosing me a Commission Under the great Seal of the United States Appointing me Commercial Agent for the United States at the Islands of Madeira & Porto Santo, to manage the occasional Concerns of Congress, to Assist the American Traders with my advice & to Solicit their Affairs with the Portugese Government.[8] I am truley Sensible of the Honour Conferred on me by this Appointment, and it Shall be my Constant Study in the execution of my office, to give General Satisfaction to my Countreymen. I am happy in the Honour of this Introduction to you and if I can be any ways Usefull to your Excy. in this Island you will Please to command me. My Relation Mr. John Searle Senr. was Suddenly Caried off with a fit of the gout in the Stomach, in February last, but his Demise will make no alteration in the firm of the House the Buisness being carried on as usual by the Surviving Partners, who will ever make it their Study to Imitate the example of their worthy Partner. Any of your Excellency's friends who may in their way from Europe to America Stop in at Madeira will be rec'd and treated with true American hospitality. The 27th. ulto. Arived here from Philadelphia the United States Indiaman Capt Thomas Bell bound for the Coast of Coromandel & Canton in China. She tooke in 125 Pipes of Wine for the India Market from Messrs. John Searle & Co. whose Vast Connections in the India trade Put it in their Power to give Some the full hints respecting the voiage.[9] The Buisness of the Imperial East India Company is conducted by Messrs. John Searle & Co. at this Place. Should Your Excellcy or friends have Intrest with the french Company Trading to the East you will render me an eternal obligation by recommending this House to them. Should Your Excy. Honour

8. Pintard was elected to the post by Congress on Oct. 31, 1783: XL, 504n.

9. Though the phrasing here is obscure—probably because of copying errors—Pintard is most likely referring to the advice that Capt. Bell received from Searle & Co. when taking on the wine. The firm recommended sailing to Pondicherry rather than Canton, as the market was more favorable there. The *United States* reached Pondicherry on Dec. 26: William B. Clark, "Postscripts to the Voyage of the Merchant Ship *United States*," *PMHB*, LXXVI (1952), 300–2.

me with an Answer to this letter you will Please forward Those [*via*] London to the Care of Messrs. Beckford & James and those via Lisbon to the Care of Messrs. Herman Cremer Van Zeller & Dorhman Merchant there. Wishing your Excy. every degree of heath I remain with every Sentiment of Esteem & Regard Your Excellencys Most Obedient Humble Servant

JOHN MARSDEN PINTARD

(Copy)

From ——— [Saimier?]

LS: American Philosophical Society

Monsieur   Paris 16. may 1784

J'ai l'honneur de vous renvoyer la lettre du Capitaine Gardner, que vous avés bien voulu me confier et la Copie de celle de M. Texier négociant à Bordeaux.[1] D'après les faits qui y sont exposés la ferme générale a écrit Sur le Champ à Bordeaux, pour qu'il ne fut donné aucune Suitte au procès verbal qui a été rendu, aussi c'est une affaire que vous pouvés regarder comme arrangée. Cependant comme il y a une contravention rèelle, puisqu'il S'est trouvé un Excédent a la quantité de Tabac déclaré, La ferme Générale, espère que vous trouverés juste que le Capitaine Gardner, paye une legère amende [*de*] 12 *l.t.* qui Sera abandonnée aux Employés qui ont fait la Vérification.[2]

1. Gardner had petitioned BF in a letter of *c.* May 4 (above); we have no record of when BF forwarded it to the farmers general. Pierre Texier's letter, dated May 4, was written to Ménage de Pressigny, a farmer general for Bordeaux (*Almanach royal* for 1784, pp. 559, 564). Texier explained that Gardner had arrived in Bordeaux on May 1, and that the amount of tobacco on board was innocently underestimated by the broker who made the declaration on behalf of the captain. He asked the indulgence of the farmers general. APS.

2. Gardner thanked BF in a letter from London dated Aug. 10. He had just learned "that the Farmers General had been pleased to remit the Fine to which I had become liable by the unlucky mistake of my Broker in reporting my Tobacco," a result that had been entirely owing to "the friendly interposition of your Excellency." APS.

Je suis avec un profond respect Monsieur Votre trés humble et
trés Obéissant Serviteur   [SAIMIER?]

From Lafayette   ALS: University of Pennsylvania Library

My dear Sir   Paris Monday Evening [May 17, 1784]³
In Case the Arrêt for our free ports Has not Yet Come to
Your Excellency's Hands, I Have the Honour to Send You one
Which I Have just Now Got— Most Respectfully and Affec-
tionately Yours   LAFAYETTE

From ———— Gaspard de Bebiniere
                    L: American Philosophical Society

M.   Ce Mardi 18. May 1784./.
Le Sr. Gaspard de Bebiniere Machiniste, a l'honneur de
vous faire part qu'il fera aujourd'hui à cinq heures du soir dans
le Jardin des Thuilleries, en présence de MM. de l'Académie des
Sciences, l'expérience d'une nouvelle Pompe de son invention
avec laquelle il monte à plus de 100. pieds un muid et un quart
d'eau en 25. secondes avec la plus grande aisance, par le moyen
d'un ajoutoir d'onze lignes de diametre et avec la moitié moins
de bras que ceux que l'on employe ordinairement.⁴ Il vous prie
de vouloir bien l'honorer de votre présence.

3. The day Calonne sent Lafayette 24 copies of the May 14 *arrêt* concerning free ports. Lafayette had tried to influence the government's selection by writing to Calonne, Vergennes, and Castries: XXXIX, 104n; XLI,
286; Giunta, *Emerging Nation*, II, 369.
    4. We have found no record of that particular demonstration, but
Gaspard de Bebiniere, "machiniste de la marine," did demonstrate his exceptionally powerful fire pump before commissioners of the academy on
Aug. 13, 1784. The commission's report was submitted on July 27, 1785;
it concluded that the machine was a vast improvement over the previous
pumps. Gaspard then demonstrated the fire engine before the king and
the royal ministers at St.-Cloud: *Jour. encyclopédique ou universel*, February, 1786, p. 523; Académie des sciences, *Procès-verbaux*, CIV (1785), 154–8;
Jour. de Paris, Oct. 16, 1785.

Addressed: A Monsieur / Monsieur francklin Ministre des Etats
/ unis de l'Amérique / A Chaillot.

Notation: Gaspard De Bebiniere 18 Mar. 1784—

From Sears & Smith[5]   ALS:[6] American Philosophical Society

Sir.   New York May 18th. 1784

We beg leave to address your Excellency upon a piece of
Business, we have by accident become engag'd in, & to ask
your Interest to get redress from the Court of France, if it is
practicable.—

The last Summer we engag'd in a Voyage to the Coast of
Africa, in full Expectation that we could effect it by bartering
away the Cargo we sent there, for Gold Dust, Ivory, & Wax,
but contrary to our Expectations those Articles could not be
had, & the Captn: of our Vessel took a Cargo of Slaves, which
he carried to Martinico, where they are landed & will be sold.
We beg leave to inclose you our Friend Mr: Mounirou's Letter to
us on the Occasion;[7] from which you will find the Revenue Officers of Martinique are contemplating to make us pay a heavy
Duty upon the Slaves, & we cannot find from the Enquiry we
have made of some French Gentln. now here from Martinique,
that such a Duty has ever been paid at that Island by any Americans, & from our Friends Letter, the Governor of Martinique
is not clear that the Duty ought to be paid, however we imagine
it will be stopd untill a Representation is made to France, & we
take the Liberty of begging your Influence (which we know to

5. New Yorkers Isaac Sears (xxix, 662–3n) and his son-in-law Paschal
Nelson Smith (xxix, 681n) operated out of Boston during the war, but
reestablished their business in New York City after independence. They
were located at 62 Water St.: *Independent Gaz.; or, the N.-Y. Jour. Revived*,
March 4, 1784.
6. Appears to be in Smith's hand. This copy, marked "Duplicate," is
addressed to BF at Philadelphia, and was sent with Sears & Smith's letter of
Oct. 13, 1785. Because they had not received BF's answer (Aug. 4, below),
they assumed that he had never received their original inquiry.
7. Not found.

be very great) in getting the Affair settled so as to prevent our paying so heavy a Duty—

We are sensible this is asking a very great favor, but from your Excellency's Character, we make no doubt you will excuse the freedom we take, & that you will get us redress if it be possible—

That you may long live & enjoy every happyness is the Sincere wish of—Your Excellencys Most Obt. very humble Servts.

SEARS & SMITH

P.S. The Vessel that has perform'd the above mentiond Voyage, is the Ship Firebrand, Phœnix Frazer Master, who took Slaves directly from the Coast of Guinea to St. Pierres Martinique[8]

Duplicate

His Excellency Benjn. Franklin Esq

Addressed: His Excellency B Franklin Esq / Philadelphia

From Anthony Todd   LS: American Philosophical Society

Sir,   General Post Office May 18th: 1784.

I received the favour of your Letter of the 15th. past[9] by the Hands of Col: Harmar, who appears to be an inteligent, amiable Man, and I am only sorry his short stay here would not allow me to shew him all the Attention I could have wished, and that he really seems to merit.

I have also been favoured with your Letter of the 3rd: Instant,[1] mentioning the Proposal from Mr: de Couteulx[2] for the Exchange of Letters which come to France for England, and to

8. Phoenix Frazier was commissioned to command the 10-gun brigantine *Firebrand* on Oct. 6, 1782: Charles H. Lincoln, comp., *Naval Records of the American Revolution, 1775–1788* (Washington, D.C., 1906), p. 293; Claghorn, *Naval Officers*, p. 115.

9. Missing.

1. Missing.

2. The banker who was administering the French packet boat service: XLI, 48n.

England for France by the Packet Boats of the respective Countries at some settled rate of Postage. A Proposal of the same kind has been received from the Baron D'Ogny in a Letter of the 30th. past, to which I beg leave to send you a Copy of my Answer for your fuller Information,[3] and hope you will both be satisfied that the only way to avoid Complication and Difficulty will be to abide by the Regulations proposed in the Advertisement which I submitted to your Consideration the 9th: of April, and therefore the sooner it is published in America the better, which will render any Articles in the Treaty with France in relation to the Correspondence with the United States unnecessary.

I feel myself exceedingly obliged to you for the Offer of your Services in that Business as well as your friendly Wishes to see me in Paris, but there are now so very few Articles to adjust and those of no great Consequence, that I expect when we have received the Project from the Baron D'Ogny, there will be no occasion to send any person to France, but that the whole may be finally settled with very little Difficulty.[4]

3. Todd's reply to the baron d'Ogny is dated May 11 and written in French: he has shown d'Ogny's April 30 letter to the joint British postmasters general, who say that they are eager to receive the draft Franco-British treaty and hope that it will not contain any articles concerning the packet boat service to America, even though the terms that d'Ogny proposes are perfectly just. The scheme communicated to BF on April 9 must be adopted: namely, that letters between North America and the European continent, sent via an English packet, be sent under cover to an individual in London, and letters between North America and Great Britain, sent via a French packet, be sent under cover to an individual in France.

4. The Franco-British postal treaty was signed in London on Aug. 4, and in Paris on Aug. 15. Ordinary post from England to France was to leave London at midnight on Tuesdays and Fridays, and be conveyed to Calais on British packet boats at British expense. Ordinary post from France to Great Britain and Ireland was to leave Paris at 10 A.M. on Mondays and Thursdays, and be conveyed to Dover on French packet boats at French expense. Once having arrived in Calais or Dover, letters and packets were to be distributed to their destinations at the expense of the post office of that country. Britain further agreed to pay France specified amounts to transport between Calais and various cities along the French borders and coasts British letters and packets destined for, or coming from, Italy, Spain, Portugal, Turkey, the Levant, and Switzerland: "Treaty between the two Post Offices of England and France, made in the year 1784 . . . " (British Postal Museum and Archive).

As you seem to think your Opinion will not have much Weight with Mr Hazard The PostMaster General of North America,[5] I have submitted to this Board the Advertisement I inclosed to you on the 20th. past[6] for receiving the Packet as well as the Inland Postage quite to New York on all Letters for America before they are forwarded, when it was thought advisable to publish it immediately, in order to remove all Difficulties and render it unnecessary to keep Accounts between the two Countries.[7]

I am, Sir, Your most obedient and most humble Servant.

ANTH TODD Secy

His Excellency Dr: Franklin Paris.

From Benjamin Webb

ALS: Library of Congress

Dear Sir,   Geneva May 18th: 1784

I received the Favour of your Letter of 22d. past last Saturday Afternoon only.[8] By some Accident the superiour pleasure I had on Its arrival was defer'd so much longer than your Goodness intended It should. I am indeed more obliged to you than I can express. The material Services It renders Me are exceedingly enchanced by your ingenious & generous Condition. It suits precisely my own Feelings—for 'tho, I am from Necessity begging of all the World—in my own Mind I esteem every Shilling I receive in this way, as Loans. Sacred as if bound by every Tye that Laws have invented to make Men honest. Should I ever be able I have no more Idea of dying, without being first out of debt, than I have of the destruction of my own Ofspring, and

5. Ebenezer Hazard had never responded to BF's letter of Dec. 26; see XLI, 352–3.

6. Letter and enclosure both missing.

7. Todd issued the advertisement on May 22, 1784. It was published immediately in Great Britain and was reprinted in American newspapers in August. See, e.g., *London Gaz.*, May 18–22, 1784; *Pa. Packet*, Aug. 12, 1784.

8. May 15.

of Course the List of those who have preserved my Charles and me from Starving must be early refer'd to. The last contracted Debts must be first discharged.

I have looked forward to such a possible Ability as productive of a Satisfaction that could admit of *no* Increase. But It belongs to you Sir, & you only I beleive, to have thought of entailing an additional Joy as the Sure produce of that happy period. Should It ever arrive I shall also avail myself of so valuable a hint to dispose, of what may be absolutely refused me, to return. In that Case I have now a Remedy. Any other appropriation of such property would be a sort of Sacrilege. But this is an Aerial Fabrick—At my Time of Life highly improbable. By the active Malice of my declared Enemies, and the indolent Attempts of some professed Friends I have been robbed of all power to attempt anything beneficial to myself or Family. I have been Kept in a State of teazing Suspence, without their having advanced One Step; as I can find. The difficulty with but One, was from the beginning, and Time has rivited that old Gentleman's prejudices against me very naturally, when he is taught to beleive that I am rioting in the Enjoyment of *his* basely secreted Property, instead of having the utmost difficulty to live, and that intirely by the Bounty of Others. We will hope the Memorial will have Its Uses, not only as It regards present Subsistance, but future. That the Light of Truth will chase away those Mists of Error & prejudice that have so long obscured my *real* Character.

I have heard three times from Mr pigott at paris. His last Letter surprized me when It informed me that the following day he should set out for London. And, his first Letter grieved me, to learn that having paid you a Visit, he was sorry to find you unwell.— And that from Circumstances It was imagined It might be the Stone or Gravel. It directly occur'd to me what I shall now take the Liberty of detaining you a little longer with. To relate the Cases of two persons in England who found the greatest releif from the most Simple Remedies possible. I have an Idea that you Knew one, if not both the parties. Mr. Horne who I think you must have seen in the Family of Messrs. Browns & Colleson[9] at

9. Browns & Collinson: XXI, 469n.

Clapham, had been many years afflicted with the Gravel, so that he could not walk without much pain. He had tried a variety of Remedies, at last a Relation who often Swerved from the beaten path in his profession, as a physician—a very honest Man—told him, invariably to remember at his Meals to drink a good draught (of his usual diluting Liquor) *before* he ate anything Solid. He did so—soon found Benefit and always continued It—without being ever more troubled with this Complaint to his Live's end. He died at an advanced Age.[1] The Other Instance—Mr Bullock of Brixton Causeway near Clapham was for a long Time tortured with the Stone, and after trying every Remedy found Releif & Cure indeed only from drinking half a Glass of Water on going to bed, & the other half on rising in the Morning.[2]

These two Instances fell so within my own Knowledge & the Remedies so intirely *Simple*, tempted me to recite them, tho I feel how impossible almost but you must have heard them recommended before.

I am with the highest Respect & Gratitude & the warmest Wishes for the Restoration of health & Continuance of your Life, Dear sir Yr: Most obliged & obedt: hble Servant

B: WEBB.

I hope your Grandson is perfectly Well. It will be one of my pleasures on mr pigott's return to hear It from his Mouth.—

Addressed: To / The Honble: B. Franklin Esqr. / at Passy / near Paris.

1. This was probably the merchant Samuel Horne, who died on Jan. 1, 1777, at the age of 77 at his Clapham home: *Gen. Evening Post,* Jan. 2–4, 1777.

2. Richard Bullock, who died at the age of 83 in June, 1779, claimed that he had been cured of the stone and gravel using rainwater from a well in his cellar: *Gazetteer and New Daily Advertiser,* Jan. 7, 1768; *Public Advertiser,* June 8, 1779.

From Philippe-Denis Pierres

ALS: American Philosophical Society

Monsieur,   Paris 19 Mai 1784.
Je vous prie de permettre à Monsr. Baradelle l'ainé porteur de
la presente de voir votre petite Presse. C'est un homme très ha-
bile & très intelligent pour toutes les pièces de mathématiques.[3]
Je serois bien aise qu'il prît le dessin des bandes,[4] &ca.—parcequ'il pourra simplifier les masses de nos presses.[5] Je suis persuadé que vous ne serez pas faché de parler avec lui; vous verrez
que c'est un homme très instruit.

3. A trade card for "Baradelle l'ainé" among BF's papers identifies him
as "Ingénieur en Instrumens de Mathematique et de Phisique. Au Quartier
Anglois Quay de l'horloge du Palais, près la Cour de la Moignon" (APS).
Of the three Baradelle brothers who were instrument makers at this time,
the most likely one is Nicolas-Eloi, who signed himself *l'aîné* in the 1780s.
Their late father, Jacques-Nicolas Baradelle (d. 1779), was himself a
prominent instrument maker and *ingénieur du roi:* Actes faits en l'hôtel du
lieutenant civil, Châtelet de Paris, Minutes, Nov. 23, 1782, and Feb. 20,
1789, Archives nationales, Paris; Jean-Dominique Augarde, "La Fabrica-
tion des instruments scientifiques du XVIIIe siècle et la corporation des
fondeurs," in *Studies in the History of Scientific Instruments . . .* , ed. Chris-
tine Blondel *et al.* (London, 1989), pp. 52, 64, 65, 66, 70; *Jour. de Paris*,
June 3, 1779.
4. This reference to "bandes"—the "ribs" or "rails"—may indicate that
BF's press featured the improved carriage system that he had described to
William Strahan in 1753: V, 83.
5. Pierres was in the process of perfecting a new kind of printing press
operated by a vertical lever and cam action, which replaced the standard
central screw mechanism operated by a bar pulled horizontally. On May 7,
1784, he presented a prototype to the king, who, after pulling a proof, ordered one for his *cabinet*. Baradelle l'aîné was hired to construct it, and the
small press was delivered to Versailles on July 2. Pierres continued to improve his design; he had a full-scale press by October, 1784, and in December, 1785, he submitted his invention to the Académie des sciences, which
approved it: Académie des sciences, *Procès-verbaux*, CIV (1785), 75; CV
(1786), 109–12. In *Description d'une nouvelle presse d'imprimerie . . .* (Paris,
1786), Pierres explained in detail the machine's development, its mecha-
nisms, and its advantages over ordinary presses. In the same work, he acknowledged BF's friendship and his expertise in the arts of printing, as well
as the debt he owed to BF's "instructions" (pp. 3–4).

Je vous renouvelle, Monsieur, les assurances de mon attachement inviolable & du respect avec lequel Je suis, Monsieur Votre très humble & très obeissant serviteur   PIERRES

M. franklin.

Notation: Pierres 9 May 1784.

Thomas Mifflin to Franklin and John Adams

Copy: National Archives

Gentlemen,   Annapolis May 20th. 1784

I have the Honor to transmit to you the following Acts of Congress relating to the formation of commercial Treaties &c Viz—

N 1. Letter to the Ministers plenipotentiary at the Courts of Versailles and Madrid dated 17th. of October 1780—[6]

N 2. Instructions to the Ministers of the United States for making Peace with Great Britain dated May 30th. 1783[7]

N 3. Instructions to the Ministers plenipotentiary of the United States of America at the Court of Versailles empowered to negotiate a Peace &c. dated the 29th of October 1783,[8] May 7th. 1784 & May 11th 1784.—

N 4. Instructions to the Ministers of the United States at the Court of Madrid dated May 3d 1784.[9]

6. A letter to Jay, then minister to Spain, with a copy to be sent to BF, explaining why the United States insisted on the Mississippi River as the western boundary and on free navigation and free ports on that river: XXXIII, 471–2; William T. Hutchinson *et al.*, eds., *The Papers of James Madison*, Congressional Series (17 vols., Chicago and Charlottesville, 1962–91), II, 127–36. Congress was still concerned about access to the Mississippi; see the June 3 portion of the instructions to the new commission, May 7[–June 3], above.

7. See the first congressional resolution of May 11, published with the instructions cited above.

8. XLI, 154–8.

9. Directing the minister to obtain compensation from Spain for South Carolina for the participation of the frigate *South Carolina* in the Spanish capture of the Bahamas: *JCC*, XXVI, 332. A copy of the instructions in BFB's hand, and a press copy of it, are at the APS. BF endorsed the copy "Resolution May 3. 1784 Relating to the South-Carolina Frigate."

I also transmit to you the Papers relating to the detention of the Schooner Nancy referred to in the Instruction of May 11th 1784.

I have the honor to be with the greatest Respect and Esteem Your Obident & humble Servant   THOMAS MIFFLIN

The Honorable John Adams & Benjamin Franklin

From Lafayette   ALS: American Philosophical Society

My dear Sir   Versailles thursday Morning [May 20, 1784][1]

I intended Having this day the pleasure to See You, But am obliged to Stay Here for the Queen's Concert, and Will do Myself the Honour to Call Upon You to Morrow Morning— Then I will lay Before You a letter I Have Received from mr. de Calonne—[2] I am glad to Hear the Washington[3] is Soon Expected, and Hope we May Get intelligences Before My departure which is fixed on the 12th of june.

There is an other point Upon Which I Beg leave to Offer my Opinion, and Since, on the Opposite Side, Under Government Banners, I perceive a Respected Veteran, to Whom I Have Had the Honour to Be a fellow Soldier, I Beat A parley and am Sure He Will like My proposition— That Mesmer is the true preacher of Magnetism Animal, to Which By the Way He Has Been Much Helped By Your electric discoveries, is a truth which No Body will deny— That deslon Has treacherously Broken His faith, trampled Upon the Most Sacred Engagements is no More disputable— That While Mesmer Intended Acquiring a

1. The first Thursday after May 17, when Calonne wrote the letter to Lafayette mentioned in the first paragraph.

2. On May 17 Calonne sent Lafayette the first printed copies of the May 14 *arrêt* announcing the French free ports, one of which the marquis immediately forwarded to BF: Lafayette to BF, [May 17], above. In his letter, Calonne assured Lafayette that all the terms specified in his Jan. 9 letter, which Lafayette had forwarded to America (see XLI, 286–7n), still applied, and that American ships now arriving in France could claim the benefits of the free ports. Regarding tobacco, the farmers general had agreed to buy tobacco only in France and the United States, and to build a depot in Lorient where merchants could store it: Giunta, *Emerging Nation*, II, 369.

3. The *General Washington*.

great glory and a great fortune, He Has not Been Such a fool as to Impart His Whole System to One Man who Might Claim a share in the Honour and profit is also pretty Clear— That Baron de Breteuil, out of a private picque to Mesmer, Has Sent to deslon, in order *to know Mesmer's doctrine Which does not Exist*, and thus what May Be known of the doctrine will Be Either Betraied By deslon, or Stolen out By private Spies, are also pretty clear to Every Mind.

Now, My dear Sir, instead of Helping to those Transactions, don't You think the Commissaries, to Whom the World Considers you as a president, Had Better Report

that What they Have Seen Gives them the idea of a Great discovery, But that Mesmer Being the Author of it, He is the Fountain Head to Which You Must Apply— That Sciences and Letters are frighted a way By the Hand of despotism— But that, in order to Come to the Whole truth, Commissaries Must plainly, and Oppenly Go to mr. Mesmer, and in the Same way as other people do, Be Regularly let By Him into His whole System.

Upon that I Have not Spoken to Mesmer— But I would Be Sorry to See a traitor triumph over an Honest man—and I am Sure You May Give a Good turn to the Affair— I was very Happy in Admitting Your Grand Son into our Society.[4]

Most affectionately and Respectfully Yours   LAFAYETTE

Notation: La Fayette

4. The Société de l'harmonie was created by Nicolas Bergasse and the banker Guillaume Kornmann. Its purpose was twofold: to regulate the dissemination of Mesmer's discovery (preventing unauthorized disclosures like Deslon's), and to provide financial security for Mesmer. For an initiation fee of 100 *louis*, members were to be instructed in the workings of animal magnetism after swearing not to reveal what they learned. Chapters of the society soon opened all over France. The names of the first hundred members, who joined between Oct. 1, 1783, and April 5, 1784, were published in May. They included prominent courtiers and nobles (Lafayette was number 91), bankers, merchants, lawyers, clergymen, and physicians. WTF became member number 163. On July 1 he received a printed invitation to a meeting of the society scheduled for the following Wednesday, July 7, at Mesmer's luxurious clinic in the rue Coq-Héron (APS): Bachaumont, *Mémoires secrets*, XXVI, 14–15; *Jour. du magnétisme*, XI (1852), 268–9; Robert Darnton, *Mesmerism and the End of the Enlightenment in France* (Cambridge, Mass., 1968), pp. 51–2, 73–7.

Commissioners to Investigate Animal Magnetism[5] to the Baron de Breteuil

Press copy of L:[6] American Philosophical Society

Monsieur Le Baron,   à Passy ce 22 Mai 1784.[7]

Nous apprenons la mort de Mr. Borie.[8] Il étoit un des Commissaires du Roi pour le magnétisme animal. C'est une Perte que fait la Commission. En le regrettant, nous pensons qu'il seroit nécessaire de le remplacer, et de completter le Nombre des Quatre médecins choisis par le Roi dans la Faculté. Nous Vous prions donc, Monsieur le Baron, de vouloir bien prendre les ordres de Sa Majesté à cet égard. Nous ne doutons pas que le Successeur de M. Borie ne soit choisi dans le nombre de ceux qui Jouissent de plus de considération et dans la Faculté et dans le Public: mais l'Unité de zéle et de Vuës étant un objet également essentiel dans ceux qui sont destinés à travailler en commun, la Compagnie des Commissaires du Roi pense que relativement à ces différens objets, personne ne paroit plus convenable que Mr. Majault;[9] et elle prend la Liberté de vous le proposer comme un des plus anciens Docteurs de la Faculté; qui a mérité la confiance de son Corps et celle du Public; et qui s'est déja acquitté avec Distinction de plusieurs commissions importantes dont il a été chargé. Nous souhaitons, Monsieur le Baron, que Mr. Majault vous paroisse propre à remplir les Intentions du Roi, et que sa Majesté l'honore de son choix.

Nous sommes avec Respect, Monsieur Le Baron, Vos très humbles et très obeissants Serviteurs.

à Mr. Le Baron de Breteuil.

---

5. *I.e.*, the joint commission of the Faculté de médecine and the Académie des sciences.

6. In the hand of L'Air de Lamotte. The press copy was made before the commissioners signed.

7. A Saturday when all the commissioners were at Passy; see the Report of the Commission on Animal Magnetism, [Aug. 11].

8. He died on May 21, but the announcement did not appear until May 23: A. Pinard *et al.*, eds., *Commentaires de la Faculté de médecine de Paris, 1777 à 1786* (2 vols., Paris, 1903), II, 1120–1; *Jour. de Paris*, May 23, 1784.

9. Michel-Joseph Majault: Pinard *et al.*, eds., *Commentaires de la Faculté de médecine de Paris*, I, 30; II, 514, 1045.

From Thomas Collinson

ALS: American Philosophical Society

My dear Friend   Southgate. May. 22.d. 1784

The Bearer of this Mr Thos Hill,[1] a Gentleman with whom I have the pleasure of being intimately acquainted; visting the Continent from motives of Curiosity, and a laudable desire of extending useful Knowledge; I have requested that he will oblige me; by the transmission of my most respectful Regards to you; & personally to enquire after your Welfare and Health; as such I therefore hope he may fortunately find you for a few moments in some measure disengaged from the many important Affairs you sustain,—so that I may have the Pleasure of receiving the agreeable Information from his Letter, that you are well and happy—

Monday last I dined with our Friends at the George and Vulture—[2] Your old Friend Mr Mitchel was there— We conversed together about you, and most cordially wish'd for your Presence. He has just finish'd the great Speculum, that has cost him so many years Labour;[3] but has been so much indisposed as to prevent his Trials of it by Night; tho he seems to be satisfied, that his Labour has not been in vain, by what he has seen by it in the Day— Herschel also I hear intends to cast his 4 feet Speculum this Summer—[4]

I beg you will believe me to remain with the utmost Respect yr affectionate Friend   THOS COLLINSON

1. Most likely Thomas Ford Hill, an antiquarian, who left for the Continent in 1784 on what would become a five-year trip. Like Collinson, he was a Quaker. Hill had toured Scotland in 1780 and collected Gaelic songs, which he then published in the *Gent. Mag.: ODNB*. He must have visited, as BF received the present letter, but we have no record of their encounter.

2. For the Monday Club see x, 250.

3. Collinson had also reported this to BF on Nov. 12: XLI, 196. Speculum mirrors, cast in metal, were extremely difficult to fabricate, and Michell's, with an aperture of 29.5 inches, was enormous for its time: Russell McCormmach, "John Michell and Henry Cavendish: Weighing the Stars," *British Jour. for the History of Science*, IV (1968), 140n, 153n.

4. William Herschel's four-foot speculum mirror was not cast until October, 1785, and had to be recast before the telescope was finally put into use in 1789: Michael Hoskin, *Discoverers of the Universe: William and Caroline Herschel* (Princeton and Oxford, 2011), pp. 110–24.

To Mesmer Copy:[5] Bibliothèque Nationale

Passy, ce 23 Mai 1784.
Copie de la Réponse de M. Franklin

J'ai reçu, Mr, la Lettre que vous m'avez fait l'honneur de m'écrire le 14 de ce mois, et le Mémoire que l'accompagnoit concernant M. D'Eslon. J'ai communiqué la Lettre ainsi que le Mémoire aux autres Commissaires, comme vous le desiriez et ils m'ont chargé de vous faire savoir, qu'en entendant M. D'Eslon, ils se bornent simplement à l'exécution de leur Commission, conformément au vœu du Gouvernement.[6]

J'ai l'honneur d'être Mr, Votre très humble et très Obeissant Serviteur,[7] Signé FRANKLIN

To Vicq d'Azyr L:[8] Yale University Library

à Passy ce 24 Mai 1784.—
M. Franklin a l'honneur de faire mille Complimens à Monsieur Vicq-d'azir, et le prie de vouloir bien lui envoyer le Rapport de Messrs. Andry et Thouret sur les Aimans présentés par

5. The third of three letters copied for Mesmer to forward to Joly de Fleury in December; see the annotation of Mesmer to BF, May 14.

6. The commissioners must have reviewed Mesmer's letter and its enclosure on May 22, when they convened at Passy; see their May 22 letter to Breteuil.

7. A tangentially related document found among BF's papers, probably dating from the end of May, 1784, is a copy in Le Veillard's hand of a poem by Cerutti (XXXIX, 235n) ridiculing all types of charlatans, including mesmerists. It was published in *Mémoires secrets* on May 25: "Portrait du Charlatanisme, fait par luy même dans un moment de franchise" (APS); Bachaumont, *Mémoires secrets*, XXVI, 5–6, 10–12. Cerutti published a revised version in *Recueil de quelques pieces de littérature, en prose et en verse* (Glasgow, 1784), pp. 37–46.

8. In the hand of L'Air de Lamotte. On the top of the page, a secretary of Vicq d'Azyr's drafted a partial reply: "La Société se fera un devoir de lui faire parvenir ceux qui sont déjà imprimés elle sera très flattée s'il Veut bien les accueillir." Beneath this, another hand noted "Bien" and "Répondu".

Mr. L'abbé le Noble,[9] il lui en sera infiniment obligé. Il desireroit aussi savoir si la Société Royale continue toujours à faire imprimer chaque Année la Collection de ses mémoires, qu'il n'a point reçue depuis l'Année 1778.[1]

From Francis Hopkinson   ALS: American Philosophical Society

Dear Friend.   Philada. 24th. May 1784—

I cannot suffer so good an Opportunity to pass without renewing my Assurances of the Love & Respect I have for you— mine & my Father's[2] steady Friend. It is indeed long since I have written to you, & much longer since I have received a Letter from you— Your more serious & important Avocations are doubtless the Occasion of both— I am unwilling to intrude upon your Time, & you are too much engaged in the embarassing & vexatious Duties of a public Station & political Character to amuse yourself with Letters of mere Friendship & private Concern.

9. This 15-page report (cited in xxvi, 523n) had been submitted to the Société royale de médecine more than a year earlier (April, 1783) and printed at that time for distribution to the members. For unknown reasons the *Jour. de Paris* brought it to the public's attention on May 4, 1784, through an article whose author is not known. Praising the report as a model study (without reference to its date), the article described the work and stated, by way of conclusion, that electricity, magnetic fluid, and animal magnetism (which had not been the focus of the report) were all worthy objects of medical investigation.

Andry and Thouret's study was made at the request of the abbé Le Noble (xxvi, 523); it tested the medical efficacy of lodestones that the abbé had donated to the society. The authors were experts in the field, having published in 1780 a massive study of the history and practice of therapeutic magnetism (for which see the following note). They found the curative powers of the abbé's magnets to be unquestionable, though they did not understand the process. Likening the potential of magnetic fluid to the promising field of medical electricity, they argued for further research.

1. Vol. 2 of *Histoire de la Société royale de médecine* . . . (10 vols., Paris, 1779–98) was published in 1780. Only one volume had appeared since then, vol. 3 for the year 1779, published in 1782. That volume contained the 1780 paper by Andry and Thouret mentioned in the previous note: "Observations et Recherches sur l'usage de l'aimant en médecine, ou, mémoire sur le magnétisme médicinale." The paper was also issued as a separate extract.

2. Thomas Hopkinson (I, 209n).

I have long look'd for the additional Volumes of the new
french Encyclodpædia— You have forwarded 3 Viz the first
Vols. of Jurisprudence, Natural History & Mechanics; but I am
told, there are several more published—[3] I requested in my last
that you would tell me in what Manner I should pay my Subscription to this Work; informing that it would be more easy for
me to pay in Portions as the Work proceeded than it might be to
furnish the full Amount at once.[4]
I have industriously applied myself to raise from a State of
Lethargy, our philosophical Society, in this I have been assisted
by the steady Abilities of Mr. Rittenhouse & the sanguine
Vivacity of Mr. Vaughan (whom you know)— To this End I
delivered a Speach to the Society last Winter—the purport of
which was to rouse their Attention to the Objects of their Institution, & to encourage a Pursuit of experimental Philosophy,
by removing what I believe to be a great Obstacle, especially
in this Country vizt: an Idea that none but Men of profound
Learning & scholastic Education ought to meddle with Pursuits of this kind—& this I did by asserting that many of the
most important Discoveries had been made by Men who had
not liberal Educations, but were led to the Discovery of Truth

3. At Hopkinson's request, BF subscribed on his behalf to publisher
Charles-Joseph Panckoucke's massive *Encyclopédie Méthodique* (XXXVII,
240–1n). He forwarded the first installment in December, 1782 (XXXVIII,
490), which consisted of the three volumes Hopkinson notes here. Since
then, seven more installments had become available: George B. Watts,
"The Encyclopédie Méthodique," *PMLA*, LXXIII (1958), 351–2; Robert
Darnton, *The Business of Enlightenment: a Publishing History of the Encyclopédie, 1775–1800* (Cambridge, Mass. and London, 1979), pp. 469–70;
Encyclopédie Méthodique, XLVI (1788), lxii–lxvii, xcvii.
4. XXXIX, 399. After writing the present letter, it seems, Hopkinson
conceived the idea of reimbursing BF with the proceeds he hoped to derive
from an improved harpsichord jack he had presented to the APS in December. On May 24 he wrote and illustrated his "Description of an Improvement in the Manner of Quilling a Harpsichord or Spinnet." The following day he wrote to TJ, then in Philadelphia en route to France, enclosing
the description and models of the jack, and asked him to show them to a
Parisian instrument maker. He requested that, if the latter should agree to
purchase the invention, TJ would arrange to pay BF for his subscription to
the encyclopedia. He also asked TJ to show BF the description and models:
Jefferson Papers, VII, 285–7; Francis Hopkinson, "An Improved Method of
Quilling a Harpsichord," APS *Trans.*, II (1786), 185–7.

by a careful Attention to Facts, & a steady Investigation of the Phœnomena of Nature— I asserted that the Book of nature was the Book of Knowledge; that it was open to all—that it was not written in Latin, Greek or Hebrew—but in a Language intelligible to every one who would take the Pains to read & observe—&a &a. This gave Offence to some of the learned Faculty, who think it impossible to attain Wisdom but by Means of Grammar Rules, a System of Logic & the whole visionary Fabric of Metaphysics— I, perhaps, carried my Doctrine a little to far; but it was with a View to encourage those who had not the means of a learned Education, to become useful by experimental Enquiries.— I would send you a Copy of this Speach, if I thought it worth your Attention— It had, however, some good Effect.—[5]

I have long thought that a great Reform is wanting in the Education of Youth— Too much of the ancient Superstitions of the Schools remain— A great deal of precious Time is spent in forcing upon young Minds logical & metaphysical Subtleties—which can never afterwards be applied to any possible Use in Life—whilst the practical Branches of Knowledge, are either slightly glanced over, or totally neglected— Even the learned Languages are, in my Opinion, taught by a wrong Method— The Grammar should be the last Book put into the Learner's Hands— No Language is built upon it's Grammar, but the Grammar is deduced from the Language— Elegance of Style in speaking or Writing can never be acquired by Rules— Conversing with Men of a polish'd Conversation & reading Books of approved Composition will insensibly lead the Ear & the Eye to an accurate Judgment of Propriety of Diction, & the Scholar will with great Facility acquire a Taste for Elegance, which no System of Rudiments can ever inculcate— More of our Knowledge is acquired by Habit than we are aware of— We attribute too much to the Understanding— As to the Translation of Latin Words into English a Vocabulary or Dictionary is

5. Hopkinson delivered this address on Jan. 16. In it, he singled out BF as a prime example of someone who made important experimental discoveries without the benefit of a formal education: Francis Hopkinson, *The Miscellaneous Essays and Occasional Writings of Francis Hopkinson, Esq.* (3 vols., Philadelphia, 1792), I, 359–71.

the only possible Resource: but the due Arrangement of these Words so as to make them elegantly expressive, this is more easily attained by the Ear than by any other Method— After the Scholar has made himself well acquainted with the Use of Latin Words, that is, can tell the English of any Latin Word that occurs, I would wish that the Teacher, not a common School-Master, but a Gentleman of refined Taste should continually read to him out of the most approved Authors, & cause the Pupil to make little Essays of his own.— My Objection to Grammar is that it's Rules are not founded in Nature— In a living Language they are ever fluctuating— General Custom makes Propriety—& even in Languages called *dead* & therefore *fixed*, the Rules of Grammar are necessarily encumber'd with so many Exceptions, that in many Instances it is immaterial whether we take the Exceptions to the Rule or the Rule itself for the Standard. But the learning a Language by means of a Grammar is not only insufficient to inculcate it's Force & it's Elegancies; but is a Bar to the Acquirement— We seldom see common Schoolmasters, those Haberdashers of Moods & Tenses, possess'd of the least Feeling or Taste for the Authors they teach, much less are they able to write with Urbanity in the Language they profess— What would Virgil think could he hear his beautiful Poem fritter'd into it's grammatical component Parts in one of our Schools:— How would Horace swear to hear one of his Odes *parsed* (as it is called) by Mood & Tense— All the Spirit of Elegance must evapourate under such an Operation— But I have inadvertently fallen upon a Subject that would require long Discussion & Argument to set in a proper Light— Let us leave it—

I enclose for your Amusement a *pettit* Piece which I published with a View of having our Streets better attended to— They had been much neglected since the War, & of Course became shamefully dirty—[6] My Performance fully answer'd my

6. This satire, "Some Account of a new Work, entituled Dialogues of the Dead," appeared in the *Pa. Gaz.* on March 10. The carcasses of a dog and cat, lying in the street, discuss the little-understood public health benefits underlying the city's policy of keeping the streets filthy and putrid, and explain how the street-cleaning taxes are being used toward that end: Hopkinson, *Miscellaneous Essays*, I, 327–39.

Intention, & above 100 Scavengers were employed in two or three days after it's Appearance—& our Streets are now kept tolerably clean— I will also (if I can get it) enclose another Squib in which I have endeavoured to ridicule *false* Learning— but no great Effect is to [be] expected from it, as rooted Prejudices are not so easily shaken.[7]

We have been diverting ourselves with raising Paper Balloons by Means of burnt Straw to the great Astonishment of the Populace— This Discovery, like Electricity, Magnetism & many other important Phænomena, serve for Amusement at first— It's Uses & Applications will hereafter unfold themselves. There may be many mechanical Means of giving the Balloon a progressive Motion, other than what the current of Wind would give it— Perhaps this is as simple as any—let the Balloon be constructed of an oblong Form, something like the Body of a Fish, or a Bird, or a Wherry—& let there be a large & light Wheel in the Stern, vertically mounted— This Wheel should consist of several Vanes or Fans of Canvas, whose Plains should be considerably inclined with respect to the Plain of it's Motion, exactly like the Wheel of a Smoak-Jack— If the navigator turns this wheel swiftly round, by means of a Winch, there is no Doubt but it would (in a Calm at least) give the Machine a progressive Motion, upon the same Principle that a Boat is *scull'd* thro' the Water— But my Paper is almost out—& perhaps your Patience— If you can spare Time, let me know that I live in your Remembrance— Any philosophical Communications will highly gratify me—& be thankfully received by our Society, who expect their President will now & then favour them with his Notice.

Are we to hope that you will revisit your native Country or not?—that Country for which you have done & suffered so much— Whilst there is any Virtue left in America the Names Franklin & Washington will be held in the highest Esteem.—

7. "Modern Learning Exemplified by a Specimen of a Collegiate Examination" was published in the *Pa. Gaz.* on May 5. Caricaturing contemporary pedagogy, Hopkinson depicted a professor systematically examining a student on the properties of a salt box: Hopkinson, *Miscellaneous Essays,* I, 340–58.

Adieu & be assured there is no one loves you more than Your faithful & affectionate   FRAS. HOPKINSON

Dr. Franklin

From the Baron d'Ogny   LS: American Philosophical Society

Paris le 25. May 1784.

Vous aurés vu, Monsieur, par la remise qui vous a déja été faite de plusieurs lettres venant de Newyorck a votre destination que le Gouvernement S'est occupé des Moyens d'établir une Correspondance fixe et réglée entre les treize Etats unis et la France par la voye des Paquebots qu'il a établis à Lorient partant une fois par Mois de ce port pour Newyorck et revenant en France aussi une fois par mois;[8] mais comme il me paraît aussi intéressant pour l'office des Postes des treize Etats unis de l'Amérique que pour celui de France de profiter de la voye de ces Paquebots pour établir une bonne correspondance entre ces différents Etats pour la remise de leurs lettres réciproques et pour celle des lettres venant des Pays par delà la France, J'ai imaginé que vous approuveriés que je vous proposâsse mes idées à ce Sujet.

C'est dans ces vües que j'ai fait rédiger un Projet de traité[9] pour assurer cette Correspondance réciproque. Je le joins ici dans la persuasion ou je suis que vous agréérés que les liens de nos deux Nations se resserent de plus en plus. Mais comme je ne présume pas avoir rempli d'avance toutes les vues que vous pourriés avoir a ce Sujet, Je vous prie de ne regarder ce projet de traité que comme une Esquisse et une donnée pour entrer en matiére, et que je vous demande en conséquence un jour ou nous puissions nous entendre Sur cette affaire. Ce Sera avec grand plaisir que je me rendrai à Passy le jour qui vous conviendra dans la Semaine prochaine, en vous observant que mes occupations me forcent a vous demander que ce Soit plustôt l'après midi que le matin; Je Saisirai avec grand empressement cette

---

8. The French packet service between Lorient and New York had begun operations the previous September: XL, 399–400.

9. Immediately below.

occasion de faire une connaissance particuliére avec vous et de vous assurer de l'estime et du Sincère attachement avec lesquels j'ai l'honneur d'être, Monsieur, votre très humble et très obéissant Serviteur. RIGOLEY DOGNY

M francklin, Ministre Plénipotentiaire des Etats unis de l'amérique Sèptentrionale à Passy.

[*In d'Ogny's hand:*] si par hasard, monsieur, l'après diné de jeudy prochain pouvoit vous convenir je serai a vos ordres sur les sept heures du soir, sinon je me trouverés forcé de vous proposer de renvoyer notre conférence au jeudy 3. juin a la même heure me proposant d'aller passer les fêtes a la campagne

From d'Ogny: Proposed Franco-American Postal Treaty

Autograph translation by Benjamin Franklin: American Philosophical Society; D: American Philosophical Society

Under cover of the May 25 letter immediately above, the baron d'Ogny sent Franklin a thirteen-page "Projet de Traité pour la Correspondance des Lettres entre l'Office des Postes de France et celui des Etats Unis de l'Amérique Septentrionale." The text published below is Franklin's translation of that document, which he may have prepared in anticipation of the meeting that d'Ogny had proposed. Franklin, like d'Ogny, wrote the articles in the right-hand column of each page and left blank the left side of the page for comments and revisions. With the one exception noted below, neither man's version has anything written in those blank columns, and the texts contain no alterations, leaving us to wonder whether they ever met to discuss the articles.

It is possible that they did not. The issue of a postal treaty was raised again the following spring, at the urging of St. John de Crèvecœur, who wrote to d'Ogny from America. D'Ogny approached Vergennes, who agreed that it would be desirable to conclude a postal convention with the United States. On May 10, 1785, d'Ogny sent Vergennes a text that was identical to the one he had sent to Franklin in 1784. Vergennes forwarded it to Marbois, the French chargé d'affaires in Philadelphia, on July 19, with instructions to send it to

Secretary for Foreign Affairs John Jay.[1] D'Ogny evidently also discussed the draft treaty with Thomas Jefferson shortly before Franklin left Paris. It seems he told Jefferson—or Jefferson understood him to say—that he had given Franklin a proposed postal convention to be submitted to Congress. Franklin, when questioned on the matter, told Jefferson that "he did not recollect any such draught having been put into his hands." Jefferson related this exchange to Jay, advising him of the arrangement that the French were proposing.[2]

When Jay and Postmaster General Ebenezer Hazard examined the French plan, they decided that several points would be difficult or unworkable, including the provision that all postage on ordinary mail sent from the United States had to be calculated in French currency. In March, 1786, with the approval of Congress, Jay submitted a counterproposal to the French chargé d'affaires in New York. The negotiations foundered thereafter, and the treaty was never concluded.[3]

[*c.* May 25, 1784]

Plan of a Treaty for the Management of Letters between the General Post-Office of France, and that of the United States of America.— per M. D'Ogny

Articles of Agreement made for the Carrying and Transporting of Letters, Dispatches, & Pacquets sent from France to New York for the U.S. of Ama. and of Letters &c. sent from N York for France;— between [*blank*] authorised for that purpose by [*blank*] of the one Part, and [*blank*] duly authorised on the other Part; who have agreed to the Articles following.

Article 1.

That there shall be maintain'd a good, firm, & mutual Correspondence, on both sides, for sending, receiving & distributing Letters, Dispatches and Pacquets.

1. D'Ogny to Vergennes, May 10, 1785, enclosing "Projet de Traité . . . "; Vergennes to d'Ogny, May 24, 1785; Vergennes to Marbois, July 19, 1785; all at the AAE.

2. *Jefferson Papers*, VIII, 453–4.

3. *Jefferson Papers*, VIII, 455–6n, XI, 274, XVI, 303–4; *JCC*, XXIX, 898n, XXX, 80–2, 141–4; Eugène Vaillé, *Histoire générale des postes françaises* (6 vols., Paris, 1947–55), VI, part 2, 648–52.

Article 2.

That the Letters, &c of France and those of Foreign Countries passing thro' France, for any Part of the U.S. shall be managed & sent at the Charge of the French Post Office only, both by Land in France and by the King's Pacquet Boats from L'Orient to N York once a Month, which are on their Arrival to deliver the Mails containing the said Letters to the Post Office of the U.S. of Ama. at N York for which the Officer of the said Post-Office shall give his Receipt to the Captain of the Pacquet Boat in presence of the Consul of France or of the Agent of the Pacquet Boats, with whom the said Office at New York shall examine and ascertain the Number of Letters, whether single double treble or Pacquets valued by the Ounce contain'd in each Mail, excepting only the Letters & Pacquets which shall be countersigned by the Ministers of France or others who have the Right of Franking, of which Letters and Packets there shall be formed a separate Parcel, to be put into the Mail by the Post Office at L'Orient.

Article 3.

The Director of the Posts at L'Orient shall send with the said Mails of Letters, a Bill signed by him, dated the Day of their Departure, directed to the Post Office of New York; which Bill shall express not only the Number of Letters contain'd, distinguish'd as single double, treble, Packets, & their Weight, but also the Value of the Postage to N York, in French Money, mark'd on the said Letters of each sort, and the Amount of the whole.

Article 4.

The Post-Office of the U.S. at N York is to engage, after the Verification of the said Bill, to be accountable to the Post-Office of France for the Amount of each of the said Mails of charged Letters, and to cause them to be distributed according to their destinations; adding to the Rates marked on them the additional Charges accruing for their port and Distribution throughout the thirteen United States.

Article 5.

In Case the said Post Office at New York shall find Errors in the Bill and as aforesaid with the Letters from L'Orient, it is agreed that on informing the French Office thereof by the first Packet after the Reception of the Mail, the said Errors shall be rectified, so that the Post Office of New York shall not be obliged to account with that of France, for more than the Amount of what was really found in each Mail.

Article 6.

It is also agreed that the Countersigning (or Franking) of French Letters, which were therefore not charged when sent from L'Orient shall not be understood to frank the said Letters, except for their Port in France and across the Seas.

Article 7.

All the Letters which shall be delivered on the Part of the French Office to that of the said U.S. and which shall fall under the denomination of dead Letters without having been opened, shall be retaken by the French Office at the Rates they were delivered, the Office of New York returning them every Six Months.

Article 8.

In like Manner the Letters and Dispatches from all Parts of the U.S. of America for France shall be managed & forwarded by & at the Expence of the Post Office of the U.S. till their Arrival at New York, and from N. York at the Expence of the Office of France, as well in respect of the Pacquet Postage to L'Orient as of the Land Postage from thence to the different Parts of France. The Mails which shall contain the said Letters receiv'd from the Post Office of New York by the Captain of each Pacquet Boat ready to depart for L'Orient, are to be delivered immediately on his Arrival to the Postmaster of the said Place, who shall give his Receipt to the said Captain, in presence of the Agent for the Pacquet Boats, with whom shall be ascertain'd the Number of Letters valu'd as single, double, triple or Pacquets by the ounce, contain'd in each Mail.

Article 9.

The said Post Office at New York shall send with the Letters of each Mail, a Bill signed, dated the Day of Departure, and addressed to the Post Office at L'Orient, which Bill like that from L'Orient to N York, shall express not only the Number of Letters distinguish'd as single, double, treble & Pacquets, but also the Amount of the whole Charge in French Money and not otherwise which shall be put on the said Letters of each kind for their Postage to New York only, & a general Account of the Total of said Charges.

Article 10.

The Post Office at L'Orient is engaged, after Verification made of the said Bill, to be accountable to the Office of the U.S. of America at New York for the Amount of the said Letters & Packets as charged in America, and to distribute them in France, adding to the American Charges those of France for the Post of said Letters from New York to the Places of their Destination.

Article 11.

It is agreed that the Clause inserted in Article 5 of this Treaty relative to Errors which may be found in the Amount of Letters sent from France to New York, shall be exactly the same respecting Errors that may be found in the Amount of Letters sent from New York to L'Orient where the Verification is to be made.

Article 12.

It is also agreed as in the 7th Article, that all the Letters which have been charged in Account by the Office of New York to that of France & which shall become dead Letters without having been opened shall be retaken by the Office of the U.S. at the Rates they had been charged, the French Office returning them to New York every Six Months.

Art. 13.

It is also agreed on both sides that all the Letters and Pacquets that are sent reciprocally, shall be exactly stamp'd in a legible manner on the Superscription with the Name of the Place where they shall be written, and the Figures of the Rates at which they shall be charged shall express Sols or Livres tournois. [*Franklin's note in the margin:* Difficult]

Art. 14.

The Accounts between the two Offices shall be rendered every six Months, by the Office that shall find itself indebted to the other, who having verified the said Accounts & allowed them to be just, shall settle them; after which, the Ballance due to the said Office shall be paid to the Person authorised to receive the same.

Art. 15.

All the Bags and Mails shall be well and duly sent from one Office to the other, sealed by the true known Seal of each Office.

Art. 16.

The Parties oblige themselves reciprocally to hinder by all possible Means, the Carrying any of the above named Letters, in any other manner than by the common Posts.

Art. 17.

It is also agreed that this present Treaty shall have its Execution, and begin to be carried into Effect, & to be executed between the said Parties, the first Packet after the Exchange of the Ratifications in form signed and sealed on the one part by [blank] and on the other by [blank] and it is moreover agreed by both the Parties that the said present Treaty shall not be broken by either, till after having given a Year's Notice.

And the Powers are to be transcrib'd and added of us the said [blank]

In faith whereof we have reciprocally signed this present Treaty, and fixed the Seal of our Arms. Done double between us at Paris this

From Henry Hunter[4]   AL: American Philosophical Society

Hotel de Russie, Rüe de Richlieu
Thursday May 27th. 1784

Dr. Hunter presents his Respects to Dr. Franklin. He this morning forwarded a Packet addressed to Mr Jay from Dr Wither-

4. The "eminent dissenting Minister" living in London whom John Witherspoon introduced to John Jay in a letter of May 7, 1784 (described below). Hunter, ordained by the Church of Scotland in 1766, received his

poon who is now at London; but is this moment informed that Mr Jay is departed for America. He is apprehensive, from a Note brought him by his Servant from Passy, that the Packet from London will be dispatched after Mr Jay, unopened; & he is well assured it contains papers of importance to Dr Witherspoon to be used at Paris.[5] It will therefore be necessary that the Gentleman who transacts Mr Jay's business should open the Packet, & act upon the information it contains.

If Dr Franklin has any thing to forward to Dr. Witherspoon, Dr. H. will be happy to carry his Commands: he sets out for England, by Way of Flanders & Holland on Monday next.—

Addressed: A Monsieur / Monsieur le Doct. Franklin / a Passy

Notation: Dr. Hunter May 27, 1784.—

Franklin and Chaumont: Agreement on Accounts and Receipt

(I) ADS:[6] Historical Society of Pennsylvania; press copy of ADS: American Philosophical Society; D (draft):[7] American Philosophical Society;

---

doctorate of divinity from the University of Edinburgh in 1771 and that year accepted a position as minister to the congregation at London Wall. He was also known for his translations of religious and scientific works: *ODNB.*

5. The packet contained Witherspoon's May 7 letter to Jay, mentioned above. That letter explained that Witherspoon had brought from America sealed letters from La Luzerne to Vergennes and to the comte de Sarsfield, and a third sealed letter from Marbois to "an Abbé." Being ill and unable to travel to France, Witherspoon was entrusting these letters to Dr. Hunter for delivery to Jay. Would Jay consider forwarding them? If they were favorably received, Witherspoon might make the trip to France; if Jay thought it improper to deliver them, he should not do so. Columbia University Library.

There is no evidence that Witherspoon went to Paris. He went to Scotland in June, and sailed from London to America in late July: Varnum L. Collins, *President Witherspoon: a Biography* (2 vols., Princeton, 1925), II, 141–3.

6. In BF's hand.

7. In the hand of Ferdinand Grand.

copy:[8] the marquis de Bausset, Ivry-sur-Seine (1961); (II) press copies of two DS:[9] American Philosophical Society

The "Experiment" that Franklin proposed to his landlord on May 2 succeeded. Chaumont finally accepted the judgment that their arbitrator, Ferdinand Grand, had drawn up two years earlier.[1] Franklin, in turn, agreed to allow Chaumont to deduct his debt in Europe from the larger sum owed to him by Congress, and, as promised, gave him another large advance: 20,000 *l.t.*

Document (I) is the agreement signed by both parties in the presence of Thomas Barclay. Drafted by Ferdinand Grand, it was written by Franklin on the verso of Grand's 1782 report.[2]

Document (II), written by Franklin for Chaumont's signature, is a receipt for the advance and an acknowledgment of their arrangement regarding payment. It, too, was attested by Barclay.

A third document, which formed the basis for the other two, was also signed on May 28 by Franklin, Chaumont, and Barclay: a one-sheet account calculating Chaumont's debt in Europe. It deducted from the 1782 total the additional rent that Franklin owed in the interim: 1,333 *l.t.* from the time of Grand's award (May 7, 1782) until January 7, 1783, and 7,500 *l.t.* from that date through April 7, 1784. The latter sum was calculated at a rate of 6,000 *l.t.* per year.[3]

Barclay reviewed all the papers relating to Chaumont's accounts over the next two weeks. He returned them to William Temple Franklin on June 13, approving the settled account but pointing out that Grand's report had made an error of one *livre* in Franklin's

8. This copy descended in the Chaumont family. Two pages in length, it consists of Grand's 1782 report, the May 28, 1784, agreement between BF and Chaumont, and the May 28, 1784, summary account described in the headnote.

9. We publish the one in BF's hand. The second, written in a hand we do not recognize, was also signed by Chaumont and attested by Barclay. All press copies of (I) and (II) are in Account XIX (XXVIII, 3).

1. On May 7, 1782: XXXVII, 279–81.

2. BF endorsed it, "Mr. Grand's Award May 1782 And the Acceptance of it May 1784". We included that endorsement when publishing the document: XXXVII, 281.

3. BF endorsed this sheet "Account with M. de Chaumont / Settled May 28. 1784" (University of Pa.). A press copy of it is in Account XIX. Rent from this time forward was paid quarterly. On July 5, 1784, BF paid Chaumont 1,500 *l.t.* for the quarter; Chaumont's signed receipt for that amount, written by WTF, is at the APS.

favor.[4] The official copy of Chaumont's account that he sent to Robert Morris was dated June 14, 1784. Franklin wrote an explanation to accompany it; that letter, addressed to Robert Morris and dated June 15, is now missing.[5]

[May 28, 1784]

I.

Nous soussignés aprés avoir bien examiné & reflechi sur l'arbitrage cy dessus, rendu par Monsieur Grand, & vu le dépouillement qu'il a fait de nos Comptes respectifs; avons unanimement & respectivement accepté le dit Arbitrage, en consequence duquel moy Le Ray de Chaumont me reconnois redevables envers M. le Docteur Franklin de la Somme de Trente cinque mille six cents trent quatre livres neuf Sols sept deniers.

Et moy Benjamin Franklin consens que la susdite Somme de 35,634.9.7 cy dessus reste entre les mains de Monsieur le Ray de Chaumont pour valoir en deduction de celle qu'il reclame du Congrés pour Marchandise livrée au General Lincoln, & Medecines livrées à Rhodeisland, conformement au Reçu separé qu'il m'en remettra en consequence.[6] Et moy le Ray de Chaumont reconnois que M. Le Docteur Franklin m'a rendu en ce moment mes deux Billets montant a cinquant mille Livres ensemble consentis cy-devant en sa faveur.[7] Au moyen de quoi nous nous reconnoissons respectivement quittes & dechargées reciproquement, renonçons en consequence à toutes pretentions quelqueconques l'un envers l'autre relativement au Compte dessus dit Arbitrage; declarons de plus que tous titres & Pièces qui pourroient etre restées entre nos mains à la charge de l'un ou de l'autre sont devenues nulles & de nulle effet, n'entendant s'il s'en trouve qu'on puisse s'en prevaloir, ni en faire aucun usage.

4. Thomas Barclay to WTF, June 13, 1784, APS. In that letter, Barclay also asked WTF to help him arrange a time to meet with Chaumont and settle his accounts with Silas Deane.

5. *Morris Papers*, IX, 541–2.

6. Document (II), below.

7. Grand's May, 1782, report reduced Chaumont's claim against BF by the amount of these two promissory notes, which BF received on Jan. 1, 1779: XXVIII, 325–6; XXXVII, 279.

En foy de quoy nous avons signé a Passy ce vingt huit Mai, 1784.

LE RAY DE CHAUMONT   B FRANKLIN

[*In Thomas Barclay's hand:*] Present THOS BARCLAY

II.

At Passy, this 28th Day of May 1784, then adjusted all Accounts between me and Mr Franklin Minister Plenipotentiary of the United States; and allowing the Ballance found to be due from me by our Arbitrator M. Grand, viz Thirty-five Thousand Six hundred and Thirty four Livres nine Sols and seven deniers, and deducting from that Sum the Sum of Eight Thousand Eight hundred and thirty three Livres since accruing to me for Rent to the seventh of April last, there remains due from me the Sum of Twenty-six Thousand Eight hundred and one Livres, nine Sols & seven deniers: But as there is a Debt due to me from the Congress, in America, M. Franklin has advanced to me Twenty Thousand Livres on that Account,[8] which with the above Ballance making in the whole Forty six thousand Eight hundred and one Livres nine Sols & seven deniers As to be deducted from the said Debt, due for Clothing delivered to General Lincoln & for Medicines. Witness my hand.

LERAY DE CHAUMONT

[*In Thomas Barclay's hand:*] Present THOS BARCLAY

From William Alexander   ALS: American Philosophical Society

My Dear Sir   Richmond Virginia 30 May 1784
I cannot let my first ship go without dropg you a few lines— Jonn woud inform you of my arrival of the severity of the Winter, & of my Journey to Philadelphia which was necessary for setling a plan for conducting my money transactions which I did

8. This advance is recorded under May 28, 1784, in Account XXVII (XXXII, 4).

to my Satisfaction—⁹ I had the pleasure of Seeing your amiable Daughter Grand Children & Mr Bache, & received every mark of kindness from all of Them— Your Town pleases me much, not merely on account of the regularity of the streets, but the seeming energy of the Inhabitants, in a word The Congress may Sit where It pleases but Philadelphia is, & always will be the Capital of America—¹ With regard to my business I have met with all the Obstructions I expected & some that I coud not forsee, particularly there is a want of order & economy in business in this State, that exceeds all Imagination— A Man must literaly do what Poor Richard Advises, to have any thing done he must *go*,² judge what follows from this for a person whose business must Lye equaly on the four great rivers, & over an Extent of 50 leagues on each of these rivers, with a very little time I hope however to have my machine mounted, to go with tolerable regularity & Some Advantage, what can be done for a litle time will be merely to keep afloat, without dammage to the Concern— This I think we shall do in all events—

I have on mature deliberation fix'd myself here for the present, it is pretty Centrical, the seat of Government & of the weekly post, but I am obliged to Contrive posts for my own business, & when I begin vigourously, must keep 7 or 8 horses running Constantly backward & forward.

The difficulties I have to encounter give me time to Lay my plan in such a way as will require less mending than if we had been hurried at first—

9. Alexander arrived in Philadelphia bearing a letter of credit from the Paris bankers Laval & Wilfelsheim, along with BF's attestation to having witnessed their signatures. After he enticed Robert Morris to sign a secret agreement on March 2 to become an equal partner with him and JW ("Jonn") in their tobacco enterprise, Morris agreed to negotiate the bills William Alexander & Co. would draw on the French bankers: XLI, 180–1; RB to BF, March 7, above; *Morris Papers,* IX, 152, 156–7; Herbert A. Johnson *et al.,* eds., *The Papers of John Marshall* (12 vols., Chapel Hill, 1974–2006), V, 94, 98–9, 106.

1. Congress had moved from Philadelphia to Princeton in June, 1783, and then to Annapolis in November: XLI, 145; *Morris Papers,* VIII, 662–5.

2. Worded in the preface to the 1758 almanac as follows: "If you would have your Business done, go; If not, send": VII, 344.

I have been very well receivd by the Governor[3] & have got acquainted & even Connected with all the Ingenious Men in this state, who make any figure, Except Mr Jefferson & two or three more yet Absent— In a word If my Constitution will stand this Climate, I can live here agreeably But unless necessity were to Oblige me, woud not think of bringing out my Family— Were Philadelphia my residence I certainly woud— At present I consider myself as in Another world, & wish to forget every thing in the old one, but my Friends & my Business.

I have met with Many very Ingenious & Worthy Men in whose society I coud pass my life with pleasure— Amongst the old race Col Geo: Mason & Mr With[4] surprised me, And there are young Men getting Forward who will yield to their predecessors in Nothing— Mr Madison, must soon have a considerable weight in this state, or in any state in which he is Employed—

Your old Colleague Arthur Lee is sent to treat with the Indians, He is at present neither in Congress nor Assembly—[5]

I beg to be rememberd to your Grand son & secretary & all our Friends with You— I hope my boy gives you & Him Satisfaction—[6] I was pleasd wt His letter to Williams about the Baloons, I sent it to Dr Foulke & it helpd to make one, which he had begun upon my Information—[7] I think the Dr will Succeed in his Business which is still more material. He & his Family did every thing possible to render my stay in Philadelphia agreeable. You have got a New Colleague of whom fame Speaks highly—[8] You will learn that we are limiting our Foreign trade

3. Benjamin Harrison.

4. George Mason, Sr. (xxix, 224), and George Wythe (xiii, 321n).

5. Alexander was mistaken. Congress had indeed appointed Lee as one of the commissioners to negotiate a peace settlement with the Iroquois, but the talks did not begin in earnest until the fall. At the end of May, Lee was in Annapolis attending Congress: Louis W. Potts, *Arthur Lee: a Virtuous Revolutionary* (Baton Rouge and London, 1981), pp. 268, 269; *Jefferson Papers*, VII, 9n; Smith, *Letters*, XXI, xxvi.

6. Robert Alexander was living with BF at Passy: XLI, 524n.

7. The Philadelphia physician John Foulke, who during his years of medical study in Europe had been a friend of WTF's, constructed a paper air balloon that was launched from the garden of the Dutch minister on May 10, 1784. Francis Hopkinson called the balloon "The first that mounted our Atmosphere": XXXII, 283n; *Jefferson Papers*, VII, 246.

8. *I.e.*, TJ.

to a few points in the Bay—[9] This will soon make Norfolk a great Mart & will I think be of general Service & of advantage to us. Let me know my Dear Sir if I can be usefull to you or yours in this Country & believe me unalterably My Dear Sir Your most devoted hble Ser W: ALEXANDER

Dr B: Franklin M: P: of the United States at Passy

From Paolo Frisi[1]

ALS: American Philosophical Society

Monsieur. à Milan ce 30 Mai 1784
Depuis mon depart de Londres je ne vous ai ecrit, Monsieur, que pour vous remercier du beau present que vous m'avez fait de vos ouvrages, et j'ai appris par le gazzettes publiques les grandes nouvelles qui vous regardoient directement, celles de la revolution de L'Amerique. J'espere cependant que vous ne m'aurez pas oublié, et je vais profiter de toute la bonté que vous m'avez temoignée autres fois en vous presentant Monsr. le Chevr. Castiglioni gentilhomme d'une maison de plus distinguées de nôtre ville qui compte de faire un tour dans L'Amerique pour voir de près cette brave et nouvelle Nation, et pour y continuer ses recherches sur L'Histoire Naturelle.[2] Je l'ai chargé de presenter mes deux premiers volumes à L'Academie de Philadelphie.[3]

9. The previous day the Va. House of Delegates had voted that a bill be introduced restricting where foreign vessels could engage in trade. The final act, passed June 26, designated Norfolk and Portsmouth, Bermuda Hundred, Tappahannock, Yorktown, and Alexandria as the only authorized ports of entry: *Jefferson Papers*, VII, 216n.
1. The well-known Italian astronomer and mathematician who began an intermittent correspondence with BF in 1756 (see VII, 12), though only two of their letters have been located: this one and BF's reply of Sept. 20 (British Library). Frisi died on Nov. 22, 1784: *Dictionary of Scientific Biography*.
2. The botanist Luigi Castiglioni (1757–1832) visited BF at Passy on Aug. 3, 1784, and was received "with all the cordiality imaginable," as he reported to Frisi. Two days before, Castiglioni had met WTF at a dinner at the comte de Mercy-Argenteau's and told him of his plans to tour the United States: *Luigi Castiglioni's* Viaggio: *Travels in the United States of North America, 1785–87*, trans. and ed. Antonio Pace (Syracuse, N.Y., 1983), pp. xii, xvii–xviii, xxvii.
3. These were probably *Algebram et geometriam analyticam continens* (Milan, 1782) and *Mechanicam universam et mechanicæ applicationem ad*

Je vous prie de le diriger. Vous aurez des nouveaux droits sur la reconnoissance comme sur le vrai le profond respect avec le quel j'ai l'honneur d'etre Monsieur Vôtre très humble très obeissant serviteur FRISI

Addressed: à Monsieur / Monsieur Franklin / Ministre Plenipe. des Etats-Unis de L'Amerique / de L'Acad. Roy. des sciences de Paris. / à Passy.

To Vergennes[4]

ALS: Gilder Lehrman Collection; copy: Archives du Ministère des affaires étrangères

Sir, Passy, May 31. 1784.

Some Inconveniencies are said to have arisen from a want of Certainty in the Powers of our Consuls. The Articles respecting that Matter have been some time prepared and agreed to between Mr de Raynevall and me.[5] If there is no Change of Sentiment respecting them, I beg leave to request your Excellency would direct such Steps to be taken as may be proper for compleating them. I am ready on the Part of the United States to sign them at any time. With great Respect, I am, Sir, Your Excellency's most obedient & most humble Servant

B FRANKLIN

His Excellency the Count de Vergennes.—

---

aquarum fluentium theoriam continens (Milan, 1783), the first two volumes of a three-volume work entitled *Opera.* Castiglioni informed Frisi that BF acknowledged this gift of books for the APS: *Luigi Castiglioni's* Viaggio, p. xviii.

4. This letter was prompted by one of the same date from Barclay to WTF, asking that when he went to Versailles the next day (Tuesday, June 1), he restart the stalled process of finalizing the "Convention Explaining the Functions of the Consul." APS. See the Editorial Note on the Consular Convention, July 29, below.

5. The draft consular convention between France and the United States had been settled the previous December; see XLI, 320–32.

From the Comtesse d'Houdetot

LS:[6] American Philosophical Society

a Sannois Le 31. may 1784.

Me permettés Vous Mon Cher Et Venerable Docteur De Vous
Demander De Vos nouvelles; Et Dans L'Eloignement ou je Suis
De Vous De M'informer au Moins Comment Vous Vous portés
Et Si Vous pensés quelques fois a la personne La plus Remplie
Des Sentimens De L'attachement Le plus tendre Et De La plus
profonde Veneration, je ne puis oublier la touchante Bonté avec
Laquelle Vous avés Bien Voulû Songer aux Moyens De Venir
Encore Embellir ma Solitude que Vous avés Deja Consacrée; Et
je n'ay Songé qu'a Vous En faciliter Les Moyens. Je me Suis assu-
rée D'un yacht Commode, Dont Vous Disposerés En prevenant
quelques jours D'avance affin qu'il Soit parfaittement En Etât. Il
apartient a Mr. De La ferté Des Menus,[7] Et il Sera a Vos Ordres
ainsy que Ses Batelliers, avec Lesquels j'ay même fait prix pour
que Vous n'en Soyés pas Oberé; ils Demandent Soixante Livres
pour L'allée Et la Venue. Ils Vous Conduiraient a Epinay, qui Est
a une petite Lieüe De Chez moy, ou j'irais Vous Reçevoir. Vous
auriés Dans Votre promenade a pied Le Thé Et Du Repos a une
Maison a Moitié Chemin. En allant par Eau jusqu'a Argenteüil
Vous auriés moins De Chemin a pied De pres De Moitié mais il
faut un peu Monter Et Le Chemin n'est pas Si doux aux pieds;
il faudrait Mon Cher Docteur que Cela S'Executât au Mois ou
nous Entrons, je quitte Sannois au Mois De juillet pour Voya-
ger Et Dailleurs La Saison Serait trop Chaude Et La Campagne
Moins Belle. Vous n'auriés qu'a M'informer Du jour ou Vous
Voudriés partir Et De Celuy De Votre Retour, il faut au moins
plusieurs jours De Sejour Chez moy, Si Cela pouvait aller a huit
ou plus, ah! Mon Cher Docteur qu'elle peine pour Moy Si je
n'ay fait la qu'un Beau Songe, je m'En Remets a Votre Bonté,

---

6. In the hand of Girard; see XXXVI, 583n.

7. Denis-Pierre-Jean Papillon de La Ferté (1727–1794) served as the
intendant of the Menus-Plaisirs du Roi, the department of the royal household in charge of organizing fêtes and ceremonies: Alain-Charles Gruber,
Les Grandes Fêtes et leurs décors à l'époque de Louis XVI (Geneva, 1972),
pp. 7–8, 235.

a Votre prudence, a La persuasion ou Vous devés Estre que je ne Voudrais pas acheter Le plus grand plaisir De ma Vie aux Risques de Vous Exposer a la Moindre incommodité. Decidés Donc De mon Sort Mon Cher Docteur Et tel qu'il Soit Rapellés Vous La tendre amitié Et L'Estime De Celle qui Vous Ecrit En particulier Et Le Respect Et La Reconnaissance qu'elle partage avec Le Reste Des hommes.

Permettés moy De Me Recommander aux Soins Et aux Souvenirs De Monsieur franklin Votre petit fils qui Vous accompagnera a Ce que j'Espere. Je Serais Bien Charmée Si Vous Vouliés aussy M'amenner Ce jeune petit fils que j'ay Vû Chez Vous Dont La figure Charmante Est Deja parée D'un Si Beau Caractere De franchise Et De Liberté   LA CTESSE. DHOUDETOT

Notation: La Cesse. d'Houdetot 31 May 1784—

Meteorological Imaginations and Conjectures

AD (draft): Library of Congress;[8] press copy of copy:[9]American Philosophical Society

The "dry fog" that blanketed much of Europe during the summer of 1783 had occasioned much scientific speculation, but its cause was as yet unknown. In this paper, written nearly a year after the fog first appeared, Franklin was less concerned with its cause (though he did propose a theory that would turn out to be correct) than with its effect, proposing a connection between the summer's fog and the exceptionally cold winter that followed.[1]

8. Also at the Library of Congress is a French translation in BFB's hand with several minor corrections by BF, and a copy of that translation in the hand of Poullard, Morellet's secretary, with corrections by BF and Cabanis. As far as we know, BFB's translation was never published.

9. The copy from which the press copy was made is in the hand of L'Air de Lamotte.

1. He was correct in this hypothesis, as well: G. R. Demarée and A. E. J. Ogilvie, *"Bons Baisers d'Islande:* Climatic, Environmental, and Human Dimensions Impacts of the *Lakagígar* Eruption (1783–1784) in Iceland," in *History and Climate: Memories of the Future?,* ed. P. D. Jones *et al.* (New York, Boston, and Dordrecht, Netherlands, 2001), pp. 219–21.

Franklin docketed this essay "May 1784," and we are unable to date it more precisely. He sent a fair copy to Benjamin Vaughan well before July 17, when he offered the piece to Thomas Percival for his newly formed Literary and Philosophical Society of Manchester and suggested that Percival get a copy from Vaughan.[2] Percival read the essay to the Manchester society on December 22, and it was published in the second volume of the society's memoirs.[3]

[May, 1784]

Meteorological Imaginations & Conjectures

There seems to be a Region high in the Air over all Countries, where it is always Winter, where Frost exists continually, since in the midst of Summer on the Surface of the Earth, Ice falls often from above in the Form of Hail.—

Hailstones of the great Weight we sometimes find them, did not probably acquire their Magnitude before they began to descend. The Air being 400 times rarer than Water,[4] is unable to support it but in the Shape of Vapour, a State in which its Particles are separated. As soon as they are condensed by the Cold of the upper Regions so as to form a Drop, that Drop begins to fall. If it freezes into a Grain of Ice, that Ice descends. In descending both the Drop of Water and the Grain of Ice, are augmented by Particles of the Vapour they pass thro' in falling, and which they condense by their Coldness and attach to themselves.

It is possible that in Summer, much of what is Rain when it arrives at the Surface of the Earth, might have been Snow when it began its Descent; but being thaw'd in passing thro' the warm Air near that Surface, it is changed from Snow into Rain.

How immensely cold must be the original Particle of Hail, which forms the Center of the future Hailstone, since it is

2. BF's cover letter has not survived. We only know of his sending it to Vaughan because of his July 17 letter to Percival.

3. Literary and Philosophical Society of Manchester *Memoirs*, II (1785), 357–61. JW, evidently unaware of this publication, submitted the MS to the APS in 1813. It was rejected on account of having been published by the Manchester society: *Early Proc. of the APS* (Philadelphia, 1884), pp. 440–1.

4. BF first wrote: "being rarer in the upper Regions". When the essay was printed in the Society of Manchester's *Memoirs*, the more accurate estimate of "eight hundred times rarer than Water" was substituted.

capable of communicating sufficient Cold, if I may so speak,[5] to freeze all the Mass of Vapour condensed round it, and form a Lump of perhaps 6 or 8 ounces in weight!

When in Summer time the Sun is high, and long every Day above the Horizon, his Rays strike the Earth more directly & with longer Continuance than in Winter; hence the Surface is more heated, and to a greater Depth by the Effect of those Rays.

When Rain falls on the heated Earth, and soaks down into it, it carries down with it a great Part of the Heat, which by that means descends still deeper.

The Mass of Earth to the depth perhaps of 30 Feet, being thus heated, to a certain degree, continues to retain its Heat for some time. Thus the first Snows that fall in the Beginning of Winter, seldom lie long on the Surface, but are soon melted & absorbed. After which the Winds that blow over the Country on which the Snows had fallen are not rendred so cold as they would have been by those Snows if they had remained. The Earth too, thus uncovered by the Snow, which would have reflected the Sun's Rays, now absorbs them, receiving and retaining the Warmth they afford.[6] And thus the Approach of the Severity of Winter is retarded; and the extreme degree of its Cold is not always at the time we might expect it, viz. when the Sun is at its greatest Distance, and the Days shortest, but some Time after that Period, according to the English Proverb which says,

As the Day lengthens,
The Cold Strengthens.—

The Causes of refrigeration continuing to operate, while the Sun returns too slowly & his Force continues too weak, to counteract them.—

During several of the Summer Months of the Year 1783, when the Effect of the Suns Rays to heat the Earth in these

5. BF inserted an asterisk here, and in the margin wrote, "A Note * *if I may so speak*, because perhaps it is not by communicating Cold to the Particles of Vapour that it freezes them; but by depriving them of their Heat.—" This note was not included in the printed version but was incorporated in the French translations.

6. This sentence was added in the margin. It does not appear in the printed version but was included in the French translation.

northern Regions should have been greatest, there existed a constant Fog over all Europe; and great Part of North America.[7] This Fog was of a permanent Nature; it was dry, & the Rays of the Sun seem'd to have little Effect towards dissipating it, as they easily do a moist Fog arising from Water. They were indeed rendred so faint in passing thro' it, that when collected in the Focus of a Burning Glass they would scarce kindle brown Paper; Of course their Summer Effect in heating the Earth was exceedingly diminished.

Hence the Surface was early frozen.

Hence the first Snows remained on it unmelted, and received continual Additions.

Hence the Air was more chilled, & the Winds more severely cold.

Hence perhaps the Winter of 1783, 4, was more Severe than any that had happened for many Years.

The Cause of this Universal Fog is not yet ascertained.[8]

7. The dry fog was observed in Paris for the first time *c.* June 18, 1783, and though its origin was then unknown, it is now believed to have been caused by the Lakagígar eruption in Iceland, which began on June 8. Much of Europe was covered by a thick haze from mid-June through at least September: XL, 353; Thorvaldur Thordarson and Stephen Self, "Atmospheric and Environmental Effects of the 1783–1784 Laki Eruption: a Review and Reassessment," *Jour. of Geophysical Research*, Atmospheres, CVIII (2003), 2–3, 6–9, 21.

Scholars have searched for evidence that the haze was observable in North America. Though recent discoveries suggest that the higher latitudes of North America may have been affected, there is no proof that the haze appeared in the more populated regions to the south: Richard B. Stothers, "The Great Dry Fog of 1783," *Climatic Change*, XXXII (1996), 81–2.

8. Speculation as to the cause of the dry fog began almost immediately, with earthquakes being the most common explanation. In August, Mourgue de Montredon presented a paper to the Académie royale de Montpellier in which he postulated that various subterranean events, including the emergence of a new volcanic island off the coast of Iceland (for which see below), were somehow connected to the appearance of the dry fog, but his explanation was far from being universally adopted. The year 1783 had been full of unusual events, and news of the Lakagígar eruption did not reach the continent until September: Demarée and Ogilvie, "*Bons Baisers d'Islande*," pp. 221–30, 237–41; Thordarson and Self, "Atmospheric and Environmental Effects of the 1783–1784 Laki Eruption," p. 2.

Whether it was adventitious to this Earth, and merely a Smoke proceeding from the Consumption by Fire of some of those great burning Balls or Globes which we happen to meet with in our rapid Course round the Sun, and which are sometimes seen to kindle & be destroy'd in passing our Atmosphere, and whose Smoke might be attracted and retain'd by our Earth:[9] Or whether it was the vast Quantity of Smoke long continuing to issue during the Summer from *Hecla* in Iceland, and that other Volcano which arose out of the Sea near that Island;[1] which Smoke might be spread by various Winds over the northern Part of the World; is yet uncertain.

It seems, however, worth the Enquiry, whether other hard Winters recorded in History, were preceded by similar permanent & widely-extended Summer Fogs.[2] Because if found to be so, Men might from such Fogs conjecture the Probability of a succeeding hard Winter, & of the Damages to be expected by the breaking up of frozen Rivers at the Approach of

9. BF is referring to meteors, then known as "fireballs." His language suggests that he subscribed to the theory advanced by both John Pringle and David Rittenhouse—a minority position at the time—that meteors were extraterrestrial in origin: XXXIV, 224–5; John G. Burke, *Cosmic Debris: Meteorites in History* (Berkeley, Los Angeles, and London, 1986), pp. 17–24.

1. Some contemporary reports put the Lakagígar eruption near Mt. Hekla: *Mercure de France (Jour. politique de Bruxelles)*, Oct. 4, 1783, p. 4.

In May volcanic activity off the coast of Iceland created a new, short-lived island called Nyey (New Island). News of this eruption was reported in the *Gaz. de Leyde* on July 18, 1783, a month after the dry fog first appeared in Paris, and two months before news of the Lakagígar eruption reached France, leading many to assume a connection between the two events: Charles A. Wood, "Climatic Effects of the 1783 Laki Eruption," in *The Year Without a Summer?: World Climate in 1816*, ed. C. R. Harington (Ottawa, 1992), p. 71.

2. While it is now accepted that volcanic activity can affect world weather patterns, the exact circumstances by which this occurs are still the subject of debate. The theory that BF advances here has been widely accepted as one possible explanation for how volcanic activity may affect climate: Demarée and Ogilvie, "*Bons Baisers d'Islande*," pp. 240–1; Haraldur Sigurdsson, "Volcanic Pollution and Climate: the 1783 Laki Eruption," *Eos*, LXIII (1982), 601–2; Wood, "Climatic Effects of the 1783 Laki Eruption," pp. 69–74.

Spring; and take such Measures as are possible & practicable to secure themselves and Effects from the Mischiefs that attended the last.—[3]

Notation by Franklin: Meteorological Paper May 1784

From John Walter[4]

ALS: American Philosophical Society

Sir,   London May [*blank*] 1784

I am oblig'd for your kind Letter,[5] & the present accompanying it, which I think of great Moment to my future Patent.— When I first apply'd to have Type cemented for the incorrect

3. In late February, when the frozen Seine broke up and the winter snow began to melt, low-lying areas were inundated. In his diary, BFB describes two houses on the left bank of the Seine, opposite Passy, that were made a temporary island by the rising water: BFB's journal, entries of Feb. 26 and 27. Similar flooding occurred all over Europe with disastrous consequences, including severe damage to infrastructure and crops: Rudolf Brázdil *et al.*, "European Floods during the Winter 1783/1784: Scenarios of an Extreme Event during the 'Little Ice Age,'" *Theoretical and Applied Climatology*, C (2010), 163, 169–81; Shelby T. McCloy, "Flood Relief and Control in Eighteenth-Century France," *Jour. of Modern History*, XIII (1941), 7–12.

4. In this rambling and occasionally incoherent letter, Walter tries to explain his involvement with logography. Over the next several years his accounts of this story would evolve; he would give increasing prominence to his own role and become increasingly vague as to chronology. By 1789, when he published his most extensive account, Walter was taking nearly full credit for the development of the logographic process, acknowledging merely that an unnamed "person" had furnished him with "the first rudiments." Included in that 1789 pamphlet were all the letters Walter had received from BF. In order to make them conform with his claim of having invented the process, he altered their texts; at least he did so in the case of BF's letter of April 17 (above), the only example for which we have the MS to compare to the published version. Walter excised all mentions of Johnson and altered pronouns so as to place himself in the role of inventor: *An Address to the Public . . . shewing the Great Improvement he has made in the Art of Printing, by Logographic Arrangements . . .* (London, 1789), pp. vi–vii, 9–12, 17, 20–1.

5. Of April 17, above.

Pamphlet I sent You,[6] Mr. Caslon[7] charg'd Me 2 s./o per Pound for them, instead of 1 s./o the common Price of Letters, but gave Me Expectation that the Demand would be lessen'd, if an Appearance of Business took place in that Way, however I find no Abatement in Price from him, though he has every Reason now to find it will be continued.— When I first publish'd that Pamphlet in the Authors Name, I threw it out into the World to court every Objection, which could possibly arise against the Mode intended for Execution— The Answers & Objections made by several Printers, in viewing the Fount, & Criticisms in the Reviews, have been so puerile to common Understanding,[8] that I have been induc'd to purchase the Kings late printing House, near Apothecaries Hall, Blackfriars, (formerly Mr. Baskets) which has been fitted up for the purpose, & will open on the 1st. Day of next Month, for conducting Business on the Plan contain'd in the Pamphlet.—[9] It has been a very laborious Work to combat a whole Language, to arrange it, & make a proper Portion of Words for general Use, but when I took it up about a Year since,[1] it was so voluminous, that though 6 Years Labor

6. Johnson's *Introduction to Logography* was marred by misspellings and misalignments that by this time had been pointed out and mocked by reviewers; see the note below. The most obvious misprint occurred on the title page itself, where, in reference to the royal letters patent for logography, "his Majesty" was rendered "his Najesty." The pamphlet had been printed by John Fleming, who continued to work for Walter for some time afterwards. Walter would later lament that he had "suffered much" from Fleming's inattention: *Address to the Public*, pp. 17–20.

7. William Caslon III: xxx, 609–10.

8. One prominent review, broadly sarcastic throughout, derided logography as both theoretically unsound and impracticable. The reviewer pointed out that the typographical errors in the pamphlet itself ("Najesty" among them) contradicted the author's bold claim that, under the logographic method, spelling errors would be impossible and basic compositors' errors would be greatly reduced: *Monthly Rev., or, Literary Jour.*, LXX (March 1784), 221–3. Subsequent imprints by Walter's Logographic Press were also criticized for such imperfections: John Feather, "John Walter and the Logographic Press," *Publishing History*, 1 (1977), 99–100.

9. Walter apparently purchased the shop in late March, 1784: *The History of the Times* (7 vols., London, 1935–2005), I, 3–4.

1. This phrase, among other evidence, convinces us that Walter did not become involved with Johnson or logography until the spring of 1783. In

had been bestow'd, & great Ingenuity mark'd the Work, Utility was yet wanting; for was a Compositor to ramble round a very extended Space, in search of the different Letters of the Alphabet, the Time taken up by such a process, would not compensate for the Number of Motions to form the Words— To correct this Evil has been the Attention of my Thoughts for a considerable Time, without much Assistance from Mr. Johnson, who I found in a short Space after his Introduction to Me, not only a very eccentric Genius, but a Man without Principle, & of unbounded Extravagance, & I have had as much Plague to render him of further Use in the Matter, as with the Work itself— You will excuse my being very minute in Description of the Arrangement, on which the Facility of the Work depends, because I mean to offer a Fount of it to the Court of France, as I have already to that of Russia by the Ambassador of that Court,[2] who did Me the Honor to view it with the Duke of Richmond on Saturday last— Thus far I may venture to inform You, that the whole English Language (except Technicals & Obsolete Words) are compriz'd in 8 Cases of 3 feet 3 Inches, by 1 foot 7 Inches each, which takes up an Extent of only 6 feet 6 Inches, because 2 Pair Cases are in Front, & 1 Pair on either Side, making a triangular Box, so that the Compositor by the Method of placing, has no more than 4½ feet to range in— One Case contains all particles, Pronouns & auxiliary Verbs, likewise Words of all Figures; 6 Cases contain the rest of the Language as simple Words, with & without the concludg. Letters where they admit of a Compound, & One Case has every Termination, so that

---

XLI, 371n, citing the *DNB*, we stated that he bought Johnson's patent in 1782. That cannot be true; he himself wrote that he turned to logography after his bankruptcy (*Address to the Public*, pp. iii–vi), which was announced in the *London Chron.* issue of Feb. 1–4, 1783. Johnson's letters to Joseph Banks about logography corroborate the timing; see Neil Chambers, ed., *Scientific Correspondence of Sir Joseph Banks, 1765–1820* (6 vols., London, 2007), II, 23–4, III, 266–7; and Johnson to Banks, May 23, 1783 (Royal Botanic Gardens, Kew, England). Walter's first known public claim to holding the patent was published in the *Public Advertiser*, April 15, 1784.

2. Ivan Matveevich Simolin was minister plenipotentiary from Russia to the British court: *Repertorium der diplomatischen Vertreter*, III, 355.

for Instance if the Word *converse* is wanted—*convers* admits of ation, ing, ed, ible &c &c— The Duke of Richmond was so well pleas'd that he has desir'd a complete Fount, which I mean to present his Grace with, after the Offer of one to his Majesty,[3] whom You may observe gave Me the Liberty to dedicate it[4] to him, & his Grace the Duke of Portland did Me the Honor of presenting it— The Madness of Parties, now War is at an End, has kept the King hitherto from attending the Subject, further than perusing the Pamphlet, but I do not despair of having his royal Presence ere long.— This important Improvement of the Press is brought forward to the World, from my having been very unfortunate as well as my Country in the Consequences of the mad War it has been engag'd— The enclos'd Paper[5] will give you a Description of a hard Case, & the prophetic Warning I gave the Duke of Grafton (after addressing Lord North on the Subject I was deeply involv'd in, without Reply) but such was the Supineness (to say no worse) of our Administration, that had an Angel from Heaven portended the Seperation which has taken place, it would not have been attended to.— The Man who first invented the Arrangement of the Language would very probably have suffer'd the patent to expire, without Assistance from the Notoriety of his Character, but from my Exertion; having been for 3 Years past treating with, & cheating a Variety of Persons, to whom he had offer'd it, & was at the Time I took it in Hand, in the most abject State.— The Pamphlet you note in your Letter of Madame de St. Paul, I am utterly

3. It seems the Duke of Richmond's font was never completed. Walter did prepare a font, housed in special cases, to be presented as a gift to George III. The king accepted the font in February, 1785. After admiring it, he ordered that it be returned: *Address to the Public*, pp. 24–38, 56–64.
4. *I.e.*, the *Introduction to Logography*.
5. Missing. At some point BF acquired a copy (APS) of *The Case of Mr. John Walter, of London, Merchant* ([London, 1784]). This three-page publication gives an account of Walter's professional misfortunes and bankruptcy through losses in maritime insurance underwriting during the recent war. These losses he blamed on failures by the British government to warn and protect British shipping. *The Case*, however, makes no mention of Grafton, refers only broadly to Lord North's wartime ministry, and contains nothing that might be termed a "prophetic Warning."

a Stranger to, but the Perusal of it, & the Mode of your casting
your Terminations sent Me, (which are not quite exact) will be
highly acceptable— I am afraid the Founders here, foreseeing
a Revolution in their Trade, & being very few in Number, re-
tard my Work, as near 4 Months since I bespoke 3000lb Weight
of Types cemented, without having yet a single Pound, which
could I get Punches & Matrices made of exactness, would oblige
Me to turn Founder; for as my ultimate Intention is, to sell the
Type, I must not be at such a State of Uncertainty— My Patent being *"for the sole Privilege of casting & cementing as well as
using &c"*— I have sent You our Letters, that You may see the
Manner of cementing them, which is with the same compound
the Letter is cast, & you will observe the common Letter runs
flush at Bottom, whereas the other is printed for the Metal to
close the Vacancy— I recollect Mr. Barclay was in haste when
I deliver'd him the Pamphlet, which occasion'd my sending no
Letter by him, which I thought the less necessary, as he saw the
Apparatus at my House, & therefore was the more fully enabled
to describe it— Either You or the Founders here are wrong, by
your supposing if a Letter is batter'd, it can be remov'd, without Prejudice to the rest, as the Word is rejected should that
happen, which makes Me very desirous of casting the Word,
entire, if it is practicable with any exactness— I have corrected
the Outlines of a grammatical Dictionary for an universal Language, so digested, that the same Writing & Character, shall
be perfectly understood in the Latin, Greek, Hebrew, English,
French, Italian, Spanish, Portuguese, German, Russian, Swedish, Danish, & Turkish Languages; with Blank Columns for
the Insertion of any other Language, & that each may be alter-
nately translated into the other, by being acquainted with one
Language only. But as yet I have the Pamphlet unfinish'd, & in
Manuscript only, as the present Work engrosses all my Attention, & Johnson is so bad a Man, & so little to be depended on,
that I despair of his Services being long continued— He is so
much in Debt here, that he is afraid of stirring out, & seldom
keeps a Lodging a Month together, & of that unbounded Expence, that no Purse is equal to his Demands, & was he in Possession of a Thousand Pounds now, a Week hence would find
him without a Shilling— I am going to publish a Newspaper by

my Plan,[6] & intend very soon bringing forward a new Edition
of the Classics— I should be glad to have my Improvement laid
before the Court of France for their Approbation, & would willingly send the King a complete printing Fount, that the Nation
might have the Benefit of it, laying myself open to the Liberal-
ity of the Monarch, perhaps you might much assist Me in this
Wish, as I find it will require a much more extensive Fortune,
than the Calamities of the late War have left Me to command,
in forwarding the plan [on] a liberal Scale, which I am ambitious
of putting it—

Your further Correspondence on this [Subject,] with Convenience to yourself, will be much esteem'd by Sir Your Much
Oblig'd & Obedt. Servt   JOHN WALTER

PS. This will be deliver'd by my Friend Robt. Hunter Esqr. an
eminent Merchant of this City, whom I beg to introduce on this
Occasion—[7]

Dr. Franklin.—

Addressed: Dr. Benjamin Franklin / at Passy near / Paris / per
Favor of Robt. Hunter Esqr

Notations in different hands: Mr Hunter No 14 Rue Caumortin /
John Walter May 1784.—

6. The *Daily Universal Register* (London) began publication on Jan. 1,
1785. Its masthead declared that it was "Printed Logographically" and "By
His Majesty's Patent." Three years later the paper was renamed the *Times
or Daily Universal Register,* and the reference to a patent was dropped. The
declaration that the paper was "Printed Logographically" was removed in
February, 1792, when, it seems, the method was abandoned. See Feather,
"Walter and the Logographic Press," pp. 100–1.

7. Probably Robert Hunter (1742–1812), a prominent British merchant
who by the latter half of the 1780s was a leading public representative of
the committee of London merchants trading to Quebec. His son Robert
Hunter, Jr. (1764–1843), may have accompanied him on this trip to France.
On Nov. 4, 1785, when Robert Jr. was in Philadelphia, he recorded in his
journal that he had "met Dr. Franklin walking to the statehouse," and "found
[him] much broke in his looks since I saw him last at Passy near Paris":
Louis B. Wright and Marion Tinling, eds., *Quebec to Carolina in 1785–1786:
Being the Travel Diary and Observations of Robert Hunter, Jr., a Young Merchant of London* (San Marino, Calif., 1943), pp. 3–4, 173, 312–13; *Dictionary of Canadian Biography* (15 vols. to date, Toronto, 1966–), VII, 522–3.

From David Hartley

Copies: National Archives (London),[8] William L. Clements Library; transcript: National Archives

Sir   Paris June 1 1784

I have the honour to inform you that I have transmitted to London, the ratification on the part of Congress of the definitive treaty of peace, between Great Britain and the united states of america. I am ordered to represent to you,[9] that a want of form appears in the first paragraph of that instrument, wherein the united states are mentioned before his majesty, contrary to the established custom in every treaty, in which a crowned head and a republic are parties.— It is likewise to be observed that the term definitive *articles* is used instead of definitive *treaty*.

The conclusion likewise appears deficient, as it is neither signed by the President, nor is it dated, & consequently is wanting in some of the most essential points of form, necessary towards authenticating the validity of the instrument.

I am ordered to propose to you, Sir, that these defects in the ratification shd be corrected, wch might very easily be done, either by signing a declaration in the name of Congress, for preventing the particular mode of expression so far as relates to precedency, in the first paragraph, being considered as a precedent, to be adopted on any future occasion, or else by having a new copy made out in America, in wch these mistakes shd be corrected, & wch might be done without any prejudice arising to either of the Parties by the delay. I am Sir with great respect and Consideration Your most obedient humble Servant

D HARTLEY

To His Excellency Benjamin Franklin Esqr. &c &c &c

Copy

[*Notations?:*] A / [*blank*] In Mr. Hartley's No. 7.

---

8. In Hartley's hand and signed by him. The other copy is in George Hammond's hand.

9. The rest of the letter follows almost verbatim Foreign Secretary Carmarthen's letter to Hartley of May 28. Carmarthen, however, had added the objection to the term "articles" in a postscript (Clements Library).

From Lord Howe[1]   L (draft):[2] National Library of Australia

[June 1, 1784]

Ld Howe desires with the Kings permission[3] to Present the History of the late Capt. Cooks last Voyage Printed under the direction of the admiralty To Dr. Franklin;[4] in acknowledgment of the Doctors Liberal Endeavors for Preventing all Obstructions Which that Celebrated circumnavigator might have been liable to from American Cruizers on his return to Europe.[5]

To David Hartley

ALS: The Scriptorium (1990); copies:[6] William L. Clements Library, National Archives (London); transcript: National Archives

1. One of three drafts, written on a single sheet, of cover letters written by Joseph Banks for Richard Howe, first lord of the Admiralty. Since 1780 Banks had supervised on behalf of the Admiralty the preparation of an extravagantly illustrated three-volume account of the late Capt. James Cook's third and final voyage. The quarto edition, including 78 engravings and charts, was completed by May, 1784, and the Admiralty ordered six sets to be elegantly bound as presentation copies for the King and Queen of England, the Prince of Wales, the King of France, the Empress of Russia, and, at Banks's suggestion, BF. George III instructed Howe to seek Banks's advice on composing the cover letters to the three foreign recipients. Banks drafted the letters on June 1: Banks to BF, Aug. 13, below; Harold B. Carter, *Sir Joseph Banks, 1743–1820* (London, 1988), pp. 167–71.

2. In Banks's hand (see the note above) and filed with his papers. On the verso of the sheet he wrote, "Letters written from the office of Admiralty with the Presents of Captn Cooks voyage."

3. Lord Howe changed this word to "Approbation"; see the July 1 entry in BF's journal, [June 26–July 27], where BF quoted the phrase.

4. James Cook, *A Voyage to the Pacific Ocean . . . for Making Discoveries in the Northern Hemisphere . . . in the years 1776, 1777, 1778, 1779, and 1780* (3 vols., London, 1784).

5. In March, 1779, BF issued a circular letter requesting all captains and commanders of American armed vessels to allow Cook and his crew to pass unmolested and, further, to offer them all possible assistance: XXIX, 86–7.

6. Both copies are in the hand of Hartley's secretary George Hammond and conform in every respect to BF's ALS except for the date, which was changed to June 8. On the first copy listed, which Hartley retained, the 8 was written over a 2; the second one, sent by Hartley to Carmarthen, is a

Sir,   Passy, June 2. 1784—

I have considered the Observations you did me the honour of communicating to me,[7] concerning certain Inaccuracies of Expression and suppos'd Defects of Formality in the Instrument of Ratification, some of which are said to be of such a Nature as to affect "the Validity of the Instrument." The first is, "that the United States are named before his Majesty, contrary to the established Custom observed in every Treaty in which a crowned Head and a Republick are the contracting Parties." With respect to this, it seems to me we should distinguish between that Act in which both join, to wit, the *Treaty*, and that which is the Act of each separately, the *Ratification*. It is necessary that all the Modes of Expression in the joint Act, should be agreed to by both Parties; tho' in their separate Acts each Party is Master of, and alone accountable for, its own Mode. And on inspecting the Treaty it will be found that his Majesty is always regularly named before the United States. Thus the "established Custom *in Treaties* between crowned Heads and Republicks," contended for on your Part, is strictly observed. And the Ratification following the Treaty contains these Words, "Now know ye, that we the United States in Congress assembled, having seen and considered the Definitive Articles aforesaid, have *approved, ratified* and *confirmed*, and by these Presents do *approve, ratify* and *confirm* the said Articles, and EVERY PART AND CLAUSE THEREOF, &c." Hereby all those Articles, Parts and Clauses wherein the King is named before the United States, are *approved, ratified and confirmed*, and this solemnly under the Signature of the President of Congress, with the public Seal affixed by their Order, and countersigned by their Secretary. No Declaration on the Subject, more determinate or more authentic can possibly be made or given; which, when considered,

---

fair copy of the first. (Note that Hartley endorsed the text published here as "June 2/8".) There is no doubt that BF delayed sending this letter, as Hartley reported to Carmarthen on June 4 that he had not yet received it (Clements Library). On June 9 Hartley sent Carmarthen both his own June 1 letter to BF and this response, which he claimed to "have received this day" (Giunta, *Emerging Nation*, I, 975–6).

7. On June 1, above.

may probably induce his Majesty's Ministers to waive the Proposition of our signing a similar Declaration, or of sending back the Ratification to be corrected in this Point, neither appearing to be really necessary. I will however, if it be still desired, transmit to Congress the Observation and the Difficulty occasion'd by it, and request their Orders upon it. In the mean time I may venture to say, that I am confident there was no Intention of affronting his Majesty by this Order of Nomination, but that it resulted merely from that sort of Complaisance which every Nation seems to have for itself, and of that Respect for its own Government customarily so express'd in its own Acts, of which the English among the rest afford an Instance, when in the Title of the King they always name Great Britain before France.

The second Objection is, "that the Term Definitive Articles is used instead of Definitive Treaty." If the Words *Definitive Treaty* had been used in the Ratification instead of *Definitive Articles*, it might have been more correct, tho' the Difference seems not great, nor of much Importance, as in the Treaty itself it is called "the present *Definitive Treaty*."

The other Objections are, "that the Conclusion likewise appears deficient, as it is neither signed by the President, nor is it dated, and consequently is wanting in some of the most essential Points of Form necessary towards authenticating the Validity of the Instrument." The Situation of Seals and Signatures in Public Instruments differs in different Countries, tho' all equally valid; for when all the Parts of an Instrument are connected by a Ribband whose Ends are secured under the Impression of the Seal, the Signature and Seal wherever plac'd, are understood as relating to and authenticating the whole. Our Usage is to place them both together in the broad Margin near the Beginning of the Piece; and so they stand in the present Ratification; the concluding Words of which declare the Intention of such Signing and Sealing to be the giving Authenticity to the whole Instrument; viz. "*In Testimony* whereof, *we have caused* the Seal of the United States to be hereunto affixed, Witness his Excellency Thomas Mifflin, Esqr President;" and the Date, suppos'd to be omitted, (perhaps from its not appearing in

Figures) is nevertheless to be found written in Words at length, viz. "this fourteenth Day of January in the Year of our Lord One thousand seven hundred and eighty four;" which made the Figures unnecessary.[8]

With great Esteem and Respect I have the honour to be, Sir, Your Excellency's most obedient & most humble Servant

B. FRANKLIN

His Excellency David Hartley, Esqr

Endorsements: DF to DH June 2/8 1784 / DF to DH June 2/8 1784

From Thomas Thompson[9]

ALS and copy: American Philosophical Society

Sir   Dover 2 June 1784—

I have the honor to inform your Excellency that Mr. Jay embark'd on board the Ship Edward, Capt. Cooper with his Lady and family the 31 Ulto in the Evening with a fair wind which has continued ever since.[1]

I am also to advice you that a Picture of the Marquis la Fayet intended for Genl. Washington in Mr Jay's care[2] was oblig'd

8. In his letter to Carmarthen of June 9, cited above, Hartley reported on the conversation he had had with BF earlier that day. BF offered further arguments in defense of the language of the American ratification, highlighting its similarity to Congress' ratifications of the preliminary articles and of the Swedish-American treaty. BF showed Hartley those documents and others. Hartley concluded by asking whether he should await further instructions or return to England as Carmarthen's letter of May 25 had instructed.

9. A Dover wine merchant. In XXVIII, 187n, we suggested that Thompson was already supplying BF with newspapers. In fact, that arrangement began only after WTF met with Thompson in Dover in August, 1784.

1. Jay sailed on June 1; see the annotation of BF to John and Sarah Jay, May 13, and Oswald to BF, June 8.

2. Lafayette entrusted to Jay a portrait of himself, his wife, and their children, which was to be a gift to GW. He informed GW of this in a letter of May 14: W. W. Abbot *et al.*, eds., *The Papers of George Washington*, Confederation Series (6 vols., Charlottesville and London, 1992–97), I, 380.

to be left on shore as the Ship was quite full and it could not be taken down the Hatchway the dementions being to large, if the ship had not been fully Laden. And it was thought very improper to take it upon Deck, the only way possible it could have been Carried, Mr Jay was very sorry to be under the necessity of leaving it behind. I promisd him to write you on this Subject and to follow any instructions you may please to give me respecting the further disposal of it. If you will prefer its going up to London it can be sent to the Kings Warehouse and waite an Opportunity of shiping it for what place and to whom you may order it to be consign'd.

But if you will Chuse to have it Returnd to Calais it can be sent back any day, I apprehend Mr Joshua Johnson in London can get it shipt almost every Week for any Port in America, If you are pleas'd to give me any instructions a Letter directed for me at Mr Laurance Isaac's at Calais will be sent me the first Vessel from that port.[3]

I have the Honor to Remain with the most perfect Respect.— Your Excellencys Most Obedient and very Humble Servant

THO THOMPSON

His Excellency Benjm. Franklin Esqr. Ambassador from the United States of America

Addressed: His Excellency B. Franklin Esqr. / Ambassador from the United States / of America / a / Paris

From George Washington

ALS: American Philosophical Society; copies: Library of Congress, Bibliothèque Municipale, Nantes

Washington here announces that his former aide David Humphreys has been elected by Congress to serve as the secretary of the new

3. When WTF arrived in Dover, he arranged for Thompson to turn the portrait over to Johnson for shipment to America: WTF to BF, Aug. 28, 1784 (APS). GW received the painting in April, 1785, and hung it at Mount Vernon: Abbot, *The Papers of George Washington,* Confederation Series, III, 154–5.

commission to negotiate commercial treaties.[4] His election crushed Franklin's hopes for a diplomatic career for his grandson William Temple Franklin. On August 15 Temple wrote his friend William Carmichael that the selection of Humphreys "was rather thought singular by most of our Sensible Men (Mr. Morris & Mr. Jefferson entre autres). We were both, you and myself, mentioned, but it seems Genl. Washington on his Return Home had left his 3 Aids as a legacy to Congress & they had promised to provide for them; & having made Registers of two, they thought they could not do better than make the third a Secy. of Legation."[5] Elbridge Gerry analyzed the choice in a June 16 letter to John Adams. Although "great Pains were taken" to retain Temple Franklin as secretary to the commission, Adams' supporters in Congress were able to convince the majority that the doctor's close relationship with Temple would interfere with the work of the commission. Franklin was not only his relative but also his "best Friend & patron," and had even expressed to Congress his desire that Temple be appointed minister to Sweden. Given that Franklin and Adams "were not on the most friendly terms," Temple would surely have a bias that would disrupt, if not "defeat," the negotiations. Gerry exulted that Franklin would feel Congress' reproach in Adams' appointment as "the Head of the Commission" and in finding that Temple had "not only no Prospect of promotion, but has been actually superseeded."[6]

Dear Sir,   Mount Vernon 2d June 1784
    Congress having been pleased to appoint Colo. Humphrys Secretary to the Commissioners, for forming Commercial Treaties in Europe, I take the liberty of introducing him to you.—[7]

4. The election was conducted on May 12, the same date a congressional committee recommended denying BF leave to retire from public service; see our annotation of BF to John and Sarah Jay, May 13. Humphreys (1752–1818), who was also a poet, joined Washington's staff in June, 1780, and served him through 1783: *ANB*.
    5. APS.
    6. *Adams Papers*, XVI, 236–7.
    7. On June 2, after writing the present letter and other letters of introduction (to TJ, the comte d'Estaing, and the chevalier de Chastellux, among others), GW wrote to congratulate Humphreys, enclosing these documents as well as a certificate of Humphreys' wartime service: W. W. Abbot *et al.*, eds., *The Papers of George Washington*, Confederation Series (6 vols., Charlottesville and London, 1992–97), I, 413, 416–19. TJ received this package on Humphreys' behalf in Boston on June 19 and carried it to France. The

This Gentleman was several years in my family as an Aid de Camp.— His zeal in the cause of his Country, his good sense, prudence, and attachment to me, rendered him dear to me; and I persuade myself you will find no confidence wch. you may think proper to repose in him, misplaced.— He possesses an excellent heart, good natural & acquired abilities, and sterling integrity—to which may be added sobriety, & an obliging disposition.

A full conviction of his possessing all these good qualities, makes me less scrupulous of recommending him to your patronage and friendship.— He will repeat to you the assurances of perfect esteem, regard, & consideration, with which I have the honor to be. Dear Sir, Yr. Most Obedt. & very Hble. Ser:

GO: WASHINGTON

The Honble. Doctr Franklin

From Lafayette   ALS: American Philosophical Society

My dear Sir   Thursday Morning [June 3, 1784][8]
Having determined to Go By the Next packet that Sails from L'orient on the 22d inst,[9] I shall Be Happy to Be Honoured With Your Commands— I don't leave Paris Before the 17th and Will in a few days Wait Upon Your Excellency— Be So kind as to let

two men planned to sail together, but instead Humphreys left New York on the *Courier de l'Europe* on July 17 or 18, almost two weeks after TJ departed from Boston. By Aug. 12, Humphreys was in Lorient, and he had reached Paris by Aug. 18: *Jefferson Papers*, VII, 301, 311–12, 321, 363–4; *Connecticut Courant and Weekly Intelligencer*, July 27, 1784; *New-Haven Gaz.*, Oct. 28, 1784; Abbot, *The Papers of George Washington*, Confederation Series, II, 32–3, 41.

8. Supplied from BF's endorsements, the first of which he wrote directly below the date.

9. Lafayette had written to GW in early March about his intention to visit the United States. He delayed his departure in anticipation of the decree establishing free ports for American shipping, which was not issued until May 14: Idzerda, *Lafayette Papers*, V, 208–9, 216–18; Louis Gottschalk, *Lafayette between the American and the French Revolution (1783–1789)* (Chicago, 1950), pp. 70–2.

me know if You Have Heard Any thing from America— The only News I Had are, 1st that the Cincinnati Affair occasiones Great debates[1] 2d that Congress Have an intention to Adjourn to Six Months and leave a Committee with Very Small Powers—[2] 3dly that the Washington Packet is offered for Sale—[3] Have You Received Any thing that Relates to Your own Motions?

Most Respectfully and Affectionately Yours   LAFAYETTE

Addressed: A Monsieur / Monsieur Franklin / A Passy

Endorsements: June 3. 1784 / Marqs de la Fayette June 3. 84

From Henry Laurens:[4] Two Letters

(I) ALS: American Philosophical Society; (II) Copy: University of South Carolina Library

I.

Dear Sir.   London 4th. June 1784.

Permit me to introduce at Passy, Mr. Parker[5] a young Gentleman of an exceeding good character Son of John Parker Esquire a respectable & valuable Citizen of the State of South Carolina.

1. For the origins of the controversy surrounding the Society of the Cincinnati in America see XLI, 502n, 504.
2. On April 26 Congress voted to adjourn from June 3 to Oct. 30 and to form a committee of states to sit during the recess: *JCC*, XXVI, 287–8, 295–6.
3. Congress announced on April 16 that the public sale of the *General Washington* would take place on June 18: *Morris Papers*, IX, 258, 333n.
4. These are Laurens' last letters to BF before he and his son Henry, Jr., left for Falmouth, where they arrived on June 12 after stopping at Bath. They sailed from Falmouth to New York, arriving on Aug. 3: *Laurens Papers*, XVI, xlv, 457, 460, 481–3.
5. John Parker, Jr. (1759–1832), was evidently completing his law studies, which had been interrupted during the war. He was in Paris by July 29, when he dined with WTF; he also consulted WTF about a servant. Upon returning to South Carolina in 1785, he was admitted to the bar, and from 1786 to 1788 he served as a delegate to Congress: Walter B. Edgar, N. Louise Bailey, *et al.*, eds., *Biographical Directory of the South Carolina House of Representatives* (5 vols. to date, Columbia, 1974–), III, 537–8; [Jean-François-Paul] Grand to WTF, July 29, 1784, APS; John Parker, Jr., to WTF, undated, APS.

Mr. Parker who is studying the Law, means to improve the next vacation by a Visit to Paris & is, as all the World are, desiros of seeing & paying Respects to Doctor Franklin.

I have the honor to be Sir Your Excellency's Obedient humble servant   HENRY LAURENS

His Excellency B. Franklin Esquire Passy.

Notation: Henry Laurens, London 4 June 1784.—

II.

Dear Sir,   London 4th. June 1784

Mr. Appleby the Gentleman who will do me the honor of presenting this, is an old friend of mine from an intimate acquaintance of thirty two Years, I pronounce him an "honest Man",— My friend who is going to France for change of Air wishes to see Doctor Franklin and desires me to give him an Introduction, persuaded Sir that you will excuse the liberty, with pleasure I comply with his request. I have the honor to be With the highest Esteem and Regard, Sir, Your obedt & most hble Servant

Left under cover for Mr. Appleby at Mr. Bridgen's.[6]

His Ey: Benj: Franklin Esqr: Passy

To the Conde de Campomanes

AL (draft): American Philosophical Society

Sir,   Passy, June 5. 1784

I have received much Instruction and Pleasure in reading your excellent Writings;[7] I wish it were in my Power to make

---

6. George Appleby was one of Laurens' former business partners. On June 3 Laurens wrote to him that he would leave the present letter in Bridgen's hands: *Laurens Papers,* XVI, 150n, 457–8.

7. At the beginning of 1784, Campomanes (XXXIV, 353n) gave William Carmichael two works to be forwarded to BF. Carmichael entrusted them to a Mr. Barry: XLI, 471, 568. An earlier shipment of books from Campomanes had been sent in 1781 through the French consul: XXXV, 487, 641; XXXVI, 465.

you a suitable Return of the same kind. I embrace the Opportunity my much esteemed Friend Mr Carmichael affords me, of sending you a late Collection of some of my occasional Pieces,[8] of which, if I should live to get home I hope to publish another Edition much larger more correct & less unworthy of your Acceptance. You are engaged in a great Work, reforming the ancient Habitudes, removing the Prejudices, and promoting the Industry of your Nation.[9] You have in the Spanish People good Stuff to work upon; and by a steady Perseverance you will obtain perhaps a Success beyond your Expectation; for it is incredible the Quantity of Good that may be done in a Country by a single Man who will *make a Business* of it, and not suffer himself to be diverted from that Purpose by different Avocations, Studies or Amusements.—[1] There are two Opinions prevalent in Europe, which have mischievous Effects in diminishing national Felicity; the one, That useful Labour is dishonourable; the other that Families may be perpetuated with Estates. In America we have neither of these Prejudices, which is a great Advantage to us. You will see our Ideas respecting the first in a little Piece I send you called Information to those who would remove to America.[2] The second is mathematically demonstrable to be an Impossibility under the present Rules of Law & Religion. Since tho' the Estate may remain entire, the Family is continually dividing. For a Man's Son is but half of his Family, his Grandson but a fourth, his Great Grandson but an Eighth, the next but a Sixteenth of his Family; and by the same Progression in only

8. *Political, Miscellaneous, and Philosophical Pieces* . . . (London, 1779): XXXI, 210–18.

9. BF may be referring to *Discurso sobre el fomento de la industria popular* (Madrid, 1774) and *Discurso sobre la educación popular de los artesanos y su fomento* (Madrid, 1775). The two discourses, which the Council of Castile distributed to public and ecclesiastical officials throughout Spain, advocated the encouragement of small-scale rural manufactures, the abolition of restrictions imposed by craft guilds, the more widespread distribution of land, and general education: Richard Herr, *The Eighteenth-Century Revolution in Spain* (Princeton, 1959), pp. 50–1, 145, 151; John Lynch, *Bourbon Spain, 1700–1808* (Oxford and Cambridge, Mass., 1989), pp. 214–15, 252.

1. BF had previously articulated this idea in a letter to Thomas Brand Hollis of Oct. 5, 1783: XLI, 75. He repeated it in *Autobiog.*, p. 163.

2. XLI, 597–608.

nine Generations the present Proprietor's Part in the then Possessor of the Estate will be but a 512th, supposing the Fidelity of all the succeeding Wives equally certain with that of those now existing:[3] too small a Portion methinks to be anxious about, so as to oppose a legal Liberty of breaking Entails and dividing Estates, which would contribute so much to the Prosperity of the Country. With great & sincere Esteem and Respect, and best Wishes for the Success of your patriotic Undertakings, I have the honour to be Sir

M. de Campomanes

From Antoinette-Thérèse Melin Dutartre[4]

ALS: American Philosophical Society

ce 6 juin 1784 à L'arbalêtre par Ris à Ris
route de fontainebleau

Je vous envoye, mon papa, une Sollicitation que le principal du college des irlandois me fait,[5] Si vous pouvez y avoir egard, vous m'obligerez infiniment. Jespere que vous ne m'avez pas totalement oublié? Les maladies cruelles nous ont Separés. Je nai été qu'une Seule fois voir nôtre charmante amie, et il ne me fut pas possible d'aller vous embrasser: ne me punissez pas, mon papa, de l'obligation ou j'ai été de me priver du plaisir de vous voir: je Suis à mon arbalêtre, en assez bonne Santé toujours possedée du desir de vous y recevoir: mais vos affaires, vôtre Santé, Sont

3. For a more elaborate version of this calculation see BF to SB, Jan. 26, 1783 (XLI, 507–9), where he also claimed that the practice of entailing entire estates to the eldest heir was responsible for "all the odious mixture of pride, and beggary, and idleness that have half depopulated and decultivated Spain."

4. Mme Brillon's cousin: XXXVI, 47.

5. Charles Kearney, an Irish ecclesiastic, became rector of the Irish College in Paris in 1783: Richard Hayes, *Biographical Dictionary of Irishmen in France* (Dublin, 1949); Patrick Boyle, *The Irish College in Paris from 1578 to 1901* (London, 1901), pp. 56–7. The enclosure may have been the unsigned, undated letter to Mme Dutartre that is now among BF's papers at the APS. The author, having heard that BF is charged with appointing an American consul in Barcelona, asks her to "Employ her Credit" with BF to persuade him to appoint Owen O'Neill to the post. O'Neill is a merchant in Barcelona and well suited to the job.

elles d'accord avec mon désir? Voila le hic! C'est ce que je veux Scavoir de vous: qu'une bonne lettre, angloise, de la main du papa me dedomage de ne le point voir j'attends cette lettre et Suis en attendant avec toutte la tendresse et l'attachement possible his Dutifull Daughter MELIN DUTARTRE

From Forster frères

ALS:[6] American Philosophical Society

Sir— Bordeaux 8th June 1784—

The inclosed letter We receiv'd under cover from our R: F[7] by Ship from Dublin with directions to forward it to your Excellency, & to request an answer through our hands which We shall take care to send by the same conveyance— We shou'd esteem ourselves happy to have it in our power to render your Excellency any service in this place: as We buy annually of the first Wines for the English Markett We can at all times supply you with them and at reasonable prices; those of the first Class from 1800 *l.t.* a 2000 *l.t.* per Tun; seconds from 1400 *l.t.* to 1600 *l.t.* & thirds from 12 to 1300 We mean for Wines from 2 to 3 years old, We have some of the latter Classes of Vintage 78 that We can give at the same prices, & which if botled here woud be fit for use soon after its arrivall in Paris—

The expeditions for America upon the Peace were so considerable, that it will still require some time for that Trade to get into its proper Channell: which for the present prevents our extending & improving the connection We wou'd wish to cultivate with our Freinds Messrs: Bache & Shee; when things change We shall be happy in giving them every proof of our attachment & confidence.

We are with the greatest respect Sir Your Excellency's Obedient & Very Hble Servts FORSTERS BROTHERS

6. Most likely in the hand of John Forster, one of the principals of the Bordeaux mercantile firm: L. M. Cullen, "The Irish Merchant Communities of Bordeaux, La Rochelle and Cognac in the Eighteenth Century," in *Négoce et industrie en France et en Irelande aux XVIIIe et XIXe siècles . . .*, ed. L. M. Cullen and P. Butel (Paris, 1980), p. 58.

7. Robert Forster. The enclosed letter was from Matthew Young, dated May 23; it is summarized above, with those of other applicants for emigration, under the date of March 12.

The writer upon receiving the letter without address, & not having read the one that inclosed it, was going to open it; but recollected in time to prevent the mistake & hopes you'll pardon his inadvertence—

From Elizabeth Grattan[8]   ALS: American Philosophical Society

Monsieur   Camden Street 37.— Dublin 8th. June 1784.
L'opinion que le Monde entretien si justement des vos talens comme Consellier d'Etat, & de votre Sapience comme un Ecolier, et si generalement connu qu'il ne'st point necessaire que je le repete.

Les gens de ce païs vous regarde avec un admiration et un estime que rein ne peut egaler, mais personne plus que Sir Edward Newenham, le vrai Patriote et Soutein de la Liberte; ce'st à son desir que je me fais l'honneur de vous envoyer l'exemple d'un Œuvrë qui à reçu l'approbation des premiers personnes du Literati ici.[9]

J'ai pris la libertè de prier votre protection comme le plus grand honneur qui puisse courronner mes travaux.[1]

8. Elizabeth Warren Grattan, wife of Dublin solicitor Colley Grattan, ran a small academy to teach young ladies French and Italian: Doris O'Keefe, "A Dublin edition of the 'Emblemata Horatiana,'" *Long Room,* XXXVI (1991), 35–7.

9. Grattan enclosed a four-page printed prospectus entitled *Proposals for Publishing by Subscription . . . a Translation from the Italian of the Morals of Horace . . . by Mrs. Eliʒabeth Grattan* (Dublin, 1784). It stated that the translation would be made from a book that Sir Edward Newenham had brought back from Florence. The volume would include 60 passages, each illustrated by an emblematic engraving executed by an Irish artist. Subscriptions were two guineas, half to be paid immediately and the rest upon completion of the project. Names of the first subscribers included Newenham and Henry Grattan (XLI, 152n), who was a relation by marriage. At the bottom of the pages, Mrs. Grattan handwrote the names of 23 additional subscribers of notable rank.

1. It seems that the subscription was never filled and the project never completed beyond the first section, which was issued in 1785. Several copies of that first number are held in libraries in Ireland. More than 80 subscribers are listed on the final sheet, but BF's name is not among them: O'Keefe, "A Dublin edition," pp. 35–40.

J'ai l'honneur d'etre Monsieur avec le plus grand respect le tres humble, et tres obeissante Servante de votre Excellence

ELIZABETH GRATTAN

Addressed: A son Excellence Monsieur Monsieur / Franklin, Plenepotentiaire aux / Etats unï d'Amerique à la Cour / de France / a Paris

From Richard Oswald

ALS: American Philosophical Society

Dear Sir London 8th June 1784—

The inclosed Letter was sent to me yesterday by Lord Howe to be forwarded to you.[2] And their Lordships of that Board having ordered a Copy of Capt Cooks Books of his last Voyage to be transmitted to you, they will be Sent in a Box by the Paris Diligence directed to the care of Monsr Pissot. Libraire, Quai des Augustines, to be delivered without expence.

Mr Jay left Dover, with a fair Wind, on the 1st Instt. I went down to that place along with Mr Laurens and Mr Vaughan, to bid him and Mrs Jay farewell. Mr Laurens left this place on Sunday last[3] to go in the Falmouth packet for New York—together with his Son. His Female Friends[4] he leaves at Bath—

I am glad of this, as I shall alwise be of every opportunity of testifying my respect and best wishes for your health and happiness, being with Sincere esteem and affection Dear Sir Your most obedient humble Servant[5] RICHARD OSWALD

I beg my kind Complimts to your young Friend.

2. The letter is missing, but the draft is above, [June 1]. Its subject is the edition of Cook's voyage, mentioned in the next sentence.
3. BF interlined here, in red ink, "the 6th".
4. His widowed sister-in-law Mary, his daughters Martha and Mary Eleanor, and granddaughter Frances Eleanor: *Laurens Papers,* XVI, 464.
5. On the verso of the sheet is a sketch of a young girl's head in profile, perhaps made by BFB.

To the Comtesse d'Houdetot
LS:[6] Vicomte Foy, Paris (1957)

Passy le 9 Juin 1784

J'ai reçu, ma chere Amie, votre Lettre infiniment obligeante,[7] et depuis ce temps Je n'ai fait que songer au charmant Projet d'aller à Sanois, passer quelques Jours avec vous. Je souhaiterois de tout mon cœur être en état de l'exécuter; mais plus J'y pense, et plus il me paroit impraticable: car Je me sens moins en état de marcher que la derniere fois que J'eus le plaisir de vous voir, puisqu'en n'allant pas plus loin que chez Made. Brillon, cela m'a fait tant de mal que J'en ai souffert pendant plusieurs Jours; ce qui m'oblige à renoncer au Bonheur qui m'attendoit dans votre agréable Societé et charmante Retraite de Sanois, et à me consoler par l'Espérance de vous voir quelques fois quand vous serez de retour à Paris. Mes petits Fils sont très sensibles à la Bonté que vous avez eue de vous ressouvenir d'eux, et de les inviter à m'accompagner. Ils se Joignent à moi pour vous en faire leurs sinceres Remercîmens. Je souhaite que la Santé et le Plaisir vous accompagnent dans votre voyage et que vous trouviez partout le même Bonheur que vous ferez éprouver à vos Amis.

B. FRANKLIN

Made. la Comtesse d'Houdetot.

From Anne-Rosalie Filleul
AL: American Philosophical Society

Ce mercredy [June 9, 1784?][8]

Mde Filleul a l'honneur d'envoyë a Monsieur francklin, Ces trois derniers Volumes des mémoires du baron de tott.[9] Elle prie de vouloir bien luy envoyë le journal d'aujourdhui 9.

6. In L'Air de Lamotte's hand.
7. Of May 31, above.
8. The earliest possible date. Mme Filleul enclosed volumes that were first published in 1784; the only Wednesday the 9th that year was in June.
9. François, baron de Tott, *Mémoires du baron de Tott sur les Turcs et les Tartares* (4 vols., Amsterdam, 1784). The baron (for whom see XXXII, 65–6) recounted his experiences as Vergennes' secretary in Constantinople and as French consul in the Crimea as well as his efforts to reform the Ottoman

Addressed: A Monsieur / Monsieur Le docteur Francklin / en son hotel / a Passy

From Lord Rosehill[1]   ALS: American Philosophical Society

Sir—   Rouen 9th. June 1784
I reced. Your Obligeing Information Concerning Your Son,[2] I am again to bege the favour of You to be so Good as to Informe me by the Return of the Post if there are *Any Gentlemen of Note*, belonging to the State of Virginia, at this time in Paris, & if there is, then Names, and Addresse.— Haveing a Very Conciderable Interest in *New Jersey*,[3] I will do my self the Pleasure of Waiting on You, the first time I come to Paris,

---

military. His denunciation of Oriental despotism (and, by implication, of fanaticism and arbitrary government closer to home) made the work both controversial and hugely successful throughout Europe. It went through five editions in two years, three published in Amsterdam in 1784–85, and two in Paris and Maestricht in 1785. See the introduction to *Mémoires du baron de Tott, sur les Turcs et les Tartares, Maestricht, 1785,* ed. Ferenc Tóth (Paris, 2004), pp. 23–45.

1. David Carnegie (1749–1788) was the heir to the earldom of Northesk but predeceased his father, the sixth earl. After resigning his commission in the British army, in 1768 he went to Philadelphia, where he entered into a bigamous marriage with Margaret Cheer, the well-known female lead of the American Theatre Company. The couple was arrested for debt, parted ways, and by early 1776 Lord Rosehill was on his way back to England. Nothing is known of him in the subsequent years except that he died in Rouen without issue: James B. Paul, ed., *The Scots Peerage* . . . (9 vols., Edinburgh, 1904–14), VI, 503; Susan Rather, "Miss Cheer as Lady Rosehill: a Real-Life Drama in Late-Colonial British America," *Theatre Notebook,* LXIV (2010), 82–95; *Pa. Gaz.,* Feb. 11, 1768; Peter Force, ed., *American Archives* . . . , Fourth Series (6 vols., [Washington, D.C., 1837–46]), V, 1375. How much BF knew of the scandal is not known, but his wife had reported the news of Rosehill's marriage and arrest in a letter to SB of Aug. 23, [1768] (Yale University Library).

2. Neither Lord Rosehill's initial letter to BF nor the reply has been located.

3. Where, in 1773, Lord Rosehill had been one of the incorporators of St. Peter's Episcopal Church of Spotswood. As royal governor of the colony, WF had signed the church's charter: W. W. Clayton, *History of Union and Middlesex Counties, New Jersey* . . . (Philadelphia, 1882), pp. 760, 778.

which I imagine will be about the, *First of Jully*— In the Mean time beleave me to be Your Most Obed Hble Sert   ROSEHILL

Notation: Hill 9 June 1784

From Edward Bridgen   ALS: American Philosophical Society

London June 10 1784
At the request of Mr Champion I forward the Accompanying Book to your Excellency.[4]
Our Mutual & Worthy friend Mr Laurens leaves Bath this day for Falmouth to go with his Son for New York. May Heaven protect them and spare your Excellency's long and useful life is the prayer of Dr Sir Yr: Excellency's obliged & Faithful
EDWD: BRIDGEN

Not a line from Congress abt: the Copper Coin.[5]

Notation: Edward Bridgen. June 10. 1784.—

From William Livingston[6]   LS: American Philosophical Society

Sir   Elizabeth Town 10th June 1784
I take the liberty of recommending to you Colonel Clarkson who is appointed by the Directors of the University of New York to solicit donations in some parts of Europe, for that Institution.[7] In this capacity I do not recommend him to your notice;

4. This was *Considerations on the Present Situation of Great Britain and the United States of America*, the second, expanded edition of Richard Champion's report on Anglo-American commercial regulations (XL, 515). BF's copy, now at the Huntington Library, was inscribed, "To His Excellency Benjamin Franklin &c &c &c. From the Author".
5. For Bridgen & Waller's proposals to supply the United States with copper coinage see XL, 629–30.
6. Livingston, governor of New Jersey, wrote letters the same day to TJ and JA that were nearly identical to the present one: *Jefferson Papers*, VII, 304; *Adams Papers*, XVI, 302n.
7. Lieut. Col. Matthew Clarkson (*ANB*), who fought at the battles of Saratoga and Yorktown, was named to the first board of regents of the

because my feelings as an American are really hurt by our turning mendicants in Europe, where I think our national glory must be greatly obscured by our appearing in so disadvantageous an attitude. But as a young Gentleman of a very amiable character; and as a late brave and excellent officer in the american army, he is worthy of esteem; and your civilities may be of signal service to him as a traveller.

I have the honor to be with great respect your most obedient and very humble servant. WIL. LIVINGSTON

[*In Livingston's hand:*] His Excellency Dr Benjamin Franklin Esqr

Map of the United States of America, Following the Peace Treaty of 1783, Dedicated and Presented to Benjamin Franklin: Announcement

Printed in *Affiches, annonces, et avis divers, ou Journal général de France,* June 10, 1784.

Carte des Etats-Unis de l'Amerique Suivant le Traité de Paix de 1783, issued by Jean Lattré in 1784, was neither the first French map of the United States published after the signing of the peace, nor an entirely accurate depiction of the boundaries of the new nation, as its title implies.[8] It was, however, the only map of the United States

---

University of the State of New York—an educational system created by the N.Y. legislature on May 1, 1784. As yet, this system of public schools and colleges included only Columbia College, the formerly private, Anglican King's College. At a meeting on May 26, the regents decided to send Clarkson to France and Holland to raise money and purchase scientific equipment: Sidney Sherwood, *The University of the State of New York: History of Higher Education in the State of New York* (Washington, D.C., 1900), pp. 52–4; *A History of Columbia University, 1754–1904* . . . (New York, 1904), pp. 59–63. Their official letter of introduction for Clarkson is below, June 12.

8. For a study of this map see Mary S. Pedley, "A Map for Benjamin Franklin," in *Die Leidenschaft des Sammelns: Streifzüge durch die Sammlung Woldan,* ed. Gerhard Holzer et al. (2 vols., Vienna, 2010), II, 425–43. See also Lester J. Cappon, *The First French Map of the United States of America* (Chicago and New York, [1973]), pp. [2–6].

Cartouche from the *Carte des Etats-Unis de l'Amerique*

of America dedicated to Benjamin Franklin. Above the dedication and title, in the cartouche, Franklin's personal coat of arms (which is being hung from the topsail yard by a sailor) appears along with the Great Seal of the United States and the emblem of the Society of the Cincinnati—an organization to which Franklin was firmly, though as yet quietly, opposed.[9] A question that cannot as yet be fully answered is when and under what circumstances Franklin granted permission for this dedication.

The one clue that has come to light suggests that the map for which Franklin originally granted permission evolved over the course of time into a conceptually different work. Lattré, a prominent Parisian engraver, publisher, and retailer of maps and atlases,[1] initially announced it in an undated sales catalog as "Nouvelle Carte des Etats Unis de l'Amérique, avec les Marches & Camps de l'Armée; dédiée à M. *Franklin*," to be published at the end of December, 1783.[2] Because Lattré's name appears nowhere in Franklin's papers, and no mention of this cartographic project has been found in the correspondence of Franklin or his colleagues, we have not been able to determine when the dedication was solicited. It could have been as early as the winter of 1782–83, when the preliminary articles were signed, the cessation of hostilities was declared, and the French troops were returning home.

As the advertisement published below indicates, Lattré at some time augmented the map with two engraved panels of text that summarized, by location and date, the principal military events of the War of Independence, beginning with the shots fired at Lexington and Concord and ending with the surrender of Cornwallis at Yorktown. Almost all the sites mentioned in the panels are shown on the map.[3]

9. See Morellet to BF, and BF's reply, both dated March 16, above; and the entry of July 13 in BF's journal, [June 26–July 27, 1784], below. The cartouche is illustrated facing page 318.

1. Lattré's career is outlined in Pedley, "A Map for Benjamin Franklin," pp. 428–30.

2. The announcement appears in *Catalogue du fonds du Sieur Lattré . . .* (Paris, n.d.), bound with Lattré's *Atlas Moderne* (Paris, [1771–83]) at the Library of Congress.

3. The panels were entitled "Principaux Evenemens Militaires entre les Americains et les Anglois." That title notwithstanding, contributions of French troops were also emphasized, with particular attention paid to Lafayette; *e.g.*, the first of his heroic feats appears under Virginia, Oct. 25, 1777, as "la Fayette bat un dètachement Anglois supérieur au sien." (See Pedley, "A Map for Benjamin Franklin," p. 436.) Now rare, a set of these side panels is attached to a copy of the map held by the APS.

Following the signing of the definitive peace treaty on September 3, 1783, as depictions of the newly defined United States became increasingly desirable, Lattré evidently decided to further shift the map's focus. He would delineate the nation's new boundaries and market the map under a title emphasizing its post-treaty relevance. In the end, the "Marches & Camps de l'Armée" promised in the prepublication announcement were represented only by a barely perceptible line tracing the route of the French army's march to and from Yorktown, with encampments indicated by tiny dotted rectangles.[4]

Lattré's map derives from John Mitchell's *Map of the British and French Dominions in North America,* which was selected for use during the peace negotiations by the British and American commissioners as the most accurate of the available maps of eastern North America. First issued in 1755, it appeared in two more English editions over the next twenty years, each bearing the original 1755 copyright date. It was the last of these, dating from *circa* 1774–75, that was used by the peace commissioners and seems to have been Lattré's source.[5]

One of the Mitchell map's many shortcomings was its failure to show the St. Mary's River, separating Georgia from East Florida, which would form part of the southeastern boundary of the United States.[6] (On the Mitchell map used in the peace negotiations, on which John Jay drew the preliminary boundaries in red ink, the St. Mary's River was added and labeled by hand.[7]) Though Lattré did not have the St. Mary's River on his map, he approximated its location when he

4. To the best of our knowledge, this is the earliest printed rendition of Rochambeau's Yorktown marches and encampments. It appears to be based on the MS plan of the route attributed to Louis-Alexandre Berthier, an assistant quartermaster-general in Rochambeau's army; for that map and its contemporary copies see Howard C. Rice, Jr., and Anne S. K. Brown, eds. and trans., *The American Campaigns of Rochambeau's Army, 1780, 1781, 1782, 1783* (2 vols., Princeton and Providence, 1972), II, 196–7, map 162. Lattré might have gained access to the map as early as February, 1783, when Rochambeau returned to Paris: XXXIX, 200n. Not all the encampments shown by Berthier are represented on Lattré's map, whose scale is much smaller.

5. XXXVIII, 266–7, 452.

6. Article 2 of the definitive peace treaty specified the boundary as extending at latitude 31 degrees due east from the Mississippi River to the Apalachicola (Catahouche) River; thence north to the junction of the Flint River; thence east in a straight line to the head of the St. Mary's River; thence, following the St. Mary's to the Atlantic Ocean: XL, 571.

7. A detail of that map, showing the northern boundary, is illustrated in XXXVIII, facing p. 382; the item is described on p. xxx.

320

drew the southern boundary. He erred, however, in delineating the western portion of that boundary, by failing to capture its jog north along the Apalachicola River to its juncture with the Flint, two rivers that did appear on his map.

If Lattré's engraving was finalized in the months following the signing of the peace treaty, then why was its publication delayed? Franklin may not have allowed a map of the boundaries established by the peace treaty to be published with his name on it until after that treaty was ratified. In the meantime, as he awaited news of the congressional ratification, the French branch of the Society of the Cincinnati was established in Paris and sanctioned by the king, giving Lattré an opportunity to engrave its emblem in his cartouche as a further allusion to his unstated theme: Franco-American military cooperation. The exchange of ratifications finally took place in Paris on May 12. To the best of our knowledge, Lattré's map was first advertised for sale on June 10, in the notice published here.[8]

[June 10, 1784]

Carte des Etats-Unis de l'Amérique, suivant le traité de paix de 1783; dédiée & présentée à Son Excellence, M. *Benjamin Franklin,* Ministre Plénipotentiare des Etats-Unis de l'Amérique près la Cour de France, ancien Président de la Convention de Philadelphie,[9] & de la Société philosophique de cette ville, &c. &c. par le sieur *Lattré,* Graveur ordinaire du Roi. On a joint à cette Carte un précis des évenémens militaires entre les Américains & les Anglois;[1] le tout sur une feuille & demie de papier grand-aigle. Prix 3 liv. lavée, & 2 liv. 10 *s.* non lavée. A Paris, chez l'Auteur, rue S. Jacques, la porte-cochère vis-à-vis la rue de la Parcheminerie, no. 20.

8. Similar advertisements appeared thereafter in other publications, including the *Gaʒ. de France* of June 15 and the *Jour. de Paris* of July 9.

9. Lattré's confusion about Pa. politics required him to issue a second state of his map, which is the one here announced. The first state had misidentified BF as "Ancien Président de la Pensilvanie": Ellen M. Clark, "Acquisitions," *Annual Report of The Society of the Cincinnati for the Year Ending June 30, 2012,* p. 34. Although the present notice cites a revised dedication, it is still inaccurate. The final, corrected version appeared in the map's second state (see the List of Illustrations) and was advertised in the July 9 *Jour. de Paris* announcement.

1. The *précis* consisted of the attachable side panels described in the headnote, engraved with a state-by-state chronology of key military events.

From Francis Childs

ALS: American Philosophical Society

Honored Sir, New York, June 12th. 1784—
Pardon the Assurance I possess, in supposing, that while I take the Liberty of troubling you with a few Lines, your generosity will admit it.— I have wrote you not long since, but, Doubtful whether they have come safe to hand,[2] I feel constrained here to make a repetition;—to express in terms the most grateful, the Singular & consequential services you have rendered, & the many Obligations I am under for them; to attempt to render praise would be to offend; but, it is my duty to thank you; and my ambition is to convince you that I wish to merit it.— While some are afflicted with the harsh & unpleasing Stings of Poverty, the Just & Allwise being places others in the Circles of affluence & ease to answer his Charitable Designs in administering comfort to the Distressed—
I feel rather unhappy, that, conscious of the want of Ability, my Spirits are damped & the ardor with which Gratitude inspires me, is extinguished, in the thought of the appearance my Lines may make in the sight of one of your unrivalled abilities,—But I veil these reflexions with the hope of your generous mind burying in oblivion every thing either insignificant or offensive—
With true Respect, I have the Honor to be, Worthy Sir, Your Most Obliged & Obedient Servant, FRANCIS CHILD—

Benj. Franklin, *Esqr.*

From Johann von Gott Nekrep

ALS: American Philosophical Society

Excellency! Vienna the 12 June 1784
Allow me to send you my most gratefull Thanks, for all the favours and politeness you show'd me at Passy. But how shall I find language to express the emotions of my Heart? When

---

2. The most recent extant letter from Childs dates from the previous October: XLI, 126–8.

ever I call to Mind the agreeable hours, I have had the Honour
to pass with you, my Heart leaps with inexpressible pleasure.
Oh! may heaven restore you Sir, to perfect Health, that you may
soon fullfil your promiss, to see your good friends, and all that
honour and esteem you.
Vienna is more than ever desirous to see so sage and so able
Statesman, and so a philosopher, to know and honour him, according to the faint picture I made of him.
How greatly your Nephews will be rejoiced? whom you intend to bring to Vienna, and to visit Italie,[3] when they see the
Honours that are paid to their meritorious Uncle. You have desired me Sir, to send you News, worthy of exciting your Curiosity. I have no other fit for you, than that after a long Journey,
having pass'd through Lisll, Ostendes, Brüssels, Kölln &c. I arrived safe at Vienna, May the 17tn., where I found a Ballon fifty
six feet high, and allmost as wide. When they extended the air
in it, according to Montgolfiers Method, it swelled beautifully,
but as the weight attach'd to it, was too heavy, he did not mount.
I was not present, when it was filled, but I fore told what hap-
pend. Now it is enlarged consequently it will mount. More over
I must tell you, they have not that Enthousiasm here for Ballons,
which reigns at Paris, nor will they contribute Meney for making them.

Pardon my troubling you for the first time with so lang a
lettre which I shall not be guilting of again. Permit me only to
repeat the assurance of the boundless Esteem, with which I have
the Honour to be, with the greatest respects Your Excellencyes
Most obeidient humble Servant   J. NEKREP

I take the Liberty to desire you the Description of Camins[4]
which you had the Kindness to promise me; my Compliments
to your Dear Nephews.

---

3. Ingenhousz believed that BF would be traveling to Italy with WTF, and
that they would visit him in Vienna on the way back to Paris: XXXIX, 218n.
Nekrep is clearly referring to WTF and BFB.
    4. Possibly BF's design for a smoke-consuming coal stove, whose French
name, "poêle-cheminée," translates as "Kamin" (chimney, fireplace) in
German. Cadet de Vaux had a prototype of the stove built shortly before
Nekrep's visit to Paris: XLI, 256–8, 534–5.

From the Regents of the University of the State of New York

LS: American Philosophical Society

Sir,   New York June 12th. 1784.

Lieutenant Colonel Clarkson will have the honor of delivering your Excellency this Letter. His business in Europe is to solicit donations for the University of the State of New York.[5] We have instructed him to consult with your Excellency on the most proper mode of effecting the Objects of his Mission And we flatter ourselves that notwithstanding the important Concerns which must constantly claim Your Excellency's Attention, you will chearfully lend your Aid and Advice to promote the Cause of Science, of which you are so distinguished an Ornament.— We have the Honor to be with the highest sentiments of Esteem and Respect, Your Excellency's Most Obedient and very humble servants

[*In Clinton's hand:*] By Order & in Behalf of the University

GEO: CLINTON
JAS: DUANE[6]

His Excellency Benjamin Franklin Esqr.—

To Charles Thomson

LS:[7] Library of Congress

Dear Sir,   Passy, June 14. 1784.

I received yours of April 19 with the Information you obtained from our old Neighbour Reuben Haines respecting Marggrander, for which I thank you. I am much pester'd with Applications to make such Enquiries, and often obliged to promise that I

---

5. See William Livingston to BF, June 10, above.

6. George Clinton (*ANB*) was governor of New York and James Duane (*DAB*) the mayor of New York City and a state senator. Clinton and Duane were the driving forces behind the 1784 reconstitution of Kings College as Columbia College, and the two men sat, *ex officio*, on the first board of regents of the University of the State of New York. Clinton also served as the first chancellor of the University: Robert A. McCaughey, *Stand, Columbia: a History of Columbia University in the City of New York, 1754–2004* (New York, 2003), pp. 51–3; State of New York, *The University Manual* (rev. ed., Albany, 1882), p. 190.

7. In BFB's hand.

will transmit them: but I would not wish you to take more Trouble than to ask Questions of the Members of Congress or others that fall in your way, and communicate to me their Answers, if of any Importance. I have also a Multitude of Projects sent to me with Requests that I would lay them before Congress; they are Plans and Schemes of Government & Legislation, Education, Defence, Manufactures, Commerce &ca. form'd by People who have great Goodwill to us, but are totally ignorant of our Affairs and Circumstances, whence their Projects are for the most part wild and impracticable; or unfit to be presented to Congress as not pertaining to their Jurisdiction. I have therefore not forwarded them; but will now and then send some of them for your Amusement if you should ever have any leisure; that you may see how People make Shoes for Feet they have never measured.

As your Letter mentions nothing of Publick Affairs I imagined I might have had by the same Conveyance some Dispatches from Congress, perhaps in the Care of some Passenger: but a Fortnight has past since the Arrival of the Packet Boat, and no Letters appear; so that I have nothing from Congress later than the 14th. of January,[8] and continue in great Uncertainty as to my Return.

Mr. Norris came here after residing some time at Liege. He staid but a Week or two at Paris, and then removed to a Country Town not far distant, where nothing but French is spoken, in order to improve himself in that Language. He seems a sensible discreet young Man, and I shall with Pleasure render him any Service that may be in my Power.[9]

The King of Sweden is now at this Court, enjoying the various splendid Entertainments provided for him.[1] The Danish Minister is astonished that the Congress are so long without taking any Notice of the proposed Treaty. With great Esteem, I am ever, My Dear Friend Yours most affectionately

B FRANKLIN

8. Thomas Mifflin's letters announcing the ratification of the peace treaty: XLI, 456–7, 464–6.

9. Norris carried a letter of recommendation from Thomson: XLI, 45–6.

1. Gustavus III was visiting Paris under the name "the comte de Haga." He arrived at Versailles on June 7 and went to Paris two days later: Gunnar von Proschwitz, ed., *Gustave III par ses lettres* (Stockholm and Paris, 1986), p. 263n.

Cha. Thomson Esqr. Secretary of Congress.

Endorsed: Letter 13 May & do 14 June 1784 Doct Franklin Recd.
8 Aug. 1784

From Dufriche de Valazé

ALS: American Philosophical Society

à Essay par le Mesle sur sarthe En normandie,
Monsieur   le 15 juin, 1784./.
Le Porteur de cette lettre Est M. Dufriche desgenettes mon
neveu qui part pour londres, où il va voir Comme on traite
la Médecine qu'il Étudie depuis quatre ans à Paris. C'Est un
jeune homme sage Et de Bonne Éspérance, à qui je m'interesse
Comme à mon fils. Permettez moi, Monsieur, de vous demander
pour lui quelques Recommandations pour votre ancienne Patrie: Rien n'Est aussi nécessaire à un jeune homme qui veut tirer
quelque fruit de ses voyages.[2]
    Je suis avec le plus Profond Respect, Monsieur, Votre très
humble Et très obèissant serviteur[3]   DUFRICHE DE VALAZÉ

2. BF wrote a now-missing letter introducing the nephew, René-Nicolas
Dufriche Desgenettes (*DBF*), to John Coakley Lettsom. As Dufriche Desgenettes recounted in his memoirs, Lettsom invited him to dine and recommended that BF take bearberry for the pain of the stone. Upon his return
to Paris in January, 1785, the young physician conveyed this advice as well
as a now-missing letter from the Royal Society. BF evidently replied that
he had used bearberry during his baths, but ascribed the relief to the bath,
not the plant. Bailly, Le Roy, and Le Veillard were at Passy during this
visit, and BF discussed with them the option of a cystotomy, relating that
d'Alembert and Buffon, who were about his age, considered themselves too
old for such an operation. Dufriche Desgenettes remembered visiting BF
occasionally throughout the spring, and being among the cortege that escorted the departing BF through the Bois de Boulogne to the St.-Germain
road: *Souvenirs de la fin du XVIIIe siècle* . . . (2 vols., Paris, 1835–36), I,
95–7, 182, 184–5, 197. In 1821 he wrote the entry on BF for the *Diction-
aire des sciences médicales. Biographie médicale.* (7 vols., Paris, 1820–25), IV,
254–60.
    3. On Dec. 29, 1784, Dufriche de Valazé sent New Year's greetings,
wishing BF a long life and the United States a prosperous future: APS.

From —————— Le Carpentier, with Franklin's Note for a Reply

ALS: Library of Congress

Monsieur   ce 15 juin 1784

Jai lhonneur de vous envoyer mon Specifique contre la gravelle.[4] Jose vous le repeter, d'apres les guerisons quil a operé, vous ne courés aucun risque d'en faire usage. Vous voudrés bien, Monsieur, pendant le tems que vous le prendrés, ne point manger de Salade Surtout le Soir Si vous Soupes, vous interdire le Laitage, non pas deux cuillerées de Lait dans votre Thé, mais fromage a la crême et meme crêmes faites avec le Lait, Si vous pouviés interdire les Epices a votre cuisinier les choses n'en vaudroient que mieux. Mais Surtout, monsieur, point de choses echauffantes, du reste vivés comme il vous plaira, mon Specifique n'exige aucun regime gênant. Faites Surtout le plus d'usage que vous pouvés d'oignons; et Soyés persuadé que cest avec connoissance de cause que jai lhonneur de vous parler; comme vous m'aves fait lhonneur de me dire que vous ne buviés point de vin, il n'y auroit rien d'extraordinaire, quand vous vous trouveriés un peu *Etonné* apres avoir pris la dose que je vous indiquerai, cela est arrivé a toutes les personnes qui en ont fait usage. Si vous vous determinés a le prendre, ce que je Souhaite extremement, je vous prie de vouloir bien me le faire Savoir, jaurai lhonneur de me transporter ches vous et de Suivre le traitement qui nest pas difficile et qui m'est parfaitement connu par experience

Je Suis avec Respect Monsieur Votre tres humble et tres obeissant Serviteur   LE CARPENTIER

quay de Bourbon isle St Louis no 17

---

4. This inventor of a cure for bladder stones was in some demand. His letter implies that he had had previous contact with BF, though we have found no trace of it. Among BF's papers, however, is a Feb. 13 letter from Le Carpentier to the abbé Laffon, responding to the abbé's request for the remedy. Le Carpentier cautions that it has not been proven to cure "la pierre," only "la gravelle." He is the sole proprietor of the remedy in Paris, and for 14 years he has used it with great success in patients of both sexes and all ages. In order to prescribe a dose, he needs to see the patient and get to know his temperament, lifestyle, and strength. He expects no compensation for his care; helping his fellow man is reward enough. Library of Congress.

Rx deux Livres doignons Blancs depouillés de leur Pellicule, coupés les en tranches minces; prenés une livre de Sucre Rapé, faites alternativement un lit doignons et un lit de Sucre tant que vous aurés de lun et de lautre dans la Bassine d'un alembic, jettés dessus une Pinte de vinaigre blanc, procedés a la distillation, et reservés la liqueur dans un Vaisseau bien fermé

La dose est pour un adulte dune cuillerée dans un petit Verre de vin Blanc. Deux heures apres on peut dejeuner comme a l'ordinaire, il est mieux de le prendre dans le lit.

Mr Moret apothicaire rue St martin vis avis la Rue jean-Robert fait fort bien ce Sirop et l'a fait pour les personnes a qui je l'ai conseillé a Paris

Endorsed: Express my thankful Acknowledgements to M. Carpentier for his Goodness in sending me his Receipt. I have not yet determined to take any Remedies. When I am, I will acquaint him.

From Vicq d'Azyr

LS: American Philosophical Society

Monsieur!   15 Juin 1784

J'ai l'honneur de vous envoyer le Rapport de Mrs. Andry & Thouret Sur les Aimans de M. L'abbé Le Noble, conformément à la Demande que vous avez bienvoulu m'en faire le 24 du mois dernier.—⁵ La Société R. de Médecine, à laquelle j'ai présenté ce Billet que Vous m'avez adressé à ce Sujet, a été on-ne-peut-pas-plus flattée du Désir que Vous témoignez avoir de recevoir la Collection de Ses Volumes. Je m'empresse donc de vous prévenir qu'Elle Se fera un Devoir de vous faire parvenir ceux qui Sont déjà imprimés, & qu'elle Sera enchantée si vous voulez bien les accueuillir.⁶

5. In fact, the report was not enclosed; see his next letter, dated [after] June [15].

6. Here Vicq d'Azyr inserted a footnote marker and added at the bottom of the page: "Je vous prie de mapprendre quelle est la date du dernier Volume de nos memoires qui est entre vos mains; je vous adresserai la Suite."

J'ai l'honneur d'être avec beaucoup de respect, Monsieur,
Votre très humble & très obéïssant Serviteur   VICQ D'AZYR

M. franklin, à Passy.

Notation: Vicq-d'azir 15 Juin 1784—

From John Witherspoon   ALS: American Philosophical Society

Sir   London June 15. 1784
The Bearer Mr William Brown has been a Teacher here & is
strongly recommended to me as an excellent Classic Scholar he
goes to Paris to finish his Knowledge & Pronounciation of the
french Language & is desirous of being introduced to you & if
you Should know of any Opportunity of directing him where
he might teach either the english or learned Languages so as to
enable him to continue the longer for his own Improvement it
would be a great favour.
I am wholly uncertain whether you can or would chuse to
do any Thing of this Kind but he is so ambitious of being introduced to You & it has been requested of me so earnestly by
a Gentleman here to whom I am much obliged that I could not
refuse him this Line.
I am Sir your most obedt humble Servant
                                JNO WITHERSPOON
Dr Franklin

Addressed: His Excellency / Benjamin Franklin Esqr / Paris /
Mr W. Brown

Notation: [*crossed out:* Jona. Williams][7] June 15 1784—

7. Corrected to "John Witherspoon" in an unknown hand.

From Vicq d'Azyr

LS: American Philosophical Society

Monsieur! [after] Juin [15] 1784.

Je m'empresse de réparer l'oubli que l'on a commis involontairement, & Je joins ici quelques Exemplaires du Rapport que Je vous avais annoncé par ma précédente Lettre.[8] J'aurai l'honneur de Vous faire parvenir sous peu de temps le troisième Volume du Recueil de la Société Royale de Médecine: c'est le Seul qui aît paru depuis ceux qui Vous ont été remis.

Permettez que Je vous fasse ici les remercimens de la Société au Sujet du Mémoire de M. Perkins, que Vous avez bien voulu m'adresser.[9]

J'ai l'honneur d'être avec respect Monsieur Votre très-humble & très obéissant serviteur VICQ DAZYR

Je joins ici le Volume, qui vient de m'être remis: La Compagnie vous prie de l'agreér.

M. franklin

Notation: Vicq-d'azir Juin 1784

To Thomas Mifflin

AL (draft): Library of Congress; transcript: National Archives

Sir, Passy, June 16. 1784

My Letter by Mr Jay acquainted your Excellency that the Ratifications of the Definitive Treaty were exchanged.[1] A Copy of the British Part was also sent by him.

Mr Hartley remained here expecting Instructions to treat with us on the Subject of Commerce. The Bustle attending a new Election & Meeting of Parliament he imagined might occasion the long Delay of those Instructions. He now thinks that

8. Of June 15, above. BF's copy of Andry and Thouret, *Rapport sur les aimans présentés par M. l'Abbé Le Noble,* is at the APS.
9. This is our only evidence that BF forwarded to the Société royale de médecine William Lee Perkins' treatise on influenza, as Perkins had requested: XLI, 335–7.
1. To Mifflin, May 12[–13], above.

the Affair of American Trade being under the Consideration of Parliament, it is probable, no Treaty will be propos'd till the Result is known.— Mr Jay who sail'd for America the 1st Inst. from Dover and who saw there several of our Friends from London before his Departure, and Mr Laurens who left London the 6th. to go in the Falmouth Packet, will be able to give you more perfect Informations than I can, of what may be expected as the Determination of the British Government respecting our Intercourse with their Islands; and therefore I omit my Conjectures; only mentioning that from various Circumstances there seems to be some lurking Remains of ill-Humour there, and of Resentment against us, which only wants a favourable Opportunity to manifest itself.— This makes it more necessary for us to be upon our guard & prepared for Events that a Change in the Affairs of Europe may produce, its Tranquility depending perhaps on the Life of one Man, and it being impossible to foresee in what Situation a new Arrangement of its various Interests may place us.— Ours will be respected in proportion to the apparent Solidity of our Government, the Support of our Credit, the Maintenance of a good Understanding with our Friends, and our Readiness for Defence. All which I persuade myself will be taken care of.

Inclose I send a Copy of a Letter from Mr Hartley to me, respecting some suppos'd Defects in the Ratification, together with my Answer which he has transmitted to London.[2] The Objections appear'd to me trivial,[3] and absurd; but I thought it prudent to treat them with as much Decency as I could, lest the ill Temper should be augmented, which might be particularly inconvenient while the Commerce was under Consideration.— There has not yet been time for Mr Hartley to hear whether my Answer has been satisfactory, or whether the Ministers will still insist on my sending for an amended Copy from America as they proposed.—

I do not perceive the least Diminution in the good Disposition of this Court towards us; and I hope care will be taken to preserve it.

2. Hartley to BF, June 1, and BF's June 2 reply, both above.
3. BF here drafted but deleted, "and without Foundation".

The Marquis de la Fayette who will have the honour of delivering this to you, has ever since his Arrival in Europe been very industrious in his Endeavours to serve us and promote our Interests, and has been of great Use on several Occasions. I should wish the Congress might think fit to express in some proper Manner their Sense of his Merit.

My Malady prevents my going to Versailles, as I cannot bear a Carriage upon Pavement; but my Grandson, goes regularly on Court days to supply my Place, and is well receiv'd there.

The last Letters I have had the honour of receiving from you are of the 14th of January.—[4]

With great Respect, I am, Sir, Your Excellency's

His Excellency Thos Mifflin Esqr President of Congress

From Bailly

AL: American Philosophical Society

ce mercredi 16 juin. [1784]

M Bailly presente ses hommages a Monsieur franklin et le prie de lui renvoier le registre original de la commission[5] qu'il a eu l'honneur de lui envoier la semaine derniere, parcequ'on a indispensablement besoin demain dès le matin, qu'on doit commencer a le copier. Si Mr franklin ne l'avoit pas encore lu, il peut le garder encore jusqu'a ce soir, pourvû qu'il ait la bonté de le renvoier ce soir a chaillot a mr Bailly.

Addressed: A Monsieur / Monsieur Franklin ministre / plenipotentiaire des etats unis de / l'amerique en son hotel / a passy

Notation: Bailly.—

---

4. One was actually dated Jan. 15: XLI, 456–7, 464–6. Mifflin's tenure as president ended on June 3, 1784: *DAB*.

5. The commission to investigate animal magnetism kept a detailed log (now missing) that was periodically sent to BF for his review and signature. All the commissioners evidently signed this official, confidential record of their ongoing experiments. In BF's case, however, the register also served as his primary means of keeping abreast of the experiments performed in Paris, which he was unable to attend.

To Jane Mecom

ALS:[6] American Philosophical Society

Dear Sister, Passy, June 17. 1784.

It is long since I have had the Pleasure of hearing from you,[7] but am glad to hear by Cousin Williams that you were well the Beginning of this Year, and about to settle in the House at Boston,[8] which you may consider as your own, and I hope you will be happy in it.—

I continue, Thanks to God, in very good Health, being at present only troubled with the Stone, which sometimes gives me a little Pain, & prevents my going in a Carriage where there are Pavements, but does not otherwise make me very unhappy; as I can take the Exercise of Walking, eat, drink, sleep, read, write and enjoy the Conversation of my Friends as usual.— Give my Love to your Daughter, and believe

Addressed: To / Mrs Mecom / Boston

From Bailly

AL: American Philosophical Society

a chaillot ce jeudi 17 juin après midi [1784]

Mr Bailly presente ses respects a Monsieur Franklin. Il est chargé de le remercier au nom de Mrs les commissaires, qui se rendront chez lui samedi avant midi, et auront l'honneur de profiter de son invitation.[9] Les commissaires sont au nombre de huit, Mrs Majault, sallin Guillotin, d'arcet medecins; Mrs lavoisier, le Roy, de Bory[1] et Bailly academiciens. La commission compte assez sur les bontés de Mr Franklin pour prendre sur elle de lui mener, non seulement Mr deslon, et le jeune homme qui a eté

6. The signature and part of the complimentary close have been cut off.

7. Her last extant letter was dated April 29, 1783: XXXIX, 532–5.

8. Jonathan Williams, Sr., had written to BF at the end of December that Mecom was planning to move into BF's Unity Street house. His next letter reported that everyone in the family was well: XLI, 372, 477.

9. BF must have invited the commissioners to dine with him that day; Bailly here announces additional guests who will need to be accommodated. For the experiments conducted at Passy on Saturday, June 19, see the second extract of the commissioners' report, [Aug. 11].

1. It is not known when Gabriel de Bory joined the commission as a fifth representative of the Académie des sciences. Bory was a marine astronomer and a former governor of St.-Domingue: XXIV, 325; *DBF.*

deja le sujet d'une experience;[2] mais encore trois dames Mad de Bory, femme de notre confrere, et mesd. de Romagni et de Moret, qui sont deux malades de mr deslon. Cela fait en tout treize personne; et la commission renouvelle ses excuses a Mr Franklin de cet embaras.

Mr Bailly se rendra a passy vers dix heures du matin samedi pour faire part a Mr Franklin du plan d'experiences projetées, et preparer sous ses yeux tout ce qui sera necessaire pour les executer.[3]

Addressed: A Monsieur / Monsieur Franklin ministre / plenipotentiaire des etats unis de / l'amerique en son hotel / a passy

Notation: Bailly 17 Juin 1784—

Noël Le Mire[4] to William Temple Franklin

ALS: American Philosophical Society

Monsieur   De Paris Le 17 Juin 84

Permettés moi de vous presenter un Portrait de, Monsieur, Le Marquis De Lafayette,[5] Et vous Suplie de vouloir bien faire

2. The boy was the subject of experiments conducted at Passy on May 22; see extract (III) of the commissioners' report, [Aug. 11].

3. The plan for these experiments is published in *Œuvres de Lavoisier* (6 vols., Paris, 1862–93), III, 511–13, and includes the names of the two patients, Mme de Roumagné and Mme Moré. The experiments bear some similarity to those described in the third extract of the commissioners' report, [Aug. 11], in which two female patients were placed in separate rooms at Passy and one of the commissioners pretended to be Deslon. However, the abbreviated names and social class of the two women in the report do not match those mentioned in the plan and the present letter. Either the experiments on June 19 did not proceed as planned, the identities of the women were obscured, or the experiments described in the report were made on a different date.

4. This engraver (1724–1801) had come to BF's attention when he engraved Le Paon's portrait of GW (for which see XXXII, 65n; XXXV, 257n). Already a member of the academies of fine arts in Vienna and Rouen, in 1783 he was made a member of the Académie de peinture et de sculpture of Lille, in part because of his GW portrait: Jules Hédou, *Noël Le Mire et son oeuvre* (Paris, 1875), pp. 5, 12–15.

5. Le Mire conceived the idea for this portrait in 1782, intending it as a companion piece to his engraving of GW. He elicited WTF's help in obtaining

a Gréer a, Monsieur, votre Pere. L'autre, J'aurois déssiré pouvoir men a quitter moi même

J'ai l'honneur dêtre avec Respect Monsieur Votre trés humble Et trés obéissant Serviteur   LE MIRE

a Monsieur franklin fils

Endorsement: Le Mire 17 Juin 1784

Charles Thomson to the American Commissioners

Copy: Historical Society of Pennsylvania

Gentlemen   Philadelphia June 18. 1784

I have the honor of forwarding three comm[issions] which were not prepared in time to go by Mr Jefferson,[6] [and] a duplicate of the instructions he carried with him.[7] I [also] enclose

---

from the marquise de Lafayette a snuffbox with an excellent likeness of her husband; this he may have loaned to Le Paon, who painted the large oil portrait from which Le Mire made his engraving. For this favor, WTF was acknowledged in Le Mire's notice to subscribers, published in the Oct. 4, 1782, *Jour. de Paris:* Le Mire to WTF, June 3 and Sept. 11, 1782; Poirey to WTF, July 12, 1782 (all at the APS).

The prints sent with the present letter must have been among the earliest ones; the engraving was not advertised for sale in the *Jour. de Paris* until June 26. BF also received the "Description de cette Estampe" that Le Mire had printed for distribution with the engraving (APS). It explained that Lafayette, holding two swords, was issuing orders to both the French and American troops at Yorktown. The engraving was dedicated (in English) to GW; Le Mire translated that dedication into French in the "Description." The text of the "Description" and a catalogue raisonnée entry are in Hédou, *Noël Le Mire,* pp. 68–9. Le Paon's oil painting is at Lafayette College, and is reproduced as the frontispiece of Idzerda, *Lafayette Papers,* IV.

6. The three additional commissions, signed by Thomas Mifflin and Charles Thomson on June 3 (the day Congress resolved to send them: *JCC,* XXVII, 530), appointed JA, BF, and TJ ministers plenipotentiary to negotiate and conclude supplements to the existing treaties of amity and commerce with France, the Netherlands, and Sweden. Mass. Hist. Soc.

7. It was not quite a duplicate. TJ had carried the instructions of May 7–11; the set sent with the present letter included the final instruction that Congress adopted on June 3: *Jefferson Papers,* VII, 261–71; Smith, *Letters,* XXI, 696.

a copy of the Journal of the last session of Congress as far as printed and a news paper containing the Ordinance for putting the treasury into commission[8] and an act defining the powers of the committee of the States during the recess of Congress.[9] On the third of this Month Congress was adjourned pursuant to an act passed the 26 April to meet at Trenton on the 30 of October next.[1] With great respect I have the honor to be Gentlemen yr. most Ob: h Servt C T.

The honble. J Adams B Franklin & T. Jefferson

From Charles Thomson

Copy:[2] Historical Society of Pennsylvania

Dear Sir, Philadelphia June 18 1784

On the third of this month Congress adjourned to meet at Trenton on the 30 of Octr. next, having first appointed a comee. [committee] of the states to sit in the recess, agreeable to the Articles of Confederation. Previous to the adjournment I had the honor to receive your letter dated, if I recollect right, on the 8 March,[3] which I immediately laid before Congress. On the

---

8. Thomson sent the *Journal of the United States In Congress Assembled: containing The Proceedings from the Third Day of November, 1783, to the Third Day of June, 1784* (Philadelphia, 1784) through signature Gg, which contains all of May 27 and the first page of May 28. Though the ordinance was passed on May 28 (*JCC*, XXVII, 469–71), it would be in signature Hh.

9. For this act of May 29 see *JCC*, XXVII, 474–7. In a June 20 letter to Samuel Hardy, Thomson listed five additional enclosures to the present document: copies of the instructions to the peace commissioners of May 30 (XL, 87–8n) and Oct. 29, 1783 (XLI, 154–8); the congressional response to a letter from the Burgomasters and Senate of Hamburg (XLI, 169–70); a resolution of Nov. 1, 1783, authorizing John Paul Jones to collect American prize money in France (XLI, 298); and a resolution of March 16, 1784, stipulating that only American citizens could serve in diplomatic positions abroad (see Mifflin to BF and JA, March 20): Smith, *Letters*, XXI, 696.

1. *JCC*, XXVI, 287–96; XXVII, 555–6.

2. In Thomson's hand.

3. BF to Thomson, March 9, above.

18th. I received the letter which you did me the honor to write on the 31 March and am glad to hear of col Harmar's safe arrival with the ratification &c I shall take the earliest opportunity of communicating this to the comee of the States. I have to inform you that on the 7 May, Congress elected Mr Jay secretary for foreign Affairs. I hope he will accept the Office as I am confident of his abilities and that you will derive advantage and satisfaction from his information and correspondence.[4] I am sorry to hear he is likely to be detained longer than he expected, as the office requires his immediate attention. On the same day Congress appointed Mr Jefferson in Addition to Mr Adams and you for the purpose of negotiating commercial treaties agreeable to instructions, a duplicate of which goes by this Opportunity. The Chevr. de la Luzerne has taken his leave and is to embark for France the beginning of next week. He has acquitted himself in his Office greatly to the satisfaction of Congress and carries with him the esteem and good wishes of all who had the pleasure of his acquaintance. He has been detained a few days longer than he intended by the marriage of Mr De Marbois, which was celebrated yesterday with a daughter of Mr William Moore.—[5] I saw Mr Bache yesterday and had the pleasure to hear that Mrs. Bache and the family who are in the Country are all well. With great respect & esteem I am Dr. Sr. what I trust you have ever found me & what I shall ever continue to be yr. sincere friend

C. T.

Doct B Franklin

4. Jay finally took office on Dec. 21, after negotiating his terms of acceptance with Congress: *Jay Papers,* III, 583–5, 587, 590–1, 596, 652–3.

5. François Barbé de Marbois, La Luzerne's secretary, served as the chargé d'affaires for a year after La Luzerne's departure. He married Elizabeth Moore (c. 1765–1834), the only daughter of William Moore, a wealthy merchant and former president of the Pa. Supreme Executive Council: *DAB;* W. W. Abbot *et al.*, eds., *The Papers of George Washington,* Presidential Series (17 vols. to date, Charlottesville and London, 1987–), VIII, 215n.

From Sarah Bache   ALS: American Philosophical Society

Honoured Sir   [before June 19, 1784][6]
   This will be handed to you by Major Du Pontier, Aid of your
Friend Baron Stuben's,[7] who I shall thank you for your attention
to, we have found him a very amiable young Gentleman, he will
tell you how the Children all look, and what a delightful retreat
I have brought them to,[8] till a few days ago I flattered myself
you would have been with us on Schuilkill Banks this Summer,
I shall in a few days write you a long letter,[9] one to my Nephew[1]
and another to my Son they must now be contented with my
Love at present, I have been very busy nursing little Richard
who has been at the point of death but is now getting quite well
and lovely came here but yesterday, and the Major has been polite enough tho going tomorow to come out to see us and take
this, so that I could not request him to stay till I wrote all I have

6. This is the first of three letters from SB that refer to one another and
follow in quick succession. Only the last one is dated, thanks to her husband's intervention; it was begun on June 20. There SB mentions that she
had just finished a letter to BF; we date that one [on or before June 20]. In
that undated letter, SB states that she had written BF "a short letter the other
day" which she entrusted to Maj. de Pontière, a clear reference to the present text. If we assume that "the other day" meant something other than
"yesterday," she had to have written the letter before June 19.
   7. Louis de Pontière, a Frenchman who had served as aide-de-camp to
Baron von Steuben starting in February, 1778, and been promoted to the
rank of brevet major by Congress in September, 1783, was by this time
retired from his service in the American military and apparently on the
verge of returning to France: Asa B. Gardiner, *The Order of the Cincinnati
in France* ... (n.p., 1905), p. 175; Heitman, *Register of Officers*, p. 332; *JCC*,
XXVI, 43, 65.
   8. The Baches were renting the Cliffs, a modest house overlooking the
Schuylkill River outside Philadelphia that the Quaker merchant Joshua
Fisher had built in 1753. Fisher died in 1783, leaving the property to his son
Samuel Rowland Fisher. On June 25, 1784, RB, drawing on BF's account,
made a £60 rent payment to the lawyer Miers Fisher, Samuel's younger
brother: Harold D. Eberlein and Cortlandt V. D. Hubbard, *Portrait of a Colonial City: Philadelphia, 1670–1838* (Philadelphia, 1939), pp. 310–12; Penrose R. Hoopes, "Cash Dr to Benjamin Franklin," *PMHB*, LXXX (1956),
64; Anna W. Smith, *Genealogy of the Fisher Family, 1682 to 1896* (Philadelphia, 1896), pp. 27, 34, 50.
   9. We date that letter [on or before June 20, 1784].
   1. SB's letter to WTF was dated June 21, 1784 (APS).

to say, I beg therefore Temple will take this as an introduction of the Gentleman to him as well as to you as much as if I wrote. Mr B: is well I expect to see him at dinner.

I am as ever your dutiful and afectionate Daughter

S BACHE

Addressed: Dr: Franklin / Passy / [Maj?] Depontiere

From Thomas Jefferson   ALS: American Philosophical Society

Dear Sir   Boston June 19. 1784.

Supposing that Congress would communicate to you directly the powers committed to yourself, mr. Adams & myself, I have delayed from day to day the honour of writing to you, in hopes that every day would open to me a certainty of the time & place at which I might sail: a French packet will leave N. York early in the next month. By her I mean to take my passage,[2] and may therefore expect in the ordinary course of things to have the pleasure of joining you at Paris in the middle or latter part of August, and of communicating the commissions & instructions under which we are to act. The latter are more special than those heretofore sent.[3] I shall then also have the pleasure of giving you more particular information of the situation of our affairs than I can do by letter. In general I may observe to you that their aspect is encouraging. Congress understanding that mr. Jay was probably on his passage to America, appointed him their Secretary for foreign affairs. It would give me peculiar pleasure to meet with him before my departure and to know that he will act in an office with which we shall be so immediately connected. Congress adjourned on the 3d of June to meet at Trenton on the

2. He did not. The *Courier de l'Europe* was not scheduled to sail for Lorient until July 15, so TJ decided to sail from Boston on July 5; see Cushing to BF, July 2. He tried in vain to coordinate his passage with that of JA's wife and daughter, who left Boston for London on June 20: *Adams Papers*, XVI, 90n, 242–3, 255.

3. TJ presumably meant that the instructions of May 7 and the commissions of May 12, both above, were more precise than the instructions of Oct. 29, 1783 (XLI, 154–8).

first Monday of November, leaving a Committee of the states at the helm during their recess.— I have the pleasure to inform you that mrs. Bache & her family were well when I left Philadelphia which was about three weeks ago. In hopes of joining you nearly as soon as you will receive this I subscribe myself with very sincere esteem & regard Dr Sir Your most affectionate humble servt TH: JEFFERSON

Addressed: The honourable / Benjamin Franklin esq. / American Minister / at Paris.

Endorsed: Thos Jefferson Esqr June 19. 84—

From Charles (C.-J.) Le Roux

ALS: American Philosophical Society

Monsieur   Paris 19. Juin 1784.

Depuis quelques années que je n'ai eû l'honneur ni de vous voir ni de vous écrire, peut-être m'avez vous perdu de vue.[4] Mr. De Gebelin que la Société et les Lettres ont perdu trop tôt[5] m'honoroit de son estime et de son amitié. Il connoissoit mes ouvrages et particulierement Mon Journal d'Education que j'ai fait autrefois par ordre du Gouvernement pour l'institution de notre Monarque. Je tenois pension au College Royal de Boncourt, montagne ste. Genevieve, maintenant je Dirige une maison d'Education avec le sr. Le cœur chez qui a demeuré mr. votre petit fils, quand ce maître demeuroit à Passi.[6]

Le Porteur de la presente, du pays de feu mr. De Gebelin, est un homme de lettres Suisse qui est fort éclairé, il venoit à Paris pour y être placé par l'entremise de m. de Gebelin mais sa mort prêmaturée et inattendue est cause que ce brave étranger n'est point placé. Vous êtes, Monsieur, l'ami des hommes et surtout le protecteur des citoyens honnêtes et savans, je vous suplie d'hon-

4. BF had been invited to witness some of Le Roux's experiments in early 1783, but we have no evidence that he attended: XXXIX, 312–13.

5. Court de Gébelin died on May 12, 1784: XLI, 221–2n.

6. BFB was enrolled at Le Coeur's school from April, 1777, to April, 1779: XXV, 91–2; XXIX, 342.

norer de votre bonté le monsieur qui vous remettra cette Lettre. Il est propre à bien des choses et il peut vous être utile ou à vos connoissances.

J'ai l'honneur d'être avec respect Monsieur Votre très humble et très obéissant Serviteur

LE ROUX instituteur

à Chaillot, rue des batailles. même Maison de m. Le cœur

Addressed: A Monsieur / Monsieur Franklin / A Passi.

Notation: Le Roux 19 Juin 1784.

From Morellet

ALS: University of Pennsylvania Library

The "fragment" that Morellet enclosed with the present letter was probably an early version of what became a fifty-nine-page manuscript titled "Apologie des papiers de credit etablis par les etats unis."[7] The first half recounted the introduction, circulation, and depreciation of paper money in the colonies. The second half defended Congress' resort to paper money during the war. It rebutted at length arguments that the Continental money's devaluation amounted to bankruptcy and that Congress needed to compensate all or some holders of paper currency. Morellet adopted and elaborated on the argument made by Thomas Paine, in his *Letter Addressed to the Abbe Raynal,*[8] that the initial stipulated value of the congressional paper money in specie was much less than its nominal dollar value. Moreover, the bills' depreciation had been accepted by the American people as a substitute for paying taxes to fund their national war. Morellet contended that the number of foreigners owning paper money was very small and their losses modest. Depreciation of paper money had to be considered a predictable risk of doing business during wartime.

7. The heavily edited text (Bibliothèque municipale de Lyon) is largely in the hand of Morellet's secretary, Poullard, but Morellet made numerous corrections and added entire sections cut from other sheets. A clean text is printed, with annotation by Manuela Albertone, in *Quaderni di Storia dell'Economia Politica,* VIII (1990), 79–106.

8. For which see XXXVIII, 102n. Morellet may have been given a copy by BF: after receiving Paine's work from Robert Livingston in late 1782, BF wrote that he "distributed [it] into good Hands" (XXXVIII, 415).

Redemption at the paper's original nominal value was not only impossible, but also unjust.

On the manuscript's cover page, beneath the title, Morellet signed his name to the following note: "J'ai soumis cette discussion au jugement de mr. Franklin avant son depart pour l'amerique. Il en a ete content. Les petites notes au crayon sont de sa main." Franklin wrote very few comments on the manuscript. In several places, he drew a line next to a passage or added a word or phrase, perhaps to mark it for discussion with Morellet.

Franklin's one substantive correction was on page three. Morellet observed that two types of bills of credit circulated in the colonies before Congress issued its first emission. The first, he wrote, were called "*Paper-bills bills of credit, Paper currency.*" Franklin corrected this, interlining "The whole was called indifferently" before the terms. Morellet, writing over the comment in pen, translated it as: "On a donné à tous indifféremment le nom de *Paper-bills bills of credit*, on peut cependant les séparer en deux classes." Franklin himself drafted a sentence in French on the blank facing page: "Nous designerons le premiere espece par le nom de Paper Currency ou *Billets monnoie*, & le seconde par le nome de Province Bills, *Billets de Province.*" Morellet adopted this description. Franklin also noted that the two kinds of paper money were distinguished "by the manner in which they were issued," a phrase that Morellet translated literally and added at the place Franklin had indicated.

Monsieur   Samedi [June 19, 1784][9]
Je vous ai parlé d'un travail que j'ai entrepris relatif aux colonies de l'amerique qui peut vous interesser par son objet en voilà un fragment.[1] Je vous supplie de le lire à vos momens perdus. Si

9. Based on Morellet's statement that he planned to spend the following week with his family near Choisy-le-Roi. On Saturday, June 19, 1784, Morellet wrote to Shelburne that the next day he was going to visit for the first time Jean-François Marmontel's country house in Grignon (Val-de-Marne), near Choisy-le-Roi, and stay there for seven or eight days. The "famille" included Morellet's niece (Marmontel's wife), one of his sisters, and another niece: Medlin, *Morellet*, 1, xxxi, 518–20.
    1. Morellet's MSS at the Bibliothèque municipale de Lyon include more than a dozen dealing with American subjects, especially with the impact of American independence on prices and wages in Europe, as well as on freedom of trade and colonial administration. Other topics include monetary policy and history and a plan for a U.S. bank. In 1797 the *Jour. d'économie publique, de morale et de politique* published two articles possibly

The Cliffs

vous en etes content je vous en donnerai le reste. L'ouvrage seroit considerable je ne me determinerois á le publier que d'après
votre suffrage s'il peut m'etre favorable en voilà un echantillon.
Juges le. Je compte aller passer la semaine prochaine avec ma
famille auprès de choisi le roi. A mon retour j'irai vous demander le resultat de votre lecture. Vous saves combien je vous suis
tendrement et respectueusement devoué. L'ABBÉ MORELLET

Addressed: A Monsieur / Monsieur Franklin / ministre plenipotentiaire des etats / unis de l'amerique / A Passy

Notation: L'abbé Morellet

From Sarah Bache

ALS: American Philosophical Society

The Cliffts, on the banks of Schuylkill
Honoured Sir [on or before June 20, 1784][2]
By Major Depontiere I wrote you a short Letter the other
day,[3] it was at the very instant of my moveing, I had neither
pen or wafer, I hope you will excuse the appearance it made, I
thought you would be happy to hear I was well even if it were
wrote in Greek Characters. My little Richard is most amaiz-
ingly recovered since we came out here and the whole little
Family in such spirits that tis' impossible to find a quiet moment
for reflection or writing, they are now all jumping and dancing
about me, and to add to the sprightlyness of the Scene Willy
has brought out two young Friends to dine with him, he will
write as soon as they leave him. The Minister will give you a

---

drawn from these manuscripts, but not the "Apologie," which we believe
was enclosed with the present letter. The journal attributed the first article to BF, before issuing a correction with the second: Alfred O. Aldridge,
Franklin and his French Contemporaries (New York, 1957), pp. 72–3; Dorothy Medlin, "Catalogue of Morellet's Works," in *André Morellet (1727–
1819) in the Republic of Letters and the French Revolution,* ed. Jeffrey Merrick
and Dorothy Medlin (New York, 1995), p. 205.

2. For the dating of this letter, see the annotation of SB's letter of [before
June 19], above.

3. [Before June 19].

decription of the delightful Place we are at, as he was particularly pleased with it,[4] but no one can paint the disapointment I have met with in your not coming this Summer, I am now sorry I ever flattered myself with the thought, nothing but the size of my Family prevents my making you a visit in France, we are much indepted to the Chavilear De La Lucerne for many polite attentions to us, ever since he first came, and part with him with regret, wishing it had been more in our power to have added to his happiness during his stay at Philad. I do not think we shall ever have a Person in his Station that will do greater honor to it, or leave behind more Friends, both to himself and to his Nation, he very politely called here the other day to take leave and offer to take any thing for you, I am sorry it is at such a Season that there is nothing to send, I cannot think of one thing that would be acceptable. Mr Marbois was married on thursday last to Miss Moore,[5] we had an invitation to Breakfast at the Ministers and see the Cerimony, it was no small mortification to me that it was not in my power to go, Mr B: [Bache] was there, I shall endeavour to get to town to wait on the Bride.

I shall write both to my Nephew[6] and Son, and if possible to Mrs Barckly and Montgomery,[7] and another to you as I promised Dr Bancroft I would, I am with great afection your Dutiful Daughter   S Bache

Addressed:[8] Dr. Franklin / Passy.

4. La Luzerne, the French minister, would leave Philadelphia to return to France on June 23: *Morris Papers,* IX, 402.
5. See the annotation of Charles Thomson to BF, June 18, above.
6. In her letter to WTF of June 21, SB asked her nephew to introduce La Luzerne to BFB, as the minister had taken an interest in Willy and would be able to characterize him for his brother. She also asked WTF to send her news of WF, from whom she had not received a single letter since the peace. APS.
7. Mary Barclay and Dorcas Montgomery, SB's friends, then in France.
8. In the hand of RB.

From Sarah Bache   ALS: American Philosophical Society

Honoured Sir   The Cliffts Sunday 20[–21] June 1784[9]
    In full expectation of Dr Bancrofts calling on me before he
embarks I write again tho I have just finished one for you, I did
expect he would dine with us tomorrow and am disapointed to
hear he cannot, for I love every one you love, and the Dr is so
agreable and sensible, that every one must think favorably of
him and like his Company, for his own sake, so that he was allways doubly welcome to us, he goes with our very best wishes
for his safe arrival, and speedy passage,[1] I wish him much to see
this place before he goes, as I think there is not a more beautiful prospect on the Schuylkill banks, tis very healthy too, the
Children look like different Creatures since they came out and
have gain'd an adittional stock of spirits little Deborah this instant ran to me and beg'd me to write her a letter, I told her I
was writing to her Grand papa, and ask'd her what I should say
to him, say to him says she why Grandpa is not in this room,
prety well for a little Girl between two and three, she is a great
mimic, Dr Bancroft can tell you how well she can take off an
Owl which the Children have for a pet, I should not forget to
mention that while I stay in the Country and the house in town
is painting, we have put Willy to board with a Mr Gamble one
of the Masters at the University,[2] a man remarkably attentive to
the morals as well as the learning of the boys, and is as mindful

9. RB added "20 June 1784" beneath where his wife wrote "Sunday".
Because she continued the letter the next day, we expand the date.
    1. Edward Bancroft was returning to France after having spent almost
nine months in the United States: XL, 16n, 331n; XLI, 434. He and La Luzerne sailed on the *St. James,* which left Philadelphia on June 23 and arrived
in Lorient *c.* July 21: *Pa. Evening Post, and Public Advertiser,* June 25, 1784;
Freeman's Jour.: or, The North-American Intelligencer, Oct. 6, 1784. The two
men were in Paris by July 29: *Adams Papers,* XVI, 286–7; *Morris Papers,*
IX, 402, 469.
    2. Archibald Gamble was appointed professor of English and oratory at
the University of the State of Pennsylvania in 1782. He died on Sept. 21,
1784, at the age of 44: University of Pa., *Biographical Catalogue of the
Matriculates of the College . . .* (Philadelphia, 1894), p. 17; Timothy Alden,
A Collection of American Epitaphs and Inscriptions . . . (5 vols., New York,
1814), I, 170.

of them out of School as in, he would else have ran riot as his Father is mostly at the Store when in town, and out here every leasure moment, Willy comes out on Saturday and goes in on Monday Morn early. Monday.[3] When Mr Jeferson went I was in great distress and tho I intended it could not write. Mrs Shee one of my best Friends lay dead, and till the funeral was over had four daughters of hers with me, beside the direction of every thing, lay on Mr Bache and me,[4] Dr Bancroft call'd while I was writing this Letter but could not stay with us long, I shall send this to town to him to day, and leave it to Mr Bache to seal and direct, & put the day of the Month for I realy do not know it, I have been so much taken up with domestic Matters since I have been here, that I have not had time for any other Idea, I am now a little setled and shall be more at leasure, my little Fellows illness and at the same time a change of servants had quite deranged the Family.

You have heard no doubt of the death of your good old Friend's Dr Bond Mr Roads and Anthony Benezet,[5] it was thought this hard winter affected them much, they were greatly lamented. Mr Roads died very suddenly, Mrs Ashmead was nursing me,[6] they sent for her but he was dead before she got there. She is in as good health as ever you saw her and as useful as ever, when I saw her last she desired to be remembered to you very particularly, Mr Bache writes, the Children are all well and love you very much as does your affectionate Daughter

S BACHE

3. "Monday" (June 21) is interlined.
4. SB's friend was Jane Nailor Shee, the second wife of RB's business partner John Shee: W. A. Newman Dorland, "The Second Troop Philadelphia City Cavalry," *PMHB*, XLIX (1925), 184. SB had evidently asked TJ to carry letters for her, but when he called for them, they weren't ready and, as she wrote, "my eyes were so sweled with crying I could hardly see." She asked WTF to apologize to TJ on her behalf: SB to WTF, June 21, 1784 (APS).
5. RB had reported the deaths of Thomas Bond and Samuel Rhoads in his letter of April 28, above. Benezet died on May 3 after a brief illness: *Pa. Gaz.*, May 12, 1784.
6. Mrs. Ashmead, who had previously served as the Bache family's nurse (XXXV, 610), was presumably hired after Richard's birth.

From the Marquis de Castries   LS: Library of Congress

Versailles le 20 juin *1784*.

J'ai l'honneur, Monsieur, de vous envoyer un Projet de répartition des Prises faites par l'Escadre aux ordres du Commodore Paul Jones dont les liquidations ont été arrettées à la somme de 386,682 *l.t.*-8-2 *d.* sauf la déduction de quelques depenses générales de peu de conséquence, et dont mr. le Rey de Chaumont doit justifier.[7]

Le Roi a decidé que la répartition de la portion de la masse revenant à chaque Batiment preneur seroit repartie, entre les Equipages, conformement à l'ordonnance du 28 mars 1778 concernant les Prises faites par les Batimens de sa majesté;[8] et qu'à l'egard du Commandant et des capitaines *seulement* ils seroient traités selon les loix americaines auxqu'elles ils se sont soumis par le concordat qu'ils ont fait entr'eux.[9]

Je vous serai obligé, en conséquence, de me faire connoitre, officiellement, les Parts qui doivent étre attribuées à Mr. Jones et aux capitaines de chaque Batiment.

Il paroit par un Extrait qui m'a été adressé par ce commodore qu'il doit avoir un Vingtieme du Produit de toutes les Prises et que les capitaines doivent partager entr'eux les deux Vingtiemes;[1] mais mr. Jones demande, en outre, les deux Vingtiemes sur la Portion qui revient au Vaisseau le Bonhomme Richard, et prétend que les deux Vingtiemes attribués aux capitaines ne doivent point étre prélevés sur la masse totale du produit des Prises; mais sur la Portion de chaque Batiment, de maniere que

7. See Jones to BF, March 23. In the meantime, on May 31 Jones wrote to WTF requesting that he deliver to Vergennes copies of Sartine's May 30, 1780, letter to Congress offering Jones the *Ordre de Mérite Militaire*, along with the congressional resolution of Feb. 27, 1781, authorizing him to accept it (XXXIV, 415–16). APS.
8. François-André Isambert, ed., *Recueil général des anciennes lois françaises* . . . (29 vols., Paris, 1821–33), XXV, 248–55.
9. The agreement of Aug. 13, 1779: XXX, 223. Congress passed regulations regarding the division of prizes in 1776, and amended them in 1778: *JCC*, IV, 36–7; VI, 913; XII, 1133.
1. As specified by Congress in January, 1776: *JCC*, IV, 36.

le capitaine de la fregate l'alliance[2] n'auroit que les deux Vingtiemes de la somme de 114,990 *l.t.*, ainsi des autres.[3]

J'ai l'honneur d'etre avec la consideration la plus distinguée, Monsieur, Votre trés humble et trés obeïssant serviteur.

LE MAL. DE CASTRIES

Mr. franklin ministre des Etats Unis de l'amerique.

Prises.

Envoi du Projet de répartition des Prises du Commodore Paul Jones.

From Richard Bache: Three Letters

(I), (II), and (III) ALS: American Philosophical Society

I.

Dear & Hond. Sir   Philadelphia 21s. June 1784.

Tho' it is long since we heard from you, we have now and then the pleasure of hearing of you— Mr. Charles Thompson told me the other day, that he had received a Letter from you dated in March,[4] and that you then were well; this is the last account we have of you— I confess I have been pleasing myself with the expectation of seeing you at home this summer, nor am I yet without such a hope; added to the desire you have of being with your Family, there will be another stimulus if my information be true, that Congress have Slighted a late application of yours, which has been very generally spoken of and Congress as generally condemned—[5] Mr. J— A's influence with

2. Pierre Landais.

3. In the enclosed "Projet de répartition entre les cinq batimens qui composoient l'éscadre du Commodore Paul Jones," the share of each ship was figured according to the number of its cannons and their calibers. Castries had adopted Jones's formula, which was patterned on that of the British navy: Morison, *Jones*, pp. 68–9.

4. BF wrote to Thomson on March 9 and March 31, above.

5. Probably a reference to BF's longstanding effort to find a diplomatic post for WTF, which Congress thwarted with its May 12 appointment of

some Congressional Members, it seems is powerfull.— I have never heard the subject of the letters transmitted by you thro' my hands to Dr. Cooper[6] spoken of, but I suppose, it has been made use of by Mr. A's friends in a certain place— The Death of your Friend the Doctor,[7] may possibly prevent those Letters being made as publick as you would wish at Boston, would it not be well to transmit Copies of them to some other friend there? Of this however you are the best Judge.— Sally has given you an account of the situation of the Family, I left them all well this Morning, on the Banks of the Schuylkill— Your House in Town is in the painters hands, it much needed their assistance[8]—if you would come and enjoy it the remainder of your days, it would add much to the happiness of your family, and particularly of Your affectionate son   RICH BACHE

I shall commit the Newspapers to Dr. Bancroft's Care—

Addressed: Dr. Franklin / Passy—

II.

Dear & Hond. Sir   Philadelphia June 21. 1784

Mr. Francis West the Bearer of this is the eldest son of the late Mr. William West of this City, whom I dare say you well remember;[9] he visits Europe principally upon a plan of business; I beg leave to introduce him to your notice & Civilities, as

---

Humphreys as secretary to the commission for commercial treaties.

On Dec. 14, RB claimed in a letter to WTF that he had been unaware until "lately" of BF's "application to [Congress] in your behalf" (APS). Because RB was excusing himself for the delay in answering WTF's letter of May 27, respecting, in part, his prospects for a government position, it is possible that RB was not being entirely truthful.

6. See RB's letter of March 7, above.

7. Cooper died on Dec. 29 (XLI, 372), before receiving BF's dispatches.

8. On Sept. 13 RB recorded a charge to BF's account of £37 10s. for painting: Penrose R. Hoopes, "Cash D^r To Benjamin Franklin," *PMHB,* LXXX (1956), 65.

9. For William West see IX, 291–3; X, 20–2, 50. His son Francis was a Philadelphia dry-goods merchant and a member of the Friendly Sons of St. Patrick: John H. Campbell, *History of the Friendly Sons of St. Patrick and of the Hibernian Society* . . . (Philadelphia, 1892), pp. 138–9.

a modest deserving young Gentleman—and am ever Dear sir
Your affectionate son   RICH BACHE
Dr. Franklin

Addressed: His Excellency / Dr. Benjamin Franklin / at / Passy.
/ Favored by Mr. West

Notation: R. Bache 21 June 84

III.

Dear & Hond Sir   Philadelphia June 21st. 1784
    This may be handed you by my worthy Friend Mr. John
Donaldson of this City, a Merchant of excellent character &
reputation;[1] should he find you at Passy, I beg leave to introduce
him to your Notice & Civilities; but I can't help flattering myself, that we shall have the pleasure of seeing you at home this
summer.
    I am ever Dear Sir Your affectionate son   RICH BACHE
Dr. Franklin

Addressed: His Excellency / Dr. Benjamin Franklin / at /
Passy— / Favored by Mr. Donaldson

From Thomas Brand Hollis

ALS: American Philosophical Society

Sir   Bruton Street June 21. 1784.
    The loss of a young person of fine dispositions and excellent
principles, & in whose education I greatly interested my self, as
intending him to be my son & heir, has prevented me attending to matters which at another time would have engaged my

---

1. John Donnaldson (as his name was more commonly spelled) was an
insurance broker as well as a merchant. He resigned his position as warden
of the port of Philadelphia in June when he traveled to Europe, apparently
in the company of West. He later became comptroller general of Pennsylvania: Gregory B. Keen, "The Descendants of Jöran Kyn, the Founder of
Upland," *PMHB,* IV (1880), 344–7; Maurice J. Bric, "Patterns of Irish
Emigration to America, 1783–1800," *Eire-Ireland,* XXXVI (2001), 16.

thoughts; was it not for this, I should justly incur the imputation of negligence, as it is some time since I received from you a medal[2] to commemorate the glorious events of the Independency of America & the total Subjugation of their enemies— events which I rejoice at as I have always detested and abhorred the principle of enslaving mankind and depriving them of the rights of human nature, under any pretence whatsoever.

The medal I esteem on all accounts is a great honor from the donor. It is a most valuable addition to my friends collection of Liberty coins as he used to call his cabinet.

The head of your Liberty would have pleased him. It is simple & noble the execution is good but I could have wished the names & dates of your victories had been wrote in capitals & also the date of your independence that every part might be intelligible.

There is a mistake in the word *Juil:* which might yet be altered.

Indeed Sir, the three noble subjects united in your medal claim each a distinct medal and had I the honor to be an American it should be done; for never in the Annals of mankind such events have had such glorious consequences. The divine rights of human nature are declared & established against all the Arts of Priests & Tyrants & there is now an Asylum for the injured & oppressed.

I hope the coinage of America will be attended too at proper time to be decimal on account change as the present roman coin is, and the copper currency to perpetuate Historical events as mentioned by Addison in the Spectator which might be done with small expence.[3]

To me it is matter of surprize, after having considered it &

2. *Libertas Americana*, sent the previous October for the collection bequeathed to Brand Hollis by Thomas Hollis: XLI, 77–8. The medal is illustrated as the frontispiece of vol. 39.

3. Addison advocated the commemoration of historical events through circulating coins, as had been the practice in ancient Rome. His piece first appeared in the *Guardian* of July 1, 1713, and was reprinted in [Louis Jobert], *The Knowledge of Medals* . . . (2nd ed., London, 1715), pp. 152–6, as well as *The Works of the Right Honourable Joseph Addison, Esq* (4 vols., London, 1721), IV, 135–7.

which I cannot sufficiently understand how the Romans struck their medals, as it is known they were often struck in the camp & of emperors who lived but three days and perhaps there are not two of the same Dye of any one Emperor. I rejoice you esteem my friends labors for the Publick. There never was a man who having the means indulged less & spent his whole time in publick services. Candor to the publick obliged the compilers of the Memoirs not to conceal any sentiment of my late friends. His anxiety for the publick weal made him suspicious of Characters eminently great but which by their strenous exertions, have demonstrated to the world how much they are superior to detraction.

The mistake about your letter attributed to Mr Adams shall be rectified in a future Edition.[4]

The first opportunity I will convey to you Milton's tractate on education which I could not induce the Booksellers, tho at my expence, to print with Johnson's poets as it always accompanied his Poeticks, tho Cowleys Proposition is published with his Poems—such is the fear of Johnson with the Booksellers who unwillingly sell The remarks on Milton's Life.[5]

May you like Timoleon, long enjoy the glorious satisfaction of having emancipated your country and established Freedom on the broad basis of equal Laws, and beleive me to be with the greatest esteem and respect for your worth & excellence Sir your much obliged humble Servant   T BRAND HOLLIS.

4. BF had pointed out the error in his letter of Oct. 5 (XLI, 77), but there were to be no subsequent editions of Blackburne's *Memoirs of Thomas Hollis* (1780), which Brand Hollis had sponsored: XLI, 75.

5. Milton's *Of Education* (1644) was not included in Samuel Johnson's *Works of the English Poets . . .* (58 vols., London, 1779–80), published by a consortium of booksellers, whereas Abraham Cowley's *Proposition for the Advancement of Experimental Philosophy* (1661) was. When one of the booksellers approached Johnson in 1778 and suggested, at the behest of an acquaintance, that *Of Education* be included in the edition, Johnson's answer was that he disagreed with Milton's views on the subject: Marshall Waingrow *et al.*, eds., *James Boswell's* Life of Johnson . . . (3 vols. to date, Edinburgh and London, 1994–), III, 264. By "remarks on Milton's Life," Brand Hollis is most likely referring to the biographical essay written by Johnson for his *Prefaces, Biographical and Critical, to the Works of the English Poets* (10 vols., London, 1779–1781), later known as *Lives of the Poets*.

From Joseph Rati   ALS: American Philosophical Society

May it Please your Excellenzy   Genoa Juin the 21st: 1784
Sir
The subscriber a Subject of the Thirteen United American States Inhabitant of Salem in New-England, having sailed from thence since the 20th: of July 1782 & been trading in the W-Indies & on the Spanish Main, upon a report that the Moors of barbary did not choose to prey upon any American Flagg[6] having attempted to Come from Martinicca to this Port with Hides; I find to my great disappointement that we are not respected by any of those Regencies, & having a rich Cargo to go back with to New England, these Seas being full of Moorish Rovers, whom on the occasion of Spain threatening Algier,[7] durst not go home & have no better cruizing ground than the Ligurian Gulf for the shelter they find in Corsica, & on the Coast of Provence so that this Coast swarms with them, all this makes it higly imprudent iff not impossible to sally out without having some means of security. Had I such a Ship as I once this last War had the honour to Comand under Continental Comission,[8] the Swarthy Moor might feel the weight of American Metall, as the proud Briton has felt at our occasionall meetings but my Vessel is now only suitable for a peaceble trade. On these Circumstances having no Consul in this Place who represents the Thirteen United States I humbly take the Liberty to apply directly to your Excellency, most respectfully begging to obtain iff possible some Means of Protection as I have heard much talk of a certain Pass given on this Account by the Court of France to our American Vessels trading in the Straights: & that it might better appear that my Vessel belongs to America. I include herein

6. On Dec. 25, 1780, the *Boston Gaz.* reported, based on information just arrived from Cadiz, that the sultan of Morocco had directed his captains not to target American ships, "under penalty of the Captain's losing his head."
7. Spain launched an attack against Algiers in early July; see our annotation of BF's journal, [June 26–July 27], entry of July 20, below.
8. Between 1779 and at least 1781, Rati served as the commander of the privateer ship *Triton:* Claghorn, *Naval Officers,* p. 251; Allen, *Mass. Privateers,* p. 305.

353

a Copy of my Register;[9] And in Case my request should not be granted I shall be then forcibly obliged to make my Vessel a British Bottom so that I might return to my Country. I earnestly begg likewise Your Excellency be pleased to lett me know the Event of this affair as soon as possible, or instruct me with your ever wise directions how to act in my critical Case. I have the honour to be: Your Excellency's Ever Dutifull Most Obbedient & Most Humble Servt: JOSEPH RATI

Notation: Joseph Raty 21, Juin 1784—

From Edward Bridgen   ALS: American Philosophical Society

My Dear Sir   London June 22 1784
Our Mutual Friend Mr Hollis has just left this with me to send to your Excellency which I inclose in a packett to Monsr: Genet and dare say that you will receive it safe.[1]

I did myself the honour to send you through the hands of Mr Hartley Mr Champions observations on Lord Sheffields book,[2] which I hope you received safe & in a few days I shall convey by the same Channel a Tract which Mr Hollis mentions in his Letter sending you.

Mr Astle moved the other day in the Council of the royal Society that your Excellency might have the Gold Medal which was Struck on Acct: of the Protection given by the King of France and the Empress of Russia to Capt: Cook, and it was carried;[3] and I suppose it will be soon sent you if not already done.

9. The register, dated July 16, 1782, and signed by William West, Jr., of Salem, identifies Rati as the master and owner of the brig *Sackarissa*.

1. The enclosure was Thomas Brand Hollis' letter of June 21, above.

2. See Bridgen to BF, June 10.

3. The Royal Society had resolved to strike these commemorative medals in 1780 (see XXIX, 86–7), and ordered five in gold to be presented to royalty who had offered Cook protection: the King and Queen of England, the Prince of Wales, the King of France, and the Empress of Russia. Sir William Jones and John Paradise nominated BF and Congress to receive the same medal in recognition of the passport BF had issued for Cook in 1779, but this was met with opposition: XXXI, 448–9, 487; XXXII, 27, 176–7, 220, 590. The medals were minted in early 1784, and once they had all been

May every blessing attend your Excellency is the hearty prayer of Dr Sir Yr: faithful & Obliged EDWD: BRIDGEN

Your Worthy Collegue[4] is still detained at Falmouth but in good Spirits.

His Excellency Benj: Franklin

Addressed: A Son Exellence / Benjn: Franklin / a Passy

Notation: E. Bridgen. 22 June 1784

From Ezra Stiles

ALS: American Philosophical Society

Sir Yale College June 22 1784.

Colo. Humphrys needs not as some others Letters of Recommendation, being himself his own Epistle to every one who would take Knowledge of real Worth & singular Merit. He was educated in this College, of which he was formerly elected a Tutor or Professor.[5] He has distinguished himself in our Army through the War, and Gen. Washington has taken him into his particular Friendship and Family as one of his Aids de Camp.— Congress has finally honored him with particular Respect, by appointing him Secretary to the illustrious Triumvirate of Ambassadors or Ministers plenipotentiary for negotiating Commercial Treaties with foreign Powers. I doubt not the Colonel will avail himself of the high Advantage & opportunity this will give him of entering into the Views & perhaps the Cabinet Councils of the several Courts in Europe, which may qualify him for still higher Service to his Country & Mankind. Your Sagacity & Discernment will instantly shew you, to what a share in your Communications whether *Literary* or *Political*

---

distributed, the council of the Royal Society resolved on June 17 to use the remaining funds from the subscription to strike additional gold medals for certain individuals, including BF: Council Minutes, Royal Society Archive.

4. Henry Laurens.

5. Humphreys, a member of the Yale class of 1771, had been offered the tutorship in 1775 but turned it down: Franklin B. Dexter, *Biographical Sketches of the Graduates of Yale College* ... (6 vols., New York and New Haven, 1885–1912), III, 414–20.

your Benevolence shall admit him. You take Pleasure in forming & patronizing younger Merit for mature Usefulness & Glory. I could wish that hereafter it might be among your other Honors said, This Gentleman, as perhaps a future Plenipotentiary, was formed by the Councils & hoary Wisdom of Dr Franklin. I have the Honor to be, Sir, Your most obedient very humble servt.   EZRA STILES

Dr Franklin

Addressed: His Excellency / Benjamin Franklin Esq LL.D. / Minister plenipotentiary from the / United States to the Court of / Versailles / Honored by / Mr Secry. Humphrys

From Wadsworth & Church[6]

AL:[7] American Philosophical Society

Thursday June 24 1784

Messrs Wadsworth & Church present their respectfull Compliments to Doctr Franklin—they much regret that it is not in their power to wait on the Doctr as they leave Paris early tomorrow Morning. If the Doctr has any commands for London they will be happy to obey them

Addressed: To / His Excellency Doctr Franklin / Passy

Notation: Wathworth & Church 24 June 1784

---

6. Business partners Jeremiah Wadsworth and John Barker Church had come to France the previous summer to collect on debts owed them by the French government: XXXVIII, 546n; XL, 263–4. At that time Church was using the alias "Carter," a practice he would continue until at least February, 1784, when he and his wife, Angelica, sent BF a dinner invitation as "Mr & Mrs Carter": XLI, 542.

On Feb. 9, 1784, in answer to a request from Angelica Carter, a M. d'Aboville sent her the address of a Turinese physician, de Perse, whose powder was reputed to cure severe gravel without causing any side effects. She must have passed on this letter to BF, as an extract of it, in L'Air de Lamotte's hand, is among his papers at the APS.

7. In Wadsworth's hand.

Loose Thoughts on a Universal Fluid

AD (draft): Library of Congress; copies:[8] Historical Society of Pennsylvania, American Philosophical Society (two); copies of French translation:[9] Library of Congress (two), Bibliothèque de l'Institut de France

In this series of speculations, Franklin tried to combine into one theory his long-held beliefs about light, heat, and fire. The concept he used to link these phenomena—the subtle fluid—had become an integral part of physics in the second half of the eighteenth century. Subtle, or "imponderable," fluids possessed and could pass on measurable physical properties, but were themselves invisible, immaterial, and weightless, and they did not cause any changes in mass in the objects they acted on. The effects of subtle fluids were believed to be observable and quantifiable in the workings of electricity, heat, gravity, light, and magnetism.[1]

Franklin had sketched out the basic ideas for this paper in a letter to Benjamin Vaughan of April 29 (above), written just as he and other court-appointed scientists were beginning to investigate the so-called magnetic fluid that Franz Mesmer termed animal magnetism. By June 25, when this piece was finished, he and his fellow commissioners had proved that Mesmer's animal magnetism did not exist.[2] Their conclusions did not negate the concept of subtle fluids, however, and Franklin clearly supposed that his ideas on the subject would be of general interest.

8. Two of these copies were made by BFB. The first (Hist. Soc. of Pa.) was written in a column on the right side of the page. BF made minor corrections to it, added the dateline "Passy June 25. 1784", and labeled it "Loose Thoughts on a universal Fluid &c &c". The second of BFB's copies (APS) incorporated all these changes; it, in turn, was copied by Benjamin Vaughan, who entitled it "Loose Thoughts on a Universal Fluid" (APS). Both copies at the APS are in the Benjamin Vaughan Papers. None of the copies that have been located, in either English or French, include the final sentence or the two wording changes noted below.

9. The copies at the Library of Congress were made by BFB and Poullard, Morellet's secretary. The Institut de France holds the copy made by the abbé de la Roche. None of the French versions have titles.

1. For an overview of BF's ideas on light, fire, and heat see I. Bernard Cohen, *Franklin and Newton* . . . (Philadelphia, 1956), pp. 320–2. For the concept of subtle fluids see Thomas L. Hankins, *Science and the Enlightenment* (Cambridge, 1985), pp. 50–3.

2. See the headnote to Poissonnier to BF, April 26, and Report of the Royal Commission, under Aug. 11.

Franklin had his grandson Benny Bache make copies of this piece in both English and French. One of the English copies was sent to Benjamin Vaughan, who in turn made his own copy.[3]

As for the French translation (the draft of which does not survive), Benny made an initial copy which Franklin corrected, and that text was then copied by Morellet's secretary, Poullard. Poullard's copy was then reviewed by Franklin and Cabanis, who refined the wording. A fair copy of that final French translation was made by the abbé de la Roche. From there, the trail grows cold; if the piece sparked a conversation within the Parisian scientific community, it does not appear to have resulted in a publication.

Before leaving France, Franklin sent this essay to Jan Ingenhousz, who had requested it.[4] Once home, he offered it and other scientific papers to James Bowdoin for the American Academy of Arts and Sciences.[5] Receiving neither an acceptance nor a rejection, in 1788 he sent the papers to the American Philosophical Society. By that time he had made a few changes to his original draft (noted in the text below), including the addition of a final sentence. He also squeezed in the following line at the top of the first page: "For the Consideration of my Dear Friend David Rittenhouse Esqr."[6] The paper was read to the American Philosophical Society on June 20, 1788. When it appeared in the society's next volume of *Transactions* (1793), it bore the title "A new and curious Theory of Light and Heat; in a letter from Dr. B. Franklin to David Rittenhouse, Esq."[7]

3. BF's cover letter has not been found. Vaughan's own copy may have been made for distribution, but it remains among his papers.

4. Ingenhousz requested several papers that he believed had been published, including this one, which he referred to as "General ideas on light heat &c." Ingenhousz to BF, June 11, 1785 (APS); BF to Ingenhousz, July 6, 1785 (Munson-Williams-Proctor Arts Institute).

5. See XXXVIII, 123n.

6. Rittenhouse was vice president of the APS and one of its paper referees: Brooke Hindle, *David Rittenhouse* (Princeton, 1964), pp. 286–7.

7. APS *Trans.*, III (1793), 5–8. By the time the volume was issued, "Loose Thoughts" had already been published as an appendix to William Smith's eulogy of BF, printed in pamphlet form by BFB in 1792: William Smith, *Eulogium on Benjamin Franklin* . . . (Philadelphia, 1792), pp. iii–iv. That 1792 text derived from the copy by BFB now held at the Hist. Soc. of Pa., and consequently did not include BF's final sentence. When WTF published the piece, including the final sentence, he ascribed to it the title "Conjectures on the Nature of Fire": WTF, *Memoirs*, III, 361–3.

[June 25, 1784]

Universal Space, as far as we know of it, seems to be fill'd with a subtil Fluid, whose Motion, or Vibration; is called Light.[8]

This Fluid may possibly be the same with that which being attracted by and entring into other more solid Matter, dilates the Substance, by separating the constituent Particles, and so rendering some Solids fluid, and maintaining the Fluidity of others: of which Fluid when our Bodies are totally depriv'd, they are said to be frozen; when they have a proper Quantity, they are in Health and fit to perform all their Functions; it is then called natural Heat; when too much it is called Fever; and when forc'd into the Body in too great a Quantity from without, it gives Pain by separating and destroying the Flesh & is then called burning,—and the Fluid so entring & acting is called Fire.[9]

While organiz'd Bodies animal or vegetable are augmenting in Growth, or are supplying their continual Waste, is not this done by attracting and consolidating this Fluid, called Fire, so as to form of it a Part of their Substance; and is it not a Separation of the Parts of such Substance which dissolving its solid State, sets that subtil Fluid at Liberty, when it again makes its appearance as Fire.

For the Power of Man relative to Matter, seems limited to the dividing it, or to mixing the various kinds of it, or changing its Form and Appearance by different Compositions of it, but does not extend to the making or creating of new Matter, or annihilating the old: Thus if Fire be an original Element or kind of Matter its Quantity is fix'd and permanent in the Universe.[1] We cannot destroy any Part of it, or make addition to it. We can only separate it from that which confines it & so set it at Liberty, as when we put Wood in a Situation to be burnt; or transfer it from one Solid to another, as when we make Lime by burning Stone, a Part of the Fire dislodg'd from the Wood being left in the Stone.

8. BF first articulated this idea in a 1752 letter to Cadwallader Colden: IV, 299–300.

9. The concepts in the preceding two paragraphs had been offered as BF's "loose Notions relating to Heat and Cold" in a 1757 letter to John Lining: VII, 184–90.

1. BF originally wrote "World", changing it to "Universe" before sending the piece to the APS in 1788.

May not this Fluid when at Liberty be capable of penetrating & entring into all Bodies organiz'd or not: quitting easily in totality those not organiz'd, and quitting easily in part those which are; the part assum'd and fix'd remaining till the Body is dissolv'd.— Is it not this Fluid which keeps asunder the Particles of Air, permitting them to approach or separating them more in Proportion as its Quantity is diminish'd or augmented?

Is it not the greater Gravity of the Particles of Air, which forces the Particles of this Fluid to mount with the Matter to which it is attach'd as Smoke or Vapour?

Does it not seem to have a great Affinity with Water, since it will quit a Solid to unite with that Fluid, & go off with it in Vapour, leaving the Solid cold to the Touch, & the degree measurable by the Thermometer?—

The Vapour rises attach'd to this Fluid but at a certain height they separate, and the Vapour descends in Rain retaining but little of it, in Snow or Hail less. What becomes of that Fluid? Does it rise above our Atmosphere and mix with[2] the universal Mass of the same kind?

Or does a Spherical Stratum of it, denser or less mix'd with Air, attracted by this Globe, & repell'd or push'd up only to a certain height from its Surface by the greater Weight of Air remain there, surrounding the Globe and proceeding with it round the Sun.[3]

In such case, as there may be a Continuity or Communication of this Fluid thro' the Air quite down to the Earth, is it not by the Vibrations given to it by the Sun that Light appears to us; and may it not be, that every one of the infinitely small Vibrations, striking common Matter with a certain Force, enters its Substance, is held there by Attraction, and augmented by succeeding Vibrations, till the Matter has receiv'd as much as their Force can drive into it?—

Is it not thus that the Surface of this Globe is continually heated by such repeated Vibrations in the Day, & cooled by the

2. BF originally wrote "mix equally with". He deleted "equally" before his 1788 submission to the APS.

3. BF first mentioned the possible existence above the atmosphere of a field of "Etherial Fire" (which he at that time still associated with electricity) in the letter to Colden cited above: IV, 298–9.

Escape of the Heat when those Vibrations are discontinu'd in the Night, or intercepted & reflected by Clouds?

Is it not thus that Fire is amass'd in and makes the greatest Part of the Substance of combustible Bodies?

Perhaps when this Globe was first form'd and its original Particles took their Place at certain Distances from the Centre in proportion to their greater or less Gravity the Fluid Fire attracted towards that Center might in great Part be oblig'd as lightest to take place above the rest, and thus form the Sphere of Fire above suppos'd Which would afterwards be continually diminishing by the Substance it afforded to organiz'd Bodies, and the Quantity restor'd to it again by the Burning or other Separating of the Parts of those Bodies?

Is not the natural Heat of Animals thus produc'd, by separating in digestion the Parts of Food, and setting their Fire at Liberty?—

Is it not this Sphere of Fire which kindles the wandring Globes that sometimes pass thro' it in our Course round the Sun, have their Surface kindled by it, and burst when their included Air is greatly rarified by the Heat on their burning Surfaces?—[4]

May it not have been from such Considerations that the antient Philosophers suppos'd a Sphere of Fire to exist above the Air of our Atmosphere?[5]

Franklin's Journal[6]

Incomplete AD supplemented by WTF's edited transcript: Library of Congress.

[June 26–July 27, 1784]

⟨1784

Passy June 26.

Mr. Waltersdorff called on me, and acquainted me with a Duel that had been fought yesterday Morg between a French

---

4. In his meteorological conjectures ([May], above), BF speculated that the burning of meteors in the atmosphere might have been responsible for the dry fog in the summer of 1783.

5. BF added this sentence before submitting the piece to the APS in 1788.

6. What remains of BF's journal for 1784 survives in pieces—five fragments and two leaves with their top and bottom margins trimmed. We

Officer, and a Swedish Gentleman of that Kings Suite, in which the latter was killed on the Spot, and the other dangerously wounded:— That the King does not resent it, as he thinks his Subject was in the Wrong.[7]

---

have determined that it was cut apart by WTF when he was preparing his 1817 edition of BF's papers: the transcript he made for the printer contains blank areas into which the slices, squares, and sheets of BF's journal pages fit perfectly. Catchwords and tiny numbers, added by WTF to both his own folio sheets and the pieces of BF's original, further confirm that all these elements at one time formed a single manuscript.

BF wrote on both sides of his sheets, and both sides of the surviving fragments bear the scars of WTF's intervention: entire sections were crossed out; individual sentences and phrases were lined through; words were changed; spelling and punctuation were altered; names and phrases were added. From this we deduce that WTF marked up the entire journal before beginning to transcribe the portions he had selected—perhaps half of what was originally there. Evidently tired of copying after having filled three folio pages, he began cutting out pieces of BF's original and tacking them onto his folio sheets, continuing the work of hand copying only when necessary—for example, when an entry he wished to publish appeared on the verso of a piece he had already placed on his sheet. For his final three pages, WTF relied entirely on sections of BF's original. Having assembled this collage, he edited it further, making changes to his own transcription as well as the original. This was the MS that WTF submitted for publication and which, with minor alterations presumably made by the printer, appeared in WTF, *Memoirs*, I, 361–8.

We publish here a text that is, by necessity, a hybrid. It includes as much of BF's original as can be retrieved from both sides of the surviving pieces, ignoring all marks made by WTF. In cases where WTF trimmed the left margin of a fragment, the corresponding right margin of its verso is also gone, and with it the last letters of many lines. In such instances, we either rely on his edited transcript for the missing letters or, when none exists, supply our best guesses in square brackets. Where nothing of BF's original journal survives, we must depend entirely on WTF's transcript, and we caution readers not to consider it either complete or totally faithful to the original.

To distinguish as clearly as possible between BF's words and WTF's edited version, we enclose in angle brackets all text supplied from WTF. This includes the whole first section and scattered text thereafter.

When introducing BF's "Private Journal" in *Memoirs*, WTF wrote that he was presenting extracts from a journal "kept about this time" that "may not be found void of interest" (p. 361). Indeed, the entire journal would not have been "void of interest," and it is a shame that after *Memoirs* was published, nearly all the sheets of this and BF's other journals vanished.

7. The French officer, whom WTF identified in a footnote, was the comte de

Published July 13, 1787, by W. Bent, London.

Gustavus III, King of Sweden

He asked me if I had seen the King of Sweeden?— I had not yet had that Honor.— He said his Behavior here was not liked: that he took little Notice of his own Ambassador,[8] who being acquainted with the Usages of this Court, was capable of advising him, but was not consulted. That he was always talking of himself, and vainly boasting of his Revolution, tho' it was known to have been the Work of M. De Vergennes.—[9] That they began to be tired of him here, and wish'd him gone: but he propos'd staying 'till the 12th. July.— That he had now laid aside his Project of invading Norway, as he found Denmark had made Preparations to receive him.[1] That he pretended

---

La Marck, proprietor of the La Marck infantry regiment in French service. His victim was Carl Adrian Peyron, a former captain of the regiment who at the time of his death was serving as Gustavus' page. Peyron is said to have provoked the quarrel and inflicted the first wound. For La Marck's career see Académie royale des sciences, des lettres et des beaux-arts de Belgique, *Biographie nationale* (44 vols., Brussels, 1866–1986), I, 432–5; see also Gunnar von Proschwitz, ed., *Gustave III par ses lettres* (Stockholm and Paris, 1986), pp. 214n, 259, 271; Marc-Marie, marquis de Bombelles, *Journal*, ed. Jean Grassion et al. (8 vols., Geneva, 1977–2013), I, 334–5.

8. Baron Staël von Holstein: XLI, 516n.

9. France had been involved in Swedish domestic politics for decades to prevent the country from falling under Russian control. In 1771 Vergennes was appointed ambassador to Sweden in order to provide advice and money to Gustavus III, the new king. In August, 1772, Vergennes secured financing for Gustavus' coup d'état, which reestablished the power of the Swedish monarchy. He received much credit in Paris for the coup's success: Orville T. Murphy, *Charles Gravier, Comte de Vergennes: French Diplomacy in the Age of Revolution: 1719–1787* (Albany, 1982), pp. 176–201.

1. Motivated in part by his hostility toward Denmark (which was reciprocated by Danes like Walterstorff), Gustavus had long harbored plans to occupy Norway, which was under Danish rule. In the spring of 1783, with Russia distracted by the Crimean crisis (XLI, 245n) and Britain weakened by political divisions, Denmark appeared temporarily unprotected, and Gustavus hoped to attack as early as the following summer. However, a Russo-Turkish war failed to materialize in 1783. In early 1784 a new Danish government mobilized its army for defense, and Russia affirmed its alliance with Denmark. Gustavus abandoned his plan while visiting Paris, as Vergennes was no longer willing to supply Sweden with the customary financial support: Stewart Oakley, "Gustavus III's Plans for War with Denmark in 1783–84," in *Studies in Diplomatic History: Essays in Memory of David Bayne Horn*, ed. Ragnhild Hatton and M. S. Anderson (London, 1970), pp. 268–86.

the Danes, had designed to invade Sweden, tho' it was a known Fact, that the Danes had made no Military Preparations, even for Defence, 'till Six Months after his began. I asked if it was clear that he had had an Intention to invade Norway? He said that the marching & disposition of his Troops and the Fortifications he had erected, indicated it very plainly. He added that Sweden was at present greatly distress'd for Provisions, that many People had died of Hunger!— That it was reported the King came here to borrow Money, and to offer to sell Gottenburgh to France; a Thing not very probable.[2]

M. Dussaulx[3] call'd, and said, it is reported there is an Alliance treating between the Emperor of Austria, Russia, & England; the Purpose not known; and that a Counter-Alliance is propopos'd between France, Prussia and Holland, in which it is suppos'd Spain will join. He added that Changes in the Ministry are talked of; that there are Cabals against M. De Vergennes, that M. De Calonne is to be *Garde des Sceaux*, with some other Rumours fabricated perhaps at the *Palais Royal*.

June 29. Mr. Hammond, Secy to Mr. Hartley, called to tell me that Mr. Hartley had not received any Orders by the last Courier, either to stay or return, which he had expected; and that he thought it occasioned by their Uncertainty what Terms of Commerce to propose, 'till the Report of the Committee of Council was laid before Parliment, and its Opinion known; and that he looked on the Delay of writing to him as a sign of their intending to do something.

He told me it was reported that the King of Sweden had granted the free Use of Gottenburg as a Port for France, which allarmed the neighbouring Powers. That in time of War, the Northern Coast of England might be much endanger'd by it.

---

2. The rumors in this entry and the following one regarding Franco-Swedish relations refer to two separate agreements. In a convention signed on July 1, France ceded the island of St.-Barthélemy to Sweden and, in return, secured commercial privileges in the port of Göteborg. On July 19 Gustavus and Louis XVI signed a secret treaty, in which France guaranteed additional subsidies to Sweden as well as military assistance in case of attack: Auguste Geoffroy, *Gustave III et la cour de France* ... (2 vols., Paris, 1867), II, 40–6.

3. Doubtless Jean-Joseph Dusaulx (XXIX, 123n).

June 30th. M. Dupont, Inspector of Commerce, came to talk with me about the free Port of L'Orient, and some Difficulties respecting it,[4] I referr'd him to Mr. Barclay, an American Agent,[5] and as he said he did not well understand English when spoken, and Mr. Barclay did not speak French, I offer'd my Grandson to accompany him as Interpreter, which he accepted.

I asked him whether the Spaniards from the Continent of America, did not trade to the french Sugar Islands? He said not. The only Commerce with the Spaniards was for Cattle between them and the French at St. Domingo. I had been told the Spaniards brought Flour to the French Islands from the Continent. He had not heard of it. If we can find that such a Trade is allow'd (perhaps from the Missisipi) have we not a Claim by Treaty to the same Privilege?[6]

4. The May 14 *arrêt du conseil* that established Lorient as a free port (XXXIX, 106) declared that the franchise, to take effect on July 1, would include both the walled port and the city itself, as was the case in Dunkirk and Marseille. In response to the vigorous protests of local officials, and over the objections of American merchants and Lafayette (who reported to Calonne that BF was very interested in the issue), on June 26 the court issued new regulations confining the franchise to within the walls of the port. The June 26 *arrêt* did state, however, that the king might expand the franchise to include lands adjacent to the port if the need arose: *Arrêt du conseil d'état du roi. Portant règlement pour la franchise du port de l'Orient. Du 26 juin 1784* (Paris, 1784). For the controversy see Gérard Le Bouëdec, "L'inquiétude et l'espoir (1769–1789)," in *Histoire de Lorient*, ed. Claude Nières (Toulouse, 1988), pp. 137–43; and for the Americans' position see the Aug. 9 letter from Cain *et al.*, below.

5. "An American Agent" is an example of a phrase that we believe was added by WTF, who then corrected "Agent" to "Merchant & Comr: for Accts." BF, writing for himself, would not have needed to identify Barclay.

6. Shortly before Lafayette left Paris in mid-June, he had asked Castries about trade regulations between the United States and the French West Indies. The *maréchal* answered on June 17 that the regulations would not be settled before Lafayette's departure, but promised to discuss the flour and sugar trade with BF and Barclay. He anticipated, at the least, that there would be one free port in each colony available to the Americans: Idzerda, *Lafayette Papers*, v, 226. An *arrêt* of Aug. 30 established seven free ports for foreign vessels: three in St.-Domingue and one in St. Lucia, Martinique, Guadeloupe, and Tobago. Foreign ships would be allowed to bring in wood, coal, livestock, salt beef and fish (but not pork), rice, corn, beans, hides, furs, resin, and tar, and carry away molasses, rum, and goods manufactured in France: François-André Isambert, ed., *Recueil général des*

July 1st. The Nuncio called and acquainted me that the Pope had, on my Recommendation, appointed Mr. John Carrol, Superior of the Catholic Clergy in America, with many of the Powers of a Bishop; and that probably he would be made a Bishop *in partibus*[7] before the End of the Year.[8] He asked me which would be most convenient for him to come to France, or go to St. Domingo for Ordination by another Bishop, which was necessary.— I mentioned Quebec as more convenient than either. He asked whether, as that was an English Province, our Government might not take Offence at his going there? I thought not unless the Ordination by that Bishop, should give him some Authority over our Bishop: He said not in the least: that when a Bishop was once ordained, he would be independent of the others, and even of the Pope, which I did not clearly

---

anciennes lois françaises . . . (29 vols., Paris, 1821–33), XXVII, 459–64; Jean Tarrade, *Le Commerce colonial de la France à la fin de l'Ancien Régime* . . . (2 vols., Paris, 1972), II, 531–47; Frederick L. Nussbaum, "The French Colonial Arrêt of 1784," *South Atlantic Quarterly,* XXVII (1928), 62–78; *Morris Papers,* VIII, 685–8.

7. Short for *in partibus infidelium,* "in the lands of unbelievers," a term applied to a nonresident or titular bishop appointed to a see in a predominantly non-Catholic country: *Catholic Encyclopedia* (16 vols., New York, 1907–14), VIII, 25.

8. For background on BF's having been consulted by the papal nuncio, Doria Pamphili, on how to minister to American Catholics after independence, see XL, 410–12, 516–18; XLI, 294, 364–5. On May 3, 1784, having learned from La Luzerne that the Catholics in America would not accept a foreign bishop (XLI, 364–5n), Vergennes conveyed this information to Pamphili, who on May 17 wrote to Cardinal Antonelli in Rome. In that letter, Pamphili reported on a visit he paid to BF *c.* May 11, during which BF warmly recommended Carroll as vicar apostolic for the United States. Pius VI made the appointment on June 6, and three days later Antonelli sent the news to Pamphili and Carroll, citing BF's recommendation as a significant factor in the decision: Jules A. Baisnée, *France and the Establishment of the American Catholic Hierarchy: the Myth of French Interference (1783–1784)* (Baltimore, 1934), pp. 79, 84–7, 97, 114–18; Carl R. Fish, ed., "Documents relative to the Adjustment of the Roman Catholic Organization in the United States to the Conditions of National Independence, 1783–1789," *American Hist. Rev.,* XV (1909–10), 811–12, 814–15, 817–19. Carroll served as superior of the Catholic mission in the United States until the American clergy elected him bishop in 1789. He was ordained in England the following year: *ANB.*

understand.[9] He said the Congregation *de Propaganda Fidei* had agreed to receive & maintain and instruct two young Americans in the Languages and Sciences at Rome: He had formerly told me that more would be educated *gratis* in France.[1] He tells me they write from America that there are 20 Priests, but they are not sufficient; some new Settlements going on near the Missisipi having need of some.

The Nuncio said we should find that the Catholics were not so intollerant, as they had been represented; that the Inquisition in Rome had not now so much Power as that in Spain; and that in Spain it was used chiefly as a Prison of State for the Use of Government. That the Congregation would have undertaken the Education of more American Youths, and may hereafter, but that at present they are overburthen'd, having some from all Parts of the World: Spoke lightly of their new Convert, *Thayers* (of Boston)[2] Conversion: That he had advised him not to go to America, but settle in France. That he wanted to go to convert his Countrymen; but he knew nothing yet of his new Religion himself. &ca.

Recd. a Letter from Mr. Bridgen of London, dated the 22 past, acquainting me that the Council of the Royal Society had voted me a Gold Medal, on Acct of my Letter in favor of Capt.

9. Doubtless Pamphili meant that as bishop Carroll would be subject only to the spiritual authority of the pope. Carroll himself emphasized that Americans would accept only a regularly elected bishop, not one *in partibus* or appointed as vicar apostolic: Baisnée, *France and the Establishment of the American Catholic Hierarchy,* pp. 65–6, 103.

1. Pamphili had proposed to Vergennes and the bishop of Autun that France train American missionaries: XLI, 294–5n. On May 3 the three men agreed that the French crown would pay for the education of eight to ten American seminarians at Bordeaux and that the Holy See would enroll two or three more at the college of the Propaganda in Rome. Pamphili informed BF of this arrangement at their meeting in mid-May, and reported to Antonelli on BF's expressions of gratitude. He later reported to Antonelli on his July 1 meeting at Passy: he had refrained from asking BF about the cost of living for a vicar apostolic in America in order to avoid the impression that "financial considerations entered into the business," but he did inquire about the cost of bringing American students to France: Baisnée, *France and the Establishment of the American Catholic Hierarchy,* pp. 84–7, 122–3; Fish, "Documents," pp. 814–15, 821–2.

2. John Thayer (XXXV, 127n).

Cook.— Lord Howe had sent me his Journal 3. Vols. 4to with a large Volume of Engravings on the same Acct. and as he writes, *"with the Kings Approbation."*[3]

July 3. Mr. Smeathman comes & brings two English or Scotch Gentlemen: one a Chevalier of some Order, the other a Physician who had lived long in Russia.[4] Much Conversation. Putrid Fevers common in Russia, and in Winter much more than in Summer: therefore suppos'd to be owing to their Hot Rooms. In⟩ a Gentleman's House there are sometimes 100 Domestics; these have not Beds, but sleep 20 or 30 in a close Room warm'd by a Stove, lying on the Floor & on Benches. The Stoves are heated by Wood. As soon as it is burnt to Coals, the Chimney is stopt, to prevent the Escape of hot [Air?]—& Entry of cold Air.— So they breathe the same Air over & over again all night.— These Fevers he cur'd by wrapping the Patients in Linnen wet with Vinegar, and making them breathe the Vapour of Vinegar thrown on hot Bricks.— The Russians have the Art of distilling Spirits from Milk.— To prepare it for Distillation it must, when beginning to sour, be kept in continual Motion or Agitation for 12 Hours. It then becomes an uniform vinous Liquor, the Cream, Curd and aqueous Part or Whey, all intimately mixt. Excellent in this State for restoring emaciated Bodies.— This Operation on Milk discover'd long since by the Tartars, who in their rambling Life often carry Milk in Leather

3. Lord Howe's letter is published above under the date of [June 1].

4. Undoubtedly Dr. John Grieve, a Scot, who in 1783 returned to Edinburgh from Russia, where he had served for five years as a military doctor. He visited Paris in mid-1784, with letters of introduction from Joseph Black, and reported to Black on French scientific discoveries, including flying machines, Lavoisier's experiments, Argand's lamp, and animal magnetism. On May 11, having visited Mesmer's clinic, he wrote that there were "seldom fewer than two hundred people in it at one time . . . from morning to night," each of whom paid "five guineas the first month and four every subsequent one." He had asked Le Roy for his opinion of Mesmer, but Le Roy, who he knew was on the commission to investigate mesmerism, gave a noncommital answer: Anthony Cross, *By the Banks of the Neva: Chapters from the Lives and Careers of the British in Eighteenth-Century Russia* (Cambridge, 1997), p. 153; John H. Appleby, "John Grieve's Correspondence with Joseph Black and Some Contemporaneous Russo-Scottish Medical Intercommunication," *Medical History*, XXIX (1985), 403–7.

Bags on their Horses, and the Motion produc'd the Effect. It may be try'd with us by attaching a large Cag of Milk to some part of one of our Mills.—⁵

[July 4] [*one to three lines missing*] of seeing me.— M. Bougon in the Evening another.— Wrote [again?] [*several words missing*].

July 5.— Madame la Duchesse d'Enville did me the honour of a Visit, bringing a [Gen]tleman with her. Some Republican Conversation. Much pleas'd with the Americans for their Disapprobation of the Cincinati Project, which she thinks must have been that of some Frenchman. Thinks we should never admit of Noblesse.

July 6. Directed WTF. who goes to Court, to mention 3 Things at the Request of M. Barclay. The Main Levé of the arrested Goods.⁶ The Port of L'Orient, & the Consular Convention⁷ which he did. The Port is fix'd & the Convention preparing. Sent to Mr Barclay the Letter of Ms. de Castries on Capt. Jones's Affair, & the Minutes of Congress relative to the Division of Prize Money, and desir'd his Opinion.—⁸ Hear that Gottenburgh is to be a Free Port for France where they may assemble Northern Stores, &c. Receiv'd a Letter from M. de Vernet, the Painter, by two Young Persons, who propose to m[arry and go?] to America, if I would assure him of some Place there. Discourag'd them.⁹

Mr Hammond came and din'd with me. He acquaints m⟨e from Mr.⟩ Hartley, that no Instructions are yet come from England. Mr Hartley [*word or words missing*] lame.—

5. Grieve had written a paper on fermented milk, or kumis, which Black read at the July 12, 1784, meeting of the Royal Society of Edinburgh: "An Account of the Method of making a Wine, called by the Tartars Koumiss, with Observations on its Use in Medicine," Royal Soc. of Edinburgh *Trans.*, 1 (1788), 178–90.

6. This concerned Puchelberg's attachment of arms in the American arsenal at Nantes. At Barclay's request, BF wrote to Vergennes about this issue on Jan. 31 (XLI, 437–42). Barclay was to deliver the letter, but did not do so until mid-May. Vergennes answered it on July 31 (below).

7. BF had pressed Vergennes to conclude the convention in a letter of May 31, above.

8. The draft of BF's letter is below, July 6.

9. Vernet's letter is below, July 6.

July 7. A very hot Day. Receiv'd a Visit from the Secretary ⟨of the⟩ King of Sueden M. Frank accompanied by the Secretary of the ⟨Embassy.⟩¹

July 8. Went to Mr Grand's to talk with him concerning the C[onsul of?] Barbary he had mention'd to me; & show'd his former L[etter?].² He told me the Gentn. was to call upon him about Noon [*word or words missing*] to come with him to me. He knows nothing of the Ge[ntleman's] Character. I told him what had been written to me fo[rmerly?] about him by M. Reyneval—³

The King of Sweden's Secretary, dines with me, ⟨in⟩ Company with Mad. Helvetius, Abbé de la Roche, M⟨. Caba⟩nis, and an American Captain Le Roy of Lorrain.⁴ ⟨The King of Sweden⟩ does not go to England.— The Consul did not come.

July 9 Receiv'd Mr Barclay's Opinion relative to Capt. J[ones] [*one to three lines missing*]

⟨July⟩ 10. Mr Grand came to propose my dining with the Suedish Court at his House which is next door, and I consented. While he was with me the Consul came. We talk'd about the Barbary Powers; they are four, Morocco, Algiers, Tunis & Tripoli. He inform'd me that Salee, the principal Port belonging to the Emperor of Morocco, had formerly been famous for Corsairs. That this Prince had discourag'd them, & in 1768 publish'd an

---

1. Ulric Gustaf Franc (1736–1811), first secretary of the Swedish chancellery, and Nils von Rosenstein (1752–1824), secretary of the embassy since 1782: Proschwitz, *Gustave III*, pp. 186n, 277–8n.

2. Audibert Caille wrote to BF on July 6 (below). BF may also have shown Grand the consul's April 14, 1778, letter to the American commissioners: XXVI, 285–6.

3. Rayneval's letter has not been located.

4. Nicolas-Georges Le Roy *dit* Lefranc, born in Lorraine, served in the Pa. line from 1779 to 1784, and Congress promoted him to the rank of captain. He returned to France in June, 1784, and on July 5 transferred his membership in the Society of the Cincinnati from the Pa. chapter to the French society: Bodinier, *Dictionnaire;* W. W. Abbot *et al.*, eds., *The Papers of George Washington*, Confederation Series (6 vols., Charlottesville and London, 1992–97), I, 150, 172–3; *JCC*, XXVI, 66, 68–9; Ludovic de Contenson, *La Société des Cincinnati de France et la guerre d'Amérique, 1778–1783* (Paris, 1934), p. 215.

Edict declaring himself in Peace with all the World, and forbid their cruising any more[5] appointing him Consul for those Christian States who had none in his Country— That Denmark pays him 25,000 *Piastres fortes* yearly in Money; Sweden is engag'd to send an Ambassador every two Years with Presents: And the other Powers buy their Peace in the same Manner except Spain and the Italian States with whom they have constant War.— That he is Consul for Sardinia & Prussia, for whom he procur'd Treaties of Peace. That he propos'd a Peace for Russia; but that the Emperor having heard that Russia was going to War with his Brother the Grand Seignior he refused it. Mr. Audibert Caille (the Consul) thinks it shameful for Christendom to pay Tribute to such Canaille, and proposes two Ways of reducing the Barbarians to Peace with all Europe, & obliging them to quit their piratical Practices. They have need of many Articles from Europe, and of a Vent for their superfluous Commodities. If therefore all Europe would agree to refuse any Commerce with them but on condition of their quitting Piracy, and such an Agreement could be faithfully observ'd on our Part it would have its Effect upon them. But if any one Power would continue the Trade with them, it would defeat the whole. There was another Method he had projected, & communicated in a Memorial to the Court here by Mr Rayneval, which was, that France should undertake to suppress their Piracies and give Peace to all Europe, by means of its Influence with the Porte.[6] For all the People of these States being oblig'd by their Religion to go at times in Caravans to Mecca, and to pass thro' the Grand Seignior's Dominions, who gives them Escorts of Troops thro' the Desert, to prevent their being plundered & perhaps massacred by the Arabs, he could refuse them Passage & Protection but on Condition of their living Peaceably with the Europeans, &c.—

5. Between 1760 and 1783 Sultan Sidi Muhammad ibn Abdallah signed treaties of amity and commerce with 13 European states. In July, 1784, five of his frigates were ordered to prepare for a cruise; in September they were dispatched to the Bay of Biscay, and within a month captured an American vessel: Roberts and Roberts, *Thomas Barclay*, pp. 198–201.

6. The Ottoman Empire.

He spoke of Montgomery's Transaction, and of Crocco, whom he understands was authoriz'd by the Court.[7] The Barbarians he observ'd having no Commercial Ships at Sea had vastly the Advantage of the Europeans; for one could not make Reprisals on their Trade. And it has long been my Opinion, that if the European Nations who are powerful at Sea, were to make War upon us; it would be better for us to renounce Commerce in our own Bottoms, & convert them all into Cruisers.— Other Nations would furnish us with what we wanted, and take off our Produce.— He promis'd me a Note of the Commerce of Barbary. & we are to see each other again, as he is to stay here a Month—

Din'd at Mr Grand's with the Swedish Gentlemen. They were Mr Rosenstein Secretary of the Ambassy, and [blank] with whom I had a good deal of Conversation relating to the Commerce possible between our two Countries. I found they had seen the Pretender at Rome: They spoke of his Situation as very hard; that France who had formerly allow'd him a Pension, had withdrawn it, and that he sometimes wanted Bread. The King talks of going on Thursday.—[8]

Sunday, July 11. Mr Walterstorff call'd to enquire if we had receiv'd any News yet from America relating to our Treaty. Finding I had none, which he thought strange, he acquainted me that he would take a Trip to Holland on some private Affairs, and return by Spa, where he might stay a few Days: And he wish'd me to write for him at Spa that I had receiv'd Advices from America; that I need not write more, in case I receiv'd any; and he would return from thence immediately. He hears that the Agreement with Sueden respecting the Port of Gottenburg is

7. For Robert Montgomery's overture to Morocco, and the sultan's response, via Crocco to BF, inviting the Americans to send an envoy, see XL, 310–12; XLI, 223, 292.

8. The unnamed guest mentioned above may have been the king himself. Gustavus had visited Charles Edward Stuart, the exiled pretender to the British throne, in Florence. Finding him gravely ill, the king promised to intercede with the French government for Stuart's financial support. He did so, and Vergennes eventually granted a pension of 60,000 *l.t.* per year: Frank McLynn, *Charles Edward Stuart: a Tragedy in Many Acts* (London and New York, 1988), pp. 530–6, 543.

not likely to be concluded. That Su⟨eden⟩ wanted an Island in the West Indies, in exchange. I think ⟨She⟩ is better without it. M. de Cornick who had been kind to our People at Morlaix, came with Mr de Chaumont,[9] to see from my Windows the great Ballon of Abbé Miolan. It was unskilfully manag'd, The disappointed [*five to six lines missing*] and gave it him to carry.[1] —13. Messrs Mirabeau & Champfort[2] came and read their Translation of Mr Burke's Pamphlet against the Cincinnati which they have much enlarg'd, intending it as a Cover'd Satyr against Noblesse in general. It is well done. There are also Remarks on the last Letter of Gen Washington on that Subject.—[3]

---

9. Mathurin Cornic *fils* and his widowed mother, principals in a Morlaix firm that had been established by Cornic *père*, were Chaumont's agents in Morlaix, and in early 1777 Chaumont recommended them to the American commissioners. The Cornics assisted the commissioners and American privateersmen until at least 1779, when their extant correspondence with BF ends. See XXIV, 4, 521; and for Cornic *fils* see Olivier Levasseur, *Charles Cornic (1731–1809): un mythe corsaire* (Rennes, 2003), pp. 8–15.

1. Miollan, a professor of physics, and his assistants had constructed a huge hot air balloon capable of lifting enormous weight and being steered by jets of hot air. After successful trials in June, Miollan scheduled a public demonstration for July 11, at noon, in the Jardin du Luxembourg. The day proved exceptionally hot and humid, and the balloon did not inflate. The crowd of paying spectators eventually stormed the machinery and ripped the balloon to shreds: Gillispie, *Montgolfier Brothers*, pp. 97–8. One of Miollan's collaborators was Henry Smeathman, whose detailed description of the experiment was published in the *Morning Chron. and London Advertiser*, Aug. 9, 1784.

2. The comte de Mirabeau was the estranged son of BF's friend the marquis; see XXIV, 335n. Sébastien-Roch Nicolas, *dit* Chamfort (*DBF*), was made a member of the Loge des Neuf Sœurs in 1778 and became a fixture at the salon of Mme Helvétius; BF must therefore have been acquainted with him. Chamfort was inducted into the Académie française in 1781, and BF owned a copy of his discourse on that occasion: XXXI, 323; XXXVI, 342; Amiable, *Une Loge Maçonnique*, pp. 311–12.

3. Mirabeau and Chamfort had in fact translated only portions of Aedanus Burke's *Considerations on the Society or Order of Cincinnati* (XLI, 502n), seamlessly inserting their own arguments denouncing hereditary nobility. In so doing, they retained Burke's conceit of using pronouncements by the Society to expose its true nature. They appended to their text the revised charter abolishing hereditary membership that the Cincinnati adopted in May, 1784, and GW's May 15 circular letter to the state societies, explaining

They say Gen. W. miss'd a beau Moment when he accepted that Order.— The same of the M. de F.—[4]
It is said that M. d'Aguesseau being dead, there is much Movement at Court respecting his Places—[5]

14.— Mr Hammond calls to acquaint me that Mr Hartley is still without any Instructions relating to the Treaty of Commerce; and supposes it occasion'd by their Attention to the India Bill.—[6] I said to him, Your Court & this seem to be waiting for one another with respect to the American Trade with your Islands. You are both afraid of doing too much for us, and yet each wishes to do a little more than the other. You had better have accepted our generous Proposal at first, to put us both on the same Footing of free Intercourse that existed before

---

the reform, which they subjected to extensive marginal commentary. (The revised charter reached France by at least June 25: *Adams Papers*, XVI, 250. L'Air de Lamotte's copies of it and GW's circular letter are among BF's papers at the APS.)

The MS that Mirabeau and Chamfort read to BF on July 13 has not been located. When published at the end of the year in London as *Considérations sur l'ordre de Cincinnatus, ou imitation d'un pamphlet anglo-américain*, the text incorporated sections of BF's private critique of the same subjects, which he had written in the guise of a Jan. 26, 1784, letter to SB; see XLI, 503–11, and the exchange between BF and Morellet, March 16 (above), in which BF promised not to publish it. Though he kept his word to Morellet, BF evidently welcomed the chance to see some of his arguments put to use. Mirabeau and Chamfort paraphrased without attribution BF's observations on ascending honor among the Chinese and on the impact on the state of ascending and descending honor. They also reproduced BF's mathematical tabulation of a knight's descendants: *Considérations sur l'ordre de Cincinnatus*, pp. 72–7. Whether BF gave them the text of his satire before or after July 13 cannot be established. Rumors linking him to an anti-Cincinnati pamphlet, however, began to circulate after that date. One, reported on July 29, was that Mirabeau was writing it at BF's request. Another, published a month later, was that BF had hosted a reading of it: Bachaumont, *Mémoires secrets*, XXVI, 123; *Gaz. de Leyde*, Aug. 27, 1784 (sup.).

4. Lafayette.

5. Aguesseau de Fresnes, the senior member of the Council of Commerce (XXXV, 373n), died on July 8: Michel Antoine, *Le Gouvernement de l'administration sous Louis XV* (2nd. ed., Paris, 2004), pp. 37–8.

6. In early July, Pitt introduced a bill to reform the East India Company. It became law on Aug. 13: John Ehrman, *The Younger Pitt* (3 vols., New York and Stanford, Calif., 1969–96), I, 188–92.

the War. You will make some narrow ⟨Regulations, and then France will go beyond you in Generosity. You never see your Follies 'till too late to mend them.— He said, Lord Sheffield was continually exasperating the house against America. He had lately been publishing an Account of Loyalists murder'd there, &ca— Probably invented.—⟩

Thursday, July 15. The Duke de Chartres's Ballon went off this Morning from St. Cloud, himself & three others in the Gallery. It was foggy, & they were soon out of sight.— But the Machine being disorder'd, so that the Trap or Valve could not be opened to let out the expanding Air, & fearing that the Balloon would burst, they cut a Hole in it which ripp'd larger, and they fell rapidly, but receiv'd no Harm. They had been a vast height, met with a Cloud of Snow, & a Tornado which frighten'd them.[7] Mr Arbuthnot dines with me.[8]

Friday, 16. Receiv'd a Letter from 2 young Gentleman in London who are come from America for Orders,[9] and complain that they have been delay'd there a Year, and that the Archbishop[1]

---

7. This hydrogen balloon was a significant advance, owing to calculations made independently by the Robert brothers, whom the duc de Chartres was sponsoring, and Meusnier (XXXIV, 239), a young engineer who had participated in Charles's hydrogen balloon experiment on Aug. 27, 1783, and was currently on a commission of the Académie des sciences to solve the problems of flight. The innovation was a method of adjusting and stabilizing altitude by means of an air bladder placed inside the balloon, which could be deflated and reinflated by a hand-driven bellows. The hydrogen vent in the main balloon would still need to be employed for the final descent. The balloon was wider than it was tall; it carried an elongated gondola with a large rudder and paddles. On the flight witnessed by BF on July 15 were the duc de Chartres, the Robert brothers, and a fourth passenger who may have been their brother-in-law. It nearly ended in disaster when the cords suspending the internal bladder snapped shortly after takeoff, and the dislodged bladder blocked the hydrogen vent. The ascent was alarmingly rapid, and, fearing an explosion, the duke punctured the balloon with a flagstaff: Gillispie, *Montgolfier Brothers*, pp. 98–103, and the illustration on p. [104]; Académie des sciences, *Procès-verbaux*, CII (1783), 222; CIII (1784), 42, 148; *Jour. de physique*, XXV (1784), 39–69.

8. He had been recommended to BF by Benjamin Vaughan: BF to Vaughan, July 26, below.

9. Mason Locke Weems and Edward Gantt, Jr. Their letter of July 9 is below.

1. John Moore, archbishop of Canterbury: XXXVI, 670n.

will not permit them to be ordain'd unless they will take the Oath of Allegiance & desiring to know if they may be ordain'd here. Enquir'd and learnt that if ordain'd here they must vow Obedience to the Archbishop of Paris.—[2] Directed my Grand-Son to ask the Nuncio if their Bishop in America[3] might not be instructed to do it liberally.

Saturday. 17. The Nuncio says the Thing is impossible unless the Gentlemen become Roman Catholicks.— Wrote them an Answer.—[4]

Sunday 18. A good Abbé brings me a large Manuscript contain[ing] a Scheme of Reformation of all Churches & States, Religion, Commerce, Laws, &c. which he has plann'd in his Closet, without much Knowledge of the World. I have promis'd to look it over, and he is to call next Thursday— It is amazing the Number of Legislators that kindly bring me new Plans for governing the United States.—

Monday July 19. The Americans at Dinner with Mr White and Mr Arbuthnot from England.— The latter was an Officer at Gibraltar during the late Siege. He says the Spaniards might have taken it.— And that it is now a Place of no Value to England. That its suppos'd Use as a Port for a Fleet to prevent the Junction of the Brest & Toulon Squadrons is chimerical. That while the Spaniards are in Possession of Algazires [Algeciras], they can with their Gun-Boats, in the use of which they are grown very expert, make it impossible for any Fleet to lie there.— Hear that a Packet is arriv'd, and hope for Letters.—

Tuesday 20.— My Grandson goes to Court. No News there, except that the Spanish Fleet against Algiers is sailed.[5] Receive only one American Letter by the Packet, which is from

2. Antoine-Eléonor-Léon Le Clerc de Juigné de Neuchelles: xxvi, 493n; *Almanach royal* for 1784, p. 58.

3. *I.e.*, John Carroll.

4. Below, July 18.

5. The armament, consisting of 130 vessels under the command of Lt. Gen. of the Fleet Antonio Barceló, sailed from Cartagena at the beginning of July and bombarded Algiers from July 12 to 21: *Gaz. de Leyde*, July 30, Aug. 6, Aug. 20, and Aug. 27, 1784. For the rekindling of the Spanish conflict with Algiers see John B. Wolf, *The Barbary Coast: Algiers under the Turks* (New York, 1979), pp. 304–5.

the College of Rhodeisland, desiring me to solicit Benefactions of the King,[6] which I cannot do for reasons which I shall give them.— It is inconceivable why I have no Letters from Congress. The Treaties with Denmark, Portugal, &c all neglected!— Mr Hartley makes the same Complaint. He is still without Orders. Mr Hammond call'd and din'd with me; says Mr Pitt begins to lose his Popularity: His new Taxes & Project about the *Navy Bills*[7] give great Discontent. He has been burnt in Effigy at York. His East-India Bill not likely to go down; and it is thought he cannot stand long. Mr Hammond is a Friend of Mr Fox;—whose Friends that have lost their Places, are called *Fox's Martyrs.*

Wednesday July 21. Count de Haga,[8] sends his Card to take Leave.— Mr Grand tells me he has bought here my Bust with that of Mr D'Alembert or Diderot to take with him to Sueden. He set out last Night.—

Thursday 22.— Comtesse de Forbach & Mad. Helvetius & Comtesse d'Andelot [d'Andlau] dine with me & M. Keralio.

Lord Fitzmaurice,[9] Son of Lord Shelburne arrives, brought me Sundry Letters & Papers—

He thinks Mr Pitt in danger of losing his Majority in the House of Commons, tho' great at present; for he will not have wherewithal to pay them.— I said that Governing by a Parliament which must be bribed, was employing a very expensive Machine and that the People of England would in time find out, tho' they had not yet, that since the Parliament must always do the Will of the Minister, and be paid for doing it, and the People must find the Money to pay them, it would be the same thing in Effect, but much cheaper, to be govern'd by the Minister at first hand, without a Parliament. Those present seem'd to think

6. The Jan. 9 letter is in XLI, 431–2.

7. Pitt's first budget as prime minister, introduced in late June, raised new taxes to reduce the public debt, but his plan to fund short-term navy bills and ordnance debentures by converting them into government stock did not succeed: Ehrman, *Younger Pitt*, I, 247–8, 250–2, 258–60.

8. The alias of the king of Sweden (whom WTF identified in a footnote).

9. John Henry Petty, Viscount Fitzmaurice, and later the 2nd Marquess of Lansdowne (1765–1809): Lewis, *Walpole Correspondence*, XXXIX, 509n; *Burke's Peerage*, p. 1486.

the Reasoning clear.— Lord Fitz M. appears a sensible amiable young Man.—

Friday 23.

Saturday 24. Breakfast with Mad. B.[1]

Sunday 25. Dine with Mad. Roger at Mad. Saurin's.—[2]

Monday 26. Mr Walterstorff being return'd call'd to see me. He is impatient that we have yet no News from Congress respecting the Treaty. He confirms what I had heard that France had ceded St. Bartholomew to Sweden. I acquain[ted] him with the Advice I had receiv'd that Mr Jefferson was on his way hither to join Mr Adams and me, and that by him I expected to have our Instructions respecting the Treaty. Wrote a Letter to Count Mercy the Emperor's Ambassador[3] communicating a former Instruction of Congress, respecting a Treaty with his Impl Majesty, which ha[d] for various Reasons been delay'd, one the not receiving the C[ongress?] [one line missing].

Tuesday, 27. Lord Fitzmaurice call'd to see me. His Father having requested that I would give him such instructive Hints as might be useful to him, I occasionally mention'd the old Story of Demosthenes' Answer to one who demanded what was the first Point of Oratory?— Action. The second? Action. The third? Action.[4] which I said had been generally understood to mean the Action of an Orator with his Hands &c. in Speaking: But that I thought another kind of Action of more Importance to an Orator, who would persuade People to follow his Advice, viz. such a Course of Action in the Conduct of Life as would impress them with an Opinion of his Integrity as well as of his Understanding. That this Opinion once establish'd, all the Difficulties, Delays & Oppositions, usually occasion'd by Doubts and Suspicions, were prevented; and such a Man tho' a very imperfect Speaker, would almost always carry his Points against the most flourishing Orator, who had not the Character of Sincerity. To express my Sense of the Importance of a good private Character in public Affairs more strongly, I said the Advantage of having it, & the disadvantage of not having it were so great,

1. Mme Brillon.
2. Mme Roger was Mme Sorin's niece: XLI, 296n.
3. The letter to Mercy-Argenteau is below, July 30.
4. Cicero, *Brutus*, XXXVII, 142.

that I even believ'd if George III had had a bad private Character, and John Wilkes a good one, the latter might have turn'd the former out of his Kingdom.— Lord S. the Father of Lord Fitzmaurice has unfortunately the Character of being *insincere*, and it has hurt much his Usefulness, tho' in all my Concerns with him I never saw any Instance of that kind.—

To John Adams

ALS: Massachusetts Historical Society

Sir, Passy, June 27. 1784.

Inclosed I have the Honour of sending to your Excellency Copies of Papers contain'd in a Dispatch just receiv'd from Congress.[5] The Affair of the Free Ports recommended to us, has been sometime settled: They are Dunkirk, L'Orient, Bayonne & Marseilles.—[6]

I wonder much that we hear nothing from Congress of their foreign Arrangements. This short Line from the President is the only one I have receiv'd since that of Jan. 14. which accompanied the Ratification.—[7]

With great Respect I have the Honour to be, Sir, Your most obedient & most humble Servant   B. FRANKLIN

His Excellency John Adams, Esqr

Endorsed: Dr Franklin 27 June

From Jonathan Williams, Jr.

ALS: American Philosophical Society

Dear & hond Sir. St Germain 27 June 1784.

Mr Barclay desired me to deposit in the Consuls Office my last public Accounts as settled with you. I shall be much obliged

5. Mifflin's letter of March 20, above.
6. The *arrêt* of May 14 also included a fifth port, St.-Jean-de Luz: XXXIX, 106.
7. XLI, 456–7.

if you will please to transmit the Originals to him where they may be always open to public Inspection.[8]
I am most dutifully & Affectionately Yours.

JONA WILLIAMS J

I return you Doctor Priestlys Paper which I have read with much pleasure.

Addressed: His Excellency / Doctor Franklin.

Notation: Williams 27 June 1784.—

From Samuel Chase

ALS: American Philosophical Society

My Dear Sir.   London. 28 June 1784.
    I beg leave to introduce to Your Notice, Civility and friendship Mr. Moss, Son of the Bishop of Bath & Wells.[9] This Gentleman is very desirous of being honoured with your Acquaintance.
    I am still detained here but shall certainly sail before the middle of next Month.[1] I shall be happy to render You any Services in America. Mr Champion,[2] requests his Compliments to You, from this Gentleman's Recommendation I have recommended Mr Moss, of whom he speaks in the most liberal and friendly Manner.
    Accept my best Wishes for your Health and Happiness. Your Affectionate Friend   SAML. CHASE

---

8. See JW's letter of Dec. 2, 1783 (XLI, 253), where he first made this request. Barclay's unexpectedly long absence from Paris, from late December to mid-April, delayed the review: XLI, 438.
    9. Charles Moss (1763–1811), son of Bishop Charles Moss (1711–1802), received his B.A. from Oxford in 1783. He would eventually be named bishop of Oxford: *ODNB*, under Charles Moss, Sr.
    1. Chase did not leave England until mid-August: James Haw *et al.*, *Stormy Patriot: the Life of Samuel Chase* (Baltimore, 1980), p. 128.
    2. Richard Champion had resigned as deputy paymaster general in January and immigrated to South Carolina the following October. He died there in 1791: XL, 515n; Hugh Owen, *Two Centuries of Ceramic Art in Bristol . . .* (London, 1873), p. 262; Dixon Wecter, "An Unpublished Letter of George Washington," *S.C. Hist. and Geneal. Mag.*, XXXIX (1938), 152–3.

Addressed: His Excellency / Benjamin Franklin Esqr / Minister of / The United States / at Paris

Endorsed: Lodges at the Hotel de Richelieu Rue Richelieu.

Notation: Samuel Chase 28 June 1784

From the Marquise de Lafayette

ALS: American Philosophical Society

paris ce 28 Juin 1784

Mr De La fayette, monsieur, m'ecrit de Lorient ou Les vents Le retenoient mardy dernier,[3] et ou il [sera?] encore retenu selon toute apparence. Il me mande qu'il a trouvé a Lorient, des arrivans damerique qui Lui ont annoncé des paquets de Lettres, qui devoient etre arrivés a paris, par la poste Dimanche 20. Je n'ai point entendu parler de ces Lettres je ne puis comprendre ce qu'elles sont devenues, elles peuvent etre interessantes pour mr De La fayette, et il desiroit vivement que Les vents ne devinssent bons, qu'aprés qu'il Les auroit recues. Mandés moy, je vous conjure monsieur si vous en saves quelque chose, ou si vous avés connoissance de quelque americain arrivé depuis une quinzaine de jours qui put Les avoir, ou me faire decouvrir ou elles sont. Mr Barclay que je viens de voir, ne ma pu donner aucune Lumiere sur cet objet. J'ai recours a votre bonté, qui mest connue, et cest avec une grande confiance. Repondes moy je vous prie tout de suite, ou monsieur votre petit fils, mais s'il est possible faites moy trouver un moyen de trouver Les Lettres de mr De La fayette ou de scavoir si elles Lui ont ete envoyées.[4]

Pardonnés, monsieur, mon importunite avec votre indulgence ordinaire et agrées Lassurance et lhommage des sentimens avec

3. June 22.
4. On June 25 Lafayette wrote to his wife that he had received neither the letters from America nor those from Paris he had been expecting by the post from Versailles. He sailed on June 29 on the *Courier de New York,* which arrived in New York Aug. 4. A fellow passenger was Josiah Harmar: Idzerda, *Lafayette Papers,* V, 229–32, 398–401; Dwight L. Smith, "Josiah Harmar, Diplomatic Courier," *PMHB,* LXXXVII (1963), 428–9. BF had issued Harmar a passport on June 17 (Clements Library).

Lesquels j'ai Lhonneur d'être votre trés humble et très obeissante servante   NOAILLES DE LA FAYETTE

Addressed: A Monsieur / Monsieur franklin ministre / plenipotentiaire des Etats unis de / Lamerique / A Passy

Notation: Mde. De La Fayette 28 Juin 1784—

From Le Maire de Gimel[5]   ALS: American Philosophical Society

Vôtre Excellence.   [June 28, 1784]

Je sens combien je Vous fatigue par mes demandes réitérées, mais comme dans tous les tems Vous avez eu des bontés pour moi, j'espere que Vous Voudrez bien encore m'apostiller ce memoire, l'etourderie du copiste m'ayant rendu inutile celui que Vous eutes la bonté de m'apostiller le 30 Maÿ dernier.[6] Le ministre nattend plus qu'après cela pour prononcer sur ce qui fait l'objet de mès desirs. Jattend de Vous cette grace Voulant repasser de suite En amérique.[7] Jaurois eu L'honneur d'aller, moi

5. Under cover of this undated letter, Le Maire sent a revised version of the petition that BF had certified on March 30. (See BF's certification, published under that date.) We date the letter based on the urgent note that Le Maire sent to WTF on June 28, 1784: the "instant" after his courier left for Passy to deliver the memoir, Le Maire received word that Castries had granted him an appointment for nine o'clock the next morning. Would WTF see that BF attested and signed the document by 8 A.M., when his servant would pick it up? APS.

The revised petition that Le Maire enclosed with the present letter, delivered to Castries on June 29, was still dated March 30, 1784, as was BF's recertification. (That recertification, signed by BF, was translated into French and written by L'Air de Lamotte): Le Maire to Castries, March 30, 1784, Archives nationales d'outre-mer. Filed with this document are French copies of its enclosures, which BF also attested. One established the authenticity of Le Maire's November, 1780, commission as colonel of artillery; the other was an article from the *Boston Gaz.*, May 15, 1780, about Le Maire's demonstration of a gun carriage he had designed.

6. *I.e.*, March 30.

7. Le Maire left for Virginia in late 1784 to obtain clear title to lands the state had granted him for his services. He later settled in St.-Domingue, where he died *c.* 1793: *Jefferson Papers*, VII, 505; VIII, 120–32; W. W. Abbot *et al.*, eds., *The Papers of George Washington*, Presidential Series (18 vols. to date, Charlottesville and London, 1987–), XIV, 529–30.

même Vous rendre mes devoirs sans une incommodité qui m'en empéche.
Je suis avec un profond Respect. Votre Excellence Votre tres humble et tres obeissant Serviteur./.   COL. LE MAIRE

Notation: Le Maire

From John Adams   Copy: Massachusetts Historical Society

Sir   The Hague June 29. 1784
The Baron de Reishack,[8] has several times said to me that his Court expected that Congress would announce formally their Independence, and asked me, if any Step of that Sort had been taken.[9] That I may be able to give him an Answer, I must request of your Excellency to inform me whether you have made the annunciation directed in the first Article of the Instructions of the 29 of October 1783[1] and what is the answer.

I have the Pleasure to learn, by report only however that Mr Jay is appointed Minister of foreign Affairs and that Mr Jefferson is appointed to Madrid,[2] and that Mr Johnson has received and transmitted to your Excellency, a Packet which

8. Franz Freiherr von Reischach, minister plenipotentiary of the Holy Roman Empire in the Netherlands: *Repertorium der diplomatischen Vertreter,* III, 82.

9. JA had written to Thomas Mifflin on June 22 that several foreign ministers, including Reischach, had informed him that with the definitive treaty ratified, Congress should send a letter to all European governments giving formal notice of American independence. This, according to the diplomats, was standard practice. JA advised Mifflin on what the letter ought to say, and noted that the answers given by the various sovereigns would cause orders to be issued to all their representatives, official, civilian, and military, "to treat all Americans, Citizens of the United States according to their Characters": *Adams Papers,* XVI, 243–4.

1. The article instructed the peace commissioners to announce to Joseph II or one of his ministers the desire of the United States to negotiate a treaty of amity and commerce: XLI, 154–5. Without waiting for BF's reply, JA sent Reischach a copy of the article the following day: *Adams Papers,* XVI, 258–9.

2. JA learned this from William Bingham, who had just received letters from Philadelphia informing him that TJ had been selected to replace Jay, who intended to return to America: *Adams Papers,* XVI, 251.

probably contains an authentic Account, as it Seems to be posteriour to the Appointment, by being addressed only to your Excellency and to me.[3] I Should be glad to know whether there is any Thing else of Consequence, and whether it appears to be the design and Expectation of Congress that I should join you, where you are.

His Excellency Benjamin Franklin

From Félix Frecon[4]   ALS: American Philosophical Society

Monsieur   Lyon le 29e. Juin 1784.

Pardonnez la Liberté que je prends de vous écrire; Auteur d'un traitté des changes de toutes le places qui négocient ou peuvent négocier avec la france, il manque á mon ouvrage de faire Connoitre au public la maniere dont la france pourrait changer avec les principales Villes des Etats unis de L'Amérique. Cette république, Monsieur, doit aux éfforts de votre Génie sa Liberté et Ses Loix. C'est par vous quelle doit entrer bientot avec avantage dans la Balance Générale du Commerce; vous avez enrichi notre Siécle d'une foule de Découverte qui exciteront L'admiration et la reconnoissance de la postérité; daignez ajouter á tant de bienfaits celui de me communiquer les instructions necessaires pour rendre mon ouvrage plus utile au public en Général et particulierement á la france et a ses nouveaux alliés.

J'ose donc vous demander,

1°. le nom, la description, le poids, mis en rapport avec celui de marc de france, le titre exprimé en fraction Générale, et la valeur, de chacune des Monnoyes réelles qui sont en usage dans les principaux endroits de L'amérique.

3. Edmund Jenings wrote JA on June 23 about the arrival of this packet: *Adams Papers*, XVI, 246. It probably contained Mifflin's letter of March 20, above, and its enclosures. Joshua Johnson had volunteered the previous year to forward mail for BF from London (XL, 424), but we have found no cover letter from him.

4. Frecon is listed in the *Almanach astronomique et historique de la ville de Lyon . . . pour l'année 1787* (Lyon, 1787), pp. 229 and 230, as a writer and master of mathematics who taught arithmetic, foreign exchange, and double and single entry bookkeeping.

2°. le nom, et la Division des monnoyes fictives ou réelles dont on se sert pour tenir les comptes des Négocians, Marchands et autres, de quelle maniere on les y employe et si cette maniere est générale.

3°. s'il y a eu des changes ouverts et établis avec londres, ou quelques autres places, et de quelle maniere on les traittoit.

4°. quels sont les usages Généraux et particuliers, soit dans les achats, et ventes de Marchandises, en gros et en details en égard aux monnoyes soit fictives, soit réelles; et dans les prets d'argent &ca., savoir quels sont les termes accordés pour le crédit, si pour titre de Créance on fait des promesses, Billets, Lettres de changes á ordre, ou non, et si aprés les Echéances fixées, il y a encore des Jours de Grace.

Voila sans doute Beaucoup de choses, mais vous Jugez Monsieur, que pour etre exact il faut être instruit; car je préférerois Laisser cet objet a traitter plutot que d'induire en erreur le public. Mon ouvrage s'achevoit au moment ou j'ai Songé á cet article éssentiel; c'est pourquoi je me suis enhardy a vous demander cette Grace à Laquelle je vous prie d'ajouter celle de me faire L'honneur d'accepter un ou deux exemplaires de mon Traitté,[5] ainsi que de me permettre de me dire avec un profond Respect.

Monsieur Votre tres humble et tres obeissant Serviteur

FELIX FRECON
Mathématicien place des Terreaux à Lyon

Notation: Felix Frecon 29 Juin 1784.

From [François de Fontanges][6]

ALS: American Philosophical Society

A nancy Le 30 juin 1784.

Le Vicomte de fontanges mon frere, Monsieur L'ambassadeur, Vient de m'ecrire touts Ses regrets de n'avoir pas été Compris

---

5. No copies of his treatise have been located.

6. François de Fontanges (1744–1806), formerly chaplain to Marie-Antoinette, was at this time the bishop of Nancy: *DBF; France ecclésiastique* for 1784, p. 200.

dans La liste des officiers français auquels Le Congrés a accordé L'ordre de Cincinnatus.[7] Comme il est a St domingue il n'a pas pu Vous exposer Les titres quil avoit pour demender Cette faveur. Permettes moi de Vous Les detailler en peu de mots. Il a été major general de Larmée de mr Le Comte D'estaing dans Lexpedition De savannah. Ce general Voudra Bien Vous dire quil a Servi pendant Cette Campagne avec quelque Distinction. À la fin du siege il a été Blessé tres grievement, de maniere a S'en ressentir toute sa vie. Il a Le Brevet de Colonel depuis pres de cinq ans et il est a present Colonel titulaire du regiment du Cap a St domingue.[8] Je pense, Monsieur Lambassadeur, que Vous trouverez qu'il reunit toutes les Conditions que Vous avez demandé dans Les officiers français que Vous avez honnoré de [*illegible*] americaine; et j'espere, de Vos Bontés, que Vous Voudrez Bien procurer a mon frere un honneur quil ne Croira pas avoir trop payé dune partie de son sang.

J'ay lhonneur detre avec des Sentiments respectueux Monsieur L'ambassadeur de Votre excellence Le tres humble et tres obeissant serviteur † FR. [W.?] DE NANCY

7. Though the Society of the Cincinnati had made eligible for membership generals and colonels who had fought under Rochambeau, it had omitted those who had fought under d'Estaing. This omission, like the exclusion of officers of the French navy, was immediately pointed out by prominent French members and was rectified at the society's general meeting in May, 1784: Asa B. Gardiner, *The Order of the Cincinnati in France . . .* (n.p., 1905), pp. 11–12, 17–22.
8. François, vicomte de Fontanges (1740–1822), entered the military in 1756 and was made a chevalier de St.-Louis in 1777; see Bodinier, *Dictionnaire*, where the information given here about his service in America is confirmed. He became a member of the Society of the Cincinnati after its charter was amended: Ludovic de Contenson, *La Société des Cincinnati de France et la guerre d'Amerique, 1778–1783* (Paris, 1934), pp. 179–80.

From the Chevalier de Chadirac,[9] with Franklin's Note for a Reply

LS: American Philosophical Society

Monsieur   Paris le 1er Juillet 1784.

Attaché au Service de France, j'ay eu L'avantage de Consacrer mes jours à la défense des côtes de votre pays dans cette derniere guerre; je me suis trouvé à tous les Combats qu'essuïa L'hermione Commandée par M Delatouche, entr'autres à celui qu'elle Soutint contre l'Iris, où j'eus Le malheur de perdre le bras droit. Arrivé à Paris depuis peu, je n'ai rien de plus a cœur que d'avoir des preuves de mes Services; et je suis on ne peut pas plus jaloux d'obtenir La croix de Cincinatus: Si cette recompense militaire depend de vous, vôtre justice me la fait esperer, Sinon, veuilléz avoir La bonté, Monsieur de m'informer, dans vôtre reponse, a qui il faut S'adresser pour cet objet.[1]

J'ay L'honneur d'être avec le plus profond respect Monsieur Vôtre très humble et très obéissant Serviteur

DE CHADIRAC
Enseigne de vaissx à l'hôtel de gaston
rue traversiere St honoré

M. Franklin

Endorsed: Answer. That the Order of Cincinnatus is established only by private Agreement among the Officers, and not by Authority of the American Government. That I have therefore no Concern in it whatsoever. That M. de la Fayette acted for that

9. Pierre-Victor-Laurent, chevalier de Chadirac, sailed to America in Ternay's squadron as an auxiliary officer in 1780. From May to July, 1780, the *Hermione,* under the command of La Touche-Tréville (xxvii, 78n), cruised along the coast of Massachusetts to defend American ships against English privateers. The battle Chadirac mentions, between the *Hermione* and the British frigate *Iris,* took place on June 7, 1780, off Long Island: xxxiii, 12n; Robert Kalbach and Jean-Luc Gireaud, L'Hermione, *frégate des lumières* (Paris, 2004), pp. 83–99, 136–7. He was wounded again in combat on July 21, 1781: Ludovic de Contenson, *La Société des Cincinnati de France et la guerre d'Amérique, 1778–1783* (Paris, 1934), p. 153; Christian de La Jonquière, *Les Marins français sous Louis XVI: Guerre d'indépendance américaine* (Issy-les-Moulineaux, France, 1996), p. 56.

1. Chadirac appears to have become a member of the Cincinnati after his promotion to *lieutenant de vaisseau* in 1786: Contenson, *Société des Cincinnati de France,* p. 153; La Jonquière, *Les Marins français sous Louis XVI,* p. 56.

387

Society when here, but he is gone & and I have not heard that there is any other left in his Place.—[2] With Complimts. &c[3]

Notation: Chadirac 1er. Juillet 1784.—

From the Conte Saluzzo di Monesiglio[4]

ALS: University of Pennsylvania Library

Monsieur   Turin le 1er. juillet 1784

L'abbé Perno Piémontois ayant réüssi à appliquer un clavier à l'harmonique de manière à pouvoir jouer des airs comme l'on feroit avec le clavecin, je m'empresse d'en faire part à vôtre Excellence et de vous prier de nous apprendre si on n'a pas encore exécuté un pareil méchanisme à Paris, à Londres ou ailleurs, car la chose étant neuve, je me ferois un véritable plaisir de vous en faire passer la description et le dessein dont l'auteur seroit très charmé de vous faire hommage.[5]

2. Lafayette was in charge of examining claims for membership from French soldiers who had served with the Continental Army. (Rochambeau and d'Estaing reviewed applications from those who had served with the French forces.) At the meeting of the French chapter on July 4, Lafayette was elected president for life. He never assumed the office, possibly because, following GW's example, he had come to oppose the society's principle of hereditary membership. D'Estaing assumed the presidency of the French chapter, but Lafayette remained active in evaluating membership applications: Minor Myers, Jr., *Liberty without Anarchy: a History of the Society of the Cincinnati* (Charlottesville, 1983), pp. 149, 155–8.

3. On July 8 the haberdasher P. B. Graft wrote to WTF (a regular customer of his: XLI, 386n) to ask where he could obtain a drawing of the insignia of the Cincinnati. This was a commission from a friend in Switzerland, which Graft had been unable to fulfill in Paris. On July 10 Graft thanked WTF "for the very obliging trouble He has taken Relating the order of the Cincinati." Both letters are at the APS.

4. Conte Giuseppe Angelo Saluzzo di Monesiglio (1734–1810) was a general of the artillery in the Sardinian army, a chemist, and a co-founder of the Turinese Academy of Sciences. He had long admired BF's work on electricity: X, 311; *Biographie universelle;* Antonio Pace, *Benjamin Franklin and Italy* (Philadelphia, 1958), pp. 65–6.

5. Perno's design has never surfaced. Previous attempts to fit a keyboard to BF's armonica did not succeed: X, 124; XXII, 49n.

Je profite De cette même occasion pour vous annoncer la détermination qu'a prise L'Académie de mettre bientôt sous presse le premier volume de ses nouveaux mémoires,[6] espérant que vous voudrés y contribuer par quelqu'un de vos ouvrages, et en vous priant d'agréer les assurances des sentimens de ma plus sincère vénération pour la supériorité de vos lumières; j'ai l'honneur d'être avec le plus parfait respect De vôtre Excellence Monsieur Vôtre trés humble Et très obéïssant Serviteur et Confrere[7]　　　　　　　　　　　　　　　LE CTE. DE SALUCES

From Bailly

L: Historical Society of Pennsylvania

Ce Vendredi 2 Juillet 1784

M. Bailly présente ses respects à Monsieur Franklin. Il a l'honneur de lui envoyer la continuation du Regître de MM. les Commissaires du Magnétisme animal. Il le prie de vouloir bien en prendre lecture, le signer et le lui renvoyer le plus tôt qu'il le pourra.

Il auroit bien desiré le lui porter lui même, mais il est obligé d'aller si fréquemment à Paris que tout son tems est pris; il s'en dédommagera incessamment et ira faire sa cour à Monsieur Franklin en l'assurant de son inviolable attachement.

Notation: Bailly 2 Juillet 1784.

---

6. *Mémoires de l'Académie royale des sciences de Turin* for 1784–85 was published in 1786. This was the first volume issued since the society had become an academy: XL, 409n.

7. The count here assumes that BF has accepted the academy's nomination as a foreign member (see XL, 409–10), though his use of the word "Confrere" could also signal a Masonic connection: Vincenzo Ferrone, "The Accademia Reale delle Scienze: Cultural Sociability and Men of Letters in Turin of the Enlightenment under Vittorio Amedeo III," *Jour. of Modern Hist.*, LXX (1998), 553–8.

From Thomas Cushing[8]   ALS: American Philosophical Society

Sir   Boston July. 2d. 1784

Governor Jefferson who sails for Europe by this Conveyance[9] will be able to afford you every necessary Intelligence relative to the State of our affairs in America, it will therefore be needless for me to say any thing upon that Subject.—

I beg leave to Introduce The Honble Nathll. Tracy to your Acquaintance, a Gentleman of good Sense & who has for some time past been largely concerned in Trade & carried it on with great Reputation; He was a member of the Senate the last year, but at the close of it was oblidged to obtain leave to retire from that Bussiness, as his affairs required him to Prepare for a Voyage to Europe, you will find him a very Agreable Gentleman, I reccommend him your friendly notice, any civility you may shew him shall be gratefully Acknowledged. I wish you much Health and Happiness & that your negotiations may Issue to your own satisfaction & contribute to the lasting welfare & happiness of your Constituents.

I remain with great Respect Your most humble Servant

THOMAS CUSHING

His Excellency Benjamin Franklin Esqr

8. The lieutenant governor of Massachusetts had last written in 1782: XXXVII, 694–5.

9. After learning that the French packet boat to Lorient would not sail until July 15 (two weeks later than he thought; see TJ to BF, June 19), TJ decided to take passage with Nathaniel Tracy on the *Ceres*, which left Boston on July 5. TJ, traveling with his daughter Martha and his slave James Hemings, landed at Cowes on July 25. After a brief stay in Portsmouth, they crossed the channel on July 30 and arrived in Paris on Aug. 6. From his accounts, it appears that TJ first visited BF at Passy on Aug. 10: *Jefferson Papers*, VII, 311, 357–8, 363–4; James A. Bear, Jr., and Lucia C. Stanton, eds., *Jefferson's Memorandum Books: Accounts, with Legal Records and Miscellany, 1767–1826* (2 vols., Princeton, 1997), I, 558.

To Frecon

LS:[1] Wyndham Robertson Library, Hollins University, Virginia; AL (draft):[2] Library of Congress

Sir,   Passy, July 3. 1784.
The following is the best Answer I can give to your Letter of the 29th. past.
I am, Sir, your humble Servant.   B. FRANKLIN

The real Money us'd in the United States is French, Spanish, Portuguese and English Coins, Gold & Silver. The most common is Spanish mill'd Dollars, worth 5 Livres 5 Sols tournois.

The nominal Money is generally Paper, reckoned in Pounds, Shillings & Pence, of different Value in the different States when compared with real Money, and that value often changing, so that nothing certain can be said of it. But every where the Accounts are kept in the nominal Pounds, Shillings & Pence, the Pound containing twenty Shillings & the Shillings twelve Pence, whatever may be the real Value.

Bills of Exchange are frequently drawn on Europe, the rate of Exchange differing in different States, & fluctuating in the same State, occasioned by the greater or less Plenty of Bills or of Demand for them. They are commonly drawn at 30 Days Sight.

The Usages in Buying & Selling Merchandizes, are much the same [as][3] in Europe, except that in Virginia the Planter carries his[4] Tobacco to Magazines, where it is inspected by officers, who ascertain its Quality and give Receipts expressing the Quantity. The Merchants receive these Receipts in Payment for Goods, and afterwards draw the Tobacco out of the Magazines for Exportation.

Weights and Measures are uniform in all the States, following the Standard of Great Britain.

1. In the hand of L'Air de Lamotte.
2. Written on the verso of BF's "Of the Paper Money of America"; see XXXIV, 228–9n.
3. Supplied from BF's draft.
4. The word "his" is what BF wrote. L'Air de Lamotte copied it as "the" and we have corrected the mistake.

Money is lent either upon Bond, or on Mortgage, payable in a Year with Interest. The Interest differs in the different States from 5 to 7 per Ct.

Goods are generally imported on 18 Months Credit from Europe, sold in the Country at 12 Months Credit.

Billets or Promisory Notes payable to the Creditor or Order are in use and demandable, when due, as well as accepted Bills of Exchange; without any Days of Grace but by particular Favour.—

M. Felix Frecon.

From Le Couteulx & Cie.

Copy and press copy of copy:[5] American Philosophical Society

Sir,   Paris July 3 de 1784.

In Answer to the Letter you favoured us with yesterday,[6] we will say, that the Ship arrived at Nantes from Virginia with Tobacco is sent to our order by Mr. Morris as Part of Funds which he was to have made to us for Amount of 300,000 *l.t.*[7] which we have paid a Month Ago for Acct. of the United States, having remain'd with Pleasure in Advance to testify our Zeal for the American Government. As to giving the farmers, the Preference for the Purchase of that Tobacco, that Step has been already done by us, thro' our Friend M. Le Normand Receiver of Finances,[8] and we have been offered only 45 *l.t.* we, then

5. In the hand of L'Air de Lamotte.

6. Not found.

7. Morris had sent tobacco to the firm in June on the *Andrew*, Capt. John Robertson, in partial payment of an outstanding American bill he had drawn on Le Couteulx intended to prevent the protest of American sovereign bills drawn on the Dutch banking consortium: *Morris Papers*, IX, 107–8, 226, 370. BF had alerted him to this funding crisis in a letter of Dec. 25, 1783: XLI, 346.

8. Simon-Emmanuel-Julien Le Normand had been appointed by the farmers general to purchase American tobacco: XXVII, 260; Price, *France and the Chesapeake*, II, 747.

thought proper to advise them of the Prices at L'orient of 50 *l.t.* & at Dunkerque of 60 to 70 *l.t.* but they did not chuse to pay more than 47 *l.t.* & in Consequence thereof we sold it immediately to the House of Berard at L'Orient[9] at the Price of 50 *l.t.* with an Intent, We believe of sending it out of the Kingdom. We suppose that Part of the Cargo is already sold again by Sd. Gentleman, however, if you desire it, & the Farmers should be willing to treat at a regular Price, We shall engage Mr. Berard to prefer them for whatever is still existing.

We remain with great Esteem, Sir, Your most obedt. hble. Servts.   (signed) LE COUTEULX & CO.

P.S. You know without doubt that the Crop has been very scarce in America & that the Price of Tobacco has increased very much.—

M. Benjn. Franklin. Passy

From [Noël-Jacques] Pissot[1]

ALS: American Philosophical Society

Monsieur,   Paris Le 3 Juillet 1784.

Vous ne devez point douter que s'il me fut resté un exe. du voyage de Cook je me Serois fait un devoir de vous echanger le volume que vous avez reçu double. Je vous envoy, Selon vos desirs, le nom des personnes de connoissance à qui j'en ai vendu. J'ose me flater que l'un de ces Messieurs se feront un vrai plaisir

9. J. J. Bérard & Cie. The "Mr. Berard" mentioned below is either Jean-Jacques Bérard or his brother Thomas-Simon: XXXVI, 344n.

1. The Paris bookseller (XL, 617n) to whom the British Admiralty had sent BF's presentation copy of its three-volume edition of Cook's *Voyage to the Pacific Ocean;* see Oswald to BF, June 8. There was a mistake in the shipment, however: the package contained a duplicate copy of the third volume, and no copy of the first. Immediately after receiving the books on July 1, BF returned the duplicate to Pissot to exchange it: BF's journal, [June 26–July 27], entry of July 1; BF to Benjamin Vaughan, July 26, below; BF to Joseph Banks, Aug. 21, 1784, British Library.

de vous prêter le vol. dont vous avez besoin en attendant que Mr. Nicoll[2] vous l'ait échangé.

Mr. Le Duc De Chaulnes, rue de Bondi.

Mr. Suard, de l'acad. françoise, rue Louis-Le Grand.

Mr. Panchaud, Banquier, rue st honoré proche st. Roch.

Mr. Panckoucke, Libraire, rue des Poitevins.

Je ne connois point les autres personnes qui m'en ont acheté.

J'ai l'honneur d'être avec respect Monsieur, Votre tres humble et tres obeissant serviteur   PISSOT

Notation: Pissot 3 Juillet 1784

To John Adams   ALS: Massachusetts Historical Society

Sir,   Passy, July 4. 1784

I have received the Letter your Excelly. did me the Honour of writing to me the 29th past.

The Annunciation directed by the Instruction you mention has not yet been made; some Circumstances and Considerations, not necessary to particularize at present, occasioned the Delay here; but it may now be done immediately by your Excellency, if you think proper, to the Imperial Minister at the Hague; or I will do it to Count Mercy, by presenting him a Copy of the Instruction itself.—[3]

I hope the Report that Mr Jay is appointed Minister of Foreign Affairs will prove true.— Such an Officer has long been wanted, and he will make a good one. It is said here that Mr Jefferson was talk'd of to succeed me, of which I shall be glad on all Accounts; but I have no Letter, nor the least Hint from any one of the Congress relating to these Matters. I wrote to you a few Days since,[4] and sent you Copy of the last Dispatch, and the only one I have received since January.— Mr Hartley who has been here more than two Months, is in a similar Situation.

2. Nicol and Cadell published the edition. George Nicol had been bookseller to the king since 1781: *ODNB.*

3. BF delayed his overture to Mercy-Argenteau until he received word of the new commission: BF's journal, [June 26–July 27], entry of July 26 (above); BF to Mercy-Argenteau, July 30 (below).

4. On June 27, above.

He has expected Instructions by every late Courier to treat with us on commercial Points; but they do not arrive. He thinks the Delay occasion'd by the Report of the Committee of Council on the Subject not having been ready to lay before Parliament.[5] The Moment he is ready to treat, I shall acquaint your Excellency with it; for I make no doubt of its being "the Design and Expectation of Congress that we should join"[6] in that Transaction.

Montgomery of Alicant appears to have acted very imprudently in writing to Morocco without the least Authority from Congress or any of their Ministers.—[7] It might be well however to treat with that Prince[8] if we were provided with the proper & necessary Presents; in which Case this Court would assist our Negociations, agreable to their Treaty with Congress.[9]

I have the honour to be, very respectfully, Sir, Your most obedient & most humble Servant   B. FRANKLIN

His Excellency John Adams Esqr

Endorsed: Dr Franklin 4. July. 1784. ansd. 19. July

From Jane Mecom   ALS: American Philosophical Society

Dear Brother   Boston July 4. 1784

I often Recolect the Advice you wonce Gave won of my Sons to do the right thing with Spirit & not to Spend time in makeing Excuses for not Doing it & I ought to have profited by it, but I have So long Delayed writing to you that I am hardly capeble of makeing any Excuse at all, & now have no time to Atempt it. I have Removed From Cambridge with my Son-in-Law Collas & his wife & Live in your House at the North-End[1]

5. For the report see the annotation of Laurens' first letter of April 18.
6. BF is quoting from JA's letter of June 29, above.
7. See XL, 311n, 369, 621.
8. Sidi Muhammad ibn Abdallah.
9. By Article 8 of the 1778 Treaty of Amity and Commerce: XXV, 602–3.
1. Living in the house on Unity Street along with Mecom, her son-in-law, Peter Collas, and her daughter, Jane, was her granddaughter Jenny

& Mr Collas being Absent[2] Sildom See any won to Inform us How the world goes, am now at Cousen Williams where I am Informed a Ship is to Sail this Day with a Gentileman in it who goes Directly to you, I can't Remember Ither His Name or office[3] by which you will see what a confused State my mind is in for I Just Heard it below, I am often Afflected with grat Dizenes & Expect or fear if I live much Longer to be in such Circumstances as Dean Swift was,[4] If it Pleases God to hear my Prayer Death will be much Preferable, but who am I to Prescribe to the Allmighty the Anguish of mind I have undergone on your acount Since I heard of the Greveous malady you are Exercised with has made me consider which of the two cases I Should Prefer & I think yours bad as it is, dont think by this that I dont feal all for you that the Intimate knolige of Such cases, all the Tendernes & Affection that is Due to won who has been as a Father, Husband, & all ways the best of Brothers deserves, but your Retaining your Intlectual Faculties & such Fortitude to bare up under it must be Preferable to a Senslis Stupidetie.

But O that After you have Spent your whol Life in the service of the Publick & have Atained So Glorious A conclution as I thought as would now Premit you to come home & Spend (as you Used to say) the Evening with you Friends in Ease & Quiete, that now Such a dreadfull maledy should Atact you; my Hart is Reddy to burst with Greaf at the thought.—

How many Hours have I Laid awake on nights thinking what Excruciating Pains you might then be Incountering while I a Poor Useles, & wrothles worm, was Premitted to be at Ease; oh that it was In my Power to mitigate or Aleviate the Anguish I know you must Endure—

I have been Flattered all the Spring & Sumer that you were

Mecom, who had lived with Collas and his wife since 1780: XXXVIII, 507; Mecom to BF, Aug. 16, 1784, in Van Doren, *Franklin-Mecom*, p. 230.

2. Shortly after the family moved, Peter Collas sailed to Nova Scotia to sell lumber: Mecom to BF, Aug. 16, 1784, in Van Doren, *Franklin-Mecom*, p. 230.

3. Most likely TJ; see Cushing to BF, July 2.

4. Beset most of his life by dizziness and other symptoms associated with Ménière's disease, Jonathan Swift suffered a sharp mental decline in the years prior to his death in 1745: *ODNB*.

coming home, I know your wisdom will Direct to Emprove all circumstances that will be most comodeious for the desiered End but I fear if you take Ship for Philadelphia I Shall never See you, traveling will be so Incomodous to you that when you are got home you will not Prevail with your Self to See New-England but If you come hear first you can go mostly if not Altogather by water as you know & it may not Be so trying to you. God grant I may See you again hear but if not that we may Spend an happy Eternity togather In His Presence.

Mr Williams has tould me he has Informed you Perticularly about my Affairs but I did not think that would Jestifie me in not writing my Self but I have now nither Leters nor Papers nor time to say any thing more than that I am your most obliged & affectionat Sister   JANE MECOM

If wind or wither should detain the Ship I will writ again at Present Pray forgive the very bad Spelling & Every other defect & dont let it mortifie you that such a Scraw came from your Sister.

Mr williams says My Love to the Docter mine to your Grand son.

Addressed: His Excellency Benjamin Franklin Esqr / In / Passy / France

To Thomas Barclay   AL (draft): American Philosophical Society

Passy July 6. 1784—

Mr Franklin presents his Compliments to Mr Barclay, and requests he would peruse the enclos'd Letter of the Marquis de Castries,[5] with the Resolutions of Congress respecting the Division of Prize Money; and favour Mr. Franklin with his Opinion. Mr F. also wishes to know whether there have been any Decisions upon a similar Case in America, or any subsequent Rules given by Congress—[6]

5. Castries to BF, June 20, above.
6. Barclay's answer has not been located, but BF received it on July 9, as he noted in his entry for that date in his journal, [June 26–July 27], above.

From Etienne d'Audibert Caille[7]

ALS: American Philosophical Society

Monsieur   Paris le 6. juillet 1784.
J'eus l'honneur de vous écrire en 1778. Pour vous informer
que L'Empéreur de Maroc, m'ayant nommé Consul de Paix
pour les Puissances Maritimes Chrétiénnes qui n'avoïent point
de Réprésentant dans Ses Etats & Médiateur entre lui & celles
de ces Puissances qui voudroïent avoir la paix avec S. M. Ma-
roccaine, j'offrois en cette qualité mes Services aux Etats Unis
de L'Amérique Septentrionale.[8] Je vous adressai ensuite, Monsieur, une Dépêche pour le Congrés par laquelle je lui rendois
compte de mes bons offices auprés L'Empéreur de Maroc pour
que Ses Corsaires n'eussent causé aucun tort aux navires Sous
pavillon des Etats Unis.[9] En 1780., par voye de Mr. Jay que
j'eus l'honneur de connoitre à Madrid, je rendis nouvellément
compte au Congrés de ce qui pouvoit l'intéresser à Maroc;[1]
par celle de Mr. Carmichaer de Madrid & de Mr. Harrisson de
Cadiz,[2] j'eus encore le même Soin jusques à ce qu'il me parût
dévoir m'en dispenser. Me trouvant icy de passage, je Sérois in-

7. A French merchant who served the sultan of Morocco in various diplomatic capacities; see XL, 310n.
    8. His letter was to the three American commissioners serving at that
time: XXVI, 285–6.
    9. Caille's Sept. 6, 1779, letter to Congress is in Wharton, *Diplomatic
Correspondence*, IV, 173–4. No cover letter to BF has been found. BF must
have forwarded the Sept. 6 letter to Congress with his own of May 31, 1780,
as they were read on the same day and Congress later noted that BF had sent
it: *JCC*, XVII, 798; XX, 553.
    1. Caille, who had not received any response from Congress, sent a copy
of his Sept. 6 letter to John Jay on April 21, 1780. He enclosed a certified
French translation of his consular appointment, copies of two declarations
made by the sultan, and printed certificates to be distributed among Moroc-
can ship captains. Jay forwarded the packet to Congress on Nov. 30, 1780:
Jay Papers, II, 66–8, 357–8. Congress instructed both BF and Jay to inform
Caille of its friendly disposition toward the sultan and its desire to establish
formal relations at some unspecified future date: XXXIV, 84; *Jay Papers*, II,
451. Neither BF nor Jay acted on these instructions.
    2. William Carmichael and Richard Harrison, the American agent at
Cadiz (XL, 311n).

finiment flaté Si vous voulés bien, Monsieur, me permêttre de vous aller présenter mes dévoirs le jour & l'heure qu'il vous plairra m'indiquer.[3]

J'ai l'honneur d'être avec la considération la plus distinguée, Monsieur Vôtre trés humble & trés obeissant Serviteur

D'AUDIBERT CAILLE
Consul de Paix & Consul Général de Prusse & de Sardaigne auprés L'Empéreur de Maroc
Hôtel d'Artois, ruë Richelieu—

Notation: D'audibert Caille 6. Juillet 1784—

From ———— Colson
Printed invitation with MS insertions: American Philosophical Society

MONSIEUR,   Paris, ce *mardi 6 Juillet 1784*
JE suis chargé par la Maison Philantropique,[4] de vous rappeller que c'est Vendredi prochain le jour de son Assemblée, à

3. Caille visited BF four days later: BF's journal, [June 26–July 27], entry of July 10 (above).
4. The Maison (Société) philantropique was founded in 1780 by a group of men led by Savalette de Langes (XXXV, 42n), for the purpose of helping deserving indigents not being served by either the Church or the government. The society's first beneficiaries were aged laborers. By the end of 1783, when it counted more than 50 members, it had expanded its *bienfaisance* to include poor blind children. BF was admitted as the 90th member on June 11, 1784. In 1785, while growing rapidly in membership and prestige, the organization added two more classes of recipients: poor women pregnant with their sixth child, and widows and widowers with at least six children: *Précis sur la Société Philantropique* (two copies owned by BF are at the Hist. Soc. of Pa.); Catherine Duprat, *Le Temps des Philanthropes: la philanthropie parisienne des Lumières à la monarchie de Juillet* (1 vol. to date., Paris, 1993), I, 65–75; A.-M. Péan de St.-Gilles, *La Maison Philanthropique de Paris: histoire de cent dix ans (1780–1890)* (Paris, 1892), p. 25; *Jour. de Paris*, issues of June 3, Aug. 30, and Dec. 20, 1783. BF's membership information was kindly provided by the late Jean-Claude David, drawing on "Tableau des membres de la Maison philantropique, établie à Paris en 1780, par rangs d'ancienneté," *Calendrier philantropique* for 1786.

5 heures & demie précises, Hôtel du Musée, rue Dauphine.[5] *On y fera lecture de ce qui a été arrêté sur les Réglemens: vous voudrez bien vous souvenir qu'on paye, á cette époque, la Cotisation du sémestre de Juillet.*[6]
Je suis avec respect, Monsieur, Votre très-humble & très-obéissant serviteur, COLSON
agent[7] de la Société.

Le scrutin[8] *se fera Pour M.M. Le Mis. de Chabrillant, Lieutenant Gal. des armées, Commandt. des Carabiniers*[9] *hérault de séchelles, 1er. avocat du Roi au Chatelet*[1] *et Mony, Notaire sécretaire du Roi.*[2]

Admission de la dernière Assemblée.
MM.
D'aguesseau de fresne[3]
D'harvelay[4]

5. The society met on the second and fourth Friday of each month: *Réglemens généraux pour la Maison philantropique de Paris* ([Paris, 1784]), p. 21. BF's copy of this pamphlet is at the Hist. Soc. of Pa.
6. The annual dues were four *louis* (96 *l.t.*), to be paid in two installments at the first meetings in January and July: *Réglemens généraux*, pp. 11–12.
7. Written above the crossed-out title "Substitut du Secrétaire & Membre".
8. All invitations listed candidates whose admission would be put to a vote at the upcoming assembly, and, in a separate list, members admitted since the last meeting. Candidates could not request admittance; they had to be proposed by a *philantrope* and could be brought to the vote of the membership only by the unanimous decision of a 30-member committee, which evaluated them on the basis of "les qualités & les vertus Philantropiques." Admission was granted to candidates who won at least 80 percent of the general vote: *Réglemens généraux*, pp. 8–10.
9. Jacques-Aymar de Moreton, marquis de Chabrillan: *DBF*.
1. Marie-Jean Hérault de Séchelles, who was also a member of the Neuf Sœurs: *DBF*.
2. Possibly Jacques-Michel Mony: Jean-Claude David, "De Voltaire à Marmontel: quelques autographes du dix-huitième siècle réunis par Jacques Charavay (1809–1867)," *Studies on Voltaire and the Eighteenth Century*, CCLXXVIII (1990), 238n.
3. D'Aguesseau de Fresnes, *conseiller du roi*.
4. Joseph Micault d'Harvelay, a royal treasurer.

Le Baron de staal[5]
De Biré[6]
De st. Mart[7]
et Pia[8]

Addressed: A Monsieur / Monsieur franklin / Ministre Plénipotentiare des / Etats Unis de l'amérique / a Passy / Colson[9]
Notation: Colson 6 Juillet 1784

From Claude-Joseph Vernet[1]

ALS: American Philosophical Society

Monsieur   a Paris mardy 6e. juillet 1784
  Vous allez voir qu'on me croit un grand saint auprés de vous,
puisque des amis de versailles m'onts prié de vous Recommander

5. Staël von Holstein, the Swedish ambassador to the French court.
6. Marie-Sébastien-Charles-François Fontaine de Biré, treasurer general for war: J. F. Bosher, *French Finances, 1770–1795: From Business to Bu-
reaucracy* (Cambridge, 1970), p. 327.
7. Comte de Saint-Mart, colonel of the regiment of l'Isle de Bourbon:
Calendrier Philantropique for 1789.
8. Philippe-Nicolas Pia, a municipal officer in Paris: Jean Sgard, ed.,
Dictionnaire des journaux, 1600–1789 (2 vols., Paris, 1991), I, 336–7.
9. Nine more invitations survive among BF's papers, all at the APS
unless otherwise noted. The first five, also signed by Colson, are dated
Sept. 7, 1784, for the meeting on Sept. 10; Dec. 6, 1784, for the meeting
on Dec. 10 (University of Pa. Library); Dec. 19, 1784, for the meeting on
Dec. 24; Feb. 22, 1785, for the meeting on Feb. 25; March 5, 1785, for the
meeting on March 11. The next four, signed by Brevost, are dated April 5,
1785, for the meeting on April 8; April 18, 1785, for the meeting on April 22;
May 9, 1785, for the meeting on May 13; and May 23, 1785, for the meeting
on May 27. Though BF's private accounts for this period do not survive, we
infer that his membership was current through the end of June, 1785, as the
following year he received a reminder notice for back dues dating to July,
1785. He paid in full: Charost *et al.* to BF, Feb. 21, 1786 (APS); Account
XVII (xxvi, 3), entry of May 11, 1786.
  1. The famous landscape and seascape painter whom BF had met in 1777
through Mme Brillon: xxiv, 491. His son Carle, also a painter, wrote to WTF
the following spring, when he completed the portrait of WTF's horse. He
announced that he would bring it by the following Saturday: Carle Vernet
to WTF, May 25, 1785, APS.

Mr. Fossard premier huissier audiancier a La Prevôté de L'hô-tel,[2] qui desireroit passer en Amerique; luy meme vous ex-pliqueroit ses intentions, et ses desirs; cela occationneroit un mariage entres Luy et Madlle. de Montauville; L'un et L'autre auront L'honneur de se presenter a vous si vous voullez bien Les Recevoir; je vous sçauray un gré infiny, Monsieur, si vous avéz La bonté de Les bien acceuïllir, Les honorer de vôtre Protection et de vos conseils.[3]

Je voudrois bien avoir des occations ou je pût vous faire connôitre La veneration et Le Tres Respectueux attachement avec Lequel je suis. Monsieur Votre Tres humble et Tres obeïs-sant serviteur   VERNET

Peintre du Roy aux galleries du Louvre

Notation: Vernet 6 Juillet 1784—

From Bertrand Du Fresne[4]   LS: American Philosophical Society

Versailles le 8 Juillet 1784.

M le Maréchal de Castries me charge d'avoir l'honneur de rap-peler à Monsieur Franklin le projèt de répartition des Prises faites par le Commodore Paul Jones, qu'il lui a communiqué par sa lettre du 20 du mois dernier.

On lui montre tous les Jours beaucoup d'empressement sur cette affaire, et il desireroit que Monsieur Franklin eut la bonté de répondre à ce qu'il lui a demandé.[5]

2. He is listed in the *Almanach royal* for 1784, p. 296.

3. The young couple went together to Passy, but BF "Discourag'd them": BF's journal, [June 26–July 27], entry of July 6.

4. An associate of Jacques Necker's at the Royal Treasury who had worked in various other positions since Necker's 1781 resignation: *DBF.*

5. BF's response, if there was one, has not been located. Jones continued to negotiate the partition of the prize proceeds, and by Oct. 23, 1784, Cas-tries had acceded to most of his claims. Further disputes prevented Jones from receiving all the American shares until Sept. 5, 1785: Jones to Robert Morris, Dec. 17, 1784, in Bradford, *Jones Papers,* reel 7, no. 1531; *Jefferson Papers,* VIII, 680n.

J'ai l'honneur de présenter à monsieur franklin l'hommage de mon respect. Du FRESNE
Intendant gal. des fonds de la marine
Prises.

Mr. Franklin Ministre des Etats Unis de l'Amerique.

Notation: Du Fresne 8 Juillet 1784—

From William Carmichael

ALS: American Philosophical Society; ALS (draft): National Archives

Dear Sir   Madrid 9th. July 1784
I arrived here the 26th of June, my first business was to present myself at Aranjuez where the Court then resided. I had in some measure engaged before my departure from Spain to return before the Royal Family left that residence. So far I have fulfilled my engagements— On this Acct I set off from Paris more abruptly than I wished to do— I do not know as yet whether I may not have given more Offence to my personal friends there by the precipitation with which I left them than I have given satisfaction to my political ones here by the desire which I have manifested to return agreable to my promise— I have however the consolation to find that I have been recived individually in a manner that is highly flattering to me— I have delayed writing to your Excy. because I expected to have an Answer to send you to the Letter which you wrote to the Ct de Campomanes by me.[6] I have the honor to inform you that you are chosen a member of the Royal Academy of history here & that I shall have that of inclosing you the Diploma & the Answer of the Ct de Campomanes to your Exy's. Letter by the next Post. The Little works you gave me will soon appear in a spanish Dress— If they lose by the change of costume I can assure you that it will not be the fault of the Translator who wishes to preserve

6. Of June 5, above.

the true sense spirit & simplicity of the Original— I have taken the Liberty to draw upon your Excy. in favor of Messrs. Etienne Drouilhet & Company for 4000 Livres Tournois at 15 days after date for my Salary since the first of April. It will be impossible for Me to submit longer to the Inconvenience of remaining ten months without receiving my appointments. I draw also in favor of Mr Jonathan Williams for two thousand Livres; I have spent on this mission more than nine hundred pounds Sterling of my own property which I destined for other purposes & unless I can receive regularly my Salary in future I shall be reduced to the necessity, (as I have been) to be Injust to Others & Myself, which I am determined not to be a year longer, if I am obliged even to retire beyond the Allegany Mountains, After having sold my little property in Maryland[7] to pay Debts contracted entirely since I have engaged in the carreer in which I find myself at present—

I have no idea that your Excy will be permitted to return to America, on the Contrary, I think you can never finish your life so gloriously or so usefully as in spending the rest of it in establishing our Other European Connections on the Same footing that you have already arranged them with the Nations with which you have treated— You Owe this to the confidence reposed in you by your Country, to its Interests, to yourself & to those whom I love in proportion to the love & respect which I entertain for your Excy—

In a few days, as I hope to have more Leisure, I shall have the honor of writing you more explicitly— You seem to be a prophet on more than one occasion, for I shall have an immediate opportunity of suggesting the Idea that you gave me with respect to China— In the meantime I beg your Excellency to mention me in the proper Manner to your grandson & to all those who do me the honor to remember me & to beleive me with the highest respect and the most sincere Affection Your Excy's. Obliged & Most humble Sert   WM. CARMICHAEL

7. Presumably the estates in Queen Anne's and Talbot counties that he and his brother Richard inherited from their great-uncle: Samuel G. Coe, *The Mission of William Carmichael to Spain* (Baltimore, 1928), p. 1.

From Mason Locke Weems and Edward Gantt, Jr.[8]

ALS[9] and copy: American Philosophical Society

No 170 Strand. July 9th. 1784

Not having the honour to be known to Your Excellency we should preface this with an *Apology*, but as it relates to a Subject of public & Important Concern, we hope your Excellency will excuse form & Ceremony.

We are Natives of America & Students of Divinity, having no form of Episcopal Ordination in our own Country[1] we Came to England more than a twelvemonth ago for Orders and have been all that time Soliciting the Arch Bishop but in vain. His Grace will not ordain us unless we will consent to take the *Oath* of *Allegiance.*[2] Mr Chase a Friend of ours advised us to

8. Episcopal divinity students from Maryland. Weems had sailed to Europe in early 1782 and disembarked in Nantes before continuing to Edinburgh for his studies. Though JW (in Nantes) wrote to BF recommending him, Weems evidently did not go to Passy: XXXVI, 669–70. Edward Gantt, Jr. (1759–1810), left Maryland late in 1783. The two men seem to have joined forces in the spring of 1784, after Weems had spent months trying to find a solution to the chief obstacle to his being ordained in England: the requirement that priests swear oaths of allegiance to the British crown: *Adams Papers*, XVI, 63–4; Walter H. Stowe *et al.*, "The Clergy of the Episcopal Church in 1785," *Hist. Mag. of the Protestant Episcopal Church*, XX (1951), 263; George B. Utley, *The Life and Times of Thomas John Claggett . . .* (Chicago, 1913), pp. 43–4; Joshua Johnson to JA, Feb. 27, 1784 (Mass. Hist. Soc.).

9. In the hand of Weems, who signed both names.

1. Though American Anglicans had reframed themselves as Episcopalians, they still had no bishop in the United States and were thus forced to seek ordination from the parent church. Efforts were under way to change that. The previous August, Gantt attended the Md. Episcopal convention in Annapolis, where he was one of the signatories to a letter to the bishop of London requesting the consecration of their newly elected bishop: Frederick V. Mills, Sr., *Bishops by Ballot: an Eighteenth-Century Ecclesiastical Revolution* (New York, 1978), pp. 158, 192; Arthur P. Middleton, *Tercentenary Essays Commemorating Anglican Maryland, 1692–1792* (Virginia Beach, 1992), pp. 48–50; Md. Protestant Episcopal clergy members to the Bishop of London, Aug. 16, 1783 (University of Pa. Archives and Records Center).

2. Weems's first applications had been to the bishop of London and the bishop of Llandaff, the latter of whom had eventually referred him to the archbishop of Canterbury, John Moore (*ODNB*). The archbishop, though sympathetic, informed Weems that only an act of Parliament could alter

405

write to your Excellency[3] and acquaint you with the Deplorable Condition of our Church. Waving all Pathetic Description, permit us to assure Your Excellency that of Sixty Churches in our *State* (Maryland) there are upwards of thirty vacant.—[4] Romish Orders are Good.— We shall take it as a great favour done to ourselves & State if your Excellency will inform us as soon as possible whether we can take Orders in France. Be pleased to Let us know very particularly what Oaths we must take and What Tenets we must subscribe. If the Arch Bishop of Paris will ordain Us we will come over most Chearfully. Your Excellency will add to the Obligation by giving us a Speedy Reply. Mr Adams has invited us to go over to Denmark,[5] but the Orders from Denmark are not so Good as we wish them to be—

---

the law that required priests of the Church of England to swear oaths of allegiance to the king. That response essentially left Weems with two alternatives: wait for Parliament to act or obtain ordination in another country from a bishop of another denomination: *Adams Papers*, XVI, 63–4.

3. The previous February, Marylanders Samuel Chase (XLI, 15n) and Joshua Johnson (XXIV, 209n), whom Weems consulted in London, also advised him to write to JA: *Adams Papers*, XVI, 63–4. The correspondence between Weems and JA, which spanned several months, is described below.

4. The decline of the American Anglican Church during the Revolution can be traced in large part to the conflicted loyalties of its clergy, who were bound by oath to support the king, and to the devastating impact of disestablishment on church finances: Mills, *Bishops by Ballot*, pp. 158–9, 168–71; Middleton, *Tercentenary Essays Commemorating Anglican Maryland*, pp. 45–6.

5. The invitation actually came from the Danish court. JA had informally (he said) queried the Danish envoy to the Netherlands, who in turn wrote to the foreign minister, Rosencrone. Based on an opinion from the University of Copenhagen's Faculty of Theology, the king ruled that a Danish bishop could not only ordain Weems but do so in Latin rather than Danish, as a convenience to the American. The profession of faith would be consonant with Anglican requirements, except for the omission of the oath of allegiance. Rosencrone instructed the Danish envoy to communicate this to JA, who, on receiving the relevant letters on April 22, immediately sent copies to Congress as well as to Weems. Weems followed up on May 14, asking JA for a letter of introduction to a Danish bishop. JA sent him a passport instead: *Adams Papers*, XVI, 72n, 173–4, 215–16; William White, *Memoirs of the Protestant Episcopal Church . . .* (New York, 1880), p. 328; Soren J. M. P. Fogdall, "Danish-American Diplomacy, 1776–1920,"

We have the honour to be Your Excellency's Most Obedt
humble—Servts.   MASON WEEMS
EDWARD GANT
No 170 Strand

Notation: Edd. Gant July 9. 1784

From Michel-René Hilliard d'Auberteuil

ALS: American Philosophical Society

Monsieur   [*c.* July 11, 1784][6]
J'envoye a votre excellence un petit ouvrage[7] auquel je n'attache aucune pretention, mais qui peut être trouvera grace à vos
yeux parcequ'il vous rapellera des lieux ou l'on ne prononce
votre nom qu'avec reconnaissance et ou vous avez commencé
d'acquerir une gloire immortelle.

Je saisis avec beaucoup de plaisir cette occasion de vous reite-
rer l'assurance de mon attachement et de mon respect
HILLIARD D'AUBERTEUIL

comme j'ai cedé le manuscrit à un libraire forain vous trouverez beaucoup de fautes d'impression mais il vous sera facile d'y
supleer.

Notation: Hilliard D'auberteuil

University of Iowa Studies in the Social Sciences, VIII (1922), 27–8; JA to
Armand F. L. Mestral de Saint-Saphorin, [April 22, 1784], JA to Weems,
April 22, 1784, JA to Weems, May 19, 1784, all three at the Mass. Hist. Soc.
As far as we can determine, BF was unaware of this previous communication with the court of Denmark.
6. The day Hilliard's *Mis Mac Rea, roman historique* (Philadelphia [*i.e.,*
Brussels?], 1784) was reviewed in the *Jour. de Paris.* Two years earlier, Hilliard had written an account of Jane McCrea's brutal murder for his *Essais
historiques et politiques;* he had now turned it into a novella: XXXVII, 420n.
7. Two clues in this undated letter point to the work being *Mis Mac Rea:*
Hilliard's allusion to an American subject and the numerous typographical errors. On account of the misprints, *Mis Mac Rea* was reissued in a
second edition; see Lewis Leary's introduction, pp. 5–6, in Michel-René
Hilliard d'Auberteuil, *Miss McCrea (1784): a Novel of the American Revolution,* trans. Eric LaGuardia (Gainesville, Fla., 1958). The enclosed work
was indeed a "petit ouvrage," printed in 18°.

From Richard Price

ALS: American Philosophical Society

Dear Sir   Newington Green July 12th: 1784

I request your acceptance of the pamphlet which accompanies this letter.[8] It is intended entirely for America, and you are one of the first persons to whom it has been communicated. Most of the few copies which I have printed will be convey'd to America; and I hope the united States will forgive my presumption in Supposing myself qualified to advise them. Indeed I almost feel myself ashamed of what I have done but the consciousness wch I have that it is well-intended, and that my address to them is the effusion of a heart that wishes to Serve the best interests of Society, helps to reconcile me to myself in this instance, and it will, I hope, engage the candour of others.

The letter from *M. Turgot* which you will receive with this Stands at present in the Press, and will Stand there till I Shall be made acquainted with your opinion concerning the propriety of making it public by conveying it to the united States with my own Pamphlet.[9] The reason of my doubts about this

8. Richard Price, *Observations on the Importance of the American Revolution, and The Means of making it a Benefit to the World* (London, 1784). The pamphlet was dedicated to "The Free and United States of America . . . as a last testimony of the good-will of The Author." As that dedication was dated July 6, the sheets must have just been printed. The pamphlet would not be issued until the following October, by which time it had been expanded to include the letter from Turgot that is the subject of Price's query in the second paragraph.

Observations offered wide-ranging and emphatic advice. Tackling the public debt should be the nation's first priority; peace between states could be secured by giving a strengthened Congress the power to form a militia; freedom of religion and of speech must be guaranteed; modes of education must be reformed; foreign trade—which inevitably led to urban luxury—should be avoided; and the slave trade had to be abolished and the slaves emancipated at once.

9. In early 1778 Price asked BF to give Turgot a copy of his newly published *Two Tracts on Civil Liberty*. Turgot responded with a long and candid letter dated March 22, 1778, which he begged Price to keep secret. Highly critical of Great Britain for its treatment of the colonies, Turgot was certain that the United States would win independence, but he wondered whether the states would be able to cohere and form a viable union. He described various obstacles the states faced and proposed solutions. At the end, he observed that England and France were causing each other great harm, to no

is the charge of Secrecy with which it concludes, and which you will find written in the margin.[1] In compliance with this charge I have hitherto kept this letter private; but lately I have consider'd that probably it was only Some apprehension of personal inconvenience that led him to give this charge, and that consequently the obligation to comply with it ceased with his life. Dreading, however, every thing that might be reckon'd a breach of confidence, my Scruples are continually returning upon me; and I feel them the more, when I think that possibly he may have left a family which may Suffer in *France* when it appears there that he was so much a friend to liberty as this letter will Shew him to be. In this State of mind I cannot make myself easy in any other way than by determining to request the favour of your judgment and to abide by it. Should you think that no ill consequences can result from publishing this letter to any family that *M. Turgot* may have left, and that his death has free'd me from any obligation to keep it Secret, I will order it to be printed off and Send it to America with my pamphlet. Should you think the contrary, it Shall be Suppress'd and I Shall depend on your being so good as to destroy the copy now Sent you. You will add much to the obligation I am under to you for all your friendship by giving me a few lines on this Subject as soon as may be convenient to you. Should you think it improper to write by the post, a letter or any parcel you may wish to convey to London, may be Sent by Miss Wilkes who is on a visit

---

advantage; neither would gain by the war. The letter is published with a 1785 English translation in Peach and Thomas, *Price Correspondence*, II, 3–19. Turgot's first sentence acknowledges having received the pamphlet from BF, at Price's request; no other evidence of this transaction has been found.

1. Price had all of Turgot's letter set in type except the final sentences, which he handwrote. In this passage, Turgot asked that Price not only keep the letter confidential but also exercise great caution when answering by post—he begged that Price not allude to any specifics—since the letter would be opened and read by the French post office. The former minister feared that he would be judged too much of an "ami de la liberté pour un ministre, même pour un ministre disgracié!" BF's Aug. 2 letter, below, gave Price the approval he was seeking to publish Turgot's letter, including the handwritten ending, which appears in the pamphlet on pp. 108–9.

with the *Dutchess de la Valliere* at Paris and will return the 2d: of August.[2]

I writ to you by the Post about three months ago,[3] and hope you received my letter. I have heard lately with pleasure that you are pretty well. May your health and life and usefulness be continued as long as the course of nature will admit. Are we never to have the Satisfaction of Seeing you again in London? I have lately been at Birmingham to visit Dr Priestley. He is very happy there and going on Successfully with his experimts:.

Mrs Price desires to be respectfully remember'd to you. She is in a very weak and low State, but not worse than She has been for Some time. We are thinking of Spending the next month at Brighthelmston. Wishing you every blessing I am, my Dear Friend, with the greatest regard ever Yours   RICHD: PRICE

Perhaps Some passages may occur to you in *M. Turgot's* letter wch: might be best omitted, Should you approve of publishing it. I have marked one in P. 91 and another in P. 102.

Addressed: To / Benjamin Franklin Esq: / a / Passy / Near Paris

Notation: Richd. Price 12 July 1784.—

To Morellet and Drago

Press copy of copy:[4] American Philosophical Society

Passy, le 13. Juillet 1784.—

Notte en reponse à celle des Negociants Morellet et Drago.[5]

Dans tous et chacun des Etats-Unis de l'Amerique, Il y a des Tribunaux de Justice établis, qui sont également ouverts aux Ci-

---

2. Mary (Polly) Wilkes (1750–1802) was John Wilkes's daughter. The duchess with whom she was staying, widow of the duc de la Vallière, was born Anne-Julie-Françoise de Crussol (1713–1793): Peach and Thomas, *Price Correspondence*, II, 219n; Lewis, *Walpole Correspondence*, III, 17n.

3. April 6, above.

4. In the hand of WTF.

5. Not found.

toyens des dits Etats, et aux Etrangers qui pourroient étre dans le Cas d'y avoir Recours. Les Affaires s'y decident, legalement et promptement.

On conseille aux Sieurs Morellet et Drago, après s'etre assurés dans quel Etat le sieur Wahrendorff fils fait sa Residence, (ce dont M. Franklin ne sauroit les instruire) d'envoyer une Procuration duement légalisée, et des Instructions detaillées, à quelque Maison Danoise etablie dans le dit Etat, ou faute d'icelle, au Vice Consul de France; le quel par ce Moyen, seroit dans le Cas d'agir en tout pour les dits Sieurs, comme s'ils etoient eux mêmes personellement presents.

M. Franklin ignore les Loix que les divers Etats ont faites a l'egard des Personnes qui pourroient s'y refugier pour Raison de Dettes contractées dans un Pays etranger. Mais les Personnes que les Srs. Morrellet et Drago chargeront de leur Procuration, pourront les en instruire.

M. Franklin se chargera volontiers de faire passer les Lettres des dits Srs., et contribuera en tout ce qui dependra de lui, à seconder leurs Vues.

From James Grubb[6]   ALS: American Philosophical Society

Sir,   Nantes, 13th. July 1784
Being on the point of forming a matrimonial Union, with a young Lady of this City, some obstacles arise relative to the difference of Religion which with the Clergy of this Country are insurmountable, unless a Man will undertake to renounce the Tenets he was brought up in, which Circumstance

6. Grubb wrote to WTF on the same date as the present letter reminding him that when they had met in Paris the previous winter, he had confided his intention to wed. Explaining to WTF the problems he here outlines to BF, he further stated that unless he received a permission from Vergennes, he would have to go either to Paris or out of the country to get married. He enclosed a petition for Vergennes, asking WTF to review and deliver it. Because Vergennes had already granted similar requests from other merchants in Nantes, and because WTF had such "weight" at court, Grubb expected his application to be successful. The present letter was shorter, he wrote, out of consideration for the many demands on BF's time: Grubb to WTF, July 13, 1784 (APS).

is repugnant to the principles of a Man of Honor; but, as these difficulties may be removed, by means of a Permission from His Majesty for said Mariage, which will prevent any trouble to the Children about inheriting, after the decease of their Parents, who were different persuations, as some Merchants of this City & other parts of the Kingdom have, under similar Circumstances, obtaind (by means of their Friends at Court) a like permission from Mr De Vergennes, and as Our Union may be a means of individually adding Links to the great Chain you have form'd between America & this Country, I flatter myself you will honor me with your protection to obtain Our Request, and the Offspring of our Union shall be taught to revere your name with as much admiration as does Your Excellency's most obedient & very humble Servant[7]   J: GRUBB

His Excellency, Benjamin Franklin Esqr.

Addressed: His Excellency / Benjamin Franklin Esqr.

Notation: Grubb 13 July 1784—

7. Though BF's role in the matter is not known, WTF did apply to Vergennes, as he reported to Grubb in a now-missing letter of July 23. Grubb replied on July 29: even though Vergennes had judged that the government could not "engage" the curate of Grubb's parish to marry them, if WTF could procure "one of those permissions that are in general granted for Protestants to marry with Catholicks," Grubb would himself undertake to persuade the curate to cooperate. APS. However it was managed, on Aug. 16, after the first publication of the banns, the couple received a dispensation from the bishop of Nantes to forgo the publication of the second and third proclamations usually required, and the following day the twenty-nine-year-old Grubb married Anne Videment: register of the parish of Saint-Nicolas for 1784, Archives municipales de Nantes.

Charles Thomson to the American Commissioners

ALS: National Archives; copy: Historical Society of Pennsylvania

Gentlemen, Philadelphia July 16. 1784

In obedience to the order of the Committee of the States, I have the honor to send you copies of the papers relating to the brig L'Amiable Elizabeth a french vessel that was deserted by her Crew at Sea and was boarded and taken up by citizens of the United States and carried into St Johns in Newfoundland, where she was seized by a public Officer and her cargo disposed of; that you may require of the british court that the full value of the said brig and her cargo be restored for the benefit of Robert Shewell by whose order she was taken up at Sea, and other just claimants according to the laws & usage of civilized commercial and friendly nations.[8]

With great respect I have the honor to be Gentlemen Your most obedient and Most humble Servt[1] CHA THOMSON

8. Over the next several months the American commissioners would receive various and contradictory accounts of this incident. The basic story, according to the enclosures sent by Thomson, is as follows. On April 5, 1783, Robert Shewell, commander of the *Nancy*, bound from Philadelphia to Lorient, responded to a distress signal from the French brigantine *Aimable Elizabeth*, bound from Lorient to Philadelphia. Shewell took the Frenchmen on board and, judging the *Aimable Elizabeth* to be still seaworthy, manned her with a crew of Americans led by Lt. John Justice and instructed them to follow the *Nancy* into Lorient. A storm separated the vessels and at the end of May the *Aimable Elizabeth* landed in St. John's, where the judge of the vice admiralty court seized the vessel and cargo and detained the Americans. Without due process, it was alleged, the judge sold the ship and some of the cargo; the rest was destroyed in a warehouse fire.

1. The present letter largely reiterates the July 10, 1784, resolution by the Committee of the States (*JCC*, XXVII, 583–4). The enclosed papers begin with a copy of that resolution, in Thomson's own hand and signed by him, followed by copies of the following documents: (1) Shewell's May 23, 1784, petition to Congress, (2) an undated certificate signed by Shewell, two of his officers, and three passengers, (3) a June 5, 1783, summons issued by the Newfoundland vice admiralty court, (4) the Oct. 14, 1783, protest by John Justice, consigned by three Newfoundland merchants, and (5) a long account of what had happened at St. John's, dated Oct. 16, 1784, written by Archibald Buchanan (evidently a native of that port), attesting to Justice's good conduct and protesting the actions of the admiralty. BF endorsed the packet "Papers Relating to the Brigantine Aimable Elizabeth / Capt. Shewell's Affair".

Addressed: The Honble / John Adams, Benj Franklin and / Thomas Jefferson, ministers plenipoy / of the United States of America

Notation: Philadelphia July 16. 1784 from The Secretary of Congress enclosing Papers relative to the brig L'amiable Elizabeth

From Jonathan Williams, Jr.

ALS: American Philosophical Society

Dear & hond Sir.   Paris 16 July 1784.

Looking over some old Papers I found the inclosed Note from our good Friend Mr Hutton. I do not remember to have seen the same Verses under your Portrait,—I think them better expressed than those in print, tho' the Idea is the same. Our good Friend labours to distinguish between Tyranny & ministereal Influence. You will judge of his Success.—[2] I send

2. JW enclosed an unsigned Sept. 5, 1775, letter from James Hutton that included an unattributed French verse intended for placement under a portrait of BF:

C'est Franklin, ce mortel dont l'heureuse industrie
Sût enchainer la foudre et lui donner des Loix.
C'est lui dont la raison affermissant la voix
Du joug de l'Injustice affranchit sa Patrie;
Il desarma les Dieux, Il reprime les Rois.

Hutton explained that Du Pont de Nemours had sent the verse to "a friend." However, Turgot must have been the author, as he sent a close variant to Du Pont on June 5, 1776, with a request that Du Pont copy it and burn the original. The latter rendition included a new first line in Latin (*Eripuit coelo fulmen, sceptrumque tyrannis*) that would gain fame as an epigram. It was the only line ever published, perhaps because the French verse was seen as too subversive: XXVI, 670–1n; Gustave Schelle, ed. *Œuvres de Turgot et documents le concernant,* (5 vols., Paris, 1912–23), V, 494, 647; Alfred O. Aldridge, *Franklin and his French Contemporaries* (New York, 1957), pp. 124–35.

Hutton wrote that the last line was "too strong." Americans continued to profess loyalty to the king, but renounced dependence on what they perceived as "unconstitutional Claims of the Ministers and their Dependants."

you Mr Eulers Book, I think his Theory of Magnetism very ingenious, but not convincing, that may be because I do not understand it.——[3]

I am as ever most dutifully & affecy Yours.   J WILLIAMS J

When you have done with the Book please to give it to my Brother in Law[4] who will send it to St Germains.

Doctor Franklin.

Addressed: Dr Franklin.

Notation: Jona. Williams 6. July 1784—

To Thomas Percival

Transcripts (two)[5] and incomplete copy: Library of Congress; copy: Lancashire Record Office

Dear Sir,   Passy, July 17th. 1784
I received yesterday by Mr. White your kind letter of May 11th. with the most agreable Present of your new Book. I read it all before I slept, which is a proof of the good effect

---

3. Leonhard Euler proposed that "magnetic fluid" flowed in one direction, through infinitesimal pores in a magnet. His "Dissertatio de magnete" shared the annual prize awarded by the Académie des sciences for 1744. By 1784, Euler's theory of magnetism was available in several different kinds of publications, and we cannot be certain which of them was being loaned here.

4. Robert (Bob) Alexander, then living with the Franklin household: XLI, 524n.

5. The MS we publish, in the hand of a copyist who worked for WTF, appears to have been made from the fair copy prepared by BFB, only the first page of which survives. BFB's copy was retained by BF, and descended to WTF as part of his inheritance. The copy at the Lancashire Record Office appears to have been made from the MS that Percival received, as it includes the address and a notation made on the address sheet. The copyist was so careless, however, that we deviate from our standard policy and publish from the transcript, adding the information from the address sheet in a footnote.

your happy Manner has of drawing your Reader on, by mixing little Anecdotes and historical Facts with your Instructions. Be pleased to accept my thankful acknowledgements for the pleasure it has afforded me.

It is astonishing that the murderous practice of Duelling, which you so justly condemn,[6] should continue so long in vogue. Formerly when Duels were used to determine Lawsuits from an opinion that Providence would in every Instance favour Truth and Right with Victory, they were more excusable. At present they decide nothing. A man says something which another tells him is a Lie. They fight, but whichever is killed, the point in question remains unsettled. To this purpose they have a pleasant little Story here. "A Gentleman in a Coffee house desired another to sit farther from him.—Why so?—Because, Sir, you stink.— That is an Affront and you must fight me.— I will fight you if you insist upon it: But I do not see how that will mend the Matter. For if you kill me I shall stink too. And if I kill you, you will stink, if possible, worse than you do at present."— How can such miserable Sinners as we are, entertain so much pride as to conceit that every Offence against our imagined Honor merits *Death*! These petty princes in their own opinion would call that Sovereign a Tyrant, who should put one of them to death for a little uncivil Language, tho' pointed at his sacred Person. Yet every one of them makes himself Judge in his own Cause, condemns the Offender without a Jury, and undertakes himself to be the Executioner.

With sincere and great Esteem I have the honor to be Sir your most obdt. &c. B. F.

P. S.
Our friend Mr. Vaughan may perhaps communicate to you some Conjectures of mine relating to the Cold of last Winter, which I sent him in return for the Observations on Cold of Professor Wilson. If he should, and you think them worthy so much notice, you may shew them to your Philosophical Society, to

---

6. In the first section of the appendix: *Moral and Literary Dissertations* . . . (Warrington, Eng., and London, 1784), pp. [291]–7.

which I wish all imaginable success.[7] Their rules seem to me excellent.[8]

Dr. Percival[9]

From Ignaz Edler von Born[1]

ALS: College of Physicians of Philadelphia

Monsieur   Vienne ce 17e Juillet 1784
Un quelqu'un qui, attaché depuis le matin jusqu'au Soir a Son bureau, et privé presque de l'usage de Ses pieds,[2] ne connoit d'autre delassement, que celui que les etudes peuvent donner, Vous offre une petite brochure, qui peut etre pourra Vous amuser dans des moments perdus.[3] Agrées Monsieur cet hommage d'un inconnu, qui admire vos connaissances et vos actions depuis long tems, et qui Vous Souhaite pour le progres des Sciences et pour le bien de l'humanité une vie immortelle. Monsieur Votre tres humble et trés obeissant Serviteur   BORN

7. Percival did convey BF's "Meteorological Imaginations and Conjectures" to the Literary and Philosophical Society of Manchester; see the headnote to that essay published under [May].

8. Percival must have also enclosed, in his May 11 letter, a copy of *Rules, Established for the Government of the Literary and Philosophical Society of Manchester* . . . (Manchester, Eng., 1782).

9. The address (according to the Lancashire Record Office copy) reads "To / Dr. Percival / Manchester" and bears the notation, "Forwarded by Sir your hble Servant Henry Smeathman."

1. A mineralogist and court counselor; see XLI, 214–15.

2. Born suffered an accident while inspecting an ore mine in Hungary in 1770, and developed chronic neuritis. In his later years he could not move without assistance: Helmut Reinalter, "Ignaz von Born—Persönlichkeit und Wirkung," in *Die Aufklärung in Österreich: Ignaʒ von Born und seine Zeit*, ed. Reinalter (Frankfurt am Main, 1991), pp. 16, 29.

3. The enclosed work was *Opuscula* . . . (Augsburg, 1784), an expanded edition of Born's *Specimen monachologiæ methodo Linnæana* . . . (Augsburg, 1783). Both were published under the pseudonym "Joannis Physiophilus." This biting satire against monks classified the various orders according to a system modeled on Linnaean taxonomy, and caused outrage among church officials in Vienna: Reinalter, "Ignaz von Born," pp. 22–3. BF signed his name on the title page and inserted the present letter into the book, writing, "Given by the Author Baron de Borne of Vienna to BF." The book, as well as the letter, is at the College of Physicians of Philadelphia library.

From Feriet AL: American Philosophical Society

Versailles le 17 juillet 1784

Mr. De Feriet a L'honneur de faire mille complimens a Monsieur Franklin, et de lui apprendre que tous Les Verres sont arrivés en bon ètat.[4] Le porteur de ce billet veut bien se charger de rapporter a versailles le Sécrétaire dans lequel L'harmonica était monté, et qu'il est nécessaire D'avoir ici pour accorder Les Verres. Dès que le tout Sera transporté ici, Mr. De feriet fera son possible pour que Monsieur franklin soit content de L'accord et du fini de L'ouvrage.

Notation: De feriet 17 Juillet 1784—

From Michel-Augustin Thouret[5]

ALS: American Philosophical Society

Monsieur et trés illustre Confrere, [*c.* July 17, 1784][6]

Permettez que jaye L'honneur de vous adresser un exemplaire de mes recherches Sur Le magnètisme animal.[7] Je desire que

4. This was welcome news. Feriet had visited the glass factory on May 26, only to be told by the directors that their best worker, an Englishman, had been continually drunk all the previous week and everything he had made was defective. They assured the outraged Feriet that the work would be redone to his satisfaction: Feriet to WTF, May 27, 1784, APS.

5. Though Thouret is here writing as the author of a work on animal magnetism that had been commissioned by the Société royale de médecine (of which he was an active member), he was also a doctor regent of the Society's institutional rival, the Faculté de médecine. He and Andry (one of the Society's commissioners to investigate animal magnetism) had written earlier studies for the Society on the therapeutic use of magnets, one of which BF had recently requested: BF to Vicq d'Azyr, May 24. By offering his new publication to BF, the head of the Faculty/Academy commission, Thouret displayed the kind of cooperation that Poissonnier had hoped would be possible; see the headnote to Poissonnier to BF, April 26. BF and his colleagues drew on Thouret's study, and mentioned him by name, in their final report, described below under the date [Aug. 11].

6. The day Thouret's book was announced for sale in the *Jour. de Paris.*

7. Thouret, *Recherches et doutes sur le magnétisme animal* (Paris, 1784). As noted on p. xxxii, the Society had commissioned him on March 12 to conduct a comprehensive review of ancient and modern works on animal

418

vous Le receviez comme une foible marque du respect et de la profonde Venération avec Lesquels je Suis, Monsieur et trés illustre confrere, Votre trés humble et trés obéissant Serviteur

THOURET

To Mason Locke Weems and Edward Gantt, Jr.

AL (draft) and transcript: Library of Congress

Gentlemen, Passy, near Paris July 18. 1784.

On receipt of your Letter,[8] acquainting me that the Archbishop would not permit you to be ordain'd unless you took the Oath of Allegiance, I apply'd to a Clergyman of my Acquaintance for Information on the Subject of your Obtaining Ordination here. His Opinion was, that it could not be done; and that if it were done you would be requir'd to Vow Obedience to the Archbishop of Paris. I next enquir'd of the Pope's Nuncio, whether you might not be ordain'd by their Bishop in America, Powers being sent him for that purpose if he has them not already. The Answer was, The Thing is impossible, unless the Gentlemen became Catholicks.—[9]

This is an Affair of which I know very little, & therefore I may ask Questions & propose means that are improper or

---

magnetism. Thouret did all that and more: he considered every proposition Mesmer had published, showed how each derived from earlier authors (thereby disproving Mesmer's claim to originality), and posed and answered a series of objections, or "doutes," that supported the conclusion that Mesmer's therapeutic results were due to "imagination." Vicq d'Azyr and five other members of the Society reported on the MS at a meeting of July 9. Their report was an extensive summary, focused on the section that Thouret had written on his own initiative, and it made clear that he had exceeded his assignment. The membership approved the work for publication and voted to include the committee's report as a preface to the book. Vicq d'Azyr certified the text of the report on July 10 (pp. xix–xxxv).

8. Dated July 9, above. BF had received it on July 16; see the entry of that date in BF's journal, [June 26–July 27].

9. Pamphili (XL, 410), the papal nuncio, had recently informed BF that John Carroll had been appointed superior of the Catholic Church's American mission, with many of the powers of a bishop. He expected Carroll to be made a bishop *in partibus* before the end of the year: BF's journal, [June 26–July 27], entries of July 1, 16, and 17.

impracticable: But what is the necessity of your being connected with the Church of England? Would it not be as well if you were of the Church of Ireland? The Religion is the same, tho' there is a different Set of Bishops and Archbishops. Perhaps if you were to apply to the Bishop of Derry, who is a Man of liberal Sentiments,[1] he might give you Orders as of that Church. If both Britain & Ireland refuse you; and I am not sure that the Bishops of Denmark or Sweden would ordain you unless you became Lutherans; what is to be done? Next to becoming Presbyterians, the Episcopalian Clergy of America, in my humble Opinion, cannot do better, than to follow the Example of the first Clergy of Scotland, soon after the Conversion of that Country to Christianity; who when their King had built the Cathedral of St Andrews, and requested the King of Northumberland to lend his Bishops to ordain one for them, that their Clergy might not as heretofore be obliged to go to Northumberland for Orders, and their Request was refused; they assembled in the Cathedral, and the Mitre, Crosier, & Robes of a Bishop being laid upon the Altar, they, after earnest Prayers for Direction in their Choice, elected one of their own Number, when the King[2] said to him, *Arise, go to the Altar, and receive your Office at the Hand of God.* His Brethren led him to the Altar, robed him, put the Crosier in his Hand, & the Mitre on his Head, and he became the first Bishop of Scotland.—[3]

If the British Islands were sunk in the Sea, (& the Surface of this Globe has suffer'd greater Changes) you would probably take some such Method as this: And if they persist in denying you Ordination, tis the same thing. An hundred Years hence,

1. Frederick Augustus Hervey (XLI, 134n).
2. BF here drafted and deleted, "who honour'd the Ceremony with his Presence".
3. BF later told Granville Sharp that he thought he had read this in Raphael Holinshed's *Chronicles of England, Scotland, and Ireland*: Smyth, *Writings*, IX, 358. However, only the kernel of this anecdote appears in the *Chronicles*. According to Holinshed, before Pope Celestine sent the first bishop from Rome to Scotland, the office had been filled by local monks and priests ordained "by the voyces or suffrages of the people": *Chronicles* (2 vols., London, 1577), I, "The Historie of Scotlande," 108. The origin of the remaining details of BF's story, some of which garble historical fact, is unknown.

when People are more enlightend, it will be wonder'd at, that Men in America, qualified by their Learning and Piety to pray for & instruct their Neighbours, should not be permitted so to do, till they had made a Voyage of 6000 Miles out & home, to ask leave of a cross old Gentleman at Canterbury: Who seems, by your Account, to have as little Regard for the Souls of the People of Maryland, as King William's Attorney General Seymour had for those of Virginia. The Reverend Commissary Blair, who projected the College of that Province, and was in England to solicit Benifactions & a Charter, relates, that the Queen in the King's Absence having ordered Seymour to draw up the Charter which was to be given with 2000 £ in Money, he oppos'd the Grant, saying that the Nation was engag'd in an expensive War, that the Money was wanted for better purposes, & he did not see the least Occasion for a College in Virginia. Blair represented to him, that its Intention was to educate & qualify young Men to be Ministers of the Gospel, much wanted there; and begg'd Mr Attorney would consider that the People of Virginia had Souls to be saved as well as the People of England. *Souls*! says he, *damn your Souls. Make Tobacco*![4]

I have the honour to be, Gentlemen, &c[5]

Messrs. Weems & Gant

---

4. BF's version of this story is highly condensed, undoubtedly embellished, and, to an extent, marred by someone's faulty memory of the particulars (perhaps BF's). The Anglican minister James Blair (1655/6–1743), Va. commissary to the bishop of London, founded the College of William and Mary and was its first president. Blair traveled to England in 1691 to obtain financing and a royal charter for the institution. It took him more than a year to achieve his goal, during which time he had to contend with opposition from the Lords of the Treasury to a key part of his funding proposal. Sir Edward Seymour (1633–1708), one of the Treasury commissioners (not, as BF says, attorney general), must have been particularly vocal. Seymour had a reputation for profanity and arrogance. Whether he said these particular words, however, is not known. No other record of this conversation survives: Parke Rouse, Jr., *James Blair of Virginia* (Chapel Hill, 1971), pp. 63–77, [267], 281n; Susan H. Godson *et al.*, *The College of William & Mary: a History* (2 vols., Williamsburg, 1993), I, 4, 8–12, 14; *ODNB*, under Seymour.

5. On Aug. 13, 1784, the Enabling Act passed in Britain, allowing ordination of non-British subjects without administration of the oath. Weems

From John Adams

ALS: Library of Congress; copy: Massachusetts Historical Society

Sir   The Hague July 19. 1784

I have the Honour of your Letters of the 27 of June and 4. July, and Should advise your Excellency to present the C. de Mercy, a Copy of the Instruction as you propose.

By the Length of Time, We have been left without Information respecting foreign Affairs, and by other Circumstances, there are greater Divisions among our Countrymen, respecting these as well as their Finances, than are Salutary. It is now near two Years that I have led the Life of a Spider after having led that of a Toad under an Harrow for four Years before. But I Swear I will not lead one nor the other much longer.[6]

I cant recollect that I have had a Letter from Congress, Since the Peace.[7]

I read Somewhere, when I was young

"Tis Expectation makes the Blessing dear
Heaven were not Heaven, if We knew what it were."[8]

But this Expectation must not be disappointed continually.

Mr Hartley will wait too, I apprehend, as long as We, and for my Part I humbly propose that We Should banish all Thoughts of Politicks, and begin a Course of Experiments in Physicks or mechanicks, of telescopical or miscroscopical observations.

---

and Gantt were ordained as deacons by the bishop of Chester on Sept. 5 and as priests by the archbishop of Canterbury on Sept. 12, making them the first Americans to become Anglican clergy following the Revolutionary War: *ANB*, under Weems; David Hein and Gardiner H. Shattuck, Jr., *The Episcopalians* (Westport, Conn., and London, 2004), p. 315.

6. On July 3 and 5 JA drafted, but appears not to have sent, two bitter letters to Congress complaining about the lack of instructions and commissions and requesting his recall from the Netherlands: *Adams Papers*, XVI, 268–9, 270–1.

7. JA had long resented that most of Congress' letters for the commissioners were sent to BF; see XLI, 289n. He is here forgetting that Boudinot wrote to him directly on Nov. 1, 1783: *Adams Papers*, XV, 335–6.

8. A loose quotation of a couplet from Sir John Suckling, "Against Fruition." See *The Works of Sir John Suckling: the Non-Dramatic Works*, ed. Thomas Clayton (Oxford, 1971), p. 38.

Bertholon and Spalanzani, and Needham have so entertained me of late, that I think to devote myself to similar Researches.[9] With great Respect, I have the Honour to be, sir your Excellencys most obedient humble servant   JOHN ADAMS

His Excellency Dr Franklin

From Andrew Huntington[1]

Two ALS:[2] American Philosophical Society

Norwich, State of Connecticut
Honourd Sir   July 19th. 1784
    I ought to begin my request by asking pardon for troubling you—but I trust you will be pleased to pardon me when you are rightly informed of my case—
    In Octor. 1778. there was a large number of French Prisoners Released from confinement at New York, and Landed at this place in order to be sent to Boston— They were in the most destressed circumstances that you can easily imagine—the greater part very Sick, and in want of every comfort & necessary of Life— Monsr. Testas de Gassies, who had the care of those Prisoners Applied to me to supply them with what necessaries they wanted, and to help them on to Boston as soon as they were able to go—[3] I told that Gentleman I was not willing

9. *De l'Electricité des végétaux* (Paris, 1783), by the abbé Bertholon (xxv, 668n), examined the impact of electricity on plant development. The works of Lazzaro Spallanzani and John Turberville Needham also dealt with organic growth and reproduction, with the former refuting the latter's theory of spontaneous generation; see the entries for the three men in the *Dictionary of Scientific Biography*.

1. A Norwich, Conn., merchant (1745–1824) who served as a commissary during the war: Huntington Family Association, *The Huntington Family in America* . . . (Hartford, 1915), p. 477.

2. The duplicate ALS, with minor variations in wording, was sent under cover of a Dec. 24 letter from Samuel Huntington (APS).

3. The prisoners, numbering around 500, arrived in New London on Oct. 21, 1778. Infected with smallpox, many of them were too weak to complete the journey to Boston: [New London] *Conn. Gaz.; and the Universal Intelligencer*, Oct. 23, 1778, Jan. 8 and 29, 1779; *Huntington Papers: Correspondence of the Brothers Joshua and Jedediah Huntington* . . . , Conn. Hist. Soc. *Coll.*, xx (1923), 418.

to Advance so much money & take his promise for payment—
He Advised Mr. Holker the Consul of France who was then
in Boston—upon which I Immediately received a Letter from
Monsr. Holker dated Octor. 6th. *1778* which I here inclose[4] earnestly requesting me to supply those men with the necessaries
they wanted and that I should be repaid with Honour— I had
conceived so high an esteem of the Honour & Generosity of
his Most Christian Majesty, that I thought I might safely trust
the Honour of one of his Principal Servants in the Civil department in the Country— Accordingly I Advanced money for the
purchase of necessaries for the poor sick and dying Men—and
furnished Teams and horses for those that survived, as fast as
they were able to go, to convey them on to Boston, where they
were ordered— I advanced all the money And even Straightned
my Circumstances to accomplish it, in full expectation of being
generously repaid by Mr. Holker as he had promised—

He was selling Bills of Exchange at four for one— I expected
and Intended to take Bills in pay, as I wanted to make Remittance
for goods—but before I could get through with the Advances
and make out my Account—I received the other letter from
Mr. Holker which I inclose dated in Decr. 4th. 1778[5]—desiring
me to send my Account to him at Philadelphia for payment—
Accordingly as soon as I had finished the Account I sent the same
to Philadelphia for payment— Mr. Holker declined settling it—
and referd. me to a Mr. Bell[6] in Boston to settle it— I was much
disappointed— However I sent to Mr. Bell at Boston in hopes to
be paid agreable to Mr. Holkers promise, but I was put of there
with very little encouragement of ever being paid—

As I had Advanced all my little stock of money in Trade and
was in destress for the want of it, I still continued my Application
for payment untill in June 1779—Mr. Bell offerd to pay me the

4. Jean Holker's letter was actually dated Nov. 6. (APS, but not filed
with Huntington's letter.)
5. Not found.
6. The Boston merchant Daniel Bell, agent for both the French naval
ministry and Jean Holker personally: John Holker, *Correspondence between
John Holker . . . and Robert Morris . . .* (Philadelphia, 1786), p. 11; Joseph de
Valnais to Jean Holker, Dec. 27, 1778 (Yale University Library).

nominal sum in continental money— The money was not then worth but one third the sum which I Advanced, as Bills were then selling at 12 for one— I did not Know of any measure to take to Oblige Mr. Holker to make me satisfaction, and did fear I might Loose the whole—which my Circumstances would not allow of— I was Advised to take what I could get—in expectation that I might in after time have Justice done me— Therefore I Received the nominal Sum which I had Advanced and gave receipt in full— I have since the Peace been Advised to Apply to the Minister of France at Philadelphia—& have Accordingly made application to him by my Attorney as per Petition dated May 4th. 1784—in full Expectiation of Redress— The Petition & the Ministers Answer to the Same I also Inclose—of the 12th. June—[7]

If I had made a Profit in selling goods to the French prisoners, or if I was able to loose so much money—I would not trouble any Body about the Matter—but that is not the case— It was money, and money only—that I Advancd— Before the War I was in good circumstances— I have been largely in advance for supplies and money to the Public to carry on the War—whereby I have been a great looser, together with Large Losses by Navigation which Renders my Circumstances Low, and difficult to continue my Business, so as to support a growing Family— I have therefore taken the Liberty to Intreat and Beseach your Interest and Attention in my Behalf at the Court of France—

The French Nation have had my money for the Support of their Troops, and I do not think that his Most Christian Majesty wishes to support his Troops at my expence, when his own Abilities are aboundantly sufficient— You will please to observe by the Copy of my Account[8] the amount would have purchased

7. The petition is in the hand of Pelatiah Webster and signed by him on Huntington's behalf. The answer, written below Webster's signature and signed by Marbois and La Luzerne, certified that both men had examined it. The petition would need to be resubmitted to Holker, who, if he could not settle the matter himself, would have to obtain orders from the minister of the marine.

8. Missing.

me upwards of Six hundred pounds in Bills of Exchange at the Rate which Mr. Holker was selling at when I Advanced it—& when I Received the money again it would not buy me but about Two hundred pounds in Bills—so that it is easy to see that the King of France did not pay but only one third of my Account in Real money— The other Two thirds is still due to me— At the foot of the Account abovementioned I have stated the Same in Lawfull Money dollars @ 6/ Each by the Scale of Congress and cast the Interest up to June *1784* which leaves a Ballance due to me of £414—6—

I only want my Just due— Mr. Holker is not willing to make me satisfaction because I cannot demand it in Law— I am sorry that any Gentleman is so void of Honesty, as only to be willing to pay a Just debt when the Law will force him to do it.— My demand appears to me so Just, that I cannot think but it will appear so to every candid Mind—and I have no doubt but his Most Christian Majesty will do me Justice—though I Cannot get it from his Servant— Your Interest and Influence at the Court of France is so great that you have Obtained many un-merrited favours for this Country— Therefore I have no doubt but your Generous Disposition will Extend to the relief of the Oppressed and that you will be pleased to Interpose in Behalf of one of your Injured Countrymen.

I neen not pretend to give you any Instruction, the Matter speaks for itself, your Wisdom will direct you to such Measures, as will be proper in the Case— I only want and ask for my Just due, which I Cannot be willing to think Will be de-nied me— I am with the greatest Esteem your Most Obedient Hble Servant   ANDW HUNTINGTON

his Excellency Benjm. Franklin Esqr

From Pierre du Calvet[1]

ALS: American Philosophical Society

a Londres le 20e. Juillet 1784—
No. 9, Cannon-Street, prés la poste générale—

Monsieur L'ambassadeur,

Avec le vulgaire des grands, on ne parle guéres de comptes et de dettes, quoi que non personnelles et de pur office pour eux; beaucoup moins en vat'on jusqu'a en Solliciter avec Succés le payement auprés d'eux; leur fierté, leur délicatesse Se formalisent de ces details triviaux, et le peu d'intérest quils prennent aux bésoins étrangers, rend infructueuse toute addresse, faite auprés d'eux pour les Soulager, ce n'est pas lá l'illustre Ambassadeur de l'amérique. Mr. le docteur Franklin est la droiture, la politesse, l'équité, la bienfaisance même: il est l'ami des hommes, et le pére tendre des opprimés. C'est Sur ce pié, que tout paris le reconnoit, l'estime et l'aime, et c'est Sous ces qualités bienfaisantes, que je me flatte de le connoître bientôt moi même, de Sçience expérimentale et d'aprés les lécons du Sentiment.

Je Suis l'infortuné canadien, qui, le 17e. et le 20e. du mois d'octobre dernier, eut l'honneur de communiquer à vôtre Excellence a passi l'histoire de Ses infortunes, a quebec. durant le Sejour des généraux Américains dans la province en 1776. Je fis par leurs ordres des fournitures de toute Espece, jusques á la concurrence de 56,394 *l.t.* 10 *s.* 1 *d.* livres tournois;[2] je lui remis aussi dans les mains les duplicatas des réconnoissances, dont les originaux Sont dans la possession, de Mr. Pierre-charles L'ambert, Banquier, vieille rue du temple prés de l'égout á Paris.—[3]

---

1. The merchant who had visited BF at Passy the previous October, and whose case BF described in detail to President of Congress Boudinot: XLI, 166–7.

2. This sum included both the unpaid value of the receipts and promissory notes he had accepted for a portion of the goods he had supplied, as well as the value of the Continental currency he had been paid for the rest. He sought payment of the former and compensation for the depreciation of the latter. Congress, in response, made clear that he could expect no greater compensation for the depreciation of this currency than was extended to U.S. citizens. So far none had been offered: XLI, 166–7; *JCC*, XXVI, 260–1.

3. Du Calvet had shown BF the originals of his receipts and promissory notes, and BF enclosed the duplicates in his letter to Boudinot: XLI, 166–7.

Le général haldimand[4] en 1780, me Suspecta de favorizer le parti Américain, et me confina pendant 948 jours dans la plus barbare captivité, Sans aucun respect pour L'humanité ni pour les loix, dont j'eus beau réclamer la protection, par mes appels. C'est Sur ce principe d'attachement présumé américain, que ce vindicatif gouverneur, me denia hautement la liberté, de passer, á mon rétour En Europe, par les êtats unis, pour y aller Solliciter en personne á philadelphie, auprés du congrés, la liquidation de la dette. Par la dignité de Sa place, le général haldimand est au dessus des loix á quebec, et depuis mon départ de paris, j'en Suis á poursuivre Son rappel á londres, ou réduit á Son inconséquente individualité, il déviendra le tributaire des loix. Il S'en faut bien que je ne Sois fort avancé vers le Succés, Malgré la vivacité non ralentie de mes instances.

Vôtre Excellence lira dans mon Memoire que j'ai l'honneur de lui addresser le détail des oppressions de cét indigne gouverneur, et dans mon appel, L'indifference et l'inactivité du gouvernement d'angleterre, á les amener Sous la jurisdiction des loix.[5] Cette double Marche d'administration ou Subalterne ou en chef ne la Surprendra pas: ce même esprit de despotisme, qui a démembré L'amérique de L'angleterre, gouverne encore de prés et de loin la province de quebec. Il est vrai que la constitution angloise offre des ressources pour n'en être pas impunement la victime et la dupe: mais ce n'est qu'au poids de l'or, qu'on peut les mettre en œuvre avec Succés. Depuis Sept mois révolus que je lutte á londres contre les obstacles, mon Séjour m'a couté des Sommes considérables, et cépendant, á proprément parler, á peine ai je commencé, je prépare un appel d'éclat au parlement,

4. Governor general of Canada: XXVI, 337n.
5. The enclosures have not been found. Du Calvet's *Appel à la justice de l'état* . . . (London, 1784) combined a statement of his own case with calls for political and judicial reform in Canada. By "Memoire," he may have been referring to *The Case of Peter Du Calvet* . . . (London, 1784), published in March. Written, it is now thought, by Francis Maseres and Peter Livius (a note on the title page explained that Du Calvet did not understand English), it included a dedication to George III written in French by Du Calvet himself: *Dictionary of Canadian Biography* (15 vols. to date, Toronto, 1966–), IV, 230–1.

qui m'entrainera dans un Surcroit de dépenses, pour m'ouvrir Seulement, le chemin de la loi; Si la justice et la générosité de l'amérique ne viennent á mon Secours, il m'est impossible de me conserver dans la passe de fournir á tout.

Je S'ai, Monsieur L'ambassadeur, qu'il est une foule de demandeurs, qui comme moi, réclament cette justice et cette générosité; mais j'ose avancer que mon cas est tout á fait privilégié. C'est Sur mon attachement présumé pour la cause de l'amérique, que j'ai été dépouillé Si longtêms de ma liberté, que durant m'a captivité, la tirannie á fait á mon patrimoine une bréche de plus de £ 20,000, Sterling, que les tristes débris de ma fortune dépérissent encore tous les jours á quebec, par L'absence de l'œil du maître, et qu'enfin le gouvernement affecte l'inaction, et fait naitre des l'enteurs, pour m'arracher de mes mains mon triomphe, en M'arrachant les ressources pour l'achêter: Si le congrés, dans le Moment actuel, pouvoit être au fait de cet assemblage de circonstances, d'une part Si critiques, et de l'autre Si favorables pour moi, la Magninimité de Sentimens, qui la toujours distingué dans Sa Marche ne balanceroit pas de me favoriser dans la poursuite de mon oppresseur par Ses générosités mêmes, et bien plus encore par la liquidation d'une dette de justice et d'honneur, contractée depuis un Si long cours d'années, par l'entremise de Ses députés.

Il n'entre pas moins de n'oblesse et délévation dans la façon de penser de Son digne réprésentant, Mr. le docteur franklin, et je Suis fondé á n'en pas attendre des traits moins éclatans de Sa part, Sur tout, S'il á la bonté d'observer en Surplus, que l'ouverture du nouveau parlement, m'entraine dans des démarches nouvelles, qu'une addition de dépenses Seule peut Soutenir. Mais peut-être, que les fonds du congrés, actuellement dans les mains de Vôtre Excellence, ne répondent pas par leur valeur, aux grandes vües de justice et de générosité qui vous animent, et que la liquidation entiere de la dette quoi qu'une pure bagatelle pour un état, est actuellement hors de Ses pouvoirs: mais en attendant je récévrois une partie du payement á vôtre choix avec des transports de réconnoissance d'autant mieux fondés, que ce début de justice, en me fournissant des aisances pour mon affaire me Seroit un gage de vôtre protection en m'a faveur. Je ne Saurois me persuader que le vertueux Ambassadeur du congrés réfuse ce juste Sécours à un infortuné qui á Souffert, et ne Souffre encore que trop injustement pour avoir été Suspecté être l'ami du congrés, et qu'il voulut par ce réfus le réduire á l'impossibilité d'obtenir jamais justice.

J'ai pris la liberté de M'appuyer auprés de vôtre Excellence de la récommandation de Mr. le comte de vergennes, que je Sais être un de Ses illustres amis, autant par inclinations que par l'unité de respectables caracteres: ce grand ministre est le protecteur déclaré de tous les français, Sous quelque climat, que la fortune de la guerre puisse les disperser, vous êtes vous, Monsieur L'Ambassadeur, le défendeur des Américains et de tous ceux qui tiennent á L'amérique par quelque rélation, je Suis né français, et c'est en consideration de l'amérique que je Souffre, voila mes titres á la double protection, et de vôtre Excellence et de Mr. le comte de vergennes, c'est á dire que voila le présage assuré du Succés de mes demandes.

Crainte d'événement contraire Sur la route, je prends la liberté d'addresser á vôtre Excellence un paquet pour Mr. l'ambert, que je charge d'aller á vôtre hotel récévoir vos ordres. J'ose me flatter en concluant, qu'ils me Seront favorables, et qu'aprés avoir commencé par être L'admirateur de Mr. le d'octeur franklin, je finirai par le compter au nombre de mes Bienfaiteurs et de mes protecteurs. Si les intentions de vôtre Excellence pouvoient m'être manifestées, par le canal de Mr. L'ambassadeur de france[6] ce Seroit le comble de la bienfaisance et de l'humanité.—

J'ai l'honneur d'être avec le respect le plus profond Monsieur L'Ambassadeur, De Vôtre Excellence Le trés hûmble et trés ôbéissant Serviteur,   PIERRE DU CALVET.

Notation: Pierre Du Calvet 20— Juillet 1784—

---

6. Jean Balthazar, comte d'Adhémar de Montfalcon, had been the French ambassador to the British court since May, 1783: XL, 14n.

From Richard Price

ALS: American Philosophical Society

Dear Sir   Newington-Green July 21st: 1784

The bearer of this, Mr Lewis, is an honest tradesman, and an attendant at the Meeting-House in Newington-Green.[7] I cannot resist his desire that I would give him a line to introduce him to you. He has always been a warm favourer of the American cause, thinks of you with veneration, and wishes just to See you. Any notice, therefore, that you may think fit to take of him will give him particular pleasure. He goes abroad with no other views than those of amusement and pleasure.

I Sent a letter to you by Ld Fitzmaurice, Ld Shelburne's eldest Son, who Set out last week for Paris in order to pay a visit to the Abbe M——x. This letter accompany'd with two pamphlets made a part of a parcel directed to Miss Wilkes at the Duchess de la Valliere's; and Miss Wilkes was to convey it to you.[8] I am now hoping for the favour of your opinion on the Subject mentioned in that letter— I have lately been informed that Mr. Turgot left no family, and this removes one of the reasons of my Scruples— With great respect and affection I am, Dear Sr, ever yours   RICHD: PRICE

Addressed: To / Dr Franklin / Passy / Near Paris

Notation: Rd. Price July 21. 1784.

7. This "honest tradesman" must have been one of the six sons of a late Dissenting minister named Lewis whom Price knew well. He described the family in a 1785 letter to James Bowdoin: they were warm supporters of the American cause; two of the sons had emigrated and were linen drapers in Boston; and their sister and her family remained valued members of his congregation: Peach and Thomas, *Price Correspondence,* II, 278; III, 12–13. Their late father may have been Israel Lewis, who preceded Price as pastor at the Newington Green church: D. O. Thomas, *The Honest Mind: the Thought and Work of Richard Price* (Oxford, 1977), pp. 15–16.

8. The letter in question was dated July 12 (above). Fitzmaurice brought BF various letters and papers from London; see the entry of July 22 in BF's journal, [June 26–July 27].

From Madame Brillon

AL: American Philosophical Society

jeudi matin 22 juillet [1784][9]

Je ne suis point anguille comme le prétend monsieur votre fils mon aimable papa, et j'avois bien le projét decidé d'aller vous voir ce matin, mais mes enfans sont partis plus tard que je ne comptois, ma fille cadétte et moi avons eté plus sottes que je ne croyois, nous étions attristées, préocupées, et tout uniment nous reméttrons a dimanche le plaisir d'aller vous voir; quand a la supposition d'un oubli, ce n'est point un ami comme vous qu'on puisse jamais oubliér un seul instant, mon seul tort est de n'avoir pas envoyé plustost vous dire mon bon papa, que j'étois trop leste ce matin pour aller vous voir, que j'aurai assés d'ésprit samedi pour vous donner a déjeuner et tout celui qu'il faudra dimanche pour vous en aller demander:

Je rouvre ma léttre pour faire réparation a mr votre fils, en relisant la vostre je vois que l'anguille est madame helvétius; si elle glisse elle en est bien la maitresse, mais jamais mon coeur ne vous échapera:

Addressed: A Monsieur / Monsieur Benjamin / Franklin / A Passy

From William Franklin[1]

ALS: American Philosophical Society

London July 22d.[–August 6], 1784

Dear and Honoured Father,

Ever since the Termination of the unhappy Contest between Great Britain and America, I have been anxious to write to you,

---

9. During BF's stay in France, July 22 fell on a Thursday in 1779 and 1784. Based on the familiar tone of the letter, we assign it to the latter year.

1. This is the first communication between WF and his father since the early days of the war. WF, then the royal governor of New Jersey, was arrested in 1776 and incarcerated until 1778. He subsequently became a leader of the Loyalists in America and in England, where he arrived in September, 1782. During the period of the peace negotiations, when WF pressed the British government for restitution on behalf of the Loyalists, BF had no sympathy for their position. BF's satire on the subject, "Apologue," likened them to mongrels, "corrupted by royal promises of great rewards": XXII, 551–2; XXVII, 90, 600–1; XXXVIII, 182n; XXXIX, 197n, 230–2, 232–4.

and to endeavour to revive that affectionate Intercourse and Connexion which till the Commencement of the late Troubles had been the Pride and Happiness of my Life. Uncertain, however, whether the decided and active Part I took in Opposition to the Measures you thought proper to adopt, might not have left some unfavourable Impressions on your Mind; or, if that should not be the Case, whether you might not have some political Reasons for avoiding such Correspondence while you retained your present Employ under the Congress, I was induced to postpone my Intention of writing till I could by some Means or other learn whether your Inclinations were likely to meet my Wishes in that respect. I was, besides, led to expect an Opportunity of a personal Interview from the Accounts I frequently heard from some of your Friends in London, and particularly from a Letter which Temple wrote to Mr. Whitefoord about a Twelvemonth ago, intimating that you had Thoughts of soon returning to America, and would probably visit England in your Way.[2] In that Letter he likewise mentioned that he should have wrote to me, but that he was apprehensive it might, if known, excite Suspicions among some jealous People for whom you acted. This was an additional Motive for my delaying to write, as the Reason he gave why it was improper for him to write to me, operated equally against my writing to you or him, while in your present Situation. There are narrow illiberal Minds in all Parties. In that which I took, and on whose Account I have so much suffered, there have not been wanting some who have insinuated that my Conduct has been founded on Collusion with you, that one of us might succeed which ever Party should prevail. Similar Collusions, they say, were known to have existed between Father and Son during the civil Wars in England and Scotland. The Falsity of such Insinuation in our Case you well know, and I am happy that I can with Confidence appeal not only to you but to my God, that I have uniformly acted from a strong Sense of what I conceived my Duty to my

2. WTF, who was responding to a letter from Whitefoord that conveyed how much WF wished to renew their correspondence, actually wrote that BF had not yet received permission from Congress to return. WTF, however, "ardently" wished to visit England and longed to see his father: XL, 441.

King, and Regard to my Country, required. If I have been mistaken, I cannot help it. It is an Error of Judgment that the maturest Reflection I am capable of cannot rectify; and I verily believe were the same Circumstances to occur again Tomorrow, my Conduct would be exactly similar to what it was heretofore, notwithstanding the cruel Sufferings, scandalous Neglects, and Ill-treatment which we poor unfortunate Loyalists have in general experienced.— On a Subject so disagreeable I have no Desire to say more, and I hope every thing which has happened relative to it may be mutually forgotten. Encouraged by what passed lately between you, and that good-hearted Man Colonel Wadsworth,[3] I flatter myself that you are actuated by the same Disposition, and that my Advances towards a Renewal of our former affectionate Intercourse will be as acceptable to you as they are agreeable to myself.

It gave me great Pleasure to hear from the Colonel, Mrs. Montgomery, and others, that my Son, who owes so much to you for his Education and other Advantages, has conducted himself to your Satisfaction. The Character given of him by a Variety of Persons who have known him at Paris does him great Credit, and cannot fail to heighten that natural Affection which always interests me in whatever concerns his Welfare. Please to give my Love to him, and let him know that I wish he would write to me soon, and inform me whether he received a Letter from Mr. Galloway some Months ago, inclosing a Paper

---

3. WF described his conversation with Jeremiah Wadsworth in a 1788 submission to the Loyalist claims commission: "I happened, in the Summer of 1784, to meet with Colonel Wadsworth, an American officer just arrived from France, who told me that he had a few Days before dined with my Father, and heard him express himself surprized that I had never wrote to him, nor made any Overtures towards a Reconciliation, and that he (my Father) had said he could not see any Reason, now all Differences between the two Countries were settled, why those of Individuals who had taken opposite Sides in the Controversy should not likewise be accommodated. Finding, from the Colonel's Account, that my Father had spoke of me with some Degree of Affection, I determined to write to him": "An Abstract of the Vouchers . . . ," Feb. 14, 1788, claim of WF (National Archives, London). Wadsworth left Paris for London at the end of June; see Wadsworth & Church to BF, June 24, above.

belonging to you, as Mr. G. is uneasy lest it has miscarried.[4] Now I have broken the Ice, many Things occur which I much want an Opportunity to mention; too many, indeed, for the Limits of a Letter, and some of them respecting private Family Affairs, of a very important Nature, that cannot well be adjusted without a personal Interview. I shall therefore, if you are not likely to be soon in England, be happy to have your Approbation to wait on you at Paris. In the mean Time I beg you to be assured of my constant Prayers for your Health and Happiness, and that I am, as ever, Your very dutiful and affectionate Son

WM: FRANKLIN

P.S. Augst. 6.— As I knew not whether the Post was a safe Mode of Conveyance of Letters to you, I have postponed sending the above, in hopes of finding a private Hand, but as no one has occurred I have at length determined to send it by this Night's Mail. If you know of a better Channel of Correspondence you will please to mention it.

Please to direct to me at No. 28 Norton Street, Marylebone, and, if you think it best to put your Letter under Cover to another Person, it may be directed to Thos. Odwin, Esqr., Hylord's Court, Crutched Friars, London[5]

Benjamin Franklin, Esqr &c. &c. &c

4. The "Paper" was a will that BF made in 1776, of which we were previously unaware. Galloway was named an executor in that document, but in 1779, after he had fled to London as a Loyalist, BF apparently replaced him with Francis Hopkinson: XXIX, 622, XXXV, 472. In May, 1781, BF, who did not have a copy of the will with him in France, asked WTF to write to Galloway in London and ask what had become of it. (In that letter, WTF referred to the document as "the Will [BF] made & left with you a short Time before his last Departure from America.") Galloway's daughter, Elizabeth, initially answered that it was in New York with her father's private papers, but in the letter mentioned here, dated Oct. 28, 1783, Galloway informed WTF that a packet of these papers, including the will, had just been sent to him. He enclosed the will with the seal intact: WTF to Joseph Galloway, May 13, 1781, Library of Congress; Elizabeth Galloway to WTF, May 28, 1781, APS; Joseph Galloway to WTF, Oct. 28, 1783, APS. In the meantime, however, BF seems to have drawn up a new will with the assistance of John Jay: XXXVIII, 113.

5. A merchant: *Bailey's British Directory; or, Merchant's and Trader's Useful Companion, For the Year 1784* . . . (4 vols., London, 1784), I, 187.

Addressed: Dr. Franklin / &c. &c. &c. / at Passy / near Paris / France / per Post / [Single]

From Mary Hewson

ALS: Addinell S. Hewson, Bryn Mawr, Pennsylvania (1957)

Dear Sir   Cheam July 22[^6] 1784

I received your packets of the 26th. of April and 14th of June, with the two little books, for which I thank you.[^7] They came to me very safe by the post and I do not grudge the postage. The Sepr. Vol. of *l'ami des enfans,* which completed the set, I also received,[^8] but I know not by what conveyance it came to Sutton, whence it was brought to me by one of the men belonging to the Inn there. It was unaccompanied by any line.

If you will order any packet to be sent to Messrs. Antrobus and Seaman, Teamen, opposite Northumberland Street, it will come to me, without fail, the thursday after it arrives there.

I had some hope of taking a little trip to see you this summer, and if I could have so managed it I would have treated all my children with the jaunt, for Mr Viny told me of a person with whom he thought we could go upon easy & convenient terms, but as I have heard no more about it I fear we must give up that pleasure, and prepare for Southamton whither I now think of taking my young ones to bathe, as I believe bathing to be very wholesome, tho' thank God! their health is so good as not to want mending. The only visible effect I wish for is a little additional height to my son Thomas, who is so much below the common size that I begin to fear he will always remain so. His make

6. Hewson amended the date with a thick pen, and while the first numeral is clear, the second is not. L'Air de Lamotte read it as a "o" when writing the notation. BF, on the other hand, referred to the date as July 22 when answering Hewson on Aug. 15, below. We use his date.

7. BF sent the first volume of *Introduction familière à la connoissance de la Nature* with his letter of April 29 (not 26), above. His packet of June 14 is missing, but it must have contained the next installment of the three-part work.

8. See Hewson's letter of April 2, above.

[^6]:
[^7]:
[^8]:

is perfect, tho' in miniature; I only wish him to reach a size that will not be remarkable, and for that I think it my duty to give him every chance I can. His sister wants no assistance that way, she is as tall as most girls of her age, and tho she does not always hold herself like those who have stays & collars, she is well shaped, and I flatter myself will look as well when grown up. William is a common size, not so thick as when you knew him, yet stout & well made. Mr Gilpin[9] gives me a very good account of both my boys, and I am pleased to find that he reads their different characters. I have been charged with partiality, but, I think, unjustly, for I never see a preference shewn to either without immediately feeling that the other deserves as much. I could bear that one should be the cleverest best boy in the world (*except his brother*). I could love any one of my children more than the others, if that could be done without loving the others less than that one. That sentence may appear nonsensical, but it is more expressive of my maternal affection than any other I can find.

Being come to the end of my paper I can give you no more of my nonsense, but must conclude with the best proof of my sense that I am with perfect esteem your affectionate

MARY HEWSON

I had hopes of sending this by Mr Vonsittart (a son of the Govr who was lost) but he went sooner than I expected. He is a young man of genius & good conduct; is just entred at Oxford after being at the head of Cheam School.[1] If he should by any means be introduced to you, I should be obliged to you for taking such notice of him as will not be inconvenient to you; and place it to my account.

Addressed: A Monsieur / Monsieur Franklin / á Passy / prés de / Paris

Notation: Mary Hewson July 20 1784.—

---

9. William Gilpin, the headmaster of Cheam School: XXXVII, 259n.

1. Nicholas Vansittart (1766–1851), a future chancellor of the exchequer, enrolled at Christ Church, Oxford, in March, 1784. His father, Henry Vansittart (1732–1770?), once the governor of Bengal, perished at sea during a return voyage to India: *ODNB*, under Nicholas and Henry.

From Jonathan Williams, Jr.

ALS: American Philosophical Society

Dear & hond Sir.—   Paris 22 July 1784.

Please to send to Mr Barclay by the return of Colll Franks's Servant, the two Bundles of Papers relating to the Ship Marquis de la Fayette, which lay on your Table near the Window in the Library, as we have occasion for them to explain some parts of that Business.[2]

I am most respectfully & affectionately Yours.

J WILLIAMS J

they are the Papers you intended as materials for a Memoire

Addressed: His Excellency Doctor Franklin.

Notation: Williams 22 Juillet 1784

From Dumas

ALS: American Philosophical Society; AL (draft): Algemeen Rijksarchief

Monsieur,   La Haie 24e. Juillet 1784

Je ne doute pas que la Lecture de l'incluse pour le Congrès ne fasse plaisir à Votre Excellence.[3] C'est pourquoi je la fais passer par vos mains, Vous priant de la fermer & acheminer ensuite,

2. JW was in the process of settling his accounts with Thomas Barclay. On Aug. 11, 1784, he submitted to Barclay a memorandum explaining his purchase of cloth from Chaumont for soldiers' uniforms, which BF had authorized (Yale University Library). That cloth was shipped in 1781 on the *Marquis de Lafayette,* which was captured en route to America. The papers mentioned in the present letter may be those of which BF sent copies to Gérard de Rayneval shortly after the capture: XXXV, 192n, 244–5, 249, 337.

3. Dumas doubtless enclosed his July 22[–23] letter to the president of Congress. This time, he wrote in English. He lamented the insufficiency of his salary and pointed out the financial sacrifices he had made in the "unsought, but cheerfully accepted, and successful service of Congress." In a postscript, Dumas reported the arrival from Paris of a draft Franco-Dutch treaty of defensive alliance (National Archives). The letter is published in *Diplomatic Correspondence of the United States,* VII, 41–2.

avec celle pour Mr. Van Berckel, soit par le Paquebot de Port Louis à N. York le mois prochain, ou par Mr. Barclay, s'il sait une occasion plus prompte. Tout est fidele, & rien d'exagéré dans cette Dépeche. Si Mr. Wm. Franklin, que je prie de recevoir mes meilleurs complimens, veut bien m'accuser la réception de la présente & de son contenu en bon état, & m'apprendre aussi votre bien-être à tous égards, je lui en serai fort obligé.[4] Je suis avec le plus respectueux attachement, De Votre Excellence, Le très-humble & très-obéissant serviteur   C. W. F. DUMAS

Passy à Son Excellence M. Franklin

Notation: Dumas 24 Juillet 1784

From the Comte de Barbançon

LS: American Philosophical Society

Monsieur   A Lille ce 25. Juillet [1784]

Que j'ai de plaisir à vous annoncer que des greffes de pommier Ananas que vous avez bien voulu me donner,[5] l'une a parfaitement réussi! Je crois pouvoir vous assurer que, l'année prochaine, J'en aurai assez pour en faire part aux personnes à qui vous voudriez en donner; mandez moi, je vous prie vos intentions à cet égard.

Je crains bien, Monsieur, que la Lettre de recommandation que vous m'aviez remise pour M. Bartram,[6] ainsi que la mienne qui y étoit jointe, ne lui Soit pas parvenue; je n'ai eu aucune

---

4. Dumas may have hoped that BF would intercede with Congress on his behalf, as JA had done on May 13 (praising his services, performed for a "Pittance"): *Adams Papers*, XVI, 210–11. If so, he was disappointed. WTF responded on Aug. 1, acknowledging the receipt of the dispatch, promising to forward it, and reporting on BF's health. He added that Congress had appointed BF to a new commission, and that they daily expected the arrival of TJ, who carried the instructions (APS).

5. The count acknowledged receipt of plant material obtained from John Bartram, Jr., on Feb. 8: XLI, 540.

6. Not found.

réponse ni, de lui ni du Sieur Villiams banquier à Nantes, à qui j'avois envoyé ce paquet par un de mes amis. Comme la Saison s'avance, je prens le parti de lui écrire de nouveau, et j'ai L'honneur de vous adresser ma Lettre. Combien je vous aurois d'obligation, Si vous aviez la bonté d'y joindre quelques mots de recommandation, et faire usage de la voie la plus prompte et la plus sûre pour faire passer ce paquet à M. Bartram. Assurez le, je vous prie, de la plus grande éxactitude dans les payemens des envois qu'il nous fera. Je vais écrire à Mr. Villiams, et le prier de nous mettre très en regle à cet égard vis à vis de Mr. Bartram.

Vous m'aviez promis, Monsieur, de m'envoyer la note de ce dont vous desirez essayer la culture chez vous.[7] Vous ne pouvez douter de tout le plaisir que j'aurois à vous le procurer. Vous Savez que nous devons à notre Gouvernement l'avantage d'avoir un paquebot qui part de L'Orient pour New-york tous les derniers lundis de chaque Mois; cette voie Seroit, je crois, extrêmement commode pour vous faire passer, lorsque vous serez de retour chez vous, tout ce dont vous aurez besoin. Il Suffiroit d'avoir une occasion de New york pour Philadelphie. J'aurai de mon côté toutes facilités par notre Ministre de La marine. Je ne Saurois trop vous le répéter, Monsieur, vous ne pourrez jamais m'offrir, autant que je Le desirerois, les occasions de vous être utile.

Si vous voulez bien m'honorer d'un mot de réponse, je vous prie de me L'adresser à mon Château de Varennes près Noyon.

Je vous demande mille pardons de ne pas avoir L'honneur de vous écrire de ma main; la fievre que j'ai depuis quelque tems m'affoiblit au point de ne pouvoir en faire usage.

Agréez, je vous prie, les assurances du très Sincere attachement avec Lequel J'ai L'honneur d'être, Monsieur, Votre très humble & très Obéissant Serviteur.   LE CTE. DE BARBANÇON

Notation: Comte de Barbançon Lille 25 Juillet

---

7. In his letter of Feb. 8, cited above, the count had offered to collect French seeds for BF's friends in Philadelphia.

To Benjamin Vaughan

LS, copy, and transcript:[8] Library of Congress

Dear Friend,   Passy July 26th.[–c. August 15][9] 1784.
I have received several Letters from you lately, dated June 16th.
June 30, & July 13.[1] I thank you for the Information respecting
the Proceedings of your West India Merchants, or rather Planters:[2] The Restraints whatever they may be upon our Commerce
with your Islands, will prejudice their Inhabitants, I apprehend,
more than us. It is wonderful how preposterously the Affairs of
this World are managed. Naturally one would imagine that the
Interest of a few Particulars, should give way to general Interest. But Particulars manage their Affairs with so much more Application, Industry and Address, than the Publick do theirs, that
general Interest most commonly gives way to particular— We
assemble Parliaments and Councils, to have the Benefit of their
collected Wisdom, but we necessarily have at the same time the
Inconvenience of their collected Passions, Prejudices & private
Interests. By the help of these, artful Men overpower the Wisdom, and dupe its Possessors; and if we may judge by the Acts,
Arrets, & Edicts all the World over for regulating Commerce,
an Assembly of wise Men is the greatest Fool upon Earth.

---

8. The LS is in BFB's hand; BF wrote the last two words of the complimentary close and the postscript. The transcript, made for WTF's edition of
BF's writings, contains the wording changes published in WTF, *Memoirs*, II,
58–63. Vaughan himself published an abbreviated version of this letter in
the *Repository*, II (1789), 185–9; he excerpted part of the first paragraph and
all of paragraphs 10 to 19.
    9. The bracketed date takes into account BF's postscript about WTF's de-
livering the letter. We know that BF and WTF had decided on the latter's trip
to London by Aug. 15, when BF wrote the first of several letters that WTF
would carry: to Mary Hewson, below.
    1. None of them has been located.
    2. Since 1783 Vaughan had been one of six members of the standing
committee of West India planters and merchants, which unsuccessfully
lobbied the British government to allow American ships full participation
in the West Indian trade: Craig C. Murray, "Benjamin Vaughan (1751–
1835): the Life of an Anglo-American Intellectual" (Ph.D. diss., Columbia
University, 1989), pp. 182–3; Lillian M. Penson, "The London West India Interest in the Eighteenth Century," *English Hist. Rev.*, XXXVI (1921),
387–90.

I have received Cook's Voyages which you put Mr. Oswald in the way of sending to me. By some Mistake the first Volume was omitted, and instead of it a Duplicate sent of the third. If there is a good Print of Cook, I should be glad to have it, being personally acquainted with him. I thank you for the Pamphlets by Mr. Estlin.[3] Every thing you send me gives me Pleasure, to receive your Account would give me more than all.

I am told that the little Pamphlet of Advice to such as would remove to America, is reprinted in London with my Name to it,[4] which I would rather had been omitted; but wish to see a Copy when you have an Opportunity of sending it—

Mr. H.[5] has long continued here in Expectation of Instructions for making a Treaty of Commerce but they do not come, and I begin to suspect none are intended; tho' perhaps the Delay is only occasioned by the overgreat Burthen of Business at present on the Shoulders of your Ministers— We do not press the Matter, but are content to wait till they can see their Interest respecting America more clearly: being certain that we can shift as well as you without a Treaty.

The Conjectures I sent you concerning the Cold of last Winter[6] still appear to me probable: the moderate Season in Russia and Canada do not weaken them. I think our Frost here began about the 24th. of December, in America the 12 of Jany.

I thank you for recommending to me Mr. Arbuthnot. I have had Pleasure in his Conversation. I wish much to see the new Pieces you had in hand. I congratulate you on the Return of your Wedding day, and wish for your Sake and Mrs. Vaughan's that you may see a great many of them, all as happy as the first.[7]

I like the young Stranger very much. He seems sensible, ingenious, & modest, has a good deal of Instruction and makes

3. Probably the Unitarian minister John Prior Estlin (*ODNB*). We have no record of either a letter from him or a visit to BF.
4. For the unauthorized reprint of BF's "Information to Those Who Would Remove to America" see XLI, 413.
5. David Hartley.
6. "Meteorological Imaginations and Conjectures," above, under the date [May, 1784].
7. Vaughan married Sarah Manning on June 30, 1781: XXXV, 572–3n.

Judicious Observations. He will probably distinguish himself advantageously.

I have not yet heard from Mr. Nairne—[8]

Dr. Price's Pamphlet of Advice to America,[9] is a good one, and will do Good. You ask "what Remedy I have for the growing Luxury of my Country, which gives so much *Offence* to all *English Travellers*—without Exception." I answer that I think it exaggerated, and that Travellers are no good Judges whether our Luxury is growing or diminishing. Our People are hospitable, and have indeed too much Pride in displaying upon their Tables before Strangers the Plenty and Variety that our Country affords. They have the Vanity too of sometimes borrowing one another's Plate to entertain more splendidly— Strangers being invited from House to House, and meeting every Day with a Feast, imagine what they see is the ordinary Way of living of all the Families where they dine; when perhaps each Family lives a Week after upon the Remains of the Dinner given. It is, I own, a Folly in our People to give *such Offence* to *English* Travellers. The first part of the Proverb is thereby verified, That *Fools make Feasts*. I wish in this Case the other were as true, *and wise Men eat them*.[1] These Travellers might one would think find some Fault they could more decently reproach us with, than that of our excessive Civility to them as Strangers.

I have not indeed yet thought of a Remedy for Luxury. I am not sure that in a great State it is capable of a Remedy. Nor that

8. This may be an allusion to the correspondence between BF and Nairne about hygrometers, which Vaughan was following with interest. On Oct. 18, 1783, BF sent Nairne a letter that he had begun three years earlier, "on the subject of hygrometers." It seems that he had shown the unfinished MS to Vaughan, who had urged him to complete it. Nairne answered BF on Dec. 2 with his own observations and two drawings, making copies for Vaughan as well. If BF commented on Nairne's design, as the latter hoped he would, that reply has not been found. Nairne and Vaughan would both make hygrometers based on BF's ideas: XLI, 118, 251–3; *Jefferson Papers*, XI, 72–3.

9. Price's *Observations on the Importance of the American Revolution*, for which see Price's letter of July 12, above, and BF's response of Aug. 2, below.

1. This proverb was one of Poor Richard's favorites: I, 297; III, 8; VII, 345.

the Evil is in itself always so great as it is represented. Suppose we include in the Definition of Luxury all unnecessary Expence, and then let us consider whether Laws to prevent such Expence are possible to be executed in a great Country; and whether if they could be executed, our People generally would be happier or even richer. Is not the Hope of one day being able to purchase and enjoy Luxuries a great Spur to Labour and Industry? May not Luxury therefore produce more than it consumes, if without such a Spur People would be as they are naturally enough inclined to be, lazy & indolent? To this purpose I remember a Circumstance. The Skipper of a Shallop employed between Cape May and Philadelphia, had done us some small Service for which he refused Pay. My Wife understanding that he had a Daughter, sent her as a Present a new-fashioned Cap. Three Years After, this Skipper being at my House with an old Farmer of Cape May his Passenger, he mentioned the Cap and how much his Daughter had been pleased with it; but says he it proved a dear Cap to our Congregation— How so? When my Daughter appeared in it at Meeting, it was so much admired, that all the Girls resolved to get such Caps from Philadelphia; and my Wife and I computed that the whole could not have cost less than a hundred Pound. True says the Farmer, but you do not tell all the Story; I think the Cap was nevertheless an Advantage to us; for it was the first thing that put our Girls upon Knitting worsted Mittens for Sale at Philadelphia, that they might have wherewithal to buy Caps & Ribbands there; and you know that that Industry has continued and is likely to continue and increase to a much greater Value, and answers better Purposes. Upon the whole I was more reconciled to this little Piece of Luxury; since not only the Girls were made happier by having fine Caps, but the Philadelphians by the Supply of warm Mittens.

In our Commercial Towns upon the Seacoast, Fortunes will occasionally be made. Some of those who grow rich, will be prudent, live within Bounds, & preserve what they have gained for their Posterity. Others fond of showing their Wealth, will be extravagant and ruin themselves. Laws cannot prevent this, and perhaps it is not always an Evil to the Publick. A Shilling spent idly by a Fool, may be picked up by a Wiser Person who knows better what to do with it. It is therefore not lost. A vain silly Fellow builds a fine House, furnishes it richly, lives in it expensively, and in a few years ruins himself; but the Masons, Carpenters, Smiths and other honest Tradesmen have been by his Employ assisted in maintaining and raising their Families, the Farmer has been paid for his Labour and encouraged, and the Estate is now in better Hands— In some Cases indeed certain Modes of Luxury may be a publick Evil in the same Manner as it is a Private one. If there be a Nation for Instance, that exports its Beef and Linnen to pay for its Importations of Claret and Porter, while a great Part of its People live upon Potatoes and wear no Shirts, wherein does it differ from the Sot who lets his Family starve and sells his Clothes to buy Drink? Our American Commerce is I confess a little in this way. We sell our Victuals to your Islands for Rum and Sugar; the Substantial Necessaries of Life for Superfluities. But we have Plenty and live well nevertheless; tho' by being soberer we might be richer. By the by, here is just issued an Arret of Council, taking off all the Duties upon the Exportation of Brandies,[2] which it is said will render them cheaper in America than your Rum, in which case there is no doubt but they will be preferred, and we shall be better able to bear your Restrictions on our Commerce. There are Views here by augmenting their Settlements of being able to supply the growing People of North America with the Sugar that may be wanted there. On the whole I guess England will get as little by the Commercial War She has begun with us as she did by the Military. But to return to *Luxury*.

The vast Quantity of Forest Lands we yet have to clear and put in order for Cultivation, will for a long time keep the Body of our Nation laborious and frugal. Forming an Opinion of our People and their Manners by what is seen among the Inhabitants of the Seaports, is judging from an improper Sample. The People of the Trading Towns may be rich and luxurious, while the Country possesses all the Virtues that tend to private Happiness & publick Prosperity. Those Towns are not much regarded by the Country. They are hardly considered as an essential Part of

---

2. These letters patent were issued on July 21: *Recueil général des anciennes lois françaises* . . . (29 vols., Paris, 1821–33), XXVII, 448.

the States. And the Experience of the last War has shown, that their being in Possession of the Enemy, did not necessarily draw on the Subjection of the Country, which bravely continued to maintain its Freedom & Independence notwithstanding—

It has been computed by some Political Arithmetician, that if every Man and Woman would work four Hours each Day on something useful, that Labour would produce sufficient to procure all the Necessaries & Comforts of Life, Want and Misery would be banished out of the World, and the rest of the 24 Hours might be Leisure and Pleasure.[3]

What occasions then so much Want & Misery? It is the Employment of Men and Women in Works that produce neither the Necessaries nor Conveniences of Life, who, with those who do nothing, consume the Necessaries raised by the Laborious.— To explain this—

The first Elements of Wealth are obtained by Labour from the Earth and Waters. I have Land and raise Corn. With this if I feed a Family that does nothing, my Corn will be consum'd and at the End of the Year I shall be no richer than I was at the Beginning. But if while I feed them I employ them, some in Spinning others in hewing Timber & sawing Boards, others in making Bricks &c. for Building; the Value of my Corn will be arrested, and remain with me, and at the End of the Year we may all be better clothed and better lodged. And if instead of employing a Man I feed, in making Bricks, I employ him in fiddling for me, the Corn he eats is gone, & no Part of his Manufacture remains to augment the Wealth and the Conveniencies of the Family. I shall therefore be the poorer for this fiddling Man, unless the rest of My Family work more or eat less to make up for the Deficiency he occasions—

3. It is possible that BF remembered a passage from Sir Thomas More's *Utopia* (he owned at least two editions: Wolf and Hayes, *Library of Benjamin Franklin*), which imagines that in Utopia, both men and women devote only six hours per day to work, eight hours to sleep, and the remaining ten hours to eating, rest, study, and recreation. Since the entire population follows this regimen, "Their working hours are ample to provide not only enough but more than enough of the necessities and even the conveniences of life": More, *Utopia*, ed. George M. Logan (3rd ed., New York and London, 2011), pp. 45–6.

Look round the World and see the Millions employ'd in doing nothing, or in something that amounts to nothing when the Necessaries and Conveniencies of Life are in Question. What is the Bulk of Commerce, for which we fight and destroy each other but the Toil of Millions for Superfluities to the great Hazard and Loss of many Lives by the constant Dangers of the Sea. How much Labour Spent in Building and Fitting great Ships to go to China and Arabia for Tea and for Coffee, to the West Indies for Sugar, to America for Tobacco! These Things cannot be called the Necessaries of Life, for our Ancestors lived very comfortably without them.

A Question may be asked, Could all these People now employed in raising, making or carrying Superfluities, be subsisted by raising Necessaries? I think they might. The World is large, and a great Part of it still uncultivated. Many hundred Millions of Acres in Asia, Africa & America, are still Forest, and a great Deal even in Europe. On 100 Acres of this Forest a Man might become a substantial Farmer; and 100,000 Men employed in clearing each his 100 Acres, (instead of being as they are French Hairdressers) would hardly brighten a Spot big enough to be Visible from the Moon, unless with Herschell's Telescope, so vast are the Regions still in [*the*] World unimproved.

'Tis however some Comfort to reflect that upon the whole the Quantity of Industry and Prudence among Mankind exceeds the Quantity of Idleness and Folly. Hence the Increase of good Buildings, Farms cultivated, and populous Cities filled with Wealth all over Europe, which a few Ages since were only to be found on the Coasts of the Mediterranean: And this notwithstanding the mad Wars continually raging, by which are often destroyed in one Year the Works of many Years Peace. So that we may hope the Luxury of a few Merchants on the Sea Coast, will not be the Ruin of America.

One Reflection more, and I will end this long rambling Letter.— Almost all the Parts of our Bodies require some Expence. The Feet demand Shoes, the Legs Stockings, the rest of the Body Clothing, and the Belly a good deal of Victuals. *Our* Eyes, tho' exceedingly useful, ask when reasonable, only the cheap Assistance of *Spectacles*, which could not much impair our Finances. But THE EYES OF OTHER PEOPLE are the Eyes that ruin us. If all but myself were blind, I should want neither fine Clothes, fine Houses nor Fine Furniture.[4]

Adieu, my Dear Friend. I am Yours ever   B FRANKLIN

[*In Franklin's hand:*] P.S. This will be deliver'd to you by my Grandson. I am persuaded you will afford him your Civilities & Counsels. Please to accept a little Present of Books I send by him, curious for the Beauty of the Impression.—

B. Vaughan, Esqr.

From Campomanes

Translation of LS in Spanish:[5] American Philosophical Society

Dear Sir   Madrid, July 26, 1784

I received the collection of miscellaneous published works by Your Excellency along with your esteemed letter of June 5 and the advice to emigrants to the United States of America: all by the hand of my friend Mr. Carmichael.

The various writings, published at different times, reveal a statesman full of foresight and vigilance for the good of his country amid the varied conjunctures, presented by the political factions and the different systems of government; shining throughout with an ardent desire for the common good, founded on political principles and calculations, carried to the highest possible degree of demonstration permitted by the vicissitudes and inconstancy of the systems adopted for the government of men.

The long train of these political reflections manifest the solidity and constancy of your principles; whether regarding the colonies of America when they were united with the metropole, or when forming thereafter an independent state.

In both situations, Your Excellency directed your efforts to

---

4. BF also touched on this theme in Part II of the autobiography, written in 1784. Remarking how "Luxury will enter Families, and make a Progress, in Spite of Principle," he recounted how DF bought him new tableware because "she thought *her* Husband deserv'd a Silver Spoon and China Bowl as well as any of his Neighbours": *Autobiog.*, p. 145.

5. The complimentary close is in Campomanes' hand, as is the postscript.

the common good without flinching or going to those extremes, which affect weak souls during a crisis as long and delicate as that which we have seen for the formation of a new state, composed of thirteen provinces with different constitutions; and in spite of this wisely united by a bond strong and beneficial to each. Nature, which Your Excellency has studied in your continual meditations, seems to owe to you the deciphering of phenomena that earlier sages had not managed to discern, while the great American philosopher Franklin not only discovers them but also suggests practical methods by which people may protect themselves against the inconveniences that beset them before your investigations.

The sincerity, with which Your Excellency in your *Aviso* dissuades emigrants from crossing over to the colonies, where they will not be welcome, is a consequence of your love for all humanity, and of the candor characteristic of a good man, true philosopher and excellent patriot.

Your Excellency extends this same kindness to Spain in your two assertions in support of the honor that is due to labor, and against the entailment of property.

The first is now found canonized among us by the recent law, of which a copy is enclosed, declaring the honor that must be given to all kinds of artisans, who are made eligible for the municipal offices of the republic:[6] laborers were always honored and favored by our laws.

As to what regards entailments, I refer you to what I wrote in the year 1765 at the end of my treatise on *Amortización*,[7] in

6. The enclosure has not been found. A direct attack on social prejudices and political customs, the *cédula* (royal decree) of March 18, 1783, declared that manual trades and crafts, including those of tanners, smiths, tailors, shoemakers, and carpenters, were honorable and did not disqualify their practitioners from holding municipal offices or from enjoying noble privileges. Campomanes had criticized what he saw as a deeply ingrained Spanish disdain for manual labor and the exclusion of manufacturers and artisans from local government in his *Discurso sobre la educación popular de los artesanos y su fomento*, which was probably among the works BF received from Carmichael: William J. Callahan, "Crown, Nobility and Industry in Eighteenth-Century Spain," *International Rev. of Social History*, XI (1966), 445, 453, 455, 459–64.

7. *Tratado de la Regalía de Amortización* ... (Madrid, 1765).

which I think I have demonstrated that this regulation should be preceded by another, which is awaiting legislation. I also add that there is in my opinion some disparity of circumstances between the monarchical and the democratic constitution, and between states of ancient and new foundation in this respect.

I would with the greatest pleasure extend these reflections if the pressure of time would permit: although I do not consider it necessary given Your Excellency's penetration and perspicacity.

The honorable notice that the Philosophical Society of Philadelphia has taken of me, in naming me on January 16 to be one of their members,[8] places on me the agreeable obligation to demonstrate my gratitude through Your Excellency as its worthy President.

Eager to reciprocate in some manner this generous courtesy, I proposed to the Royal Academy of History, of which I am the Director, to add Your Excellency to their organization as an honorary member. To this the assembly assented immediately and gladly by universal acclamation;[9] glorying to have on its roll the name of a gentleman so distinguished in letters, and who played the role of prime mover in one of the most memorable revolutions of our time.

With such just motives I offer myself affectionately and cordially to Your Excellency's service, praying that God may preserve your Life for many years.

Your attentive servant kisses Your Excellency's hand

EL CONDE DE CAMPOMÁNES

P.S.

May Your Excellency excuse my delay in responding and the hand of a secretary: both stem from the multitude of my

8. Campomanes' election is recorded in *Early Proceedings of the American Philosophical Society* ... (Philadelphia, 1884), pp. 121–2. In March and July, 1783, Carmichael had written to Livingston urging that Campomanes be nominated as an honorary member of the APS, as "the nomination of the most distinguished literary characters in the different countries of Europe" would "secure useful connexions to our ministers": Wharton, *Diplomatic Correspondence*, VI, 297–8, 573–4.

9. BF was elected on July 9, 1784: *Memorias de la Real Academia de la Historia* (14 vols., Madrid, 1796–1910), I, clviii.

occupations. Nothing will prevent my being ever Your Excellency's passionate admirer yearning to prove himself worthy

Sr. Dr. Benjamin Franklin

From John Adams   Copy: Massachusetts Historical Society

Sir   The Hague July 27th 1784

I embrace the opportunity, by Mr: Bingham,[1] to enclose to your Excellency, Copy of a Letter from Mr: Jefferson,[2] by which it appears that we are joined in some affairs which will give me the Occasion to visit Paris once more, and reside there for some little time at least.

As Mr: Jefferson will not probably arrive before the latter End of August, and nothing can be done before he comes, I shall wait at the Hague for my Wife and Daughter, who are happily arrived in London,[3] and endeavour to go with them, in Time to meet your Excellency and Mr: Jefferson upon his arrival at Paris.

The Philosophers are speculating upon our Constitutions and I hope will throw out Hints, which will be of Use to our Countrymen. The Science of Government as it is founded upon the genuine Principles of Society, is many Centuries behind that of most other Sciences, that of the fine Arts, as well as that of Trades and Manufactures. As it is the first in Importance it is to be hoped, it may overtake the rest, and that Mankind may find their Account in it. The Berlin Academician has set an Example, which if liberally followed, may produce great Effects, for I dont believe that many will find with him upon Examination that Despotism or even Monarchy is the best possible form of Government.[4]

1. Richard Bingham, the son of Charles Bingham, Baron Lucan, whom JA recommended to Barclay as a "worthy youth": *Adams Papers*, XVI, 284–5.

2. TJ to JA, June 19: *Adams Papers*, XVI, 242–3. TJ's letter to BF of the same date is above.

3. They were in London by July 23: *Adams Correspondence*, V, 397–9.

4. A reference to *Sur la Forme des gouvernemens, et quelle en est la meilleure?* ([Berlin], 1784) by the Prussian minister of state Ewald Friedrich Graf von Hertzberg, a member of the Prussian Academy of Sciences: Rudolf Vierhaus, ed., *Deutsche Biographische Enzyklopädie* (2nd ed.; 12 vols., Munich, 2005–8).

They have sent me from Amsterdam, Copies of a Translation, of the Abby de Mably's Letters, made by an English Episcopal Clergymen, at Amsterdam, whom I don't know.[5] I enclose one to your Excellency and have the Honour to be, with great Respect &c

Dr: Franklin.

From Benjamin Harrison[6]   LS: American Philosophical Society

Sir,   Virginia Richmond July 27th 1784—

The Assembly of this State have voted a Statue of our late worthy Commander in Chief General Washington, and have directed one side of the Pedestal to be filled with an inscription, the other three with the Dress are left for the exercise of the genius of your humble Servant & his Council, who are all too little acquainted with a business that requires such a refinement of genius & Taste to venture any thing of their own to the Eyes of the critical world,—it was natural therefore for us to look round for the assistance of some of our friends, and we unanimously pitched on yourself and Mr. Jefferson as the most likely to come up to our wishes and the expectations of the Assembly. The friendship you have honored me with gave me the confidence to assure the Gentlemen that they might depend on your complying with the request, and I am sure you will not disappoint me. I have written fully to Mr. Jefferson on the Subject—have enclosed him a Copy of the resolution of Assembly,[7] and or-

5. The work in question was *Observations on the Government and Laws of the United States of America, Translated from the French, of the Abbé de Mably, with a Preface by the Translator.* JA asked the publisher for the name of the translator, whose preface he admired, and on the copy JA sent to BF (now at the Houghton Library of Harvard University) he wrote it as "Mr Sowden": *Adams Papers,* XVI, xiii, 280; and see BF's reply of Aug. 6. Mably's work consisted of four letters addressed to JA, commenting on the American state constitutions: *Adams Papers,* XIV, 165–7, 172–81.

6. Harrison was serving his third and final term as governor of Virginia: John W. Raimo, *Biographical Directory of American Colonial and Revolutionary Governors, 1607–1789* (Westport, Conn., 1980), pp. 506–7.

7. Gov. Harrison's letter to TJ, dated July 20, enclosed a June 26 resolution calling upon the executive branch to procure a marble statue of GW

dered Mr. Peale to send to his address a full length Picture of the General & have requested the favor of him to confer with you on the whole of this business.[8]

I have had the pleasure of Several of your recommendations and have on every occasion paid that attention to them you had so good a right to expect. If in this or any other way I can be of use to you, you'l please to command me for be assured nothing will make me happier than to have it in my power to render you service.

I have the honor to be with the most perfect respect & Esteem Dear Sir Your most obedient & Most humble Servant

BENJA HARRISON

From David Hartley

ALS: Library of Congress

My Dear friend   Rue Caumartin July 27 1784

I have thought it a long while that my Confinement has prevented my seeing you. I was in hopes to have had the pleasure of seeing you to day, but I was indiscreet in going out the night before last, wch has encreased the pain & swelling of my foot. My foot is again rather better than it was yesterday, but I am afraid to venture out to day. I hope still to see you on Thursday.—[9] I received no letters by the messenger of last night from the Secretary of State, but I understand that the report of the privy council & other documents respecting American trade are

---

with the inscription written by the assembly. Harrison delegated full responsibility for the overall design of the statue to TJ and BF, and asked them to engage the best sculptor in Europe. He assured them that the necessary funds were forthcoming: *Jefferson Papers*, VII, 378–9.

8. Harrison commissioned this portrait by Charles Willson Peale on July 1. Peale completed the painting in October, and TJ acknowledged receipt of it the following April. By that time, however, TJ and BF had arranged for Jean-Antoine Houdon to go to America and sculpt GW's likeness from life: Lillian B. Miller *et al.*, eds., *The Selected Papers of Charles Willson Peale and His Family* (5 vols. to date, New Haven and London, 1983–), I, 413–14, 422–3.

9. July 29.

laid before Parliament. I presume therefore that that Subject will soon be taken into Consideration.[1]

Yours most affecly

D H

To Dr Franklin &c &c &c

Editorial Note on the Consular Convention between France and the United States, July 29, 1784

The consular convention that Franklin and Vergennes signed on July 29, 1784, was based on the draft they had agreed to the previous December. Castries had initially objected to aspects of that draft convention, but his opposition had subsided by mid-February.[2] There matters lay until May 31, when Franklin, prompted by the American consul, Thomas Barclay, wrote Vergennes that he was eager to sign the articles if there should be no further objections. Vergennes sent a translation of Franklin's letter to Castries, asking for his views; the latter replied that as Vergennes had supplied no new information, he himself had nothing further to say.[3] When and by whom the changes to the convention described below were introduced is not known. On July 6, Franklin directed his grandson Temple to inquire about the convention during that day's meeting of foreign ministers at Versailles; the answer came back that the convention was being prepared.[4] On July 29, Franklin himself made the journey to Versailles.

1. For the report see the annotation of Henry Laurens' first letter of April 18, above. On July 27 Pitt introduced a bill in the House of Commons for maintaining the restrictions on American trade with the West Indies. By July 30 it had passed and received royal assent: *London Chron.*, July 27–29 and July 29–31, 1784. The Order in Council of July 2 continued to be renewed every six months until 1788: John Ehrman, *The Younger Pitt* (3 vols., New York and Stanford, Calif., 1969–96), I, 335.

2. The text of the draft convention and an explanation of the negotiations surrounding it are in XLI, 320–32.

3. Vergennes to Castries, June 6, 1784; Castries to Vergennes, June 13, 1784; both at the AAE.

4. BF had written to Vergennes on Dec. 6, 1783, that his bladder stone made travel excruciatingly painful, and that henceforth he would occasionally send WTF to court as his proxy: XLI, 265. For the July 6 visit see the entry of that date in BF's journal, [June 26–July 27], above.

It may have been the first time he had traveled to court since the day the peace treaty was signed.[5]

The final convention differed from the draft in only a few ways. The wording of Articles 4 and 6 was slightly modified. Article 3 was amended to give vice-consuls as well as consuls the power to appoint agents. Article 8 was revised in two respects. Consuls and vice-consuls were permitted to submit to the courts acts and declarations in assessing damages to cargoes in which both French subjects and American citizens had an interest. Moreover, the right to appoint arbitrators in cases in which only one of the parties had an interest was expanded to include consular agents as well as consuls and vice-consuls.[6]

For reasons unknown to Franklin, or to us, the copy of the convention that was initially sent to Congress never arrived. This became clear the following February, when the minister plenipotentiary received a congressional resolution dated December 14, 1784, ordering him not to sign the consular convention if he had not yet done so, and to await further orders. He immediately dispatched a duplicate of the signed convention, puzzled as to why two years of negotiations were being nullified.[7] As he would learn much later, it was John Jay who had written the resolution and Jay who, as secretary for foreign affairs, analyzed the convention when the duplicate arrived. Jay's report, dated July 4, 1785, objected to many of the articles and accused Franklin of having deviated from his instructions.[8]

While it was clear that Congress would not ratify the convention after Jay's report, it took Congress over a year to formally approve that report and order Jay to send new instructions to Thomas

5. After the British-American peace treaty was signed in Paris on Sept. 3, 1783, Vergennes hosted a dinner at Versailles for the negotiators of all the treaties signed that day: XL, 568–9.

6. As with the draft convention, this document was written in French. The two official copies, signed and sealed by Vergennes and BF, are at the National Archives and the AAE. An English translation and the French original are printed in Linda G. De Pauw et al., eds., *Documentary History of the First Federal Congress of the United States of America* (20 vols. to date, Baltimore and London, 1972–), II, 328–40, 341–6.

7. Richard Henry Lee to BF, Dec. 14, 1784 (National Archives); BF to Richard Henry Lee, Feb. 8, 1785 (Smyth, *Writings*, IX, 289).

8. Jay's report is published, with an editorial note explaining its background and aftermath, in *Jay Papers*, IV, 112–34. We agree with the editors of the *Jefferson Papers* that Jay's criticism of BF was unfounded; see *Jefferson Papers*, XIV, 73–6, for a critique of the report.

Jefferson.[9] On November 14, 1788, Jefferson and Foreign Minister Montmorin signed a much revised consular convention. The U.S. Senate ratified it the following year, just as the turmoil of the revolution in France began to render the convention obsolete.[1]

To the Comte de Mercy-Argenteau

LS:[2] Library of Congress; copy:[3] Massachusetts Historical Society; transcript: National Archives

Sir,   Passy July 30th. 1784[4]

I have the honour to communicate to your Excellency an Extract from the Instructions of Congress to their late Commissioners for treating of Peace, expressing their Desire to cultivate the Friendship of his Imperial Majesty and to enter into a Treaty of Commerce for the mutual Advantage of his Subjects and the Citizens of the United States; which I request you will be pleased to lay before his Majesty. The appointing and instructing Commissioners for Treaties of Commerce with the Powers of Europe generally, has by various Circumstances been long delayed, but is now done; and I have just received Advice that Mr. Jefferson late Governor of Virginia, commissioned with Mr. Adams our Minister in Holland, & myself for that Service, is on his way hither and may be expected by the End of August, when we shall be ready to enter into a Treaty with his Imperial Majesty for the above Purpose, if such should be his Pleasure—

With great and sincere Respect, I am, Sir, Your Excellency's most obedient & most humble Servant,   B. FRANKLIN

His Exy. the Count de Mercy &ca. &ca.—[5]

9. *Jefferson Papers*, VIII, 383; X, 430–1; *JCC*, XXXI, 712–13.

1. For a detailed history of the consular convention of 1788 see the editorial note in *Jefferson Papers*, XIV, 66–92.

2. In the hand of BFB. BF added the complimentary close before signing.

3. Also in BFB's hand. WTF forwarded it to JA on Aug. 1, along with a copy of Mercy-Argenteau's response of July 30, below: *Adams Papers*, XVI, 287–8.

4. BF drafted this letter on July 26; see the entry of that date in BF's journal, [June 26–July 27], above.

5. Notations in French, made by Mercy-Argenteau's secretary on the verso, recorded all the salient information about this letter and its enclosure,

From Mercy-Argenteau

L (draft): Haus-, Hof- und Staatsarchiv; copy: Massachusetts Historical Society; transcript:[6] National Archives

Monsieur [July 30, 1784]

J'ai reçu la lettre que vous m'avez fait l'honneur de m'ecrire ce matin, et je ne tarderai pas d'en transmettre le contenu à ma Cour.

Les Sentimens de l'Empereur pour les Etats unis d'Amérique me font prévoir la Satisfaction, que Sa Majesté aura d'entrer avec eux dans des liaisons reciproquement convenables et utiles; je ne doute pas qu'il ne soit pris incessamment á cet egard les mesures nécessaires pour se concerter avec vous, Mr. et avec Mrs. les Ministres Plénipotentiaires designés, et aussitot que la réponse de ma Cour me sera parvenue je m'empresserai à vous la communiquer.[7]

J'ai l'hr. d'etre avec le plus parfait et sincere attachement.

à m. Francklin Ministre plénipotentiaire des Etats unis d'amérique à la Cour de france en date de Paris le 30. Juillet 1784. Expe.

From Etienne-Alexandre-Jacques Anisson-Duperon, *dit* Anisson fils[8]

L: American Philosophical Society

A Paris le 31 Juillet 1784.

M. Anisson a l'honneur d'assurer de ses devoirs Monsieur Franklin. Il est bien fâché de ne pas s'être trouvé chez lui, lorsque

---

summarized the letter, and noted that the minister answered it the same day and sent a translation to Vienna on Aug. 1. Mercy-Argenteau must have enclosed this LS, as well, as it bears the stamp of the Haus-, Hof- und Staatsarchiv, Vienna.

6. The transcript is accompanied by an English translation, which is published in *Diplomatic Correspondence of the United States*, II, 32–3.

7. On Aug. 1 Mercy-Argenteau sent the emperor BF's July 30 letter, along with a translation, and requested instructions. A copy of his covering letter is at the Haus-, Hof- und Staatsarchiv, Vienna.

8. Son and designated successor of Jacques Anisson-Duperon, director of the Imprimerie royale (XXVI, 519). Though Etienne-Alexandre-Jacques

M. son fils lui a fait l'honneur d'y passer de sa part; mais il étoit a faire un voyage dont il est revenu hier au soir. Il aura le plus grand empressement d'offrir à Monsieur franklin l'exemplaire qu'il desire, de son ouvrage auquel il fait peut-être trop d'honneur.[9]

M. Anisson desirant en conférer avec Monsieur franklin, il le prie de lui faire savoir le jour et l'heure où il pourra avoir l'honneur de le rencontrer chez lui. Il lui portera lui-même un exemplaire pour lequel il fait faire des dessins sur ceux qui servent à la gravure dont il n'a pu encore voir une seule épreuve./[1]

---

would not formally become director until his father's death in 1788, he appears to have acted as co-director beginning in 1783: *DBF;* Frédéric Barbier *et al.,* eds., *Dictionnaire des imprimeurs, libraires et gens du livre à Paris, 1701–1789* (1 vol. to date, Geneva, 2007–); both under Anisson-Duperron.

9. The work in question was likely a description of Anisson's new printing press, which Anisson had declined to show BF in November, 1782, before it was finished: xxxviii, 307–8n. The press was completed by March, 1783, when Anisson presented an illustrated memoir to the Académie des sciences. The academy's commission approved the invention in May, and in the fall of 1783 the Imprimerie royale issued *Description d'une nouvelle presse exécutée pour le service du roi.* The pamphlet included a brief description of the press and its advantages, an extract of the commissioners' report, and an item-by-item comparison of the press's improved components with their counterparts in the current standard press. In 1785 the academy published the full text of Anisson's 1783 memoir as a freestanding pamphlet, and in *Mémoires de mathématique et de physique* . . . , x (1785), 613–50. Entitled *Premier mémoire sur l'impression en lettres, suivi de la description d'une nouvelle presse* . . . , it also included essentially everything published in the 1783 *Description.* If Anisson had page proofs for this pamphlet by July 1784, as is possible, he may have been offering a set to BF.

1. Some copies of the 1783 *Description* (among them the one held by the Bibliothèque Nationale) featured four plates of watercolor illustrations and a detailed key to the parts of the press they depicted. The 1785 *Premier mémoire* (both versions) incorporated this key to accompany a set of copperplate engravings corresponding closely to the earlier illustrations. It is evidently to these engravings, not yet completed, that Anisson refers in the present letter. Anisson did visit BF sometime in the next several months (see BF to Anisson, Nov. 10, 1784, Bibliothèque Nationale), but what, if anything, he may have ultimately brought to Passy on that occasion is not known.

M. Anisson fils, Directeur de L'Imprimerie Royale demeure Rue des orties du Louvre, au coin de la rue du Doyenné./.

Notation: Anison 31 Juillet 1784

From Vergennes

Copy: Archives du Ministère des affaires étrangères

Vlles le 31. Juillet. 1784

J'ai communiqué, M. à M. le mal. de Castries la lettre que vous m'aviez fait l'honneur de m'ecrire relativement à la mainlevée que vous aviez demandée des Saisies faites Sur les deniers provenans des prises de la fregate l'alliance.[2] Ce ministre m'a fait la reponse dont vous trouverez ci joint la copie. Vous y verrez M la maniere dont il pense que cette affaire doit etre envisagée et les moyens qu'il indique pour la mettre en etat de recevoir une decision.[3]

M. Franklin

---

2. BF's letter, written on Jan. 12 (XLI, 437–42), was delivered to Vergennes by Thomas Barclay, whom Vergennes knew to be in charge of settling the dispute over Forster frères' attachment of the proceeds of prizes taken by the *Alliance;* see XXXIX, 308. Barclay was not in Paris when BF wrote the letter, and was delayed far longer than he expected. He did not deliver it until *c.* May 11: Idzerda, *Lafayette Papers,* V, 215; Roberts and Roberts, *Thomas Barclay,* pp. 138–9, 322.

3. Vergennes sent Castries a translation of BF's letter, with a request to know the current state of affairs, on May 28. Castries replied on July 3. He reminded Vergennes that according to Vergennes' directions, the dispute over Forster frères' attachment had been transferred to the Conseil royal in June, 1783. It had not been decided there because neither party had provided the necessary documentation. BF was now requesting ministerial intervention, but surely Vergennes would agree that once the Conseil had assumed jurisdiction over the case under its power of evocation, ministerial action would be inappropriate. (Both letters are at the AAE.) After reading the present letter and its enclosure, Barclay wrote to WTF on Aug. 4 that he had forwarded all the documentation he had to Castries and had run out of ideas on how to settle the matter. APS. The dispute was still unsettled when Barclay left France in 1787: Barclay to TJ, July 16, 1787, in *Jefferson Papers,* XI, 593.

From ——— Beyer[4]   ALS: American Philosophical Society

Monsieur   ce 1 Aout [1784]
    Une indisposition m'ayant empeché de vaquer a mes affaires
depuis 8 a 10 jours Je n'ai pas pû m'occuper du portefeuil[5] ni de
mon instrument[6] etant obligé de garder la chambre mais jespere
que les premiers Jours de la Semaine le tous poura âitre fini j'aurai lhonneur de vous en faire part aussitot que Sa Sera pret.
    J'ai l'honneur d'etre avec un profond respet Monsieur votre
tres humble Et tres obeissent Serviteur   BEYER

Notation: Beyer[7]

4. A German-born natural philosopher and inventor, residing in Paris,
whose acquaintance with BF predated the present letter (the first in their extant correspondence) and continued until BF's departure from France in July,
1785. In addition to conferring with BF about the inventions he discusses
here, Beyer evidently also learned from him the art of building and install-
ing lightning rods. In 1800 the French government commissioned him to set
up lightning rods on public buildings and monuments in Paris, and to repair
those already in place. Beyer's lightning rods were distinguished by a point
made of platinum and a pliable wire, covered with a layer of varnish, that
aligned with the contours of the structure it protected. In 1804 Beyer devised
a conductor that could be grounded or insulated at will, so that it not only
offered protection from lightning; it also facilitated experiments with electricity: F.-J. Fétis, *Biographie universelle des musiciens . . .* (2nd. ed.; 8 vols.,
1873–75; reprint, Brussels, 1963); Beyer, *Aux Amateurs de physique, sur l'utilité des paratonnerres* (Paris, 1806), frontispiece and pp. 2, 15–16n, 42–3n.
    5. Beyer wrote that he had invented this tablet in response to BF's de-
sire to be able to write without being observed: Beyer, *Aux Amateurs de
physique*, p. 56. In the *Jour. de Paris* of Nov. 18, 1785, Beyer advertised his
"Portefeuille," a portable writing device that made it possible to write in
straight lines even in one's "poche" or in the dark. It was useful for men of
letters who wanted to be able to jot down their ideas discreetly at all times,
whether at night or while walking and traveling. Moreover, the device featured a mechanism that moved the paper along during the process of writing, allowing the writing of up to 100 lines.
    6. This was the glass-chord, a variation of the forte-piano, using glass
bars instead of strings. It would not be ready until the following January,
when Beyer presented a prototype to the Académie des sciences. After it
received the academy's approbation, BF obliged Beyer by giving the instrument its name: Beyer to BF, Jan. 17, and April 6, 1785 (APS); Beyer, *Aux
Amateurs de physique*, p. 48.
    7. On the verso of the sheet is an arithmetical calculation in BF's hand.

Matthew Ridley to William Temple Franklin[8]

ALS: American Philosophical Society

Dear Sir   Paris August the 1st. 1784—
You will oblige me by getting an Order from the Minister to
let my Baggage pass[9] a Note of which you have underneath &
also for the Furniture I propose sending to America—[1]
I shall have the pleasure of seeing you on Wednesday.—
Capt: Hughes a Relation of mine is with me, if agreeable I propose bringing him; but should you wish it not so, or that there
will be any impropriety in it be free enough to let me know by a
Line.— With best wishes I am Dear Sir Yr. Obed hble sert
                                                    MATT: RIDLEY

To Richard Price

ALS: Mrs. J. W. Williams, St. Andrews, Fife, Scotland (1955)

My dear Friend,   Passy, Augt. 2. 1784.
I received your Favour of the 12th past with the Pamphlet of
Advice to the Americans, for which I thank you much; it is excel-
lent in itself, and will do us a great deal of Good. I communicated

---

8. Ridley was packing his household in preparation for leaving France.
His wife and their infant son had died in January, and he planned to return to Maryland as soon as he settled his financial affairs in London. That
took him until 1786: XXXIX, 599n; Roberts and Roberts, *Thomas Barclay*,
pp. 137, 141, 321n, 323n.
    9. The request, dated Aug. 2, came from BF. Vergennes replied on Aug.
7 that regulations did not permit forgoing an inspection of the contents
of Ridley's trunks, but Ridley could avoid inspections by having his baggage sealed at the Paris customs office. The farmers general could then
issue a permit that would protect his belongings from further inspection.
Vergennes made this request of the farmers general the same day (Aug. 7),
enclosing a copy of BF's request. The farmers answered on Aug. 9 that the
necessary orders had been given at customs regarding Ridley's belongings.
Abstracts of all these now-missing letters are at the AAE.
    1. Ridley evidently appended to this letter two lists: what he was ship-
ping to England and what was going to America. A press copy of them,
translated into French and in the hand of L'Air de Lamotte, is at the APS.

immediately to Mr Dupont the Letter of Mr Turgot, thinking him the properest Person to consult on the Subject, as he has the Care of the Papers left by that great Man.[2] He sent me thereupon the Note enclos'd dated July 26.[3] and this Day brought me the Proof corrected, which I enclose; and gave me his Opinion that the whole Letter may well be printed, even with the manuscript part at the End, you only adding a Note to the purpose of what he has written.[4] He only desires two small Omissions, which are mark'd and the Place of the words omitted to be fill'd with Points or Stars, to show that something is omitted.[5] It will be well to send him if you please a few Copies, & I wish to have two or three myself.

M. Dupont waits while I write, so that I cannot enlarge.[6] I receiv'd the former Letter you mention, and purpose writing to you soon. My best Respects to Mrs Price, & believe me ever, with sincere and great Esteem, Dear Sir, Your most obedient humble Servt.   B FRANKLIN

Revd Dr Price

2. Du Pont de Nemours had published an account of Turgot's life and works in 1782, which BF sent to James Hutton: XXXIX, 543. Du Pont was planning an edition of his friend's works and correspondence, but the first volumes did not appear until 1809: Ambrose Saricks, *Pierre Samuel Du Pont de Nemours* (Lawrence, 1965), pp. 74–5, 314–15.

3. No copy of this has been located.

4. Price did so: the footnote he appended to the final paragraph explained that he had kept the letter private during Turgot's lifetime but now "thought the publication of it a duty which I owe to his memory, as well as to the United States and the world." He added that BF and some of Turgot's closest friends had concurred with his view: Price, *Observations on the Importance of the American Revolution* . . . (London, 1784), pp. 108–9.

5. Neither passage occupied more than a single line. The first was Turgot's erroneous statement that New Jersey required officeholders to profess their faith in Christ (*Observations*, p. 95). The second was Turgot's assertion that Anglo-French hostility could lead to the bankruptcy of one nation or the other (p. 107). The deleted phrases are indicated in Peach and Thomas, *Price Correspondence*, II, 4, 8.

6. Price had suggested that BF entrust his reply to Mary Wilkes, who would be leaving Paris on Aug. 2: Price to BF, July 12, above.

From Dumas ALS: American Philosophical Society

Monsieur, Lahaie 2e. Aout 1784.
Ce paquet parviendra à V. E. dans celui de M. le Cte. de Vergennes, par le Courier qui porte à Mrs. les Plénipo: Hollandois
la magnifique Epée destinée à Mr. De Suffren.[7]
J'espere que V. E. trouvera l'incluse pour le Congrès très-
interessante, & digne par son importance de lui être promptement acheminée;[8] ainsi que celle à Mr. Van Berckel, qui lui fera
grand plaisir par la même raison. Après la révolution Américaine, le plus grand évenement, par les suites qu'il aura, c'est
l'Alliance prête à se conclure entre la Fce. & la Rep. des Pays-
Bas Unis. C'est ce qu'il me seroit aisé de prouver, si le départ du
Courier ne m'imposoit la nécessité de couper court, en me disant
avec grand respect, De Votre Excellence Le très-humble & très-
obeissant serviteur C. W. F. DUMAS

Paris à Son Excellence Mr. Franklin M.P.

From John Paul Jones AL: University of Pennsylvania Library

Paris Augt. the 2d. 1784
Mr Paul Jones has the Honor to accept Doctor Franklin's kind
Invitation for Dinner on Wednesday the 4th. Instant[9]

Addressed: A son Excellence / Monsieur Franklin Ministre / Ple-
nipotentiere des Etâts-Unis / en son Hotêl à Passy / près Paris.

7. The sword was presented to the great French admiral Suffren on
Aug. 12 by the Dutch ambassadors. Valued at 50,000 *l.t.*, it was a gift from the
States General of the Netherlands in recognition of Suffren's wartime services to the Dutch Republic in the East Indies: *Gaz. de Leyde*, Aug. 20, 1784.
8. The enclosure was surely Dumas' July 28[–30] dispatch to the president of Congress, which contained a copy of the draft Franco-Dutch treaty
of defensive alliance and Vergennes' explanation of its Article 2 in response
to a request by the Dutch ambassadors (National Archives). Before forwarding them to Congress, BF had L'Air de Lamotte copy the draft treaty
and Vergennes' explanation (APS). An English translation of Dumas' letter and its enclosures is in *Diplomatic Correspondence of the United States*,
VII, 49–57. For the treaty see *Adams Papers*, XVI, 212–13n.
9. The Duke of Dorset was also among the "grande Compagnie" dining with BF on this date: BFB's journal, entry of Aug. 4, 1784.

To Sears & Smith

Press copy of ALS: American Philosophical Society

Gentlemen   Passy, Aug. 4. 1784.

Upon Receipt of yours relating to your Cargo of Slaves at Martinico,[1] I endeavour'd to inform myself what was the Law in such Cases, and I found that by an *Arrêt du Conseil d'Etat du Roi,* of the 28th of June 1783, there is a Duty laid of 100 Livres per head on all Negroes imported in foreign Ships, and this Duty is granted and is to be paid as a Premium to the French Importers of Negroes, as an Encouragement to their own African Trade.[2] Under these Circumstances I am advis'd, that it cannot be expected that a general national Law should be set aside in favour of a particular foreign Ship, especially as the King, if he forgives the Duty to the Stranger, must thereby do Injustice to his own Subjects to whom he had promised the Pardon of that Duty, unless he pays it to them out of his own Money, which one cannot decently request him to do. I do not therefore see any Possibility of your avoiding the Payment. I have the Honour to be, Gentlemen, Your most obedient & most humble Servant

B. FRANKLIN

Messrs Sears and Smith.

From David Hartley

ALS: Library of Congress

Rue Caumartin Wednesday morning Aug 4 1784

My Dear friend

I have not recd any letters from England—but I hear that a continuation of the Amern bill is passed.[3] That is all the news

1. Sears & Smith's of May 18.
2. The *arrêt* opened the slave trade of the French Lesser Antilles to foreigners in order to encourage a better supply of slaves to markets long neglected in favor of St.-Domingue, and to bring the existing contraband trade under French regulation. The measure included a number of restrictions and required a 100 *l.t.* per head duty, revenue from which was used to subsidize the trade of French slavers to the same ports: Jean Tarrade, *Le commerce colonial de la France à la fin de l'Ancien Régime: l'évolution du régime de "l'Exclusif" de 1763 à 1789* (2 vols., Paris, 1972), II, 517–21.
3. It had; see the annotation of Hartley's letter of July 27.

that I hear— My leg has been very bad again. I now write in bed. I have been confined for these last four days almost entirely to my bed & mattrass. The pain now begins again to abate.— Your ever affecte   D H

To Dr Franklin &c &c &c

Addressed: To Dr Franklin / &c &c &c / Passy

Endorsed: D Hartley Esqr Aug. 4. 84 to BF.

From Jean-Charles-Pierre Lenoir

LS: American Philosophical Society

Ce 4. août 1784

J'ai L'honneur de vous envoyer, Monsieur, la permission, que vous desirez, pour que Le paquet de livres et gravures arrivé d'angleterre à votre adresse, Soit delivré à la douane à la personne Chargée de le retirer, Sans passer à la chambre Syndicale.

J'ai L'honneur d'être avec un respectueux attachement, Monsieur, votre très humble et tres obéissant serviteur.   LENOIR

M franklin.

Notation: Le Noir 4 août 1784

To John Adams

ALS: Massachusetts Historical Society

Sir,   Passy, Aug. 6. 1784.

Mr Bingham sent me last Night from Paris, your Excellency's Letter of the 27th past, inclosing a Copy of one from Mr Jefferson. I had before sent you a Copy of one from the same to me, which I hope you receiv'd.[4] I enclose herewith Copies of a Letter from Mr Thomson, some new Instructions, and one of the Commissions;[5] the other two are in the same Words, except

4. Undoubtedly TJ to BF, June 19 (above). We have not found a cover letter.

5. Thomson to the commissioners, June 18, and the new instructions of May 7[–June 3] are both above. For the June 3 commission to negotiate a supplementary treaty with the Netherlands see the annotation of Thomson's letter.

that instead of the Words [*the United Netherlands*][6] there is, in one, *France*, and in the other, *Sweden*. These came by M. de la Luzerne, but it was not before Wednesday last that I receiv'd them.[7] You will see that a good deal of Business is cut out for us, Treaties to be made with I think twenty Powers, in two Years, so that we are not likely to eat the Bread of Idleness;[8] and that we may not surfeit by eating too much, our Masters have diminish'd our Allowance.[9] I commend their Oeconomy, and shall imitate it by diminishing my Expence. Our too liberal Entertainment of our Countrymen here has been reported at home by our Guests to our Disadvantage, and has given Offence. They must be contented for the future, as I am, with plain Beef and Pudding.— The Readers of Connecticut Newspapers ought not to be troubled with any more Accounts of our Extravagance. For my own part, if I could sit down to Dinner on a Piece of their excellent Salt Pork and Pumpkin, I would not give a Farthing for all the Luxuries of Paris.

I am glad to hear that your Family are safely arrived at London, and that you propose to bring them here with you.[1] Your Life will be more comfortable.—

6. The brackets, as well as the italics here and below, are in the MS.

7. The previous Wednesday was Aug. 4. For La Luzerne's return voyage see the annotation to SB to BF, June 20[–21].

8. Proverbs 31:27.

9. In early May, as it struggled to find savings by eliminating superfluous positions and reducing salaries of essential government personnel, Congress voted to set the annual salary of its ministers abroad at $9,000, a reduction of more than $2,000. An earlier vote had set the salaries at $8,000, but that was reversed. BF could have followed the votes on pp. 199–204 of the incomplete *Journal* of Congress that Thomson enclosed in his June 18 letter. See also *JCC*, XXVI, 349–50, 353–4.

1. JA met his wife and daughter in London, where he had already sent JQA, on Aug. 7. The following day the family left for Paris, where they arrived on Aug. 13. Four days later they moved into the Hôtel de Rouault in Auteuil, which would be their residence for the duration of their stay in France: Taylor, *J. Q. Adams Diary*, I, 207–8n; Butterfield, *John Adams Diary*, III, 170–1; *Adams Correspondence*, V, 399–400, 416, 419n, 430n.

I thank you much for the Translation of Abbé Mably's Letters. The French Edition is not yet publish'd here.[2] I have as yet only had time to run over the Translator's Preface, which seems well-written. I imagine Mr Sowdon to be a Presbyterian Minister, as I formerly corresponded with one of that Name in Holland, who I suppose might be his Father.—[3] I have not seen the Piece you mention of a B——n Academician.— I should not object to his Enjoyment of the Discovery he has made that *Despotism* is the best possible Form of Government, by his living under it as long as he pleases: For I admire the Decision of his Prince in a similar Case, the Dispute among his Clergy concerning the Duration of Hell Torments.[4]

With great Respect I have the honour to be, Sir, Your Excellency's most obedient & most humble Servant   B. FRANKLIN

His Excellency John Adams, Esqr

Endorsed: Dr Franklin Aug. 6. 1784

2. In the fall of 1783, JA requested Vergennes' help in getting Mably's *Observations sur le gouvernement et les loix des Etats-Unis de l'Amérique* published in France. However, he then chose to have the pamphlet published in Amsterdam: *Adams Papers,* XV, 312–14, 367–8. Importing *Observations* into France proved to be difficult, despite official permits for distribution and reprinting. It would not be printed in Paris until 1791: Métra, *Correspondance secrète,* XVII, 173; Durand Echeverria and Everett C. Wilkie, Jr., comps., *The French Image of America . . .* (2 vols., Metuchen, N.J., and London, 1994), II, 794–5.

3. The translator was indeed Rev. Benjamin Choyce Sowden, son of the late Benjamin Sowden, a Presbyterian minister in Rotterdam with whom BF had corresponded. The son became an Anglican priest and was named chaplain of the Episcopal Church in Amsterdam in 1782. His writings, apart from some sermons published in English, were largely anonymous: XXVII, 203–4. Johannes van den Berg and Geoffrey F. Nuttall, *Philip Doddridge (1702–1751) and the Netherlands* (Leiden, 1987), pp. 82–3, 88–9; *Gent. Mag.,* LXVI (1796), 356, 385.

4. BF's reaction was the same as that attributed by Voltaire to Frederick II in a theological dispute in Neuchâtel that David Hume reported to BF in 1762. For those clergy who insisted on the doctrine of eternal damnation, Frederick was quite content that they should suffer it: x, 81, 83; Voltaire, *Quatorzième lettre à l'occasion des miracles . . .* ([Geneva, 1765]), pp. 7–8.

Certification of Bills

Press copy of DS[5] and copy: College of William and Mary Library

[August 8, 1784][6]

I do hereby Certify whom it may concern, that the following Certificates of Money, due from the Treasury of the United States of America, to the following Officers, have been by them lodged in my Hands,[7] Viz:—

Dollars

To Major Genl DuPortail,	One dated 24 Novr. 1781. for 5,255: One dated 4 Novr 1783. for 9960: One dated 4 Novr. 1783 for 3047 58/90ths.
To Col. Gouvion.	One dated 24 Novr. 1781. for 3262. 89/90ths. One dated 4 Nov. 1783 for 1161 24/90ths One dated 4 Nov. 1783. for 4500.—
To Genl Laumoy	One dated 16 Jan 1782 for 3835.— One dated 4 Nov. 1783. for 6000.— One dated 4 Nov. 1783. for 2006. 18/19ths

5. In WTF's hand.

6. The day Jean-Baptiste de Gouvion, one of the officers named in this certificate, sent his servant to BF to collect a letter that BF had promised that morning to write to Robert Morris: Gouvion to BF, Aug. 8, 1784 (APS). The letter was probably intended to cover this certification.

7. On Oct. 10, 1783, Congress ordered Robert Morris to settle the accounts of the three officers mentioned below: Gouvion, Duportail (XXIII, 93–4), and Laumoy (XXIII, 160n). Unable to advance cash, Morris issued treasury certificates for the balance owed, and the three men were given passage back to France on the *General Washington*, which sailed *c.* Nov. 8, 1783. In April, 1784, in response to another resolution of Congress dated Jan. 22, warrants for payment were issued to Gouvion and his fellow engineers. The paymaster general, however, refused to release the funds until the treasury certificates that had already been issued to the men were returned and the new payments deducted. As the Frenchmen were no longer in America, a compromise appears to have been reached whereby the certificates would be lodged in BF's office until new ones could be issued: *Morris Papers*, VIII, 617, 626–7, 646n, 677–8; IX, 294–5, 362, 876.

All bearing Interest at 6 per Cent, and signed, by Joseph Nourse, Register, and which are to remain in my Office, or in the Office of the Consul of the said States, until duly exchanged for others.—[8] Given at Passy this 8th. Day of Augt. 1784

B FRANKLIN
Minister Plenipotentiary from the
United States of America.—

Notation by Thomas Jefferson: Copy of Dr. Franklin's receipt for certificates. These were delivered to me, and by me inclosed to Jas. Millegan (by Mr. Otto) and instead thereof I gave to the parties those I had received from Millegan viz Duportail 15967 15/90 D. Gouvion 7994 84/90 D Laumoy 10,283 33/90 D all dated Nov. 16. 1784[9]

From Luke Ryan

ALS: American Philosophical Society

May it please your Excellency—   August the 8th. 1784
To Except of my gratefull acknowledgments and everlasting thanks, for beaing So good as to give me a letter of Recommendation to his Excellency the Marchal de Castries,[1] may pease, unety, traffick, and freaindship, reaighn in your Undependent States of north America, to Compleat that great work, that you in your wisdom So happely begun; that through all futer ages it may be an everlasting Memorial to your Excellenceys name; is My prayrs and wishes—
    I have delivered your letter, along with my petishon to his Excellency On Sunday last, but as yett Receaived no Ansr,

8. The replacement certificates did not arrive until June, 1785. Knowing that BF would soon be leaving for America, Comptroller of the Treasury James Milligan sent the new treasury certificates to TJ along with a copy of this certification: *Jefferson Papers*, VIII, 87–8.

9. TJ's letter to Milligan, enclosing the original treasury certificates obtained from BF, is dated June 17, 1785. It was delivered by Louis-Guillaume Otto, who left Paris shortly thereafter to assume his role as the newly appointed chargé d'affaires in the United States: *Jefferson Papers*, VIII, 227; Giunta, *Emerging Nation*, II, 659.

1. Not found. In 1779 BF had given Ryan, an Irishman who had captained a privateer sailing under American colors out of Dunkirk, a night-glass as a reward for his services: XXIX, 571; XXX, 431, 499.

but through your Recommendation I have the greatest hopes of Sucsess, god Send it May Come Soon, as the lenth of time that I have been Confind, as well the Cruel treatment that I have Expereinced from my Eagent Mr. John Torris makes me anktious to Obtain Justis, which if neglected by his Excellency the Marchal de Castries, I may Expect no Justis from the preaincables of my Eagent John Torris;[2]

I humbly Solecit your Excellency; if you Could find it Convenient, Onst More to Remind the Minnester of My afair and if you in your great goodness would be pleased to Send me a fue Lines to the Hoatel de nismes, Rue de Grenele St. Honore at parris, you will allways Merritt the blessings of god, and the prayrs of your Most Humble Servant—   LUC RYAN

Addressed: To His Excellency— / Benjeman *Frankelin*— / Minnester to the Uneited / States of Northamerica / at *Passy*—

Notation: Ryan 8 Aout 1784

To the Regents of the University of the State of New York

LS:[3] Columbia University Library; copy: New York Society Library

Gentlemen,   Passy Augt. 9th. 1784
I received the Letter you did me the honour of writing to me by Lieut. Col. Clarkson, respecting the Purpose of his Mission, viz Soliciting Donations in Europe for the University of the State of New York.[4] Yours is the fourth American Seminary

2. During the war Ryan had been convicted of piracy and sentenced to death, but George III stayed his execution and on March 2, 1783, issued him a pardon: XXXVIII, 99n. Debts incurred during his incarceration kept him in prison until Feb. 9, 1784, when he was released on account of the intervention of the French naval ministry. Torris, Ryan's former partner in privateering ventures, never paid the money Ryan claimed he was due, and on Feb. 25, 1789, Ryan was once more imprisoned for debt. He died in prison a few months later: Donald A. Petrie, "The Piracy Trial of Luke Ryan," *American Neptune*, LV (1995), 199, 204.
3. In BFB's hand. BF added the complimentary close before signing.
4. Above, June 12.

that since the Peace has sent Persons hither, or empower'd Persons here to make such Solicitations, all of which I have declined being concern'd in;[5] tho' I should certainly be exceedingly glad if I could by any proper Means be serviceable to the Interests of Learning in our Country. The Letter I wrote to Dr. Witherspoon on the Subject, (of which I enclose a Copy)[6] will show the Reasons I then had for not encouraging his Application here for Benefactions to the College of New Jersey. The Necessity we still are under for Credit in Europe where we have Loans opened, the Success of which may be hurt by Declarations of Poverty, (the only excuse for Mendicity) make this Mode of procuring Money at this Time exceedingly improper: as do also the Orders just received by your Ministers to offer Treaties to twenty different European Powers, with whom it is fit we should stand in as respectable a Light as possible, and not appear a Nation that is either unable or unwilling to support among ourselves the common Expence of Education. I am making a large Collection of such French Books as I think may be serviceable in America, where I hope that Language, which contains abundance of useful Learning, will be more and more cultivated. I intend a Part of these Books as a Present to your University, and shall be glad of any Opportunity of promoting its Interests & Prosperity: but in the Mode proposed I hope you will excuse my not acting with Mr. Clarkson, to whom the only Advice I can give is, not to attempt here any such Solicitation.[7]

5. The first three were Dartmouth College (XXXVIII, 134–5; XXXIX, 176–7n; XL, 154–5, 322), Rhode Island College (XLI, 431–2), and the College of New Jersey (XLI, 270n; Witherspoon to BF, March 27, 1784, above).

6. The copy, by BFB, was of BF's April 5 letter to Witherspoon, above.

7. On Aug. 11, 1784, Clarkson reported to Gov. Clinton on his lack of success thus far. He had met with BF on Aug. 2, and found that "his sentiments were intirely unfavorable to my mission." When Clarkson returned to Passy a second time, BF was unchanged in his views and gave him a copy of the letter to Witherspoon cited above. Clarkson also reported on his meeting with a French noble, in which he explained the regents' plan to establish "Academies" throughout N.Y. state that would make the teaching of French a priority. The goal was to break the bond of language that cemented the relationship between Britain and the United States. Columbia University Library.

With great Respect, I have the honour to be, Gentlemen, Your most obedient & most humble Servant   B. FRANKLIN

To The Regents of the University of New York.

Endorsed:[8] 9 Augt. 1784. Benjn. Franklin

From Bailly

AL: American Philosophical Society

ce lundi 9 aout. [1784]

Mr Bailly presente ses hommages a Monsieur Franklin. Il a l'honneur de lui envoier premierement la suite du registre. Mr Franklin voudra bien le lire et le signer a l'endroit où il est dit qu'il a signé.

Secondement le rapport qui doit etre signé mercredi par les commissaires et presenté au roi vendredi.[9] Mr Bailly le lui envoie aujourd'hui, afin que Mr Franklin ait le tems de le lire. Il suffira qu'il ait la bonté de lui renvoier le tout ou demain mardi au soir, ou mercredi matin avant huit heures, a chaillot comme a l'ordinaire près la cazerne des suisses.[1]

Il n'a pû lui communiquer encore la note parcequ'il y a quelque petit changement a y faire.

On a mis ces papiers dans la boette pour que le rapport ne soit ni chiffonné, ni sali; le porteur remettra en meme tems la clef. mr Franklin est prié de renvoier le tout de même et cacheté

Mr Franklin n'oubliera pas de signer le rapport, et de menager la place, car elle est petite pour neuf signatures[2]

Notation: M. Bailly—

---

8. In the hand of James Duane.

9. The report is dated Paris, Aug. 11 (a Wednesday). It is summarized, with excerpts interspersed, under that date, below.

1. The barracks for the first company of grenadiers of the Swiss Guards. It was located at what is now the place d'Iéna: Alfred Fierro, *Dictionnaire du Paris disparu: sites & monuments* (Paris, 1998), p. 79.

2. The MS has not been located. In the official published version, BF's signature comes first.

From Alexander Cain, Mark Collins, and William Jones

LS and copy: American Philosophical Society; copies: Archives du Ministère des affaires étrangères, Archives départementales d'Ille-et-Vilaine

Sir,   L'Orient 9. August 1784.

We take The Liberty To address your Excellency on a Subject extremely interesting to us & many other persons concern'd in The Trade between This kingdom & The united states of america, The extention or diminution of which we will venture To Say depends in a great degree on your Excellency's answer.

For some Time before we left America it was currently reported & Even publish'd in most of The News papers That The Town & port of L'orient were to be declar'd free. Many private Letters from very respectable Persons in This Country, who said They had good authority for what They wrote, announc'd The same, & gave Their Correspondents The strongest assurances That on The arrival of Their Ships here They would find Magazines establish'd of all kinds of goods suitable for The different American Markets. Many of The most considerable Merchants in Philadelphia & Elsewhere in The united States, who had constantly Traded with This kingdom during The late war (and who would have Still continued To do So, had not The extreme Scarcity & high Price of almost every article of The Manufactures of This kingdom, & The Little demand They found for american Produce, oblig'd Them To Turn Their Views Elsewhere) were induc'd by These prospects To Try once more if it was possible to Establish a commercial Connection with This kingdom as advantageous as That which They carried on with England, Holland &a., & The Vessels which we command Together with Several others expected daily, were Sent To This Port rather Than to London or Amsterdam for The above reasons. The Prospect of a good return freight, which The freedom flatter'd us with, was another strong Inducement. On our arrival here, we found That agreable To what was publish'd in America before our departure This Town & Port had in reality been declar'd free by an Edict dated The 14th. of May, but were greatly surpris'd & disappointed To find That by a second Edict The freedom was restrain'd To The

473

Port alone,[3] & even That under such restrictions as appear To us altogether incompatible with a free port, & which cause us more Trouble Than we experienc'd formerly, because The freedom does not extend to The Road, where for many reasons we often prefer loading our Vessels. We have been likewise greatly disappointed in not finding Such magazines of goods as we were given reason to Expect, & when we demand The cause of This, The Merchants & Shop keepers answer us That They countermanded Their orders to The manufacturers on finding That The Edict of The 14th. of May was not allow'd to Take place, because They did not expect any considerable demands. Thus we find it impossible To get any returns That will answer for The little adventures we brought with us, for we have not Time to write To The Manufactures, besides we always choose to See the goods before we purchase Them, & we shall be oblig'd to return with our Ships in Ballast & a Small quantity of Brandy to The Ports from Whence we came; for we have not discretionary orders, whilst Those Vessels which went To London will find Suitable goods in return for the proceeds of their Cargoes, besides valuable freights back to America. But for This Voyage The Evil is without remedy, & to Complain of our present Loss & that which our Owners may Sustain, is not our principal motive for Troubling your Excellency. Many people flatter us That The Edict of The 14th. May is only Suspended for a short Time, & That This Town, Port & Road will again be declar'd To all intents & purposes free The same as dunkirk.[4] As The St. James & Eagle will Sail for Philadelphia in about a fortnight, we would wish To know from your Excellency, before they depart, how far we can depend on These assurances, & what we may venture To report To our fellow-citizens, when we arrive; for altho'

3. This second edict was dated June 26; see the annotation of BF's journal, [June 26–July 27], entry of June 30.

4. Article 1 of the June 26 edict stated that the king might extend slightly the boundaries of the franchise if it became necessary: *Arrêt du conseil d'état du roi. Portant règlement sur la franchise accordé au port & à la ville de l'Orient. Du 26 juin 1784.* Based on the protests of the American captains and local merchants, however, a new *arrêt du conseil* was issued on Oct. 3 that reinstated the more generous limits of the May 14 edict: *Arrêt du conseil d'état du roi. Portant règlement pour la franchise du port de l'Orient. Du 3 octobre 1784.*

Magnetic Tub

The late change in publick measures may in Some degree damp The Spirits of Those That wish well to The Commerce of This kingdom & be cause of Triumph To The few remaining friends of great Britain, yet we are of opinion That, was The Trade Entirely free, a very great number of our Vessels would be induc'd To visit This port next season. Indeed we would always give it The preference in The fall & winter months, because There is no danger of beeing frozen up, as sometimes happens at London, Amsterdam, &a.

Should your Excellency have any Letters or packets for America, you may depend on our utmost Care of Them. We have The honor To remain with great respect, Your Excellency's most obedient & Very humble Servants

> ALEXR. CAIN Commander of the Ship St. James
> MARK COLLINS comander of the Ship Heer Adams
> WM. JONES. Commd. of the Eagle

His Excellency Benjamin Franklin Esqr. (Paris)

Report of the Royal Commission to Investigate Animal Magnetism: Résumé with Extracts[5]

Rapport des commissaires chargés par le Roi, de l'examen du magnétisme animal (Paris, 1784)[6]

The commissioners of the Faculté de médecine and the Académie des sciences—with the exception of Franklin—met in Paris on

5. Because no reprint of this 66-page report is available we summarize it here, printing in full the conclusion and interspersing extracts of the four sections that describe experiments and conversations that took place at BF's residence at Passy. These are the only ones in which he is known to have participated and, according to Sallin, dean of the Faculty, they were the most important experiments of the series. Sallin made this statement when countering a charge, made by an unrepentant mesmerist after being expelled from the Faculty, that BF had been a member of the commission in name only: *Mémoire pour Me. Charles-Louis Varnier . . .* (Paris, 1785), p. 8; A. Pinard *et al.*, eds., *Commentaires de la Faculté de médecine de Paris, 1777 à 1786* (2 vols., Paris, 1903), II, 1276–7.

6. The title reads as though the undersigned commissioners were the only ones appointed by the king. They were not, though by August it was

Wednesday, August 11, to sign the report of their four-month investigation. Franklin, unable to travel, had signed in advance, having received the pristine manuscript in a locked box two days earlier with instructions to keep his signature small enough to leave room for the others.[7] As head of the commission, his signature came first.

It is not known when Franklin was chosen to head this joint commission, but it may have been at its initial meeting on May 8. Though the discussions were confidential, news of the appointment quickly circulated. Mesmer sent his May 14 letter of protest to Franklin individually, declaring him to be the head of the commission. (Franklin's reply did not deny it.) A week later Lafayette, writing on Mesmer's behalf, appealed to the man whom the world considered to be the commission's "president."[8]

The American minister's prestige and reputation as both a scientist and a diplomat, as well as his being the sole foreign member, must have made him an obvious choice to lead what might have been a contentious coalition. His election to the Académie des sciences had been based on his having proved the existence of a supremely powerful, invisible force—atmospheric electricity— whose therapeutic applications had been compared to magnetic treatments and were a promising field of study. He could be seen as impartial, having never taken part in any previous attempt to investigate Mesmer or Deslon. The views he had recently expressed about Mesmer's "cures," which he guessed were psychological in nature, had been almost benign.[9] Moreover, although the members of the Faculty had initially resisted the government's injunction to work with members of the Academy, none of them seemed opposed to collaborating with Benjamin Franklin. As Lavoisier wrote of the commissioners, "Leurs lumières,

---

generally acknowledged that their report would be the more significant one. The Society's report was signed on Aug. 16. Breteuil considered it repetitive and too technical to be understood by the public, and insisted on its being substantially revised before publication: Poissonnier to unnamed correspondent, [Aug. 15, 1784], Bibliothèque de l'Académie nationale de médecine; Bachaumont, *Mémoires secrets*, XXVI, 176. When issued, its title included the name of the institution: *Rapport des commissaires de la Société royale de médecine, nommés par le Roi pour faire l'examen du magnétisme animal* (Paris, 1784).

7. See Bailly to BF, Aug. 9. As announced there, the report was due at Versailles on Aug. 13.

8. Mesmer to BF, May 14; Lafayette to BF, [May 20]; BF to Mesmer, May 23. (All are above.)

9. To La Condamine, March 19, above.

leurs qualités morales, le nom du célèbre Franklin placé à la tête, tout, dans cette Commission, paraissait propre à imprimer le respect et à inspirer la confiance."[1] If the government's purpose in expanding the commission beyond the Faculty of Medicine was to instill public confidence in its findings,[2] then the commissioners could have chosen no better person to represent them.

What were Franklin's actual contributions? We know that he hosted experiments at Passy and was himself magnetized. Finding travel prohibitively difficult, he did not attend the meetings and experiments that took place in Paris, which accounted for more than half of the commission's work. He followed its progress, however, as recorded in the confidential log ("registre") that was sent to him periodically for his review and signature. He must also have been briefed by his friend, neighbor, and co-commissioner Jean-Baptiste Le Roy.

As the "registre" has been lost, it is all but impossible to tease out the individual contributions of any of the commissioners. The notes of only one, Lavoisier, survive; from these writings, it is clear that he designed at least some of the key experiments. It seems unlikely that Franklin did not have a hand in designing experiments as well. Without the commission's log, however, none of the internal discussions and debates, or even the dates of individual experiments, is retrievable. The only surviving account of the commissioners' work is their official report, which was careful to present the group as a unified, cooperative body. The appointment of a "president" was never mentioned. The members' names were listed in the opening paragraph, but thereafter they were characterized almost exclusively in the collective third person. An individual was mentioned only when his house was the scene of an experiment (Franklin's residence being the most frequent of these), and, in one case, when a renowned ophthalmologist was described as examining a patient's diseased eye as a means of distracting her attention as she was being magnetized.[3] Otherwise, the commissioners were anonymous. They proceeded as a group, made decisions "unanimement," and in presenting their conclusions spoke with a "voix unanime."[4] Even the order of their signatures signaled their integration: the five members of the Academy and the four members of the Faculty signed in strict alternation. When Bailly addressed the Académie des sciences on September 4

1. *Œuvres de Lavoisier* (6 vols., Paris, 1862–93), III, 515.
2. See the headnote to Poissonnier to BF, April 26.
3. This was Majault, in the eleventh experiment.
4. *Rapport des commissaires chargés par le Roi, de l'examen du magnétisme animal,* p. 16 and the conclusion published below.

about the commission's work, he stressed its unity. Their efforts had been motivated by a mutual desire for truth, and the results belonged to all of them: "rien n'a été distingué, le travail appartient à tous . . . nous avons été toujours unis, toujours unanimes."[5]

The eagerly anticipated *Rapport des commissaires chargés par le Roi, de l'examen du magnétisme animal* was published by the Imprimerie royale around August 21[6] and, at 66 pages, was the size of a small book. A preview of its conclusion was made public on August 20 in the *Mémoires secrets*. Reminding readers that the commissioners had investigated Deslon, not Mesmer, the article reported that they had found animal magnetism to be "une invention illusoire, vaine & funeste."[7]

Knowing that their report would be published and that the task of convincing the public lay wholly in their hands, the authors produced an account that was both scientifically sound and accessible, making for compelling reading. Chronology was unimportant; few dates were specified. The rationale for every decision and the details of every experiment, however, were explained in terms that anyone could understand. *Rapport des commissaires* was immediately reprinted in France by private publishers. Before the year was out, an English translation was issued in London by Joseph Johnson, who placed Franklin's name in the title and identified him in the introduction as the head of the commission: *Report of Dr. Benjamin Franklin, and other Commissioners, Charged by the King of France, with the Examination of the Animal Magnetism, as now Practiced at Paris*.[8] The report would become famous for the originality and rigor of the experiments, which led systematically to conclusions that the authors considered irrefutable.

On the advice of Breteuil, the commissioners reserved some of their observations for a second, secret report, also signed on August 11, which would be for the king's eyes only.[9] Its message was

5. Jean-Sylvain Bailly *et al.*, *Exposé des expériences qui ont été faites pour l'examen du magnétisme animal* (Paris, 1784), p. 4.

6. BF to Banks, Aug. 21, 1784, in Neil Chambers, ed., *Scientific Correspondence of Sir Joseph Banks, 1765–1820* (6 vols., London, 2007), II, 299–300.

7. Bachaumont, *Mémoires secrets*, XXVI, 155.

8. Although its title page cites the year of publication as 1785, the booklet was announced for sale in the *St. James's Chron.; Or British Evening-Post* of Dec. 16–18, 1784.

9. The background presented here comes from the opening of the report itself. Published some fifteen years later, it was entitled *Rapport secret sur le mesmérisme* and attributed to Bailly: Nicolas François de Neufchâteau, *Le Conservateur, ou recueil de morceaux inédits d'histoire, de politique, de littérature et de philosophie* (2 vols., Paris, An VIII [1799–1800]), I, 146–55.

blunt: the practice of animal magnetism was a threat not only to health, as the official report had stated, but also to morality, especially in the case of weak, virtuous women. The commissioners offered a medical explanation of why the nerves and imaginations of women were more easily excited than those of men. They provided an explicit description of a certain kind of prolonged "convulsion" that resulted not from the alleged healing power of animal magnetism but rather from the close physical contact and mutual arousal of male magnetizers and female patients who did not fully understand what was being done to them.[1] Deslon himself had admitted, under interrogation by Lenoir, how easy it would be to abuse a woman in such a state. Many women had been in treatment for years without being cured. Most of them were not ill to begin with, but had been drawn to the clinic for the amusement it provided, attending regularly as a relief from boredom. Around the tub, the ease with which symptoms spread from person to person was striking. The commissioners reiterated the health risks of inducing full-blown crises, a dangerous practice that any responsible physician would shun. They implied the possibility that magnetic seances were a deliberate fraud. The uniformly critical tone of this private document was in stark contrast to the scrupulously evenhanded voice of the official report.

In the end, the commissioners of the Faculty of Medicine obtained what they had initially requested in their April 3 letter to Breteuil:[2] a group of elite scientists had undertaken a systematic, logical series of experiments to prove whether animal magnetism existed. Contrary to their original proposal, however, their own investigation had not waited until after the academicians' work had concluded; they had become integral participants. The scientists of the Academy had insisted on this, deeming the doctors' expertise indispensable. In a statement that appears to have been read at one of the commission's first sessions, Lavoisier eloquently outlined the distinct roles of scientists versus doctors, and proposed a way to proceed.[3]

1. There had long been rumors about the sensual pleasures offered by magnetic therapy; see for instance Bachaumont, *Mémoires secrets*, XXIII, 17–18; *Courier de l'Europe*, XV (1784), 315. Deslon's published description of a typical treatment included a section relating that his knees enclosed those of the patient while he massaged and stroked different areas, moving according to nerve pathways and polarities: *Le Magnétisme dévoilé* (Paris, [1784]), pp. 3–4.
2. Described in the headnote to Poissonier to BF, April 26, above.
3. *Œuvres de Lavoisier*, III, 499–500.

To all outward appearances, the group coalesced quickly. Franklin's hospitality at Passy seemed to have helped foster the spirit of cooperation that ultimately characterized the Faculty/Academy commission. Its first meeting was convened around his table. The experiments performed at Passy were preceded by dinners at that same table, to which all the participants, from the investigators down to the humblest patients, were invited. Even after the report was published Franklin continued to host the commissioners, and these new friendships were further cultivated.[4] His scientific contributions to the investigation may never be known, but Franklin's role as head of the commission was rendered iconic when the print *Le Magnétisme dévoilé* depicted him leading the charge against mesmerist superstition and vice.[5]

[August II, 1784]

⟨Paris, August II, 1784, in French: On March 12 the king appointed four physicians of the Faculty of Medicine—Borie, Sallin, d'Arcet, and Guillotin—to examine and report on animal magnetism as practiced by Deslon. At their request, the king appointed five members of the Academy of Sciences to join them: Franklin, Le Roy, Bailly, Bory, and Lavoisier. When Borie died at the outset of their work, the king appointed Majault to replace him.

The agent that Mesmer claims to have discovered is defined, in his own words, this way:[6] it is a universal fluid that facilitates a mutual influence among celestial bodies, the earth, and all living beings, and exhibits two distinct, opposite poles, like those of a magnet. Its effect can be transmitted from one animate or inanimate body to another, even over long distances, without an intermediary. The effect is intensified when the fluid is reflected in a mirror and transmitted through sound. Magnetic fluid can be collected, concentrated, and transported. In the human body it affects the nerves particularly. Animal magnetism can cure nervous disorders, improve the effect of medications, and induce salutary crises. It enables physicians to assess an individual's health and determine with certainty the cause and

4. Guillotin recalled these post-commission conversations in his letter to BF, June 18, 1787 (APS).
5. That engraving is reproduced as the frontispiece to this volume.
6. The commissioners here quoted and paraphrased Mesmer's *Mémoire sur la découverte du magnétisme animal* (Geneva, 1779), pp. vi, 74–82.

course of even the most complicated diseases. Magnetism provides a universal means of healing and preserving mankind.

Deslon endorses all of Mesmer's principles. On May 9 the commissioners and Lenoir, lieutenant of police, assembled at Deslon's house and listened to him read a memoir. He claimed that there is one nature, one disease, and one cure: animal magnetism. He then demonstrated how he directed magnetic fluid in his patients. Deslon pledged to cooperate with the commissioners to ascertain the existence of animal magnetism, to make known his knowledge of it, and to prove the usefulness of animal magnetism in the curing of disease.

The commissioners repeatedly visited Deslon's clinic and observed group therapy sessions around a *baquet*, a circular, covered wooden tub from which protrude bent, movable iron rods.[7] Patients are arranged in rows around this tub and press an iron rod to their afflicted body part, while holding each other by the thumbs or being tied together with a cord. In the corner sits a pianoforte on which different kinds of melodies are played, occasionally accompanied by singing. The magnetizer holds a metal rod 10 to 12 inches long. Deslon told the commissioners that the rod and music both conduct magnetism; that the rope and chain of thumbs both augment the effect; and that the inside of the tub concentrates magnetism. Patients receive magnetism simultaneously by these means. They are also directly magnetized when the magnetizer passes a finger and metal rod in front of their face or around their afflicted part, stares into their eyes, and applies pressure with his hands and fingers to the lower abdominal area, maintaining contact for as much as several hours.

While some patients remain calm, the more common effect of this treatment is what is called, in animal magnetism, the crisis: fits of violent convulsions and seizures that can last for hours, accompanied by screams and laughter, followed by exhaustion and lethargy. These so-called crises are considered salutary. The power wielded by the magnetizer over his patients is extraordinary. Most patients who experience crises are women, and the crises appear to be contagious among them.

After the commissioners observed the effects of these mag-

---

7. The only surviving *baquet* is illustrated facing page 475.

netic treatments, their next task was to determine the causes and to search for proof of the existence and utility of magnetism. The question of existence had to come first, for animal magnetism can certainly exist without being useful, but it cannot be useful if it does not exist.[8] Deslon insisted that the commissioners investigate the curative powers of magnetism, but they did not believe that they had to do so. Because magnetic fluid was acknowledged to be undetectable by the senses, and the commissioners considered any gradual improvement of symptoms to be inconclusive evidence of the efficacy of any particular treatment,[9] they determined to focus on immediate, physical effects attributable to no other cause than animal magnetism.

The commissioners resolved to perform the first experiments on themselves, so that they could experience the sensations. They agreed unanimously to conduct these trials as a group, in private, so that they could freely discuss their observations. Deslon set up for them a separate room with a tub, and they went there once a week; they were magnetized by either Deslon or one of his disciples for two and a half hours each time. None felt any symptoms ascribable to animal magnetism. In order to test whether sequential days of treatment would make a difference, some commissioners went three days in a row, but the effect was the same.

The commissioners next determined to experiment on subjects who were actually sick, chosen from the lower classes. This second experiment was conducted at Franklin's home.

> Sept malades ont été rassemblés à Passy chez M. Franklin; ils ont été magnétisés devant lui & devant les autres Commissaires par M. Deslon.
> La veuve Saint-Amand, asthmatique, ayant le ventre, les cuisses & les jambes enflées; & la femme Anseaume, qui avoit une grosseur à la cuisse, n'ont rien senti; le pe-

8. This oft-quoted line reads, in the original, "Le Magnétisme animal peut bien exister sans être utile, mais il ne peut être utile s'il n'existe pas."
9. The commissioners' reasons for excluding the treatment of diseases were explained at length. This concept was key to their decision to change the focus of their investigation from a narrow examination of Deslon's patients (which is what the doctor had expected) to a general investigation of animal magnetism.

tit Claude Renard, enfant de six ans, scrofuleux, presque étique, ayant le genou gonflé, la jambe fléchie & l'articulation presque sans mouvement, enfant intéressant & plus raisonnable que son âge ne le comporte, n'a également rien senti, ainsi que Geneviève Leroux, âgée de neuf ans, attaquée de convulsions & d'une maladie assez semblable à celle que l'on nomme *chorea sancti Viti*. François Grenet a éprouvé quelques effets; il a les yeux malades, particulièrement le droit, dont il ne voit presque pas, & où il a une tumeur considérable. Quand on a magnétisé l'œil gauche en approchant, en agitant le pouce de près & assez longtemps, il a éprouvé de la douleur dans le globe de l'œil, & l'œil a larmoyé. Quand on a magnétisé l'œil droit, qui est le plus malade, il n'y a rien senti; il a senti la même douleur à l'œil gauche, & rien par-tout ailleurs.

La femme Charpentier, qui a été jetée à terre contre une poutre, par une vache, il y a deux ans, a éprouvé plusieurs suites de cet accident; elle a perdu la vue, l'a recouvrée en partie, mais elle est restée dans un état d'infirmités habituelles; elle a déclaré avoir deux descentes, & le ventre d'une sensibilité si grande, qu'elle ne peut supporter les cordons de la ceinture de ses jupes: cette sensibilité appartient à des nerfs agacés & rendus très-mobiles; la plus légère pression faite dans la région du ventre, peut déterminer cette mobilité & produire des effets dans tout le corps par la correspondance des nerfs.

Cette femme a été magnétisée comme les autres, par l'application & par la pression des doigts; la pression lui a été douloureuse: ensuite en dirigeant le doigt vers la descente, elle s'est plainte de douleur à la tête; le doigt étant placé devant le visage, elle a dit qu'elle perdoit la respiration. Au mouvement réitéré du doigt de haut en bas, elle avoit des mouvemens précipités de la tête & des épaules, comme on en a d'une surprise mêlée de frayeur, & semblables à ceux d'une personne à qui on jetteroit quelques gouttes d'eau froide au visage. Il a semblé qu'elle éprouvoit les mêmes mouvemens ayant les yeux fermés. On lui a porté les doigts sous le nez en lui faisant fermer les yeux, & elle a dit qu'elle se trouveroit mal si on continuoit. Le septième malade, Joseph Ennuyé, a éprouvé des effets du même genre, mais beaucoup moins marqués. Sur ces sept malades, il y en a quatre qui n'ont rien senti & les trois autres ont éprouvé des effets. Ces effets méritoient de fixer l'attention des Commissaires, & demandoient un examen scrupuleux.

The third series of experiments was conducted with patients chosen from the aristocracy. In one experiment, four of them, two women and two men, were admitted to the commissioners' private tub; two felt minor effects. Other patients were tested in other circumstances. Deslon magnetized one commissioner suffering from acute migraine, but the pain did not abate. The doctor also went to Passy to magnetize Franklin and members of his household.

M. Franklin, quoique ses incommodités l'aient empêché de se transporter à Paris, & d'assister aux expériences qui y ont été faites, a été lui-même magnétisé par M. Deslon, qui s'est rendu chez lui à Passy. L'assemblée étoit nombreuse; tous ceux qui étoient présens ont été magnétisés. Quelques malades qui avoient accompagné M. Deslon, ont ressenti les effets du Magnétisme, comme ils ont coutume de les ressentir au traitement public; mais Mme de B**, M. Franklin, ses deux Parentes, son Secrétaire, un Officier Américain, n'ont rien éprouvé, quoiqu'une des Parentes de M. Franklin fût convalescente, & l'Officier Américain alors malade d'une fièvre réglée.[1]

Collecting and analyzing the data gathered so far, the commissioners concluded that magnetic treatments had the capacity neither to detect illnesses nor to alleviate them. The fact that the most pronounced symptoms were experienced by lower-class patients, who were presumed to be more credulous and more eager to please their examiners, while the more educated and

---

1. The test subjects were most likely Mme de Bory, BF, WTF, BFB, L'Air de Lamotte, and David Salisbury Franks, who was ill with a fever during his time in Paris: Oscar S. Straus, "New Light on the Career of Colonel David S. Franks," *American Jewish Hist. Quarterly*, X (1902), 103.

skeptical subjects felt little or nothing, led them to suspect that the patient's imagination played a part in producing symptoms. At this stage of the investigation, the commissioners learned that a medical doctor named Jumelin[2] was conducting experiments with animal magnetism at the home of the dean of the Faculty. Though Jumelin was not a disciple of Mesmer or Deslon, he magnetized patients as they did, using his fingers and an iron rod and laying his hands on affected parts of the body. He did not, however, make any distinction between poles. Jumelin agreed to perform a series of experiments (the fourth series) at the home of commissioner Majault. First, he magnetized eleven patients, eight men and three women. As only one woman felt effects—intense heat directly beneath where Jumelin's hand floated above her body—the commissioners proposed blindfolding her so that she could not see where the magnetism was being directed. Under those conditions, she felt no effects in the places being magnetized. They removed the blindfold and had Jumelin place his hand on her abdomen; then, she again felt heat and even fainted. The blindfold was reinstated, and the commissioners led her to believe that Jumelin was magnetizing her once more (which he was not). She felt the same effects, with the same intensity. After some time, Jumelin was silently directed to magnetize her over her stomach and back; she felt nothing. These experiments led the commissioners to conclude that the method of magnetizing and the distinction between poles were irrelevant. They then tested the supposition that the patients' reactions were caused by their imaginations, by having Jumelin conduct similar experiments (the fifth series) on other patients. Once again the blindfolded patients felt sensations according to where they believed the magnetism to be directed.

In the sixth series of experiments, conducted at M. Jumelin's home, the commissioners used his servant to test a blindfold they had designed, which, being padded with goose down, was comfortable and admitted no light whatsoever. The commissioners, especially the doctors among them, conducted an

2. Jean-Baptiste Jumelin was a doctor regent of the Faculty who was interested in physics and chemistry: *Nouvelle biographie*.

"infinite" number of experiments on patients who either were or were not being magnetized, with and without their knowledge. The results were always the same: effects were felt only when patients believed that magnetism was being applied, and patients could induce these sensations in themselves.[3] Having determined that imagination, on its own, can produce sensations and make a patient feel pain and heat, the commissioners wanted to test whether the imagination by itself was powerful enough to induce actual crises. The seventh, eighth, and ninth experiments, designed to provide an answer, were performed at Passy on different days with subjects chosen by Deslon: a boy and two women.

Lorsqu'un arbre a été touché suivant les principes & la méthode du Magnétisme, toute personne qui s'y arrête doit éprouver plus ou moins les effets de cet agent; il en est même qui y perdent connoissance ou qui y éprouvent des convulsions. On en parla à M. Deslon, qui répondit que l'expérience devoit réussir pourvu que le sujet fût fort sensible, & on convint avec lui de la faire à Passy, en présence de M. Franklin.[4] La nécessité que le sujet fût sensible, fit penser aux Commissaires que pour rendre l'expérience décisive & sans réplique, il falloit qu'elle fût faite sur une personne choisie par M. Deslon, & dont il auroit éprouvé d'avance la sensibilité au Magnétisme. M. Deslon a donc amené avec lui un jeune homme d'environ douze ans, on a marqué dans le verger du jardin, un abricotier bien isolé, & propre à conserver le Magnétisme qu'on lui auroit imprimé. On y a mené M. Deslon seul, pour qu'il le magnétisât, le jeune homme étant resté dans la maison & avec une personne qui ne l'a pas quitté. On auroit desiré que M. Deslon ne fût pas présent à l'expérience, mais il a déclaré qu'elle pourroit manquer s'il ne dirigeoit pas sa canne

3. Here, a footnote in the report quotes a July 30 letter the commissioners had received from Dr. Sigault of the Faculty, who had been pretending to magnetize people on the street. By giving out that he was trained, he was able to induce symptoms in numerous individuals who believed him to have special powers.

4. The experiment took place on Saturday, May 22, as recorded in BFB's journal.

& ses regards sur cet arbre, pour en augmenter l'action. On a pris le parti d'éloigner M. Deslon le plus possible, & de placer les Commissaires entre lui & le jeune homme, afin de s'assurer qu'il ne feroit point de signal, & de pouvoir répondre qu'il n'y avoit point eu d'intelligence. Ces précautions, dans une expérience qui doit être authentique, sont indispensables sans être offensantes.

On a ensuite amené le jeune homme, les yeux bandés, & ou l'a présenté successivement à quatre arbres qui n'étoient point magnétisés, en les lui faisant embrasser, chacun pendant deux minutes, suivant ce qui avoit été réglé par M. Deslon lui-même.

M. Deslon présent, & à une assez grande distance, dirigeoit sa canne sur l'arbre réellement magnétisé.

Au premier arbre, le jeune homme interrogé au bout d'une minute, a déclaré qu'il suoit à grosses gouttes; il a toussé, craché, & il a dit sentir une petite douleur sur la tête; la distance à l'arbre magnétisé étoit de vingt-sept pieds.

Au second arbre, il se sent étourdi, même douleur sur la tête; la distance étoit de trente-six pieds.

Au troisième arbre, l'étourdissement redouble ainsi que le mal de tête; il dit qu'il croit approcher de l'arbre magnétisé; il en étoit alors environ à trente-huit pieds.

Enfin au quatrième arbre non magnétisé, & à vingt quatre pieds environ de distance de l'arbre qui l'avoit été, le jeune homme est tombé en crises; il a perdu connoissance, ses membres se sont roidis, & on l'a porté sur un gazon voisin, où M. Deslon lui a donné des secours & l'a fait revenir.

Le résultat de cette expérience est entièrement contraire au Magnétisme. M. Deslon a voulu expliquer le fait, en disant que tous les arbres sont magnétisés par eux-mêmes, & que leur Magnétisme étoit d'ailleurs renforcé par sa présence. Mais alors une personne sensible au Magnétisme, ne pourroit hasarder d'aller dans un jardin sans risquer d'avoir des convulsions; cette assertion seroit démentie par l'expérience de tous les jours. La présence de M. Deslon n'a rien fait de plus que ce qu'elle a fait dans le carrosse où le jeune homme est venu avec lui, placé vis-à-vis de lui, & où il n'a rien éprouvé. Si le jeune homme n'eût rien senti, même sous l'arbre magnétisé, on auroit pu dire qu'il n'étoit pas assez sensible, du moins ce jour-là: mais le jeune homme est tombé en crise sous un arbre qui n'étoit pas magnétisé; c'est par conséquent un effet qui n'a point de cause physique, de cause extérieure, & qui n'en peut avoir d'autre que l'imagination. L'expérience est donc tout-à-fait concluante: le jeune homme savoit qu'on le menoit à l'arbre magnétisé, son imagination s'est frappée, successivement exaltée, & au quatrième arbre elle a été montée au degré nécessaire pour produire la crise.

D'autres expériences viennent à l'appui de celle-ci, & fournissent le même résultat. Un jour que les Commissaires se sont réunis à Passy chez M. Franklin, & avec M. Deslon, ils avoient prié ce dernier d'amener avec lui des malades, & de choisir dans le traitement des pauvres, ceux qui seroient le plus sensibles au Magnétisme. M. Deslon a amené deux femmes; & tandis qu'il étoit occupé à magnétiser M. Franklin & plusieurs personnes dans un autre appartement, on a séparé ces deux femmes, & on les a placées dans deux pièces différentes.

L'une la femme P**, a des taies sur les yeux; mais comme elle voit toujours un peu, on lui a cependant couvert les yeux du bandeau décrit ci-dessus. On lui a persuadé qu'on avoit amené M. Deslon pour la magnétiser: le silence étoit recommandé, trois Commissaires étoient présens, l'un pour interroger, l'autre pour écrire, le troisième pour représenter M. Deslon. On a eu l'air d'adresser la parole à M. Deslon, en le priant de commencer, mais on n'a point magnétisé la femme; les trois Commissaires sont restés tranquilles, occupés seulement à observer ce qui alloit se passer. Au bout de trois minutes la malade a commencé à sentir un frisson nerveux; puis successivement elle a senti une douleur derrière la tête, dans les bras, un fourmillement dans les mains, c'est son expression; elle se roidissoit, frappoit dans ses mains, se levoit de son siège, frappoit des pieds: la crise a été bien caractérisée. Deux autres Commissaires placés dans la pièce à côté, la porte fermée, ont entendu les battemens de pieds & de mains, & sans rien voir, ont été les témoins de cette scène bruyante.

Ces deux Commissaires étoient avec l'autre malade, la demoiselle B**, attaquée de maux de nerfs. On lui a laissé la vue libre & les yeux découverts; on l'a assise devant une porte fermée, en lui persuadant que M. Deslon étoit de l'autre côté, occupé à la magnétiser. Il y avoit à peine une minute qu'elle étoit assise devant cette porte, quand elle a commencé à sentir du frisson; après une autre minute, elle a eu un claquement de dents, & cependant une chaleur générale; enfin après une troisième minute, elle est tombée tout-à-fait en crise. La respiration étoit précipitée; elle étendoit les deux bras derrière le dos, en les tordant fortement, & en penchant le corps en devant: il y a eu tremblement général de tout le corps; le claquement de dents est devenu si bruyant, qu'il pouvoit être entendu de dehors; elle s'est mordu la main, & assez fort pour que les dents y soient resté marquées.

Il est bon d'observer qu'on n'a touché en aucune manière ces deux malades; on ne leur a pas même tâté le pouls, afin qu'on ne pût pas dire qu'on leur avoit communiqué le Magnétisme, & cependant les crises ont été complètes. Les Commissaires qui ont voulu connoître l'effet du travail de l'imagination, & apprécier la part qu'elle pouvoit avoir aux crises du Magnétisme, ont obtenu tout ce qu'ils desiroient. Il est impossible de voir l'effet de ce travail plus à découvert & d'une manière plus évidente, que dans ces deux expériences. Si les malades ont déclaré que leurs crises sont plus fortes au traitement, c'est que l'ébranlement des nerfs se communique, & qu'en général toute émotion propre & individuelle est augmentée par le spectacle d'émotions semblables.

The tenth and eleventh experiments were performed on the highly susceptible dame P***, who suffered from filmy eyes and who, at Passy, had fallen into a crisis. This time she was tested at the home of Lavoisier, with Deslon present, to determine the extent to which her imagination was engaged. After recovering from the swoon she experienced when entering the house, she was shown a group of cups filled with liquid and asked to select the one that had been magnetized. She fell into a crisis after having been shown four non-magnetized cups, but afterwards, when given a cup of water to drink that had been magnetized by Deslon himself, she felt nothing. Next, Majault examined the film on her eyes while, unbeknownst to her, the magnetized cup was held for twelve minutes behind her head. Distracted and comforted by the eye exam, she was calmer than at any other time.

The twelfth experiment tested the power of sight to stimulate the imagination. One of Jumelin's patients, who had lost the power of speech when he magnetized her, agreed to be magnetized again at his house in the presence of the commissioners. Her extreme reaction could be reproduced only when she was able to see Jumelin.

The thirteenth experiment explored the role of the magnetizer's gaze, which, it was agreed, was far more powerful than any other kind of sign or gesture. A new patient at Deslon's clinic, coming out of a crisis, was transfixed by her magnetizer's gaze, and reported that she carried it in her mind's eye for three days, asleep or awake.

The fourteenth and fifteenth experiments tested whether animal magnetism could produce any effects *without* the imagination being engaged. As magnetic fluid was said to pass through walls and heavy wooden doors, and as Deslon himself had asserted that it passed through paper, the commissioners removed a door between two chambers and replaced it with a paper partition. From behind that partition, at a distance of eighteen inches, one of the commissioners magnetized Mlle. B** for thirty minutes without her knowledge, as she chatted with the others. Although when magnetized at Passy she had fallen into a violent crisis within minutes, this time she felt nothing. The magnetizer then entered her chamber, stood in front of her at precisely the same distance, and magnetized her in a manner that, unbeknownst to her, should have produced no effects, according to Mesmer's doctrine of polarity. Within minutes she fell into a convulsive crisis complete with headache, hiccups, teeth-chattering, foot-tapping, twisting limbs, and pain in her lower back.

The sixteenth experiment, also conducted on Mlle. B**, proved that imagination could end a crisis as well as instigate it. As the magnetizer told her that it was time to stop, he crossed his index fingers in a way that should have continued the flow of magnetism exactly as before. He then told her that each of her symptoms would abate. Within only three minutes, his voice directing her imagination, the pain in her head, neck, chest, and arms disappeared.

Having proven that animal magnetism did not exist and that all the symptoms they had observed were attributable to the imagination, the commissioners discussed the physical effects and how they were augmented in group sessions. They pointed out the potentially harmful consequences of prolonged pressure, either light or deep, on the colon, diaphragm, stomach, and uterus during magnetic treatments. They noted the phenomenon of mutual incitement and imitation of symptoms in group sessions, particularly among women, that often led to the proliferation of crises.[5] And they discussed how hysterical symptoms could become habitual, and could be easily induced by the repetition of certain triggers.

The real causes of the effects ascribed to animal magnetism, they determined, were touch, imagination, and imitation. Among these, imagination was the most important. Even Deslon agreed in some measure with this assessment.

M. Deslon ne s'éloigne pas de ces principes. Il a déclaré dans le Comité tenu chez M. Franklin le 19 juin, qu'il croyoit pouvoir poser en fait que l'imagination avoit la plus grande part dans les effets du Magnétisme animal; il a dit que cet agent nouveau n'étoit peut-être que l'imagination elle-même, dont le pouvoir est aussi puissant qu'il est peu connu: il assure avoir constamment reconnu ce pouvoir dans le traitement de ses malades, & il assure également que plusieurs ont été ou guéris ou infiniment soulagés. Il a observé aux Commissaires que l'imagination ainsi dirigée au soulagement de l'humanité souffrante, seroit un grand

5. Here, a footnote describes an incident of mass hysteria among teenage girls in 1780.

bien dans la pratique de la Médecine (*h*);[6] & persuadé de cette vérité du pouvoir de l'imagination, il les a invités à en étudier chez lui la marche & les effets. Si M. Deslon est encore attaché à la première idée que ces effets sont dûs à l'action d'un fluide, qui se communique d'individu à individu par l'attouchement ou par la direction d'un conducteur, il ne tardera pas à reconnoître avec les Commissaires qu'il ne faut qu'une cause pour un effet, & que puisque l'imagination suffit, le fluide est inutile. Sans doute nous sommes entourés d'un fluide qui nous appartient, la transpiration insensible forme autour de nous une atmosphère de vapeurs également insensibles; mais ce fluide n'agit que comme les atmosphères, ne peut se communiquer qu'infiniment peu par l'attouchement, ne se dirige ni par des conducteurs, ni par le regard, ni par l'intention, n'est point propagé par le son, ni réfléchi par les glaces, & n'est susceptible dans aucun cas des effets qu'on lui attribue.

Finally, the commissioners considered whether the crises and convulsions produced around the tub could ever be useful in curing patients. They concluded that they could not; these convulsions were violent and harmful, capable of causing lasting physical and neurological damage. Wise doctors attempted to quiet such convulsions, not induce them. Suffering them regularly could only be fatal.

The commissioners unanimously concluded that animal magnetism did not exist and a belief therein constituted a regression to the superstitions of a less enlightened age.

6. The footnote quotes Deslon, writing in 1780, to the effect that if Mesmer had discovered no other secret than how to make the imagination improve one's health, it would have been a marvelous good in itself: Deslon, *Observations sur le magnétisme animal* (London, 1780), pp. 46–7. However, Deslon's acknowledgment that animal magnetism might be harnessing the powers of the imagination was based on the assumption, common in 18th-century physiology, that the imagination was an insensible fluid flowing through the fibers of the nervous system. By contrast, the commissioners treated the imagination not as a material force but as a "moral," or psychological, factor. This unusual understanding of the imagination received much criticism from the proponents of animal magnetism: Jessica Riskin, *Science in the Age of Sensibility: the Sentimental Empiricists of the French Enlightenment* (Chicago and London, 2002), pp. 219–22.

Les Commissaires ayant reconnu que ce fluide magnétique animal ne peut être apperçu par aucun des nos
sens, qu'il n'a eu aucune action, ni sur eux-mêmes, ni sur
les malades qu'ils lui ont soumis; s'étant assurés que les
pressions & les attouchemens occasionnent des change-
mens rarement favorables dans l'économie animale; & des
ébranlemens toujours fâcheux dans l'imagination; ayant
enfin démontré par des expériences décisives que l'imagination sans Magnétisme produit des convulsions, & que
le Magnétisme sans l'imagination ne produit rien; ils ont
conclu d'une voix unanime, sur la question de l'existence
& de l'utilité du Magnétisme, que rien ne prouve l'existence du fluide magnétique animal; que ce fluide sans existence est par conséquent sans utilité; que les violens effets
que l'on observe au traitement public, appartiennent à
l'attouchement, à l'imagination mise en action, & à cette
imitation machinale qui nous porte malgré nous à répéter
ce qui frappe nos sens. Et en même temps ils se croient
obligés d'ajouter, comme une observation importante, que
les attouchemens, l'action répétée de l'imagination, pour
produire des crises, peuvent être nuisibles; que le spectacle
de ces crises est également dangereux à cause de cette imitation dont la nature semble nous avoir fait une loi; & que
par conséquent tout traitement public où les moyens du
Magnétisme seront employés, ne peut avoir à la longue que
des effets funestes (*i*).[7]

A Paris, ce onze Août mil sept cent quatre-vingt quatre.
Signés, B. FRANKLIN, MAJAULT, LE ROI, SALLIN, BAILLY,
D'ARCET, DE BORY, GUILLOTIN, LAVOISIER.)

7. The footnote anticipated the objection from Mesmer and his follow-
ers (which Mesmer and Lafayette had already raised in their letters to BF
of May 14 and [May 20], respectively) that the commission should have
examined Mesmer's theory and practice rather than Deslon's. The commissioners argued that Deslon was clearly capable of producing the effects
generally ascribed to animal magnetism, regardless of the theory explaining them. They also pointed to his longstanding association with Mesmer
prior to their falling-out.

From William Carmichael

ALS: American Philosophical Society

Dear Sir   St. Ildefonso Augt. 11th 1784

I received some days ago a Letter from the Cte de Campomanes[8] in answer to the one which your Excellency put into my hands for him; As I had in prospect an occasion of sending it by an extraordinary Courier I have taken the Liberty to detain this Letter until the moment of the Departure of the Courier— The packet would have cost your Excellency an extraordinary postage, & As I had been instrumental in bringing you into this Correspondence, I did not wish to engage your Excellency to pay more than was necessary for the proofs of my desire to contribute to your satisfaction— It is with the highest pleasure I can assure you that your Name is in Veneration here, your confidence & esteem are my passeports to all the Literati. I beg your Exy to answer Campomanes as soon as your Leisure will permit you & to answer *generally* as a well wisher to every measure taken for the encouragement of Agriculture & the Sciences here. If my information from America is just, I hope your Excellency will have the satisfaction of concluding a Treaty with this Country as much to your honor as those to which you have already given your signature. I hope from the friendship which your Excy has so often declared to me that you will have the goodness to make me the instrument of notifying the Intentions of Congress to this Court. The Silence of that Body afflicts & Surprises me. I do not know what to think of this Silence which distresses me to the last degree— *Patience* you have been my example & I love & respect you too much not to follow it. I drew upon you the ninth of last month in favor of Messrs Drouilhet for 4000 Livres Tournois, I wished not to be too pressing & altho I wrote your Excellency that I should draw in favor of Mr Williams for 2000 Livres Tournois I shall not do it until next week—

I beg & entreat your Excellency to charge My Namesake[9] to have the goodness to write me from time to time. Situated as I am & as I have been here I cannot remain longer spending

8. Campomanes to BF, July 26, above.
9. WTF.

494

money for Others & my own Time more precious still without having it in my power to serve others or myself essentially. On My return to America I may possibly be of use to my friends & to myself & certainly I have had no motive to induce me to remain here because, I have not consulted my own Interests but those of the States— I always regarded them as inseraparable, but I am afraid I shall sooner or later experience that Ostracism has not existed only in Athens— I should not complain of this, If I had only a shirt of your garment to give me some claim to merit, but as this gift cannot be bestowed without your ascencion to *another World*[1] I will consent to suffer every *thing* in this provided Your Excellency will also determine not to leave us, even Tho' Madame Helvetius should invite you to Elysium to revenge herself of the indifference of her Caro Esposo & you of the Inconstancy of your Gaia,[2] until you shall see us hors d'Affaire with all the potentates of Europe— I cannot tell your Exy How we shall be *here*, but this week I shall have an opportunity of writing you more fully by a private hand— With affectionate remembrance to my Namesake I have the honor to be with the highest regard & Affection Your Excys most Obliged & Most Humble Sert   WM CARMICHAEL

From Dumas   ALS: American Philosophical Society

Monsieur,   Lahaie 12e. Aout 1784
     Dans l'espérance que ma derniere, avec les incluses, est bien parvenue, voici No. 44 pour le Congrès, qu'il trouvera sans doute très interessante.[3] Je la recommande à V. E. pour la fermer

1. A reference to the biblical story of Elijah's ascension, after which Elisha took up the prophet's mantle, literally and figuratively: 2 Kings 2:14.
2. BF's inconstant Gaia, the earth goddess of Greek mythology, is DF, whom he finds married to Mme Helvétius' "Caro Esposo" (dear husband) in "The Elysian Fields": XXXI, 322–7.
3. Dumas' Aug. 10 letter to the president of Congress reported, among other political news, that the States General of the Netherlands had accepted without changes the draft Franco-Dutch treaty of defensive alliance

& acheminer, comme aussi celle pour Mr. Van Berkel, & celle pour Mr. le D. de la V [Vauguyon]—
Je présente mes complimens à Mr. Wm. Franklin, & suis avec grand respect De Votre Excellence Le très-humble & très obéissant serviteur   C. W. F. DUMAS

Passy à Son Exce. Mr. Franklin M. Pl. des E. U.

Charles Thomson to the American Commissioners

ALS: Massachusetts Historical Society; copy: Historical Society of Pennsylvania

Gentlemen,   Philadelphia 13 Aug. 1784

In pursuance of the Orders of the Committee of the States,[4] I have the honor to transmit to you the copy of a letter signed T. Gilfillan, dated London the 19 feby 1784 with a copy of an inspection roll of Negroes taken on board certain vessels at anchor near Staten Island on the 30 of November 1783, to be made use of in any negotiations you may have with the court of Great Britain agreeably to the instructions heretofore transmitted to you.[5]

----

as proposed by Vergennes. In a postscript, Dumas noted JA's departure for London and Paris and his own precarious situation. National Archives.

Earlier on Aug. 10, Dumas had written a long letter to WTF that he also enclosed with the present letter. He thanked WTF for the news contained in his of Aug. 1, reported that he knew of TJ's arrival, asked WTF to forward an enclosed letter to La Vauguyon, and promised to write to BF as soon as he learned the outcome of the treaty negotiations. APS.

4. This July 22, 1784, resolution (*JCC*, XXVII, 596) directed that a copy of the enclosures Thomson describes be sent to the joint commissioners.

5. The American commissioners had already protested to David Hartley the British evacuation of fugitive slaves in violation of Article 7 of the preliminary peace treaty; see XXXIX, 579; XL, 192, 284–5, 315–16. The letter in question was by Thomas Gilfillan, a British army captain who was inspecting "Negroes" embarked at Staten Island with the departing British garrison of New York. The recipient was William S. Smith, appointed by GW to supervise the evacuation (XLI, 127n). It enclosed an inspection roll describing each person in detail. (Both documents are at the National Archives; see Smith, *Letters*, XXI, 771n.)

James Cook Gold Medal

With great Respect I have the honor to be Gentlemen Your most obedient and most humble Servt   CHAS THOMSON.

The Honbl. John Adams Benj Franklin & Thomas Jefferson

Notations:[6] Philad Augst. 13. 1784 from The Secretary of Congress / Papers relating to Negroes carried from New York

From Joseph Banks

ALS: University of Pennsylvania Library; AL (draft): Royal Society

Dear Sir   Soho Square Augst. 13 1784
    Willing as much as is in my Power to Clear the R. Society & myself from our share of the Charge of Illiberal treatment towards you with which I fear this Countrey may too justly be accusd, I take my Pen with no small Pleasure to inform you that I am instructed by the Council of the Royal Society to Present to you in their name the Gold medal they have struck in honor of Captn. Cook[7] as a testimony how truly they respect those liberal Sentiments which inducd you when his return to Europe was expected to Issue your orders to such American Cruizers as were then under your direction to abstain from molesting that great Circumnavigator an act worthy those sentiments of General Philanthropy by which I have observd your Conduct ever actuated since I have had the honor of your acquaintance. At the Same time give me leave to Congratulate you on the honorable manner in which you receivd a Copy of Captn. Cooks voyage sent to you by his Britanic Majesties orders as a testimony of his Royal approbation of the same liberal Conduct.[8]
    As I suppose you would wish to know to whom you are obligd for the representation which inducd his Majesty to Send it I can Inform you that it was Ld Howe, when I, who by desire of the Admiralty conducted the General Business of that Publication reported the names of those to whom Presents of the work ought in my opinion to be sent I did not venture to insert your

6. In the hand of David Humphreys.
7. See Bridgen to BF, June 22.
8. See Lord Howe to BF, [June 1].

497

name in the List but when Ld Howe on hearing my reasons for Sending one to his Most Christian Majesty approvd of them in warm Terms I thought it proper to acquaint him that you had an equal right to the same compliment a circumstance of which he was ignorant on which his Lordship of his own mere motion & without hesitation orderd your name to be inserted in the List & Obtaind his Majesties Royal assent with as little difficulty.

We have at last began to Exhibit Ballons as a matter of Profitable shew two days ago a French man who Calls himself Chevr. Moret advertisd that he would ascend at Chelsea in a machine made on Mont Golfiers Principles, Tickets were sold for a Guinea half & half a Crown & a most numerous assembly got together especialy on the outside of the Enclosure it seemd however that the Chevr. knew by Previous experiment that his Machine was so ill Constructed & so heavy that it Could not raise even its own weight above 10 feet from the Ground this at best was the result of the Experiment & the Company Finding reasons to beleive that the Chevr. never meant to ascend which they deduced from the fire pla[ce?] within being held up by wyers so thin that they soon burnd off but more especialy by a Dram bottle which they had examind in his Gondola & found empty became quite outrageous & tore to peices in a few minutes the whole apparatus.[9]

To day a Montgolfier is to ascend in which we are told a Major Gardiner who came here from America as a Loyalist about 3 or 4 years ago is to go up with another Gentleman whose name is secret[1] in a few days more a Globe of 32 feet filld with Gas &

9. In January, 1784, London newspapers announced the construction and imminent ascent of "the largest balloon ever made in this country," which was in the form of a "Chinese Temple." This hot-air balloon was the brainchild of the chevalier de Moret, whose flair for drama exceeded his competence as an engineer. Moret's oft-postponed exhibition finally took place on Aug. 10 at Five Fields Row, Chelsea. The temple-shaped balloon, made of coarse, porous cotton covered by thin paper, was reportedly 65 feet high and 120 feet in circumference. After watching for three hours as a mass of burning straw failed to budge the colossal edifice, the angered crowd stormed the balloon and shredded it, while Moret, hidden by the thick smoke, made his escape. A few days later he apologized and offered various excuses: J. E. Hodgson, *The History of Aeronautics in Great Britain* ... (London, 1924), pp. 111–13.

1. "Major Gardiner" was probably Valentine Gardner, a British army officer who went to America in the 1750s, at the beginning of his military

well made is to Carry up a Mr. Lunardi a writer in the office of
the Neapolitan minister & a Mr. Biggins who seems a well Educated young man who lives upon his Means.[2]

Adieu dear sir beleive me Your Obedient & Faithfull servant

JOS: BANKS

P.S. I will send the Gold medal by the first safe opportunity &
the bronze one with it which you receive from the Soc. as one
of the fellows

Addressed: Dr. Franklin / Passy / near / Paris

---

career. In 1769 he married Alida Livingston, daughter of Robert Livingston of New York. His regiment was thereafter transferred for a time to
the British Isles, but he returned to America in 1775 as an aide-de-camp of
Gen. Burgoyne, and in 1776 was promoted to a major in the 16th Regiment
of Foot, which occupied Philadelphia in 1777. He seems to have returned
to London *c.* January, 1782, whereupon he was elected to the Coffee House
Philosophical Society: Whitfield J. Bell, Jr., *Patriot-Improvers: Biographical
Sketches of Members of the American Philosophical Society* (3 vols., Philadelphia, 1997–2009), II, 293–5; T. H. Levere and G. L'E. Turner, eds.,
*Discussing Chemistry and Steam: the Minutes of a Coffee House Philosophical
Society* (Oxford and New York, 2002), p. 23. Gardner collaborated with the
anatomist John Sheldon and the merchant Allen Keegan on the construction of a hot-air balloon that was 84 feet high and 80 feet wide. Sheldon was
to perform various scientific experiments during the balloon's voyage, but
the launch, originally scheduled for early August, was postponed several
times. During an attempted launch on Sept. 29, the balloon was destroyed
by fire, for which the three participants blamed one another: Hodgson, *History of Aeronautics*, pp. 113–16; *ODNB*, under Sheldon.

2. Vincenzo Lunardi staged the first successful manned balloon flight
in England on Sept. 15 before thousands of spectators on the Artillery
Ground at Moorfields. Banks had contributed to the public subscription
for this hydrogen balloon, which was distinguished from its predecessors
by the addition of oars and wings, intended to make it steerable. The balloon's launch had been scheduled for August, but the permission to use the
grounds of Chelsea Hospital was revoked after the riot attending Moret's
failed demonstration. On the day of the experiment, Lunardi discovered
that he had overestimated the balloon's lift, forcing him to leave behind his
collaborator, George Biggin. Lunardi's flight from London to Hertford-
shire, which made him famous, inspired a popular tune and a fashion trend,
and prompted the striking of a commemorative medal: Hodgson, *History
of Aeronautics*, pp. 117–25; *ODNB*, under Lunardi.

From the Comte de la Morliere[3]

LS: American Philosophical Society

Au Chateau de Lussiennes par Marly

Monsieur,   Le Roy le 13 Aoust 1784

J'ai des regrets infinis de ne pouvoir accompagner mon fils qui aura L'honneur de vous remettre ma Lettre pour vous engager à lui prêter vôtre attention sur la demande que je pense que ses services méritent; j'avois engagé Mr. Le Cte. D'estaing sur L'amitié qu'il à de tous temps pour moi de lui fournir, oú de lui procurer les occasions de Se distinguer; Mon fils s'est trouvé sous ses ordres á L'affairré de Savanha; il lui remit après cette expédition nos blessés et nos malades pour les jetter dans Charlestown; il en a soutenu le Siege en commandant tout ce qui lui restoit de français en état de porter les armes; il y a été fait prisonnier de guerre ainsi que la garnison; Les Certificats qu'il mettra sous vos yeux vous paroîtront, je l'espere, Dignes, de la grace honoraire qu'il vous demandera, dont ont été pourvus tant d'officiers françois, et j'ai à vous Supplier de vouloir bien la lui procurer,[4] comme de m'accorder celle de me croire avec autant de respect que de considération, Monsieur, Vôtre très humble et très obéissant Serviteur

LE CTE DE LA MORLIERE

lnt general des armées du Roy

From Charles Thomson

ALS: American Philosophical Society; AL (draft): Historical Society of Pennsylvania

My dear friend,   Philadelphia August 13. 1784

The renewal of our ancient correspondence and the receipt of your letters excited those sensations, which real friends feel

---

3. The count wrote to BF once before. In October, 1778, he requested a meeting to discuss the desire of his son Louis-Antoine Magallon de la Morliere du Tillet to join the American forces. When summarizing that letter, we wrote that Morliere asked BF to grant "them" an audience (XXVII, 104–5); actually, he wrote in the first person singular, as his son was in St.-Domingue.

4. Louis-Antoine was now seeking membership in the Society of the Cincinnati. He was made an honorary member of the French branch on Sept. 20, 1789: Asa B. Gardiner, *The Order of the Cincinnati in France* . . . (n.p., 1905), p. 211; Bodinier, *Dictionnaire*, under Magallon.

on meeting unexpectedly after a long separation. As Mr Jefferson, who I hope is by this time safe arrived will explain matters to you and make you fully acquainted with the state of our affairs I shall no longer conceal from you the circumstance of the Omission of the signature of the letter of the 5 Jany last, which procured me the favour of hearing from you.[5] The letter was to have been signed by the President. As the vessel was on the point of sailing and the captain only waiting for the dispatch, I copied the letter in Congress and delivered it to the President, who sealed it in a hurry without putting his Name to it. So that my letters to you are all private, and this will explain why they generally contain "nothing of public Affairs."[6] I am sensible you must, for a considerable time past, have been greatly at a loss for want of official communications. And though I often wished to give you some yet I forbore, for reasons, which if ever I am so happy as to have a personal interview I can assign and which I am persuaded you will deem satisfactory. But this Inconvenience will be obviated, if Mr Jay who with his family is arrived at New York and who as I mentioned to you in a former letter, is appointed Secretary for foreign affairs, accepts that Office, as I hope he will: Though I must confess my hope is founded more on my wishes than on any solid reason. I have written and informed him of his appointment & urged his acceptance, but have not yet received his Answer.[7]

Col Harmar who arrived with the Marquis de la Fayette after a fine passage of 35 days delivered me on the eighth your letter of the 14 June with a copy of that of the 13 May, the original of which I had received before, announcing the exchange of the ratifications of the definitive treaty of peace: On this happy completion of our hazardous enterprize I most sincerely congratulate you. It is an event, which I have devoutly wished and yet I cannot but say, the prospect of it has often excited many uneasy apprehensions. From the first appeal to arms, through the whole contest, I never had a doubt of the issue; but I was afraid it would come upon us before we had acquired national

5. See BF to Thomson, March 9, above.
6. Quoted from BF's June 14 letter to Thomson, above.
7. Thomson wrote twice, on June 18 (the day he informed BF) and again on July 29, after Jay reached New York: *Jay Papers,* III, 583–4, 590–1.

principles habits and sentiments, which would enable us to improve it to advantage and to act becoming our station and dignity. I need not mention to you who know so well the peculiar circumstances of America at the commencement of this revolution. The several colonies were distinct and separate governments, each jealous of another and kept apart by local interests and prejudices. Being wholly dependent on Great Britain they were secluded from all Negotiations with foreign courts and almost from all intercourse with foreign Nations. Having never been much taxed, nor for any length of time, they had no funds, whereon to ground public credit. Those who know the difficulty which old established nations experience in their attempts to introduce new arrangements either in government, police or finance, will readily conceive what we have had to encounter; more especially when it is considered, that the ancient governments being dissolved, the people were thrown into a state of nature, that property being equally divided and the feudal system unknown in this country, there were no individuals to whom the people were accustomed to look up and who could influence their conduct or Opinions. And even when new governments were adopted, the ideas of liberty which prevailed threw the whole power into the hands of the people And the rotation which took place in the legislatures and executives of the several states afforded little Opportunity of acquiring National sentiments. Notwithstanding all this we have made considerable progress in the short period of eight years; the time elapsed since we became a Nation; And I am happy to think that the people every day become more and more impressed with the necessity of honorably paying our debts, supporting public credit and establishing a national character. And though Rhode island still holds out and refuses her assent to the impost of 5 per cent, yet as all the other states have agreed to the measure I have strong hopes that she may be induced to come into it, or that some means will be devised to overcome the obstacle which her refusal throws in the way.[8] In like manner I am persuaded the

8. Disputes among the states regarding whether and on what terms to ratify the impost persisted, and the measure was never enacted: XL, 65n; *JCC*, XXVIII, 198n; XXX, 7–8; Ferguson, *Power of the Purse*, pp. 239–42.

people of these states will quickly find it to be their interest as well as of absolute necessity to be faithful in the Observance of treaties and to avoid internal contentions and divisions.

There is no doubt but Britain will watch for advantages, if not to recover what she has lost, at least to be revenged for what she has suffered; and that every thing will be attempted and every artifice used, which Malice can suggest, to break our Connection with France and to sow dissensions among the states. The easy access which foreigners have to these states and the ready reception they meet with afford favourable opportunities of putting their arts in practice. And it is worthy of Observation, that it is strangers lately come among us, whom we know nothing of, joined with Men, who, to say the least of them, were lukewarm in our cause and of doubtful Characters, who are now most active in sowing jealousies of France, from an affected regard for our liberty and a zeal to preserve this country from foreign influence. I think it therefore highly necessary both for France and America to be on their guard and not suffer themselves to be duped by the arts of their common enemy.

The atrocious and unprovoked outrage lately committed in this city by one Longchamps a vagabond frenchman seems to carry strong marks of a premeditated design to embroil us with France:[9] And what makes this still more probable is the palliating

9. Charles-Julien de Longchamps arrived in Philadelphia in September, 1783, and married a wealthy Quaker against the will of her guardians, who disparaged in the press his claim to high social standing. When La Luzerne and Marbois refused to certify documents allegedly proving his nobility and military record, Longchamps first threatened Marbois on May 17 and then, two days later, assaulted the consul in public. Citing the law of nations, La Luzerne demanded that Longchamps be turned over to the French legation so that he could be sent to France for punishment. On June 7, however, the justices of the Pa. Supreme Court advised the Supreme Executive Council that, in the absence of a consular treaty, Longchamps had to be tried in Philadelphia under state law: La Luzerne to Vergennes, June 19, 1784, in Giunta, *Emerging Nation*, II, 393–9; G. S. Rowe and Alexander W. Knott, "Power, Justice, and Foreign Relations in the Confederation Period: the Marbois-Longchamps Affair, 1784–1786," *PMHB*, CIV (1980), 275–89.

By the time Thomson wrote the present letter, WTF had already received an account of the Longchamps affair from George Fox, whose June 16 letter (APS) was carried by Edward Bancroft. Bancroft had arrived in Paris by July 29.

account given of this affair in a paper newly set up here, as if for the purpose, entitled "Courier de l'Amerique," and which is conducted by Boinod and Gaillard, two strangers, who came to this place last fall about the same time as Longchamps.[1] The complexion of this paper evidences a marked inveteracy against France and a strong desire to excite fears and jealousies or at least to give an unfavourable impression of her: I am glad to find that the zeal of the Authors has hurried them into so palpable a manifestation of their design and that suspicions are already raised which I trust will guard against the influence of the poison they mean to convey.

I send you the Courier de l'Amerique as far as published and some other papers of the day. I also enclose the copies of some originals, which will explain the circumstances of the outrage committed by Longchamps and the Measures taken by Government in Consequence thereof.[2] I must inform you that the judges have not yet given an Answer to the last letter of the President. The question "Whether Longchamps can be legally delivered up by the Council according to the claim made by the late Minister of France" was publickly argued by lawyers before the Judges, who still have it under advisement.[3] In the mean

1. Daniel Boinod and Alexandre Gaillard operated a bookstore in Philadelphia. Their semi-weekly *Courier de l'Amérique* began publication on July 27. It was not alone in denouncing the French for demanding that Longchamps be turned over to French jurisdiction; other Philadelphia newspapers and pamphlets also depicted the French position as a threat to American sovereignty and to fundamental American rights, laws, and liberties: Jean Sgard, ed., *Dictionnaire des journaux, 1600–1789* (2 vols., Paris, 1991), I, 278–81; Rowe and Knott, "Power, Justice, and Foreign Relations," pp. 93–4, 294–5, 297–9.

2. The enclosures, which run to 20 pages, are titled "Papers relative to the outrage and violation of the law of Nations committed by Longchamps." They are listed in Smith, *Letters*, XXI, 775–6n.

3. The trial of Longchamps in the Court of Oyer and Terminer at Philadelphia, which was presided over by the justices of the Supreme Court, began on June 24. He was found guilty, but on June 26 the Supreme Executive Council asked the justices to delay sentencing until they had considered three questions (including the one Thomson quotes) aimed at allowing French authorities to help determine Longchamps' punishment. The court delivered its judgment on Oct. 7; it ruled that the council had no authority to hand over Longchamps to the French government

while Longchamps is confined in prison and the matter is laid before the legislature, who have now under consideration a bill, which I have no doubt they will pass for effectually securing the rights and immunities of public Ministers and punishing the violators of them.—[4]

It may not be amiss to acquaint you that from his own shewing it appears that Longchamps had been an Officer in the french service; that in 1775 he came to America and went to our camp then before Boston, where he was cordially received; that after being in our camp and about head quarters for some weeks he took the advantage of a pass given for the purpose of going into the country, to slip into Boston, which we were beseiging; that he wanted permission of genl Gage to come again into our camp; But for some reason that does not appear it was not granted; That in our camp he passed by the name of Longchamps and in Boston by that of Blutiere.[5] In short from many circumstances there is reason to suspect that at that time he either was or wished to be employed as a spy of the british general. Whether his late crime is the effect of sudden passion

---

and that the state could not sentence Longchamps to indefinite imprisonment, to last until Louis XVI deemed that adequate "reparation" had been made. However, because Longchamps had violated both state law and the law of nations, the court imposed what it considered a harsh sentence of 100 "French Crowns" and trial costs, two years of prison, and security for seven years of good behavior. Marbois regarded the sentence as too lenient and believed that the court had been intimidated by public opinion: Alexander J. Dallas, *Reports of Cases Ruled and Adjudged in the Courts of Pennsylvania* . . . (4 vols., Philadelphia, 1790–1807), I, 111–18; Marbois to Vergennes, Nov. 10, 1784, in Giunta, *Emerging Nation*, II, 491; Rowe and Knott, "Power, Justice, and Foreign Relations," pp. 289–94, 300.

4. The "Act for preserving the privileges of public Ministers of foreign Princes and States" was introduced on Aug. 7 and debated in August and September, but never came up for a vote. It was read twice more before the Assembly in November, but further consideration was postponed: *Minutes of the First Session of the Eighth General Assembly of the Commonwealth of Pennsylvania* . . . (Philadelphia, 1783[–1784]), pp. 268, 283, 359; *Minutes of the First Session of the Ninth General Assembly of the Commonwealth of Pennsylvania* . . . (Philadelphia, 1784[–1785]), pp. 22, 35, 38.

5. This description resembles the story related in 1778 to the American commissioners by a "Longchamp": XXVI, 208–9.

or the result of some premeditated design may possibly in time be manifested. There is a circumstance in the Conduct of Longchamps not mentioned in any of the papers, which it may not be improper to inform you of. On the 17 he committed the first insult. On the 18 he went to a justice of the peace and took an Oath of allegiance to the state, after which he perpetrated the outrage of the 19th. His views in taking the oath have been variously interpreted, some imagining that he meant thereby to secure himself from the french laws and from the power and resentment of the Consul; others that his design was by becoming a citizen to involve the state in his crime and interest the populace in his favour. But whatever might have been his views, even the lawyers who undertook his defence laid little stress upon it in their pleadings And the Bench seemed to be decidedly of opinion that the oath he had taken was of no effect and that he was only to be considered in the light of an alien stranger.

The Commissions which Mr Jefferson carried with him and which I hope you have received befor this will not only inform you of the purpose of Congress respecting your request of recal, but enable you to satisfy the Danish Minister and to proceed on commercial treaties with Great Britain and other powers. I wish I were able to give you any pleasing expectations with respect to some employment for your secretary W. T. F, against whose conduct or abilities while in public service I have never heard the least Objection. On the contrary I have always heard them well spoken of. But to me it appears that it will be injuring your grandson to delay making some other provision for him in hopes of an employment from Congress and of this I am persuaded you are already convinced by the Appointment of Col Humphreys. And yet I have seen such changes in the conduct of public affairs occasioned by the change of men entrusted with the direction of them, that there is always room left for hope. But he who has other means of support is less affected by a disappointment in meeting with public employ and if his Country stands in need of his services and calls upon him to fill any office, he seems to confer rather than to receive an obligation by accepting it.—

I have taken some steps but they have hitherto been fruitless to find out Philip Hearn. Upon Enquiry I learn that capt. Holland came to this Country in 1775 and was employed as adjutant to a regiment; that in 1776 he was promoted to the rank of a captain in the Delaware and was killed in the battle of Germantown in 1777; that he had married a daughter of Parson Ross of the Delaware state by whom he left issue and that his widow & children enjoy a pension from the Assembly of that state agreeably to a recommendation of Congress.[6]

I need not mention with what marks of cordiality and Affection the Marquis de la Fayette, who came to this place last Monday, was received by all ranks of people. His stay was but short as he was anxious to see general Washington. He left town this Morning and expects to return in three or four Weeks.[7]

Mr Laurens is arrived at New york, but not yet come forward.

I intended to have troubled Mr Jefferson with a line by this Opportunity, but my letter to you has insensibly become so long, that I shall not have time. You will please to make my respectful compliments to him and Mr Adams. I thank you for the notice you have taken of Mr Isaac Norris. From what I hear I am afraid he is too fond of the company of "Moines crasseux." Is there no way of reclaiming the son of our common and worthy friend?[8]

With sincere affection and esteem I am Dear Sir Your old and constant friend   CHAS THOMSON

P.S Pray what is the nature of this new discovery called Animal Magnitism of which we have such strange Accounts?[9] Is it a real

6. We have not found a letter requesting information about Hearn, but Elizabeth Holland's letter seeking information about Capt. Holland is in XL, 57–9. Shortly after the definitive peace treaty was signed, BF forwarded to Thomson a batch of inquiries that he had accumulated; it may have contained letters other than the ones we were able to identify: XL, 625–6.

7. Lafayette's festive reception in Philadelphia included visits from the officers of the Pa. line and from a committee of the Pa. legislature: Louis Gottschalk, *Lafayette between the American and the French Revolution (1783–1789)* (Chicago, 1950), pp. 85–8.

8. Norris converted from Quakerism to Catholicism during his stay in France: Taylor, *J. Q. Adams Diary*, I, 236; "Extracts from the Diary of Ann Warder," *PMHB*, XVIII (1894), 54.

9. The previous day Lafayette had addressed a specially called meeting of the APS on "the wonderful effects of a certain invisible power, in nature, called *animal magnetism* lately discovered by Mr. Mesmer." Lafayette also carried a personal letter he had solicited from Mesmer to GW which authorized him to describe animal magnetism to the general: *Early Proceedings*

arcanum of nature lately discovered? is the old magic revived? or is it quackery and a sporting with the imagination?

Honble B Franklin

From Jonathan Williams, Jr.

ALS: American Philosophical Society

Dear & hond Sir.   Havre de Grace 13. Augt 1784.

I should have called on you before my Departure if I had not been detained so long in Paris, that I expected to find you in bed and I was determined not to Stop myself 'till I came hither.[1] The inclosed from my Father in Law will give you an Idea of his Business & Situation.[2] I hope to have the pleasure of seeing you in about 15 days in the mean Time I remain as ever yours most dutifully & affectionately Yours.   J WILLIAMS J

Addressed: A Son Excellence / Monsr Le Docteur Franklin / Ministre des Etats Unis / en son Hotel A Passy / prés Paris.

Notation: Williams 13 Augt.— 1784.—

---

of the American Philosophical Society (Philadelphia, 1884), pp. 126–7; W. W. Abbot *et al.*, eds., *The Papers of George Washington*, Confederation Series (6 vols., Charlottesville and London, 1992–97), I, 380, 454; II, 151.

1. JW was in charge of receiving tobacco sent from Virginia by William Alexander under the contract with the farmers general signed the previous autumn: XLI, 180n. The partnership's first shipment, carried by the *Mariamne* (or *Marianne*), Capt. Archibald Carrol, arrived in Le Havre on Aug. 9: *Jefferson Papers*, VII, 395; Carrol to BF, Oct. 4, 1784 (AAE).

2. Although William Alexander's May 30 letter, above, was optimistic, he realized by October the impossibility of fulfilling the contract with the farmers general. Market conditions in both the United States and France were unfavorable; tobacco prices in the United States were too high, and it was impossible to turn a profit on what the farmers had agreed to pay. Despite being supported by Robert Morris' credit, and his own best efforts at finding bargains, Alexander was able to purchase only about 7 percent of the amount specified in the tobacco contract, and he sent even less to France. He later calculated that the partnership's losses on the contract amounted to more than 4,000 pounds in Virginia money: Price, *France and the Chesapeake*, II, 743–6, 1088; Le Couteulx & Cie. to BF, July 3, above; *Morris Papers*, IX, 470.

To Mary Hewson

ALS: Katherine N. Bradford, Philadelphia, Pennsylvania (1956)

Dear Friend,   Passy, Augt. 15. 1784—
I received your kind Letter of July 22. I wish you had executed your Project of taking a little Trip to see me this Summer.
You would have made me very happy,—and might have bath'd
your Children here as well as at Southampton, I having a Bath
in my House, besides the River in view.— I like your motherly
Account of them, and in Return send you my Daughter's Account of my Grandchildren at Philadelphia.³ You will see she
expected me home this Summer; but my Constituents have sent
me a new Commission, and I must stay another Winter. Can
you not come and pass it with me here? Temple who purposes
to have the Pleasure of delivering this, will explain to you how
you may be accommodated; and if you can resolve to come, will
conduct you. Except being at home, which I begin now to fear I
never shall be, nothing could give me greater Pleasure. Come,
my dear Friend, live with me while I stay here, and go with me, if
I do go, to America. Believe me ever, Yours most affectionately
                                                    B FRANKLIN

My Love to the dear Children particularly my Godson,⁴ for
whom Temple has a little Present of French Books

Mrs Hewson

---

3. The enclosure is missing. SB often wrote about her children; see her
letter of Nov. 5, 1783 (XLI, 178–9) and hers of [on or before June 20] and
June 20[–21], both above.
    4. William Jr.

Index

Compiled by Philipp Ziesche.

(Semicolons separate subentries; colons separate divisions within subentries. A volume and page reference in parentheses following a main entry refers to an individual's first identification in this edition.)

Franklin, Benjamin—books (*continued*) work to journal, 138–9: to intercede to have Hartley's pamphlet printed in Paris, 245–6; Gourdon returns borrowed books to, 79; sells *Encyclopédie* to Ridley, 113–14; orders pirated Lausanne edition of *Encyclopédie*, 114n; sends books to Hewson, 116, 198, 436, 509: *Pieces*, "Information" to Campomanes, 310, 403, 448: books to B. Vaughan, 448; owns two pamphlets by Graham, 138n: poem ridiculing mesmerists, 267n; references poem by Watts, 175–6; influence of Mather's *Essays to Do Good* on, 236; thanks Mather for *Dying Legacy*, 236; subscribes to *Encyclopédie méthodique* for Hopkinson, 269; Hopkinson sends newspaper essay to, 271–2; presents his works to Frisi, 286; acknowledges works of Campomanes, 309; comments on Morellet's manuscript, 342: Hertzberg's book, 467; article by Morellet erroneously attributed to, 343n; promises to read reform project by abbé, 376: donation of French books to University of the State of N.Y., 471; wants to exchange duplicate copy of Cook's *Voyage*, 393–4, 442; and Price's publishing of letter from Turgot, 408–10, 431, 461–2; forwards pamphlet from Price to Turgot, 408n, 409n; relates anecdote from Holinshed's *Chronicles*, 420; commends Price's *Observations*, 443, 461; Anisson wants to present book to, 457–9; Chambre syndicale does not inspect books shipped to, 465; receives book shipment from England, 465
—business and financial affairs: pays rent for Bache family's country house, xxv, liv, 338n: bill from Drouilhet & Cie., 168n: for painting of his Philadelphia house, 349n: dues to Maison philantropique, 401n; settles accounts with Chaumont, l, 203–6, 280–3; contract with Finck, 3; accounts of, 3–4, 140n, 168n, 203–6, 281n, 283n, 338n, 349n, 401n; gives BFB allow-

ance, 3n: advance to Chaumont, 281, 283; asks Hodgson to pay Withering, 5–6n, 64; writes name of London bankers on letter, 14n; supports renewal of *arrêt de surséance* for JW, 17–19; allowed free postage, 21, 22; recommends Alexander, 21: Bache & Shee, 21: Mühlberger, 57; and depreciation of American paper money, 31, 341–2, 425–6, 427n: Thomas' complaint against Bache & Shee, 227–9: JW's public accounts, 379–80, 438; agrees with Laurens on American national debt, 47; cannot help Carmichael pay bills of exchange, 47–8, 83; wishes Laurens success with restitution claims, 48; inquires into price of church bells, 65n, 148n; bills of exchange, loan office certificates drawn on, presented to, cashed by, 114n, 174; owed money by Shaffer, 128; provides financial assistance to Webb, 174–5, 258–9; approves Grand's paying back salary to Laurens, 212n; assists Bridgen to recover property confiscated by N.C., 232; attests signature on letter of credit for Alexander, 284n; provides Frecon with information about money, exchange, and credit in U.S., 384–5, 391–2; describes method of trading tobacco in Virginia, 391; provides Frecon with information about weights and measures, 391; informed of sale of tobacco by Le Couteulx & Cie., 392–3; will (1776) of, 434–5; will (1782) of, 435n; authorizes JW's purchase of cloth from Chaumont, 438n; wants to settle accounts with B. Vaughan, 442; certifies receipt of treasury certificates from Gouvion, Duportail, and Laumoy, 468–9; promises to write to Morris on behalf of Gouvion, 468n
—character and reputation: accusations in America against, li, 20n, 49, 306, 348–9; reputed to be a philanthropist, 35; child named after, 69; Laurens comments on infallibility of, 85; rumored to be returning to America,

INDEX

Poirey, Joseph-Léonard (Lafayette's secretary), 335n
Poissonnier, Pierre-Isaac (physician, chemist, XIX, 328n; XXVII, 559n): and royal commissions on animal magnetism, 184–90, 418n, 476n; sends report on Albert's bathhouse for BF's signature, 246; letters from, 184–90, 246
Poissonnier-Desperrières, Antoine (Pierre-Isaac's brother), 185n
Polhill, Nathaniel, 142
Pontière, Louis de, 338–9, 343
Porteus, Beilby (bishop of Chester), 422n
Port Louis: packet boats between New York and, 439
Portugal: Congress instructs commissioners to conclude treaty with, li, 217. *See also* Trade; Treaty of Amity and Commerce, proposed Portuguese-American
Postage: L'Air de Lamotte keeps records of, 3–4; RB complains about American, 20–2; BF allowed free, 21, 22; for mail between France, England, 130–1, 256–7: France, U.S., 275–9; Todd complains about French, 130–1
Postal Treaty, British-French: of 1713, 129–31: 1784, 129–31, 256–8
Postal Treaty, proposed Franco-American, 273–9
Post Office: American, 20–2, 130–1, 273, 274–9; British, 129–31, 256–8; French, 129–31, 256–8, 273, 274–9, 409n
Post Office Acts: of 1711, 130: 1765, 130
Poullard, —— (Morellet's secretary), 289n, 341n, 357n, 358
Pouponeau, Mlle ——, 29n
Powder magazines: commission examines proposal for installation of lightning rods on, 164n, 179–84
Praslin, César-Gabriel, comte de Choiseul, duc de, 187
Pratt, Sir Charles, Earl Camden (VIII, 3n), 203
Prefaces, Biographical and Critical, to the Works of the English Poets (Johnson), 352

Preliminary Articles of Peace, British-American, xxv, 191, 218n, 222, 304n, 319, 496n
Premier mémoire sur l'impression en lettres, suivi de la description d'une nouvelle presse ... (Anisson fils), 458n
Presbyterians, 420
Price, Richard (clergyman, XI, 100n): supports king in conflict with Commons, 65; BF sends engravings of balloon experiments to, 122: sends small balloon to, 122: sends "To the Royal Academy of Brussels" to, 122: recommends Chateaufort to, 251; comments on discord in Royal Society, 122: election in England, 123; considers invention of balloons as marking new epoch, 122; and BF's planned trip to England, 122–3, 231, 410: Paradise, 124–5: Percival, 235; concerned about BF's stone, 123, 410; favors parliamentary reform, 123–4; sends greetings to JA, Jay, 124; writes, sends *Observations on the Importance of the American Revolution*, 124, 408, 431, 443, 461; asks BF's opinion on publishing letter from Turgot, 408–10, 431, 461–2; visits Priestley, 410; recommends Lewis, 431; sends letter, pamphlets with Fitzmaurice, 431; letters from, 122–5, 408–10, 431; letter to, 461–2
Price, Sarah Blundell (Richard's wife), 123, 410, 462
Prielmayr, Franz Ferdinand von, 53
Priestley, Joseph (scientist, XIII, 185n), 122–3, 124n, 235, 380, 410
Primogeniture: BF criticizes, 310–11, 449–50
Princeton, N.J.: Congress meets at, 284n
Pringle, John (physician, VI, 178n), 234, 235n, 293n
Printing. *See* Franklin, Benjamin—printer
Prisoners, American: assisted by Coffyn, 4, 18: Leveux, 15, 22, 90: Hodgson, 68–9n: Pecquet, 225; at Dunkirk, 4, 18: Calais, 15, 22, 90; English-

United States (*continued*)
162, 163, 198–9, 212, 213, 238, 331,
374–5, 441, 445, 454n, 464–5; rumors
about, in Great Britain, 46, 163, 199,
375, 443; religious freedom in, 53,
222, 408n; emigration from Ireland
to, 54: Germany to, 158–9; high price
of labor in, 67; unfavorable conditions for winegrowers in, 67; wheat
farming in, 67; British public not in
favor of reconciliation with, 80n; Lafayette visits, 81, 263, 307, 332, 365n,
381, 388, 501, 507; dispute over when
armistice takes effect on coast of,
115, 145–6, 167; will be considered
too poor to support colleges, fears
BF, 120, 471; Price offers advice to,
124, 408, 431, 443, 461; Doyle's plan
for union of Canada and, 159; Laurens warns of new conflict between
Britain and, 163; reports, rumors
of disunion in, 163, 199, 244; Hartley proposes naval alliance between
Britain and, 192–4; border between
Canada and, 194; mutual denization,
naturalization with Britain, in proposed British-American commercial
treaty article, 194; Congress debates
whether to consider as one nation in
foreign treaties, 217, 218; citizens of,
need more time to pay English creditors, 222, 262, 336n; establishment
of Catholic Church in, 222, 366–7;
France restricts trade between French
West Indies and, 238–9, 365–6n,
374–5; Castiglioni plans tour of, 286;
named before British king in congressional ratification of peace treaty, 300,
302–3; boundaries of, delineated in
definitive peace treaty, 320–1; Morellet's writings on, 342–3n; arsenal of,
at Nantes, 369n; abundance of land
in, 445; Thomson fears British plot
to break alliance between France and,
503. *See also* Army, American; Continental Congress; Currency; Debt;
Duties; Loans; Packet boats; Peace
Treaty, Definitive British-American;

Post Office; Preliminary Articles
of Peace, British-American; States,
American; Trade; Treaties (various)
United States (merchant ship), 251n, 252
United States Chronicle, 131n
University of the State of New York,
317–18, 324, 470–1
University of the State of New York, Regents of the: ask BF to help Clarkson
raise funds, 324; BF discourages from
fund-raising in Europe, 470–2: promises donation of French books to, 471:
sends copy of letter to Witherspoon
to, 471; plan to establish schools for
teaching French, 471n; letter from,
324; letter to, 470–2
University of the State of Pennsylvania,
345
Utopia (More), 446n

Vallet, ———, 202n
Vallière, Anne-Julie-Françoise de Crus-
sol, duchesse de la, 410, 431
Valnais, Henry Quincy Joseph Dupas de
(Joseph's son), 121, 137
Valnais, Joseph (Jean) Dupas de Iden de:
announces birth of his son, 121; BF
misaddresses letter to, 137; thanks BF
for good wishes, 137; Bayard's claims
against, 224; letters from, 121, 137
Van Schellebeck, ——— (merchant), 32
Vansittart, Henry, 437
Vansittart, Nicholas, 437
Van Zeller, Herman Cremer, & Dohrman
(Lisbon firm), 253
Varnier, Charles-Louis, 475n
Vatican. *See* Holy See
Vaughan, Ann (Benjamin's sister), 27, 207
Vaughan, Barbara (Benjamin's sister), 27,
207
Vaughan, Benjamin (BF's editor, xxi,
441): asks BF about remedy for luxury,
lii, 443; and Withering, 5, 148–9n,
152: Jay, 152n: Laurens, 162n: Limon,
215: Arbuthnot, 375n, 442: commit-
tee of West Indian merchants, plant-
ers, 441: Estlin, 442: BF-Nairne correspondence on hygrometers, 443n;